Alternative Medicines: On the Way towards Integration?

Stefano Maddalena

Alternative Medicines: On the Way towards Integration?

A Comparative Legal Analysis in Western Countries

PETER LANG
Bern · Berlin · Bruxelles · Frankfurt am Main · New York · Oxford · Wien

Bibliographic information published by Die Deutsche Bibliothek
Die Deutsche Bibliothek lists this publication in the Deutsche Nationalbibliografie; detailed bibliographic data is available on the Internet at ‹http://dnb.ddb.de›.

British Library and Library of Congress Cataloguing-in-Publication Data:
A catalogue record for this book is available from The British Library, Great Britain, and from The Library of Congress, USA

Presented to the School of Law (University of Neuchâtel) to obtain the degree of PhD in Law.

Published with support of the Swiss National Science Foundation.

ISBN 3-03910-812-3
US-ISBN 0-8204-8029-0

Hochfeldstrasse 32, Postfach 746, CH-3000 Bern 9, Switzerland
info@peterlang.com, www.peterlang.com, www.peterlang.net

Printed in Switzerland

To Marie-Laure, my family

Special Thanks

I discovered the discipline of Health Law in the course of Professor Olivier Guillod. Through him, I learned to appreciate this branch of law; he later accepted to be the director of my thesis. My research would have been impossible without his support, availability and open-mindedness. I realise that I have been lucky to have such a guide.

During my studies at Columbia University, I was fortunate to have Prof. William Sage supervising my research. His expertise in both legal and medical fields was always helpful, and his advice and suggestions have contributed to the quality of this work.

I also want to thank Professor Pascal Mahon who kindly accepted to be a member of the jury. The dissertation has benefited from his scrupulous correction and constructive critics.

My research was also facilitated and made more effective by the people working at the Institute of Health Law at the University of Neuchâtel. I want to thank all members of this friendly team for their help and competence.

Many persons and institutions have helped me to gather, verify and correct information from more than twenty countries. I want to thank them and especially: Roscam Abbing, Dosa Agnes, Anne-Mielke Alkemade, Carles Amengual i Vicens, Kirsten Been, Christine Bohnet, Rosemary Boothman, Nathalie Brunner, Giancarlo Buccheri, Chandler Burr, Mr. Cherpillod, Albert Chevalley, Mr. Colin, Gilberto Colussi, Jean-François Dumoulin, Motzi Eklöf, Dennis Falzon, Annet Frijlink, Sylvia Füszl, Mr. Gaffner, Christian van Gessel, Daniel Grunwald, Rainer Gstöhl, Jasminka Goldoni, Anna-Karin Gullberg, G. J. Hamilton, Alexandra Hmelewskaja, Jacques Léo Hirsch, Laurent Jomé, Charles Joyce, Marili Juell, Viktor Jaksons, Edwald Kaufmann, Damian König, Willem Kramers, Laila Launsö, May Margot, Antti Marttila, Jeffrey Martins, Jonathan Monckton, Margot Muller, Claire Neyrinck, Nickolay A. Nikolaev, Oskar Ospelt, Mrs Pisano, Magalie Ramillien, Vasco Pinto Reis, Jacques Renk, Bruno Riek, Harald Schmadlbauer; Mr. Schnapp, Kari Bente Sorlie, Dominique Sprumont, A. Stacher, Julie Stone, Tiina Telekavi, Margit Ulmer, Tuula Vaskilampi, Fernando A. Verdú Pascual, Jaime Vidal Martinez, Jan Stepan, Pierre Villeneuve, Michael Wagner, Michel van Wassenhoven, Raymond Xerri, Andrej Zbonikowski and Xiaorui Zhang.

Furthermore, I want to thank the Swiss National Fund for Scientific Research which made this study possible, the Caisse Vaudoise and Les

Instituts Boiron who financially helped me, as well as the School of Law at Columbia University in New York who provided me with an academic home for almost two years. The COST B4 program at the European Commission as well as the Traditional Medicine Program at the World Health Organisation provided support and contacts to gather and verify the information.

I would like also to thank François Bohnet, Catherine Chandler and Christophe Müller for their careful reading, and last but not least Marie-Laure, who encouraged and supported me with tenderness during all these years.

Spring 2005 Stefano Maddalena

Table of Contents

Most Used Abbreviations

A.	Atlantic Reporter (US)
A.2d	Atlantic Reporter, Second series (US)
A.L.R.	American Law Reports (US)
A.L.R.3d	American Law Reports, Third series (US)
ABGB	Allgemeines Bürgerliches Gesetzbuch (Austria)
aCst	Former Constitution (Switzerland)
AH	Federal Act on "Heilpraktikers" (Germany)
AIM	Act on the Internal Market (Switzerland)
AJP	Aktuelle Juristische Praxis (Switzerland)
Ala.	Alabama (US)
AM	Alternative Medicines
Am.	American (US)
AMA	American Medical Association (US)
Ann.	Annoted
App.	Appeal
Apr.	April
Ariz.	Arizona (US)
Ark.	Arkansas (US)
Assoc.	Association
ATF	Arrêt du Tribunal Fédéral (Switzerland)
Aug.	August
BGBL	Bundesgesetzblätter (Austria)
BMJ	British Medical Journal (Great Britain)
BMS	Bulletin des Médecins Suisses (Switzerland)
BOE	Boletin Oficial del Estado (Spain)
Bus. & Prof.	Businesss and Professions (US)
BverfG	Bundesverfassungsgericht (German Supreme Court)
C.F.R	Code of Federal Regulation (US)
Cal.	California (US)
Cal. Rptr.	West's California Reporter (US)
CAM	Complementary and Alternative Medicines
Can.	Canadian
CAS	Commission on Alternative Medicine (Netherlands)
CCDHA	Conference of Cantonal Directors of Health Affairs (Switzerland)
CDS	Conférence des Directeurs Cantonaux des Affaires Sanitaires (Switzerland)
CEA	Cost-Effectiveness Analysis
Chap.	Chapter
CHSAFS	Conference of Health and Social Affairs of French Swiss speaking Cantons (Switzerland)
Cir.	Circuit (US)

Civ. App.	Court of Civil Appeals (US)
CMS	Cahiers Médicaux Sociaux
Co.	Company
Colo.	Colorado (US)
Cong.	Congress
Conn.	Connecticut (US)
CPE	Code of Professional Ethics
Crim. App.	(Court of) Criminal Appeals (US)
Cst	New (Swiss) Constitution
Ct.	Court
D.	District (US)
DC	Doctor of Chiropractic
Dec.	December
Del.	Delaware (US)
Dist.	District (US)
Div.	Division (US)
DO	Doctor of Osteopathy
DUMENAT	"Diplôme Universitaire de Médecines Naturelles" (University Diploma in Natural Medicine) (France)
E.	Eastern (US)
e.g.	For example
EBM	Evidence Based Medicine
Educ.	Education
ERISA	Employee Retirement Income Security Act (US)
EU	European Union
F.	Federal Reporter (US)
F. Supp.	Federal Supplement (US)
F.2d	Federal Reporter, Second Series (US)
F.3d	Federal Reporter, Third Series (US)
F.C.R.	Federal Court Report (US)
FAHI	Federal Act on Health Insurance (Switzerland)
Fam.	Family
FC	Federal Court (Supreme Court) (Switzerland)
FCB	Federal Commission on Benefits (Switzerland)
FDA	Federal Drug Administration (US)
Feb.	February
FF	Feuille Fédérale (Switzerland)
FFDCA	Federal Food, Drug, and Cosmetic Act (US)
Fla.	Florida
FMH	Foederatio medicorum Helveticorum (Federation of Swiss Physicians)
FOSI	Federal Office of Social Insurance (Switzerland)
GKV-NOG	Gesetzliche Krankenversicherung (Germany)
GMC	General Medical Council (Great Britain)
GP	General Practitioner (physician)
GPC	German Penal Code (Germany)

GPC	German Penal Code
GSC	German Social Code (in German: "Sozialgesetzbuch")
HMO	Health Maintenance Organisation
Hosp.	Hospital
HPUS	Homeopathic Pharmacopeia of the United States
i.e.	namely
Ill.	Illinois (US)
Ind.	Indiana (US)
Ins.	Insurance
J.	Journal
J.T.S.	Jurisprudencia del Tribunal Supremo (Spain)
JAMA	Journal of the American Medical Association (US)
Jan.	January
Kan.	Kansas (US)
L. Rev.	Law Review (US)
La.	Louisiana (US)
LAMal	In French: "Loi sur l'Assurance Maladie" (Swiss Federal Act on Health Insurance (FAHI))
LMI	Loi sur le Marché Intérieur (Switzerland)
M.D.	Medical Doctor
Mar.	March
Mass.	Massachussets (US)
MB/KK	Musterbedingungen des Verbandes der privaten Krankenversicherungen (Germany)
Md.	Maryland (US)
Me.	Maine (US)
MedR	MedizinRecht (Germany)
MEP	In French: "Médecin à Mode d'Exercice Particulier" (French physicians with a particular mode of practice)
Mich.	Michigan (US)
Minn.	Minnesota (US)
Miss.	Mississippi (US)
Mo.	Missouri (US)
Mont.	Montana (US)
N.	North(ern)
N.C.	North Carolina (US)
N.D.	North Dakota (US)
N.E.	Northern Reporter (US)
N.E.2d	Northern Reporter, Second Series (US)
N.H.	New Hampshire (US)
N.J.	New Jersey (US)
N.M.	New Mexico (US)
N.W.	North Western Reporter (US)
N.W.2d	North Western Reporter, Second Series (US)

N.Y.	New York (US)
N.Y.S.	New York Supplement (US)
N.Y.S.2d	New York Supplement, Second Series (US)
n°	number
NCCAM	National Centre for Complementary and Alternative Medicine (US)
Neb.	Nebraska (US)
Nev.	Nevada (US)
NHS	National Health System
NJW	Neue Juristische Wochenschrift (Germany)
Nov.	November
NZZ	Neue Zürcher Zeitung
OAM	Office of Alternative Medicines (US)
Oct.	October
OFAHI	Order of the Federal Act on Health Insurance (Switzerland)
Okla.	Oklahoma (US)
OOGKK	In German: "Oberösterreichische Gebietskrankenkasse" (Austrian public insurance fund)
Or.	Oregon (US)
P.	Pacific Reporter (US)
P.2d	Pacific Reporter, Second Series (US)
Pa.	Pennsylvania (US)
PARCA	Patient Access to Responsible Care Act
PPO	Preferred Provider Organisation
Prac.	Practice
Prim.	Primary
Promot.	Promotion
Pub.	Public (US)
R.I.	Rhode Island (US)
RCT	Randomised Controlled Trial
Reh'g	Rehearing (US)
Rev.	Revised (US)
RMSR	Revue Médicale de la Suisse Romande
RS	Recueil Systématique du Droit Fédéral (Swiss Federal Law)
RSJ	Revue Suisse de Jurisprudence
S.	South(ern)
S.C.	South Carolina (US)
S.D.	South Dakota (US)
S.E.2d	Southeastern Reporter, Second Series (US)
S.W.	South Western Reporter (US)
S.W.2d	South Western Reporter, Second Series (US)
SCAM	Swedish Commission on Alternative Medicine (Sweden)
SCC	Swedish Commission on Competence (Sweden)
Sept.	September
SGB	In German: "Sozialgesetzbuch" (German Code of Social Statutes)
SII	Social Insurance Institution (Finland)

SMC	Spanish Medical Council (Spain)
SNM	Société Neuchâteloise de Médecine (Switzerland)
So.	Southern Reporter (US)
So.2d	Southern Reporter, Second Series (US)
SPC	Swiss Penal Code (Switzerland)
ss	pages
Stat.	Statute (US)
Sup. Ct.	Supreme Court (US)
TEC	Treaty instituting the European Economic Community (EU)
Tenn.	Tennessee (US)
Tex.	Texas (US)
U.S.	United States
U.S.C.A.	United States Code Annotated
US	United States (of America), or American
Va.	Virginia (US)
vol.	Volume
Vt.	Vermont (US)
Wash.	Washington
WHCCAMP	White House Commission on Complementary and Alternative Medicine Policy
WHO	World Health Organisation
Wis.	Wisconsin (US)
Wyo.	Wyoming (US)

Introduction

During the past few decades, alternative medicines have gained increasing importance within Western countries. There are various reasons for the emergence of alternative medicines as a viable alternative to evidence-based medicine including the failure of allopathic medicine to treat specific illnesses, the disillusionment of patients with their physicians, the lower costs and risks of alternative techniques and the sense of well-being experienced by patients from alternative treatments. The inherent failure of evidence-based medicine to address these problems indicates both its limits and inability to respond effectively to the dissatisfaction felt by patients.

Faced with the demand of patients for a different medicine, alternative medicines have had to develop, within a framework not originally designed for them. Indeed, these techniques are usually not investigated or taught in medical schools, and the practice of such techniques has often been unregulated or even banned. They have also traditionally been excluded from insurance schemes. As a result, the market offers an array of alternative medicines that vary widely in quality, cost and effectiveness.

The recent evolution of these alternative techniques is considered from the perspective of their integration within Western medical systems, which presupposes the existence of an integrated system of medicine. The primary aim behind this focus on the integration of alternative medicines is to highlight and discuss the concept of a unique medicine, whose purpose is not only to relieve pain but to predict, prevent and cure illness and disease. As a result, all available methods must be employed to reach these objectives, irrespective of whether such methods are considered as being allopathic or alternative. However, this view is not shared by the strong proponents of evidence-based-medicine who have argued against the integration of any technique whose efficacy has not been demonstrated.

The purpose of this research is not only to investigate the extent and meaning of such integration but also to offer some proposals for the regulation of alternative medicines. Given that the debate goes further than a discussion concerning the problems of integrating alternative medicines within the current strict legal framework, a comparative and interdisciplinary approach has been chosen. It is hoped that such an approach will not only provide a more interesting and critical insight into the nature of the barriers that still exist to integration but also provide some response to questions that may arise such as what is an integrated system of medicine? Are we moving towards such a system? If so, what are the reasons? And is such a shift suitable or even feasible? It is apparent that providing complete answers to these questions would require not one but several dissertations on the legal, scientific, ethical, sociological and economical issues that such questions raise. It is proposed instead to limit our contribution to putting into evidence some interesting features noted during our research and by offering some general proposals as to the regulation of alternative techniques. These proposals are made more as policy recommendations than as precise suggestions within a defined legal framework.

The first part of the research is an overview of the current position of alternative medicines in some Western countries. The main topics are the licensing to practise alternative medicines and the coverage of alternative medicines by social and private insurance. Definitions and concepts are provided in order to delimit the object of our research. Finally, some sociological elements are presented regarding the extent of alternative medicines as well as various research and education issues in order that the reader understands the current environment surrounding alternative medicines.

On this basis, the second part of the study focuses on the most important regulatory mechanisms which are analysed and questioned from a comparative perspective. As scientific arguments play a crucial role in this set of problems and given that scientific approval may provide solid validation for regulation, some important points that such arguments raise are discussed. The last chapter focuses on the concept of an integrated system of medicine. The main components of such a system are presented with a comparison made between current trends and a theoretical model. This chapter also provides a summary of the research made and opens the door to future discussions.

To the best of our knowledge, this is the first extensive comparative study on the subject. For this reason, it seemed necessary to clearly distinguish the factual from the analysis and to propose several levels of readings to further aid understanding of the issues raised. The presentation of the facts, which fill a significant part of this research, was necessary as there was no data available to make a serious analysis before this research was undertaken. The purpose behind this factual approach is to allow access to the information gathered in order that an informed evaluation and critique can be made of our analysis. The second part of the research will be of more interest to those who wish to examine the current scientific debate surrounding alternative medicines, or who are interested in the analysis made of the process by which alternative medicines are regulated. Finally, the last chapter provides a broad overview of those issues that are discussed in more detail in previous chapters and, as such, may be of appeal to those who wish to have only a general picture of the situation or who are interested in the outline presented for an integrated system of medicine.

Methodology and Warnings

In 1991, National Research Program Number 34 (PNR 34) on Alternative Medicines was launched by the Swiss National Fund for Scientific Research (SNFSR). The aim of the program was to understand more fully the impact of alternative medicines on society through studies in various fields. Several studies in the medical, sociological and health law fields were completed within the framework of PNR 34.[1] In 1996, at the end of PNR 34, a mandate was given to the Institute of Health Law at the University of Neuchâtel (IHL) to provide an overview of the legal status of alternative medicines in Europe.[2]

A decision was made to continue the research not only because of the interesting nature of the topic but also because it was apparent that a more in-depth investigation was needed. The research was conducted at the University of Neuchâtel (Switzerland) and Columbia (New York/USA) without, initially, any clear idea of exactly where the research would end. However, as the research continued it became clear that the concept of an integrated system of medicine was able to incorporate and address all the main issues raised in relation to alternative medicines.

Only those countries for which sufficiently reliable information was received were reported. In order to obtain the data, we worked closely with several correspondents all over Europe, in particular with delegates of the COST B4 Program of the European Commission, correspondents of the Traditional Medicine Program of the World Health Organisation[3] and contacts of the IHL. We also had the opportunity to meet with important participants on the alternative medicine scene in various European countries.

1 For the presentation of the studies conducted during PNR 34, see FREY F. (coeditor: BAUMANN P. H.), *Supplementum 62, FNRS-PNR 34: Médecines complémentaires*, Schwabe, 1994, Basel.

2 A book was published that presents the results of the research: MADDALENA S., *The legal status of complementary medicines in Europe*, Stämpfli, 1999, Bern.

3 A collaboration with the Traditional Medicine Program and other participants resulted in the publication of a book that presents a summary of the legal status of alternative medicines in the World: WHO (V), *Legal status of traditional medicine and complementary/alternative medicine – A World overview*, WHO, 2001, Geneva.

We have attempted to gather the same type of information for all the countries studied in this research, in order to obtain the most accurate comparison possible between them. However, the means and time we had at our disposal limited our ability to present a complete picture. Thus, the information that is provided must be treated with caution as the only data that we could gather and control was up to and including October 1, 2001. However, updates have been made with regard to the evolution until October 2004, especially for Switzerland and the US.[4]

The consistency of the law in the field of alternative medicines varies widely. Sometimes, there is a considerable difference between theory ("the law in the books") and practice ("the law in action"). The legal situation may also quickly change. Although we have tried to provide the most realistic image for each country, some gaps may still exist. We have tried to remain as objective as possible, and to this end, we have avoided taking any of the partisan positions so common in this field which have the effect of limiting the scope of the discussion.

The analysis made in the second part of this study is mainly based on the facts presented in the first part. We have avoided making, wherever possible, cross-references between the first and second parts of this study in order to render the text more fluid. Readers may refer to the relevant section in part 1 if they need the complete information on the facts presented. For ease of reference, an index has been placed at the end of the study, with a glossary containing the main terms employed. Bibliographies for each chapter or section have also been included, to which the footnotes refer.

4 In order to have access to international legislation, go to http://www.who.int/idhl. To have access to Swiss legislation, go to http://www.admin.ch/ch/f/as/index.html, all accessed February 1, 2005.

Part I

The Current Position of Alternative Medicines in Western Countries

1. Concepts and Definitions

Bibliography

ANDERSEN J. O., *Health seeking in pluralistic health care systems*, in: JOHANNESSEN H. (co-authors: LAUNSO L., OLESEN S. G., STAUGARD F.) (I), *Studies in alternative therapy 1 – Contributions from the Nordic countries*, Odense University Press, 1994, Gylling: 114–25; ANGELL M. (co-author: KASSIRER J. P.), *Alternative medicine – The risks of untested and unregulated medicine*, in: New England Journal of Medicine, 1998, vol. 339, n° 12: 839–41; BENFELD H. (co-author: KORNGOLD E.), *Between heaven and earth: A guide to Chinese medicine*, Ballantine Books, 1991, New York; BERNER D., *L'exercice illégal de la médecine ou les problèmes juridiques posés par les médecines parallèles*, in: *Aspects du droit médical*, Editions universitaires, 1988, Fribourg: 155–58; BORGHI M. (co-editor: GASSMAN J.), *Thérapies complémentaires ou alternatives en psychiatrie: Un défi? Un droit?*, Schriftenreihe der Schweizerischen Stiftung Pro Mente Sana n° 20, 1999, Zürich; BOUCHAYER F., *Alternative medicines: A general approach to the French situation*, in: LEWITH G., *Complementary medicine and the European Community*, CW Daniel, 1991, Saffron Walden: 45–48; BRITISH MEDICAL ASSOCIATION (LAMONT T.), *Complementary medicine – New approaches to good practice*, Oxford University Press, 1993, Oxford/New York: 5–8; COHEN M. H. (I), *Complementary and alternative medicine – Legal boundaries and regulatory perspectives*, The Johns Hopkins University Press, 1998, London & Oxford; CREMONINI D., *La salute nelle diverse tradizioni mediche*, in: BORGHI M., *op. cit.*: 37–41; DITTMANN V., *Schulmedizin und Alternativmedizin – unüberbrückbare Gegensätze?*, in: BAUHOFER S. (co-editors: BOLLE P.-H., DITTMANN V.), *Sectes et occultisme – Aspects criminologiques*, Verlag Rüegger, 1996, Zürich: 333–49; DONDEN Y., *Health through balance: An introduction to Tibetan medicine*, Snow Lion, 1986, New York; EISENBERG D. M. and co-authors (I), *Trends in alternative medicine use in the United States, 1990–1997*, in: JAMA, 1998, vol. 280, n° 18: 1569–75; DOSSEY L. (co-author: SWYFERS J. P.), in: *Alternative medicine: Expanding horizons,* NIH publication n° 94–066, 1994: XXXIX–XLI; ESKINAZI D. P., *Factors that shape alternative medicine*, in: JAMA, 1998, vol. 280, n° 18: 1621–23; FEUARDENT R., *Qu'entend-on par médecines alternatives?*, in: RMSR, 1986, vol. 106: 93–95; FREUDENBERG U., *Der Leitstungsanspruch bei alternativen Heilmethoden gegenüber der gesetzlichen Krankenversicherung, der privaten Krankenversicherung und der Beihilfe*, Dissertation, 1994, Bonn: 4–8; GRUNWALD D., *Pratiques médicales non éprouvées*, Session de l'Ordre des médecins, September 1997, Paris; GRUPP K., *Rechtliche Probleme alternativer Behandlungsmethoden*, in: MedR, 1992, vol. 5: 256–57; GUILLOD O., *Rebouteux, naturopathes et guérisseurs: Pour un traitement légal alternatif*, Recueil de Jurisprudence Neuchâtelois, 1989, Neuchâtel: 7–12; HARALDSSON E. (I), *Research on alternative therapies in Iceland*, in: JOHANNESSEN H. (co-authors: LAUNSO L., OLESEN S. G., STAUGARD F.) (I), *Studies in alternative therapy 1 –*

Contributions from the Nordic countries, Odense University Press, 1994, Gylling: 46–50; HARALDSSON E. (II), *Spiritual healing in Iceland*, in: JOHANNESSEN H. (co-authors: LAUNSO L., OLESEN S. G., STAUGARD F.) (I), *Studies in alternative therapy 1 – Contributions from the Nordic countries*, Odense University Press, 1994, Gylling: 103–13; HERNESNIEMI A., *Co-work between a medical doctor and a traditional healer*, in: JOHANNESSEN H. (co-authors: LAUNSO L., OLESEN S. G., STAUGARD F.) (I), *Studies in alternative therapy 1 – Contributions from the Nordic countries*, Odense University Press, 1994, Gylling: 126–38; HEUSSER P., *Kriterien zur Beurteilung des Nutzens von komplementärmedizinischen Methoden*, Bundesamt für Sozialversicherung, Mar. 1998, Bern: 3–4; HILL A., *A visual encyclopaedia of unconventional medicine*, Crown publishers inc, 1974, New York; JOHANNESSEN H. (co-authors: LAUNSO L., OLESEN S. G., STAUGARD F.) (I), *Studies in alternative therapy 1 – Contributions from the Nordic countries*, Odense University Press, 1994, Gylling; JOHANNESSEN H. (II), *Alternative therapies as social cultural and therapeutic phenomena*, in: JOHANNESSEN H. and co-authors (I), *op. cit.*: 13–23; KUHN T. S., *La structure des révolutions scientifiques*, Flammarion, 1983, Manchecourt; KÜNZI M., *Komplementärmedizin und Gesundheitsrecht*, Helbing & Lichtenhahn Verlag AG, 1996, Basel: 1–13; LAPLANTINE F. (co-author: RABEYRON P.-L.), *Les médecines parallèles*, PUF, collection Que sais-je?, 1987, Paris; LEWITH G. (co-author: ALDRIDGE D.), *Complementary medicine and the European Community*, Saffron Walden, CW Daniel, 1991; Merriam-Webster's Collegiate Dictionary, 10th ed., Meriam-Webster, 1993, Springfield; MICOZZI M. S. (ed.), *Fundamentals of alternative medicine*, Churchill Livingstone, 1996, New York; MINISTRY OF HEALTH AND SOCIAL AFFAIRS, *Report on alternative medicine – English summary*, Norges Offentliche Utredniger NOU 1998: 21, 1998, Oslo: 266; NATIONAL INSTITUTES OF HEALTH, OFFICE OF ALTERNATIVE MEDICINE, *Alternative medicine: Expanding medical horizons: A report to the MH on alternative medical systems and practices in the United States*, National Institutes of Health, Office of Alternative Medicine, 1995, Washington; O'CONNOR B. B. and co-authors, *Defining and describing complementary and alternative medicine*, in: Alternative Therapies, Mar. 1997, vol. 3, n° 2: 49–57; OMS, *Médecine traditionnelle et couverture des soins de santé*, OMS, Genève, 1983; *The Oxford English Dictionary*, 2nd ed., Clarendon Press, 1989, Oxford; PÉNTEK M., *Die Leistungspflicht der Gesetzlichen Krankenversicherung bei der Anwendung von Aussenseitermethoden in der Medizin*, Dissertation, 1996, Konstanz: 11–26; ROBARD I., *La santé hors la loi: Les hors la loi de la santé*, 4th ed., Ed. de l'Ancre, 1994, Suresnes: 8–9; RÖSCH B., *Die Stellung der Erfahrungsheilkundigen aus verfassungs- und verwaltungsrechtlicher Sicht, dargestellt am Beispiel der geistig Heilenden*, Helbing & Lichtenhahn Verlag AG, 1994, Basel: 1–63; ROSSI I. (I), *Médecine, médecines: Parallélisme ou complémentarité*, in: CMS, 1996, vol. 40: 17–24; ROSSI I. (II), *Pluralisme médical: Les enjeux des corps possibles*, in: CMS, 1995, vol. 39: 25–31; SALE D. M., *Overview of legislative developments concerning alternative health care in the United States*, 1995: iii; SALMON J. W. (eds), *Alternative medicines – Popular and policy perspectives*, Tavistock Publications, 1984, New York; SELECT COMMITTEE ON SCIENCE AND TECHNOLOGY, *Complementary and alternative medicine*, House of Lords – Session 1999–2000 6th Report, The Stationary Office, 2000, London: 11, 22–23; SHAPIRO A. K. (co-author: SHAPIRO E.),

The powerful placebo – From ancient priest to modern physician, The Johns Hopkins University Press, 1997, Baltimore/London: 43–73; STAUGARD F. (I), *Introduction*, in: JOHANNESSEN H. and co-authors (I), *op. cit.*: 27–29; STONE J. (co-author: MATTHEWS J.), *Complementary medicine and the law*, Oxford University Press, 1996, Oxford: 87–90, 244; THOMAS K. J. (I), *Non-orthodox health care in the UK*, in: LEWITH G., *op. cit.*: 125–27; THOMAS R. W. (II), *Evidence for an energy model-based paradigm for health and healing – Two examples*, in: JOHANNESSEN H. and co-authors (I), *op. cit.*: 240–52; VISSER G. J., *Alternative medicine in the Netherlands*, in: LEWITH G., *op. cit.*: 114–15; WARDWELL W. I., *Alternative medicine in the United States*, in: Social Science and Medicine, 1994, vol. 38, n° 8: 1061–68; WHO REGIONAL OFFICE FOR AFRICA, *African traditional medicine: Report of an expert group*, WHO, AFRO Technical Report Series, n° 1, 1976, Brazzaville; WICKI M., *Komplementärmedizin im Rahmen des Rechtes*, Dissertation, Stämpfli, 1998, Bern: 204–07; WISE T. A., *Origin and history of medicine*, in: WISE T. A., *The Hindu system of medicine*, Mittal Publications, 1986, New Delhi.

There have already been several publications discussing the etymology and providing a definition and description of alternative medicines and alternative practitioners. The purpose of this chapter is not to provide an exhaustive summary of these studies but rather to provide the reader with the necessary concepts in order that the set up problems analysed in this research may be fully understood.

First, the basic concepts underlying the development of medicine, biomedicine and alternative medicine will be explained. Second, a definition of alternative medicine will be given. Finally, attention will be focused on the distinction between the various providers of alternative medicines.

1.1 Basic Concepts: Medicine, Biomedicine and Alternative Medicine

The Oxford English Dictionary defines medicine as being

> that department of knowledge and practice which is concerned with the cure, alleviation, and prevention of disease in human beings, and with the restoration and preservation of health. Also, in a more restricted sense, applied to that branch of this department which is the province of the physician, in the modern application of the term: the art of restoring and preserving the health of human beings by the administration of remedial substances and the regulation of diet, habits, and conditions of life; distinguished from surgery and obstetrics.[1]

As this definition suggests, the term "medicine" has two meanings. In its more restrictive sense, the definition is limited to the medicine provided by an academic doctor in the course of medical treatment, such medicine being termed "biomedicine", "evidence-based-medicine",[2] or "allopathy".[3] In its broader sense medicine is a holistic whole including both "biomedicine" and "alternative medicines".[4]

Biomedicine is based on materialism, being the theory that "physical matter is the only or fundamental reality, and that all beings and processes and phenomena are manifestations or results of matter".[5] According to the biomedical paradigm,[6] biological entities are considered more or less equal to the sum of their anatomic parts (in opposition to holism) and this model endeavours to demonstrate the molecular, physiological and pathological mechanisms that form the structure of the biological processes. In this model, disease is viewed as a biochemical phenomenon that can be classified into diagnostic categories through scientific methods and, as such,

1 *The Oxford English Dictionary*, *op. cit.*
For a definition of "Health" and "Illness" in Swiss law and according to the World Health Organisation, see RÖSCH B., *op. cit.*: 28–31.
For an overview regarding the concept of "health" in several cultures, see CREMONINI D., *op. cit.*: 37–41.

2 In reference to double-blind testing or randomised controlled trials that are commonly used in clinical testing.

3 This term was employed by homeopaths to describe the ordinary medical practice.

4 O'CONNOR B. B., *op. cit.*: 51; RÖSCH B., *op. cit.*: 4. For the development of the concept of "integrated system of medicine", see chap. 8.2.

5 Merriam-Webster's Collegiate Dictionary, *op. cit.*

6 For the development of the notion of "paradigm", see COHEN M. H. (I), *op. cit.*: 2–3; KUHN T. S., *op. cit.*; WICKI M., *op. cit.*: 204–07. See also chap. 8.3.2.

it is treated according to standardised, objectively validated mechanisms, which interfere with identified pathological molecular processes.[7]

The term "biomedicine" has been extended so as to define the dominant medical system in Western countries. Such dominance may be explained by its

> reputation for efficacy and broad cultural authority as well as dominant (or perhaps even exclusive) access to legislative and social institutional supports such as medical practice laws, legally recognised accreditation and rights of self-regulation, third-party payment, privileged access to public research monies and to prestigious publication venues, high status, and so forth.[8]

The term "alternative medicine(s)" usually includes all medical care methods, which do not depend on biomedicine. They may be used for diagnosis (e.g., iridology, chirology), therapy (e.g., phytotherapy, mesotherapy), or both (e.g., acupuncture, reflexology, homeopathy, osteopathy, chiropractic).[9] Some alternative techniques are also used in psychiatry.[10]

Various terms have been used to describe these techniques, the most common being "complementary" and/or "alternative".[11] The term "alternative medicine", has been chosen as it is more representative of the status of these techniques within Western heath care systems. Indeed, as Eskinazi notes, "the origin of a practice may be alternative (e.g., culturally or economically different), while its use can be complementary with biomedicine (or other alternative therapies)".[12]

7 The biomedical model became prominent in the late nineteenth century, when Newtonian physics and Cartesian philosophy dominated the intellectual world.

8 O'CONNOR B. B., *op. cit.*: 51.

9 As there are innumerable alternative medicines, the decision was made to focus on the most widespread and teachable methods. The intention was not to include "magical" techniques or therapies requiring supernatural forces. However, they are sometimes mentioned. One must be aware that several alternative treatments have been considered or still are considered as being quackery. The importance of religious treatment is also not to be underestimated. For a useful discussion on this subject, see SHAPIRO A. K., *op. cit.*: 43ss.
For a description of the most common used techniques, see the glossary at the end of the book.

10 For studies on the subject, see BORGHI M., *op. cit.*

11 They are also defined as "natural", "non-allopathic", "unconventional", "non-orthodox", etc. Sometimes the term "traditional" is also employed. As it has a cultural component and is linked with the medical history of countries, it may design biomedicine as well as alternative medicine.

12 ESKINAZI D. P., *op. cit.*: 1622.
Some authors use a combination of terms, such as "alternative and complementary" suggesting that these techniques may be used as a substitute for biomedical

Alternative techniques may be comprised of either a single consistent technique (such as chiropractic), or a comprehensive medical system that includes several techniques (such as naturopathy,[13] or traditional Chinese medicine). Some similarities may be observed.[14]

First, these techniques represent a philosophical approach to managing health and disease that differs from that of Western biomedicine.[15] For example, spirituality usually plays an important role.[16, 17]

Second, the primary explanation for biological phenomena is often based on the existence of a "vital energy".[18] This concept must be

---

care or in combination with biomedicine (Cohen M. H. (I), *op.cit.*: xii–xiii; O'connor B. B., *op. cit*: 51).
On the subject, see also, e.g., Bouchayer F., *op.cit.*: 47–48; British Medical Association, *op.cit.*: 5–8; Eskinazi D. P., *op.cit.*: 1622; O'connor B. B., *op.cit.*: 51–53; Robard I., *op.cit.*: 8–9; Rösch B., *op.cit.*: 35–37; Rossi I. (I), *op.cit.*: 17–24; Rossi I. (II), *op.cit.*: 25–26; Thomas K. J. (I), *op.cit.*: 125–27.

13 Like homoeopathy, naturopathy holds that the best therapy consists of mobilising the body's capacity to heal itself. Naturopaths stress that a major cause of illness is imbalance within the body especially the accumulations of toxins. They use a range of therapeutic programmes, not only dietary adjustment and fasting, but hydrotherapy and exercise regimes as well.

14 For a presentation of the parameters used to describe alternative systems, see Dossey L., *op.cit.*: XXXIX–XLI; O'connor B. B., *op.cit.*: 53–56. See also Heusser P., *op.cit.*: 3–4; Stone J., *op.cit.*: 87–89. For a presentation of an alternative medicine such as Ayurveda, see Patel V., *op.cit.*: 61–65.

15 However, some authors are of the opinion that alternative medicines "have a diagnostic, investigative and therapeutic understanding which share some similarities with orthodox medicine" (Stone J., *op.cit.*: 87).
For a discussion regarding the relationship and the differences between the biomedical and holistic healing paradigm, see Cohen M. H. (I), *op.cit.*: 1–8; Hernesniemi A., *op.cit.*: 126–38; Rossi I. (I), *op.cit.*: 17–24; Rossi I. (II), *op.cit.*: 25–31; Staugard F. (I), *op.cit.*: 27–29. See also chap. 8.3.2.

16 E.g., several spiritual schools influenced the ancient Chinese medical system, in particular, Taoism. Similarly, the Traditional Hindu world view has influenced the Ayurveda, which is the traditional Indian medical system. Buddhist meditation is an integral part of the training of Tibetan physicians.

17 Andersen J. O., *op.cit.*: 114–25; Benfeld H., *op.cit.*; Bouchayer F., *op.cit.*: 47–48; Donden Y., *op.cit.*; Eskinazi D. P., *op.cit.*: 1621; Haraldsson E. (I), *op.cit.*: 46–50; Haraldsson E. (II), *op.cit.*: 103–13; Hill A., *op.cit.*; Micozzi M. S. (ed.), *op.cit.*; National Institutes of Health, Office of Alternative Medicine, *op.cit.*; OMS, *op.cit.*; Rösch B., *op.cit.*: 22–23, 47–59; Select Committee on Science and Technology, *op.cit.*: 22–23; Stone J., *op.cit.*: 87–90; Wardwell W. I., *op.cit.*; Wise T. A., *op.cit.*

18 "Qi" in China, "Ki" in Korea, "prana" in India, and "vital forces" in Western countries.

approached with care, however, as no empirical evidence exists as to the nature of this "energy".[19]

Finally, holism is common to most alternative techniques. It implies a belief in the unity underlying all diversity in that no one thing can be considered in isolation. This principle leads towards the consideration of the individual as an indivisible whole rather than as separated, anatomic parts.[20] Furthermore, a proper interaction with the environment is supposed to influence the maintenance of health. Disease is viewed as having multiple causes (biological, environmental, psychological, and social). Thus, therapeutic interventions include stimuli (e.g., colour, taste and sound) for any of the five senses which interrelate the individual with his or her environment including, among others, intervention on multiple levels through pharmaceutical, individual or family counselling, support groups, nutrition, exercise and relaxation techniques.[21] On the same basis, means of communication with the "invisible" environment form an integral part of the therapeutic approach, for example the use of meditation or prayer.[22]

Given that biomedicine and alternative medicines are based on such different philosophical approaches, the latter is predictably not usually (well) recognised in Western countries. Indeed, they are usually not able to satisfy classic scientific standards.[23] As a result, supporters of alternative medicines must face the scepticism and antagonism of Western biomedicine supporters and, in particular, medical doctors.[24]

19 ESKINAZI D. P., *op. cit.*: 1621. For a scientific discussion regarding the energy phenomenon, see THOMAS R. W. (II), *op. cit.*: 240–52.

20 As an author notes, "a whole is more that the sum of its parts because the whole is not purely mechanical but has inner tendencies and interrelationships between the parts which give rise to something 'more'" (COHEN M. H. (I), *op. cit.*: 7).

21 Some therapies emphasise the body's self-healing capacity, which is stimulated to regain anatomical and functional integrity. Thus, disease is seen as a weakening of the body's own healing proporties rather than as a colonisation by bacteria or virus. Development of disease from an acute to a chronic phase is seen as a gradual weakening of the self-healing power.

22 COHEN M. H. (I), *op. cit.*: 3–8; ESKINAZI D. P., *op. cit.*: 1621; MINISTRY OF HEALTH AND SOCIAL AFFAIRS, *op. cit.*: 266; RÖSCH B., *op. cit.*: 23; SELECT COMMITTEE ON SCIENCE AND TECHNOLOGY, *op. cit.*: 22; THOMAS K. J. (I), *op. cit.*: 126–27.

23 For that reason, some authors define alternative medicines in contradiction to biomedicine (see below).

24 For developments regarding research in alternative medicines, see chap. 3.2, and for developments regarding scientific evaluation, see chap. 6.3. See also, e.g., COHEN M. H. (I), *op. cit.*: 10–13.

In respect of widely taught and used therapies such as chiropractic, osteopathy or hypnotism there is still little consensus as to whether these techniques are alternative, complementary or mainstream.[25] Indeed, in some Western countries, alternative medicines have been granted official status and are currently included in mainstream medicine. For example, chiropractic, in the USA, in Scandinavian countries and in Switzerland, is a well-organised profession with recognised training, licences to practise, extensive coverage and good relationship with physicians.[26] Therefore, one could consider chiropractic as no longer being an "alternative".[27] However, as this research is conducted from a comparative perspective and since these techniques are still not integrated in primary health care services in all Western countries (at least for the moment), they shall be considered and treated as "alternative".

25 Bouchayer F., *op. cit.*: 47–48; Cohen M. H. (I), *op. cit.*: 4–5; Eskinazi D. P., *op. cit.*: 1621; Künzi M., *op. cit.*: 1–13; Office of Alternative Medicine home page, *What is CAM?*, available at: http:nccam.nih.gov/nccam, accessed Oct. 1 2001; OMS, *op. cit.*: 245; Péntek M., *op. cit.*: 11–26; Rosenthal Center for Complementary and Alternative Medicine, *Information Sheet: What is alternative medicine?*, available at: http://www.rosenthal.hs.columbia.edu/, accessed Sept. 1 2001; Rösch B., *op. cit.*: 3; Wardwell W. I., *op. cit.*

26 E.g., in Switzerland, chiropractic has the same status as other biomedical professions. In fact, the technique will be included in the proposed Federal Act Regulating the Exercise of the Professions of Physicians, Pharmacists, Veterinarians, and Chiropractors. For more details, see chap. 4.3.6.1.

27 E.g., the American Chiropractic Association states that: "we do not wish to belittle any other professions that will come under study at the Office of Alternative Medicine. While some have and others will doubtlessly make significant contributions to human health, as a group they have not yet reached the level of broad acceptance achieved by the chiropractic profession. Considering the fact that 19 million patients visit D.C.s yearly, that 85% of major employers cover chiropractic services under their employer health plans and that most major federal, state and commercial health care programs cover chiropractic services, it becomes clear that chiropractic does not belong in the same category as these other professions" (cited in: Sale D. M., *op. cit.*: iii).
On that subject, see also, e.g., O'connor B. B., *op. cit.*: 52; Johannessen H. (II), *op. cit.*: 13–14; Wardwell W. I., *op. cit.*: 1065.

1.2 Definition of Alternative Medicine

It remains difficult to provide a clear definition of "alternative medicine". When definitions are proposed, they normally include either lists of practices felt to be complementary or alternative or consists of categorical criteria that may be subject to change. Therefore, such definitions do not allow for a lasting definition of alternative medicine.[28]

Lists of alternative medicines are generally disparate and often include complex traditional medical systems,[29] as well as their components provided as distinct entities.[30] Usually, a wide variety of discrete modalities and other products more difficult to categorize are also included in these lists.[31]

Alternative medicines are also often defined in a negative way. For example, they gather techniques that are not taught in medical schools, not covered by insurance, not available in hospitals, not scientifically proven, or not allowed.[32] However, these reference criteria are not only changing

28 For an interesting study on this question, see Cohen M. H. (I), *op. cit.*: xii–xiii; Eskinazi D. P., *op. cit.*; Hill A., *op. cit.*; Johannessen H. and co-authors (I), *op. cit.*; Laplantine F., *op. cit.*; Péntek M., *op. cit.*: 11–26; Salmon J. W., *op. cit.*; Select Committee on Science and Technology, *op. cit.*: 11; Stone J., *op. cit.*: 87–89; Wardwell W. I., *op. cit.*

29 Such as Chinese (traditional Chinese medicine), Indian (Ayurveda), or Native American.

30 E.g., acupuncture, medicinal herbs, dietary principles, and spiritual practices.

31 Micozzi M. S., *op. cit.*; National Institutes of Health, Office of Alternative Medicine, *op. cit.*

32 E.g., Angell M., *op. cit.*: 839–41 ("Untested and unregulated medicine"); Grunwald D., *op. cit.* ("unproven medical practices"); Freudenberg U., *op. cit.*: 7 ("Alle auf einem rationalen, intersubjektiv nachvollziehbaren Erklärungsansatz beruhenden diagnostischen und therapeutischen Verfahren, deren Wirksamkeit zwar von der herrschenden wissenschaftlichen Auffassung bezweifelt wird, deren Unwirksamkeit oder gar Schädlichkeit aber nicht nachgewiesen"). Similarly, the US Oregon statute describes alternative medicine as techniques "that the treating physician, based on the physician's professional experience, has an objective basis to believe has a reasonable probability for effectiveness in its intended use even if the treatment is outside recognised scientific guidelines, is unproven, is no longer used as a generally recognised or standard treatment or lacks the approval of the United States Food and Drug Administration; [as long as that therapy] [...] is supported for specific usage or outcomes by at least one other physician licensed by the Board of Medical Examiners [...]" (Or. Rev. Stat. § 677.190 (1)(b)(A)).

rapidly but also remain inconsistent and are across Western countries. For example, medical schools in several countries offer courses in alternative medicine.[33] Similarly, the coverage of alternative medicines as well as the availability of alternative medicines in hospitals also varies widely.[34] Perhaps for that reason, some authors define alternative medicines as the techniques, which are not widely available in hospitals and are not widely taught in medical schools.[35]

In this research, it is proposed that the definition of alternative medicines suggested by Eskinazi be adopted, namely

> a broad set of heath care practices (i.e., already available to the public) that are not readily integrated into the dominant health care model, because they pose challenges to diverse societal beliefs and practices (cultural, economic, scientific, medical, and educational).[36]

The author characterises some elements of the definition as being:

1. cultural: the technique or medical system may have been developed outside the mainstream Western culture and, as a consequence, may not be consonant with its cultural values;
2. economic: the technique or medical system tends to be developed by private practitioners, bypassing established economic networks (such as pharmaceutical industry, research institutions, and hospitals) and there are difficulties going through the path generally required to achieve acceptance in conventional medical practice;

33 E.g., in Austria, France, Switzerland, United States. For more details, see chap. 3.3.

34 For more details, see chap. 5.

35 Bouchayer F., *op. cit.*: 47–48; British Medical Association, *op. cit.*: 7–8; Dittmann V., *op. cit.*; Eisenberg D. M. (I), *op. cit.*: 1569; Eskinazi D. P., *op. cit.*: 1621; Feuardent R., *op. cit.*: 93; Freudenberg U., *op. cit.*; Grupp K., *op. cit.*: 256–57; Guillod O., *op. cit.*: 7–9; Péntek M., *op. cit.*: 11–26; Rösch B., *op. cit.*: 33–44; Visser G. J., *op. cit.*: 114.

36 Eskinazi D. P., *op. cit.*: 1621. Another good definition was provided by a Panel on Definition and Description which met in April 1995, at the Office of Alternative Medicine of the National Institutes of Health: "Complementary and alternative medicine (CAM) is a broad domain of healing resources that encompasses all health systems, modalities, and practices and their accompanying theories and beliefs, other than those intrinsic to the politically dominant health system of a particular society or culture in a given historical period. CAM includes all such practices and ideas self-defined by their users as preventing or treating illness or promoting health and well-being. Boundaries within CAM and between the CAM domain of the dominant system are not always sharp of fixed" (O'connor B. B., *op. cit.*: 50). See also Select Committee on Science and Technology, *op. cit.*: 11.

3. scientific beliefs: there is no scientific explanation for how some techniques (for example, homeopathy or Reiki) could possibly work. The lack of research data is most likely due to such techniques being alternative;
4. medical: the technique or medical system often focuses on the preventive and therapeutic enhancement of existing biological mechanisms, rather than on following the allopathic model;
5. educational standards: the technique or medical system is passed on from generation to generation primarily through oral tradition rather than through classic training at a specific school.

The advantage of this definition is that, unlike other current definitions, it remains valid as long as deep societal changes do not occur. Furthermore, it encompasses all kinds of alternative medicine no matter the actual level of integration of these techniques into Western health care systems. Therefore, as soon as a technique "poses challenges" to one of the elements of the definition (cultural, economic, scientific, medical, or educational), it should be considered as alternative.[37]

An additional problem that arises when defining alternative medicines is the determination of when an act (or a health care practice) can be classified as medical. In other words, what is the boundary between medicine (or therapeutic practice) and lifestyle practice.[38] As it is particularly difficult to find objective criteria in order to make this distinction, authors usually circumvent the difficulty by using subjective criteria.[39] This problem will not be addressed here. However, the definition proposed by Eskinazi is sufficient for the purpose of this research whilst being aware that all definitions of alternative medicines remain unclear as to their ambit.

37 ESKINAZI D. P., *op. cit.*: 1622; O'CONNOR B. B., *op. cit.*: 52.

38 See STONE J., *op. cit.*: 244 (on the question as to whether relaxation or advice to take herbal preparations be considered medical acts).

39 E.g., according to O'Connor "the definition addresses the issue of the boundary between medicine or therapeutic practice and lifestyle with respect to complementary and alternative medicine by specifying that the domain includes all actions and choices 'self-defined by their users as preventing or treating illness or promoting health and well-being'. It follows from this formulation that the distinction is not a constant, but rather a situation-specific determination that necessarily involves the intentions of the person taking the action" (O'CONNOR B. B., *op. cit.*: 53).

1.3 Alternative Practitioner

Providers of alternative medicines are generally called "alternative practitioners". The various distinctions between alternative practitioners are set forth below:[40]

1. "alternative physicians", i.e. medical doctors (with a PhD in academic (bio-) medicine) who use alternative medicine with or without additional training in alternative medicine;
2. "alternative ancillary practitioners", i.e. ancillary staff (nurses, physician assistants, physiotherapists, etc.) with a biomedical training, usually working under the instructions of a doctor in medicine, and using alternative medicine with or without an additional training in alternative medicine;[41]
3. "non-allopathic practitioners", i.e. providers of alternative medicines, who have not attended a biomedical training and who have undergone, or not, a training in alternative medicine. In order to provide a consistent definition, a health care practitioner without biomedical training shall be considered a "non-allopathic practitioner" as soon as he or she provides an "alternative medicine" under the above adopted definition.[42] This remains true even if the profession itself has already gained a certain degree of incorporation into the national health system.

   This category includes practitioners who have solely a training in alternative medicines provided by a school (chiropractors, osteopaths, acupuncturists, homeopaths, etc.), and "traditional practitioners" (or "folk healers", "magical healers"), who performed a traditional apprenticeship under a practitioner or who have a natural talent.[43]

40 For a different categorisation of non-allopathic practitioners and a historical study regarding the terms employed to define alternative practitioners since the 18th century, see WARDWELL W. I., *op. cit.*

41 Berner defines paramedical professionals as medical practitioners whose practice is limited as to the techniques they may use or as to the illnesses they may treat (BERNER D., *op. cit.*: 155–56).

42 See above, chap. 1.2.

43 The term "traditional practitioner" must be understood as "a person who is recognised by the community in which he lives as competent to provide health care by using vegetable, animal and mineral substances and certain other methods based on the social, cultural and religious background as well as on the knowledge, attitudes and beliefs that are prevalent in the community regarding physical, mental and social well-being and the causation of disease and disability" (WHO REGIONAL OFFICE FOR AFRICA, *op. cit.*: 4). For a discussion of the last category of traditional healers, see OMS, *op. cit.*; WARDWELL W. I., *op. cit.*

2. The Extent of Alternative Medicines

Bibliography

See ALDRIDGE D. (I), *Unconventional medicine in Europe*, Advances, 1994, vol. 10, n° 2: 55–56; ALDRIDGE D. (II), *Pluralism of medical practice in Germany*, in: LEWITH G. (co-editor: ALDRIDGE D.), *Alternative medicine and the European Community*, CW Daniel, 1991, Saffron Walden: 75–83; ANDREWS L. B., *The shadow health care system: Regulation of alternative health care providers*, in: Houston Law Review, 1996, vol. 32: 1276, 1280, 1312; ASTIN J. A., *Why patients use alternative medicine – Results of a national study*, in: JAMA, 1998, vol. 279, n° 19: 1548–53; BERMAN B. M. and co-authors, *Physicians' attitudes toward complementary or alternative medicine: A regional survey*, in: J. Am. Board Fam. Prac., 1995, vol. 8: 361ss; BETTSCHART R. (co-authors: GLAESKE G., LANGBEIN K., SALLER R., SKALNIK C.), *Bittere Naturmedizin – Wirkung und Bewertung der alternativen Behandlungsmethoden, Diagnoseverfahren und Artzneimittelrecht*, Kieper & Witsch, 1995, Köln: 15–17; BOOZANG K. M., *Western medicine opens the door to alternative medicine*, in: American Journal of Medicine, 1998, vol. 24, n° 2/3: 185–212; BORCHGREVINK C. F., *Alternative medicine in Norway*, in: JOHANNESSEN H. (co-authors: LAUNSO L., OLESEN S. G., STAUGARD F.) (I), *Studies in alternative therapy 1 – Contributions from the Nordic countries*, Odense University Press, 1994, Gylling: 51; BOUCHAYER F., *Alternative medicines: A general approach to the French situation*, in: LEWITH G. (co-ed.: ALDRIDGE D.), *Alternative medicine and the European Community*, CW Daniel, 1991, Saffron Walden: 45–55; BRITISH MEDICAL ASSOCIATION (LAMONT T.), *Complementary medicine – New approaches to good practice*, Oxford University Press, 1993, Oxford/New York; BUDD S. (co-author: MILLS S.), *Professional organisation of complementary and alternative medicine in the UK 2000: A second report to the Department of Health*, University of Exeter, 2000, London; BURG M. A. and co-authors, *Personal use of alternative medicine therapies by health science center faculty*, in JAMA, 1998, n° 280: 1563; BÜRGI M. (co-authors: SOMMER J. H., JÜRG H. et THEISS R.), *Alternative Heilmethoden – Verbreitung in der Schweiz*, Verlag Rüegger; 1996, Zürich; CMS, vol. 40, n° 1, 1996, *Médecines plurielles*; CARTER J. P., *Racketeering in medicine – The suppression of alternatives*, Hampton Roads Publishing Co., 1993, Norfolk: 234–45; COHEN M. H. (I), *Complementary and alternative medicine – Legal boundaries and regulatory perspectives*, The Johns Hopkins University Press, 1998, London & Oxford: 2–3, 67; CONFÉRENCE DES DIRECTEURS CANTONAUX DES AFFAIRES SANITAIRES (I), *Rapport du groupe de travail "Autorisations de pratiquer les professions du domaine de la santé"*, CDS, 2000, Bern, available at: http://www.sdk-cds.ch/fr/berufsbildung-f.html: 22, accessed Feb. 1 2005; COST ACTION B4, *COST action B4 unconventional medicine – Final report of the management committee, 1993–1998*, European Communities, 1998, Luxembourg: 18–22; CRAMER R., *Strafrechtliche Grenzen der Therapiefreiheit und der Heilbehandlung durch den Heilpraktiker*; Dissertation, 1995, Köln: 11–12; DAGUET R., *Per una cura integrata: Riflessioni su medicina moderna e terapie alternative*, in: BORGHI M. (co-ed.: GASSMAN J.), *Thérapies complémentaires ou alternatives en psychiatrie: Un défi? Un droit?*, Schriftenreihe der Schweizerischen Stiftung Pro Mente Sana n° 20, 1999, Zürich: 15–21; DOMENIGHETTI G. (co-authors: GRILLI R., GUILLOD O., GUTZWILLER F., QUAGLIA J.), *Usage personnel de pratiques relevant des médecines douces ou alternatives parmi les médecins suisses*, in: Médecine et Hygiène, 2000, vol. 58, n° 2291: 570–72; DUTCH HEALTH COUNCIL, *Report on complementary therapies and research*, Dutch Health Care Council, 1993, The Hague; EHLERS A. P. F., *Medizin in den Händen von Heilpraktikern – "Nicht-Heilkundigen"*, Springer Verlag, 1995, Berlin/Heidelberg: 29–40, 59–65; EISENBERG D. M. and co-authors (I), *Trends in alternative medicine use in the United States, 1990–1997*, in: JAMA, 1998, vol. 280, n° 18: 1569–75; EISENBERG D. M. and co-authors (II), *Unconventional medicine in the USA*, in: The New England Journal of Medicine, 1993, n° 328: 246–52; EKLÖF M. (co-author: TEGERN G.), *Stockholmare och den komplementära medicinen: Befolkningsstudie angaende inställning till och användning av komplementär medicin genomförd under ar 2000 i Stockholms läns landsting*, HSN rapport nr 12/00, Stockholm läns landsting, 2001, Stockholm; ERNST E. (co-author: WHITE A.) (II), *The BBC survey of complementary medicine use in the UK*, in: Complementary Therapies in Medicine, 2000, n° 8: 32–36; FEUARDENT R., *Qu'entend-on par médecines alternatives?*, in: RMSR, 1986, vol. 106: 93–95; FISHER P. (co-author: WARD A.), *Alternative medicine in Europe*, in: BMJ, vol. 309, July 7 1994: 107–11; FROST AND SULLIVAN Ltd, *Alternative medical practices in Europe*, Report n° E874, Sullivan House, Grosvenor Gardens, 1987, London SW1; GOLDBECK-WOOD S. and co-authors, *Alternative medicine is booming worldwide*, in BMJ: 1996, n° 313: 131–33; GROUPE DE RÉFLEXION "MÉDECINES DIFFÉRENTES", *Evaluer les médecines différentes, un défi? – Rapport aux ministres des affaires sociales et de la solidarité nationale et au secrétaire d'Etat chargé de la santé*, La documentation française, 1986, Paris: 20–21; GRUNWALD D., *Pratiques médicales non éprouvées*, session de l'Ordre des médecins, Sept. 1997, Paris; GUILLOD O., *Rebouteux, naturopathes et guérisseurs: Pour un traitement légal alternatif*, Recueil de Jurisprudence Neuchâtelois, 1989, Neuchâtel: 35–36; JOHANNESSEN H. (co-authors: LAUNSO L., OLESEN S. G., STAUGARD F.) (I), *Studies in alternative therapy 1 – Contributions from the Nordic countries*, Odense University Press, 1994, Gylling; JOHANNESSEN H. (III), *Research on alternative therapy in Denmark*, in: JOHANNESSEN H. and co-authors (I), *op. cit.*: 30–32; JUNG H. (co-author: NEUMANN J. N.), *Alternative Behandlungsmethoden*, in: ESER (co-authors: LUTTEROTTI, SPORKEN), *Lexikon Medizin – Ethik – Recht*, Freiburg, 1989: 48–63; LAPLANTINE F. (co-author: RABEYRON P.-L.), *Les médecines parallèles*, PUF, collection Que sais-je?, 1987, Paris: 3, 17–18, 45; LAUNSO L. (co-author: BRENDSTRUP E.) (I), *People choose alternative therapies – The consequence for future pharmacy practice*, in: Journal of Social and Administrative Pharmacy, 1995, vol. 12, n° 1: 46–49; LEMAL I., *Le succès des médecines parallèles prescrit une loi*, in: Le Soir, Jan. 23, 1998; LEWITH G. (co-author: ALDRIDGE D.), *Complementary medicine and the European Community*, Saffron Walden, CW Daniel, 1991; MACLENNAN A. H. (co-authors:

WILSON D. H., TAYLOR A. W.), *Prevalence and cost of alternative medicine in Australia*, in: Lancet, 1996, n° 347: 569–73; MELCHART D. (co-authors: LINDE K., WEIDENHAMMER W., WORKU F., WAGNER H.), *The integration of natural healing procedures into research and teaching at German universities*, in: Alternative Therapies, 1995, vol. 1, n° 1: 30; MILLAR W. J., *Use of alternative health care practitioners by Canadians*, in: Can J. Public Health, 1997, n° 88: 155–58; MINISTRY OF HEALTH AND SOCIAL AFFAIRS, *Report on alternative medicine – English summary*, Norges Offentliche Utredniger NOU 1998: 21, 1998, Oslo: 266; PORTELLI N., *Le délit d'exercice illégal de la médecine*, mémoire, 1994, France: 7; OSTENDORF G.-M., *Probleme der Alternativmedizin in der privaten Personenversicherung*, in: Versicherungsmedizin 47, 1995, n° 6: 224–31; RASMUSSEN N. (co-author: MORGALL J.), *The use of alternative treatments in the Danish population*, in: LEWITH G., *op. cit.*: 83–99; ROBARD I., *La santé hors la loi: Les hors-la-loi de la santé*, 4th ed., Ed. de l'Ancre, 1994, Suresnes; RÖSCH B., *Die Stellung der Erfahrungsheilkundigen aus verfassungs- und verwaltungsrechtlicher Sicht, dargestellt am Beispiel der geistig Heilenden*, Dissertation, Helbing & Lichtenhahn Verlag, 1994, Basel: 3–63; ROSSI I. (I), *Médecine, médecines: Parallélisme ou complémentarité?*, in: CMS, 1996, vol. 40: 17–24; ROSSI I. (II), *Pluralisme médical: Les enjeux des corps possibles*, in: CMS, 1995, vol. 39: 25–31; SAKS M. (I), *Alternative medicine in Britain*, Clarendon Press, 1992, Oxford; SAKS M. (II), *The changing response of the medical profession to alternative medicine in Britain: A case of altruism or self-interest?*, in: JOHNSON T. (co-authors: LARKIN G, SAKS M.), *Health professions and the State in Europe*, Routledge, 1995, London/New York: 103–15; SANGARE H. C., *Les déterminants de la demande des médecines alternative en Suisse*, IEMS, 2001, Lausanne; SANTOS-EGGIMANN B., *Le recours aux médecines non-conventionnelles en Suisse*, CMS, 1996, vol. 40: 11–16; SCHÄR A. (MESSERLI-ROHRBACH V., SCHUBART P.), *Schulmedizin oder Komplementärmedizin: Nach welchem Kriterien entscheiden sich die Patientinnen und Patienten?*, in: FREY F. (co-ed.: BAUMANN P. H.), *Supplementum 62, FNRS-PNR 34: Médecines complémentaires*, Schwabe, 1994, Basel: 18–27; SELECT COMMITTEE ON SCIENCE AND TECHNOLOGY, *Complementary and alternative medicine*, House of Lords – Session 1999–2000 6th Report, The Stationary Office, 2000, London; SERMEUS G., *Alternative health care in Belgium: An explanation of various social aspects*, in: LEWITH G., *op. cit.*: 61–74; SHARMA U., *Alternative medicine today; practitioners and patients*, Routledge, 1995, London; SWEDISH COMMISSION ON ALTERNATIVE MEDICINE, *Report on alternative medicine*, Regeringskansliet, 1989, Stockholm: 25–26; THOMAS K. J., *Non-orthodox health care in the UK*, in: LEWITH G., *op. cit.*: 125–34; VASKILAMPI T. (I), *The role of alternative medicine: The Finnish experience*, in: LEWITH G., *op. cit.*: 101–12; VASKILAMPI T. (II), *The role of alternative medicine: The Finnish experience*, in: Complementary Medical Research, 1990, vol. 4, n° 2; VISSER G. J. (co-author: PETERS C.) (II), *Alternative medicine and general practitioners in the Netherlands: Towards acceptance and integration*, in: Family Practice, 1990, vol. 7, n° 3: 227–32; WHITE HOUSE COMMISSION ON COMPLEMENTARY AND ALTERNATIVE MEDICINE POLICY, *Final report*, Mar. 2002, available at http://www.whccamp.hhs.gov/pdfs/fr2002_document.pdf, accessed Feb. 1 2005: 15–19; WHO (V), *Legal status of traditional medicine and complementary/alternative medicine – A World overview*, WHO, 2001, Geneva:

148–49; WIESENDANGER H., *Das grosse Buch vom geistigen Heilen*, Scherz Verlag, 1994, Bern/München/Wien: 340; WICKI M., *Komplementärmedizin im Rahmen des Rechtes*, Dissertation, Stämpfli, 1998, Bern: 36.

2.1 Introduction

In order to understand the set of problems linked with alternative medicines a knowledge of the sociological environment surrounding alternatives medicines is essential. The purpose of this chapter is to provide the reader with this necessary information.

To the best of our knowledge, a serious comparative study as to the extent of alternative medicines (world-wide or European) does not exist.[1] Therefore, the results of researches undertaken in several countries are presented which must be viewed with caution.[2] Indeed, the techniques used to gather, interpret and present the information vary widely from one study to another. Furthermore, the design, purpose, approach and context of each such research differ and, as such, may be questionable. The literature under review rarely refers to cultural and social aspects as possible factors. However, these studies do allow identification of the main trends and provide a general picture of the situation.

The extent of alternative medicines shall be presented under several categories, with a summary included at the beginning of each one. A comparative chart is also added to give a more schematic view.[3]

2.2 Rate of Use

The use of alternative medicines is no longer marginal in Western countries and, indeed, is increasing. Some techniques have been, at least to some extent, integrated into the medical tradition of various countries.

1 A limited comparative study has been done by the COST ACTION B4, *op. cit.*: 18–22; SHARMA U., *op. cit.*; and by GOLDBECK-WOOD S., *op. cit.*: 131–33.

2 Unfortunately, some of those were conducted in the 1980s without any recent updating.

3 For a presentation of the methodology employed during this research, see Methodoly and Warnings.

The recourse to alternative medicines is approximately equivalent in both monopolistic (i.e. having a hostile legal framework) and tolerant (i.e. legally open to these techniques) countries.[4]

According to a 1998 poll,[5] between 40% and 70% of the Belgian population had used alternative medicines at least once. According to another study, roughly 24% had used alternative medicines in the last twelve-month period preceding the study.[6]

In Denmark, alternative medicines have become an integrated part of the health care culture.[7] They are considered a legitimate form of treatment and only some groups of allopathic professionals consider alternative medicines as something they must compete with.[8]

A 1987 study showed that, during a twelve month period, between 10% and 20% of the population used one or more of these various treatments and almost one quarter of the population had used at least once one or more methods of alternative medicines.[9] According to a 1991 study, 37% of the population received alternative therapies either from an alternative practitioner, a chiropractor, or as a self-treatment. Even with the exclusion of chiropractic,[10] 25% of the population still used alternative therapies.[11] Another study conducted in 1994 showed that 33% of the adult population used alternative therapies in that same year.[12]

In Finland about 32% of the adult population used alternative medicines at least once.[13]

4 For the presentation of the existing general policies towards the regulation of alternative medicines, see chap. 4.2.
5 The study was undertaken by Market Analysis & Synthesis. It was ordered during the debate concerning the creation of a law on alternative medicines.
6 Lemal I., *op. cit.*; Sermeus G., *op. cit.*: 65–68.
7 Frost and Sullivan, *op. cit.*: 249; Johannessen H. (III), *op. cit.*: 31.
8 Aldridge D. (I), *op. cit.*: 55; Rasmussen N., *op. cit.*: 83.
9 In 1987, the Danish Institute for Clinical Epidemiology published the results of the first comprehensive national study on health and morbidity in the adult Danish population. For a complete summary of this study, see Johannessen H. (III), *op. cit.*: 30–32; Rasmussen N., *op. cit.*: 83–98.
10 In Denmark, chiropractors are not considered as alternative therapists but as conventional practitioners.
11 Launso L. (I), *op. cit.*: 46.
12 Danish Institute for Clinical Epidemiology (DIKE), 1995, Copenhagen.
13 Vaskilampi T. (I), *op. cit.*: 109–10 (contains a summary of the studies conducted in 1982).

In France, a 1985 survey people showed that 49% of the persons of the 1000 questioned used alternative medicines at least once and 16% had used them during the past twelve months.[14]

In Germany, a 1992 poll showed that between 20% and 30% of the population used alternative medicines at least once and between 5% and 12% had used them during the past year.[15] According to another source, 71% of the population had already had some experience of some form of alternative medicine.[16] In 1992, 20 million patients contacted alternative practitioners.[17]

In Great Britain, the transfer of patient care from allopathic practitioners to non-allopathic practitioners has always existed. However, it has increased during the last decades.[18] In 1982, the British Research Council on Alternative Medicines was formed in response to the increasing use of alternative medicines by the public, and the government's concern over their effectiveness.[19]

According to a survey conducted by the BBC in 1999, 20% of the British population used alternative medicines during that year.[20] That same year, up to 5 million patients consulted an alternative practitioner.[21] Prior studies had showed a lower use of between 8% and 10%.[22]

14 BOUCHAYER F., *op. cit.*: 45, 53; GROUPE DE RÉFLEXION, *op. cit.*: 20–21; LAPLANTINE F., *op. cit.*: 3; SHARMA U., *op. cit.*: 16.
15 EHLERS A. P. F., *op. cit.*: 33; SHARMA U., *op. cit.*: 17.
16 MELCHART D., *op. cit.*: 30.
17 CRAMER R., *op. cit.*: 11; WIESENDANGER H., *op. cit.*: 340.
18 For a sociological study regarding the change of attitude towards alternative medicines in Great Britain, see SAKS M. (I), *op. cit.*; SAKS M. (II), *op. cit.*: 103–15. For a discussion concerning the relationship between physicians and non-allopathic practitioners, see BRITISH MEDICAL ASSOCIATION, *op. cit.*: 38–39.
19 The British Research Council noted that allopathic medicine had made possible remarkable technological advances, and noticed the major role that alternative medicines may play to reduce the costs of the health care system.
The Council's achievements during its five years of activity were numerous and varied (twelve research projects in hospitals and universities, holding of seminars and conferences, production of various publications, the establishment of a Fellowship in Research Methodology at Glasgow University, etc.). Its final objective is to encourage the incorporation of alternative medicines in the mainstream of modern medical practice. The Council plans also research to investigate the efficacy of alternative medicines (CARTER J. P., *op. cit.*: 243, 245).
20 ERNST E. (II), *op. cit.*: 32–36. For a presentation of other studies, see SELECT COMMITTEE ON SCIENCE AND TECHNOLOGY, *op. cit.*: 12–16.
21 BUDD S., *op. cit.*
22 SHARMA U., *op. cit.*: 16.

In Italy, 24% of the adult population had used alternative therapies at least once.[23]

In the Netherlands, according to a 1985 survey, 18% of the 1000 people questioned used alternative medicines at least once, and between 6% to 7% used them during the last twelve months period.[24, 25] Figures released by the Central Bureau of Statistics showed that over 900,000 people had consulted alternative practitioners (other than their own general practitioner) in 1990.[26] It also observed that the yearly percentage of the population consulting alternative practitioners (other than the patient's own GP) rose from 4.5% in 1985 to 5.9% in 1990.[27] A further study conducted in 1995 showed that 6% of the total population had seen an alternative practitioner at least once a year.[28]

In May 1994, the Opinion AS Institute carried out a poll in Norway.[29] The study showed that 27% of people had tried alternative medicines at least once. The respondents were asked if at any time during the last 12 months they had consulted various kinds of health practitioners. The affirmative answers concerning alternative medicines were the following: 4.27% used chiropractic,[30] 2.53% acupuncture, 1.89% homeopathy, 1.81% reflexology and 2.41% other types of "natural medicine". According to another study, 51% of patients used these practices and between 80% and 90% of the population had used them at least once.[31]

In Sweden, studies undertaken by the Swedish Commission on Alternative Medicines in collaboration with the Central Bureau of Statistics in

23 ROBARD I., *op. cit.*: 210.
24 SHARMA U., *op. cit.*: 16; VISSER G. J., *op. cit.*: 227.
25 According to another source, in 1979, the proportion of the Dutch population who, at one time or another, consulted an alternative practitioner was around 20% (CARTER J. P., *op. cit.*: 239).
26 DUTCH HEALTH COUNCIL, *op. cit.*
27 By comparison, the percentage of the population who visited their own GP rose from 71.9% in 1985 (52 million contacts) to 75.4% in 1990 (56.2 million contacts).
28 According to other studies, in 1981, between 4 and 6% of the Dutch population consulted with an alternative practitioner. This percentage has increased to 9.1% in 1985 and 15.7% in 1990 (BORCHGREVINK C. F., *op. cit.*: 51; FISHER P., *op. cit.*: 107).
29 Opinion AS: Institut for meningsmalinger og markedsanalyse (Institute for public opinion poll measurements and market analysis).
30 One should note that chiropractic is not considered an alternative medicine in Norway as chiropractors are regulated as an authorised health care profession (see chap. 4.3.3.8).
31 FROST AND SULLIVAN, *op. cit.*: 251; ROBARD I., *op. cit.*: 226.

1989 showed that one in five adults had, at one time or another, received an alternative treatment.[32]

In 2000, a regional study conducted in the county of Stockholm showed that 49% of the citizens of that county had visited some kind of alternative practitioner in their lifetime with 20% having done so in the previous year. These studies indicate an increase in use during the past fifteen years.[33]

In 1993, the percentage of the Swiss population using alternative medicines was estimated as being between 41% and 44%.[34] A further study revealed that users of alternative medicines were split into two categories. The first category was made of those with complementary health insurance policy and the second category was made of those without it.[35, 36] A summary of these findings is set forth below.

1. First category: 20.7% did not use alternative techniques, 18.9% had used one technique, 21.5% two techniques, and 39% three or more techniques. Thus, in total 79.4% used at least one technique. The average number of techniques used was 2.3.
2. Second category: 56.4% did not use alternative medicines, 20.5% had used one technique, 13.4% two techniques, and 9.7% three or more techniques. Thus, in total 43.6% used at least one technique. The average number of techniques used was 0.8.

A former study had shown that between 13% and 40% of the population had used alternative medicines at least once.[37] Therefore, one can assume that the use of alternative medicines has probably increased since 1993.

In the United States, the probability of users visiting an alternative practitioner during a twelve months period increased from 36.3% in 1990 (i.e., 60 million people) to 46.3% in 1997 (i.e., 83 million people). One should note a 47.3% increase in total visits to alternative practitioners, from 427

32 SWEDISH COMMISSION ON ALTERNATIVE MEDICINE, *op. cit.*: 25–26.

33 EKLÖF M., *op. cit.*

34 At that time, the basic compulsory social insurance did not cover the five most used alternative therapies. For more details, see chap. 5.3.5.14.B.

35 There are several levels of health care protection in Switzerland. Insured persons have the freedom to either the minimum basic coverage or an extensive coverage provided through complementary health insurance policies. The latter may also provide coverage for alternative medicines. For more details, see chap. 5.3.5.14.

36 BÜRGI M., *op. cit.*: 21–23, 26–27. See also SANTOS-EGGIMANN B., *op. cit.*: 11–16.

37 SHARMA U., *op. cit.*: 17.

million in 1990 to 629 million in 1997, thereby exceeding total visits to all US primary care physicians (estimated to 386 million).[38]

This substantial increase in the use of alternative medicines between 1990 and 1997 is primarily attributable to an increase in the proportion of the population seeking alternative therapies, rather than from increased visits per patient.[39]

2.3 Most Employed Techniques

Since the mid-nineteenth century biomedicine has slowly integrated the medical tradition to become the standard in Western health care systems.[40] However, despite the emergence of allopathic medicine, the practice of alternative medicines has survived. Today, some societies have, in some cases recently, integrated a number of alternative practices, even in hostile environments. This has led to medical pluralism, being the expression of socio-cultural values specific to a period.[41]

In Western countries, the most widely used alternative techniques are (in alphabetical order): acupuncture, chiropractic, herbal remedies (including phytotherapy), homeopathy, naturopathy and osteopathy. Other techniques such as alternative massages, anthroposophic medicine, hypnotherapy, neuraltherapy and relaxation therapy are also commonly used, but their popularity varies from one country to another. In addition, indigenous forms of treatment (or "folk medicine")[42] may be popular among the resident population.[43]

To the best of our knowledge, there is no recent sociological study on the use of alternative medicines in Austria. However, one should note that

38 Eisenberg D. M. (I), *op. cit.*: 1569, 1571–72.
39 Eisenberg D. M. (I), *op. cit.*: 1569, 1575.
40 For a development regarding the historical evolution of alternative medicines, see Rösch B., *op. cit.*: 3–63.
41 The coexistence of several forms of health care is a constant in Western medical history. For a study, see Laplantine F., *op. cit.*; Rossi I. (I), *op. cit.*: 17–18.
42 Such as cupping and bone setting in Finland, kinesiology in Norway, magnetotherapy in Switzerland, etc.
43 This popularity stresses the importance of cultural elements in the medical practice.

homeopathy is widely practised as well as other techniques including acupuncture, neuraltherapy and bioresonance.[44]

The most widely used alternative medicines in Belgium are, in decreasing order of frequency: homeopathy (81% of users), acupuncture (38%), osteopathy (27%), phytotheraphy (25%), chiropractic (21%) and a moderate use of other therapies.[45]

In Denmark, the most widely used alternative treatments are chiropractic, acupuncture, hypnotherapy, reflexology and other alternative massages, iridology and homeopathy.[46]

Alternative medicines have a strong foundation in Finland.[47] For example, both the Ministry of Social Affairs and Health and the academic community recognise the increasing contribution of these therapies to the Finnish health care system.[48]

The Finnish people use folk medicines such as massage, bone setting and cupping and other therapies such as natural medicine or alternative manipulation techniques. Acupuncture and hypnosis have recently been introduced. While traditional medicines are used by the older, less educated rural population, the new forms of alternative medicines are used by the younger urban population.[49]

In France, the most popular forms of alternative medicines are homeopathy (36% of users), acupuncture (21%), herbal medicines (12%), water cures (8%), chiropractic (4%), thalassotherapy (3%), osteopathy (3%), and iridology (2%).[50]

Homeopathic and herbal health care products are highly popular in France.[51] They are available in pharmacies and are attractively advertised and presented.[52]

44 Prof. Stacher, at the Wiener Internationale Akademie für Ganzheitmedizin, July 2001, Vienna.

45 FROST AND SULLIVAN, *op. cit.*: 192; LEMAL I., *op. cit.*

46 JOHANNESSEN H. (III), *op. cit*: 30–32; LAUNSO L. (I), *op. cit.*: 47; RASMUSSEN N., *op. cit.*: 87.

47 Popular medicine research in Finnish ethnology also has a long tradition in the country. For more details, see VASKILAMPI T. (I), *op. cit.*: 107–08.

48 BRITISH MEDICAL ASSOCIATION, *op. cit.*: 23–24; FROST AND SULLIVAN, *op. cit.*: 250; VASKILAMPI T. (II), *op. cit.*: 26.

49 ALDRIDGE D. (I), *op. cit.*: 55; SHARMA U., *op. cit.*: 17, 19; VASKILAMPI T. (I), *op. cit.*

50 ALDRIDGE D. (I), *op. cit.*: 55; FISHER P., *op. cit.*: 107; GROUPE DE RÉFLEXION, *op. cit.*: 20–21; SHARMA U., *op. cit.*: 16.

Frost and Sullivan note that, despite the official rejection of alternative medicines, they remain very popular and form part of the practice of many allopathic medical practitioners. Manipulative methods are also widely used within health care services.[53]

There is a long tradition of alternative medicines in Germany. The majority of them have been accepted, at least partially, by the medical establishment.[54] The interest of public authorities in alternative medicines within Germany is illustrated by the issuance in 1992 by the Federal German Ministry of Research and Technology of an extensive research program on alternative medicines coordinated by the University of Written/Herdecke.[55]

The most frequently used alternative medicines remain: homeopathy (27% of users), acupuncture (15%), procaine injection therapy, chiropractic, ozone and oxygen therapy, herbal medicines, humoral pathology, massage, and cell therapy.[56]

The market for herbal medicines is also expanding, for example, phytopharmaceuticals accounted for 7.7% of the total pharmaceutical market in 1985 and 10% in 1990.[57]

The most widely used alternative medicines in Great Britain are: herbal medicines, osteopathy, homeopathy, acupuncture, chiropractic, spiritual healing and hypnotherapy.[58]

The British market for alternative medicines is growing by 20% every year. In particular, homeopathic products and other natural remedies are becoming increasingly popular and are now widely available in health food stores and pharmacies. Herbal and other natural remedies are produced by a variety of small companies, which have received a considerable boost in recent years.[59]

51 Leading manufacturers are Boiron, Dolisos and Laboratories Lehning. Vitamin and mineral supplements are represented by leading producers such as Laboratoire Herbaxt.

52 FROST AND SULLIVAN, *op. cit.*: 222.

53 FROST AND SULLIVAN, *op. cit.*: 221–22.

54 ALDRIDGE D. (II), *op. cit.*: 75–85; BETTSCHART R., *op. cit.*: 15–17; FROST AND SULLIVAN, *op. cit.*: 209; MELCHART D., *op. cit.*: 30; OSTENDORF G.-M., *op. cit.*: 224–31.

55 FISHER P., *op. cit.*: 109.

56 EHLERS A. P. F., *op. cit.*: 35; MELCHART D., *op. cit.*: 30; FROST AND SULLIVAN, *op. cit.*: 209; SHARMA U., *op. cit.*: 17.

57 FISHER P., *op. cit.*: 107.

58 BRITISH MEDICAL ASSOCIATION, *op. cit.*: 36; ALDRIDGE D. (I), *op. cit.*: 55–56; SELECT COMMITTEE ON SCIENCE AND TECHNOLOGY, *op. cit.*: 11; SHARMA U., *op. cit.*: 16; THOMAS K. J. (I), *op. cit.*: 129–30.

59 FISHER P., *op. cit.*: 107; FROST AND SULLIVAN, *op. cit.*: 240, 246.

In Italy, the most common forms of alternative medicines are: homeopathy, acupuncture, herbal remedies, prana therapy, anthroposophic medicine, and chiropractic.[60]

Recently, several methods of alternative medicines have become more popular in Latvia. According to Dr. Nicolaev,[61] the cooperation between medical traditions of both East and West has been a notable success in the fields of medical postgraduate education, legal clinical application and integration into the state system of social welfare. The most commonly used techniques in the country are homeopathy and acupuncture.[62]

To the best of our knowledge, there are no recent official statistics or studies on the use of alternative medicines in Malta. However, one should note that Chinese medicine, chiropractic and osteopathy are widely practised.[63]

The most current forms of alternative medicines in the Netherlands are homeopathy, herbal medicines, manual therapies (chiropractic, osteopathy, etc.), paranormal healing, acupuncture, diet therapy, naturopathy and anthroposophical medicine.[64]

In Norway, the most commonly used alternative techniques used at least once by the population are acupuncture (35%), homeopathy (33%), reflexology (29%), naturopathy (29%), chiropractic (16%), kinesiology (7%), healing (3%) and iridology (3%).[65]

Until 1987, alternative medicines played only a minor role in the Spanish health care system, with the exception of homeopathy, which has a long tradition and is widely practised. Other alternative therapies commonly used are acupuncture, auriculotherapy, and neuraltherapy.[66]

60 SHARMA U., *op. cit.*: 17.
61 Dr. Nickolaev N. A., Professor and Director of the Association for Medical Acupuncture and Related Techniques of the Republic of Latvia, Sept. 2001, Riga.
62 Dr. Nickolaev N. A., Professor and Director of the Association for Medical Acupuncture and Related Techniques of the Republic of Latvia, Sept. 2001, Riga.
63 Dr. D. Falzon, Principal Medical Officer at the Department of Public Health, Mar. 1998, Valletta; Dr. Gafa, Legal Office, Department of Health, Mar. 1998, Valletta.
64 DUTCH HEALTH COUNCIL, *op. cit.*; ROBARD I., *op. cit.*: 241; SHARMA U., *op. cit.*: 16.
65 MINISTRY OF HEALTH AND SOCIAL AFFAIRS, *op. cit.*: 266; Opinion AS: Institut for Meningsmalinger og Markedsanalyse (Institute for Public Opinion Poll Measurements and Market Analysis).
66 Dr. Juan R. Villaverde, Aug. 2001, Spain.

Chiropractic is the most commonly used alternative medicine in Sweden where 13% of the population have used it at least once, followed by homeopathy (4%), acupuncture, naturopathy, and herbal medicine.[67]

Alternative medicines are widely used in Switzerland, which has a long tradition as a world centre for medical treatments.[68]

Research shows that users of complementary medicines are split into two categories: the first category was made of those with complementary health insurance policy and the category was made of those without it.[69] The most frequently used forms of alternative medicines are:[70]

1. homeopathy (63% first category, 26% second category);
2. alternative massages (41% first category, 19% second category);[71]
3. phytotherapy (27% first category, 14% second category);
4. nutrition therapy (22% first category, 9% second category);[72]
5. acupuncture (18% first category, 4% second category);
6. anthroposophic medicine (13% first category, 3% second category);
7. magnetotherapy (8% first category, 3% second category).

By taking into consideration the percentage of the population using alternative medicines,[73] most employed techniques were as follows:[74]

1. homeopathy: 49% (0.79 x 0.63) first category and 11% (0.44 x 0.26) second category;
2. Chinese medicine: 14% (0.79 x 0.18) first category and 1.76% (0.44 x 0.04) second category;
3. anthroposophic medicine: 10% (0.79 x 0.13) first category and 1.3% (0.44 x 0.03) second category;
4. phytotherapy: 21% (0.79 x 0.27) first category and 6% (0.44 x 0.14) second category;
5. neural therapy: 3% (0.79 x 0.04) first category and 0,2% (0.44 x 0.006) second category;

67 Frost and Sullivan, *op.cit.*: 253; Swedish Commission on Alternative Medicine, *op.cit.*: 25–26; Carter J. P., *op.cit.*: 234.

68 Frost and Sullivan Ltd, *op.cit.*: 254–55; Rossi I. (I), *op.cit.*: 17–24.

69 At that time the basic compulsory social insurance did not cover the five most commonly used alternative therapies.
For more details, see chapter 5.3.5.14.

70 Bürgi M., *op.cit.*: 28–31. See also Sangare H. C., *op.cit.*: 14–17; Santos-Eggimann B., *op.cit.*: 11–16.

71 E.g., reflexotherapy or acupressure/shiatsu.

72 E.g., Budwig diet.

73 See above, chap. 2.3.

74 The following rate is an estimation.

In the United States, national surveys conducted on the prevalence, costs and patterns of use associated with alternative medicines demonstrate their substantial presence in the US health care system.[75]

The most commonly used alternative medicines are:[76]

1. relaxation techniques (16.3% in 1997 vs. 13.1% in 1990);
2. herbal medicine (12.1% in 1997 vs. 2.5% in 1990);
3. massage (11.1% in 1997 vs. 6.9% in 1990);
4. chiropractic (11.0% in 1997 vs. 10.1% in 1990);
5. spiritual healing by others (7.0% in 1997 vs. 4.2% in 1990);
6. megavitamins (5.5% in 1997 vs. 2.4% in 1990);
7. self-help group (4.8% in 1997 vs. 2.3% in 1990);
8. imagery (4.5% in 1997 vs. 4.2% in 1990);
9. commercial diet (4.4% in 1997 vs. 3.9% in 1990);
10. folk remedies (4.2% in 1997 vs. 0.2% in 1990);

The use of alternative medicines increased from 33.8% in 1990 to 42.1% in 1997. The most rapid rise in popularity has been in therapies such as herbal medicine, massage, megavitamins, self-help groups, folk remedies, energy healing and homeopathy.[77]

In 1997, about 15 million adults took prescription medications concurrently with herbal remedies and/or high-dose vitamins representing 18.4% of all prescription users.[78]

2.4 Profile of Users

Users of alternative medicines do not constitute a homogeneous group. Instead, such users are represented in all ages and social groups. However, it is possible to discern some common features. Generally, users tend to be women rather than men, between the ages of 30 to 50 and city dwellers,

75 Eisenberg D. M. (I), *op. cit.*: 1569, 1574.

76 Eisenberg D. M. (I), *op. cit.*: 1572.
Astin provides an alternative ranking of the most commonly used alternative medicines: 1. Chiropractic; 2. Life-style diet; 3. Exercise-movement; 4. Relaxation (Astin J. A., *op. cit.*: 1550). For a survey of the most frequently used alternatives according to health problems, see the same author, at 1550.

77 Eisenberg D. M. (I), *op. cit.*: 1569, 1571–72.

78 Eisenberg D. M. (I), *op. cit.*: 1569.

with a high level of education and upper middle class.[79] Furthermore, they have often first been treated with allopathic medicine. As a Swiss author notes, users of alternative medicines have post-materialistic value priorities, holistic interpretative models of health and disease, and want to share in decision-making on treatment questions.[80]

An interesting feature is the attitude of patients towards their regular physician. The latter are usually not asked about alternative possibilities to biomedical treatments, neither are they informed about the visits made by their patients to alternative practitioners. Generally, patients are afraid to be ridiculed by their physicians. This illustrates the considerable gap still existing between patients ready to use any form of treatment that is available to improve their health and the widespread rejection of alternative medicines by physicians using exclusively biomedicine.[81]

A recent study indicated that Belgian women use alternative medicines more often than men. Moreover, a survey indicated that patients of alternative medicines have more complaints on average than patients of specialist doctors.[82]

In Denmark, studies show that users of alternative medicines are represented in all age and social groups with women using alternative medicines more frequently than men. In addition, studies show that users have become increasingly younger in the period from 1970 to the present day.[83]

Surveys have also shown that the use is higher among hospitalised patients, than among the general population.[84] Regarding children, 12% of hospitalised children and 21% of children treated on an out-patient basis had tried alternative medicine.[85] A study showed that 28% of all school-children from 6th to 10th grade have tried alternative medicines, including chiropractic.[86]

In Finland, women tend to use alternative medicines more frequently than men. Studies show that there exist several subcultures of users. A commentator notes that one such group consists of "health conscious middle-class

79 However, a Finnish study showed that users of "folk medicine" tend to be the elderly living in rural areas.

80 SCHÄR A., *op. cit.*: 18. See also ANDREWS L. B., *op. cit.*: 1312, footnote 275.

81 See also below, chap. 2.5.

82 LEMAL I., *op. cit.*; SERMEUS G., *op. cit.*: 61, 64–65.

83 JOHANNESSEN H. (III), *op. cit.*: 31; LAUNSO L. (I), *op. cit.*: 48.

84 JOHANNESSEN H. (III), *op. cit.*: 31.

85 A study focusing on the use of alternative therapy among children with chronic diseases showed that 28% had tried mineral therapy and 25% reflexology.

86 JOHANNESSEN H. (III), *op. cit.*: 31; LAUNSO L. (I), *op. cit.*: 49.

middle-age women who are well educated and innovators of social trends looking for new methods and new life styles".[87] Homeopathic, anthroposophical and some oriental medicines are more common among high social class groups. Folk medicine (massage, bone setting, cupping, herbs, naturopathy, spiritual and psychological approaches, life style advice) is used by elderly rural dwellers.[88]

In France, recourse to alternative medicines appears to be particularly high among top executives (68%), mid-rank executives (60%), artisans, traders, company managers (57%), and other employees (52%). Farmers (40%) use alternative medicines the least.[89]

Users are more often women (53%) than men (44%). People between 35–45 years old (59%) are the most frequent users of alternative medicines, followed by the 50–64 years (50%) and the 25–34 years ranges (45%).[90]

In Germany, users are mostly female, between 18–65 years old with a relatively high educational level. Often, they have first been treated in a hospital.[91]

In Great Britain, typical users of alternative medicines are middle-aged, middle-class women.[92] Generally, patients having recourse to these techniques also use allopathic medicine. Therefore, the majority of patients seem to use alternative medicines as a supplement to, rather than a substitute for, allopathic medicine. Treatment of chronic diseases are the habitual work of alternative practitioners.[93]

Of interest is the fact that 70% of the general public is in favour of alternative medicines becoming widely available on the National Health Service (NHS), in particular, osteopathy, acupuncture, chiropractic and homeopathy.[94]

In Italy, users are mainly female between the ages of 25 to 50.[95]

87 VASKILAMPI T. (I), *op. cit.*: 110.
88 VASKILAMPI T. (I), *op. cit.*: 110.
89 BOUCHAYER F., *op. cit.*: 53; GROUPE DE RÉFLEXION, *op. cit.*: 20–21; SHARMA U., *op. cit.*: 20.
90 BOUCHAYER F., *op. cit.*: 53; SHARMA U., *op. cit.*: 20.
91 EHLERS A. P. F., *op. cit.*: 35; SHARMA U., *op. cit.*: 21.
92 The profile of users of allopathic medicine is similar.
93 ALDRIDGE D. (I), *op. cit.*: 55–56; SHARMA U., *op. cit.*: 18; ROBARD I., *op. cit.*: 219; THOMAS K. J., *op. cit.*: 125, 129–31.
94 BRITISH MEDICAL ASSOCIATION, *op. cit.*: 32–33; FISHER P., *op. cit.*: 107, 109.
95 ROBARD I., *op. cit.*: 210; SHARMA U., *op. cit.*: 21.

In the Netherlands, studies show that more women than men use alternative medicines and that people from 35 to 50 years of age are the most frequent users.[96] Furthermore, recourse to these techniques appears to be particularly frequent among executives and the intellectual professions, except for herbal medicines and paranormal healing, which are used by people of low education.[97]

In Norway, more women (30% of the population) use alternative medicines than men (23%); and users are more middle-aged than young and old. However, in recent years, use among the elderly has increased, as well as use by men. While recourse to alternative medicines was once greatest in cities, it is now essentially the same in both cities and rural areas. In addition, the correlation once present between the level of education of a person and his or her reliance on alternative techniques is fading, although people with a better education still use alternative therapies more than other groups.[98]

Furthermore, even if there is an increasing tendency for patients to inform their doctor of their use of alternative medicines, many of them still feel that they cannot discuss such issues with their doctor.[99]

Two-thirds of Norwegian are in favour of a refund scheme for alternative medicines and four out of five people favour a licensing or authorisation scheme for alternative practitioners. Moreover, a majority of users would like hospitals to offer alternative medicines.[100]

In Switzerland, users of alternative medicines are not a homogeneous group. Nonetheless, studies show that alternative medicines are more frequently used in the German and French parts of Switzerland than in the Italian part. Users tend to be female, with a higher level of education, from the upper middle class, living in cities, and aged between 30 and 50.[101]

In the United States, according to one study, the use of alternative medicines is prevalent among women (52%) than men (48%) and less common among African Americans (33.1%) than members of other racial groups

96 Sharma U., *op. cit.*: 20.

97 Sharma U., *op. cit.*: 20.

98 Frost and Sullivan, *op. cit.*: 251; Ministry of Health and Social Affairs, *op. cit.*: 266; Robard I., *op. cit.*: 226.

99 Ministry of Health and Social Affairs, *op. cit.*: 266.

100 Ministry of Health and Social Affairs, *op. cit.*: 266.

101 Bürgi M., *op. cit.*: 22–23; Santos-Eggimann B., *op. cit.*: 11–16; Schär A., *op. cit.*: 18–27.
For a recent study on the profile, behavior and satisfaction of users of alternative medicines in Switzerland, see Sangare H. C., *op. cit.*: 23–43.

(44.5%). People aged between 35 and 49 years of age reported higher rates of use (50.1%) than either younger (41.8%) or older (39.1%) age groups. People with some college education (50.6%) were found to use alternative medicines more often than those with no college education (36.4%). Use of alternative medicines is also more common among people with annual incomes above $50,000 than those with lower incomes. Finally, the population in the Western regions of the United States (50.1%) use alternative medicines more often than elsewhere in the United States (42.1%).[102]

The percentage of individuals consulting a medical doctor for a primary condition who also use an alternative therapy increased from 19.9% in 1990 to 31.1% in 1997. Furthermore, the percentage of people who see a medical doctor and who also seek the services of an alternative therapist increased from 8.3% in 1990 to 13.3% in 1997. Finally, in 1990, 96% of patients who saw an alternative practitioner for a primary condition also consulted a medical doctor during the preceding 12 months, but only a minority of the alternative medicines used were actually discussed with a medical doctor.[103]

Eisenberg notes that "despite the dramatic increase in use and expenditures associated with alternative medical care, the extent to which patients disclose their use of alternative therapies to their physicians remains low. Less than 40% of the alternative therapies used were disclosed to a physician in both 1990 and 1997".[104]

102 ASTIN J. A., *op. cit.*: 1550–51; EISENBERG D. M. (I), *op. cit.*: 1571.
Astin notes "users tend to be better educated and to hold a philosophical orientation toward health that can be described as holistic (i.e. they believe in the importance of body, mind, and spirit in health). They are more likely to have had some type of transformational experience that has changed their worldview in some significant way, and they tend to be classified in a value subculture as cultural creatives" (ASTIN J. A., *op. cit.*: 1552).

103 EISENBERG D. M. (I), *op. cit.*: 1572–73.

104 EISENBERG D. M. (I), *op. cit.*: 1569.

2.5 Reasons to Seek Alternative Medicines and Patient Satisfaction

The symptoms leading patients to use alternative medicines can be divided into two main categories. The first category encompasses chronic, recurrent and minor diseases and other problems, such as muscoskeletal difficulties (e.g., back and neck problems, rheumatism), nervous illnesses (headaches, migraines, stomach pain), allergies, fatigue, insomnia, etc. The second category includes those serious illnesses that biomedicine is not always able to treat, such as, among others, specific forms of cancer and sclerosis.

Patients have reported that their main reasons for consulting alternative practitioners and using alternative medicines are:[105]

1. the failure of medicine to treat specific problems which typically are serious illnesses. As patients become dissatisfied with biomedicine, they seek alternative medicines as the last recourse;[106]
2. the disillusionment of patients with their physicians. Patients often argue that their physicians do not listen to them and have a mechanical approach toward their health problems.[107] They also report that their problems have not been taken seriously or physicians are arrogant.[108] These patients prefer their relationship with alternative practitioners. An important aspect of this preference is the length of the consultation, which is longer with alternative practitioners than with

105 The list is presented according to author's interpretation of the main reasons leading to the use of alternative medicine. For a US study on the subject, see ASTIN J. A., *op. cit.*: 1548–53. For a British study, see SELECT COMMITTEE ON SCIENCE AND TECHNOLOGY, *op. cit.*: 24ss. See also COHEN M. H. (I), *op. cit.*: 2–3; DAGUET R., *op. cit.*: 15–21; COST ACTION B4, *op. cit.*: 18–22.

106 One must, however, stress that alternative medicines are often used in conjunction with biomedicine.

107 As an example of this mechanisation of the human being, Daguet mentions the case of the male impotence treated with Viagra. He argues that this ethiological complex phenomenon is reduced to an ordinary hydraulic problem. The author adds that this vision is predominant in medicine (DAGUET R., *op. cit.*: 17).

108 In the United States, the development of new systems, particularly within managed health care systems, has even suppressed the physical contact between practitioners and patients. For example, when asking for a referral, patients must explain the reasons that led them to see a certain practitioner through an automatic answering machine. Then, the physician sends the requested patient the referral by regular mail, thus avoiding any personal contact.

regular physicians.[109] In other words, they seem to prefer the holistic approach of alternative practitioners that takes into consideration other aspects traditionally lacking in biomedicine;[110]

3. the lower costs and risks. Patients consider alternative techniques as less expensive and less harmful than biomedicine (including medication);
4. the search for well-being improvement and the prevention of illnesses.

Patients are usually satisfied when using alternative medicines. In particular, the satisfaction is high for chronic, recurrent and minor diseases, but less so for the treatment of serious illnesses. Furthermore, the number of patients who did not experience any effect is not negligible. Finally, only a few patients had a negative experience, such as the worsening of their health.

It is noticeable that alternative medicines are often seen as the response to "civilisation diseases" such as psychosomatic disorders, adaptation problems, depression, immune system debility and degenerative illnesses. These are generally the consequence of tense and twisted relationships as a result of conflict between individuals and their social environment.[111] Therefore,

109 A British author notes that "Increasing pressure on an under doctored National Health Service (NHS) are now such that the average primary care physician has very little time to spend with each patient in consultation in order to offer the attention and 'tender loving care' which were important therapeutic weapons for his predecessors" (SELECT COMMITTEE ON SCIENCE AND TECHNOLOGY, *op. cit.*: 10). See also COHEN M. H. (I), *op. cit.*: 67.

110 Cohen observes that "the biomedical model's orientation is frequently distant, detached, and deficient in empathy and warmth. The model alienates patients from their own being when their mental, emotional, and spiritual realities are seen as having little bearing on disease or healing. Feelings of depression, rage, social isolation, and bewilderment, and other subjective, but significant, experiences often are discounted, invalidated, or denied as hallucinatory. [...] Biomedicine created feelings of dependence and personal estrangement as individuals 'exchange the status of person for that of patient'. [...] Hospitalisation leaves patients surrounded by charts, tubes, and monitors, being spoken about rather than to, in incomprehensible debates among strangers" (COHEN M. H. (I), *op. cit.*: 3). See also, e.g., DOMENIGHETTI G., *op. cit.*: 570; SELECT COMMITTEE ON SCIENCE AND TECHNOLOGY, *op. cit.*: 10–11. See also chap. 1.1.

111 Among the 30 most frequently sold drugs in France, 10 are tranquillizers or sleeping tablets, 8 analgesics, and 5 are more or less placebos (GUILLOD O., *op. cit.*: 35–36).

the search for other forms of health care by patients may be viewed as a spontaneous social response.[112]

In Belgium, research shows that many patients made use of alternative treatments for problems with limbs, muscles and joints, as well as problems with the stomach, abdomen and digestive system. Recourse to alternative medicines was, however, rare for acute symptoms, infectious diseases and malignant tumours. In addition, 85% of users had first consulted an allopathic provider.[113]

A 1987 study indicated that 77% of Belgian users were satisfied with alternative treatments.[114] Sermeus notes that

> once the patient has crossed the threshold of alternative medicine, he is more and more attracted and convinced by the absence of iatrogenic effects. In addition, the patient is drawn very strongly by the open and comforting relationship with the practitioner and by the fact that the practitioner takes time to tell the patient about his condition and the proposed treatment.[115]

In Denmark, the most common health issues leading people to seek alternative therapists are joint and muscular problems, headaches, migraines, allergies, asthma and tension. Patients suffering from cancer, rheumatism and sclerosis also tend towards a relatively high usage of alternative therapies. Respectively, 34%, 47% and 50% of patients use alternative medicine.[116]

With respect to the satisfaction experienced by users, 77% reported they had been cured, 17% did not experience any effect and 1% had experienced a worsening of their health problems.[117]

In Finland, between 60% and 80% of users were satisfied when using alternative medicines.[118]

112 Some authors consider that the use of alternative medicines is a reaction by part of the population to the evolution of scientific medicine, in particular, to its current boundaries in the manipulation of the body and human beings. It is also seen as a response of individuals to the politico-financial "powers" linked to the health care system. For a study, see ROSSI I. (I), *op. cit.*: 21. See also GUILLOD O., *op. cit.*: 35–36.

113 LEMAL I., *op. cit.*; SERMEUS G., *op. cit.*: 61, 64–65.

114 SERMEUS G., *op. cit.*: 61, 64–66.

115 SERMEUS G., *op. cit.*: 65–66.

116 JOHANNESSEN H. (III), *op. cit.*: 31; LAUNSO L. (I), *op. cit.*: 49.

117 LAUNSO L. (I), *op. cit.*: 49.

118 Users expressed their satisfaction towards biomedicine as well. For more details, see VASKILAMPI T. (I), *op. cit.*: 109.

In France, 54% of patients used alternative medicines for chronic symptoms, 49% for minor diseases, 17% for preventive medicine and/or a healthy lifestyle, and 3% for serious illness.[119]

A survey on the level of patients' satisfaction when using alternative medicines found that 70% of users considered them efficient for minor diseases such as flu, colds, general fatigue and headaches, 65% found them effective for chronic diseases such as sleeplessness, rheumatism, digestive problems and allergies. However, only 9% of patients found alternative medicines effective for serious diseases such as cancer or cardiac problems. Overall, 11% of users considered these therapies as inefficient for minor diseases, 15% found them so for chronic diseases and 38% for serious illnesses.[120]

In Germany, there are various reasons for the recent increasing interest shown by patients in alternative medicines. One is the disillusionment of patients regarding their physicians. Patients claim that their physicians do not really listen to them and that they employ a mechanical approach when treating them. As such, their relationship becomes anonymous. In contrast, "Heilpraktikers"[121] have a different, holistic, approach. Such practitioners are more responsive and open to listening their patients, and, overall, the relationship is less anonymous. Second, patients consider alternative medications as being less expensive and less harmful than classic ones. Finally, and importantly, biomedicine has failed to treat specific illnesses.[122]

According to a recent poll, 52% of the population think that alternative medicines are effective.[123]

In Great Britain, a survey[124] found that patients sought alternative health care for:

119 BOUCHAYER F., *op. cit.*: 55.
The National Order of Physicians, however, considers that users of alternative medicines are essentially cancer victims with some punctual cases of chronic diseases (GRUNWALD D., *op. cit.*).

120 For each of these categories, respectively 19%, 20% and 53% of respondents had no opinion (BOUCHAYER F., *op. cit.*: 54–55; GROUPE DE RÉFLEXION, *op. cit.*: 20–21; ROBARD I., *op. cit.*: 8).

121 Heilpraktikers are the German non-allopathic practitioners allowed to provide alternative treatments. For more details, see chap. 4.3.3.2.

122 CRAMER R., *op. cit.*: 11–12; EHLERS A. P. F., *op. cit.*: 33, 59–65; JUNG H., *op. cit.*: 48–63.

123 MELCHART D., *op. cit.*: 30.

124 ERNST E. (II), *op. cit.* For recent developments regarding other possible explanations for the use of alternative medicines, see SELECT COMMITTEE ON SCIENCE AND TECHNOLOGY, *op. cit.*: 15. These include current popularity dictated by fashion, cultural change with a renewed interest in the paranormal and increased anxiety about health across society.

1. helping or relieving a injury or existing condition. This applied to 25% of those patients using alternative medicines;
2. a liking and attachment to alternative therapies (20%);
3. relaxation. This applied to 19% of users;
4. good health and general well-being (14%);
5. preventive purpose (12%);
6. lack of belief in the efficacy of conventional medicine (11%);
7. reasons relating to a doctor's recommendation or referral (11%);
8. curiosity and interest in other ways of life, new experiences (11%), or as a lifestyle choice (8%);
9. reasons relating to lack of access to NHS treatment or conventional medicine (7%).

Prior surveys show that 90% of users, such users comprising one eighth of the British population, were willing to try alternative therapies again.[125] One should note that consultations with alternative practitioners last eight times longer than those with general practitioners and, as such,[126] the level of satisfaction experienced by patients when undergoing alternative treatments is high.[127]

There are four general categories of users: patients rehabilitating after an accident, patients with chronic diseases, older patients wishing to maintain their health and retired patients needing a rest-cure.[128]

In the Netherlands, the most common complaints patients bring to alternative practitioners are nervous complaints such as a serious headache or pain in the muscoskeletal system including back pains or a stiff neck.[129] The most frequently cited reason given by patients for seeking alternative treatment was that orthodox methods had no effect on their chronic disorders. Only a small proportion (14%) chose an alternative treatment at first.[130]

A further survey showed that 56% of respondents had experienced major improvement in their overall health due to their having received alternative treatment, 22% had experienced some improvement and 22% had experienced no improvement at all.[131]

125 BRITISH MEDICAL ASSOCIATION, *op. cit.*: 32; ROBARD I., *op. cit.*: 219.

126 ROBARD I., *op. cit.*: 220.

127 SELECT COMMITTEE ON SCIENCE AND TECHNOLOGY, *op. cit.*: 24. For a development on the subject, see the same author at 24ss.

128 EHLERS A. P. F., *op. cit.*: 36; ALDRIDGE D. (II), *op. cit.*: 79.

129 CARTER J. P., *op. cit.*: 240; VISSER G. J., *op. cit.*: 117.

130 CARTER J. P., *op. cit.*: 240; ROBARD I., *op. cit.*: 240.

131 FISHER P., *op. cit.*: 109; ROBARD I., *op. cit.*: 240; VISSER G. J., *op. cit.*: 118.

In Norway, people seek alternative medicines for the following reasons:[132]

1. lack of response from the official health care system;
2. a feeling that they have not been taken seriously and encounters with arrogant doctors;
3. media influence;
4. fear of side effects and/or adverse effects of drugs;
5. as a last hope;
6. effectiveness.

The Committee on Alternative Medicines noted that persons suffering from chronic or serious disease are particularly likely to make use of alternative medicine. However, there is also an increasing tendency to apply them for the purpose of relieving other ailments, such as headache, migraine and back and neck problems. Even though patients generally consult a medical doctor before consulting an alternative practitioner, there are increasing numbers of patients who consult an alternative practitioner directly.[133]

Patient satisfaction is evidenced by the fact that more than two-thirds of those people using alternative medicines stated that their health had improved.[134]

In Sweden, 40% of users stated that they had chosen alternative medicines treatment because of dissatisfaction with the National Health Service. Overall, 70% of users that considered themselves cured of their illness or said that their health had improved, only 1% thought their health had deteriorated.[135]

In Switzerland, the most commonly mentioned health conditions leading to use of alternative medicines are chronic problems.[136]

The use of alternative medicines by the sick is for the following reasons:[137]

1. the ability to receive a treatment without drugs or chemistry;
2. the lack of side effects of alternative medicines;
3. the unsuccessful treatment of specific illness by allopathic medicine.

132 BORCHGREVINK C. F., *op. cit.*: 51.
133 MINISTRY OF HEALTH AND SOCIAL AFFAIRS, *op. cit.*: 266.
134 MINISTRY OF HEALTH AND SOCIAL AFFAIRS, *op. cit.*: 266.
135 SWEDISH COMMISSION ON ALTERNATIVE MEDICINE, *op. cit.*: 25–26.
136 SCHÄR A., *op. cit.*: 18–27.
137 BÜRGI M., *op. cit.*: 47–63. See also, e.g., SANGARE H. C., *op. cit.*: 18–22.

The use of alternative medicine by healthy people is generally:

1. to improve their well-being; and
2. as a preventive measure.

A more exhaustive study showed that recourse to alternative medicines was not necessarily due to a patient's personal disappointment with biomedicine but rather an endeavour to do everything possible for one's health.[138] Patients seem to regard alternative medicines as a complement to conventional medicines. The longer-lasting nature of the consultation and the better doctor-patient relationship are also mentioned as being favourable aspects of alternative medicine. Other reasons included a critical attitude to modern civilisation and the growing symbolic value of health. Generally, however, the choice between biomedicine and alternative medicines is usually linked to the nature of the disease.[139]

In the United States, the highest condition-specific rates of CAM use are the following:[140] back problems, allergies, fatigue, arthritis, headaches, neck problems, high blood pressure, sprains or strains and insomnia.

Consumers seek services from alternative providers rather than physicians for several reasons including greater accessibility, better communication, lower cost, and the possibility of a service more in keeping with the consumer's personal desires, cultural beliefs or other health care needs.[141] Astin notes that

> the majority of alternative medicines users appear to be doing so not so much as a result of being dissatisfied with conventional medicine but largely because they find these health care alternatives to be more congruent with their own values, beliefs, and philosophical orientations toward health and life.[142]

The use of alternative medicines seems to be a complement to, rather than a replacement of conventional treatments.[143]

Eisenberg observes that

> in 1990, a full third of respondents who used alternative therapy did not use it for any principal medical condition. From these data, we inferred that a substantial amount of alternative therapy was used for heath promotion or disease prevention.

138 See, however DOMENIGHETTI G., *op. cit.*: 570.

139 SCHÄR A., *op. cit.*: 18–27.
For a recent development on this subject, see DAGUET R., *op. cit.*: 15–21.

140 EISENBERG D. M. (I), *op. cit.*: 1572–73. See also WHITE HOUSE COMMISSION ON COMPLEMENTARY AND ALTERNATIVE MEDICINE POLICY, *op. cit.*: 15–19.

141 ANDREWS L. B., *op. cit.*: 1276, 1280.

142 ASTIN J. A., *op. cit.*: 1548.

143 ASTIN J. A., *op. cit.*: 1551.

In 1997, 42% of all alternative therapies used were exclusively attributed to treatments of existing illness, whereas 58% were used, at least in part, to "prevent future illness from occurring or to maintain health and vitality".[144]

2.6 Alternative Practitioners

The number of providers of alternative medicines, including those having or not having an allopathic background, is increasing. These providers are usually well organised. They often create organisations in order to gain credibility in the eyes of the public and the authorities, for example by establishing training requirements and standards of practice. Sometimes, membership of an association for an alternative practitioner may be a decisive condition in allowing a practitioner to practise in a specific country.

In Austria, a 1997 study on the use of alternative medicines by physicians in Vienna found that there were 100 physicians practising acupuncture, 87 homeopathy, 87 neuraltherapy, 40 bioresonance, and 200 using other forms of alternative medicines.[145]

In Belgium, according to recent studies, one out of four physicians uses alternative medicines, the most commonly used being homeopathy (59% of doctors using alternative medicines), acupuncture (40%) and phytotherapy (28%).[146]

The categories of medical practitioners who use acupuncture are not clearly defined. Some authors[147] claim that physicians provide most of the acupuncture treatments while others[148] claim that physiotherapists provide most of these treatments.

The use of manipulative treatments is divided between physiotherapists (33%) and non-allopathic practitioners (34%).[149]

In Denmark, approximately 700 physicians are members of the Danish Society for Medical Acupuncture and 116 of these have recently finished

144 EISENBERG D. M. (I), *op. cit.*: 1575. For information regarding the first study, see EISENBERG D. M. and co-authors (II), *op. cit.*: 246–52.

145 Prof. Stacher, at the Wiener Internationale Akademie für Ganzheitmedizin, July, 2001, Vienna.

146 LEMAL I., *op. cit.*

147 FISHER P., *op. cit.*: 108; SERMEUS G., *op. cit.*: 61, 67.

148 ROBARD I., *op. cit.*: 213.

149 ROBARD I., *op. cit.*: 213.

the diploma course in acupuncture. However, only 20 doctors approximately practise acupuncture in full-time medicine.[150]

In France, the social security system qualifies physicians using alternative medicines as "doctors with a particular type of practice (MEP)". In 1993, physicians registered as MEP represented 6.2% of the whole medical corpus. In the respect of the techniques provided by MEP, acupuncture and homeopathy are used by respectively 30% and 20% of the MEP.[151] According to Bouchayer, a rising number of paediatricians are turning to homeopathy and rheumatologists are becoming increasingly interested in acupuncture and manual medicines.[152]

More specifically, acupuncture has been estimated to be practised by approximately 10,000 doctors in France, of whom about half are reported to have undertaken acupuncture training.[153]

In addition, it has been estimated that between 2,000 and 4,000 kinesitherapists use alternative therapies.[154]

Research on non-allopathic practitioners shows that approximately 50,000 of them provide alternative medicines in France including magnetism, hypnotism, parapsychology.[155]

In Great Britain, non-physicians provide the largest proportion of alternative medicines. From about 2,000 non-allopathic practitioners in 1987, they have increased sizeably to around 8,000 in 1994. The number of non-medically qualified practitioners is estimated to be growing by about 10% each year.[156] According to a survey conducted in 1999, there were approximately 50,000 alternative practitioners in the country with 10,000 of these being statutorily registered health professionals.[157]

In Italy, 5,000 of 250,000 physicians use alternative techniques. Within this group circa 1,300 physicians practise acupuncture.[158] Another commentator notes that 4,000 Italian doctors use acupuncture.[159]

150 Langgaard H., M.D. researcher into complementary cancer therapies, Aug. 2001, Copenhagen.
151 Portelli N., *op. cit.*: 7.
152 Bouchayer F., *op. cit.*: 51.
153 Frost and Sullivan, *op. cit.*: 222.
154 Bouchayer F., *op. cit.*: 51.
155 Aldridge D. (I), *op. cit.*: 55; Bouchayer F., *op. cit.*: 51; Laplantine F., *op. cit.*: 3, 45.
156 British Medical Association, *op. cit.*: 28; Fisher P., *op. cit.*: 108.
157 Budd S., *op. cit.*
158 Robard I., *op. cit.*: 210.
159 Frost and Sullivan, *op. cit.*: 232.

In the Netherlands, there is no precise figure for the number of alternative practitioners. This is due to the fact that many practitioners do not belong to any professional association. However, a 1985 survey showed that there were more than 4,000 alternative practitioners: 735 naturopaths, 300 paranormal healers, 220 homeopaths, 475 anthroposophical professionals, 945 acupuncturists and 1,450 manual therapists.[160]

According to another survey conducted in 1992, almost half of the Dutch GPs provided alternative medicines once or more, the most commonly prescribed being homeopathy (40%). Only 9% of the respondents to the survey used manipulative medicine, 4% acupuncture and 4% naturopathy.[161] According to another source, there were 10,000 alternative practitioners in the Netherlands, in 1986.[162]

In Norway, research has shown that alternative medicine is practised by practitioners from very different backgrounds ranging between those with no prior education in alternative medicine to those with a lengthy training in alternative medicines, and those with or without a background in the public health service. Generally, authorised health personnel do not use alternative medicines in their professional practice. However, some medical doctors and other health personnel do use some forms of alternative medicine, such as acupuncture and/or homeopathy as an integrated part of their practice. There are also some practitioners who are authorised health personnel, for example nurses, who set up a practice in alternative medicine.[163]

In Switzerland, alternative medicines are provided by physicians, non-allopathic practitioners,[164] pharmacists and by the patients themselves. Studies show that between 11 to 21% of physicians provide homeopathy services and between 10 to 13% perform acupuncture. These physicians are mainly general practitioners (22% of them in canton Vaud, 7% in canton

160 Visser G. J., *op. cit.*: 119.

161 Fisher P., *op. cit.*, 109; Visser G. J., *op. cit.*: 119.

162 Robard I., *op. cit.*: 240.

163 Been K., Secretary for the Alternative Medicine Commission, Feb. 1998, Oslo; Vegar Nore, Norwegian Ministry of Health and Social Affairs, Sept. 2001, Oslo.

164 In 1995, between 3,000 and 5,000 naturopaths were practising in Switzerland. According to more recent statistics, more than 12,000 are registered by insurance companies.

Fribourg) but they can also be specialists (11% of specialists in canton Vaud, and 7% in canton Fribourg).[165, 166]

According to a further study, 46% of Swiss physicians have used alternative medicines. The most commonly used techniques have been homeopathy (55% of users), acupuncture (45%), various manual therapies (22%) and other practises (33%).[167]

In the US, a study on the attitude of physicians towards alternative medicines revealed that more than 90% of those surveyed considered diet and exercise, behavioral medicine, biofeedback and counselling or psychotherapy to be legitimate medical practices. The figures showed that 50% of physicians considered acupuncture, massage therapy and hypnotherapy a legitimate medical practice but this endorsement fell to less than 27% for herbal medicine, homeopathic medicine, Native American medicine, traditional Oriental medicine, and electromagnetic applications.[168]

In contrast, there are approximately 350,000 staff working at more than 2,500 traditional medicine hospitals in China. In addition, 95% of general hospitals in China have established traditional medicine units and 50% of rural doctors have the choice of using both traditional and Western medicine.[169]

2.7 Organisations

All of the countries surveyed possess organisations linked to alternative medicines. These organisations usually consist of patients using alternative medicines or alternative practitioners providing them. These organisations and, particularly, associations consisting of non-allopathic practitioners often play a role in the development of new training and also act as lobby groups with the aim of influencing government policies in favour

165 In 1994, 2.6 million insured people (40% of the entire Swiss population) had a complementary insurance covering some alternative medicines.

166 BÜRGI M., *op.cit.*: 32–42; CONFÉRENCE DES DIRECTEURS CANTONAUX DES AFFAIRES SANITAIRES (I), *op.cit.*: 22; SANTOS-EGGIMANN B., *op.cit.*: 15; WICKI M., *op.cit.*: 36.

167 DOMENIGHETTI G., *op.cit.*: 570–72.

168 BERMAN B. M. et al., *op.cit.*: 362ss; BOOZANG K. M., *op.cit.*: 188.

169 WHO (V), *op.cit.*: 148–49.

of the mainstreaming of alternative medicines. They also play an important role in the distribution of information about alternative therapies to the general public.

For example, there is an academy of holistic medicine in Austria.[170] In Belgium, there are several patients, physicians and pharmacists associations linked with homeopathy.[171] In Denmark, there are several associations of non-physicians providers of alternative medicines as the Danish Chiropractic Association.[172] In Finland, some organisations support alternative medicines.[173] In Great Britain, a survey revealed a wide spectrum of organisational and administrative development. In Italy, the SIO (Societa Italiana di Omeopatia) links the different societies and schools of homeopathy.[174] International congresses in Medical Acupuncture and Alternative medicines are also often organised in Latvia.[175] In Spain, a new society founded in 1996, the Spanish Society of Homeopathic Medicine, represents all homeopathic associations.[176]

170 In German "Wiener Internationale Akademie für Ganzheitmedizin" (Prof. Stacher, at the Wiener Internationale Akademie für Ganzheitmedizin, Aug. 2001, Vienna).

171 Liga Medicorum Homeopathica Internationalis, Mallorca, 1996.

172 The association has 300 members (there are 16,000 medical doctors in Denmark) and its objective is to obtain full reimbursement of chiropractic treatments from the social insurance as well as to gain official recognition (Langgaard H., M.D. researcher into complementary cancer therapies, Sept. 2001, Copenhagen).

173 VASKILAMPI T. (I), *op. cit.*: 108.

174 Liga Medicorum, *op. cit.*

175 There are also several associations of alternative practitioners in the country (acupuncture, phytotherapy, resonance therapy, acupuncture, iridology, etc.).
Dr. Nickolaev N.A., Professor and Director of the Association for Medical Acupuncture and Related Techniques of the Republic of Latvia, March 1998, Riga.
WHO liaison Officer, Riga, 2000.

176 Dr. Amengual I Vicens C., Liga Medicorum Homeopathica Internationalis, Mallorca, Sept. 2001.

2.8 Comparative Chart

The comparative chart set forth below provides a schematic overview of the extent of alternative medicines within the various countries addressed in this chapter.

The first two lines show the proportion of the population who have used alternative medicine. A distinction is made between those who used at least once in their lives an alternative medicine ("used once") and those who have used alternative medicines at least once during a twelve months period ("last year").[177] The most frequently occurring forms of alternative medicines are presented in decreasing order of frequency (when numbered).[178] In addition, the profile of users of alternative medicines ("users' profile")[179] and the reasons for recourse to alternative medicines and the satisfaction level of patients post-treatment ("reasons to seek and satisfaction") has been compiled according to the author's own methodology.[180]

177 People questioned during polls are usually asked if they used an alternative medicine during the last twelve months period. Approximate ranges are calculated by the author, using available data.

178 The percentages indicate the proportion of users. The term "massage" means alternative forms of massage.

179 Although the age of users of alternative medicines is homogeneous, the chart indicates the category of users who mostly use alternative medicines.

180 The abbreviation "AM" means alternative medicines, "BM" biomedicine, and "NHS" National Health Service.

	Belgium	Denmark	Finland
"Used once" "Last year"	40–70% 24%	25% 10%–37%	40–60% 15–20%
Most frequently used forms of alternative medicines	1. homeopathy 2. acupuncture 3. osteopathy 4. phytotherapy 5. chiropractic	1. chiropractic 2. acupuncture 3. hypnotherapy 4. reflexology massage 5. iridology	1. herbal remedies 2. massages 3. chiropractic, naprapathy and bone setting 4. acupuncture 5. homeopathy 6. cupping 7. faith healing
Users' profile	– more women than men – users of AM have more complaints than patients of specialist MDs	– more women than men – all age and social groups – users have become younger – use higher among hospitalised patients	– more women than men – middle-aged – well educated – elderly rural dwellers use folk medicine
Reasons to seek alternative medicines and satisfaction	– limbs, muscles, joints, stomach, abdomen and digestive, but no acute symptoms (e.g. cancer) – use as a complement – better relationship – users are satisfied	– joint and muscular problems, rheumatism, headaches, migraines, allergies, asthma, cancer and sclerosis – 77% satisfied, 17% no effect and 1% negative effects	

	France	Germany	Great Britain
"Used once" "Last year"	49% 16%	20–30% 5–12%	26–30% 8–10%
Most frequently used forms of alternative medicines	1. homeopathy 2. acupuncture 3. herbal medicines 4. water cures 5. chiropractic 6. thalassotherapy 7. osteopathy 8. iridology	1. homeopathy 2. acupuncture 3. procaine injection therapy 4. chiropractic 5. ozone and oxygen therapy 6. herbal medicines 7. humoral pathology 8. massage 9. cell therapy	1. herbal remedies 2. osteopathy 3. homeopathy 4. acupuncture 5. chiropractic 5. spiritual healing 6. hypnotherapy
Users' profile	– more women than men – aged 35–45 – executives and higher intellectual as well as intermediate professions	– more women than men – high educational level – often first been treated in hospital	– more women than men – middle-aged – middle class – in favour of integration of AM in the NHS (osteo., chiro. and homeo.)
Reasons to seek alternative medicines and satisfaction	– chronic symptoms (54%), minor disease (49%), prevention (17%), serious illnesses (3%) – minor and chronic (70–65% satisfied, 11–15% not satisfied), serious disease (9% satisfied, 38% not satisfied)	– rehabilitation, chronic diseases, elderly, and rest-cure – disillusionment of patients regarding MDs – AM less expensive and less harmful – failure of biomedicine to treat – 52% of the population think that AM are effective	– use as a complement – 90% of users are ready to try them again

	Italy	Netherlands	Norway
"Used once" "Last year"	24%	18% 6–7%	80–90% 10%
Most frequently used forms of alternative medicines	1. homeopathy 2. acupuncture 3. herbal remedies 4. prana therapy 5. anthroposophic medicine 6. chiropractic	1. homeopathy 2. herbal medicines 3. manual therapies 4. paranormal healing 5. acupuncture 6. diet therapy 7. naturopathy 8. anthroposophical medicine	1. acupuncture 2. homeopathy 3. reflexology 4. naturopathy 5. chiropractic 6. kinesiology 7. healing 8. iridology
Users' profile	– more women than men – aged 25–50 years	– more women than men – aged 35–50 years – executives and higher intellectual professions	– more women than men – middle-aged – equal in towns and country – relatively more people with higher education – increasing tendency to tell MDs about the use of AM – users positive for licensing, refunding, and delivering at hospitals
Reasons to seek alternative medicines and satisfaction		– nervous illnesses, muscoskeletal system – failure of biomedicine – small proportion use AM at first – improvement of condition (56%), some improvement (22%), no improvement (22%)	– little help from biomedicine – not taken seriously, have met arrogant MDs – influence of media – afraid of drugs' side effects – AM as the last hope – effectiveness of AM – for chronic and serious diseases – 66% were satisfied

	Sweden	Switzerland	USA
"Used once"	20%	45–80%	
"Last year"			46%
Most frequently used forms of alternative medicines	1. chiropractic 2. homeopathy 3. acupuncture 4. naturopathy 5. herbal medicine	1. homeopathy 2. alternative massages 3. phytotherapy 4. nutrition therapy 5. acupuncture 6. anthroposophic medicine 7. magnetotherapy	1. relaxation techniques 2. herbal medicine 3. massage 4. chiropractic 5. spiritual healing 6. megavitamins 7. self-help group 8. imagery 9. commercial diet 10. folk remedies (4.2%)
Users' profile		– no homogenous group – more women than men – aged 30–50 – superior education – upper middle class – living in towns – more in German and French part	– more women than men – aged 35–49 – college education – annual income above 50,000 – less common among Afro-americans – more often in West states
Reasons to seek alternative medicines and satisfaction	– no satisfaction with biomedicine – improvement for 70%, deterioration for 1%	– treatments without drugs or chemistry – no side effects of AM – failure of biomedicine – improvement of well-being – preventive measure – AM as a complement – better relationship	– back problems, allergies, fatigue, arthritis, headaches, neck problems, high blood pressure, sprains or strains, insomnia – greater accessibility – lower cost – better communication – more congruent with own values – use of AM in conjunction with BM – increase of use of AM as principal medical condition

2.9 Conclusion

The sociological overview of alternative medicines presented here demonstrates a clear trend toward increasing use of alternative medicines in current medical practice. The use of alternative medicines and the role they play in modern Western society is already important and shall probably increase in the future. One may predict that as long as biomedicine and its providers remain unable to satisfy patients' needs, the success of alternative medicines is bound to continue, and that fresh attempts to suppress them shall certainly fail.[181] In this respect, the crucial elements continue to be the inability of biomedicine to treat specific illnesses particularly given that alternative medicines may sometimes be a solution in these cases combined with the prevailing dissatisfaction felt by patients towards their regular physicians. Nor shall such criticisms of biomedicine cease to be valid in the future as biomedicine shall continue to confront serious challenges in its efforts to find a cure for various diseases, in particular diseases with psychological factors.

Today, simple ignorance, rejection or prohibition of alternative medicines is no longer a viable alternative. A more sensible approach consists in understanding the reasons for the success attained by alternative medicines, and in considering the benefits these techniques may bring to medicine. As one author notes, it is important not to disregard the dynamics induced by non orthodox medicines; because in ignoring these dynamics the potential benefits of alternative medicine would be lost for patients, health care providers, hospitals and scientific research.[182]

181 The suppression of alternative medicines would, in any case, be particularly difficult since some alternative medicines are already deeply integrated and entrenched in mainstream medicine (see SANTOS-EGGIMANN B., *op.cit.*: 11; BOOZANG K. M., *op.cit.*: 185–212).

182 In French: "Hors de toute allégeance à une mode ou à une école, il importe de ne pas négliger les dynamiques induites par les médecines non orthodoxes; car ignorer ces approches viendrait à méconnaître le potentiel et les contenus qu'elles véhiculent pour les patients et les soignants, ainsi que pour la clinique et la recherche scientifique" (ROSSI I. (I), *op.cit.*: 17).
See also DOMENIGHETTI G., *op.cit.*: 570. The author states that, on the basis of a sociological study of the use of alternative medicines by the Swiss population and among Swiss physicians, a restrictive policy towards alternative medicines, as well as their (non-)coverage by insurance seems unacceptable, not only to consumers, but also to a great proportion of the medical profession.

3. Research and Education

3.1 Introduction

Research and education are fundamental elements to consider[1] in any decision to regulate alternative medicines.[2] During the past two decades, education and research on alternative medicines have significantly developed. While initially alternative medicines were taught only outside universities in an unregulated environment, they start to be better organised and paralleled with fundamental and clinical research. The recent increased interest focused on alternative medicines by public authorities has undoubtedly played a role in this evolution, with a subsequent effect on training for both physicians and non-physicians, as well as on thc establishment of new research programs.

This chapter shall provide an overview of recent developments concentrating on the research and education environment of alternative medicines.

3.2 Research

Bibliography

ANGELL M. (co-author: KASSIRER J. P.), *Alternative medicine – The risks of untested and unregulated medicine*, in: New England Journal of Medicine, 1998, vol. 339, n° 12: 839–41; ANONYMOUS (IV), *Integrated healthcare – A way forward for the next five years?*, Foundation for Integrated Medicine, 1997: 8–18, 57–59; BALON J. and co-authors, *A comparison of active and simulated*

1 Research and education are strongly linked. Discoveries are made by researchers, which are then demonstrated and developed as physical and natural laws, and then are subsequently taught as part of the academic curriculum.

2 For a development regarding the scientific background when regulating alternative medicines, see chap. 6. See also chap. 8.3.4. For a presentation of the importance of education when regulating alternative medicines, see chap. 7.3.5.2 (licensing), and 7.4.2 (coverage). For proposals regarding education, see chap. 7.5.2.

chiropractic manipulations as adjunctive treatment for childhood asthma, in: New England Journal of Medicine, 1998, vol.338, n° 15: 1013–27; Beck A., *La chaire de médecine complémentaire à l'Université de Berne: Une création récente*, in: CMS, 1996, vol.40: 55–62; Boozang K. M. (I), *Western medicine opens the door to alternative medicine*, in: American Journal of Medicine, 1998, vol.24, n° 2/3: 189–90; Boozang K. M. (III), *National policy on CAM: The White House Commission report*, in: The Journal of Law, Medicine and Ethics, 2003, vol.31, n° 2: 251–61; Borghi M. (co-editor: Gassman J.), *Thérapies complémentaires ou alternatives en psychiatrie: Un défi? Un droit?*, Schriftenreihe der Schweizerischen Stiftung Pro Mente Sana n° 20, 1999, Zürich; Brody J. E., *Evaluating acupuncture: Medical profession is divided*, in: International Herald Tribune, Nov. 20, 1997; Bruset S., *Holism and individualism – The Yin and Yang in complementary medicines*, in: Johannessen H. (co-authors: Launso L., Olesen S. G., Staugard F.) (I), *Studies in alternative therapy 1 – Contributions from the Nordic countries*, Odense University Press, 1994, Gylling: 186–96; Chez R. (co-author: Jonas W.), *The challenge of complementary and alternative medicine*, in: American Journal of Obstetrics and Gynecology, 1997 Nov. vol.177, n° 5: 1156–61; Cost Action B4, *COST action B4 unconventional medicine – Final report of the management committee, 1993–1998*, European Communities, 1998, Luxembourg: 64–81, 108–09; Dayer P., *Le groupe multidisciplinaire d'étude des médecines non-conventionnelles de Genève*, in: CMS, 1996, vol.40: 67–69; Dejung B., *Manuelle Triggerpunktbehandlung bei chronischer Lumbosakralagie*, in: Frey F. (co-editor: Baumann P. H.), *Supplementum 62, FNRS-PNR 34: Médecines complémentaires*, Schwabe, 1994, Basel: 82–87; Deluze C. (co-author: Vischer T.-L.), *Interactions entre médecine académique et médecines non conventionnelles*, in: CMS, 1996, vol.40: 33–40; Ernst E. (ed.) (I), *Complementary medicine: An objective appraisal*, Butterworth Heinmann, 1996, Oxford; Eskinazi D. P., *Factors that shape alternative medicine*, in: JAMA, 1998, vol.280, n° 18: 1621–23; European Committee for Homeopathy, *Homeopathy in Europe – Developing standars for professionnal practice of homeopathy in the European Union*, European Committee for Homeopathy, 1994, Rotterdam: 16–21; Frey F. (co-editor: Baumann P. H.), *Supplementum 62, FNRS-PNR 34: Médecines complémentaires*, Schwabe, 1994, Basel; Gysin T. (co-author: Ziegler C.), *Klinische Hypnotherapie/Selbsthypnose für unspezifische chronische und episodische Kopfschmerzen ohne Migräne und andere definierte Kopfweharten bei Kindern und Jugenlichen*, in: Frey F., *op.cit.*: 64–66; Hochstrasser B. (co-author: Mattmann P.), *Homöopathie und Schulmedizin in der Schwangerschafts- und Geburtsbetreuung*, in: Frey F., *op.cit.*: 28–35; Hürny C. and co-authors, *Verbessern nicht-konventionelle Zusatztherapien die Lebensqualität von Krebspatienten?*, in: Frey F., *op.cit.*: 55–63; Johannessen H. (co-authors: Launso L., Olesen S. G., Staugard F.) (I), *Studies in alternative therapy 1 – Contributions from the Nordic countries*, Odense University Press, 1994, Gylling; Launso L. (co-author: Brendstrup E.) (III), *Headache and reflexogical treatment*, The Council Concerning Alternative Treatment, The National Board of Health, 1997, Copenhagen; Margolin A., *Investigating alternative medicine therapies in randomized controlled trials*, in: JAMA, 1998, vol.280, n° 18: 1626–28; Marwick C., *Alterations are ahead at the OAM*, in: JAMA, 1998, vol. 280, n° 18: 1553–54; MEDICIS T. C., *Akupunktur und Bronchialasthma*, in: FREY F., *op. cit.*: 39–48; MELCHART D. (co-authors: LINDE K., WEIDENHAMMER W., WORKU F., WAGNER H.), *The integration of natural healing procedures into research and teaching at German universities*, in: Alternative Therapies, 1995, vol. 1, n° 1: 30–33; MINISTRY OF HEALTH AND SOCIAL AFFAIRS (I), *Report on alternative medicine – English summary*, Norges Offentliche Utredniger NOU 1998: 21, 1998, Oslo; MINISTRY OF HEALTH AND SOCIAL AFFAIRS (II), *Chinese-Norwegian Health Seminar*, Ministry of Health and Social Affairs, 2001, Oslo; MONTAKAB H. (co-author: LANGEL G.), *L'effet de l'acupuncture dans le traitement de l'insomnie*, in: FREY F., *op. cit.*: 39–48; PERREZ M., *Möglichkeiten und Grenzen der Evaluation von alternativen Behandlungsmethoden*, in: BORGHI M., *op. cit.*: 141–56; ROBARD I., *La santé hors la loi: Les hors la loi de la santé*, 4th ed., Ed. de l'Ancre, 1994, Suresnes; SELECT COMMITTEE ON SCIENCE AND TECHNOLOGY, *Complementary and alternative medicine*, House of Lords – Session 1999–2000 6th Report, The Stationary Office, 2000, London; TRADITIONAL MEDICINE PROGRAMME AND GLOBAL PROGRAMME ON AIDS, *Report of a WHO consultation on traditional medicine and AIDS: Clinical evaluation of traditional medicines and natural products*, WHO, 1990, Geneva; WEIBO L., *Research in traditional Chinese medicine*, in: AKERELE O. (co-editor: STOTT G., WEIBO L.), *The role of traditional medicine in primary health care in China*, WHO, 1985, Geneva: 48–53; WHITE HOUSE COMMISSION ON COMPLEMENTARY AND ALTERNATIVE MEDICINE POLICY, *Final report*, March 2002, available at http://www.whccamp.hhs.gov/pdfs/fr2002_document.pdf, accessed Feb. 1 2005: 19–20, 30–50; WHO (I), *WHO monographs on selected medicinal plants*, vol. 1, WHO, 1999, Geneva; WHO (III), *Report of the working group on auricular acupuncture nomenclature*, WHO, 1990, Lyon; WHO (V), *Legal status of traditional medicine and complementary/alternative medicine – A World overview*, WHO, 2001, Geneva; WHO REGIONAL OFFICE FOR WESTERN PACIFIC (I), *Research guidelines for evaluating the safety and efficacy of herbal remedies*, WHO, 1993, Manila; WHO REGIONAL OFFICE FOR WESTERN PACIFIC (II), *Guidelines for clinical research on acupuncture*, WHO, 1995, Manila; WHO SCIENTIFIC GROUP, *A proposed standard international acupuncture nomenclature*, WHO, 1991, Geneva.

For decades alternative medical research and practice have been excluded from Western academia.[3] This explains the paucity of data in this area. Individuals with limited research training and resources have conducted most alternative medical research outside the universities. Conversely,

3 In particular, threats were made by supporters of mainstream medicine to people and institutions associated with alternative practitioners. Established academic researchers have also been discredited and have had difficulties when attempting to conduct alternative medical research (ESKINAZI D. P., *op. cit.*: 1622 and cited references. See also ROBARD I., *op. cit.*: 177–78).

studies with serious methodology may lack comparability and replication.[4] As a result, the development of high-quality academic research has been particularly difficult until now.[5]

Although the situation remains unsatisfactory, there is an increase of studies undertaken all over Western countries,[6] for several reasons.[7] For example, in the United States, the National Center for Complementary and Alternative Medicines (NCCAM) was created, with one of its objectives being the legitimisation of alternative medical research.[8] In Norway,

4 E.g., differences among individual investigators' resources, lack of funding, personal research interests have limited replication of studies in homeopathy and acupuncture.

5 Angell M., *op. cit.*: 839–40; Anonymous (IV), *op. cit.*: 10; Beck A., *op. cit.*: 56–57; Boozang K. M., *op. cit.*: 189–90; Bruset S., *op. cit.*: 186–96; Chez R., *op. cit.*: 1156–61; Eskinazi D. P., *op. cit.*: 1622; Cost Action B4, *op. cit.*: 77, 79–80; Johannessen H. (I), *op. cit.*; Margolin A., *op. cit.*: 1626–28; Ministry of Health and Social Affairs (I), *op. cit.*: 269; Select Committee on Science and Technology, *op. cit.*: 8–9, 30, 64–65, 76ss.

6 These studies on alternative medicines include:
1. general alternative medical research: see Anonymous (IV), *op. cit.*: 8–18, 57–59; Ernst E. (I), *op. cit.*; Cost Action B4, *op. cit.*: 64–81, 108–09; Johannessen H. (I), *op. cit.* (research in Scandinavia); Melchart D, *op. cit.*: 30–33 (research in Germany);
2. acupuncture: see Brody J. E., *op. cit.*; Deluze C, *op. cit.*: 33–40; Medicis T. C., *op. cit.*: 39–48 (acupuncture and bronchial asthma); Montakab H., *op. cit.*: 39–48 (acupuncture and insomnia);
3. homeopathy: see European Committee for Homoepathy, *op. cit.*: 16–21; Hochstrasser B., *op. cit.*: 28–35;
4. chiropractic treatment for asthma: see Balon J., *op. cit.*: 1013–27;
5. clinical hypnotherapy and self-hypnosis for headache: see Gysin T., *op. cit.*: 64–66;
6. manual trigger points treatment for chronic lumbosacral pain: see Dejung B., *op. cit.*: 82–87;
7. reflexology for headache treatment: see Launso L. (III), *op. cit.*;
8. use of alternative medicines in psychiatry: see Borghi M., *op. cit.*;
9. alternative treatments to improve the life quality of cancer patients: see Hürny C. and co-authors, *op. cit.*: 55–63;
10. presentation of natural remedies: see WHO (I), *op. cit.*

7 E.g., governments noticing the increasing use of alternative medicines mandated studies to investigate the effectiveness of specific therapies to potentially cover them.
As Margolin says, "because alternative medicine therapies are used by a significant number of Americans [...] and people worldwide [...], there is an urgent need for their efficacy to be evaluated formally" (Margolin A., *op. cit.*: 1626–28).

8 For more details regarding the NCCAM, see chap. 4.3.6.2. For recent developments regarding the NCCAM, see Boozang K. M. (III), *op. cit.*: 251–61;

Switzerland and Germany, extended national programs have been conducted[9] and articles in well-known allopathic medical journals have been published.[10] There are now a variety of scientific journals dealing with alternative medicines.[11] In other countries, the government supports research in alternative medicines.[12] At the international level, the European Commission[13] and the World Health Organisation have also been active, proposing a unification of nomenclatures, guidelines and standards in research and evaluation of alternative therapies.[14]

MARWICK C., *op. cit.*: 1553–54; WHITE HOUSE COMMISSION ON COMPLEMENTARY AND ALTERNATIVE MEDICINE POLICY, *op. cit.*: 31.

9 DAYER P., *op. cit.*: 67–69; FREY F., *op. cit.*; MINISTRY OF HEALTH AND SOCIAL AFFAIRS (II), *op. cit.*

10 See the New England Journal of Medicine, 1998, vol. 338, n° 15; the Journal of the American Medical Association (JAMA), 1998, vol. 280, n° 18; the Lancet, 1996, n° 347. The fact that these medical journals have published articles regarding alternative medicines and their testing is strong evidence of a change of attitude towards alternative techniques.

11 E.g., the Journal of Alternative and Complementary Medicine: Research on Paradigm, Practice, and Policy; Alternative in Health and Medicine; Alternative Health Practitioner: The Journal of Complementary and Natural Care, etc.

12 E.g., in Great Britain, the Secretary of State can allocate funds to medical faculties in order to allow physicians to study thoroughly their medical knowledge, as for example in homeopathy. According to the Institute of Alternative Medicines, both Houses of Parliament support these therapies (ROBARD I., *op. cit.*: 222).

13 The European Cooperation in the field of Scientific and Technical research (COST) of the European Commission conducted the COST project B4, an European initiative for a comprehensive research program on alternative medicines. The goals of the project were to demonstrate the possibilities, limitations, and significance of unconventional medicines by establishing a common scientific background, to help to control health care costs and to harmonise legislation.

14 COST ACTION B4, *op. cit.*: 64–81, 108–09 (research guidelines); TRADITIONAL MEDICINE PROGRAMME AND GLOBAL PROGRAMME ON AIDS, *op. cit.* (clinical evaluation of traditional medicines and natural products); WHO (I), *op. cit.* (medicinal plants); WHO (III), *op. cit.* (auricular acupuncture nomenclature); WHO REGIONAL OFFICE FOR WESTERN PACIFIC (I), *op. cit.* (safety and efficacy of herbal remedies); WHO REGIONAL OFFICE FOR WESTERN PACIFIC (II), *op. cit.* (guidelines for clinical research on acupuncture); WHO SCIENTIFIC GROUP, *op. cit.* (propositions for an international standard regarding acupuncture nomenclature).
The British Select Committee on Science and Technology has determined as important the following areas for research in the alternative medical field: 1. research into the effects of each individual therapy; its efficacy, its safety and its cost-effectiveness; 2. research into the mechanisms of action of each individual therapy, including patterns of response to treatment and research into the placebo

Similarly, in China, numerous research institutions also exist with perhaps the most prestigious being the Academy of Traditional Medicine in Beijing. In 1984 a Bureau of Traditional Medicine was set up as part of the central health administration.[15]

One of the primary objectives of medical research is to evaluate the efficacy, safety, biological plausibility, and any other factors that are especially relevant to the provision of medical treatments. In order to conduct this evaluation effectively, any research undertaken must define the most appropriate methods of accomplishing such research. However, research in alternative medicines is currently facing several problems. In particular, the common criteria used in biomedicine – the so-called *"evidence based medicine"* – employed to demonstrate the mechanisms of action (usually with bio-chemistry) or to establish the effectiveness of medical treatments (typically the double-blind testing or randomised controlled trials) are not easily applicable to alternative treatments.[16] An effort is currently being made to find new ways to asess the scientific validity of alternative techniques.[17]

---

effect; 3. research into the CAM genre itself, including social research into the motivation of those patients seeking CAM and the usage patterns of CAM; 4. research into new research strategies which are sensitive to the CAM paradigm; 5. research into the efficacy of the diagnostic methods used; 6. research into the implementation and effects of CAM in specific healthcare settings (SELECT COMMITTEE ON SCIENCE AND TECHNOLOGY, *op. cit.*: 76). For more on these developments, see the same author at 76ss.

15 WHO (V), *op. cit.*: 148–52; WEIBO L., *op. cit.*: 48–53.

16 See also BRUSET S., *op. cit.*: 186–96 (lack of scientific tools, lack of qualified supervisors, problems regarding standardisation of patients and treatment, individualisation of treatments); MARGOLIN A., *op. cit.*: 1626–28 (basis to undertake a controlled trial, codification and acceptance of treatments, identification of objective outcomes, difficulties of blinding procedures); PERREZ M., *op. cit.*: 141–56 (standardisation of patients and of the method, criteria to evaluate effectiveness, placebo effect).

17 Regarding the situation of research in alternative medicines, an author notes, "although various reports have set out guidelines for CAM research methodology in some details, there is still widespread ignorance on the subject, among both practitioners and researchers. There are also some clear indications that the 'gatekeepers' to funding for research are not fully aware of the current debate on research methods. Background information and agreed guidelines on current issues in research into CAM therefore need to be prepared, and communicated to all 'gatekeeper' organisations and to researchers. When funding organisations consult with referees they should ensure that they are appropriately experienced and informed" (ANONYMOUS (IV), *op. cit.*: 10–12). For a recent development

3.3 Education and Training

Bibliography

ALDRIDGE D. (I), *Unconventional medicine in Europe*, Advances, 1994, vol. 10, n° 2: 55; AMBÜHL I., *Naturheilkunde auf dem Weg zur Annerkennung*, in: Basler Zeitung, Mar. 22, 1994; ANONYMOUS (IV), *Integrated healthcare – A way forward for the next five years?*, Foundation for Integrated Medicine, 1997; ANONYMOUS (V), *La formation postgraduée de deux ans selon la LAMal*, in: BMS, 1997, vol. 78, n° 25: 943–44; ANONYMOUS (VI), *Nouvelle systématique des titres de spécialiste*, in: BMS, 1997, vol. 78, n° 39: 1426–27; ARJALAGUER X., *Los médicos daràn reconocimiento oficial a homeopatìa, acupuntura y medicina naturista*, in: La Vanguardia, Sep. 24, 1996: 25; BECK A., *La chaire de médecine complémentaire à l'Université de Berne: Une création récente*, in: CMS, 1996, vol. 40: 55–62; BOUCHAYER F., *Alternative medicines: A general approach to the French situation*, in: LEWITH G. (co-editor: ALDRIDGE D.), *Complementary medicine and the European Community*, CW Daniel, 1991, Saffron Walden: 51–52; BRITISH MEDICAL ASSOCIATION (LAMONT T.), *Complementary medicine – New approaches to good practice*, Oxford University Press, 1993, Oxford/New York:

---

regarding proposed guidelines in alternative medical research, see the same author, at 12ss. See also SELECT COMMITTEE ON SCIENCE AND TECHNOLOGY, *op. cit.*: 8–9, 77–82.

Of note are the general principles developed by the Foundation for Integrated Medicine (ANONYMOUS (IV), *op. cit.*: 8):

1. "if CAM are to be more closely integrated, they must both be subject to rigorous scrutiny. The methods employed should be appropriate to the task and should embrace a wide spectrum, both quantitative and qualitative;
2. CAM research will frequently involve expert researchers from outside CAM practice, but CAM practitioners should be actively involved or consulted in the design and execution of a study;
3. Collaboration between patients, practitioners and researchers is required;
4. Priorities need to be set. They should include, for example, systematic literature reviews of published studies, further investigation where there is some evidence of effectiveness, where the wide use of a therapy indicates that further investigation is warranted, where the nature of the health problem is of importance, and where there are major potential benefits (either health and/or economic);
5. The perspectives of different groups will need to be taken into account. In particular, while a substantial amount of research will necessarily follow tried and tested methods, there is a need to develop innovative approaches appropriate to CAM. This might lead to new methods of value also to orthodox medical approach."

For developments regarding parameters to establish scientific legitimacy, see chap. 6.3.

22, 24, 41–43; Chapman-Smith D. A., *Legislative approaches to the regulation of the chiropractic profession*, in: J. Can. Chiropractic Assoc., 1996 June; vol. 40, n° 2: 113; Cherkin D. C. (co-editor: Mootz R. D.), *Chiropractic in the United States: Training, practice and research*, Agency for Health Care Policy and Research, 1997, Rockville; Cohen M. H. (I), *Alternative medicine – Legal boundaries and regulatory perspectives*, The Johns Hopkins University Press, 1998, London & Oxford; Committee on Traditional Chinese Medicine, *Traditional Chinese Medicine*, Ministry of Health, 1995, Singapore: 35; Conférence des Directeurs Cantonaux des Affaires Sanitaires, *Rapport annuel 1998*, CDS, 1998, Bern: 6–7; Cramer R., *Strafrechtliche Grenzen der Therapiefreiheit und der Heilbehandlung durch den Heilpraktiker*, Dissertion, 1995, Köln: 35–40, 47–48; Dayer P., *Le groupe multidisciplinaire d'étude des médecines non-conventionnelles de Genève*, in: CMS, 1996, vol. 40: 67–69; Deluze C. (co-author: Vischer T.-L.), *Interactions entre médecine académique et médecines non conventionnelles*, in: CMS, 1996, vol. 40: 33–40; Diezi J., *L'enseignement informatif sur les médecines parallèles à la faculté de médecine de Lausanne*, in: CMS, 1996, vol. 40: 63–65; Dutch Health Council, *Report on complementary therapies and research*, Dutch Health Care Council, 1993, The Hague; Ehlers A. P. F., *Medizin in den Händen von Heilpraktikern – "Nicht-Heilkundigen"*, Springer Verlag, 1995, Berlin/Heidelberg: 143–45, 148; Fisher P. (co-author: Ward A.), *Complementary medicine in Europe*, in: BMJ, vol. 309, July 9, 1994: 110; Friedman R. (co-authors: Sedler M., Myers P., Benson H.), *Behavioral medicine, complementary medicine and integrated care: Economic implications*, in: Prim. Care 1997 Dec., vol. 24, n° 4: 950; Frost and Sullivan Ltd, *Alternative medical practices in Europe*, Report n° E874, Sullivan House, Grosvenor Gardens, 1987, London SW1: 210, 232, 245–46; Gaier H. (II), *Reveille for biocentric medicine*, in: Lewith G. (co-editor: Aldridge D.), *Complementary medicine and the European Community*, CW Daniel, 1991, Saffron Walden: 9–34; General Osteopathic Council, *Standard 2000 – Standard of Proficiency*, General Osteopathic Council, March 1999; Giger M., *Les médecines parallèles dans le réseau de la Fédération des Médecins Suisses*, in: CMS, 1996, vol. 40: 53–54; Goodwin J., *A health insurance revolution*, in: New Age Journal's Guide to Holistic Medicine, 1997–1998: 66; Hänggeli C. (I), *Une étape décisive pour la FMH*, in: Bulletin des Médecins Suisses: 1998, vol. 79, n° 48: 2447–48; Hänggeli C., *La formation postgraduée en pleine mutation: Chance ou risque?*, in: BMS: 2000, vol. 81, n° 35: 1896–98; Hoff W. (I), *Guidelines for training traditional health practitioners in primary health care*, Divison of Strengthening of Health Services and Traditional Medicine Programme, Geneva 1995; Hoff W. (II), *Traditional practitioners as primary health care workers*, Divison of Strengthening of Health Services and Traditional Medicine Programme, Geneva 1995: 111–18; Kilgore C., *Expanding coverage signals growing demand, acceptance for alternative care*, in: Medicine & Health Perspectives, May 4 1998: 3; Künzi M. (II), *Komplementärmedizin und Gesundheitsrecht*, Helbing & Lichtenhahn Verlag AG, 1996, Basel: 24–25, 29–37, 68–71; Lechat P., *A propos du projet de création d'un diplôme interuniversitaire d'homéopathie dans les facultés de médecine*, in: Bulletin de l'Académie Nationale de Médecine, 1998, vol. 182, n° 4: 889; Lewith G. (co-editor: Aldridge D.), *Complementary medicine and the European Community*, CW Daniel, 1991,

Saffron Walden; MCCARTHY M. (co-author: REES S.), *Health systems and health medicine in the European Community*, Royal College of Physicians of London, 1992, London: 21–22; MELCHART D. (co-authors: LINDE K., WEIDENHAMMER W., WORKU F., WAGNER H.), *The integration of natural healing procedures into research and teaching at German universities*, in: Alternative Therapies, 1995, vol. 1, n° 1: 30–33; MINISTRY OF HEALTH AND SOCIAL AFFAIRS (I), *Report on alternative medicine – English summary*, Norges Offentliche Utredniger NOU 1998: 21, 1998, Oslo: 267; PETIT-PIERRE M.-C. (I), *L'homéopathie et la médecine chinoise décrochent le titre envié de spécialité*, in: Le Temps, Oct. 24 1998; ROBARD I., *La santé hors la loi: Les hors la loi de la santé*, 4th ed., Ed. de l'Ancre, 1994, Suresnes; ROEMER M. I., *National health systems of the world*, vol. 1, Oxford University Press, 1992, New York: 73, 590; ROSENTHAL M. M., *Modernization and health care in the people's republic of China: The period of transition*, in: ROSENTHAL M. M. (ed.), *Health care systems and their patients: An international perspective*, Westview Press, 1992, Boulder: 302; SAGE W. M. (co-author: AIKEN L. H.), *Regulating interdisciplinary practice*, in: JOST T. S., *Regulation of the healthcare professions*, Health Administration Press, 1996, Chicago: 82–83; SALLER R., *Médecine naturelle (Naturheilkunde) à l'Université de Zürich*, in: CMS, 1996, vol. 40: 71–74; SERMEUS G., *Alternative health care in Belgium: An explanation of various social aspects*, in: LEWITH G., *op. cit.*: 63; THOMAS K. J., *Non-orthodox health care in the UK*, in: LEWITH G., *op. cit.*: 129; VASKILAMPI T. (I), *The role of alternative medicine: The Finnish experience*, in: LEWITH G., *op. cit.*: 101, 108; VISSER G. J. (I), *Alternative medicine in the Netherlands*, in: LEWITH G., *op. cit.*: 119; WALDBURGER N. (co-author: MARCER N.), *Définition d'un niveau de formation adéquat – Exigences d'un examen final pour l'obtention d'un diplôme reconnu par le Service de la Santé Publique*, 2001, Lausanne; WARDWELL W. I., *Alternative medicine in the United States*, in: Social Science and Medicine, 1994, vol. 38, n° 8: 1065–66; WETZEL M. S. (co-authors: EISENBERG D. M., KAPTCHUK T. J.), *Courses involving alternative medicine at US medical schools*, in: JAMA, 1998, vol. 280, n° 9: 784–87; WHITE HOUSE COMMISSION ON COMPLEMENTARY AND ALTERNATIVE MEDICINE POLICY, *Final report*, Mar. 2002, available at http://www.whccamp.hhs.gov/pdfs/fr2002_document.pdf, accessed Feb. 1 2005: 51–67; WHO REGIONAL OFFICE FOR WESTERN PACIFIC (II), *Technical briefing on traditional medicine*, WHO, Manila: 3, 22; YOUBANG C., *Education and training in traditional Chinese medicine*, in: AKERELE O. (co-editor: STOTT G., WEIBO L.), *The role of traditional medicine in primary health care in China*, WHO, 1985, Geneva: 37–40.

3.3.1 Education and Training for Allopathic Practitioners

Once only available outside medical schools, educational courses and internships are now being proposed for some medical schools. Education in alternative medicines is varied in the forms it takes, being either part of the general curriculum, in a series of optional courses, or post-graduate training. The following sections demonstrate the variety of approaches taken by various Western countries towards training in alternative medicine.

3.3.1.1 Austria[18]

During the past few years, the Council of the Order of Physicians has created training programmes in acupuncture, homeopathy, manual therapies and neuraltherapy, lasting between two and three years (from 140 to 350 hours). The training culminates in a diploma,[19] which is officially recognised as a medical qualification.

3.3.1.2 Belgium

As the Belgian Royal College of Physicians considers alternative medicines as being insufficiently proven or impossible to prove, they are still not taught in Belgian medical schools. This is true both for the basic curriculum and for post-graduate training.[20] However, the Belgian Medical Faculty of Homeopathy does organise courses for physicians, surgeons, dentists, pharmacists and veterinarians, following the standards of the European Committee for Homeopathy.[21] Furthermore, there are two associations of acupuncturists which hold training courses in the evening and during week-ends.[22] The program lasts for three years.[23]

It is important to notice that recent developments regarding the licensing to practise alternative medicines may influence the teaching of alternative medicines in university faculties.[24]

18 Prof A. Stacher, Wiener Internationale Akademie für Ganzheitmedizin, Mar. 1997, Vienna; H. Schmadlbauer, oberösterreichische Gebietskrankenkasse, Linz, Aug. 2001.

19 In German: "Spezial-Diplome der Österreichischen Ärztekammer".

20 SERMEUS G., *op. cit.*: 63.

21 LIGA MEDICORUM HOMEOPATHICA INTERNATIONALIS, Mallorca, 1996.

22 However, practitioners using acupuncture are generally trained in East-Asia or in France.

23 ROBARD I., *op. cit.*: 214.

24 Details of the new statute are outlined in chap. 4.3.3.1.

3.3.1.3 *Denmark*

The Danish Society for Medical Acupuncture has proposed a 120 hour diploma course in acupuncture for physicians.

3.3.1.4 *Finland*[25]

Acupuncture is accepted as part of orthodox medical practice and it has been included in the medical curriculum since 1975.

3.3.1.5 *France*

Medical training at the undergraduate level lasts seven years. In the fifth year students may choose a specialty, which may include general practice. Specialty training includes four terms of clinical practice, one of which must be done outside the hospital.[26]

Up until 1990, some medical schools offered a few courses on alternative medicines, in particular, acupuncture and homeopathy[27], leading to a certificate.[28] In 1982, the Department of Natural Medicines was created within the University of Bobigny. Since then, the University has awarded diplomas in acupuncture, homeopathy, phytotherapy,[29] osteopathy, auriculotherapy, naturopathy, oligotherapy and mesotherapy.[30] In 1990, the DUMENAT[31] was created, being a continuous education program leading to an inter-university diploma.[32]

25 ALDRIDGE D., *op. cit.*: 55; BRITISH MEDICAL ASSOCIATION, *op. cit.*: 24; VASKILAMPI T. (I), *op. cit.*: 101.
26 MCCARTHY M., *op. cit.*: 21–22.
27 At the Universities of Marseille, Bordeaux, Lille, Besançon and Bobigny.
28 Of note is that during the nineteen eighties a large number of physicians in France chose alternative medicines as a new way of practising medicine. One of the reasons for this interest was the increasing number of GPs who were (and still are) looking for new ways to practise medicine (ROBARD I., *op. cit.*: 48).
29 Phytotherapy is also taught during the basic curriculum in pharmacy.
30 The typical profile of students attending the DUMENAT is comprised of physicians between 35 and 40 years of age (Prof. Cornillot P., University of Bobigny, Oct. 1997, Paris).
31 In French: "Diplôme Universitaire de Médecines Naturelles" (university diploma in natural medicine).
32 ALDRIDGE D., *op. cit.*: 55; ROBARD I., *op. cit.*: 48; Prof. Cornillot P., University of Bobigny, Oct. 1997, Paris.

The DUMENAT in acupuncture and osteopathy is recognised by the French National Order of Physicians.[33] The Order is also considering the recognition of the DUMENAT in homeopathy.[34]

It should be stressed, however, that the DUMENAT diplomas are not yet considered as new specialties, but merely as recognised diplomas. In order to obtain the recognition as a medical specialty,[35] the training should fulfil the same criteria as an allopathic specialty, i.e. it must be full-time and include periods of clinical practice.[36]

On the subject of chiropractic, a Decree of February 11 1953 stated that chiropractic should be taught in medical schools. The recognition of chiropractic as a medical specialty was apparently confirmed by not only two ministerial decrees but also by the Council of State as well as the French Courts. However, the 1953 Decree was never applied and chiropractic has never been taught in medical schools. Indeed, the medical corpus did not consider the technique serious and was opposed to its recognition.[37]

3.3.1.6 Germany

In 1989, a project for "Integration of Natural Healing Procedures into research and teaching" commenced at the Ludwig-Maximilian University in Munich. Its objective was to improve research and teaching of some alternative medicines and to provide the infrastructural and conceptual prerequisites for the establishment of an independent academic institution. In the years 1989 to 1992, pre-graduate courses on alternative medicines

33 The decisive criterion for the recognition of a new diploma is that the training must be available in several universities, which is precisely the case for inter-university diplomas.

34 In Apr. 1998, the French National Academy of Medicine opposed the creation of a new inter-university diploma in homeopathy (LECHAT P., *op. cit.*: 889). One should note that homeopathy is refunded by social security when provided by a physician. For more details, see chap. 5.3.5.4.

35 The National Order of Physicians is also responsible for recognising new medical specialties.

36 The DUMENAT training is more theoretical and less practical than training in allopathic specialties. The present DUMENAT training schedule encompasses 12–16 hours per month over a period of three years. This equates to total of 300–400 hours and includes only limited practical training (Prof. Cornillot P., University of Bobigny, Oct. 1997, Paris; Dr. Grunwald M., vice-general secretary of the National Order of Physicians, Oct. 1997, Paris).

37 ROBARD I., *op. cit.*: 49–50.

were organised.[38] Parts of these courses have now been integrated into the regular undergraduate education. In fact, since 1993, medical schools are now obliged to test students on their knowledge of alternative medicines. Various guidelines in relation to postgraduate education have also been set up. There are also some post-graduate specialisations in alternative medicines for physicians.[39]

In 1993, a network of clinics using alternative medicines developed a comprehensive quality assurance project which included observational studies and conducting controlled clinical trials. In recent years, two chairs of alternative medicine have also been established in Ulm and in Berlin.[40] However, as Melchart notes, alternative medicines "are still inadequately represented in academic medicine, teaching, and research".[41]

3.3.1.7 Great Britain

In 1995, three medical schools were providing education in alternative medicine. According to a survey, another three medical schools were planning to introduce the same type of education.[42]

Additionally, the homeopathic faculty of the Royal London Homeopathic Hospital organises courses for physicians, but these, however, are not integrated into a recognised training. Some private schools have also

38 The course was mainly to provide information. Teaching objectives centred on the basic knowledge regarding diagnostics, indications and contra-indications for specific techniques, and the ability to communicate between biomedicine and alternative medicines, as well as the acquisition of basic practical skills in at least one specific technique. There were also lectures on general subjects, introductions to specific alternative medicines, weekend study groups, self-analysis seminars and practical courses. Students had to choose at least one optional course in either acupuncture, diagnostic-therapeutic local anaesthesia and manual medicine, health food nutrition, homeopathy, hydro- and climatherapy, physiotherapy, phytomedicine or traditional Chinese medicine.

39 Cramer R., *op. cit.*: 47–48; Melchart D., *op. cit.*: 30–32.

40 The German Medical Association prescribes at least 4 weeks of a basic training course covering specific topics and 3 months of internship or practical work under the supervision of a physician licensed for postgraduate education in the field. Since 1993, the Münchener Modell has run a pilot postgraduate training optimised every year, with testing focused on theoretical knowledge, competence, and performance skills in practice.

41 Melchart D., *op. cit.*: 30. See also British Medical Association, *op. cit.*: 22.

42 Anonymous (IV), *op. cit.*: 19. For a critical appraisal of education in alternative medicines in Great Britain, see the same author, at 20–21, 67.

proposed a comprehensive course leading to a certificate. For example, the London College of Classical Homeopathy offers a four-year training course.[43, 44]

There are 54 professional associations representing therapists within Great Britain. These associations offer comprehensive full time courses in anthroposophy, chiropractic, phytotherapy, naturopathy and osteopathy lasting for a minimum of three years.[45]

3.3.1.8 Italy[46]

There are serious training courses for physicians in acupuncture. In some post-university courses on anaesthesiology, acupuncture is a facultative course. Other universities, such as the University of Catania in Sicily, have organised a post-graduate course in acupuncture.

3.3.1.9 Latvia[47]

The Council of Ministers of the Republic of Latvia has delegated its power to regulate and supervise all medical specialties to the Medical Society of the Republic.[48] In addition, acupuncture and homeopathy received the same legal status as clinical allopathic specialties.

Since 1990, over 300 physicians from the Scandinavian and Baltic countries have already attended the training in acupuncture and traditional Chinese medicine.

3.3.1.10 Netherlands

A survey conducted by the Dutch National Advisory Council for Public Health showed that approximately 60% of the members of alternative professional organisations had undergone a classic medical training that did

43 This includes 1,440 hours of theory and 300 hours of practice.

44 BRITISH MEDICAL ASSOCIATION, *op. cit.*: 41, 43; ROBARD I., *op. cit.*: 224–25.

45 ANONYMOUS (IV), *op. cit.*: 19; BRITISH MEDICAL ASSOCIATION, *op. cit.*: 41–42; FROST AND SULLIVAN, *op. cit.*: 245–46; ROBARD I., *op. cit.*: 223; THOMAS K. J., *op. cit.*: 129.

46 FROST AND SULLIVAN, *op. cit.*: 232.

47 Dr. Nickolaev N. A., Professor and Director of the Association for Medical Acupuncture and Related Techniques of the Republic of Latvia, Sept. 2001, Riga.

48 The licensing procedure is provided in the regulations of certification of health professionals (cabinet of Ministers, 1995).

not include alternative medicines.[49] Their regular education was generally as a medical doctor, physical therapist or nurse.[50]

In 1993, the Dutch Health Council pointed out that alternative institutions had organised a number of training courses and that appropriate steps had been taken to develop a training curriculum and national registration systems. The intention was to establish standards.[51]

Medical doctors requiring a training in alternative medicines can attend a part-time course in anthroposophical medicine, acupuncture, homeopathy or manipulative therapy. These courses last from one to four years.[52] One should note that the new Health Care Professionals Act defines the necessary training requirements as the necessity to be registered as a medical professional and also introduces the possibility of creating new medical specialties, under specific conditions.[53] However, as of yet, there are no specialties in alternative medicines yet.

3.3.1.11 *Norway*[54]

Education in alternative medicines is offered for a range of treatments, including acupuncture, acupressure, aromatherapy, holistic therapy, osteopathy and yoga/breathing exercises. Furthermore, some schools offer courses on basic medical subjects which includes some courses on alternative medicines.

The schools that offer training in alternative medicines are private and, as such, are not entitled to give examinations under the Universities and Colleges Act. The length of the education varies from brief courses to several years of full-time study. All such courses of education contain a mandatory practice period.

49 Several Dutch medical schools include a familiarization with alternative medicines in their curriculum (FISHER P., *op. cit.*: 110).

50 The number of GPs in the Netherlands in 1987 was about 6,200, physiotherapists 9,000 and medical specialists 11,000. The number of non-organised alternative practitioners is not known (VISSER G. J., *op. cit.*: 119).

51 DUTCH HEALTH COUNCIL, *op. cit.*

52 These courses are usually organised outside universities.

53 For more details, see chap. 4.3.3.7.

54 MINISTRY OF HEALTH AND SOCIAL AFFAIRS (I), *op. cit.*: 267.

3.3.1.12 *Spain*[55]

The Universities of Barcelona, Valladolid and Murcia organise postgraduate training in homeopathy, acupuncture and naturopathy for physicians. In addition, professional colleges and some universities offer basic and advanced homeopathic courses for pharmacists and veterinarians. Several universities also provide certificates in alternative medicines.

So far as education in acupuncture is concerned, two societies (Sociedad Española Acupunctura and Sociedad Española de Medicos Acupunctores in Madrid) organise initiation courses of two weeks, three training courses of 90 days and a complete training of three years. There are also other professional organisations that organise training courses.

3.3.1.13 *Sweden*[56]

There are no training courses in alternative medicines at the University level in Sweden. However, at the academic level, there are some short orientation courses in alternative medicines. Since 2000, such course has been offered at the medical school Karolinska Institutet in Stockholm.[57] Furthermore, there are private schools for education in homeopathy, naprapathy, and acupuncture.

3.3.1.14 *Switzerland*

During the past few decades, training in alternative medicines has been developed outside universities.[58] For example, since the beginning of the 1990s, introductory courses on alternative medicines have been included in the academic curriculum for physicians. The Swiss Interfaculty Medical Commission recommended that the medical faculty create a new body specifically to deal with alternative medical issues. Further recommendation were that this body insure that information regarding the most widespread

55 ARJALAGUER X., *op. cit.*: 25; Dr. Amengual I. Vicens C., Liga Medicorum Homeopathica Internationalis, Mallorca, Aug. 2001.

56 Dr. Motzi Eklöf, at the Department of Physical Education and Health, Örebro University, Örebro, Sept. 2001.

57 These courses should shortly also be offered at other schools for health care personnel.

58 Several medical associations have set up training in alternative medicines. These include the Swiss association of homeopaths physicians ("Schweizerische Vereinigung homöopatischer Ärzte"), the Swiss medical society for acupuncture and traditional Chinese medicine ("Schweizerische Ärztegesellschaft für Akupunktur und Traditionell-Chinesische Medizin"), etc.

alternative techniques be provided to medical students and that studies regarding the evaluation of alternative medicines be conducted.[59]

Until June 2002,[60] the FMH has been the association responsible for medical specialities. It was aware of the need for post-graduate training in alternative medicine,[61] and between 1999 and 2000, it established a new training regime for homeopathy, Chinese medicine (including acupuncture), anthroposophic medicine and neural therapy.[62] These courses do not lead to a specialty degree but rather to a diploma,[63] awarded in various certification attesting that the practitioner successfully attended the training. Physicians providing alternative medicine must hold these diplomas to be able to have the medical acts they provide be covered under the compulsory social insurance.[64]

The universities of Zürich and Bern[65] include courses on alternative medicines in their medical curricula. Four main departments in the medical faculty in Bern were created; anthroposophical medicine, homeopathy,

59 BECK A., *op. cit.*: 57; GIGER M., *op. cit.*: 53.

60 When the modification of the Federal Act regulating the Exercice of the Professions of Physicians, Pharmacists and Veterinarians entered into force. For more details, see chap. 4.3.6.1.

61 The FMH considered that the 4,500 alternative physicians members of the FMH have the right to be considered seriously by their professional organisation. Furthermore, it considered that it had a duty to introduce post-graduate training in alternative medicines in order to ensure the quality of provided services.
A survey among physicians in the canton Bern showed that 40% of them had used alternative techniques or had referred patients to alternative practitioners. Students also expressed their interest in alternative medicines (BECK A., *op. cit.*: 58).

62 For an overview of the content of the training, go to http://www.fmh.ch, accessed July 30 2001. For example, the training in acupuncture lasts 360 hours.

63 The FMH set up two categories of diplomas, namely certificates of complementary training and certificates of technical capacity.

64 One must notice that these diplomas attesting a two-year post-graduate training comply with EU law regarding the recognition of training.
ANONYMOUS (V), *op. cit.*: 943–44; ANONYMOUS (VI), *op. cit.*: 1426–27; AMBÜHL I., *op. cit.*; GIGER M., *op. cit.*: 53–54; HÄNGGELI C. (I), *op. cit.*: 2447–48; HÄNGGELI C. (II), *op. cit.*: 1896–98; KÜNZI M. (II), *op. cit.*: 24–25; PETIT-PIERRE M.-C. (I), *op. cit.*

65 The statute of Feb. 7 1954 on the University of Bern was modified. The new article 4 (2) specifies that at least one chair in alternative medicines must be attached to the faculty of medicine. According to Beck, the objective is to consider alternative medicines as an integral part of the physician professional training (BECK A., *op. cit.*: 58ss).

neuraltherapy and Chinese medicine (including acupuncture).[66] In addition, there is an interdisciplinary Commission in charge of supervising research projects in alternative medicines. Since 1995, the medical official schedule has included two days of introduction to alternative medicines and a bimonthly course provided by four teachers. Furthermore, several lectures are organised. Students may also acquire diagnostic and therapeutic knowledge in alternative medicines through internships with four teachers during the optional year.[67]

On May 1 1995, the government of canton Zürich created a new chair in natural medicine within the university of Zürich. This new division consists of several departments including research, teaching and providing care. Courses, seminars and lectures are optional for students in the fourth year. An introductory course was proposed (2–4 hours per week during one year).[68] In addition, continuous education for physicians and pharmacists is organised in cooperation with non-physician alternative practitioners.[69]

In 1992, a multidisciplinary study group on alternative medicines was created at the university of Geneva. A data center was set up and several research projects are now in progress. Furthermore, an optional course (introduction to non-conventional medicine) is organised every year. It consists of 4 to 6 seminars in fields including acupuncture, homeopathy, natural medicine, chiropractic, phytotherapy and anthroposophical medicine.[70]

66 The objectives of the chair are: 1. the development of a theoretical scientific basis to understand the mechanism of several alternative techniques; 2. to supervise and coordinate research projects; 3. to gather and interpret scientific literature in the field; 4. to give scientific data to the media; 5. to promote interdisciplinary works within and outside the university; 6. to verify the quality of alternative medicines; 7. the teaching of specific knowledge to students and physicians, in cooperation with specialists in alternative medicine; 8. the information to patients about alternative medicines during clinical studies; 9. the setting up of a concept in the long term; [...].

67 AMBÜHL I., *op. cit.*; BECK A., *op. cit.*: 57–62; KÜNZI M. (II), *op. cit.*: 24–25; PETIT-PIERRE M.-C. (I), *op. cit.*

68 The course includes fundamental questions such as definitions, concepts, theoretical representations, nosologies, diagnostic questions, as well as diagnostic and therapeutic techniques in natural medicine, comparison with other techniques, and research in natural medicine. Beside courses, seminars and lectures are organised. Internships are also organised in Switzerland and in Germany. PhD dissertations are in progress.

69 SALLER R., *op. cit.*: 71–73.

70 DAYER P., *op. cit.*: 67–69.

Since 1992, the university of Lausanne has also offered an introductory course on alternative medicine.[71]

3.3.1.15 *Ukraine*[72]

The Academy of Physicians Postgraduate Education and the Ukrainian National Medical Association, both under the supervision of the Ukrainian Ministry of Public Health, offer special educational courses for physicians. These associations organise and provide training in homeopathy, iridology, reflexology, aromatherapy and phytotherapy.

3.3.1.16 *United States*

During the last few years, education in alternative medicine has become an area of interest. In 1997, for example, the Group on Educational Affairs of the Association of American Medical Colleges, the American Public Health Association and the Society of Teachers of Family Medicine formed special interest groups focusing on alternative therapies. In addition, the Federation of State Medical Boards has urged the development of educational opportunities for licensees, consumers, and legislators. The American Medical Association (AMA) has also recognized the need for medical schools to respond to the growing interest in alternative health care practices.[73, 74]

A 1998 survey over 125 US medical schools showed that 64% reported offering one or more courses in alternative medicines or including the topic in required courses. The majority (63%) of schools, (including those at

71 DIEZI J., *op.cit.*: 63–65.

72 Dr. Hmelewskaja A., Aug. 2001, Kiew.

73 A 1997 report on "Encouraging Medical Student Education in Complementary Health Care Practices" responded to a request for the AMA to "study the development of a model elective curriculum for increasing awareness of the prevalence and potential impact of various complementary/alternative health care practices on patients' health" by concluding that "medical schools should be free to design their own required or elective experience related to alternative/complementary health care practices" (WETZEL M. S., *op.cit.*: 784–87).
A survey exploring the attitudes of family physicians and primary care internists showed that physicians have a high degree of interest in alternative medicine, that more than half indicated that they would encourage patients who raise the possibility of alternative medicine, and that 57% were willing to refer their patients for treatment for 6 or more alternative therapies (WETZEL M. S., *op.cit.*: 784–87).

74 KILGORE C., *op.cit.*: 3; WETZEL M. S., *op.cit.*: 784–87. See also WHITE HOUSE COMMISSION ON COMPLEMENTARY AND ALTERNATIVE MEDICINE POLICY, *op.cit.*: 51ss.

Harvard and Columbia), offered a single course and 37% offered two or more courses. A total of 123 courses was reported.[75, 76]

All of the free-standing alternative medicines courses are currently offered as electives. Thirty-one schools (41% of those schools reporting courses) reported that 38 courses included alternative medicine topics as a component of a required course. These topics are frequently taught in an introduction to clinical medicine or in patient-physician communication courses in the first or second year, with electives typically offered in the third and fourth years.[77]

The amount of time scheduled for elective courses ranged from 6 to 160 hours, with only 9 schools reporting courses of more than 100 hours.[78, 79] Nine courses were offered by separate institutes or centers affiliated with universities or medical schools.[80] Extensive postgraduate programs hare held at the University of Arizona or at the New York's Beth Israel Medical Center.[81]

The average number of students per elective course was 16, ranging from 5 students in clinical electives to 40 or more in several well-established courses.[82]

The most frequently cited educational features include visits to centers offering alternative medical therapies and observational or preceptorial

75 Another 1998 survey conducted by the Liaison Committee on Medical Education indicated a notable increase in instruction in alternative medicine. It showed that, although no medical school reported offering a separate required course in alternative medicines, medical schools covering these areas as part of a required course increased to 63 (from 46 in 1996–1997) and medical schools offering a separate elective course increased to 54 (from 47 in 1996–1997). In the 1996–1997 academic year, 34 medical schools offered instruction as part of an elective course, and 28 offered other educational experiences.

76 Wetzel M. S., *op. cit.*: 784–87. See also Cohen M. H. (I), *op. cit.*: 8; Friedman R., *op. cit.*: 950; Goodwin J., *op. cit.*: 66; Kilgore C., *op. cit.*: 3.

77 Wetzel M. S., *op. cit.*: 784–87.

78 E.g., the University of Cincinnati College of Medicine, Cincinnati, Ohio; Cornell University Medical College, New York, NY; The Johns Hopkins University School of Medicine, Baltimore, Md; and the University of Maryland School of Medicine, Baltimore were listed as having 3- or 4-week electives with up to 7 hours of class per day.

79 Hours devoted to alternative medical topics in required courses ranged from 2 to 10, with an average of 4.5 hours.

80 Wetzel M. S., *op. cit.*: 784–87.

81 White House Commission on Complementary and Alternative Medicine Policy, *op. cit.*: 53–54.

82 Wetzel M. S., *op. cit.*: 784–87.

experiences with providers of these treatments. Several unique teaching methods were also reported in addition to the predominant lectures, case studies and discussions.[83] Course requirements varied greatly among the 61 schools reporting these details.[84]

With respect to the topical content of the courses, most medical schools include acupuncture, chiropractic, massage, therapeutic touch, homeopathy, nutrition, herbal medicine and mind-body techniques. Several courses focus on faith and spirituality. Other courses have a public health, biostatistical or epidemiological perspective, with their principal focus on rules of evidence and critical reading of relevant medical literature. Native American and Asian ethnomedicine is well represented in several courses, while other courses are based on a humanistic or human potential viewpoint. Several schools have courses designed and taught by faculty with a folklore background. Many courses appear to have the objective of introducing the student to the diverse forms of alternative medicines.[85]

It appears that students have had an enormous influence on the development of alternative medicines courses.[86]

One should also note that the publisher of *Gray's Anatomy*, the medical students' bible, recently published *Fundamentals of Complementary and Alternative medicine*, one of the first extensive books covering alternative medicine.[87]

3.3.1.17 China

Alternative and allopathic medical education are part of an integrated system in China. Every Western-style medical school in China has a department of traditional medicine. Similarly, traditional medicine schools contain a department of Western medicine.[88] Thus, students learn both traditional and modern medicine. After graduation they can practise both systems of medicine.[89]

83 Thirty-five schools (56%) required a paper or project, and forty-five schools (74%) assigned required readings. Only 19% of schools gave a final examination.
84 Wetzel M. S., *op. cit.*: 784–87.
85 Wetzel M. S., *op. cit.*: 784–87.
86 Wetzel M. S., *op. cit.*: 784–87.
87 Goodwin J., *op. cit.*: 66.
88 Roemer M. I., *op. cit.*: 590.
89 Committee on Traditional Chinese Medicine, *op. cit.*: 35; WHO Regional Office for Western Pacific (II), *op. cit.*: 22; Youbang C., *op. cit.*: 37.

Thirty traditional medical schools provide formal education at bachelor, master and doctoral levels.[90] These universities bear the major responsibility for human resource development in traditional medicine.[91]

The total period of study to qualify as a Chinese medical physician is between five and seven years. Admission standards to colleges or universities generally require completion of middle school (seven grades), but some flexibility exists. In some colleges, a primary school education (four grades) is sufficient.[92]

Between ten to twenty percent of the teaching in modern medical schools is allocated to traditional medicine. A somewhat rather greater emphasis is placed on modern medicine in colleges of traditional Chinese medicine.[93, 94]

3.3.2 Education and Training for Non-Allopathic Practitioners

In Western countries, education for non-allopathic practitioners is almost exclusively organised by private schools which were the first to encourage education in alternative medicines for physicians and non-physicians. Their influence has been important in setting up programs in medical schools and they remain active in the development of teaching for non-physicians.

Set forth below, the education and training for non-allopathic practitioners in some Western countries as well as China and India are presented, in order to give a point of comparison with developments outside Western countries. Proposals of the World Health Organisation on the subject will close this section.

3.3.2.1 Austria

In 1996, the legislature adopted a new statute on the training of authorised medical professions, which came into force on August 1, 1996.[95] One

90 There were 39,700 students enrolled in 1997.
For an overview regarding the content of the education, see YOUBANG C., *op. cit.*: 37–40.

91 WHO REGIONAL OFFICE FOR WESTERN PACIFIC (II), *op. cit.*: 3.

92 COMMITTEE ON TRADITIONAL CHINESE MEDICINE, *op. cit.*: 35; ROEMER M. I., *op. cit.*: 590; YOUBANG C., *op. cit.*: 38.

93 The Division of Traditional Medicine, at the Ministry of Public Health, suggests that thirty percent of teaching should be orientated towards Western medicine.

94 ROSENTHAL M. M., *op. cit.*: 302; YOUBANG C., *op. cit.*: 37–40.

95 BGBL n° 378/1996.

of the main objectives of this regulation was to prohibit the creation of new schools of alternative medicines. Violators of the statute can be prosecuted and fined up to 500,000 Shillings. As a consequence, education for non-allopathic practitioners is almost non-existent, and any development of alternative education for non-allopathic practitioners will be difficult in the future.

3.3.2.2 Denmark[96]

The Danish Chiropractic Association has established its own training for non-physicians. In order to become a member of the Association, candidates first have to be trained in a college accredited by the American Council of Chiropractic Education. Then, the candidates have to follow an internship for a period of six months with a member of the Association. Finally, they have to pass an exam organised by the Association.

According to recent information, there is now an authorised Danish chiropractic education.

3.3.2.3 Finland[97]

Three professions, chiropractors, naprapaths and osteopaths are officially recognised as health care providers.[98] The formal education for these professions consists in a training consisting of at least four consecutive years. This training must be approved by the National Board of Medico-legal Affairs (art. 3 of the Decree 564). Chiropractors are generally trained in the US whereas some therapists are trained in alternative medical schools in Sweden.

3.3.2.4 France

France permits the teaching of alternative medicines to non-allopathic practitioners.[99]

96 Langgaard H., M.D. researcher into complementary cancer therapies, Mar. 1998, Copenhagen; Andreas Jull Sorensen, Ministry of Health, Copenhagen, Sept. 2001.

97 VASKILAMPI T. (I), *op. cit.*: 108.

98 For more details, see chap. 4.3.3.8.

99 In November 1977, the Constitutional Council confirmed that freedom of teaching is a fundamental freedom having a constitutional value. However, when practitioners trained in alternative schools start to practise, they may be prosecuted under art. L 372 of the Code of Public Health (ROBARD I., *op. cit.*: 44–45). See also chap. 4.3.2.2.

The French State has a monopoly in issuing specific grades and diplomas such as baccalauréat,[100] bachelor's degree or doctorate.[101] As a consequence, private schools are not allowed to issue this kind of diplomas.[102]

During the past few decades, there has been an explosion in the use of alternative medicines and, consequently, of training programmes in alternative medicines.[103] However, since there are no recognised diplomas in alternative medicines for non-physicians, the quality of training varies widely. For instance, some schools train people for only one week-end and then deliver "pseudo-diplomas". As a result, this kind of school has brought discredit upon the very techniques they were supposed to teach and promote. Other practitioners declare that they were trained on a "compagnonage" basis, being work undertaken as an apprentice with a qualified and experienced practitioner. This type of apprenticeship may or may not be a complement to a classical training.[104]

Some ancillary practitioners using alternative medicines are trained in foreign schools. For example, kinesitherapists (i.e. physiotherapists) who also provide chiropractic treatments are usually trained in Great Britain or in Germany and then work discreetly in France.[105] Most non-allopathic practitioners also complete their training in foreign schools, for example in Germany ("Heilpraktiker"), in the USA (chiropractors) or in China (acupuncturists). However, the diplomas in alternative medicines gained in foreign countries are not legally recognised in France.

3.3.2.5 Germany

"Heilpraktiker" candidates do not have to follow any standardised training regime in order to pass the exam allowing the practice of alternative medicine. Many courses are organised during weekends or in the evening. The methods of teaching as well as the length and quality of the training vary widely.[106] For example, the German Federal Association of

100 Being is the secondary school examination qualifying for entry to university.
101 Art. 4 of the Act of 18 Mar. 1880, which is still in force.
102 ROBARD I., *op. cit.*: 45–46.
103 Naturopathy and manipulative techniques seem to be the best organised alternative techniques.
104 BOUCHAYER F., *op. cit.*: 51–52; ROBARD I., *op. cit.*: 41–42.
105 Frossard M., General Direction of Health at the Ministry of Social Welfare, Paris, Jan. 1998; Mr. R., a physiotherapist using chiropractic, Oct. 1997, Paris; Prof. Cornillot P., University of Bobigny, Oct. 1997, Paris. To the best of our knowledge, the situation has not changed since then.
106 For more details, see CRAMER R., *op. cit.*: 36–40; EHLERS A. P. F., *op. cit.*: 143–45.

"Heilpraktikers" organises training in 29 cities in Germany for those who wish to obtain a "Heilpraktiker" licence. Some training courses last for 3 years (3,500 hours). Today, even the most extensive "Heilpraktiker" training lasts only half the length of medical students' internships.[107] Thus, there can be no comparison made with the length of a physician's training.[108] However, as "Heilpraktikers" have to respect certain rules laid down by law[109] serious training is needed in order to acquire the necessary knowledge to practise medicine. According to a recent poll, only 10% of "Heilpraktikers" had no training at all, whereas 88% had had some training of between one to four years.[110]

3.3.2.6 Great Britain

There are dozens of professional associations representing therapists within Great Britain. These associations offer comprehensive full-time courses in anthroposophy, chiropractic, phytotherapy, naturopathy and osteopathy to non physicians lasting for a minimum of three years.[111]

The quality and length of training varies widely from one school to another. Whether some commentators consider that non-allopathic practitioners generally have a very good training,[112] others such as the Select Committee on Science and Technology, consider that training courses in alternative medicines "vary unacceptably in content, depth and duration".[113] Thomas adds that professional organisations proposing to train

107 E.g., the "Heilpraktiker" school in München lasts two years. This includes an internship within a hospital and an additional one-year internship as a "Heilpraktiker's" or physician's assistant (EHLERS A. P. F., *op. cit.*: 148).

108 CRAMER R., *op. cit.*: 35–37; FROST AND SULLIVAN, *op. cit.*: 210; ROBARD I., *op. cit.*: 252–53.

109 E.g., they must be able to recognise the different illnesses they are not allowed to treat.

110 CRAMER R., *op. cit.*: 35–36, 40; EHLERS A. P. F., *op. cit.*: 143; ROBARD I., *op. cit.*: 252–53.

111 BRITISH MEDICAL ASSOCIATION, *op. cit.*: 41–42; FROST AND SULLIVAN, *op. cit.*: 245–46; ROBARD I., *op. cit.*: 223; THOMAS K. J., *op. cit.*: 129; WALDBURGER N., *op. cit.*

112 E.g., Robard. The author mentions the training in phytotherapy at the School of Herbal Medicine that proposes a comprehensive training lasting for four years (ROBARD I., *op. cit.*: 224).

113 SELECT COMMITTEE ON SCIENCE AND TECHNOLOGY, *op. cit.*: 8. Similarly, Frost notes that a considerable number of diplomas are available today in a variety of healing therapies, and that training courses are not always serious, leading to inexperienced and dishonest practice (FROST AND SULLIVAN, *op. cit.*: 246).

potential therapists are under a legal obligation to keep registers. Therefore, it becomes difficult for the general public to assess the formal status of practitioners.[114] The General Osteopathic Council[115] has, however, defined and set minimum standards for osteopathy and out of 25 existing schools it has only recognised 5 as reaching these minimum standards. The European School of Osteopathy received the best ranking.[116] Also of note is the

114 One of the purposes of the new Chiropractor and Osteopath Acts is to ensure a high quality level of in education.

115 For more details, see chap. 4.3.3.3.

116 The training lasts for four years. It includes the following modules:
- Year 1: basic science (251 hours); osteopathic principles (207 hours); complementary studies (39 hours); physiology/neural science (60 hours); pre-clinical studies (93 hours);
- Year 2: basic science (247 hours); osteopathic principles (219 hours); complementary studies (73 hours); physiology/neural science (140 hours); pre-clinical studies (300 hours);
- Year 3: clinical science (185 hours); osteopathic principles (347 hours); complementary studies (160 hours), clinical studies (180 hours);
- Year 4: clinical science (480 hours); osteopathic principles (168 hours); complementary studies (69 hours); research methodology (180 hours);

Basic science/clinical science includes applied anatomy, anatomy of the automatic nervous system, general anatomy, orthopaedics, pathological principles, physiological principles, neural science, prosection observation, radiology, paediatrics, medical imaging in the practice of osteopathy, osteopathic care of children, pharmacology;

Osteopathic principles include biomechanics, fundamentals of osteopathy, general osteopathic treatment, history of osteopathy, language of osteopathy, osteopathic technique, patient handling, physiological relationships within osteopathy, what is an osteopath, introduction to cranial, structural articulation, applied biomechanics, peripheral biomechanics, peripheral techniques, balanced ligamentous tension, involuntary mechanism, muscle energy technique, principles of osteopathy, visceral osteopathy;

Complementary studies include anthropology, library induction, research methodology, study skills, an introduction to Tai Chi, introduction to patient handling, communication skills, ethics, psychology, introduction to computing, clinical sociology, audit/management systems as part of patient evaluation, audit management of the osteopathic process, other alternative therapies, introduction to statistics, complementary healthcare and disease, first aid, research project, nutrition and dietetics, health and welfare services, business studies, practice management, accounting, jurisprudence, professional life, continuing professional development;

Physiological/Neural science includes physiological principles and neural science;

Pre-clinical studies include: clinical neurology, palpation and clinical anatomy, clinical osteopathic examination, clinic observation and case history skills;

curriculum available at the University of Exeter, which includes Complementary Health Studies as a subject even in its PhD programs.[117]

Currently, the Institute of Alternative Medicines is working with the Training Desk seeking to establish national standards of training, acceptable to both the general public and government.[118] In the same spirit, the British Medical Association has recommended that alternative medicines be incorporated into the undergraduate curriculum for medical students and that accredited postgraduate training be established.[119]

3.3.2.7 Hungary

A new statute on natural medicine provides training requirements including examinations for "natural doctors", that physicians and non-physicians alike must complete in order to practise as an alternative practitioner.[120]

Annexe 4 of the new statute states all the theoretical and practical requirements for the examination of a candidate in the following natural medicines: acupuncture, massage techniques, lifestyle counsel, reflexology, alternative physiotherapy, bioenergy, physiotherapy, auriculotherapy, kinesitherapy and eye rehabilitation. For each technique, the annexe specifies the practical and theoretical requirements to be taught and to be the object of the examination.

3.3.2.8 Italy

In Italy, non-physicians have access to serious training courses in acupuncture such as, for example, the courses organised by the Society of Italian Acupuncturists and the Paracelse Institute. The latter is a member of the World Federation of Acupuncturists and the Moxibustion Society.

Clinical studies include case history skills, clinical neurology, sports strapping and sports medicine.

For a comparison between this school and other osteopathic schools, see WALDBURGER N., *op. cit.*

117 GAIER H. (II), *op. cit.*: 9–34; GENERAL OSTEOPATHIC COUNCIL, *op. cit.*; THOMAS K. J., *op. cit.*: 129; WALDBURGER N., *op. cit.*

118 ROBARD I., *op. cit.*: 225.

119 BRITISH MEDICAL ASSOCIATION, *op. cit.*: 59; FISHER P., *op. cit.*: 110.

120 However, physicians do not have to pass the examination in order to be allowed to use the title of "natural doctor".

For a presentation of the new statute, see chap. 4.3.3.4.

3.3.2.9 Latvia[121]

There are a few special courses for non-doctors which are intended to provide them with at least some limited medical knowledge. This would equate to approximately one to two years of a traditional medical course in a medical school. There are also some qualification courses in Reiki-method and medical astrology among others.

3.3.2.10 Malta[122]

In Malta, bonesetters are usually trained through family-teaching, while chiropractors and osteopaths may be certified by overseas teaching institutions. As there is still no local registration of these practitioners, their level of proficiency is not standardised and remains difficult to assess.

3.3.2.11 Netherlands

A survey conducted by the Dutch National Advisory Council for Public Health showed that approximately 60% of members of alternative professional organisations had undergone some classic medical training that did not include alternative medicines.

In 1993, the Dutch Health Council pointed out that alternative institutions had organised a number of training courses and that steps had been taken to develop professional and training profiles as well as national registration systems in order to establish standards in this field.[123]

There are post-graduate courses for physical therapists; most of them qualify for acupuncture or manipulative therapy.[124]

Without any medical or paramedical training, individuals may also register in one of the three Academies for Naturopathy offering 3–4 years full-time courses.[125]

121 Dr. Nickolaev N.A., Professor and Director of the Association for Medical Acupuncture and Related Techniques of the Republic of Latvia, Sept. 2001, Riga.

122 Dr. D. Falzon, Principal Medical Officer at the Department of Public Health, Mar. 1998, Valletta; Dr. Gafa, Legal Office, Department of Health, Mar. 1998, Valletta; and Mr. Wismayer, Director Government Pharmaceutical Services at the Ministry of Health, 2000, Valletta. The situation does not appear to have changed since then.

123 DUTCH HEALTH COUNCIL, *op. cit.*

124 VISSER G. J., *op. cit.*: 119.

125 VISSER G. J., *op. cit.*: 119.

3.3.2.12 *Norway*

In Norway, the chiropractic profession is regulated. However, there are no recognised schools of chiropractic in the country.

There are, however, private schools offering training in a wide range of treatments including acupuncture, acupressure, aromatherapy, holistic therapy, osteopathy and yoga/breathing exercises.[126] These schools are not entitled to give examinations under the Universities and Colleges Act and most study options are intended as part of the basic education. The entrance requirements vary widely, from no formal educational requirement to completion of a health education.[127] The length of the education varies also from brief courses to several years of full-time study. All of these training courses, regardless of length, carry a practice period requirement.

3.3.2.13 *Switzerland*

Many private institutions offer training in alternative medicines. Examples include the Swiss association of natural doctors,[128] the school for natural medicine of Zürich,[129] the academy for natural medicine of Basel,[130] and the Swiss school for osteopathy of Belmont/Lausanne.[131, 132]

126 MINISTRY OF HEALTH AND SOCIAL AFFAIRS (I), *op. cit.*: 267.
127 MINISTRY OF HEALTH AND SOCIAL AFFAIRS (I), *op. cit.*: 267.
128 The complete training consists of four parts:
1. introduction with basic knowledge on anatomy, physiology and biochemistry;
2. physiology and pathology seminars;
3. diagnosis possibilities seminars;
4. treatments possibilities seminars.
The complete training lasts six semesters and is taught during week-ends.
For more information regarding schools of naturopathy, see http://www.rme.ch/ecoles.htm, accessed on July 19 2001.
129 Two training programs are available. Both programs include basic courses on anatomy, physiology and pathology. Students may further choose between a specialisation on homeopathy and traditional Chinese medicines (program 1) and several forms of alternative massages (program 2).
The complete training lasts four years.
130 The school offers first a basic common course (anatomy, physiology, pathology, psychiatry, neurology and physical diagnosis), and then three specialisations:
1. homeopathy, phytotherapy and natural medicine;
2. traditional Chinese medicine;
3. acupuncture.
The complete training lasts four years. In addition, a four months internship is required.
131 The complete training lasts six years (five years for the diploma and six for the doctorate). The school is trying to obtain the same status as a university faculty.

With respect to chiropractic training there is still no recognised school in Switzerland, even though it is a recognised profession.[133] Practitioners who wish to train in chiropractic must attend courses in foreign countries. However, chiropractors still have to pass an examination regulated by the Swiss Cantonal Conference of Directors of Health Affairs (CCDHA).[134]

According to Künzi, training provided by these schools, excepting the school of Belmont, can not be compared to academic education.[135]

Some of the tolerant cantons[136] have specific rules concerning the exam that candidates have to pass before being allowed to practise alternative medicine.[137]

In 1998, the CCDHA rejected the demand from the Swiss Homeopathic Society that it recognise a specific training in homeopathy. The CCDHA argued that homeopathy was only one of several techniques available in natural medicine, and that without a unified curriculum it would be impossible to regulate effectively alternative professions in Switzerland.[138]

3.3.2.14 Ukraine

The Academy of Physicians Postgraduate Education and the Ukrainian National Medical Association are under the supervision of the Ukrainian Ministry of Public Health and both offer special educational courses for non-physicians. These institutions organise and offer courses in homeopathy, iridology, reflexology, aromatherapy and phytotherapy.[139]

For developments on the subject, see WALDBURGER N., *op. cit.* (including a comparison between the several training courses available in osteopathy at the EU level).

132 KÜNZI M. (II), *op. cit.*: 29–30.

133 For more details regarding the regulation of chiropractic in this country, see chap. 4.3.6.1.

134 CONFÉRENCE DES DIRECTEURS CANTONAUX DES AFFAIRES SANITAIRES, *op. cit.*: 7.

135 KÜNZI M. (II), *op. cit.*: 31.

136 Such as Appenzell external Rhodes, Basel Landschaft, Graubünden, Obwalden, St. Gallen, Shaffhausen and Thurgau.

137 For more details, see KÜNZI M. (II), *op. cit.*: 31–37.

138 CONFÉRENCE DES DIRECTEURS CANTONAUX DES AFFAIRES SANITAIRES, *op. cit.*: 6–7.

139 Dr. Hmelewskaja A., Aug. 2001, Kiew.

3.3.2.15 United States

There are several schools that teach alternative medicines in the US. For example, chiropractic and osteopathic colleges and schools are usually private and are accredited under standards set by the United States Office of Education.[140] The quality of training provided is generally considered to be good, even if such courses are not, yet, as considered as to have achieved the same level of education as classic medical faculties.

An example of an alternative school of medicine in the US is the North-Western College of Chiropractic. The school offers three degree courses: the doctor of chiropractic degree program, the bachelor of sciences in human biology degree program, and the postgraduate and continuing education program. The doctor degree curriculum consists of five academic years of chiropractic college instruction. Each academic year is composed of two 15-week trimesters. The curriculum is made up of courses in basic science, chiropractic science, clinical science and clinical experience. A 12-month public clinical internship and preceptorship constitutes the last three trimesters. The bachelor of science degree may be earned simultaneously with the doctor of chiropractic degree. It provides a strong foundation in the mechanics of the human body, and represents an important professional tool for chiropractic.[141] Postgraduate training in several specific fields is also available.[142]

Until about 1950, several chiropractic schools also offered naturopathic degrees. Today, only two naturopathic colleges remain, in the States of Washington and Oregon, and both require 2 years of pre-professional college work plus four years in a naturopathic college.[143]

140 Chapman-Smith D. A., *op. cit.*: 113; Wardwell W. I., *op. cit.*: 1066.

141 The bachelor of science degree is a requirement for a licence to practise in some states. It is granted to those candidates who have completed the necessary credits by fulfilling the following requirements: 1. Prerequisites: complete a specific courses with success including general education, natural and physical sciences and electives. For example, at North Western College the training program includes: complete a specific course with success including biochemistry, central nervous system, community health, clinical nutrition, embryology, gross anatomy, histology, infection disease, microbiology, pathology, peripheral nervous system, physiology, as well as human biology and physiology emphasis, research and development emphasis biomechanics, rehabilitation, and ergonomics emphasis.

142 Http://www.nwchiro.edu accessed Aug. 1 2001.
See also http://dir.lycos.com/health/alternative/chiropractic/colleges/ accessed Aug. 1 2001.

143 Künzi M. (I), *op. cit.*: 68–71; Wardwell W. I., *op. cit.*: 1066.

3.3.2.16 *China*[144]

In China, there are two non-university degrees available for the training of alternative practitioners. The basic level is an apprenticeship to a traditional practitioner.[145]

The secondary level leads to a diploma and the training lasts between three to four years. There are 51 secondary level medical schools of traditional medicine with approximately 50,000 students. The objective of these schools is to train mid-level practitioners in traditional Chinese medicine.[146]

3.3.2.17 *India*

The required courses of study for a diploma in traditional medicine vary in length, with an upper limit of five years in post secondary education. Three further years of study are required to qualify as a specialist.[147]

In most schools, although teaching is still predominantly oriented towards traditional systems, some aspects of modern medicine are incorporated into the curriculum.

3.3.2.18 *World Health Organisation*

From 1974 until 1994, a study was conducted by the WHO to evaluate the effectiveness of projects where traditional practitioners were being trained to provide various primary health care services to communities. The objectives were to evaluate the impact the projects had upon the communities they served, to determine which materials and training approaches were most effective and to develop training guidelines to assist others in replicating similar projects. Guidelines for training traditional health practitioners in primary health care were also proposed.[148, 149]

144 For a survey of the current training system in China, see YOUBANG C., *op. cit.*: 37–40.

145 COMMITTEE ON TRADITIONAL CHINESE MEDICINE, *op. cit.*: 35; YOUBANG C., *op. cit.*: 38–39.

146 COMMITTEE ON TRADITIONAL CHINESE MEDICINE, *op. cit.*: 35.

147 ROEMER M. I., *op. cit.*: 590.

148 The guidelines are divided in six parts (which are also steps in the creation of guidelines):

1. Planning for the training (to review existing policies and regulations, to involve traditional practitioners and community members in the planning, to identify the health conditions of communities, to identify the types of health practitioners available, to identify important characteristics of health practitioners);

3.4 Summary and Conclusion

Key figures in several Western countries have recognised the importance of alternative medicines in modern society and they have also understood the basic reasons why alternative medicines have enjoyed such a success. This recognition has also brought a realisation that fundamental clinical research in alternative medicines must be undertaken and that the standards of teaching must be improved.

Even if, initially, research on alternative medicines had been excluded from Western academia, this is no longer the case. Various countries have been actively conducting national programs and they have also been active in creating the appropriate structures to investigate varying aspects of alternative medicines. More specifically, efforts are being made to establish new ways of evaluating the scientific validity of alternative techniques.

There is an evolution in the education of physicians in alternative medicines as well. Education is slowly shifting from private organisations, previously linked to alternative medicines, to medical schools.[150] Some medical schools are now testing students on alternative medicines during graduate training and there is a trend towards establishing postgraduate training for some techniques, including internships and research programs.[151]

---

2. Determining the content of training (to identify what trainees need to know, to train to alleviate social and economical need, to write specific training objectives);
3. Determining the training methods (to develop a training plan, to group the knowledge and skills to be taught in a logical pattern, to integrate the teaching of new ideas about health with indigenous beliefs about health and illness, to choose appropriate training methods);
4. Selecting training materials (to review the needs for audio-visual materials in the curriculum, to select AV matierials that already exist locally, to prepare your own material, to pretest materials before using, use AV materials effectively);
5. Training the trainers;
6. Evaluating the training.

149 HOFF W. (I), *op. cit.*; HOFF W. (II), *op. cit.*: 111–18.

150 The most taught techniques (for non-allopathic practitioners also) are chiropractic, osteopathy, acupuncture, homeopathy, iridology, massage techniques, naturopathy, phytotherapy and anthroposophy.

151 Medical students seem to be interested in alternative medicines and their influence has played a role in the development of new courses.

However, the movement toward further integration of alternative medicines into the medical school curriculum is at an early stage of development. Furthermore, there is considerable heterogeneity in the quality and length of courses provided to physicians.

Some organisations and schools provide serious training for non-physicians. Some of these training courses are even recognised in foreign jurisdictions as being the principal requirement necessary to obtain a licence to practise. However, the quality and length of the training for non-allopathic practitioners as for physicians varies widely from one school to another.

Thus, although research in alternative medicines is improving and some schools provide high-level training, the situation remains unsatisfactory. There is no doubt that standardised training, particularly in medical schools, based on serious research would improve and ensure the quality and safety of care, thus providing the necessary prerequisite to the regulation of alternative medicines.

4. Licensing to Practise Alternative Medicines

4.1 Introduction

The licensing to practise alternative medicines is a cornerstone of the regulation of alternative techniques. Therefore, the current position for licensing in some representative Western countries shall be developed below.

First, the various options available to the lawmaker when deciding to license the practice of alternative medicines shall be presented.

Second, an overview of the current position at the European Union level and in several Western countries shall follow.[1] The countries have been divided into four pre-defined categories, which correspond to the typical approach taken by the lawmaker in any regulation of practice of alternative medicines. In some federal countries, more than one approach towards the regulation of alternative medicines may exist. As a result, these countries shall be presented later in this chapter.

Finally a schematic overview of the situation shall be presented in the form of some comparative charts.

4.2 Classification

Bibliography

De Bijl N. (co-author: Nederveen-van de Kragt I.), *Legal safeguards against medical practice by not suitably qualified persons: A comparative study in seven EU-countries*, 1997, in: European Journal of Health Law, vol. 4: 5–18; Rösch B., *Die Stellung der Erfahrungsheilkundigen aus verfassungs- und verwaltungs-*

1 The Western countries analysed in this study are the following: Austria, Belgium, Denmark, Finland, France, Germany, Great Britain, Hungary, Italy, Latvia, Liechtenstein, Luxembourg, Malta, Netherlands, Norway, Spain, Switzerland, Ukraine and the United States of America.
The position in some non-Western countries, such as China and India has also been addressed, to provide the reader a point of comparison.

rechtlicher Sicht, dargestellt am Beispiel der geistig Heilenden, Dissertation, Helbing & Lichtenhahn Verlag AG, 1994, Basel: 70–73; STEPAN J., *Traditional and alternative systems of medicine: A comparative review of legislation*, in: International Digest of Health Legislation, 1985, vol. 36, n° 2.

In all the countries studied, access to medical practice is, by law, permitted on certain conditions, which are broadly the same: the possession of a certificate or qualification from a recognised school and a registration or authorisation.[2] Other requirements may include, for example, taking the Hippocratic oath or being physically and mentally fit for practice.[3]

While the conditions may be quite similar, the actual approach used to regulate access to medical practice can vary widely.[4] Stepan was the first to categorise these legislative approaches into four different systems:[5]

1. the monopolistic system, where only the practice of scientific medicine by professionals and auxiliaries is recognised as lawful, to the exclusion of and sanctions against all other forms of healing. Countries having this system usually have an exclusive biomedical approach and defend the monopoly of physicians in this field. The actual enforcement of such stringent legislation varies from one state to another. There is, however, no country completely closed to alternative medicines;
2. the tolerant system, where only the practice of scientific medicine is recognised although, at least to some extent, practitioners of various forms of alternative medicines are tolerated by law. Some acts are, however, strictly reserved for physicians, such as surgery, obstetrics or gynaecology;
3. the inclusive system, in which systems other than biomedicine are not only merely tolerated, but recognised as forming a special part of the structure of health care such as ayurvedic medicine in India. However, they work as two parallel systems, being independent one from the other;

2 Registration implies entering a register and authorisation implies permission/licensing by a competent body.

3 For further development regarding the conditions to obtain a licence to practise, see chap. 7.3.5. See also, e.g., DE BIJL N., *op. cit.*: 5–18.

4 The conditions necessary to fulfil in order to practise as a physician shall be presented for each country, subject to availability of information, in order to provide a point of comparison.

5 STEPAN J., *op. cit.* For a classification, see also RÖSCH B., *op. cit.*: 70–73, 118–22.
For a presentation of the several licensure modalities at the disposal of the lawmaker when deciding to enact a regulation on the subject, see chap. 7.3.2.

4. the integrated system, where official promotion of the integration of two or more systems exists within a single recognised service; integrated training of health practitioners is the official policy. Only a few countries have adopted this integrative health care policy such as China, Nepal and North Korea.

In Western countries, only monopolistic and tolerant systems are represented. However, these two systems can overlap forming a combination of the two. For this reason, De Bijl and Nederveen-Van de Kragt introduced a new category, which they called the mixed system.[6] In this system, only health care professionals are allowed to perform specific medical acts and any violation of this limited monopoly results in an offence. For the remaining medical acts, persons who are not qualified as physicians are tolerated.

There is no clear distinction between tolerant and mixed systems. Indeed, the regulations of countries generally considered as tolerant, generally enact specific rules to protect patients, creating what is, in effect, a limited monopoly. Germany, for example, which is considered as a typical tolerant country, has rules restricting the use of specific medical acts to physicians,[7] and any persons violating these rules may be sentenced. According to a strict interpretation of De Bijl's categorisation, Germany should be considered as a mixed country. However, the author does not consider that Germany has a mixed system. It is apparent that the creation of this additional category creates additional difficulties of categorising countries. Therefore, in order to maintain a clear classification of the legislative approaches, only the categories defined by Stepan shall be considered.

The following countries studied in this research have adopted a monopolistic approach: Austria, France, Italy, Latvia, Luxembourg, Spain and the Ukraine.

The tolerant countries are Belgium, Denmark, Finland, Germany, Great Britain, Hungary, Liechtenstein, Netherlands, Malta, Norway, and Sweden.

In countries having a federal system, such as Switzerland or the US, each state or canton has its own regulation on the subject. As a result, both tolerant and monopolistic systems can be found.

Within the European Union (EU), the free movement of persons and services within the medical sector has been achieved by a mutual recognition of medical qualifications and diplomas. However, there are still differences

6 DE BIJL N., *op. cit.*: 5–18.

7 E.g. to practise in dentistry or to treat sexual and communicable diseases.

between Member States regarding access to the profession of medical doctor and the performance of medical acts. Therefore, even though the free movement of physicians is relatively effective, non-allopathic practitioners do not benefit from this freedom. Indeed, while they may be legally recognised in their own country, they are usually not allowed to provide treatments in other country members of the EU.

4.3 Overview[8]

4.3.1 European Union

Bibliography

Bonnamour M.-C. (co-author: Granturco T.), *The Lannoye report on non-conventional medicines was adopted by the European Parliament*, CP Info, June 1997, Bruxelles; British Medical Association (Lamont T.), *Alternative medicine – New approaches to good practice*, Oxford University Press, 1993, Oxford/New York: 9–18; Conférence des Directeurs Cantonaux des Affaires Sanitaires (I), *Rapport du groupe de travail "Autorisations de pratiquer les professions du domaine de la santé"*, CDS, 2000, Bern, available at: http://www.sdk-cds.ch/fr/berufsbildung-f.html, accessed July 30 2001: 14–15; De Bijl N. (co-author: Nederveen-van de Kragt I.), *Legal safeguards against medical practice by not suitably qualified persons: A comparative study in seven EU-countries*, 1997, in: European Journal of Health Law, vol. 4: 5–6; Dommers J., *An introduction to European Union health law*, in: European Journal of Health Law, vol 4, n° 1, 1997: 19–41; Dumoulin J.-F. (co-authors: Guillod O., Méroz J.-C.), *L'impact d'une adhésion suisse à l'Union Européenne sur le droit de la santé*, in: Cottier T. (co-editor: Kopse A. R.), *L'adhésion de la Suisse à l'Union Européenne – Enjeux et conséquences*, Schulthess, 1998, Zürich: 925–48; Fisher P. (co-author: Ward A.), *Alternative medicine in Europe*, in: BMJ, vol. 309, Jul. 9 1994: 107–11; Friedel E. (co-author: Freundlich M.), *European community harmonisation of the licensing and manufacturing of medicinal products*, in: Food and Drug Law Journal, 1994, vol. 49: 141–70; Grunwald D., *Pratiques médicales non éprouvées*, session de l'Ordre des médecins, 1997 Sept., Paris; Haehnel P., *Les médecines parallèles au Parlement Européen: Un projet voué à l'échec*, Bulletin de l'Ordre, Sept. 1996; Kahil-Wolff B., *L'accord sur la libre circulation des personnes Suisse-CE et le droit des assurances sociales*, in: Semaine Judiciaire, 2001, vol. 123, n° 4: 81–135; Lannoye P., *Is there a future*

8 Recent regulations of various Member States may be found in the international digest of health legislation edited by the World Health Organisation at http://www.who.int/idhl/, accessed July 17, 2001.

for complementary medicine in Europe? – European report on the status of non-conventional medicine, The Natural Medicines Society, 1996, Heanor; MULAS S., *Freizügikeit freier Berufe im europäischen Binnenmarkt*, Dissertation, 1995, Tübingen; PLOTKE H., *Gegenseitige Anerkennung von Diplomen und Berufserfahrung in der EWG und Auswirkungen aud die Schweiz*, Helbing & Lichtenhahn, 1991, Basel; PROCOMED, *Lettre d'information de l'Association pour la reconnaissance et la promotion des médecines complémentaires en Europe*, Bulletin n° 2, Dec. 1997, Bruxelles; ROBARD I., *La santé hors la loi: Les hors la loi de la santé*, 4th ed., Ed. de l'Ancre, 1994, Suresnes: 283, 296–301; SCHNEIDER H., *Die Annerkennung von Diplomen in der Europäischen Gemeinschaft*, Maklu, 1995, Uitgevers Antwerpen; SEGEST E., *Consumer protection and the free movement of medical practitioners in the European Union*, in: European Journal of Health Law, 1997, n° 4: 267–72; TRIBUNE POUR L'EUROPE, *Médecines non conventionnelles*, in: Tribune pour l'Europe, June 1997, Antwerpen.

4.3.1.1 General principles

A. General remarks

On November 1, 1993, the Treaty on the European Union[9] came into force. The objective of the Treaty instituting the Economic Community (TEC) was the creation of a large market zone without borders, through the free movement of persons, goods, services and capital.[10]

The competences of the European Community in the field of public health were not clearly determined until after the Maastricht treaty was concluded. Competences derive from rules aimed at regulating specific fields such as, among others, the protection of workers,[11] the protection of the environment[12] and research.[13, 14]

9 The so-called "Maastricht Treaty".

10 According to art. 2 TEC, the task of the European Union is to promote a harmonious and balanced development of economic activities, a high degree of convergence of economic performance, a high level of employment and of social protection, the raising of the standard of living and quality of life, and economic and social cohesion and solidarity among Member States.
The contribution to the attainment of a high level of health protection is one of the common activities provided by art. 3 (o) TEC.
For more details, see ROBARD I., *op. cit.*: 283; DOMMERS J., *op. cit.*: 19–21; KAHIL-WOLFF B., *op. cit.*: 86.

11 Art. 117ss TEC; art. 55 CECA Treaty; title II, chapter III Euratom Treaty.

12 Art. 130Rss TEC.

13 Art. 8a TEC.

14 The Community first tried to ensure the protection of workers. Then it attempted to eliminate national barriers that could hinder the workers' freedom of movement.

With the adoption of the Treaty on the European Union, a general competence on public health was introduced under Article 129 of the Treaty stating that the aim the EU is to guarantee a high level of human health protection by encouraging cooperation between the Member States. The same article states that EU action is focused on the prevention of illnesses, and the fight against scourges such as drug addiction. The EU must also favour research and information in this field.[15, 16]

In the new Amsterdam treaty,[17] art. 129 has become art. 152. Since then, the EU has competence to control human organs and substances, as well as blood and its derivates (art. 152 (4) (a)), and take measures in the veterinarian and phytotherapeutic field (art. 152 (4) (b)). Furthermore, the European Council may adopt measures, such as Directives, and not only encourage actions by the Member States. Article 152 now obliges the EU not only to contribute to ensure a high level of human health protection, but also to ensure such level of protection.[18]

Today, EU policy in public health is focused mainly on four topics:

1. the free movement of persons;
2. the free movement of goods in particular, drugs and medical equipment;
3. the coordination of social security including health insurance;
4. the coordination and encouragement of measures aiming to reach specific objectives such as protection and promotion of health, prevention of illnesses and accidents, and encouragement of research.

B. Free movement of persons

The Maastricht Treaty introduced the concept of Citizenship of the Union (art. 8–8 (e) TEC)[19] and concretised the free movement of persons. Citizens

---

Finally, it tried to set up some coordination between the several systems of social security.

For more details, see DUMOULIN J.-F., *op. cit.*: 925–26.

15 Requirements regarding health protection have also been the subject of a Council resolution (Resolution of the Council of Nov. 12, 1996, regarding the integration of EU policies on health protection requirements, JOCE C 374/3 of Dec. 11, 1996).

16 DUMOULIN J.-F., *op. cit.*: 926.

17 Signed on Oct. 2 1997.

18 DUMOULIN J.-F., *op. cit.*: 926.

19 For a retrospective regarding the development of the freedom of movement see KAHIL-WOLFF B., *op. cit.*: 87–90.

of the Union enjoy the rights conferred by the EC Treaty such as the right to move and take up residence freely within the territory of the Member States. More specifically, articles 39, 48–66 TEC provide that citizens have the right to move freely within the EU and the right to establish residence in another Member State for the purpose of engaging in activity as an employee or self-employed person.[20]

Under the Maastricht Treaty Member States may also limit the right of free movement justifying such a restriction on the grounds of public health (art. 6, 48 (3), 56, and 66 TEC).[21] For example, Directive 64/221/EEC[22] co-ordinates by special measure the movement and residence of nationals from the Members States, on the grounds of public policy, public security or public health.[23, 24]

The EU Community has adopted two types of Directives in order to regulate the exercise of medical, pharmaceutical, and related professions: sectorials and generals Directives.[25]

The first type of Directives were adopted to regulate the classic medical professions such as physicians, nurses, dentists, midwifes, veterinarians

20 DOMMERS J., *op. cit.*: 26–27; KAHIL-WOLFF B., *op. cit.*: 86–108.

21 On this subject, see SCHNEIDER H., *op. cit.*

22 Official Journal EC n° 850/64, Apr. 4, 1964, Directive 75/35/EEC amending Directive 64/221/EEC, Official Journal EC n° L. 14, 1975.

23 Articles 8 and 9 of the Directive guarantee the right of appeal to a court of the refusing Member State in the case of a refusal of entry or of residence. In this respect, Dommers notes that "considering, however, that everyone has the right to respect for his private and family life (art. 8 ECHR), and considering Directive 95/46/EEC on the protection of privacy to individuals with regard to the processing of personal (medical) data and the free movement of data, Member States should be very careful in applying this Directive (Official Journal EC n° L. 281, Nov. 23, 1995)" (DOMMERS J., *op. cit.*: 29).

24 DOMMERS J., *op. cit.*: 29; KAHIL-WOLFF B., *op. cit.*: 86, 98–99.

25 Concerning the adoption of these Directives, Egest states that "the EU has maintained its position with regard to important goals, i.e. to facilitate the free movement of medical practitioners on basis of mutual recognition of diplomas, and at the same time to protect patients against possible harm caused by substantial medical practice, whether they be unauthorised, unqualified or incompetent. Or in other words: EU citizens have a right to medical treatment and care which is of good quality in all Member States, in accordance with the accepted standards of the medical profession, regardless of whether this right is exercised in the patient's own country or in another EU Member State" (SEGEST E., *op. cit.*: 268).
For a further development, see DE BIJL N., *op. cit.*: 5–6; DOMMERS J., *op. cit.*: 27; DUMOULIN J.-F., *op. cit.*: 930–31; SCHNEIDER H., *op. cit.*

and pharmacists.[26] These Directives contain precise rules on training[27] and coordination between Member States for a mutual recognition of diplomas. The Directives usually establish several steps that need to be fulfilled before there is complete mutual recognition of a diploma.[28, 29]

The difficulty attached to establishing and implementing specific Directives led the EU to the decision to adopt "general" Directives, which regulate all the remaining regulated professions.[30] These Directives are based on the principle of mutual trust. The EU having considered that national training was similar in the Member States, Directives regulating only the process of issuing licences to practise were adopted. The first of these

26 77/452/453/EEC; 78/686/687/EEC; 78/1026/1027/EEC; 80/154/155/EEC; 78/1026/1027/EEC; 85/432/433/EEC; and 97/50/EU.

27 Several criteria have been developed regarding the equivalence of diplomas, in particular, concerning:
1. the conditions to have access to training, in particular, the type of diploma previously obtained;
2. the type of institution delivering the training;
3. the type of training (theoretical and practical-clinical training);
4. the content of training;
5. the length of training (minimum number of hours).

28 E.g., for physicians, the first step concerns the necessity to have some coordination of requirements for training in medicine and specialised medicine. A complete period of medical training should comprise of at least a six-year course or 5,500 hours of theoretical and practical instruction given in a university or under the supervision of a university (Art. 23 (2) of the Directive). According to art. 26 of the Directive, Member States are obliged to ensure a minimum length for specialised courses such as five years for general surgery and four years for psychiatry. There are also qualitative requirements; for example, physicians must be able, at the end of their training, to understand the structure, the functions, and the behaviour of healthy and sick persons (art. 23 (2) (b) of the Directive).
The second step is the mutual recognition – without any limitation – between the Member States of diplomas, certificates and other formal qualifications in medicine and specialised medicine as listed in Directive 93/16/EEC.
The third step consists in creating a system to facilitate the exchange between the Member States of relevant information regarding disciplinary action of a professional or administrative nature taken in respect of persons concerned or criminal penalties imposed on them when pursuing their profession in the Member State of origin or in the Member State from which they came (art. 12 (1) of the Directive).

29 DE BIJL N., *op. cit.*: 5–6; DOMMERS J., *op. cit.*: 27–28; DUMOULIN J.-F., *op. cit.*: 930–31; SCHNEIDER H., *op. cit.*: 464–65.
For a study on the effects of the mutual recognition of medical professions, see: ABBING R., *op. cit.*; SEGEST E., *op. cit.*; SCHNEIDER H., *op. cit.*

30 89/48/CEE; 92/51/CEE; 2001/19/UE.

general Directives concerns chiropractic, physiotherapy and psychologist-psychotherapists. One of the general conditions requires a diploma attesting that three years of university training has been successfully completed. The other conditions for mutual recognition are the following, namely that:[31]

1. the diploma was delivered by the competent service of the Member State;
2. the holder of the diploma is an EU citizen;
3. the diploma attests an equivalent level of training;
4. the training that led to the diploma was mainly undertaken in the EU;
5. the diploma or proof of capacity is a condition to practise in the country of origin.[32]

The Directives concern only "regulated" professions,[33] being only those activities whose access to, exercise of, and coverage by social insurance[34] are regulated by the State.[35] However, although the purpose of these Directives is to facilitate the free movement of people within the EU, Member States may create exceptions for public order reasons.[36]

C. Attempts at harmonisation

The licensing and manufacturing of medical products at the EU level is regulated at two levels, for while manufacturing authorisations remain under the aegis of national authorities, common standards of good manufacturing products practice have been established by the Commission, to ensure harmonisation in this area. Furthermore, the development and

31 Conférence des Directeurs Cantonaux des Affaires Sanitaires (I), *op. cit.*: 14; Dumoulin J.-F., *op. cit.*: 931; Mulas S., *op. cit.*: 137, 139; Schneider H., *op. cit.*: 465ss.
32 Differences between licensing conditions may be smoothed by satisfying additional requirements of the destination country, such as professional experience, internships, ability tests, etc.
33 This concept is similar to the "profession requiring an authorisation" (or "licensed professions" (in French: "profession soumise à autorisation"), under Swiss law.
34 The third condition applies only to health care activities.
35 See the Council Directive regarding a general regulation of the recognition of university diplomas attesting three years professional training (89/48/CEE), art. 1 (e), (f) 2nd Directive 92/51/CEE (complement of Directive 89/48/CEE).
36 Conférence des Directeurs Cantonaux des Affaires Sanitaires (I), *op. cit.*: 14–15; Mulas S., *op. cit.*: 141; Plotke H., *op. cit.*: 16.

implementation of pharmaco-vigilance activities among EU Member States serve the protection of public health.[37]

The principle of subsidiarity[38] is also important in the area of health policy. Indeed, in areas that do not fall within the exclusive competence of the EU, such as health, the EU shall take action only when and so far as the objectives cannot be sufficiently achieved by the respective Member States. The content, organisation and financing of the health care systems of the Member States remain a national competence. There is, however, EU co-operation in the fields of human health protection and prevention of diseases.[39]

4.3.1.2 Position of Alternative Medicines

At the end of the 1980s, a debate was initiated concerning the recognition of alternative medicines and alternative practitioners.[40] The three main problems were the creation of Directives on alternative medicinal products (homeopathic and phytotherapeutic products), on the free movement of patients and practitioners, and on the coverage of alternative medicines by national health care systems.[41]

In April 1994, before the Committee on the Environment, Public Health and Consumer Protection of the European Parliament, the European Deputy Paul Lannoye presented a proposal on the status of alternative medicines. The objectives were

> on the one hand, to respond to the demand of the Treaty on European Union and the legitimate claims of non conventional medical practitioners, and, on the other, to respond to a growing demand from patients. It is therefore a question of matching supply and demand, on the basis of a principle of double freedom: freedom for patients to choose the medical therapy of their choice, and freedom for practitioners to exercise their professions.

37 For a development regarding the harmonisation of regulations of medical products at the EU level, see Friedel E., *op. cit.*: 141–70. Also, for further development, see chap. 7.2.4.

38 This principle has been applied throughout the entire European integration process.

39 Furthermore, EC laws such as the common rules on competition or the EC Directives on public procurement and working time must be taken into account when developing health care policy and legislation (Dommers J., *op. cit.*: 34–35).

40 British Medical Association, *op. cit.*: 9–18; Robard I., *op. cit.*: 296–301.

41 For further development regarding the possibility to set up a Directive on the coverage of alternative medicines, see chap. 5.3.1. For a development regarding the creation of Directives on herbal and homeopathic products, see chap. 7.2.4.

He added that "it goes without saying that this double principle involves guaranteeing the patient both safety and quality of treatment".[42] In addition, Paul Lannoye asked for alternative medicines to be provided for within social security systems, the incorporation of complementary systems in the European Pharmacopoeia and a research budget of 10 millions euro per year for five years. He also included a demand to end prosecutions of non-allopathic practitioners in monopolistic countries such as France or Spain, and for a pan-European system of recognition and regulation of these practitioners along the lines of the British Osteopath and Chiropractor Acts.[43] At the last moment, the European Parliament cancelled the vote on the proposal.[44]

At the end of 1995, the Conference of Presidents of the European Parliament decided to propose a new report. The objective of the report was to engage the Commission in the process of recognising alternative medicines. There were obviously objections to the content of the report, particularly from physician members of the European Parliament.[45, 46]

On February 27, 1997 the Commission on Welfare, Public Health and Consumers' Protection adopted a project. Finally, the European Parliament came forward with a resolution on May 29, 1997,[47] stating that:[48]

> The European Parliament
> 1. calls on the Commission, if the results of the study allows, to start the process for the recognition of non-conventional medicine and, for this purpose, to take the necessary steps to encourage the establishment of appropriate committees;

42 LANNOYE P., *op. cit.*: 4.

43 Paul Lannoye founded the proposal also on the principle of free movement of persons.

44 BONNAMOUR M.-C., *op. cit.*: 2; FISHER P., *op. cit.*: 109; LANNOYE P., *op. cit.*: 1; PROCOMED, *op. cit.*: 1.

45 E.g., the French National Order of Physicians was opposed to Lannoye's report, considering that the propositions enclosed in the report would not ensure a sufficient quality of cares (GRUNWALD D., *op. cit.*: 27–28).

46 PROCOMED, *op. cit.*: 2.

47 As the original proposition for the establishment of a legal regime regulating alternative medicines at the pan-European level had been rejected, the modifications from the initial proposal were such that Mr Lannoye resigned from his assignment as "rapporteur". The report was finally published in the name of the President of the Commission on Welfare, Mr. Ken Collins.
One should note that there were supporters and detractors of alternative medicines in each political party (PROCOMED, *op. cit.*: 3).

48 BONNAMOUR M.-C., *op. cit.*: 2; GRUNWALD D., *op. cit.*: 28; PROCOMED, *op. cit.*: 2–3; TRIBUNE POUR L'EUROPE, *op. cit.*

2. calls on the Commission to carry out a thorough study on the safety, effectiveness, scope of application and the complementarity and alternative nature of all non-conventional medicines, and to prepare a comparative study of the various national legal models to which non-conventional medical practitioners are subjected;
3. calls on the Commission, in formulating European legislation on non-conventional forms of medicine, to make a clear distinction between non-conventional medicines which are "complementary" in nature and which ones are "alternative" in the sense that they replace conventional medicine;
4. calls on the Council, after completion of the preliminary works referred to in paragraph 2 above, to encourage the development of research programmes in the field of non-conventional medicines covering the individual and holistic approach, the preventive role and the specific characteristics of the non-conventional medicine, undertakes to do likewise;
5. urges the Commission to submit as soon as possible a report to the Council and European Parliament on the results of the studies and research already carried out under budget item B-7142 which, since 1994, has been earmarked for research on the effectiveness of homeopathy and other non-conventional medicines;
6. calls on the Commission, in examining the effectiveness of forms of therapy used in non-conventional medicine, to ensure that none of the treatments used in Member States makes use of medicines made from the organs of protected animal species, which would constitute an involvement in illegal trafficking;
7. calls on the Commission to submit a proposal for a Directive on food supplements, which are frequently situated on the boundaries between dietary and medicinal products. Such legislation should help guarantee good manufacturing practices to secure consumer protection without restricting freedom of access or choice and ensure the freedom of all practitioners to recommend such products;
8. calls on the Commission to remove trade barriers between Member States by giving manufacturers of health products free access to all markets in the EU;
9. instructs its President to forward this resolution to the Council, the Commission and the governments of the Member States.

On June 11, 1999, the Council of Europe adopted a further resolution reinforcing and stressing the earlier resolution of May 29, 1997. This later resolution called for the integration of alternative medicines at the European level to be achieved through a better coordination between Member States and stated that both practitioners and patients must have access to alternative medicines and further, that research must be undertaken in the field.[49]

However, as a European Resolution is not a binding act, these acts must generally be considered only as declarations of policy. Nevertheless, the

49 The document is available at http://stars.coe.fr/index_e.htm, accessed on July 18, 2001.

Maastricht Treaty added a new article, 138B TEC, which gave the European Parliament a "power of initiative".[50] Thus, in 1992, it was decided to provide European MPs with the same power. In essence, this means that although the resolution is not binding, it can nevertheless lead to the use of the provisions of article 138B TEC and an application addressed by the European Parliament to the European Commission to undertake deliberations in the field of alternative medicines.[51]

According to Paul Lannoye and the lobbying group PROCOMED[52] the final vote was a disappointment. However, they considered that the adoption of the resolution was an important step, which could open up new perspectives to be explored. They also stressed that the European Commission must continue to work in this field. Bonnamour considers that "although the perspective of recognition of complementary medical practices is postponed until the results of an 'in-depth study on the harmlessness, timeliness, scope of application and the complementary or alternative nature of each discipline' are given, the objective of a recognition nevertheless remains".[53]

With regard to the content of the resolution, Granturco mentions that

> the European Parliament has taken care not to include considerations on reimbursement of the 'health care' provided by these professionals, doctors or not, in their concerns. On the contrary, they emphasized difficulties that could arise from refusing free movement and free establishment of these health care professionals within the European Union (art. 52–55 TEC) and, on the other hand, from not supervising their training at a time when there is talk about defining a Community health policy and increasing consumer protection.[54]

50 Art. 138 TEC is similar to art. 152 EC which enables the Council of Ministers to ask the European Commission to make proposals, in particular legislative proposals, in fields where it considers it necessary.

51 Bonnamour M.-C., *op. cit.*: 4.

52 This group organised different propositions on the recognition of alternative medicines in Europe (PROCOMED, *op. cit.*).

53 Bonnamour M.-C., *op. cit.*: 2. See also the opinion of PROCOMED (PROCOMED, *op. cit.*: 2–3) and the French National Order of Physicians (Grunwald D., *op. cit.*: 28).

54 Bonnamour M.-C., *op. cit.*: 3. See also the opinon of the French National Order of Physicians (Grunwald D., *op. cit.*: 28; Haehnel P., *op. cit.*).
With regard to the several studies that the European Commission must undertake the author adds that "it seems that in this way, the MPs want to underscore the fact that the international medical community does not agree on the question of recognition of these practices (exercised in some countries and not in other,

Even though the adoption of the resolution did not create the effect of free movement for alternative practitioners it had several other effects. Some countries, such as France, Italy or Austria decided to examine the position of alternative medicines within their borders more closely and other countries, such as Belgium, decided to modify their legislation in response to the resolution.[55]

In summary, the adoption of Directives on the free movement of alternative practitioners appears difficult to implement. Even though the principle of free movement of persons within the European Union is one of the cornerstones of the Treaty of Rome, it appears that the diversity of national systems precludes such free movement for alternative practitioners in the foreseeable future.[56] In this respect, it is noticeable that rules have been established regarding the mutual recognition within the EU of diplomas leading to the licensing to practise specific professions, but the practice of alternative medicines is neither allowed, nor regulated in several EU Member States, and cannot, therefore, be subject to any such Directives. However, the adoption of a General Directive on Chiropractic will, perhaps, provide an impetus for further regulation of other alternative professions and, as a test case, should provide much information for supporters of the regulation of alternative practitioners.[57]

---

when one type of practice is considered rather than another) and, secondly that the Member States have adopted very different legislative provisions in this field. This study, if it were effectively to be done, could be a dangerous weapon since it could show major scientific divergences within the international medical community" (Bonnamour M.-C., *op. cit.*: 3–4).

55 PROCOMED, *op. cit.*: 2–3.

56 When considering the case of a non-medically qualified acupuncturist practising in France, (Case n° 61/89), the European Court of Justice confirmed the right of Member States to reserve the practice of the healing art to doctors, in accordance with their own legislation.
Such issues were raised at the European Parliament and, in response, the European Commission stated that it was not planning any specific proposals in this area (Written question by Mrs Ursula Braun-Moser in: Official Journal EC n° L. 102, 22.4.1992/23–24; 92/C 102–55).
As one author notes "The Commission has consistently stated its belief that the delivery of health care, including non-conventional therapies, is outside its remit [...]. The Commission clearly believes that it should be up to each Member State to establish its own legal framework regulating the practice of non-conventional medicines, and it seems almost certain that the practice of these professions will continue to be governed by national law in the foreseeable future" (British Medical Association, *op. cit.*: 12). See also the same author at 15–16, 27.

57 Fisher P., *op. cit.*: 109; Grunwald D., *op. cit.*: 27; Schneider H., *op. cit.*

4.3.2 Monopolistic Countries

4.3.2.1 Austria

Bibliography

FROST AND SULLIVAN LTD, *Alternative medical practices in Europe*, Report n° E874, Sullivan House, Grosvenor Gardens, 1987, London SW1: 248; SCHICK P. J., *Die kriminologische und arztrechtliche Problematik unwisserschafltischer Heilmethoden*, in: BAUHOFER S. (co-editors: BOLLE P.-H., DITTMANN V.), *Sectes et occultisme – Aspects criminologiques*, Verlag Rüegger, 1996, Zürich: 351–73; SCHWARTZ W., *Von Exorzisten und Heilpraktkern: Geistheilungen rechtlich betrachtet*, in: Recht der Medizin, 1999, n° 1: 13–19; STEPAN J., *Traditional and alternative systems of medicine: A comparative review of legislation*, in: International Digest of Health Legislation, 1985, vol. 36, n° 2, Genève: 288.

A. General principles

The legislature in Austria has chosen a monopolistic approach to licensing medical professions. Indeed, only authorised medical professionals are permitted to perform medical acts and the practice of medicine without an authorisation is an offence.

There is no specific legal or para-legal regulation nor a draft on the use of alternative medicines in the country.[58] However, Austria is fairly broad-minded in its approach to alternative medicines and physicians are implicitly allowed to use alternative treatments. Furthermore, there are newly recognised post-graduate diplomas on alternative medicines for physicians and Austrian courts have been relatively tolerant in their attitude towards non-allopathic practitioners.

58 Schwartz views alternative medicine as an alien body in the Austrian legal framework (in German: "Dem österreichischen Recht sind rechtsmässige Geistheilungen fremd; es stellt solche Behandlungen unter strenge verwaltungsrechtliche und gerichtliche Strafdrohungen" (SCHWARTZ W., *op. cit.*: 19)). For a development regarding the notion of "Heilkunde" and "Geistheilung", see the same author at 13–15 (making an evaluation with religious concepts).

B. Characteristics of the country

Under the Physicians Act of 1984[59] and the Federal Medical Act of 1964[60] medical acts[61] that are not provided by authorised medical professionals such as, for example, midwifes, medical-technical services and nurses, are reserved for physicians.[62, 63]

According to the Health Services Act, only methods that are scientifically recognised can be provided in hospitals. However, acupuncture,[64] neuraltherapy and chiropractic are recognised,[65] but not homeopathy. In practice, physicians are allowed to use any medical technique, even if not scientifically proved, as long as they receive an informed consent from their patients. Therefore, physicians may have recourse to alternative medicines, but any use of such medicine is their own responsibility.[66]

Any practice of medical acts, by any person other that an authorised medical practitioner is an offence and can be prosecuted.[67] According to art. 184 of the Penal Code, those who practise medical acts or activities reserved for physicians, without having the necessary skills, create an abstract, dangerous situation. The offence carries a penalty of a term of imprisonment lasting up to three months or a fine.[68] The subject of the

59 In German: "Ärztegesetz" 1984, BGBl n° 373, modified in BGBl n° 378/1996.

60 Federal Law n° 50 of Mar. 18, 1964, in: IDHL, 15: 735–765 (1964).

61 Medical acts are restrictively defined. Under the Federal Medical Law (section 1(2)), the practice of medicine "includes all activities based on medico-scientific knowledge carried out directly or indirectly on human beings" performed for the purposes of diagnosis, treatment, prophylaxis, etc.

62 Section 1a (1) of the Federal Medical Law lays down that "the independent practice of medicine shall be the exclusive right of general practitioners and specialists".

63 STEPAN J., *op. cit.*: 288. See also SCHICK P. J., *op. cit.*: 357–58; SCHWARTZ W., *op. cit.*: 15–16; Ministry of Work, Health and Social of Austrian Republic, July 1997, Vienna; H. Schmadlbauer, oberösterreichische Gebietskrankenkasse, Aug. 2001, Linz.

64 Acupuncture achieved special recognition through the teaching activities of the Ludwig Boltzmann Institute.

65 Neuraltherapy and chiropractic are taught within universities.

66 FROST AND SULLIVAN LTD, *op. cit.*: 248; SCHICK P. J., *op. cit.*: 358–59; SCHWARTZ W., *op. cit.*: 15–16; Ministry of Work, Health and Social of Austrian Republic, July 1997, Vienna and Prof A. Stacher, Wiener Internationale Akademie für Ganzheitmedizin, Mar. 1997, Vienna.

67 SCHICK P. J., *op. cit.*; SCHWARTZ W., *op. cit.*: 15–16.

68 The conditions to be prosecuted are: 1. to practise in a professional way, 2. to have at least treated 10 people; and 3. to practise without a diploma from a medical school.

infringement is the creation of an abstract, dangerous situation[69] and medical practice is restricted to physicians because the legislature considers that non-physicians are not able to make correct diagnosis and provide complex treatments.[70] Furthermore, there is a potential risk of negligence if non-doctors provide medical treatments without an allopathic training.[71]

Austrian courts have, however, been tolerant in their interpretation of the law.[72] For example, art. 184 is not enforceable when practitioners use methods that are considered non-scientific,[73] as the elements of art. 184 are not fulfilled.[74]

Schick considers that the definition of art. 184 of the Penal Code would have to be changed, in order to protect patients against the practice of medicine by non-physicians and to prevent physicians providing quackery treatments.[75, 76]

Possibly, non-allopathic practitioners providing care may be prosecuted under art. 80, and 88 of the Penal Code dealing with criminal negligence (death and physical injuries).

69 E.g., when a practitioner does not use an allopathic treatment deemed necessary or when he does not pass over the patient to an allopathic doctor when necessary.

70 Schick notes that, according to a strict interpretation of art. 184 of the Penal Code, tooth technicians providing dental care as acupuncturists should also be prosecuted (SCHICK P. J., *op. cit.*: 360).

71 SCHICK P. J., *op. cit.*: 357, 360; SCHWARTZ W., *op. cit.*: 16–18.

72 Some authors propose the suppression of art. 184 of the Penal Code (SCHICK P. J., *op. cit.*: 357).

73 E.g., the use of a mystic water treatment.

74 SCHICK P. J., *op. cit.*: 361.

75 In a famous Austrian case, a physician advised the parents of a six-year child who had cancer not to use allopathic medicine and try the so-called "new medicine". After the "new medicine" treatment which lasted a few months, the condition of the child worsened and she finally had to be treated with chemotherapy. As the "new medicine" physician was a physician, art. 184 of the Penal Code could not be applied. However, he was held civilly liable because he gave false and bad advice, which resulted in health damages being imposed (art. 1300 (2) ABGB).

76 SCHICK P. J., *op. cit.*: 364.

4.3.2.2 France

Bibliography

ALBER J. (co-author: BERNARDI-SCHENKLUHN B.), *Westeuropäische Gesundheitssysteme im Vergleich, Bundesrepublik Deutschland, Schweiz, Frankreich, Italien, Grossbritanien*, Campus Verlag, 1992, Frankfurt: 323–413; ALMÉRAS J.-P. (co-author: PÉQUIGNOT H.), *La déontologie médicale*, Litec, 1996, Paris; BOUCHAYER F., *Alternative medicines: A general approach to the French situation*, in: LEWITH G. (co-editor: ALDRIDGE D.), *Alternative medicine and the European Community*, CW Daniel, 1991, Saffron Walden: 45–60; BRITISH MEDICAL ASSOCIATION (LAMONT T.), *Alternative medicine – New approaches to good practice*, Oxford University Press, 1993, Oxford/New York: 226; DE BIJL N. (co-author: NEDERVEEN-VAN DE KRAGT I.), *Legal safeguards against medical practice by not suitably qualified persons: A comparative study in seven EU-countries*, 1997, in: European Journal of Health Law, vol. 4: 5–18; DE FORGES J.-M. (I), *Le droit de la santé*, PUF, Collection que sais-je?, 1997, Paris; DE FORGES J.-M (co-authors: TRUCHET D., PENNEAU J., VIALA G.) (II), *Codes de la santé publique de la famille et de l'aide sociale,* 10e éd., Dalloz, 1993, Paris; FROST AND SULLIVAN LTD, *Alternative medical practices in Europe*, Report n° E874, Sullivan House, Grosvenor Gardens, 1987, London SW1: 221–22; GROUPE DE RÉFLEXION "MÉDECINES DIFFÉRENTES", *Evaluer les médecines différentes, un défi? Rapport aux ministres des affaires sociales et de la solidarité nationale et au secrétaire d'état chargé de la santé*, La documentation française, 1986, Paris; GRUNWALD D., *Pratiques médicales non éprouvées*, session de l'Ordre des médecins, 1997 Sept., Paris; GUILLOD O., *Rebouteux, naturopathes et guérisseurs: Pour un traitement légal alternatif*, Recueil de Jurisprudence Neuchâtelois, 1989, Neuchâtel: 9–45; LE GALLOU A., *Responsabilité pénale médicale*, in: Médecine et droit, 1997, n° 24: 26–30; MÉMETEAU G., *The new code of medical deontology*, in: European Journal of Health Law, 1996, n° 3: 75–84; PELLERIN D., *Sur la pratique de l'acupuncture par les sages-femmes*, in: Bulletin de l'Académie Nationale de Médecine, 1997, vol. 181, n° 9: 1909–10; PORTELLI N., *Le délit d'exercice illégal de la médecine*, mémoire, 1994, France; ROBARD I., *La santé hors la loi: Les hors la loi de la santé*, 4th ed., Ed. de l'Ancre, 1994, Suresnes; STEPAN J., *Traditional and alternative systems of medicine: A comparative review of legislation*, in: International Digest of Health Legislation, 1985, vol. 36, n° 2, Genève: 287–88, 316, 320; VÉRON M., *L'exercice illégal de la médecine*, in: AUBY J.-M., *Droit médical et hospitalier*, Litec, 1993, Paris.

A. Historical evolution of the licensing to practise

Until recently, alternative medicines have been operating within a hostile environment in France, resulting from two factors: first, a panoply legal regulations and court cases; and second, the development of the medical corporation that has benefited from a monopoly over the provision of health care.[77]

Until the French Revolution, several schools and universities teaching medicine were organised as corporations.[78] The French Revolution outlawed all corporations and associations and, consequently, universities and schools of medicine. As a result, the practice of medicine became free, but it lasted only a short time. In 1795, the Schools of Health were created and, later, the Act of March 10, 1803, regulating the practice of medicine, was enacted. The Act fundamentally modified the organisation for the teaching and licensing of medical practitioners. Since that time, the State has been responsible for organising medical education and delivering medical diplomas. Thus, only persons holding the title of doctor were allowed to provide medical care. In addition, medical diplomas had to be registered by prefectures. Finally, the illegal practice of medicine was defined.[79]

In 1892, the adoption of a new Act marked a second step in the evolution of the licensing to practise medicine within France. According to the new Act, only physicians were allowed to practise medicine, with the exception of dentistry. Moreover, art. 13 of the 1892 Act entitled medical corporations to bring a civil suit for damages[80] against people illegally practising medicine.[81] However, actual prosecution for the illegal practice of medicine was rare and the sentences levied were lenient.[82]

Since 1892, new regulations have increased the protection of the medical corporation. The Act of 26 July, 1935, consecrated the monopoly of doctors and the Vichy Act of 7 October, 1940, introduced new structures in the form of professional orders. Finally, the Order of 24 September, 1945, established the organisation of the medical profession. It encompassed

77 De Forges J.-M. (I), *op. cit.*: 108; Robard I., *op. cit.*: 19.
78 Robard I., *op. cit.*: 22–26.
79 De Forges J.-M. (I), *op. cit.*: 108; Robard I., *op. cit.*: 29–30.
80 This principle has been upheld until the present regulation.
81 Art. 16 regulated anew the illegal practice of medicine, the definition of which has been revived by the present Code of Public Health.
82 Robard I., *op. cit.*: 30–31.

two forms of regulation: the first set of rules determined the requirements for the licence to practise medicine, while the second provided that the practice of medicine would take place under the authority of the Order of Physicians, which was itself placed under the supervision of the Council of State. Art. 66 of the Act of 1945 laid down that a Professional Code of Ethics[83] had to be adopted, which would then be officially recognised by disciplinary courts.[84, 85]

In short, from the Middle Age until today, the (fiercely allopathic) medical profession has never stopped regulating its own practice in order to eliminate allegedly incompetent or non-allopathic practitioners. The inevitable consequence has been the implementation of a monopolistic system of licensing medical professionals.[86]

B. General principles

France has a typical monopolistic regulation structure regarding the licensing to practise alternative medicines.[87] Health care professionals have been subjected to specific surveillance for a long period. Currently, according to the Code of Public Health, only doctors in (allopathic) medicine and recognised ancillary professionals are permitted to provide medical care, thus excluding non-allopathic practitioners.[88]

The Code of Public Health contains rules regarding the licensing to practise medicine as well as the illegal practice of medicine. The Code of Professional Ethics also plays an important role, particularly in spelling out the rights and duties of physicians, such as the forbidding to provide alternative medicines.[89]

83 After several amendments since 1945, the latest Code of Professional Ethics was adopted on Sept. 6, 1995.

84 The Council of State and the Order of Physicians were designated as disciplinary authorities.

85 Alber J., *op. cit.*: 368; Mémeteau G., *op. cit.*: 75–79; Robard I., *op. cit.*: 31–34.

86 De Forges J.-M. (I), *op. cit.*: 108; Robard I., *op. cit.*: 34.

87 As in other countries influenced by the French Civil Code, the so-called "Code Napoleon", such as in Belgium, or Italy.

88 British Medical Association, *op. cit.*: 26; Le Gallou A., *op. cit.*: 28; Robard I., *op. cit.*: 58–60; Stepan J., *op. cit.*: 287–88, 316, 320.

89 Mémeteau G., *op. cit.*: 75–79.

The licensing to practise medicine is subject to several conditions, namely the possession of a State certificate,[90] citizenship[91] and registration by a professional body such as the National Order of Physicians.[92, 93]

The scope of practice of medical doctors is widely defined and, in effect, a monopoly is created whereby physicians occupy the whole field. According to art. L. 372 of the Code of Public Health and art. 17 of the Code of Professional Ethics, the practice of medical doctors covers the diagnosis and treatment of human diseases. This is the principle of "universality" animating the physician's diploma,[94] which allows medical doctors to perform all medical acts, excepting a few procedures restricted to pharmacists.[95, 96]

90 Art. L. 356 of the Code of Public Health. See art. L. 478 Code of Public Health for physiotherapists.
State certificates for doctors have existed since 1803. In 1947, the State certificate for physiotherapists was created, in 1952 for dieticians, in 1970 for ergotherapists and in 1962 for speech therapists.

91 Candidates must be French, Tunisian, Moroccan or citizens of a Member State of the EU. However, there are possible exceptions, under specific conditions.

92 The National Order of Physicians registers newly licensed physicians after making sure that all requirements are met, e.g., the authenticity of the certificate and the verification of the good mental and physical health. It also verifies that doctors, in accordance with the Code of Professional Ethics, have shown sufficient morality and professional independence. In 1945, for example, an administrative judge considered that the last condition had not been met by a doctor who had administered quack treatments (Council of State, Feb. 14, 1945, *Benrekdjan*).

93 DE BIJL N., *op. cit.*: 7–8; DE FORGES J.-M. (I), *op. cit.*: 109–11; DE FORGES J.-M. (II), *op. cit.*: 173–82, 200, 203; GUILLOD O., *op. cit.*: 22; ROBARD I., *op. cit.*: 62–67; VÉRON M., *op. cit.*: 16–17.

94 Some authors use the term "omnivalence" (in French: "le principe d'omnivalence du diplôme médical") (ALMÉRAS J.-P., *op. cit.*: 128; PORTELLI N., *op. cit.*: 18 and DE FORGES J.-M. (I), *op. cit.*: 113).

95 In comparison, the scope of other medical professions is more restrictively defined. For example, dentistry covers the diagnosis and treatment of mouth-related ailments, while the profession of midwife encompasses doing deliveries and providing a strictly defined number of medical acts.
According to Robard, the medical monopoly had undesirable side effects. Indeed, since physicians hold a monopoly in the practice of medicine, they are allowed to administer any kind of treatment, even when they do not have sufficient skills in a specific field (ROBARD I., *op. cit.*: 107–12). However, rules dealing with malpractice liability could be enforced in such cases.
For more details and examples, see DE FORGES J.-M. (I), *op. cit.*: 112.

96 ALMÉRAS J.-P., *op. cit.*: 128; DE FORGES J.-M. (I), *op. cit.*: 111–12; PORTELLI N., *op. cit.*: 15–16.

Two jurisdictions play an important role in the field of alternative medicines within France: the criminal jurisdiction[97] and the disciplinary jurisdiction.[98]

Professional medical orders, such as the National Medical Council,[99] have also played an active role in public health. Indeed, in order to guarantee public health, the legislature has empowered professional medical orders with a number of important functions, such as the elaboration of general rules of practice,[100] the enforcement of professional rules through administrative controls and the representation of medical professions before public authorities. Such professional medical orders also have the power to initiate prosecutions against illegal practitioners of medicine.[101] The State itself has two essential roles in the field of medical professions. First, it organises the medical professions by controlling their training and the issuance of diplomas. Secondly, it provides a framework for the prosecution illegal practices.[102]

C. Particularities of the country

The position of non-allopathic practitioners

General remarks

French law is very repressive with regard to the illegal practice of medicine. Under the Code of Public Health (articles L.372–L.376), persons other than licensed physicians who, usually or continuously, diagnose or treat

97 With respect to the provisions of the Code of Public Health and of other public laws.

98 With respect to the provisions of the various Codes of Professional Ethics. The Order of 1945 makes up the legal basis for this jurisdiction, which may only consider violations of the Code of Professional Ethics (ROBARD I., *op. cit.*: 79. See also below, same chapter).

99 In French: "Ordre National des Médecins". Usually, there are a number of regional orders and a national order for each profession. Professions that are not organised in orders come under the surveillance of public authorities, which have the same functions and play the same role as the orders.

100 Particularly the Professional Code of Ethics. These codes are more than a professional document since they are published by governmental decree.

101 The National Council of the Order may decide sanctions including fines, temporary suspension or withdrawal of licences to practise.

102 ALMÉRAS J.-P., *op. cit.*: 158; DE FORGES J.-M. (I), *op. cit.*: 116–20; GUILLOD O., *op. cit.*: 22–23; MÉMETEAU G., *op. cit.*; ROBARD I., *op. cit.*: 59.

illnesses, real or supposed, or who perform medical acts and procedures, commit the offence of the illegal practice of medicine.[103]

According to article L. 372 of the Code of Public Health, the offence of the illegal practice of medicine is committed where four elements are established:[104]

1. Performing a medical act reserved to medical doctors;
2. Performing such acts on a regular basis;
3. Not holding a State certificate;
4. Absence of justification.

The elements of the offence of illegal practice of medicine are set forth below.

1. Performing a medical act reserved to medical doctors[105]

The first element refers to the making of a diagnosis, the prescribing of a treatment, and the performance of medical acts reserved to doctors in medicine, medical assistants and pathology laboratories.

The scientific value, efficacy and innocuousness of the medical technique is irrelevant. It is also irrelevant if practitioners have requested that their patients first receive an allopathic diagnosis.[106] The position for other various forms of treatment is similar; all medical acts belonging either to preventive or to reconstructive medicine come within the ambit of the code. The Decree of January 1962 further provides (art. 2) that, in addition to

103 GUILLOD O., *op. cit.*: 20; PORTELLI N., *op. cit.*: 2; VÉRON M., *op. cit.*: 2.

104 DE FORGES J.-M. (II), *op. cit.*: 205–07; GUILLOD O., *op. cit.*: 21–22; LE GALLOU A., *op. cit.*: 28–29; PORTELLI N., *op. cit.*: 10–26; ROBARD I., *op. cit.*: 95–151; VÉRON M., *op. cit.*: 2.

105 DE FORGES J.-M. (II), *op. cit.*: 202–05; ROBARD I., *op. cit.*: 95–97; PORTELLI N., *op. cit.*: 15–18; VÉRON M., *op. cit.*: 2–5.

106 Therefore, practitioners using "magnetism", i.e. observing variations of length of electro-magnetic waves revealing deficiencies in the organism, and who make a diagnosis using a machine measuring the length of waves commit the offence of illegal practice of medicine. Acupuncture, which is partially recognised, is also restricted to physicians.

the medical acts usually reserved to physicians, there is a list of medical acts strictly reserved to medical doctors.[107, 108]

French Courts have also considered various non-allopathic methods of treatment:[109]

- In one case, magnetism and spiritualism were considered an illegal practice of medicine. It was irrelevant whether there was a previous diagnosis or not. As a result, when a healer seeks to ascertain the origin of the disease by utilising a pendulum or when he lays his hands upon a patient, he commits an offence. In contrast, religious as well as "supernatural" treatments are permitted, provided that they do not consist of physical interventions. However, these practices could amount to fraud;
- The use of dowsing, being the examination of the radiation emanating from the patient's organs, is allowed for physicians as a method of diagnosis. Non-allopathic practitioners can assist physicians during the making of the diagnosis, but they commit an offence if they make a diagnosis on their own or if they are assisted by physicians and share the fees. Other courts have, however, expressed a different view, holding that dowsing is not a method of diagnosis and that the rules pertaining to practitioners using dowsing should be relaxed;
- Courts regularly sentence non-allopathic practitioners using acupuncture;

107 The acts restricted to physicians are the following: 1. all manipulations of joints, enclosing slipped disc, osteopathy, vertebrotherapy and chiropractic; 2. prosthetic massages; 3. gynaecologic massages; 4. specific physiotherapeutic acts; 5. methods for removal of hair, except for methods using tweezers and wax; 6. abrasion of teguments; 7. handling of a machine determining the ocular refraction; 8. tonal audiometry.
The duties of the pharmacist profession have also been subjected to criticism because pharmacists often need to make a simple diagnosis in order to satisfy those clients who had gone directly to drugstores for treatment of some minor illnesses.
The scope of practice of the profession of beautician was also the subject of controversy. Indeed, the limit between therapeutic and cosmetic treatments is not clear. Nevertheless, the courts are rather tolerant in this respect. Some legal writers have also noted that the term of therapy is losing its meaning and therefore, it may be used to designate both medical and non-medical treatments

108 DE FORGES J.-M. (II), *op.cit.*: 202–05; GUILLOD O., *op.cit.*: 21; ROBARD I., *op.cit.*: 121–29, Addendum: 9–11; STEPAN J., *op.cit.*: 287–88, 316; VÉRON M., *op.cit.*: 3, 11–14.

109 DE FORGES J.-M. (II), *op.cit.*: 203–05; GUILLOD O., *op.cit.*: 21–22; LE GALLOU A., *op.cit.*: 29; ROBARD I., *op.cit.*: 121, 125, Addendum: 9–12; STEPAN J., *op.cit.*: 288; VÉRON M., *op.cit.*: 12–15.

- Courts have not been consistent in their attitude towards psychological methods, even though today psychologists are authorised to practise psychology and psychoanalysis. Indeed, in the past, they considered that psychoanalysis was a medical act within the monopoly of medical doctors. Psychologists could, therefore, be prosecuted if they provided psychiatric treatments to mentally ill patients;
- Recently, several tribunals have relaxed their rules for practitioners using iridology and osteopathy. The reasons were first, that iridology was not included in the list of the Act of January 6, 1962, and, second, that the latter Act did not provide a sufficiently precise definition to enable judges to unmistakeably recognize treatments included in the law from those other treatments not restricted to physicians;
- Two more cases demonstrate the difficulty of finding consistency among French courts in this area: in 1993, a Tribunal released a naturopath whereas a sophrologist who had opened an anti-tobacco centre was sentenced.

2. *Performing such acts on a regular basis*

Alternative practitioners are subject to punishment as soon as they perform any medical act reserved to doctors twice.[110]

3. *Not holding a State certificate*

In accordance with article 356 of the Code of Public Health, only those persons[111] holding a French diploma, or a diploma recognised in France are permitted to practise medicine.[112]

Essentially, there are three categories of persons who may commit the offence: physicians in some specific cases, other allopathic health practitioners holding a recognised diploma but exceeding their field of knowledge,[113] and non-allopathic practitioners without any recognised title practising medicine.[114]

110 DE FORGES J.-M. (II), *op. cit.*: 205; PORTELLI N., *op. cit.*: 15; VÉRON M., *op. cit.*: 3–4.

111 I.e., EU citizens, as well as Tunisian and Moroccan citizens.

112 For further analysis concerning the relationship between French and European law, see PORTELLI N., *op. cit.*: 19–26; ROBARD I., *op. cit.*: 94–95; VÉRON M., *op. cit.*: 5–15.

113 E.g., dentists, midwives, nurses, opticians, kinesitherapists, speech therapists, audio-prothesists, dieticians and pharmacists performing medical acts going beyond their competence.

114 DE FORGES J.-M. (II), *op. cit.*: 203, 205–07; PORTELLI N., *op. cit.*: 27–51; ROBARD I., *op. cit.*: 64–67; VÉRON M., *op. cit.*: 5–16.

Thus, practitioners who have obtained a foreign certificate recognized in the country where they underwent the training are not allowed to practise in France, as long as that training or profession has not been recognised in the country.[115] This category of practitioners may not rely on the principle of free movement within the EU.[116]

4. Absence of justification

Article L. 372 of the Code of Public Health does not apply to medical students, midwives, nurses and paramedic professionals if they act on the recommendation of a physician and under his surveillance. The motive for the act is unimportant. Indeed, article L. 372 of the Code of Public Health protects not only the medical monopoly, but also public health. Therefore, elements such as the sincere wish to help others or the provision of free care do not justify what remains an illegal act. In exceptional circumstances, the courts will allow for the providing of assistance in an emergency.[117]

Persons sentenced for the illegal practice of medicine risk a fine of up to 10,000 Euros and/or imprisonment for up to six months. The number of court cases on this topic is impressive. According to Guillod, the strict repression of illegal practice of medicine in France is directly related to the vigour of medical corporatism.[118]

The current trend is to move towards lighter sentences. The regional professional medical Orders often receive only 1 symbolic franc as compensatory damages, and courts have started relaxing their approach to alternative practitioners or renouncing harsh penalties. Today, the Orders hesitate to initiate prosecution[119] because in most cases the trial results in positive publicity for the prosecuted practitioner.[120]

115 The offence is committed even if they perform the act in the presence of a physician.

116 PORTELLI N., *op. cit.*: 20–23; VÉRON M., *op. cit.*: 3, 16.

117 DE FORGES J.-M. (II), *op. cit.*: 202; VÉRON M., *op. cit.*: 18–19. For more details, see chap. 4.3.1.

118 See DE FORGES J.-M. (II): GUILLOD O., *op. cit.*: 21–23; LE GALLOU A., *op. cit.*: 29; STEPAN J., *op. cit.*: 288; PORTELLI N., *op. cit.*; GROUPE DE RÉFLEXION, *op. cit.*: 28; VÉRON M., *op. cit.*: 19–20.

119 Article L. 375 of the Code of Public Health provides that the prosecution can start through two means: the direct summons or the introduction of a civil suit by the victim. Both actions begin at the same time. Doctors, the Council of the Order and the trade bodies can lodge a complaint as soon as a practitioner interferes with the interests of the profession. They may also sue and ask illegal practitioners for damages.

Some observers consider that the number of quacks has increased and that courts should be more severe, even given the current trend is towards leniency.[121]

The position of allopathic practitioners

Physicians may encounter the following situations: where they assist persons illegally practising medicine, or they themselves practice alternative medicines. In both examples, they run the risk of being tried by penal and disciplinary jurisdictions.

In the first hypothesis, physicians may be disciplinarily prosecuted according to art. 30 of the Code of Professional Ethics (CPE), which forbids the provision of help to any person practising medicine illegally. Such persons may also be criminally prosecuted, under art. L. 372 (3) of the Code of Public Health.[122]

In the second hypothesis, namely when physicians use insufficiently proved methods, they may be prosecuted under the CPE, which may lead to disciplinary sanctions.[123] Even though art. 8 CPE establishes the principle of freedom of prescription, other provisions restrict this guiding principle.[124] For example, art. 30 and 39 CPE state that physicians may not propose to their patients cures that are illusory or insufficiently proved as such practices would be charlatanism.[125] Art. 32–34 CPE would also

Some legal writers consider that the disciplinary jurisdiction is not impartial, because the Order of Physicians are both "judge and jury" (Portelli N., *op. cit.*: 54–58; Robard I., *op. cit.*: 112).

120 Bouchayer F., *op. cit.*: 50; British Medical Association, *op. cit.*: 26; Groupe de réflexion, *op. cit.*: 28; Portelli N., *op. cit.*: 2, 62–69; Robard I., *op. cit.*: 120–21; Véron M., *op. cit.*: 2; Dr. Grunwald D., at the National Council of Order of Physicians, considers that the number of prosecutions has not decreased, Oct. 1997, Paris.

121 Le Gallou A., *op. cit.*: 29.

122 Robard I., *op. cit.*: 97; Portelli N., *op. cit.*: 30–33; Véron M., *op. cit.*: 17–18.

123 The National Order of physicians reported 3 relaxes, 2 warnings, 7 reprimands and 58 suspensions in relation with the use of alternative medicines by physicians. Unfortunately, the Order does not mention for which period these sanctions have been taken nor its sources (Grunwald D., *op. cit.*: 21).

124 The Constitutional court refused to express its opinion regarding the freedom of prescription for medical practitioners. However, according to several authors, this freedom results from the individual freedom (Robard I., *op. cit.*: 69–70).

125 An appropriate use of alternative medicine is not considered as charlatanism.

be applicable in that they provide that physicians must use scientifically proven methods of treatment and must inform patients of the pertinent characteristics of alternative medicines.[126]

In contrast, civil jurisdictions have extensively interpreted the concept of freedom of prescription, considering that the use of an alternative method should not be condemned merely because the medical establishment rejects it. They consider that applying these rules strictly would make it impossible to undertake new research for the purpose of discovering new treatments. However, this has not been the opinion of the Council of State and the disciplinary jurisdiction as both have interpreted the concept more restrictively. This has resulted in a very strict legal framework for the use of new medical treatments.[127]

The National Medical Council is gradually becoming more tolerant regarding the practice of alternative medicines when provided by physicians. In December 1997, it adopted a report on homeopathy which contained information on the practice of homeopathy, and the current research in homeopathy.[128]

The position of kinesitherapists[129] is representative of the legal status of ancillary practitioners providing alternative medicines. They are allowed to work only on the recommendation of a physician, and the practice of medical acts, other than massages and gymnastics, amounts to the illegal practice of medicine. However, on January 9, 1987, a court held that kinesitherapists are allowed to provide chiropractic under the surveillance of a physician.[130]

There is a large body of court rulings concerning kinesitherapists performing various medical acts that are, as stated in art. 2 of the Decree of January 6, 1962, restricted to physicians. These medical acts include performing any joint manipulations, working on slipped discs, osteopathy, vertebral therapy, chiropractic, prosthetic and gynaecologic massages. As for physicians, the present trend is towards lighter sentencing ancillary

126 BOUCHAYER F., *op. cit.*: 50; GRUNWALD D., *op. cit.*: 22; ROBARD I., *op. cit.*: 67, 100–02.

127 ROBARD I., *op. cit.*: 75–85.

128 For the National Medical Council, homeopathy is a therapeutic medical method, the use of which must be reserved to medical doctors. However, homeopathy is not recognised as a speciality. Furthermore, doctors practising homeopathy must abide by the same code of conduct as other doctors.

129 I.e., French physiotherapists. The profession of kinesitherapist is regulated under articles L. 487–503 of the Code of Public Health.

130 ROBARD I., *op. cit.*: 118; VÉRON M., *op. cit.*: 9.

professional convicted of the illegal practice of medicine. Since 1976, 18 chiropractors convicted of the illegal practice of medicine were not given to any penalty. Similarly, two kinesitherapists using sympathicotherapy and iridology were released.[131] Other paramedic professionals can be prosecuted too, such asopticians measuring the ocular refraction, adapting contact lenses or prescribing ocular gymnastics, or dental technicians taking dental impressions.[132]

The Minister of Work and Social Affairs asked for the opinion of the Medical National Academy on the provision of acupuncture by midwives. The Academy refused to include acupuncture as part of the techniques at the disposal of midwifes, observing that there had been no recent developments regarding the anatomo-physiological basis of the technique.[133]

4.3.2.3 Italy

Bibliography

BRITISH MEDICAL ASSOCIATION (LAMONT T.), *Alternative medicine – New approaches to good practice*, Oxford University Press, 1993, Oxford/New York: 26; FROST AND SULLIVAN LTD, *Alternative medical practices in Europe*, Report n° E874, Sullivan House, Grosvenor Gardens, 1987, London SW1: 225–33; MCCARTHY M. (co-author: REES S.), *Health systems and health medicine in the European Community*, Royal College of Physicians of London, 1992, London: 34–38; MATTOLI P., *La legislazione omeopatica in Italia*, in: AUSSER O., *Handbuch zu den natürlichen Heilweisen und besonderen Therapierichtungen*, Alfred & Söhne, 1992, Meran; ROBARD I., *La santé hors la loi: Les hors la loi de la santé*, 4th ed., Ed. de l'Ancre, 1994, Suresnes: 210–12; STEPAN J., *Traditional and alternative systems of medicine: A comparative review of legislation*, in: International Digest of Health Legislation, 1985, vol. 36, n° 2, Genève: 288.

131 They informed their patients that they were not doctors in medicine, and warned them that the treatment they provided did not replace allopathic medicine.

132 DE FORGES J.-M. (II), *op. cit.*: 203; GROUPE DE RÉFLEXION, *op. cit.*: 28; GUILLOD O., *op. cit.*: 21; LE GALLOU A., *op. cit.*: 29; ROBARD I., *op. cit.*: 103; STEPAN J., *op. cit.*: 288; VÉRON M., *op. cit.*: 9

133 PELLERIN D., *op. cit.*: 1909–10.

In Italy, the legislator has chosen a monopolistic system for licensing medical professions. Only registered physicians[134] can use alternative medicines, but courts have been relatively tolerant with non-physician alternative practitioners. Furthermore, some therapies are recognised or are in the process of being recognised.

There is no specific regulation on alternative medicines in Italy, apart from an exception for homeopathy and anthroposophic medicine.[135]

In a decision of the Criminal Supreme Court of Appeal in Perugia, the court held that the practice of alternative medicines is allowed, but only by registered physicians.[136] The court noted that, even though acupuncture is not taught in Italian Universities, only physicians or surgeons are allowed to practise it. It further considered that a medical and/or surgical expertise is necessary to establish an exact diagnosis and avoid prejudicial consequences for patients. However, physicians using these techniques have to assume any consequences that may arise from taking patients away from allopathic medicine.[137]

Similarly, art. 82 of the Code of Professional Ethics of 1995 stipulates that physicians are responsible for their choice to use innovative or alternative methods rather than consolidated scientific experiences. Furthermore, physicians may not cooperate with, or help non-allopathic practitioners illegally practising medicine, even in the field of alternative medicines.[138]

134 In order to practise as an allopathic physician, candidates must:
1. be graduated in medicine or surgery;
2. pass the corresponding state exam;
3. be registered in a professional register.

Physicians can specialise after graduation without any formal clinical experience. If a doctor works for five years in a specialist post, whether he or she has been formally trained or not, he or she is automatically recognised as a specialist. Over 100 different specialities are recognised. The law 175 of Feb. 5, 1992, expressly prohibits the use of titles that are not recognised by the State. No alternative medicines are recognised as medical specialities by this law. Thus, any courses organised, even at the university level, such as acupuncture, are not legally recognised (McCarthy M., *op. cit.*: 38).

135 Robard I., *op. cit.*: 210.

136 Decision sect. 6, n° 7176 of July 19, 1982. This decision regards acupuncture but is valid for all alternative medicines. A circular of the Italian Health Ministry followed this position and certified that acupuncture was a medical act.

137 British Medical Association, *op. cit.*: 26; Frost and Sullivan Ltd, *op. cit.*: 232; Mattoli P., *op. cit.*: 40; Robard I., *op. cit.*: 211; Stepan J., *op. cit.*: 288.

138 According to this article, ancillary practitioners are not allowed to provide alternative medicines.

The Commentary of the Code (art. 31) specifies that physicians, knowing the limits and the non-scientifically proven efficacy of alternative medicines, may use them only for patients' benefits.

Practitioners treating patients without the appropriate authorisation can be prosecuted under art. 348 of the Italian Penal Code for the illegal practice of medicine. However, non-allopathic practitioners are seldom prosecuted. Robard notes that, for the time being, there is a peaceful cohabitation between non-physicians and physicians.[139]

Furthermore, chiropractors are tolerated when they work under the supervision of a doctor, even though the practice of this technique is theoretically not allowed.[140]

Homeopathy, as an alternative discipline, has also enjoyed a long tradition in Italy and, since 1841, there have been several attempts to regulate homeopathy through the licensing to practise and through the training of homeopathy and pharmacopoeia.[141] On March 17, 1995, Decree n° 185 was adopted, incorporating Directive 92/73/CEE, which regulates the marketing and the registration of homeopathic and anthroposophic products.[142]

Currently, the climate in Italy is evolving in favour of alternative medicines.[143] Furthermore, legislation on homeopathic products has been adopted and several projects on the regulation of alternative medicines are in progress.[144]

4.3.2.4 Latvia[145]

Latvia has a monopolistic system for the licensing of the medical professions. Medical treatments may only be performed by physicians but alternative practitioners are relatively well accepted, even if practising outside the legal regime.[146]

139 ROBARD I., *op. cit.*: 211.
140 ROBARD I., *op. cit.*: 212.
141 For a historical development of homeopathy in Italy, see MATTOLI P., *op. cit.*
142 MATTOLI P., *op. cit.*; ROBARD I., *op. cit.*: 212. For more details, see chap. 7.2.4.
143 E.g., Italian regions such as Lombardy, have commenced rigorous research into alternative medicines, which demonstrates the interest of the Italian authorities in this field.
144 ROBARD I., *op. cit.*: 211; MATTOLI P., *op. cit.*: 38.
145 The information regarding Latvia was provided by Nickolay A. Nickolaev, Traditional Chinese Medicine and Acupuncture Department at the Ministry of Social Welfare, Riga, Mar. 1998; WHO liaison Officer, Riga, 2000.
146 In order to practise legally as a recognised physician, the following conditions must be met:

Physicians must, in order to be legally allowed to provide alternative medicine, attend special multi-step training courses.[147] The certification process and the supervision of these practitioners is led by a commission of experts, which consists of members of medical associations, in cooperation with representatives of the Medical Society of the Republic of Latvia.

For example, the Association of Medical Acupuncture and Related Techniques is responsible for the certification of physicians in the field of acupuncture. The certification commission includes 10 professional-experts and is headed by the president of the association. Other similarly constructed commissions provide certification for other methods of alternative medicines.[148]

The state certificate is valid for a period of five years. A new authorisation is then necessary, which requires attending new courses and passing related exams.

Non-allopathic practitioners are not allowed to practise alternative medicines, even if they work under the supervision of a recognised health professional. Indeed, the Administrative Codex provides for a penalty for unauthorised medical practice. However, in practice, patients very seldom sue healers, even when their health has been compromised. Therefore, several non-allopathic practitioners do provide health care.

4.3.2.5 Luxembourg

Bibliography

ROBARD I., *La santé hors la loi: Les hors la loi de la santé*, 4th ed., Ed. de l'Ancre, 1994, Suresnes: 216–17; STEPAN J., *Traditional and alternative systems of medicine: A comparative review of legislation*, in: International Digest of Health Legislation, 1985, vol. 36, n° 2, Genève: 288.

1. to graduate from the local Medical Academy or from any other Medical College delivering a recognised diploma;
2. to obtain the authorisation according to the local legislation.

147 Local legislation provides such rules.

148 E.g., auriculotherapy, iridology, magnetotherapy, osteoreflexology, phytotherapy, naturopathy, lasertherapy, bio feed-back, Qigong, and Su-Jok.

Luxembourg is a monopolistic country which has a very strict position towards alternative medicines; medical acts are restricted by law to certified physicians[149] and alternative practices are prohibited.[150]

Currently, there is no legal regulation or draft of regulation specifically regulating alternative medicines.[151]

Article 7 of the Act of April 29, 1983, concerning the illegal practice of medicine, stipulates that persons without the required qualifications who practise or participate in the diagnostic or the treatment of real or supposed pathological disorders, or in a delivery through personal acts, verbal or written consultations or other methods, can be prosecuted. Thus, treatment, diagnosis and prevention are restricted to members of the medical corpus. Non-allopathic practitioners using alternative medicines are regularly prosecuted.[152]

According to the Code of Professional Ethics, physicians may not suggest the use of therapies to their patients or their circle of acquaintances, as being salutary and harmless, when such therapies are based on an illusory method or are not scientifically proven.[153]

The Medical College is unequivocally opposed to the practice of alternative medicines in Luxembourg. It considers alternative practitioners to be quacks. Nevertheless, members of Parliament favour official recognition of alternative professionals and techniques.[154]

149 The conditions to fully practise medicine as a physician are first, the holding of a university certificate and second, the authorisation from the Minister of Health together with the consent of the Medical College (ROBARD I., *op. cit.*: 216).

150 ROBARD I., *op. cit.*: 216; STEPAN J., *op. cit.*: 288.

151 ROBARD I., *op. cit.*: 217; Jomé L. at the MINISTRY OF HEALTH, Mar. 1998, Luxembourg; Schleder-Leuck A., at the MINISTRY OF HEALTH, Sept. 2001, Luxembourg.

152 ROBARD I., *op. cit.*: 216; Schleder-Leuck A., at the Ministry of Health, Sept. 2001, Luxembourg.

153 In French: "le médecin ne peut pas proposer aux malades ou à leur entourage comme salutaire et sans danger un remède ou un procédé illusoire ou non scientifiquement éprouvé".

154 ROBARD I., *op. cit.*: 216–17.

4.3.2.6 *Spain*

Bibliography

ARJALAGUER X., *Los médicos daràn reconocimiento oficial a homeopatìa, acupuntura y medicina naturista*, in: La Vanguardia, Sept. 24, 1996: 25; LAGUNA T., *El quiromasajista no representa competencia deleal para el fisioterapeuta, según la Audencia*, in: Las Provincias, Mar. 19, 1997, Valencia; MCCARTHY M. (co-author: REES S.), *Health systems and health medicine in the European Community*, Royal College of Physicians of London, 1992, London: 49–54; ORGANIZACIÓN MEDICA COLLEGIAL, *Regulación de las medicinas alternativas – Documento de la OMC sobre la proposición de la Ley socialista*, in: Organización Medica Collegial, n° 25, Febr. 1, 1993; PÉREZ OLIVIA M., *El código de los médicos catalanes da más poder de decisión a los pacientes*, in: El Pais, June 17, 1997; ROBARD I., *La santé hors la loi: Les hors la loi de la santé*, 4th ed., Ed. de l'Ancre, 1994, Suresnes: 233–38; ROMERO-CASABONA C. (co-authors: HERNANDEZ-PLASCENCIA J., SOLA-RECHE E.), *Spain* in: *International Encyclopedia of Laws – Medical Law*, Kluwer Law International, The Hague/London/Boston.

A. General principles

Spain has a monopolistic system for the licensing of the medical professions. The practice of medicine is the exclusive competence of doctors[155] and, as of yet, alternative medicines are not recognised. However, the State medical authorities are open-minded in their attitude towards them.[156]

Alternative medicines were not included within the Royal Decree 127/1984 regarding medical specialities.[157] Thus, there are no specific regulations nor recognition of these disciplines.[158]

155 There are three categories of conditions necessary to satisfy before the right to practise medicine is obtained: legal, administrative and ethical.
1. The legal conditions are the following: first, the holding of an academic degree in medicine. Second, physicians have to obtain an authorisation from a medical college. Finally, doctors are submitted to professional secrecy;
2. The administrative condition is the accomplishment of fiscal duties;
3. The ethical condition is respect for the Spanish Code of Professional Ethics of 1990. The Statutes of the Collegial Medical Organisation provide an official basis to the obligation to follow ethical rules. Duties, rights and prohibitions are specified in art. 41–44 of the Statutes.

156 ROBARD I., *op. cit.*: 233.

157 A physician's postgraduate qualifications require an initial academic year followed by a two-year service training (MCCARTHY M., *op. cit.*: 53).

158 ROBARD I., *op. cit.*: 233. However, a Royal Decree of Mar. 27, 1926, on naturopathy establishes that only licensed physicians may practise naturopathy.

Physicians are, in principle, legally allowed to practise in any branch of medicine, and therefore to provide alternative methods. However, art. 44 of the Statutes of the Collegial Medical Organisation states that non-scientifically proven techniques including the simulation of the making of a diagnosis, or the application of therapeutic treatments, are prohibited. It is, however, true to say that State authorities are relatively tolerant with private doctors using alternative medicines.[159]

On June 16, 1997, the new Code of Medical Professional Ethics was adopted in Catalonia.[160] It provides that physicians using alternative medicines must inform their patients of the necessity to continue a medical treatment and of the non-conventional character of the treatment. Furthermore, they must co-ordinate their actions with the physician in charge of the basic treatment.[161]

Authorised ancillary professionals[162] are only permitted to perform medical acts under the supervision of a physician.[163] However, some provide alternative medicines in an independent, and therefore illegal way.[164]

According to Robard,[165] alternative medicines are semi-recognised in Spain. The reasons being first, the existence of court rulings legitimating non-physicians and, second, a royal Decree 1175/1990 of September 28, 1990, which expressly states that naturopaths and acupuncturists are health professionals subject to taxation for economic activities.[166]

B. Characteristics of the country

Illegal practice of medicine

The illegal practice of medicine is regulated by art. 403 of the Penal Code, modified in 1996, which focuses on intrusions committed in the medical

159 Robard I., *op. cit.*: 235.
160 The Council of Medical Colleges of Catalonia wants to make official homeopathy, acupuncture and naturopathy.
161 La Vanguardia, Sept. 24, 1996; Dr. Amengual I Vicens C., Universidad de Valencia, Aug. 2001; Liga Medicorum Homeopathica Internationalis, Mallorca, Mar. 1998.
162 There are three categories of ancillary professions: 1° odontology practitioners, 2° psychologists and 3° university graduates in nursing (such as physiotherapists).
163 Art. 62 concerning the legal status of medical personnel of the social security 3166/1966 of Dec. 23, 1996.
164 Prof. Med. F. A. Verdú, University of Valencia, Sept. 2001.
165 Robard I., *op. cit.*: 238.

field. Article 403 states that persons practising acts specific to a profession, without relevant academic certificates, risk imprisonment for a period of up to twelve months. This definition covers all intrusions made by non-physicians in the field of medicine.[167]

Today, court rulings favour non-allopathic practitioners. On January 23, 1984, the Spanish Supreme Court ruled[168] that it was not necessary to have a degree in medicine in order to provide health care. However, when practitioners, prior to applying alternative techniques, make a diagnosis, a clinical or medical examination, or decide to apply a specific therapy, they go beyond the area reserved to recognised medical professionals. Thus, the Supreme Court makes a distinction between alternative medicines not requiring allopathic medical knowledge and those requiring university studies.

More recently, on June 19, 1989,[169] the Supreme Court found a non-allopathic practitioner practising acupuncture-moxibustion to be not guilty. The arguments were the following:

1. the practitioner held several foreign certificates and was a member of the Latin-American Association of Research on Acupuncture-Moxibustion;
2. alternative medicines are not taught within Spanish medical faculties and there are no official certificates authorising and legitimating these

166 This Decree came into force on Jan. 1, 1991.

167 The Penal Code was approved on Nov. 23, 1995 (BOE of Mar. 2 1996).
In Spanish, art. 402: "El que ilegitimamente ejerciere actos proprios de une autoridad o funcionario publico atribuyendose caracter oficial, sera castigado con la pena de prision de uno a tres años".
Art. 403: "El que ejjerciere actos proprios de una profesion sin poseer el correspondiente titulo academico expedido o reconocido en Espana de acuerdo con la legislación vigente, incurrira en la pena de multa de seis a doce meses. Si la actividad profesional desarrollada exigiere un titulo oficial que acredite la capacitacion necesaria y habilite legalmente para su ejercicio, y no se estuviere en posesion de dicho titulo, se impondra la pena de multa de tres a cinco meses.
Si el culpable ademas, se atribuyese publicamente la cualidad de profesional amparado por el titulo referido, se le impondra la pena de multa de tres a cinco meses".
Until 1973, non-allopathic practitioners could not be prosecuted under penal law. The reason was that the offence was considered only when practitioners claimed to be doctors, while non-allopathic practitioners never did so (Prof. Med. F. A. Verdú, Mar. 1999, University of Valencia).

168 The case concerned the techniques of acupuncture and reflexology. See J.T.S. 1984 200.

169 See J.T.S. 1989 421.

> professions. It is difficult therefore to argue that these practices are the object of intrusion, since they do not legally exist, and consequently do not correspond to determined professions.[170]

According to Robard,[171] this decision is fundamental and describes perfectly the absurdity of the legal position in Spain and in France. Indeed, it seems paradoxical to qualify health practices, which are ignored and rejected by medical faculties and medical organisations, as being an illegal practise of medicine or as an intrusion in the medical profession. The Supreme Court confirmed its decision in January 1993, when it released a non-physician acupuncturist. The argument was the same, namely that alternative medicines were not included within medical specialities.[172]

Chiropractic has followed the same way as acupuncture.[173]

Alternative techniques[174]

Public authorities are tolerant towards acupuncture, Despite a lack of legislation regulating the technique.[175]

170 Currently, several medical schools (Madrid, Seville, Nurcia, Zaragoza, Valladolid, Barcelona, and Santiago) provide certificates on homeopathy, naturopathy and acupuncture but only to physicians.

171 ROBARD I., *op. cit.*: 237.

172 ROBARD I., *op. cit.*, addendum: 17.

173 The Spanish Association of Physiotherapists has denounced certain chiropractors for intrusion. However, the regional Court of Valencia considered, in a decision of Mar. 18, 1997, that chiropractors and other practitioners using alternative medicines did not have to be considered as persons who commit the offence of intrusion. The Court pointed out that society has evolved more quickly than legal rules, which have remained excessively protectionist. For example, today, there are professions close to the profession of barrister (in social or fiscal law), which are not considered intrusions. Therefore, allopathic medicine must accept technological advances and the competition of alternative medicines. The Court added that society required new medical specialities and that several medical practitioners were studying in order to obtain a specialisation in alternative medicine (LAGUNA T., *op. cit.*).

174 ARJALAGUER X., *op. cit.*: 25; ORGANIZACIÓN MEDICA COLLEGIAL, *op. cit.*: 17; ROBARD I., *op. cit.*: 235–38.

175 In 1990, during the European Forum in Rome where the role of alternative medicines was discussed, the Spanish Teaching Centre of Chinese Traditional Medicine proposed a project for training practitioners under the aegis of the Council of Europe and co-sponsored by the World Health Organisation. The objective was to give access to a professional status in acupuncture for both physicians and non-physicians, with the condition that the training should be serious and comprehensive.

Meanwhile, professional associations registered by the Ministry of Interior are attempting to gain recognition from the Spanish government for graduate practitioners using these techniques.[176]

In 1996, an expert committee proposed that the Medical Council of Barcelona recognise three alternative medicines as medical specialities, namely homeopathy, acupuncture, and naturopathy. The objective was to regularise the practice of alternative physicians providing these techniques, and to establish certain standards in the field.

Opinion of the Spanish Medical Council

In Spain, the opinion of the Spanish Medical Council (SMC) is one of the most significant in the medical field.[177] The attitude of the SMC regarding alternative medicines has changed. Once clearly opposed to alternative medicines,[178] the SMC now supports alternative medicines when practised by licensed physicians.

According to the SMC, the current objectives are as follows:[179]

1. to guarantee patients a minimum standard of quality in provided health care;
2. to regulate the legal status of alternative medicines in Spain as well as at the European level;
3. to ensure the integration of alternative medicines into the allopathic medical system, with a guarantee on the effectiveness and the security of the treatments;
4. to promote a good relationship between alternative medicines and medical specialities.

4.3.2.7 Ukraine[180]

Ukraine has chosen a monopolistic approach for the licensing of its medical professions. Only physicians are permitted to provide medical treatments[181] but the authorities are relatively tolerant with non-allopathic practitioners.

176 Naturopaths, acupuncturists, chiropractors and osteopaths are particularly active.

177 ROBARD I., *op. cit.*: 233.

178 ROBARD I., *op. cit.*: 233–34.

179 ORGANIZACIÓN MEDICA COLLEGIAL, *op. cit.*: 16.

180 Dr. Hmelewskaja A., Sept. 2001, Kiew, gave the information.

181 To obtain a licence to practise medicine as a physician, several documents are required from the Ministry of Health which delivers the authorisation:

There is no specific regulation on alternative medicines and their legal status is regulated according to general regulations.

The illegal practice of medicine in the Ukraine includes the activity of those people who do not hold documents confirming that they completed the appropriate training and acquired the required professional skills for the accomplishment of medical activity as a physician.

Today, courts are tolerant towards non-allopathic practitioners, when such practitioners hold a diploma attesting a successful training provided by the Academy of Physicians Postgraduate Education or by the Ukrainian National Medical Association.

In order to be registered as a legal non-allopathic practitioner, it is necessary to be graduated either from a special educational course headed by the Academy of Physicians Postgraduate Education or from the Ukrainian National Medicine Association, which is under the supervision of the Ukrainian Ministry of Public Health.[182]

4.3.2.8 Other countries

Bibliography

WHO (V), *Legal status of traditional medicine and complementary/alternative medicine – A World overview*, WHO, 2001, Geneva.

Other countries having a monopolistic system are, divided by continent:

1. Africa: Algeria, Cape Verde, Comoros, Côte d'Ivoire and Seychelles;
2. Americas: Cuba, Ecuador, Honduras and Venezuela;
3. Eastern Mediterranean: Afghanistan and United Arab Emirates;
4. Europe: Greece and Portugal;
5. Asia: none;
6. Western Pacific: some Australian States.

---

1. an authenticated copy of documents attesting the level of education and necessary qualifications for the practice of medicine (medical diploma or certificate of specialisation);
2. a letter of reference issued by the former employer;
3. an approval from local authorities.

182 These associations organise courses in homeopathy, iridology, reflexology, aromatherapy and phytotherapy.

4.3.3 Tolerant countries

4.3.3.1 Belgium

Bibliography

British Medical Association (Lamont T.), *Alternative medicine – New approaches to good practice*, Oxford University Press, 1993, Oxford/New York: 26; De Bijl N. (co-author: Nederveen-van de Kragt I.), *Legal safeguards against medical practice by not suitability qualified persons: A comparative study in seven EU-countries*, in: European Journal of Health Law, vol. 4, 1997: 5–18; Nys H. (I), *La médecine et le droit*, Kluwer, 1995, Diegem; Nys H. (II), *Belgium*, in: International Encyclopedia of Laws – Medical Law, Kluwer Law International, The Hague/London/Boston; Robard I., *La santé hors la loi: Les hors la loi de la santé*, 4th ed., Ed. de l'Ancre, 1994, Suresnes: 213–15; Schepers R., *The Belgian medical profession since the 1980s: Dominance and decline?*, in: Johnson T. (co-authors: Larkin G., Saks M.), *Health professions and the State in Europe*, Routledge, 1995, London/New York: 162–77; Sermeus G., *Alternative health care in Belgium: An explanation of various social aspects*, in: Lewith G. (co-editors: Aldridge D.), *Alternative medicine and the European Community*, CW Daniel, 1991, Saffron Walden: 61–74; Stepan J., *Traditional and alternative systems of medicine: A comparative review of legislation*, in: International Digest of Health Legislation, 1985, vol. 36, n° 2, Genève: 288; Swennen H., *The medical profession in Belgium*, in: Fure M. (co-authors: Finsinger J., Siegers J., van den Bergh R.), *Regulation of professions, a law and economics approach to the regulation of attorneys and physicians in the US, Belgium, the Netherlands, Germany and the UK*, 1993, Maklu Antwerpen: 129.

A. Current regulation

On April 29, 1999, the Belgian Parliament adopted a new and tolerant Act on the providing of alternative medicines.[183] This constituted a dramatic change from the former (monopolistic) approach.[184]

183 Moniteur Belge, 1999, vol. 169, n° 124, June 24. Available at http://just.fgov.be/html/fd2_w3.htm, accessed Sept. 1, 2001. In French: "Loi du 29 avril 1999 relative aux pratiques non conventionnelles dans les domaines de l'art médical, de l'art pharmaceutique, de la kinésithérapie, de l'art infirmier et des professions médicales".

184 After the intervention of the European Commission concerning the (non-) enforcement of the European Directive on homeopathic products, the Belgian government asked the Federal Department of Public Health to elaborate draft legislation on alternative medicines. The government considered that it should offer the population the most extensive choice of therapeutic treatments, as long as they were safe, structured, and controlled. It added that the current situation, namely

According to the new Act, the practice of registered alternative medicines by non-allopathic practitioners is permitted when practitioners obtain a registration linked to the specific practice (art. 3 and 8 (1) of the Act).[185] The registration is delivered by the Ministry of Social Affairs, Public Health and Environment, according to the advice of the affected chamber, and only when all the requirements of art. 3 are satisfied (art. 8 (2) of the Act). Violations may result in the suspension or the withdrawal of the registration (art. 8 (3) of the Act).

A commission with parity of representation[186] advises the government regarding the practice of alternative medicines (art. 3 of the Act),[187] in particular, the conditions to receive and suspend a licence to practise.[188]

The Act already regulates the practice of homeopathy, chiropractic, osteopathy and acupuncture and allows for the recognition of other alternative techniques (art. 2 of the Act).[189]

---

the practice of alternative medicines without a structured legal framework, contained numerous risks.

According to a 1998 poll, the population wanted the four most important alternative medicines, i.e. homeopathy, acupuncture, osteopathy and chiropractic to be recognised by the MINISTRY OF HEALTH. In contrast, the medical profession was divided: 43% of physicians were in favour of this law and 43% were opposed to it (LEMAL I., *op. cit.*).

185 In order to be able to fully practise allopathic medicine, the holding of an academic degree in medicine is necessary. Registration on the List of the Order of Physicians is also mandatory. In order to obtain this registration, a certificate of good character and repute must be provided. Furthermore, doctors have to submit their diploma for inspection to the Medical Commission (Art. 7 (1) Practice of Medicine Act of 1967).

186 The commission with parity of representation instituted by the Ministry is composed of 5 members proposed by medical faculties and 5 members proposed by the chambers. All members must practise either biomedicine (GPs or specialists) or alternative medicine (art. 5 of the Act). Each chamber is composed of 5 members proposed by medical faculties allowed to practise medicine (with at least one GP) and 5 members practising alternative medicines proposed by a recognised professional organisation (art. 6 (1) of the Act).

Each chamber proposes standards of practice. Furthermore they also advise the government on the organisation of a peer review system, and on a code of professional ethics (art. 6 (2) of the Act).

187 Such as professional insurance, the membership of a recognised professional organisation, the system of registration, advertising and the list of medical acts forbidden to non-physicians.

188 In particular, the basic training of practitioners and continuous education.

189 The criteria necessary to fulfil prior to having the opportunity to register alternative medicines are the quality of care, its accessibility and positive influence on patients' health (art. 3 (2) of the Act).

More specifically, to be allowed to practise acupuncture, practitioners must be members of a professional organisation.[190] In order to become a member and to be registered as qualified acupuncturist, candidates must have the title of MD, dentist, physiotherapist, qualified nurse or midwife. In addition, the candidate must have studied at least 750 hours of acupuncture, including 250 hours on the basic principles of traditional Chinese medicine, 250 hours of pathology and 250 hours of clinical practice. The acupuncture training must be completed with a dissertation.[191]

The Act provides some rules regarding the general framework of practice. For example, prior to treatment, non-physicians alternative practitioners must obtain from their patients a recent diagnosis from a physician. However, patients may also decide not to consult a physician before seeking a non-allopathic practitioner. In this case, the patient must make his or her wishes known be in writing (art. 9 (2) of the Act).

According to art. 9 (3) of the Act, registered alternative practitioners must take precautions to prevent patients being deprived of biomedical treatments. As a result, practitioners must inform physicians of their evaluation of the health condition of patients.[192]

Furthermore, alternative practitioners must keep a file for each patient (art. 9. (1) of the Act).

Any person infringing the Act risks a fine. For example, a person is liable under art. 11 of the Act if he or she practises alternative medicines without having first obtained the proper registration or starts a treatment without having first obtained the diagnosis from a physician or obtains a patient's written consent to avoid such diagnostic.

B. Former regulation

The evolution of the Belgian regulation of alternative medicines reflects the current trend in Western countries. The former position of alternative medicines in the country is presented hereafter.

Previously, Belgium had a monopolistic approach towards licensing medical doctors.[193] The practice of medicine was exclusively reserved for doctors, including diagnosis, treatment, prescriptions, surgery and

190 For the moment, only the Belgian Acupuncture Federation is recognised as a professional organisation of acupuncturists by the State Council of Belgium.

191 This information was provided by Mr. Vanlaethem, Belgian Acupuncturists Federation, during the International Congress on Traditional Medicine in Beijing, 2000.

192 The consent of the patient is necessary for all exchanges of information.

193 For a historic approach see: Sermeus G., *op. cit.*: 61–63.

preventive medicine. The performance of medical acts without a legal qualification was an offence.

Access to medical practice was previously primarly regulated by the Practice of Medicine Act of 1967. The Act introduced a monopoly in this field. The consequences were similar to those in France, namely the practice of medicine was restricted to physicians.[194]

Although doctors were, in principle, legally able to practise in any branch of medicine, they could find themselves in conflict with their professional organisation when providing alternative medicines. Indeed, the Code of Professional Ethics, applied by provincial councils, practically banned the use of alternative medicines.[195, 196]

Ancillary professionals were permitted to provide alternative medicines but only if they worked under the supervision of a physician. For example, physiotherapists regularly provided osteopathy.[197]

The practice of alternative medicine by any person who was not a registered medical practitioner was outlawed,[198] and non-allopathic practitioners were sometimes prosecuted for the illegal practice of medicine.[199] The three conditions rendering the practice of medicine illegal were:

1° the practice of a medical activity;
2° by an unauthorised person;
3° on a regular basis.

The enforcement of the law was reputedly very strict in Belgium. Lately, however, public prosecutor offices prosecuted only those charlatans who had knowingly deceived and financially exploited the public, and non-allopathic practitioners who had prescribed "treatments" leading to an accident, which was, sometimes, lethal.[200]

194 De Bijl N., *op. cit.*: 7–11; Nys H. (I), *op. cit.*: 9–23; Nys H. (II), *op. cit.*: 37–41; Robard I., *op. cit.*: 213; Schepers R., *op. cit.*: 163, 166; Swennen H., *op. cit.*: 129.

195 Only allopathic practitioners were elected to the disciplinary courts. Therefore, they did not have specific knowledge on complementary medicines and, consequently, were unable to judge their correct application. They were, in any case, opposed to these practices (Hirsch J. L., barrister in Belgium, Sept. 2001, Bruxelles).

196 Sermeus G., *op. cit.*: 61.

197 Robard I., *op. cit.*: 213.

198 The misuse of the title of physician was also (and still remains) punishable.

199 See Nys H., *op. cit.* (I): 30–95; Nys H. (II), *op. cit.*: 41–48; Sermeus G., *op. cit.*: 63.

200 Stepan J., *op. cit.*: 288; Hirsch J. L., Barrister in Belgium, Mar. 1998, Bruxelles.

4.3.3.2 Germany

Bibliography

ALDRIDGE D., *Pluralism of medical practice in Germany*, in: LEWITH G. (co-editor: ALDRIDGE D.), *Alternative medicine and the European Community*, CW Daniel, 1991, Saffron Walden: 75–83; ARNDT K. F., *Heilpraktikerrecht – Entstehung, Funktionswandel, Berufszulassungsregelung*, Alfred Metzner Verlag, 1985, Frankfurt am Main; BRITISH MEDICAL ASSOCIATION (LAMONT T.), *Alternative medicine – New approaches to good practice*, Oxford University Press, 1993, Oxford/New York: 21; CRAMER R., *Strafrechtliche Grenzen der Therapiefreiheit und der Heilbehandlung durch den Heilpraktiker*, Dissertation, 1995, Köln; DE BIJL N. (co-author: NEDERVEEN-VAN DE KRAGT I.), *Legal safeguards against medical practice by not suitably qualified persons: A comparative study in seven EU-countries*, 1997, in: European Journal of Health Law, vol. 4: 5–18; EHLERS A. P. F., *Medizin in den Händen von Heilpraktikern – "Nicht-Heilkundigen"*, Springer Verlag, 1995, Berlin/Heidelberg; GRUPP K., *Rechtliche Probleme alternativer Behandlungsmethoden*, in: MedR, 1992, vol. 5: 256–63; GUILLOD O., *Rebouteux, naturopathes et guérisseurs: Pour un traitement légal alternatif*, Recueil de Jurisprudence Neuchâtelois, 1989, Neuchâtel: 13–15; JUNG H. (co-author: NEUMANN J. N.), *Alternative Behandlungsmethoden* in: ESER (co-authors: LUTTEROTTI, SPORKEN), *Lexikon Medizin – Ethik – Recht*, Freiburg, 1989: 48–63; LAUFS A. (co-author: UHLENBRUCK W.) (I), *Handbuch des Arztrechts*, C.H. Beck'sche Verlagbuchhandlung, 1992, München: 75–79; LAUFS A. (II), *Sorgfaltspflichten des Heilpraktikers*, in: MedR, 1991, n° 4: 195–98; NARR (I), *Ausübung der Heilkunde*, in: MedR, 1990, n° 5: 283–85; NARR (II), *Werbeverbot für Heilpraktiker*, in: MedR, 1990, n° 2: 82–83; NARR (III), *Das Heilpraktikergesetz ist auf psychotherapeutisch tätige Diplompsychologen anwendbar*, in: MedR, 1988, n° 6: 299–304; REILING E. (I), *Ausübung der Heilkunde durch Heilmagnetiseur*, in: MedR, 1992, n° 1: 52–53; REILING E. (II), *Ermächtigungsgrundlagen im Heilpraktikergesetz; Heilkundebegriff*, in: MedR, 1992, n° 1: 54–58; ROBARD I., *La santé hors la loi: Les hors la loi de la santé*, 4th ed., Ed. de l'Ancre, 1994, Suresnes: 250–54; TAUPITZ J. (I), *Arzt und Heilpradtiker im Doppelberuf?*, in: MedR, 1993, n° 6: 219–24; TAUPITZ J. (II), *"Geistheilen" und Heilpraktikergesetz*, in: MedR, 1994, n° 9: 369–72; TAUPITZ J. (III), *Erlaubnispflichtige Ausübung der Heilkunde*, in: MedR, 1998, n° 12: 571–75; WICKI M., *Komplementärmedizin im Rahmen des Rechtes*, Dissertation, Stämpfli, 1998, Bern: 92–96.

A. Historical evolution of the licensing to practise

The coming into force of the Order on Trade (the Order) in 1869 created in Germany a complete freedom regarding medical practice, the so-called "Kurierfreiheit". This freedom was absolute; there were no medical exams, nor any controls over training. Medical practitioners were free to do anything, irrespective of their actual training and knowledge.[201]

The former "Kurierfreiheit" consisted of two principles: first, the freedom for everyone to practise medicine and second, the freedom for patients to choose the type of treatment and practitioner they desired.[202]

In 1883, a modification of the Order on Trade banned the wandering practice of "Heilpraktikers". Even at this stage, however, an official licence to practise medicine was not introduced. Consequently, non-physicians could continue to freely treat patients without public authorisation. The sole obligation of "Heilpraktikers" was to advise their patients of life-threatening treatments.[203, 204]

As the Order did not clearly define the "Heilpraktiker" profession, courts had to clarify certain notions. For example, the term "medicine" was defined as the activity which presupposes certain specific knowledge, which is carried out by doctors or laymen, and whose objective is to observe, cure and relieve ill persons and animals.[205] Despite the legal modification, charlatans and fraudsters continued practising, pretending they had no knowledge in medicine.[206]

The "Kurierfreiheit" created some problems. There were abuses from charlatans and the competition between physicians and "Heilpraktikers" engendered a conflict between allopathic and non-allopathic practitioners.[207]

201 ARNDT K. F., *op. cit.* 19–21; CRAMER R., *op. cit.*: 16; EHLERS A. P. F., *op. cit.*: 7–10; WICKI M., *op. cit.*: 94.

202 ARNDT K. F., *op. cit.* 19–21; CRAMER R., *op. cit.*: 18; EHLERS A. P. F., *op. cit.*: 7–10.

203 In 1930, the Supreme Court sentenced, a "less intelligent" healer who had provided homeopathy to a child who died instead as the result of a diphtheria.

204 GUILLOD O., *op. cit.*: 13; EHLERS A. P. F., *op. cit.*: 11–12; ROBARD I., *op. cit.*: 252–53.

205 In German: "eine besondere, ärtzliche Fachkenntnis voraussetzende Tätigkeit zu verstehen war, die auf Feststellung, Heilung oder Linderung von Krankheiten bei Menschen und Tieren gerichtet ist, möchte sie von einem wissenschaftlich gebildeten Arzt oder einem Laien vorgenommen werden".

206 ARNDT K. F., *op. cit.*: 24–25; CRAMER R., *op. cit.*: 16–17; EHLERS A. P. F., *op. cit.*: 10–12; GUILLOD O., *op. cit.*: 13.

207 CRAMER R., *op. cit.*: 18–19; EHLERS A. P. F., *op. cit.*: 12–13.

During the early twentieth century, the legislature attempted several times to regulate medical practice. In 1909, a draft was proposed to maintain the "Kurierfreiheit", with some restrictions.[208] However, the draft was finally not adopted by the legislature.[209]

After 1930, there was a movement to restrict "Heilpraktikers"' activities. There were violent oppositions to the adoption of a statute restricting the freedom to practise medicine. Eventually, in 1939, the current Act on "Heilpraktikers" (AH) and an Order concerning its enforcement were adopted.[210]

The five principal characteristics of the AH of 1939, modified in 1945, were the following:[211]

1. the abolition of general "Kurierfreiheit";
2. the abolition of the "Heilpraktiker" profession through the establishment of controls for access to the profession (with transitional measures);
3. the introduction of a monopoly for physicians;
4. the legal recognition and regulation of the "Heilpraktiker" profession during the transitional period;
5. the creation of the German association of "Heilpraktikers".

B. General principles

Germany is the typical tolerant system. All authorised medical practitioners are permitted to use alternative medicines. Furthermore, there is no legal monopoly in medical practice and, in principle, it is not an offence for non-registered practitioners to engage in healing.[212]

The keystone of the German system is the legal status of "Heilpraktikers". An exception to the protected status of authorised medical

208 According to the draft, "Heilpraktikers" had to announce when they commenced their activity as practitioners. They had to give information regarding their personal situation and detail their methods. Furthermore, some activities were still restricted to physicians. It was also possibile to forbid "Heilpraktikers" to practise medicine, under certain conditions.

209 ARNDT K. F., *op. cit.*: 21–22; CRAMER R., *op. cit.*: 19.

210 ARNDT K. F., *op. cit.*: 27–28; CRAMER R., *op. cit.*: 20; EHLERS A. P. F., *op. cit.*: 13–14; GUILLOD O., *op. cit.*: 14; JUNG H., *op. cit.*: 58–59; WICKI M., *op. cit.*: 94.

211 ARNDT K. F., *op. cit.*: 46; LAUFS A. (I), *op. cit.*: 75.

212 DE BIJL N., *op. cit.*: 10.

practitioners is made for them.[213] They may, with public approval, practise medicine without holding an allopathic diploma, except for certain medical acts, which are restricted to physicians.[214] Even though their training is not regulated, they have to qualify for a licence and an examination is carried out by health authorities for the sole purpose of establishing that treatments do not negatively affect the public health.[215]

As the legal status of "Heilpraktikers" is the most important particularity of the German system, it is addressed in greater detail below.

C. Specificities of the system

Conditions to practise as "Heilpraktiker"

Despite the permissiveness of the current regulation, the first objective of the AH of 1939[216] was to put an end to the "Kurierfreiheit". As a result, the AH introduced a licensing system (art. 1 (1) AH). The primary aim, in the long term, was to eliminate "Heilpraktikers" through the establishment of a monopoly of physicians and the banning of new schools of "Heilpraktikers". Persons practising could continue their activity but new licenses did not have to be issued.[217]

Today, the AH is still in force but its interpretation and enforcement differ greatly from the legislature's original intention in 1939.[218] After the coming into force of the new Constitution of 1949, the Constitutional

213 The system leading to the licence to practise medicine for physicians differs radically from the system for "Heilpraktikers". The qualifying requirements to practise medicine as a physician are the following: 1. the possession of an academic degree in medicine; 2. a practical experience; 3. a licence from public authorities; 4. a medical certificate confirming that there are no indications of physical or mental disability or addiction to drugs.
For a presentation of the differences between the physician and "Heilpraktiker" professions, see LAUFS A. (I), *op. cit.*: 77–79, and TAUPITZ J., *op. cit.* (I).

214 In Germany, physicians must be registered and it is an offence when a person wrongly pretends to be registered (DE BIJL N., *op. cit.*: 10, 13; LAUFS A. (I), *op. cit.*: 79).

215 DE BIJL N., *op. cit.*: 7–8; FROST AND SULLIVAN, *op. cit.*: 210.

216 The AH was modified in 1945.

217 ARNDT K. F., *op. cit.* 31–35; CRAMER R., *op. cit.*: 21; EHLERS A. P. F., *op. cit.*: 13–15; GUILLOD O., *op. cit.*: 14; LAUFS A. (I), *op. cit.*: 75; ROBARD I., *op. cit.*: 251.
For an extensive presentation and criticism of the AH, see ARNDT K. F., *op. cit.* 26 30, 47–99; CRAMER R., *op. cit.*: 45–49; EHLERS A. P. F., *op. cit.*: 98–124.

218 The AH was also into force in East Germany until 1989. However, in this country, no authorisation has been delivered since 1949 (GUILLOD O., *op. cit.*: 14).

Court interpreted the AH in such a way that a restriction to the access to the "Heilpraktiker" profession would violate art. 12 of the Constitution. Indeed, this article guaranteed the freedom to choose a profession, and the providing of licences only in exceptional circumstances, brought in by the AH of 1939 was considered a numerus clausus.[219]

According to Art. 1 of the AH, "Heilpraktikers" were defined as non-physicians, namely non-allopathic practitioners providing medical acts[220] in a professional manner.[221]

As the intention of the legislature in 1939 had been to eliminate "Heilpraktikers" completely, there were no precise rules regarding the requirements of training, knowledge and skills for these practitioners and, in fact, the only conditions were administrative. In 1941, however, a new Order was issued that incorporated the conditions necessary to attain the basic knowledge needed to obtain a licence and other requirements regarding the enforcement of the AH.[222]

Since then, a licence is refused only when candidates do not have sufficient skills and knowledge to avoid a danger to the public health. A danger to the public health occurs when there is a risk that patients may be physically or mentally injured in relation to the providing of a treatment, or when there is delay in recognising the necessity of an allopathic medical treatment.[223] This protection not only covers the population as a whole, but also specific patients. However, in practice, rejections are rare.[224]

219 ARNDT K. F., *op. cit.*: 55–63; CRAMER R., *op. cit.*: 22–23; EHLERS A. P. F., *op. cit.*: 15–16; GRUPP K., *op. cit.*: 257–63; GUILLOD O., *op. cit.*: 14; LAUFS A. (I), *op. cit.*: 75; ROBARD I., *op. cit.*: 252.

220 For a development regarding the concept of medicine, see below.

221 CRAMER R., *op. cit.*: 20; EHLERS A. P. F., *op. cit.*: 106; LAUFS A. (I), *op. cit.*: 75.

222 CRAMER R., *op. cit.*: 21; EHLERS A. P. F., *op. cit.*: 14–15, 125–35; GUILLOD O., *op. cit.*: 14; LAUFS A. (I), *op. cit.*: 75; ROBARD I., *op. cit.*: 251.

223 In German: "Die sogenannte Volksgesundheit ist nach der zitierten Entscheidung des BverwG gefährdet, wenn befürchtet werden muss, dass infolge der Behandlung durch den Heilpraktiker unmittelbar oder durch ein nicht rechtzeitigen Erkennen der Notwendigkeit einer ärtzlichen Behandlung für den Patienten ernsthafte Gesundheitsschäden eintreten können; den Schutz vor Gesundheitsgefährdungen geniesse nicht nur die Bevölkerung als Ganzes, sondern auch und gerade der einzelne".

224 CRAMER R., *op. cit.*: 21; EHLERS A. P. F., *op. cit.*: 14; GUILLOD O., *op. cit.*: 14; LAUFS A. (I), *op. cit.*: 75.
For a study on the conditions leading to the licence to practise between 1939 and 1945, see ARNDT K. F., *op. cit.*: 35–46.

The conditions to obtain a "Heilpraktiker" licence are as follows (art. 2 (1) of the Order on the AH). A person must:[225]

1. be at least 25 years old;
2. have German or EU citizenship;
3. have completed primary school;
4. have a good reputation (meaning that the candidates have sufficient guarantees for a normal professional practice);[226]
5. have a medical certificate confirming that there are no indications of physical or mental disability or addiction to drugs;
6. pass an examination before a health commission, to prove that the candidate has sufficient knowledge and ability in order to practise as a "Heilpraktiker" and that he or she does not constitute a public health risk.[227]

The content of the exam consists of verifying basic knowledge about health regulations, in particular, the statute on epidemic diseases. Candidates must also have a basic knowledge of anatomy, physiology, hygiene measures, pathology, sterilisation, disinfection and diagnosis. However, the questions must be framed in such a way so as to be easy and understandable.[228, 229]

The State Department of Health responsible for the examination of "Heilpraktiker" candidates must also verify that "Heilpraktikers" do not

225 ARNDT K. F., *op. cit.*: 68–91; CRAMER R., *op. cit.*: 24–28; EHLERS A. P. F., *op. cit.*: 135–62; GUILLOD O., *op. cit.*: 14; LAUFS A. (I), *op. cit.*: 77–78.

226 This condition is not fulfilled, for example, when a practitioner practised medicine without a "Heilpraktiker"'s licence and caused a physical injury.

227 For a study on this concept, see ARNDT K. F., *op. cit.*: 79–85.

228 There are some differences concerning the exams for "Heilpraktikers" within Germany. Even if the AH is uniform throughout the whole country, each "Land" (State) issues its own rules with regard to the enforcement of the law (i.e., procedure, form, and content of the exam).
To eliminate the differences between German "Länder", the central government wanted to issue an order establishing a uniform exam throughout the country. However, this proposition was rejected by the Geraman Parliament. It argued that such a regulation could give the appearance that "Heilpraktikers" would be officially recognised as allopathic medical practitioners, thus giving them a stronger position within the health care system. For a study on the subject, in particular a draft of the unified regulation, see ARNDT K. F., *op. cit.*: 92–99, 102–05.
As a comparison, the complete academic medical education is regulated by federal laws and controlled by state authorities.

229 ARNDT K. F., *op. cit.*: 92–99, 100, 102–05; CRAMER R., *op. cit.*: 27, 37–39; EHLERS A. P. F., *op. cit.*: 19–24, 97; LAUFS A. (I), *op. cit.*: 76.

use the title of physician, do not treat illnesses the treatment of which is restricted to physicians and do not make unauthorised advertising.[230]

The "Heilpraktikers"' associations have issued a Professional Code of Practice demonstrating their effort to set up ethical rules for their members.[231] However, the Code has not incorporated any rules establishing minimum standards of training or the necessary skills required to practise medicine diligently.[232]

"Heilpraktikers" are, however, allowed to advertise publicly, which is forbidden to physicians.[233]

Criminal liability when practising medicine

The practice of medicine is illegal when practitioners provide health care without holding a licence from public authorities, which may be either a licence as a physician, ancillary professional or "Heilpraktiker".[234]

Furthermore, while conducting their professional activities, "Heilpraktikers" may be liable for two types of offences: voluntary offences and offences due to negligence.[235] Within the perspective of this research, two voluntary offences are particularly interesting, namely the practice as "Heilpraktiker" without a public licence (1) and the providing of medical treatments restricted to recognised health care professionals (2).[236, 237]

230 CRAMER R., *op. cit.*: 28–29.

231 Article 2 of the Professional Code of Practice provides that "Heilpraktikers" have to be conscious of the limits of their knowledge and skills. Art. 3 concerns professional secrecy, and art. 4 the obligation to give patients clear explanations concerning their illnesses, the treatments that the "Heilpraktikers" provide as well as the length and dangers of the treatment. Art. 4 also incorporates the obligation to refer patients to a specialist when "Heilpraktikers" are not competent to treat them. According to Cramer, this code of practice is not comparable to professional public regulations for allopathic medical professionals.

232 CRAMER R., *op. cit.*: 42.

233 GUILLOD O., *op. cit.*: 16; LAUFS A. (I), *op. cit.*: 78; NARR (II), *op. cit.*: 82–83.

234 BRITISH MEDICAL ASSOCIATION, *op. cit.*: 21; CRAMER R., *op. cit.*: 65–181; EHLERS A. P. F., *op. cit.*: 237–61; GUILLOD O., *op. cit.*: 14–15; ROBARD I., *op. cit.*: 253–54.

235 For a development of criminal liability when causing an injury or death, see chap. 7.2.3.3, and for a development of civil liability, see chap. 7.2.3.2.

236 The other infringements are the following:
1. to infringe on professional secrecy according to art. 203 of the Penal Code;
2. to commit a fraud according to art. 263 of the Penal Code;
3. to commit a physical injury according to art. 223 of the Penal Code. "Heilpraktikers" are rarely sentenced for voluntary physical injury because they usually obtain the consent of their patients beforehand. However, they may

A practitioner may be liable for the first offence (1), if he or she fails to obtain a licence that must be delivered by the public authorities (art. 1 AH). A licence is obligatory to practise medicine and any person practising medicine without such licence risks a fine or prison sentence (art. 4 AH).

It is apparent that a major problem has been to expand the concept of "Heilkunde" (medicine). Art. 1 of the AH defines medicine as a professional activity whose objective is to observe, cure and relieve ill persons or persons suffering from physical injuries.[238] Courts have defined which activities must be considered as "Heilkunde" (art. 1 AH) and which must therefore be restricted to physicians and "Heilpraktikers".[239] According to

be sentenced according to rules regarding causing physical injury through carelessness;

4. to cause a dangerous physical injury according to art. 223 a of the Penal Code;
5. to cause a physical injury by omission according to art. 223, 13 of the Penal Code.

237 British Medical Association, *op. cit.*: 21; Cramer R., *op. cit.*: 183–84; Guillod O., *op. cit.*: 14–15; Robard I., *op. cit.*: 253–54.

238 In German: "jede Tätigkeit umfasst, die berufs- oder gewerbmässig zur Feststellung, Heilung oder Linderung von Krankheiten, Leiden oder Körperschäden bei Menschen ausgeübt wird".
Some consider this definition as insufficient. Indeed, according to a strict interpretation, it excludes prophylactic means, cosmetic and surgical interventions. Furthermore, medical assistants could be criminally prosecuted because they practise medicine without state authorisation. Finally, this definition does not exclude the practice of quacks. Indeed, they could pretend to be practising outside the medical field. However, in such cases, art. 263 of the Penal Code concerning swindling could be enforced (Cramer R., *op. cit.*: 20–21; Ehlers A. P. F., *op. cit.*: 106–07).

239 Psychotherapy if practised by a psychologist without an academic degree; dietetic advising; cauterisation of naevus and verrucas; providing of some forms of massage; chiropractic if practised by a practitioner without a recognised certificate; preventive treatments provided to health persons and plastic surgery.
On the other hand, the measurement of eyesight as well as the detection of telluric currents or the setting of a protection system are not considered medical acts because they are not concrete treatments of an illness. Thus, the treatment of small cut treatments, the providing of logopedy, some blood analysis, and health advice, are not considered as medical activities. Consequently, they do not require public authorisation.
Regarding magnetism (laying on of hands) and use of supra-natural forces, there is some controversy. Some authors are of the opinion that this kind of treatment should be considered as "Heilkunde" only in accordance with the "Eindruckstheorie".

the Supreme Court, only activities requiring medical knowledge, in contrast to technical knowledge, are considered as "Heilkunde". Therefore, activities giving only the impression that they may contribute to recovery (the so-called "Eindruckstheorie") are not considered as "Heilkunde".[240]

The second offence (2) concerns the providing of treatments restricted to recognised health care professionals. Licensed "Heilpraktikers" are, in principle, allowed to provide any medical treatment, save for a series of potentially dangerous medical acts. These latter are restricted to specific allopathic practitioners. Furthermore, some courts have considered specific medical activities constituting a risk to a patient's health as being forbidden to "Heilpraktikers".[241] For the rest, Heilpraktikers are allowed to practise all the medical acts they wish.[242] One should also note that incidents involving "Heilpraktikers" are quite rare.[243, 244]

Some authors consider that, since "Heilpraktikers" are completely free to choose the type of treatment they wish to practise (as are physicians), a good level of training is always recommended to avoid the risk of physical injury. Furthermore, they must clearly inform their patients about their knowledge, skills and the risks of treatments in order to obtain a patient's informed consent and to avoid the risk of prosecution as well as potential criminal and civil sentences.[245]

240 CRAMER R., *op. cit.*: 29–33; EHLERS A. P. F., *op. cit.*: 106–24; GUILLOD O., *op. cit.*: 15; JUNG H., *op. cit.*: 58–59; LAUFS A. (I), *op. cit.*: 76; NARR (I), *op. cit.*: 283–85; NARR (III), *op. cit.*: 299–304; REILING E. (I), *op. cit.*: 52–53; REILING E. (II), *op. cit.*: 54–58; ROBARD I., *op. cit.*: 252; TAUPITZ J. (I), *op. cit.*: 369–72; TAUPITZ J. (III), *op. cit.*: 571–75. For a extensive study on this problem, see CRAMER R., *op. cit.*: 29–35.

241 E.g., "Heilpraktikers" are not allowed to: 1. practise dentistry; 2. treat sexual diseases; 3. treat communicable and epidemic diseases; 4. deliver certain medications (drugs); 5. give or provide anaesthetics and narcotics; 6. practise obstetrics and gynaecology. Only physicians, midwives and relieving male nurses are allowed to practise obstetrics and gynaecology, except under exceptional circumstances; 7. Only physicians and dentists are allowed to X-ray. However, "Heilpraktikers" have the opportunity to acquire the necessary knowledge and to pass an exam to legally X-ray; 8. practise autopsies and to deliver death certificates.
These acts are restricted to physicians, possibly dentists and veterinarians. The violation is usually prosecuted. Those persons committing such acts risk a fine or a prison sentence.

242 In particular, they are allowed to: do injections; practise surgery; do narcosis; do psychotherapies; work as a lab assistant.

243 EHLERS A. P. F., *op. cit.*: 84–87. For more details, see chap. 6.5.

244 CRAMER R., *op. cit.*: 28–29; DE BIJL N., *op. cit.*: 10; FISHER P., *op. cit.*: 210; GRUPP K., *op. cit.*: 257–58; GUILLOD O., *op. cit.*: 15; ROBARD I., *op. cit.*: 253–54.

245 CRAMER R., *op. cit.*: 183–84, 189; GRUPP K., *op. cit.*: 258–60; JUNG H., *op. cit.*: 59–61; LAUFS A. (II), *op. cit.*: 195–98.

4.3.3.3 Great Britain

Bibliography

See: ANONYMOUS (IV), *Integrated healthcare – A way forward for the next five years?*, Foundation for Integrated Medicine, 1997: 27–34; BRITISH MEDICAL ASSOCIATION (LAMONT T.), *Alternative medicine – New approaches to good practice*, Oxford University Press, 1993, Oxford/New York; DE BIJL N. (co-author: NEDERVEEN-VAN DE KRAGT I.), *Legal safeguards against medical practice by not suitability qualified persons: A comparative study in seven EU-countries*, in: European Journal of Health Law, vol. 4, 1997: 5–18; FISHER P. (co-author: WARD A.), *Alternative medicine in Europe*, in: BMJ, vol. 309, July 9 1994: 107–11; FROST AND SULLIVAN LTD, *Alternative medical practices in Europe*, Report n° E874, Sullivan House, Grosvenor Gardens, 1987, London SW1: 235–47; GENERAL OSTEOPATHIC COUNCIL, *Standard 2000 – Standard of proficiency*, General Osteopathic Council, Mar. 1999; MCHALE J. (co-authors: FOX M., MURPHY J.), *Health care law: Text, cases and materials*, Sweet and Maxwell, 1997, London: 258; MONTGOMERY J., *Health care law*, Oxford University Press, 1997, Oxford: 161–63; ROBARD I., *La santé hors la loi: Les hors la loi de la santé*, 4th ed., Ed. de l'Ancre, 1994, Suresnes: 218–25; SAKS M. (I), *Alternative medicine in Britain*, Clarendon Press, 1992, Oxford; SAKS M. (II), *The changing response of the medical profession to alternative medicine in Britain: A case of altruism or self-interest?*, in: JOHNSON T. (co-authors LARKIN G, SAKS M.), *Health professions and the State in Europe*, Routledge, 1995, London/New York: 103–15; SELECT COMMITTEE ON SCIENCE AND TECHNOLOGY, *Complementary and alternative medicine*, House of Lords – Session 1999–2000 6th Report, The Stationary Office, 2000, London: 36ss; STEPAN J., *Traditional and alternative systems of medicine: A comparative review of legislation*, in: International Digest of Health Legislation, 1985, vol. 36, n° 2, Genève: 287–88; STONE J. (co-author: MATTHEWS J.), *Alternative medicine and the Law*, Oxford University Press, 1996, Oxford; TAYLOR R. C. R., *Alternative medicine and the medical encounter in Britain and the United States*, in: SALMON J. W. (eds), *Alternative medicines – Popular and policy perspectives*, Tavistock Publications, 1984, New York: 191–229; THOMAS K. J., *Non-orthodox health care in the UK*, in: LEWITH G. (co-editors: ALDRIDGE D.), *Alternative medicine and the European Community*, CW Daniel, 1991, Saffron Walden: 125–34.

A. General principles

Great Britain is a good example of a tolerant country. Only medical practitioners holding a university degree in medicine are officially allowed to practise medicine,[246] but the law tolerates those persons who practise alternative medicines without a medical degree.

Under the terms of the National Health Service Act of 1977, the Secretary of State for Health is responsible for safeguarding the health of the nation. The General Medical Council (GMC), a statutory body that regulates the medical profession, maintains the register in which persons first have to be recorded in order to be qualified as a doctor. Its primary role is to maintain the required standards for registered doctors. In terms of its disciplinary function, the GMC has jurisdiction over all medical specialities. The conditions under which doctors are admitted to the Registers are governed partly by regulations and decisions of the GMC.[247]

The right to practise without formal recognition is established under British common law.[248] Provided that an individual being treated has given an informed consent, he or she can be treated by any person whatsoever, even if such person has no training of any kind in health care. However, persons exercising this right must not identify themselves by any of the titles protected by statute and they cannot prescribe medicines that are regulated prescription-only drugs. Thus, as long as such persons do not claim to be a medical practitioner registered[249] under the Medical Act of 1983,[250] then they can offer medical advice and treatment and can purport to treat a

246 To obtain the title to fully practise medicine as a physician, it is necessary to possess of a certificate or a qualification from the faculty of medicine of a university. Furthermore, doctors have to obtain provisional registration on graduation and full registration after satisfactorily completing a year of general clinical training (De Bijl N., *op. cit.*: 7).

247 De Bijl N., *op. cit.*: 8, Stone J., *op. cit.*: 49–51.

248 For a historical approach, see British Medical Association, *op. cit.*: 25; Saks M. (I), *op. cit.*: 25–135; Stone J., *op. cit.*: 19–36.

249 Being a registered medical practitioner confers other privileges and responsibilities, namely: to use the title or describe oneself as a registered practitioner, or be recognised by law as a physician or surgeon; to recover one fees for medical attendance or advice in a court of law; to hold specific posts; to provide general medical services in the NHS and to give some statutory certificates (Stone J., *op. cit.*: 47).

250 In principle, non-registered persons are even allowed to perform surgical acts with the consent of patients.
Robard notes that, in practice, persons who practise alternative medicines usually have a professional training (Robard I., *op. cit.*: 219).

range of diseases, provided that they do not claim to cure or treat certain specified diseases as proscribed by law. The common law right to practise springs from the fundamental principle that everyone can choose the form of healthcare that they require. Thus, although statutory regulation can award protection of title to a therapy, it cannot stop the employment of the techniques of that therapy under a slightly different name.[251]

In addition, alternative practitioners are subject to a wide range of statutory and non-statutory controls, the most important being:

1. the Health and Safety at Work Act of 1974 and its associated regulations, which place a statutory duty on employers and the self-employed to ensure the health and safety of people affected by activities undertaken on their premises;
2. the provisons of the Trade Descriptions Act 1968 and the Consumer Protection Act 1987, which are enforced by local authority Trading Standards Officers, and apply to professions which make claims for the goods or services they sell, including alternative practitioners;
3. legislation relating to specific illnesses and medical conditions which prohibits non-medically qualified practitioners from purporting to treat;[252]
4. many organisations representing alternative practitioners, which are registered charities or limited companies (or both) under the Charities and Companies Acts, and are subject to the provisions of those Acts;
5. the London Local Authorities Act 1991, which requires the licensing of premises used for activities that include acupuncture, massage, and other special treatments;
6. the common law, where all practitioners have a duty of care towards their patients;
7. the private sector, where there is a contractual relationship between therapists and customers, which is legally enforceable.

Even if there is no actual regulation on the licensing to practise alternative medicines, the government supports both the Osteopath and Chiropractor Acts, enacted respectively in 1993 and 1994. Thus, these two professions are partially recognised, with their members enjoying special rights.[253]

251 ANONYMOUS (IV), *op. cit.*: 27; BRITISH MEDICAL ASSOCIATION, *op. cit.*: 24, 42; ROBARD I., *op. cit.*: 218; SELECT COMMITTEE ON SCIENCE AND TECHNOLOGY, *op. cit.*: 40; STONE J., *op. cit.*: 47, 207, 285–331; THOMAS K. J., *op. cit.*: 127.

252 For more details, see below.

253 For more details, see below.

They are not, however, recognised as official health care providers and, as such, usually cannot work within NHS hospitals.

Even if physicians[254] decide to refer patients to non-allopathic practitioners during the period of treatment, they still retain clinical responsibility for their patients. As the Parliamentary Secretary of State for Health stated in 1991, alternative medicines may be provided either by physicians themselves, or may be delegated to therapists who remain clinically accountable to registered medical practitioners responsible for patients' care.[255] Thus, when employing auxiliary staff, doctors have to ensure that they work with practitioners having academic and vocational qualifications.[256] These principles are meant to safeguard the patients' interests. Furthermore, alternative practitioners are not permitted to countermand instructions or prescriptions given by physicians.[257]

B. Characteristics of the country

Restrictions to the freedom to practise medicine

Despite the principle of freedom to carry out medical acts, there are in place certain controls that restrict this principle.[258] Indeed, certain acts are restricted to physicians.[259] For the rest, non-allopathic practitioners may execute medical acts. However, if such acts result in death[260] or injury, these practitioners are subject to criminal or civil liability.[261, 262]

254 Regarding the providing of alternative medicines by physicians, the GMC's Blue Book, which reflects the attitude of the British Medical Association, states that "a doctor persisting in unsupervised practice of a branch of medicine without having the appropriate knowledge and skills or having acquired the experience which is necessary may risk a finding of serious professional misconduct. This would suggest that if registered medical practitioners are to practise any of the major therapies, they should receive the appropriate training from a recognised registering professional body" (BRITISH MEDICAL ASSOCIATION, *op.cit.*: 58; STONE J., *op.cit.*: 55).

255 Until 1977, the General Medical Council considered that, according to the Code of Professional Ethics, physicians could not advise patients to consult with non-allopathic practitioners. Now, the position is the reverse.

256 Art. 28 of the latest NHS (General Medical Services) Regulations 1992.

257 BRITISH MEDICAL ASSOCIATION, *op.cit.*: 43, 47.

258 Under the terms of Section 4 of the Cancer Act 1939 and under the Venereal Disease Act of 1917.

259 Thus, only registered doctors may: 1. treat cancer, diabetes, epilepsy, glaucoma and tuberculosis; 2. prescribe controlled drugs; 3. perform specific medical acts such as abortion or treat venereal diseases.

260 If a patient dies, the practitioner may be criminally prosecuted for involuntary homicide, while registered physicians cannot be prosecuted.

Furthermore, unqualified practitioners may not claim to be, or actually practise as pharmacists, midwives or dentists, or imply that they are state-registered practitioners whose legal status is regulated by the Professions Supplementary to Medicine Act of 1960.[263] Moreover, the law prohibits the commercial use of the term "health care centre" in relation to any premises where no doctors and nurses are employed.[264]

Osteopath and Chiropractor Acts

Although there is no specific legislation on the licensing to practise alternative medicines, the government has supported two private members' bills.[265] the Osteopath Act 1993 and the Chiropractor Act 1994.[266] According to Stone

> the willingness of the Government to pass these two Acts, which creates the first two autonomous statutorily protected complementary health professions, has

261 Currently, individuals are protected under British law from incompetent or unskilled therapists by the tort-based common law of negligence.
Concerning the effectiveness of common law on the subject, see STONE J., *op. cit.*: 184–87. In particular, she notes that "despite the massive increase in cases against medical practitioners there has been no corresponding rise in cases against alternative practitioners" (STONE J., *op. cit.*: 189).

262 BRITISH MEDICAL ASSOCIATION, *op. cit.*: 25; DE BIJL N., *op. cit.*: 10; ROBARD I., *op. cit.*: 219; STEPAN J., *op. cit.*: 287; STONE J., *op. cit.*: 164–72, 183, 188; THOMAS K. J., *op. cit.*: 127.

263 This Act covers the following professions: dieticians, medical-laboratory technicians, occupational therapists, physiotherapists, radiographers and orthoptists.

264 STONE J., *op. cit.*: 59.

265 According to Montgomery "the Government view is that statutory regulation is appropriate where the therapies can be shown to be based on a systematic body of knowledge, where a voluntary registration scheme already exists, where there is a code of professional conduct, where the profession itself seeks a statutory regime, and where the medical profession is supportive of that project" (MONTGOMERY J., *op. cit.*: 162).

266 Excepting these two Acts, which are essentially the same, there is still an almost total absence of statutory regulation concerning alternative medicine. These Acts are modelled very closely on the Medical Act of 1983 (STONE J., *op. cit.*: 37, 153).
Prior to the adoption of the Chiropractor Act, an association with members practising full time laid down its own rules regarding training and discipline. Since 1925, it has managed a register of chiropractors having a recognised training (in accordance with rules of the American Council of Chiropractic Education). All members are subject to the Code of Professional Ethics (ROBARD I., *op. cit.*: 224).

> been interpreted as a highly significant development in alternative medicine. [...] various other therapies are now vigorously pursuing the same level of recognition. Acupuncturists, homeopaths and herbalists, and possibly other therapies are now actively considering statutory regulation.[267, 268]

The organisation of the profession under the Chiropractor Act is such that, in contrast to other professions, there is a significant number of members outside the profession in the General Chiropractic Council.[269] The regulation of chiropractic is based upon a register of allopathic professions. The right to use the title of chiropractor is restricted to registered chiropractors and the registration depends upon a recognised qualification.[270]

The General Chiropractic Council has published a Code of Professional Ethics, similar to those of other professional and equivalent bodies. Any departures from the Code does not, in itself, constitute "unacceptable professional conduct", but will be taken into account in disciplinary proceedings.[271] Under the Chiropractor Act, the principal criteria for disciplinary jurisdiction are professional incompetence, conduct that falls short of the standard required from a registered chiropractor, conviction of a criminal offence, and serious health impairment affecting the ability to work as a chiropractor.[272, 273]

267 STONE J., *op. cit.*: 126.
268 STONE J., *op. cit.*: 145–60.
269 According to the Chiropractor Act 1994, Chap. 1 (1), (11) there are twenty members. Six do not have to be chiropractors and at least one has to be a registered medical practitioner.
270 *Idem*, s. 32.
271 *Ibidem*, s. 19 (4).
272 *Ibidem*, s. 20 (1), (2).
273 According to Montgomery "these texts are different from the older formulations in at least two respects. First, there is specific reference to incompetence, ensuring that the General Chiropractic Council is able to deal with malpractice. Secondly, the change from 'professional misconduct' to that which 'falls short of the standard required' may reduce the relevance of the practitioner's culpability. Misconduct implies something more wilful than the more external and objective criterion used in the new statute. This change suggests a greater concern for protecting the public in difficult cases rather than protecting the chiropractor from an 'unfair' restriction on business. A further indication of the importance given to safeguarding the public is the fact that the Council will be able to require chiropractors to carry professional indemnity insurance" (Chiropractor Act 1994, art. 1, (1), (32), (37)) (MONTGOMERY J., *op. cit.*: 163).
On the standards of professional misconduct in chiropractic, see also MCHALE J., *op. cit.*: 258.

The sanctions available to the Professional Conduct Committee are varied. It may admonish, suspend or dismiss practitioners. The right to practise is initially granted for a period of up to three years, then such right is reviewed on subsequent occasions on the basis of the necessity to protect the public, usually every two or three years.[274]

As far as osteopathy is concerned, the General Osteopathic Council has defined minimum standards and has officially recognised five schools from the 25 existing ones.[275]

Other alternative techniques[276]

There are five associations representing non-statutory registered acupuncturists. Some of these, such as the British Acupuncture Council, are seen as having led the way in establishing verifiable standards of education for their profession. These include the appointment of a professional Chief Executive, the adoption of a core curriculum and a revised code of ethics and practice. The Council has also set up an acupuncture resource centre to encourage undergraduate and post-graduate research.

Homeopathy is practised by two separate groups; medical homeopaths are medically qualified practitioners regulated by the General Medical Council, non-medical homeopaths are professionals who use homeopathy only. Four main bodies representing the non-medical homeopaths[277] are attempting to create a single register of homeopaths. So far, however, there has been little communication between these groups and the official bodies representing medical homeopaths.

Naturopaths are currently represented by two main voluntary bodies. The largest of these two, the General Council and Register for Naturopaths is actively seeking a consensus on regulation in this field. Similarly, nutritional therapists have created a new umbrella body, the Nutritional Therapy Council, which aims to establish common education and national occupational standards.

Position of State authorities, The British Select Committee on Science and Technology, and the British Medical Association

Successive governments have ensured that access to alternative medicines will be guaranteed, for as long as patients require. The government and

274 MONTGOMERY J., *op. cit.*: 163.

275 GENERAL OSTEOPATHIC COUNCIL, *op. cit.*

276 SELECT COMMITTEE ON SCIENCE AND TECHNOLOGY, *op. cit.*: 38ss; For an extensive presentation of the regulatory situation, see the same author at 38ss.

277 The most important is the Society of Homeopaths.

the two Houses support patients' freedom of choice in the medical field, requiring that medical treatments be harmless and of good quality, and that unjustified therapeutic requests be avoided.[278]

According to the British Select Committee on Science and Technology, "there is considerable variation in the levels of professionalisation within the CAM world. Even within some therapeutic disciplines there is considerable fragmentation, sometimes resulting in several bodies, each with different training and educational requirements, codes of practice and complaints procedures, representing therapists in the same field".[279] The Committee considered that the experience of the osteopathic profession demonstrates not only the benefits the public has gained from the use of osteopathy, but also demonstrates ultimately, the well-organised and coherent regulatory structure the profession has acquired. It added that one serious problem for therapies represented by several professional bodies is that the disciplinary procedures of those bodies have little weight. As a result the Committee recommended that "in order to protect the public, professions with more than one regulatory body make a concerted effort to bring their various bodies together and develop a clear professional structure".[280]

The British Medical Association has identified certain fundamental features deemed necessary in order to ensure effective regulation that may protect the public, namely:[281]

1. to provide a code of conduct, a disciplinary procedure and a complaints procedure;
2. to provide minimum standards of training and to supervise training courses and accreditation;
3. to understand and advertise areas of competence, including limits of competence within each therapy;
4. to keep an up-to-date register of qualified practitioners;
5. to provide and publicise information on alternative medicines.

278 Robard I., *op. cit.*: 221–22.

279 Select Committee on Science and Technology, *op. cit.*: 40.

280 Select Committee on Science and Technology, *op. cit.*: 41. For a development regarding proposals of the British Select Committee on Science and Technology, see the same author at 41–57, 112–13.

281 British Medical Association, *op. cit.*: 46.

4.3.3.4 Hungary

In February 1997, the Hungarian legislature adopted a new tolerant regime for alternative medicines.[282, 283] These Decrees clearly and officially recognise alternative practitioners, both physicians and non-physicians. Indeed, even though physicians still have a wide predominance in that field, non-physicians and recognised non-allopathic practitioners are also allowed to practise specific alternative medicines.

The most important characteristics of these new Decrees are the laying down of precise rules for the training of alternative practitioners, and for the providing of alternative medicines. The Decrees contain a list of authorised alternative medicines, as well as a list of the medical practitioners who are allowed to provide them.[284]

The Decree n° 47 is divided into two parts. The first part (art. 1–7) regulates the general conditions necessary to fulfil in order to practise alternative medicines, while the second part (annexes 1–4) contains specific requirements for each type of alternative medicine.

Annexe 4,[285] which focuses on the training and examination of alternative practitioners, states all the necessary theoretical and practical requirements for an examination in the following natural medicines: acupuncture, massage techniques, lifestyle counsel, reflexology, alternative physiotherapy, bioenergy, physiotherapy and auriculotherapy.[286]

The Decree n° 47 contains the list of authorised medical practitioners:[287] physicians, practitioners with a non academic but high health qualification, and other practitioners (non-allopathic practitioners). The term "natural

282 Government Decree n° 40/1997 (IV 5) Korm. r. on Natural Medicine and Decree of the Minister of Welfare n° 11/1997 (V 28) on some aspects of the practice of Natural Medicine. These Decrees came into force on July 1, 1997 (art. 6).

283 The new law also contains some rules for the providing of drugs.

284 E.g., there is a basic education program in homeopathy of three years for physicians (LIGA MEDICORUM HOMEOPATHICA INTERNATIONALIS, 1996, Mallorca).

285 The structure of the annexe is always the same:
1. the definition of the technique;
2. practical requirements;
3. ethical rules;
4. a description of theoretical requirements;
5. the specific requirements for the examination.

286 Two allopathic techniques are put in the same category, namely kinesitherapy and eye rehabilitation.

287 Art. 1, and annex 1 of the Decree.

doctors" refers to authorised practitioners from the above three categories who are also permitted to use alternative medicines.

Physicians with an academic degree in medicine may ask for a licence to practise as natural doctors without having to take another specific exam. They are also allowed to use the title of natural doctor (art. 7). In contrast, psychologists with a high health qualification, have to take a specific examination on natural medicine, which if successful, means that they are allowed to use the title of natural doctor. The regulatory regime is the same for other practitioners; they are authorised to use the title of "natural doctor" once they have passed the examination on natural medicine.

The scope of practice of these practitioners is defined by art. 2 and 3 of the Decree n° 47. The main principle is that physicians are in charge of illness diagnosis, therapy planning and the follow-up of patients (art. 2 (1)). According to patients' wishes or upon a physician's referral, other authorised practitioners may participate in the providing of care. Non-physician "natural doctors" are allowed to practise independently when they work under the supervision of a physician, or when they intervene after a physician's diagnosis. They may also directly examine patients if they have the necessary qualifications.[288] If a patient wants to be treated by a "natural doctor", his or her consulting physician may not oppose the choice that is made. Therefore, the right to choose one's medical practitioner is guaranteed by law.

The Act contains some restrictions made to non physician natural doctors. They may not, for example, administer a treatment prescribed by a physician (art. 2 (2)). Thus, if a patient is under treatment, the natural doctor has first to consult with the consulting physician.

Article 1 also contains some restrictions to the use of alternative medicines. For example, only physicians are permitted to practise certain therapies.[289] Practitioners with a (non academic) high health qualification may also provide manual therapies. Other practitioners not holding a high health qualification are allowed to provide a whole range of techniques.[290]

Another restriction is articulated in art. 2 (3); only qualified psychologists or physicians with a qualification as psychotherapists are permitted to provide psychotherapeutic care based on natural medicine.

288 Unfortunately, there is no data available regarding these qualifications.

289 Namely, homeopathy, manual therapies, Chinese and Tibetan medicine (in particular acupuncture), biologic dentistry, therapies using oxygenation, neuraltherapy, anthroposophy and magnetic bio-resonance.

290 Such as acupressure, alternative massage therapies, lifestyle counsel, reflexology, bio energy, phytotherapy and auriculotherapy.

According to art. 3, "natural doctors" are subject to the same obligations and ethical rules as the other medical practitioners. They must, for example, keep a file for each patient.[291]

According to art. 5, the Ministry of Social Welfare is the authority responsible for the Institute of Health. The Institute of Health is responsible for the training of "natural doctors" and is authorised to examine the candidates. There is a register of "natural doctors", and a special commission is responsible for the surveillance of natural doctors.

4.3.3.5 Liechtenstein

Bibliography

Schädler P., *Die "Götter in Weiss" sollen eine Kammer bekommen*, in: Liechtensteiner Vaterland, July 22, 1997; Stotter H. J., *Das neue liechtensteinische Strafgesetzbuch*, ex jure Verlagsanstalt, 1988, Vaduz: 301–03.

Liechtenstein illustrates the paradoxical situation that several Western countries are facing currently. Officially, the country has a monopolistic system for the licensing medical professions, in that only physicians are allowed to provide medical acts and non-allopathic practitioners may be criminally prosecuted.[292] However, the monopoly does not include "natural medicine" and, in practice, the system is tolerant towards non-allopathic practitioners as such practitioners are free to practise alternative medicines.

291 Art. 6 and annex 3 also contain directives in connection with the setting up of a natural doctor's practice. Annex 2 includes data that has to be collected by "natural doctors", such as anamnesis or description of the current treatment.

292 According to article 49 of the Health Law and according to Order I, the conditions to practise medicine in Liechtenstein are the following: 1. to hold the citizenship of Liechtenstein or of a country member of the European Economic Space and to live in Liechtenstein; 2. to graduate from a Swiss, German or Austrian school of medicine; 3. to complete the requirements of capacity, repute, hygiene measures and to respect the general physician's duties; 4. to obtain a government's licence to practise.
The right to work as an independent GP as well as the obtaining of a specialist title requires postgraduate studies followed by an internship (the whole training lasts from three to five years (articles 49 and 54 of Health Law and articles 9–22 of Order I). A new medical department is responsible for the above mentioned conditions and issues licences to practise (Schädler P., *op. cit.*).

There are two Acts responsible for the regulation of alternative medicines. The first is the Health Act of December 18, 1985,[293] which regulates the health care professions. Art. 24 (a) (I) of the Act provides that the following acts are not considered acts of health care professions: natural medicine, being only health care that does not consist of bodily intrusions, child birth, the treatment of infectious diseases and the prescription of medication.[294]

Article 184 of the Penal Code which regulates the illegal practice of medicine specifies that a person who performs medical acts which are legally reserved for medical doctors,[295] in a professional way, without having the necessary training for the practice of medicine, may be subject to imprisonment for a period of up to three months, or may be fined.[296] Thus, non-allopathic practitioners could theoretically be prosecuted under article 184 of the Penal Code when providing alternative care. However, until now, alternative practitioners have never been subjected to prosecutions under article 184. Ancillary professionals are tolerated when providing alternative medicines and non-allopathic practitioners only need a trade licence in order to provide medical acts.[297]

The State health authorities are considering two ways to resolve the perceived contradiction between article 24 (a) (I) of Health Act, and article 184

293 Gesetz über das Gesundheitswesen vom 18. Dezember 1985, in: Liechtensteinisches Landesgestzblatt (n° 12, 1986).

294 In German: "Die nachfolgenden Tätigkeiten gelten nicht als Berufe der Gesundheitspflege: Naturheilkunde, verstanden als Heilkunde, die keine körperlichen Eingriffe, geburtshilfiche Verrichtungen und keine Behandlungen infektiöser Krankheiten vornimmt und keine rezeptpflichtige Substanzen sowie giftige Heilmittel verwendet".
According to art. 22 of the Health Act, chiropractors are considered medical professionals.

295 All medical acts included in art. 24 (a) (I) of the Health Law (in particular natural medicine) do not have to be considered as being reserved for physicians. However, there are no court rulings on this point.

296 In German, "Wer, ohne die zur Ausübung des ärtzlichen Berufes erforderliche Ausbildung erhalten zu haben, eine Tätigkeit, die den Ärzten gesetzlich vorbehalten ist, in bezug auf eine grössere Zahl von Menschen gewerbmässig ausübt, ist mit Freiheitsstrafe bis zu drei Monaten oder mit Geldstrafe bis zu 180 Tagessätzen zu bestrafen".

297 One should note that, although non-allopathic practitioners are tolerated, they are not allowed to provide care in the national health care system.

of the Penal Code; either the introduction of an Act on Natural Medicine Practitioners,[298] or the abolition of article 24 (I) of the Health Act.[299]

The Act on Public Health does not regulate the providing of alternative medicines by physicians. Therefore, physicians are allowed to use alternative medicines without having to pass a supplementary exam. However, article 9 of Order I states that "physicians must practise only in their speciality, and according to their knowledge, with the exception of emergencies".[300]

4.3.3.6 *Malta*[301]

The Maltese regulation on alternative medicines is a mixture of a monopolistic and tolerant system.[302] The legislature chose a monopolistic system of licensing medical professions, in that only registered medical professionals are allowed to practise medicine. However, some alternative professions are regulated together with the allopathic professions.

The medical professions are regulated by the Medical and Kindred Professions Ordinance[303] and, in particular, by Part II of the Ordinance and Part IV of the Department of Health Ordinance.[304] The fundamental conditions for the practice of medicine are:

298 In German: "Naturheilpraktikergesetz". There is currently a draft law on Natural Medicine, which is the subject of controversy. While some people are opposed to the free practise of non-allopathic practitioners, others opt for an extension of the right to practise medical acts.
For more details, see STOTTER H. J., *op. cit.*: 302–03.

299 Cornelia Marxer-Broder, collaborator at the Liechtenstein Government, Vaduz, Sept. 2001.

300 In German: "Der Arzt darf sich nur im Kompetentenbereich seines Faches betätigen, ausgekommen während seiner Tätigkeit im Notfalldienst".

301 The information was provided by Dr. D. Falzon, Principal Medical Officer at the Department of Public Health, March 1998, Valletta; Dr. Gafa, Legal Office, Department of Health, March 1998, Valletta; and Mr. Wismayer, Director Government Pharmaceutical Services at the Ministry of Health, 2000, Valletta. To the best of our knowledge, the position has not changed since then.

302 As Malta is fairly broad-minded concerning alternative medicines, it was decided to place it in the category of tolerant systems.

303 Chap. 31 of the Laws of Malta.

304 Chap. 94 of the Laws of Malta. Part IX of Chap. 31 of the Laws of Malta provides rules regarding ancillary professions.

1. a licence issued by the President of Malta;[305] and
2. the registration of the practitioner in the Medical Register.[306]

Physicians are permitted to provide alternative treatments whereas the legal status of non-allopathic practitioners is still unregulated. There is no registration system for such practitioners and, therefore, non-allopathic practitioners are not allowed to practise within the scope of practice of listed professions, such as physiotherapists, physicians or pharmacists (Chapter 31 of the Laws of Malta). A breach of the provisions contained in Chapter 31 usually constitutes a criminal offence, and is punishable by a fine, imprisonment or both. Furthermore, there are restrictions on advertising treatment[307] and clinics.[308]

The law does not address alternative medicine specifically and until now the only alternative premises licensed by the Minister of Health were moxibustion and traditional Chinese medicine clinics.[309]

Traditional Chinese Medicine is widely practised in Malta and, as such, has a special place within the Maltese health care system.[310] Acupuncture

305 Art. 5 of Chap. 31 of the Laws of Malta. The minimum requirement for obtaining this licence is the successful completion of a university course leading to a MD or other equivalent degree.

306 Art. 6 of Chap. 31 of the Laws of Malta.

307 Chap. 31, Sect 90 A provides that:
(1) "no person shall advertise or permit or suffer to be advertised in any manner whatsoever, any medical or health service or treatment, not being a service provided by Government, or any other service or treatment which is or is described as being of a medical, therapeutic or curative value or effect, or in any other way beneficial to health, without the approval of the council of Health."
(2) "For the purpose of subsection (1) of this section, 'treatment' shall include any form of advice relating to the treatment or cure of maladies or ailments, or any advice relating to health."

308 Chap. 31, Sect 98 provides that "no person shall use any premises as a hospital, clinic, maternity home, home for the aged, medical diagnostic laboratory, X-Ray department, or any other similar established or institution, by whatever name called, unless there is in respect of such premises a valid license for the purpose issued by the minister responsible for public health, and no person may open or carry on any establishment or institution for any of the purposes aforesaid unless he is in possession of a valid license for the purpose issued by the said Minister."

309 Art. 98 of Chap. 31 of the Laws of Malta.

310 As part of the cooperation between the governments of Malta and China, the Chinese Government has sent a number of medical experts on acupuncture and moxibustion to work with the government health services in Malta. This led to further collaboration between the two governments, resulting in the establishment

clinics are locally licensed under section 98 of Chapter 31, and the Minister imposes conditions of licence as he deems fit. The licence is conditional upon proof provided of adequate training and experience[311] and must be renewed every year (art. 10 of the Provisions).[312]

Article 3 of the Provisions restricts the practice of Chinese Medicine, providing that "the medical care provided at the clinic shall be limited to the practice of traditional Chinese medicine (including Acupuncture). Patients diagnosed as suffering from an infectious disease are to be referred to a registered medical practitioner for treatment, and no treatment for infectious diseases can be given at the clinic".

Article 6 of the Provisions stipulates the appropriate hygiene conditions, and according to art. 7 "all persons attended to for traditional Chinese medicine (including acupuncture) must be referred by a doctor registered to practise in Malta".

Malta has also considered the possibility of allowing other specific alternative disciplines, in particular chiropractors and osteopaths, to be registered together with other conventional professions by the local Board of Professions Supplementary to Medicine, as provided for in the Medical and Kindred Professions Ordinance.[313]

4.3.3.7 *Netherlands*

Bibliography

BRITISH MEDICAL ASSOCIATION (LAMONT T.), *Complementary medicine – New approaches to good practice*, Oxford University Press, 1993, Oxford/New York: 18–22; CARTER J. P., *Racketeering in medicine – The suppression of alternatives*, Hampton Roads Publishing Co., 1993, Norfolk: 237–39, 241; DE BIJL N. (co-author: NEDERVEEN-VAN DE KRAGT I.), *Legal safeguards against medical practice by not suitably qualified persons: A comparative study in seven EU-countries*, 1997, in: European Journal of Health Law, vol. 4: 6, 11, 13; FISHER P.

---

of the Mediterranean Regional Center for Traditional Chinese Medicine in Malta, in 1993. The Center serves a dual purpose: 1. as a training center and; 2. as a center for treatment.

311 In effect, acupuncturists employed by the Mediterranean Centre for Traditional Chinese Medicine are usually qualified doctors as well as acupuncturists.

312 The Public Health Department must be kept informed of the name and qualifications of every person employed under licence (art. 4 of the Provisions). It also carries out inspections (art. 9 of the Provisions).

313 Chap. 31 of the Laws of Malta, Section 84 (1).

(co-author: WARD A.), *Complementary medicine in Europe*, in: BMJ, vol. 309, July 9, 1994: 108; FULDER S., *The handbook of complementary medicine*, 2nd edition, Oxford University Press, 1988, Oxford/New York: 92–94; MINISTRY OF HEALTH, WELFARE AND SPORT, *The Individual Health Care Professional Act*, Ministry of Health, Welfare, and Sport, 1997, Rijswijk; ROBARD I., *op. cit.*: 239, 242–45; STEPAN J., *Traditional and alternative systems of medicine: A comparative review of legislation*, in: International Digest of Health Legislation, 1985, vol. 36, n° 2, Genève: 288; VISSER G. J., *Alternative medicine in the Netherlands*, in: LEWITH G. (co-editor: ALDRIDGE D.), *Complementary medicine and the European Community*, CW Daniel, 1991, Saffron Walden: 115–16, 119.

A. Historical evolution of the licensing to practise[314]

In the past, there were three main categories of medical practitioners. First, there were medical doctors trained at Universities. Second, a group trained at *"Clinical Schools"*. Finally, a third group that provided medical care without any medical training.[315]

In order to put an end to this situation, the Act on Medical Practice was adopted in 1865. It introduced a monopoly for university-trained qualified practitioners. Thus, only doctors and midwives were permitted to perform medical procedures. The scope of the Act was subsequently widened to allow dentists and, since 1964, physiotherapists,[316] to perform medical acts as legally specified.

Subsequent changes in the field of medicine, and public perception made the monopoly no longer acceptable.[317] Even though the practice of medicine by non-recognised health care professionals was illegal, the police did not prosecute, unless there was clear evidence of harm to patients.[318] Public

314 For an historical development see CARTER J. P., *op. cit.*: 237–39; DE BIJL N., *op. cit.*: 6; FULDER S., *op. cit.*: 92–94; VISSER G. J., *op. cit.*: 115–16.

315 VISSER G. J., *op. cit.*: 115.

316 On a referral from a doctor.

317 Indeed, large numbers of patients were turning to practitioners other than doctors, especially when registered practitioners had failed in their efforts to help them (CARTER J. P., *op. cit.*: 238). According to the Ministry of Health, Welfare and Sports "Mature adults should as patients be able to consult the care provider they feel can do them the most good, no matter whether he or she practices conventional or alternative medicine. Any restrictions on this freedom must be limited to those, which are necessary in the interest of the patient. [...] Furthermore, there were a number of matters, which had hitherto largely escaped the attention of the law. For example medical specialisms were not regulated by law, and it was difficult to promote professional standards by means of peer review and continuous training" (MINISTRY OF HEALTH, *op. cit.*: 2).

318 Professor Muntendam, the head of the Commission, pointed out that "The consensus of public opinion is no longer behind the monopoly, and the law is broken

pressure and the expansion of alternative medicine forced the authorities to set up the Commission on Alternative Medicine (CAS) and finally,[319] to review the regulation on medical practice.[320]

The CAS noted that official recognition of an alternative form of treatment invariably means the statutory regulation of the practitioners using it. Indeed, the recognition of the profession precedes the inclusion of the treatment in health insurance schemes. It also observed that alternative medicines may be said to have gained official recognition when both the government and the medical world no longer regard them as undesirable. Therefore, the CAS advised the Ministry of Health to include practitioners trained in alternative medicines as one of the qualified classes of health professionals, as defined in the 1977 bill. Practitioners providing an alternative therapy without having an adequate training could not be deemed qualified. Therefore, they would not be prevented from practising, but they could not use some appellations. The CAS suggested the progressive idea of organising sponsored courses in basic medicine for these practitioners, in order to reduce any potential risks for the public. In effect, it saw the expansion of training as the key to a successful integration of alternative medicines.[321]

The medical profession was opposed to any end to the monopoly. It attempted to keep the legal monopoly arguing that the effectiveness of alternative therapies was not scientifically proven. However, the Minister of Health stated that the argument was not a compelling one, as the public demand for freedom of choice in medicine was more important than scientific arguments.[322]

After taking into consideration the conclusions of the CAS report, the government elaborated a new Individual Health Care Professions Act, which, in 1993, replaced the Medical Practice Act of 1865.[323]

---

a thousand times a day as sick and disabled people seek the help of people who are not legally authorised to provide it" (Fulder S., *op. cit.*: 93).

319 According to Fulder: "The Commission was the end result of a runaway public campaign for freedom of choice in medicine, a campaign helped, unwittingly, by the Government itself through its health centres. The public made clear to the Government the anomaly of the promotion of natural health in a society that bans natural medicine" (Fulder S., *op. cit.*: 93).

320 British Medical Association, *op. cit.*: 18; Carter J. P., *op. cit.*: 237; Fisher P., *op. cit.*: 108; Fulder S., *op. cit.*: 93; Robard I., *op. cit.*: 239, 242, 243–44; Stepan J., *op. cit.*: 288; Visser G. J., *op. cit.*: 116.

321 Carter J. P., *op. cit.*: 241; Fulder S., *op. cit.*: 93–94; Robard I., *op. cit.*: 245.

322 Fulder S., *op. cit.*: 93–94; Robard I., *op. cit.*: 245.

323 British Medical Association, *op. cit.*: 18–22; De Bijl N., *op. cit.*: 6, 11, 13.

B. General principles

The purpose of the new Individual Health Care Professions Act is to foster and monitor high standards of professional practice, and to protect patients from professional carelessness and incompetence.[324]

The guiding principle of the new legislation is that everyone is allowed to provide medical care.[325] However, in order to prevent unacceptable health risks for patients, resulting from a lack of professional competence, specific procedures are restricted to authorised professional practitioners.[326] Furthermore, the Act limits medical freedom by considering any injury to a person's health as an offence.[327]

In order to set up appropriate standards of professional practice, the Act contains provisions relating to the protection of titles, registration, reserved procedures, and medical discipline. Thus, the new Act effects a shift from the unqualified practice of medicine to the unqualified use of title.[328, 329, 330]

C. Characteristics of the country

Licence to practise

The new Act put an end to the professional monopoly. Thus, the performance of medical procedures is no longer restricted to specific medical practitioners. However, the Individual Health Care Professions Act has

324 MINISTRY OF HEALTH, *op. cit.*: 1.
325 According to the Ministry of Health, Welfare and Sports, "it takes a fresh approach to the provision of care by professional practitioners. It basically opens up the practice of medicine instead of restricting it, thus lifting the ban on the unauthorised practice of medicine and giving people more freedom to choose the care provider they want" (MINISTRY OF HEALTH, *op. cit.*: 2).
326 See below.
327 MINISTRY OF HEALTH, *op. cit.*: 2.
328 Orders in Council and implementation decrees can be issued to regulate additional aspects of quality in the area of professional practice, such as continuous training, peer review, locum arrangements, and consulting-room equipment.
329 BRITISH MEDICAL ASSOCIATION, *op. cit.*: 18; MINISTRY OF HEALTH, *op. cit.*: 2.
330 The Dutch government believes that the introduction of training requirements in order to obtain the registration, and therefore the right to use a specific title, is a good mechanism to ensure a high level of quality of health care.
According to the British Medical Association "this would alter radically the existing legislation governing the practice of health care and would allow patients to choose for themselves not only the type of medical treatment they receive but also from who they obtain it" (BRITISH MEDICAL ASSOCIATION, *op. cit.*: 18).

introduced a system protecting the titles of a limited number of professional groups.[331] Those persons practising a medical profession, which is regulated by law, are entitled to have any entry in the legal registers. This registration gives them the right to practice under a protected title, with the aim of insuring they are qualified in a specific field of health care.[332] The purpose is to make it clear to the public, and to the insurance companies whose fields in which they are expert.[333] In order to be registered,[334] professional practitioners have to meet some legal requirements, the most important being that the practitioner has successfully completed the appropriate training.[335]

The Individual Health Care Professions Act also contains measures against practitioners who are unfit to practise[336] which applies to all registered professional practitioners.[337]

For example, eight professions are regulated by section 3 of the Act.[338] However, the Individual Health Care Professions Act makes it possible for

331 The criteria for registering a profession are the need for disciplinary procedures and the need for direct authorisation to carry out reserved procedures. The criteria applicable to a profession are the need for public information (protected title), the need to regulate the independent providing of reserved procedures, and the need to regulate a specific training (MINISTRY OF HEALTH, *op. cit.*: 2).

332 Registered medical practitioners and third parties are entitled to know the content of their registration and the remarks.

333 MINISTRY OF HEALTH, *op. cit.*: 2.

334 The registration is valid only for a limited period. Applications for re-registration are assessed mainly on the basis of individual competence. If this requirement is not met, the applicant will not be re-registered thus losing the right to use a legally protected title.

335 BRITISH MEDICAL ASSOCIATION, *op. cit.*: 21; MINISTRY OF HEALTH, *op. cit.*: 3.

336 Unfitness must be the result of the mental and/or physical condition of the person concerned or of his or her habitual misuse of alcohol or drugs.

337 The board may decide to impose restrictions concerning professional practice, partially withdraw the authorization to practise under a title or strike the person's name off the register. For more details, see MINISTRY OF HEALTH, *op. cit.*: 6.

338 Namely medical doctor, dentist, pharmaceutical chemist, health care psychologist, psychotherapist, physiotherapist, midwife and nurse.
Educational requirements are laid down for each of these professions and their area of professional competence is defined.
Regulations pursuant to secondary legislation such as Orders in Council are likely to be used mainly for the ancillary professions, such as speech therapist, dental hygienist and dietician.

other specialities to be regulated.[339] Professional bodies may themselves introduce rules and request the Minister of Public Health, Welfare and Sport to give legal protection to specialist titles.[340]

Regarding alternative medicines, the Act contains rules allowing new professions to be regulated by law (section 3) or by Order of Council (section 34), under specific conditions. In the near future, only a few more professions are expected to be regulated by Order of Council. The Dutch government encourages and stimulates practitioners using alternative medicines and their professional organisations, both non-allopathic and allopathic, to meet certain standards of quality, to develop training courses and to set up professional codes of practice and procedures for peer review.[341]

Reserved procedures

Although the basic principle behind the new Act is freedom to practise, some procedures are restricted to specific categories of practitioners (art. 36).[342] The performance of any such procedure by an unauthorised practitioner is a criminal offence.[343]

Such orders contain rules concerning training and define the area of professional competence. Those meeting these requirements are entitled to use a professional title, but will not be registered by the government. However, professional bodies may institute registration themselves (BRITISH MEDICAL ASSOCIATION, *op. cit.*: 21; MINISTRY OF HEALTH, *op. cit.*: 3).

339 Non-allopathic practitioners are not included in the above mentioned "protected" professions. According to the British Medical Association "clearly, the Dutch legislation will have profound implications for the practice of non-conventional medicine in the Netherlands. In order to register, professional groups such as acupuncturists, osteopaths, chiropractors, and homeopaths will have to provide a clear professional profile of their scope of practice and skills" (BRITISH MEDICAL ASSOCIATION, *op. cit.*: 21).

340 MINISTRY OF HEALTH, *op. cit.*: 3.

341 Although there are training courses for non-allopathic practitioners, until now, no official status may be derived from the certificates (VISSER G. J., *op. cit.*: 119).

342 1. surgical procedures, 2. obstetric procedures, 3. catheterisations and endoscopies, 4. punctures and injections (according to the definition of the above-mentioned medical acts, the practice of acupuncture is not restricted to physicians), 5. general anaesthetic, 6. procedures involving the use of radioactive substances and ionising radiation, 7. cardioversion, 8. defibrillation, 9. electroconvulsive therapy, 10. lithotripsy and 11. artificial insemination.

The list of reserved medical acts is not exhaustive and further additions are possible when two criteria are satisfied: first, when there is a risk of considerable damage in the case of unqualified treatment and second, when there is a real

There are two groups of medical practitioners who may provide reserved procedures: those with direct authorization,[344] and those who may perform the procedure under the instructions of the former and are thereby authorised.[345, 346]

Disciplinary Code

Regulated professions are subject to a disciplinary code. The primary aim of the disciplinary code is to guarantee proper standards of professional practice in order to protect patients' interests.[347]

When a disciplinary board considers a complaint justified, it must always take action. The zero-tolerance system applies and, as a result, a penalty must be pronounced when a practitioner is found to be guilty. There are several disciplinary measures, on a rising scale of severity.[348] A practitioner who has been struck off as a disciplinary measure may not

likelihood that unqualified persons would be practising in that area (BRITISH MEDICAL ASSOCIATION, *op. cit.*: 19).

343 BRITISH MEDICAL ASSOCIATION, *op. cit.*: 19–20; DE BIJL N., *op. cit.*: 6; MINISTRY OF HEALTH, *op. cit.*: 3–4.

344 Namely doctors, dentists and midwives. The law specifies which group is authorised for each category of reserved procedures. This entitles them to perform reserved procedures on their own initiative, as long as they are competent in the field (BRITISH MEDICAL ASSOCIATION, *op. cit.*: 19–20; DE BIJL N., *op. cit.*: 6; MINISTRY OF HEALTH, *op. cit.*: 3–4).

345 Namely, nurses and nursing assistants. These practitioners are not allowed to determine whether a procedure is indicated, and must follow instructions of practitioners with direct authorization. The performance of such procedures under supervision is not restricted to registered practitioners. In effect, anyone who has been instructed to perform a reserved procedure and is proficient is thereby authorised to do so. The most important requirement is that the practitioner having direct authorization must have reasonable grounds for assuming that the medical practitioner to whom he or she is giving the order is capable of performing the procedure properly (MINISTRY OF HEALTH, *op. cit.*: 3–4).

346 BRITISH MEDICAL ASSOCIATION, *op. cit.*: 19–20; DE BIJL N., *op. cit.*: 6; MINISTRY OF HEALTH, *op. cit.*: 3–4.

347 The new Act lays down two disciplinary norms. The first relates to the principle of due care when providing treatment. The second covers all other activities which conflict with the proper practice of individual health care. The disciplinary code and the criminal and civil law can be used in conjunction with one another. The new Act strengthens in many respects the position of the patient in the disciplinary code. For more details, see MINISTRY OF HEALTH, *op. cit.*: 5.

348 Namely, warning, reprimand, a fine not exceeding 6,000 Euros, temporary suspension for a maximum period of one year, partial withdrawal of the authorization to practise under a professional title, being struck off the register.

be re-registered, and is no longer allowed to use the legally protected professional title. This also means that doctors, dentists and midwives who are struck off are no longer authorised to perform reserved procedures for which they have direct authorization.[349]

Penal provisions

The new Act includes penal provisions in addition to disciplinary measures. These provisions apply to anyone, namely all medical practitioners, whether registered or not, who do not comply with the obligations laid down in the Act.[350]

The Act specifies three penalties: detention for up to three months, a fine or debarment from the profession.[351] They may be imposed on a practitioner who:[352]

1. harms a person's health or acts in such a way as to create a significant risk of harm being done;
2. performs reserved procedures without being legally authorised to do so or on a practitioner with direct authorization who orders them to be carried out without observing the statutory requirements;
3. fails to observe the restrictions imposed on the practice of the profession;
4. wrongfully uses a legally protected professional title or specialist title;
5. provides inaccurate and/or incomplete information when applying for registration.

4.3.3.8 Scandinavian countries and Finland

Bibliography

See ALDRIDGE D., *Unconventional medicine in Europe*, Advances, 1994, vol. 10, n° 2: 55; BRITISH MEDICAL ASSOCIATION (LAMONT T.), *Alternative medicine – New approaches to good practice*, Oxford University Press, 1993, Oxford/New York: 22–24; CARTER J. P., *Racketeering in Medicine – The suppression of alternatives*, Hampton Roads Publishing Co., 1993, Norfolk: 235, 37; DE BIJL N. (co-author: NEDERVEEN-VAN DE KRAGT I.), *Legal safeguards against medical*

349 BRITISH MEDICAL ASSOCIATION, *op. cit.*: 21; MINISTRY OF HEALTH, *op. cit.*: 5.
350 BRITISH MEDICAL ASSOCIATION, *op. cit.*: 19; MINISTRY OF HEALTH, *op. cit.*: 6.
351 Art. 96 to 103 of the Individual Health Care Professions Act.
352 MINISTRY OF HEALTH, *op. cit.*: 6–7; BRITISH MEDICAL ASSOCIATION, *op. cit.*: 19.

practice by not suitability qualified persons: A comparative study in seven EU-countries, in: European Journal of Health Law, vol. 4, 1997: 5–18; FROST AND SULLIVAN LTD, *Alternative medical practices in Europe*, Report n° E874, Sullivan House, Grosvenor Gardens, 1987, London SW1: 249; MINISTRY OF HEALTH AND SOCIAL AFFAIRS (I), *Report on alternative medicine – English summary*, Norges Offentliche Utredniger NOU 1998: 21, 1998, Oslo: 135–76, 268–69; MINISTRY OF HEALTH AND SOCIAL AFFAIRS (II), *Chinese-Norwegian health seminar*, Ministry of Health and Social Affairs, 2001, Oslo; RASMUSSEN N. (co-author: MORGALL J.), *The use of alternative traetments in the Danish population*, in: LEWITH G. (co-author: ALDRIDGE D.), *Alternative medicine and the European Community*, CW Daniel, 1991, Saffron Walden: 84–85; ROBARD I., *La santé hors la loi: Les hors la loi de la santé*, 4th ed., Ed. de l'Ancre, 1994, Suresnes: 225–32; STEPAN J., *Traditional and alternative systems of medicine: A comparative review of legislation*, in: International Digest of Health Legislation, 1985, vol. 36, n° 2, Genève: 294–95; SWEDISH COMMISSION ON ALTERNATIVE MEDICINE, *Report on alternative medicine*, Regeringskansliet, 1989, Stockholm; SWEDISH COMMISSION ON COMPETENCE TO PURSUE A PROFESSION WITHIN THE HEALTH AND MEDICAL SERVICES, *Report on the new legislation on competence to pursue a profession within the health and medical services*, in: Statens offentliga utredningar 1996: 138, Socialdepartementet, 1996, Stockholm: 29–44; VASKILAMPI T., *The role of alternative medicine: The Finnish experience*, in: LEWITH G. (co-author: ALDRIDGE D.), *Alternative medicine and the European Community*, CW Daniel, 1991, Saffron Walden: 101–12.

A. General principles

Scandinavian countries and Finland have a similar tolerant approach towards the licensing of alternative medicines.

Norway

Norway has the oldest tolerant regulation on medical practice by non-physicians. The first legislation of this kind dates back to 1619 and new Acts were adopted in 1871 and 1936. The Act n° 9 of June 19, 1936, on the limitations of the right of persons who are not physicians or dentists to undertake treatment of ill persons was used as a model by both Sweden and Denmark. As such, there is a marked similary between these Scandinavian countries.[353]

353 MINISTRY OF HEALTH AND SOCIAL AFFAIRS (I), *op. cit.*: 268; ROBARD I., *op. cit.*: 226.
The Ministry of Health and Social Affairs has proposed a revision of the Act. For more details, see below.

Under the Norwegian Act of 1936, any person is allowed to provide treatments to patients, although some medical acts are restricted to physicians.[354] Any violation of this limited monopoly is an offence. The Act does not regulate the providing of alternative medicines by allopathic practitioners who may practise alternative medicines, as long as they provide them in a diligent manner. Since 1990, only chiropractic is officially recognised as a health care profession.[355]

Denmark

The situation is similar in Denmark where the Practice of Medicine Act of 1970 allows physicians[356] and ancillary professionals to use all the techniques they desire, including alternative medicines. Non allopathic practitioners may also freely provide care, whatever their training, and without previous authorisation.[357] In effect, there are no official approval mechanisms for these practitioners. However, they are not recognised as official health care providers, their title is not protected by law, and they are not integrated within the national health system apart from one exception made for chiropractors. In fact, the treatments provided by the members

354 An official registration by the Norwegian authorities is needed to practise medicine in Norway. To receive an authorisation as a medical doctor it is necessary to: 1. have a medical degree from a Norwegian or otherwise recognised university; 2. have undergone 18 months of compulsory internship.

355 See the new Act of July 2, 1999, no 64 relating to Health Personnel etc. (The Health Personnel Act).

356 In Denmark, two conditions are necessary to fully practise medicine as a physician; 1. hold an academic degree in medicine and 2. take the Hippocratic Oath before a faculty of Medicine. The National Health Service grants the authorisation. It is not necessary to have an authorisation for medical practice to undertake subordinate functions in hospitals or to act as assistants or substitutes of general practitioners.
The title of physician is protected. As a result, persons who are not granted an authorisation as physicians may not call themselves physicians.

357 According to Rasmussen "this legal approach (i.e. not forbidding the practice of alternative treatment but regulating its scope) is based on the premise that no one should be hindered in seeking help where they can find it, while at the same time protecting the health status of the general population" (RASMUSSEN N., *op. cit.*: 84–85).
The conclusion of a Danish study on alternative practitioners' treatments was that the legislation in this field is considered as sufficient, and therefore limitations are not necessary (RASMUSSEN N., *op. cit.*: 85 and references).

of the Danish Chiropractic Association are partially reimbursed by the social security.[358]

Sweden

In Sweden, the former so-called "Quackery Act" of 1960 is now included in a new Act promulgated in 1998 and in force since January 1, 1999.[359] It includes rules for the whole health care personnel, as well as providing a list of restricted activities. Licensed chiropractors and naprapaths are now included in the categories of recognised health care personal.[360]

Finland

The situation in Finland is slightly different. Generally speaking, there is no regulation on the licensing to practise alternative medicines. At first sight, only medically qualified doctors are allowed to practise medicine,[361] namely, to diagnose and take fees. However, although the Finnish law generally does not recognise the practice of alternative medicines by any individuals other than registered medical professionals, there are three exceptions. The Decree 564/1994[362] stipulates that the protected title of professional person, referred to in the Act 559, includes trained chiropractors, naprapaths and osteopaths.[363] According to this legal regulation, only those who have received a formal training are permitted to use the title of "trained" therapist, but any other person can use the plain name of chiropractor.[364]

Medical professional practitioners who fulfil the required conditions have different rights, such as the right to use an occupational title (art. 7 and 34–35 of the Act 559). As a result, under the Act 559, non-allopathic practitioners are allowed to treat patients if they do not practise within

358 DE BIJL N., *op. cit.*: 11; RASMUSSEN N., *op. cit.*: 84–85; ROBARD I., *op. cit.*: 231–32.

359 Lag (1998: 531) om yrkesverksamhet pa hälso-och sjusvardens omrade.

360 Dr. Motzi Eklöf, at the Department of Physical Education and Health, Örebro University, Örebro, Sept. 2001. To the best of our knowledge, the situation has not changed in the meantime.

361 The right to practise as an independent medical doctor can be granted to practitioners who have completed the basic medical training, as well as an additional training in primary health care or a special training in some of the medical specialities (art. 4 of the Act 559).

362 The Act concerning Health Care Professionals 559/1994 of June 28, 1994.

363 Art. 1 of the Decree.

364 ALDRIDGE D., *op. cit.*: 55; BRITISH MEDICAL ASSOCIATION, *op. cit.*: 23; VASKILAMPI T., *op. cit.*: 101; Vaskilampi Tuula, Kuopio, Finland, Sept. 2001. To the best of our knowledge, the situation has not changed in the meantime.

the public services and do not pretend to be health care professionals. Thus, any person is permitted to provide alternative medicines, but only the medical authorities may supervise the practice of registered medical practitioners.[365] Therefore, in Finland, there is not a limited monopoly on medical acts restricted to physicians, but a limited monopoly regarding the use of professional medical titles.

B. Restrictions to medical practice

Norway

In Norway, any person wishing to practise alternative medicines, apart from medical doctors or dentists, is subject to the Act of June 19, 1936. This statute limits the rights of non-allopathic practitioners. In particular, these practitioners are not allowed to provide a wide range of medical acts, which are instead restricted to physicians, dentists, and persons "assisting the physician" who are considered the responsibility of the physician.[366, 367]

The Act of June 19, 1936, provides for a jail sentence of up to three months if a patient's life or health was exposed to serious danger, irrespective of whether the danger resulted from a treatment or from the absence of treatment.[368] Criminal sanctions are rarely used, however, except in the most serious cases.[369] According to the Ministry of Health, the Act is today more or less dormant, and is considered as out of date.[370]

365 BRITISH MEDICAL ASSOCIATION, *op. cit.*: 24

366 Namely, 1. to use the title of doctor in medicine, or to use the title of specialist for a specific illness; 2. to advertise. However, announcements in the press with only the indication of name, address, consultation-hours and general information on the activities are permitted; 3. to use medications (in the treatment) which are not freely sold; 4. to perform surgical operations; 5. to give an injection; 6. to practise general or local anaesthesia; 7. to apply diagnosis or therapeutic methods restricted to physicians; 8. to treat cancer, diabetes, dangerous anaemia, struma/goitre with sticky forms, and some contagious/infectious diseases mentioned in a regulation given under Act n° 55 of 5 Aug. 1994 on contagious/infectious diseases (including venereal diseases, tuberculosis, infectious hepatitis, HIV infection, poliomyelitis, infectious meningitis and others); 9. practise in an itinerant way.

367 MINISTRY OF HEALTH AND SOCIAL AFFAIRS (I), *op. cit.*: 268; Vegar Nore, Norwegian Ministry of Health and Social Affairs, Sept. 2001, Oslo.

368 People who are sentenced to imprisonment for such practices are not permitted to practise medicine again. The maximum sentence is 2 years of imprisonment.

369 E.g., a non-medically trained person "treating" terminally ill patients by telephone at a hefty price has recently been prosecuted.

370 Vegar Nore, Norwegian Ministry of Health and Social Affairs, Sept. 2001, Oslo. To the best of our knowledge, the situation has not changed in the meantime.

Denmark

In Denmark, only physicians are allowed to practise specific acts,[371] according to art. 23–26 of the Danish Order concerning the Practice of Medicine Act.[372]

The illegal practice of medical acts is an offence and may result in penal sanctions such as imprisonment for a period of up to twelve months. However, non-allopathic practitioners are only prosecuted in the event of death or serious deterioration of the patient's medical condition and for the sale of harmful products.[373] In addition, non-allopathic practitioners are not allowed to expose patients to a provable danger.[374, 375]

Sweden

In Sweden, only physicians are allowed to practise specific acts, according to the Swedish Act.[376] Violation of restrictions on medical practice is an offence and may be prosecuted. Furthermore, non-allopathic practitioners who, by inappropriate healing, damage a person's health may be charged with the criminal offence of "charlatanism constituting a danger to health".[377] Practitioners found guilty are liable, in addition to punishment under the penal law, to be prohibited thereafter from working in the field of health care.[378]

371 Namely 1. to treat persons for venereal diseases, tuberculosis, or any other infectious disease; 2. to perform surgery, to administer total or local anaesthetics or to provide obstetric aid; 3. to apply medicines which may be dispensed only with physician's prescriptions; 4. to use X-ray or radium treatments or therapies using electrical machines.

372 Order n° 426 issued by the Minister of the Interior on Aug. 19, 1976.

373 Launso L., PhD in sociology, Sept. 2001, Copenhagen; Langgaard H., M.D. researcher into complementary cancer therapies, Mar. 1998, Copenhagen.

374 In the event of prosecution, the sentence is particularly severe if the practitioners treated insane or mentally deficient patients or persons less than eighteen years of age, or those declared incapable to manage their own affairs.

375 Langgaard H., M.D. researcher into complementary cancer therapies, Mar. 1998, Copenhagen.

376 In Sweden, 1. to pretend to be a doctor in medicine; 2. to practise general or local anaesthesia; 3. to provide care with radiological methods; 4. to practise in an itinerant way; 5. to treat specific contagious diseases; 6. to treat cancer, diabetes, epilepsy or pathological conditions associated with pregnancy or childbirth; 7. to treat a child who is less than eight years old; 8. to issue written recommendations or instructions for the treatment of patients who were not personally examined by them; 9. to provide acupuncture; 10. to test or supply contact lenses.

377 In Swedish: "kälsofarligt kvacksalver".

378 ROBARD I., *op. cit.*: 229–30; STEPAN J., *op. cit.*: 295.

Finland

The definition of illegal practice of medicine can be found at art. 34, being illegal practice as a health care professional and art. 35, being illegal professional practice as a health care professional, of the Act 559.[379]

Such cases, as defined above, are quite rare in courts.[380] It seems apparent that there is a problem regarding the elements of legal versus illegal practice, and it is unclear whether specific acts undertaken, during the treatment of patients, should be considered as the practice of medicine or not.[381]

C. Specific techniques

Manual methods

In Norway, chiropractic has gradually been recognised within the health care system. Since 1979, chiropractors upon the satisfaction of certain conditions, are permitted to use X-ray machines.[382] In 1990, a regulation on licensing to practise chiropractic was adopted. Only those persons registered as chiropractors are entitled to use the title of chiropractor.[383]

379 Under art. 34.1, "anyone practising as a health care professional as referred to in the Act without a right based on the act [...] shall be subject to a fine" and under the art. 34.2, "anyone who gives treatment that may prejudice the life or health of the person receiving treatment in connection with activity as referred to the art. 34.1 [...] shall be subject to a fine or to a sentence of imprisonment not exceeding six months".
According to art. 35.1 "anyone who pretends to be a professional in the activity referred to in art. 34.1 [...] shall be subject to a fine or to a sentence of imprisonment not exceeding six months". Art. 35.1 specifies that "if in addition activity as referred to in art. 35a is of kind referred to in art. 34.2, [...] the person concerned shall be convicted of 'illegal professional practice as a health care professional endangering the safety of the person being treated' and shall be subject to a fine or to a sentence of imprisonment not exceeding six months".

380 Antti Marttila, Director at the National Board of Medicolegal Affairs, Mar. 1998, Helsinki, Tarja Holi, Director at the National Authority for Medicolegal Affairs, Sept. 2001.

381 There is no jurisprudence or case law on actions considered to be the practice of medicine (Antti Marttila, Director at the National Board of Medico legal Affairs, Sept. 1997; Tarja Holi, Director at the National Authority for Medico legal Affairs, Sept. 2001).

382 Art. 1 of Prescription of Nov. 2, 1979.

383 The requirements to be registered are the following:
1. education and passing examinations at an institution for education of chiropractors, which is considered by the Norwegian health authorities good enough

In Denmark, the chiropractic profession is regulated by a 1992 Act. Whenever patients consult a chiropractor without an allopathic physician's referral, chiropractors must inform their patients' practitioners, whether allopathic physicians or not, of their diagnosis and treatment.[384]

In Sweden, since 1989, chiropractors satisfying the standards laid down by the Council of Chiropractic Education are officially recognised. Since then, chiropractors who have completed studies as doctors of chiropractic have the right to obtain an authorisation and to be registered under the National Health Service.[385] In 1998, the Swedish School for Chiropractic (Skandinaviska kiropraktorhögskolan) was the first to be granted such authorisation. Several practitioners, who have obtained a registration, continue to be trained abroad.[386]

The Swedish Commission on Competence (SCC) is of the opinion that because of the importance and the extent of manual methods such as, for example, chiropractic or osteopathy, a uniform regulation is necessary and has proposed that a special Commission on manual methods of treatment be appointed.[387]

In Sweden, in 1994, an authorisation became available for naprapaths. Therefore, the SCC saw no need for any amendments to be made to the rules of authorisation for naturopaths.[388]

There are no special regulations on the competence required by osteopaths, and the SCC does not have, at present, any proposals concerning this profession.[389]

---

for practising chiropractic in Norway (currently, there is no chiropractor education institution in Norway);
2. additional education on Norwegian health law and chiropractic disciplines;
3. practical training (one year);
4. the person must not be in a position that would lead to withdrawal of the authorisation (i.e. that he or she is not suitable for practising due to old age, illness, alcohol or drug abuse or other circumstances).
5. in order to become a member of the Norwegian Association of Chiropractors, candidates must have a certificate approved by the American Council on Chiropractic Education, and undergo three months of clinical training.

384 World Chiropractic Alliance, July 2000.

385 Government bill 1988/89: 96 on the certification of some chiropractors.

386 BRITISH MEDICAL ASSOCIATION, *op. cit.*: 23; SWEDISH COMMISSION ON ALTERNATIVE MEDICINE, *op. cit.*: 29; SWEDISH COMMISSION ON COMPETENCE, *op. cit.*: 37; Dr. Motzi Eklöf, at the Department of Physical Education and Health, Örebro University, Örebro, Sept. 2001.

387 SWEDISH COMMISSION ON COMPETENCE, *op. cit.*: 38. For more details regarding the Commission, see below.

388 SWEDISH COMMISSION ON COMPETENCE, *op. cit.*: 38.

389 SWEDISH COMMISSION ON COMPETENCE, *op. cit.*: 38.

Acupuncture

In Norway, the legal situation is unclear for acupuncture as it is uncertain whether this technique must be considered a surgical intervention in the sense of the Act of 1936 or not. As a result of this dilemna, there is no criminal prosecution currently for those non-physicians who provide acupuncture. The Committee on Alternative Medicine[390] is of the opinion that considering acupuncture as a surgical intervention under the Medical Quackery Act is "stretching the word of the law rather too far, and that there are good reasons for claiming that acupuncture involving no serious risk is legal also for practitioners other that doctors and dentists".[391]

In Denmark, the insertion of a needle breaking the patients' skin was declared in 1981 by the Supreme Court to be a surgical operation. As a consequence, acupuncture can be performed only by physicians or by non-allopathic practitioners or paramedic practitioners working under the supervision of a doctor.[392]

D. The Reports

The Norwegian Report on Alternative Medicines

In April 1997, the Ministry of Health and Social Affairs appointed a Committee to report on the various legal, educational, sociological and economical aspects of alternative medicines. The report was delivered on December 15 1998. The main conclusions of the report are set forth below.[393]

At the sociological level, the Committee noted that practitioners associations, schools and patient organisations desire more co-operation and fuller integration between alternative medicines and the health care service.[394] It also considered that "the patient's best interests, including concerns of self-determination, protection of patient security and the need for treatment, are paramount".[395]

The Committee also noted that many people consult alternative practitioners and that generally the majority is satisfied, but that sometimes patients are misled and exploited. Therefore, it was in the patients' interests

390 For more information regarding the Committee, see below.
391 MINISTRY OF HEALTH AND SOCIAL AFFAIRS (I), *op. cit.*: 268.
392 FROST AND SULLIVAN, *op. cit.*: 249; RASMUSSEN N., *op. cit.*: 85; ROBARD I., *op. cit.*: 232.
393 For a complete presentation of the report, see MINISTRY OF HEALTH AND SOCIAL AFFAIRS (I), *op. cit.*
394 MINISTRY OF HEALTH AND SOCIAL AFFAIRS (I), *op. cit.*: 269.
395 MINISTRY OF HEALTH AND SOCIAL AFFAIRS (I), *op. cit.*: 272.

to expand the total knowledge on treatment methods and recommended further research on the efficacy of treatments.[396]

The Committee did not make any general proposals for the inclusion of alternative medicine within the established health care services. It preferred instead to "propose measures that can help bring alternative medicine and conventional medicine closer together in a way that the people involved consider fruitful". Thus, the Committee considered that the health authorities should encourage alternative medicines and increase co-operation between alternative practitioners and the established health care services. The Committee proposed that the following measures be implemented:[397]

1. education. For example, the establishment of an "information bank" and the promotion of research efforts and dissemination of knowledge by general information and educational activities. Furthermore, health personnel education should also incorporate an introduction to alternative medicines, so that health personnel could become acquainted with the field;
2. organisation. For example, setting up local collaboration projects and projects in institutions and public health;
3. economics. For example, providing funds for local government and county councils, for general public information, for research purposes, and for co-operative projects between the health service and alternative therapists.

The Committee also suggested the repeal of the Medical Quackery Act and certain criminal provisions applicable to non-health personnel practitioners. The Committee did not propose changes in other criminal rules of significance for alternative practitioners, or changes in current compensation law. However, it did propose weakening the doctors' monopoly on treatment of serious complaints and illnesses, since it recognised a patient's

396 MINISTRY OF HEALTH AND SOCIAL AFFAIRS (I), *op. cit.*: 272.
397 MINISTRY OF HEALTH AND SOCIAL AFFAIRS (I), *op. cit.*: 271–72, 274. The Committee added that "in the Committee's evaluation, the measures should be designed such that they reflect the varying needs, and such that a large range of good treatment offers is available. They should be flexible and suitable for researching the utility of new co-operation forms and alternative medicine treatments. They should therefore be directed at concrete projects or limited trials and be suited to local conditions, including the patient's needs and desires, available personnel resource, and willingness to work together between health personnel and alternative medicine practitioners" (MINISTRY OF HEALTH AND SOCIAL AFFAIRS (I), *op. cit.*: 272).

right to self-determination.[398] In all cases, treatments should take place in co-operation with, or in mutual understanding with, a doctor.[399]

The Committee further suggested the establishment of a register for alternative practitioners, which should be open to all people wishing to apply alternative medicines. The purpose of such register is to distinguish practitioners having developed criteria of professionalism from others. The criteria would be:[400]

1. membership of a professional organisation for alternative practitioners. The Ministry of Health and Social Affairs should accredit organisations where membership would provide grounds for registration. However, these organisations must make qualification requirements for membership, have professional ethical rules and a disciplinary system for considering complaints about members' professional conduct, with the option of exclusion, and have a minimum of 30 members. The Committee rejected the enforcement of a requirement for a minimum competency level in basic medical subjects, and/or of a competency level in the relevant alternative medical treatment.
2. the taking out of a liability insurance to ensure that injured patients receive economic settlement if the injury triggers compensation;
3. documentation of the business for the past year to be included in the annual report, or general business report, or in a declaration from an employer.

The revocation or non-award of registration or of licence would represent a sanction.[401]

According to the Committee, some groups of alternative practitioners could be regulated under the proposed new Health Personnel Act. It found that the creation of a special licensing scheme for alternative practitioners was unnecessary and unfruitful, because such a scheme would create uncertainty and confusion, and help sustain the perception that there was a distinction between such practitioners and conventional health care

398 The Committee considered that adults, who are competent to give consent and reject medical treatments, should personally be able to choose alternative treatment without this triggering criminal liability for the practitioner. For children and others who are incompetent to give such consent and are suffering from serious disease, the Committee proposeed that alternative medicine treatment be given without prosecution if conventional medicine was not able to cure or alleviate the disease.

399 MINISTRY OF HEALTH AND SOCIAL AFFAIRS (I), *op. cit.*: 271–73.

400 MINISTRY OF HEALTH AND SOCIAL AFFAIRS (I), *op. cit.*: 273.

401 MINISTRY OF HEALTH AND SOCIAL AFFAIRS (I), *op. cit.*: 271.

practitioners.[402] However, the Committee did not decide whether, and if so, which groups of alternative practitioners should be given authorisation under this Act.[403]

On the basis of the report, the Ministry of Health and Social Affairs proposed the following measures to be implemented that:[404]

1. "the government will facilitate a further strengthening of research within the field of alternative medicines;[405]
2. the government aims to amend the legislation relating to this field, by among other things, proposing to repeal the Act of 19 June 1936 [...];
3. The Ministry will consider the establishment of an 'information bank' (database) which can be made available to the public;
4. The Ministry will promote contact between the different branches within the community of alternative medicine and the health authorities for instance, through the establishment of a contact group for alternative medicine;[406]
5. Increased knowledge of alternative medicine may stimulate understanding and appreciation. The Ministry will therefore consider measures to ensure that health personnel gain more knowledge within this field".

The reports from the Swedish Commissions on Alternative Medicine and on Competence

The Swedish Parliament gave a mandate to the Commission on Alternative Medicine (SCAM) to examine issues concerning the position of alternative

402 Similarly, the Committee suggested that licensed alternative practitioners under the proposed new Health Personnel Act be submitted to the same oversight regulation covering health personnel.

403 Ministry of Health and Social Affairs (I), *op. cit.*: 271, 273.

404 Ministry of Health and Social Affairs (II), *op. cit.*

405 In addition to a program for research in the field of alternative medicines, the Norwegian Research Council has signed a contract with the University of Tromso on the establishment of a competence centre on alternative medicine in Norway. The center was opened in 2001.

406 Of particular interest was the agreement signed between China and Norway in 1999 in order to increase the knowledge and understanding of traditional Chinese medicine among health personnel, and to better integrate traditional Chinese medicine within the Norwegian health care system. Vegar Nore notes that, in practice, traditional Chinese medicine has become an important part of the health care system in Norway (Vegar Nore, Norwegian Ministry of Health and Social Affairs, Sept. 2001, Oslo).

medicines in Swedish society.[407] The SCAM emphasised that "everyone should have the freedom to choose those forms and methods of treatment available, as long as attention is paid to his or her needs and safety".[408]

The task of the Swedish Commission on Competence (SCC) was to undertake a comprehensive review of the principles governing authorisation and competence. In the light of this review, the SCC had to put forward proposals concerning, for example, rules of authorisation and competence for various professional categories in the medical care area, which includes the "Quackery Act". The Report of the SCC was published in 1996.[409]

The content of the SCAM and the SCC reports can be summarised as follows:[410]

1. the creation of a new statute on the practice of alternative medicines;
2. the creation of a group of non-allopathic practitioners having one year of training and who are registered by the National Social Welfare Board;[411]
3. the creation of a State register in which all non-allopathic practitioners who passed a recognised exam could be registered;
4. the creation of professional titles. The SCC stresses that, for instance, some authorised professions are excluded from the list of protected titles. Furthermore, currently, practitioners with professional titles such as physiotherapists or nurses, for example, are not necessarily trained and authorised in that profession. However, they are allowed to exercise and use professional titles as long as it is not combined with the term "authorised". In order to obtain a title, one should demonstrate having the sufficient qualification to ensure a good quality of care;[412]

407 SWEDISH COMMISSION ON ALTERNATIVE MEDICINE, *op. cit.*: 25.
408 SWEDISH COMMISSION ON ALTERNATIVE MEDICINE, *op. cit.*: 25.
409 SWEDISH COMMISSION ON COMPETENCE, *op. cit.*
410 SWEDISH COMMISSION ON ALTERNATIVE MEDICINE, *op. cit.*; SWEDISH COMMISSION ON COMPETENCE, *op. cit.*
411 This measure would improve the skills and proficiency required for practitioners allowing them to make general assessments regarding the health condition of their patients, and to possibly refer such patients to the appropriate health services (CARTER J. P., *op. cit.*: 235; SWEDISH COMMISSION ON ALTERNATIVE MEDICINE, *op. cit.*: 27).
412 The SCC mentions that "Regulation of this kind would have the general effect of strengthening the safety of patients and of making the rules of competence more informal and distinct [...]. The right to a protected title of this kind is not linked to authorisation but to a particular degree or course matriculation certificate" (SWEDISH COMMISSION ON COMPETENCE, *op. cit.*: 36).

5. the upholding of restrictions regarding medical acts restricted solely to physicians;[413]
6. the introduction of some alternative medicines into the NHS, which fulfil the requirements laid down for registration (i.e. to guarantee a good level of skills and professional knowledge);
7. the providing of specific alternative medicines within National Health Services only if specific conditions are fulfilled.[414] Furthermore, medical professionals working in the National Health Service could refuse to provide alternative treatments;
8. a strict control with regard to advertising for natural remedies;
9. the planning of scientific studies on the effectiveness of alternative medicines;
10. the creation of channels of contact between allopathic and alternative medicines.

In relation to the first three proposals, Eklöf notes that there has never been a new statute on the practice of alternative medicines, there is no group of non-allopathic practitioners registered by the National Social Welfare Board (with the exception of chiropractic and naprapathy), and there is no State register.[415]

In conclusion, the SCAM stated that the increasing freedom of patients and the reduction of the physicians' monopoly, resulting from the recognition of non-allopathic practitioners, would be a benefit for both patients and for future scientific development.[416]

413 The SCAM and SCC added a new limitation: non-allopathic practitioners could treat psychoses provided that patients had first consulted a registered doctor. Furthermore, only registered alternative practitioners should be allowed to treat children. The age level at which children can be treated by untrained persons was subject to discussion. The SCC opted for maintaining the age at eight years, while the SCAM opted for raising the age from eight to fifteen years.

414 Namely, 1. the patient expressed a consent for such treatment; 2. the treatment is not dangerous; 3. the treatment given is in accordance with generally accepted methods (SWEDISH COMMISSION ON ALTERNATIVE MEDICINE, *op. cit.*: 28).

415 Dr. Motzi Eklöf, at the Department of Physical Education and Health, Örebro University, Örebro, Sept. 2001.

416 CARTER J. P., *op. cit.*: 237.

4.3.3.9 *Other countries*

Bibliography

WHO (V), *Legal status of traditional medicine and complementary/alternative medicine – A World overview*, WHO, 2001, Geneva.

Other countries having a tolerant system, or tending towards such system, are, by continent:

1. Africa: Angola, Botswana, Burkina Faso, Burundi, Central African Republic, Chad, Democratic Republic of Congo, Equatorial Guinea, Ethiopia, Gabon, Gambia, Ghana, Guinea, Guinea-Bissau, Kenya, Liberia, Madagascar, Malawi, Mali, Mauritania, Mauritius, Mozambique, Namibia, Niger, Nigeria, Rwanda, Sao Tomé, Senegal, Sierra Leone, South Africa, Swaziland, Tanzania, Togo, Uganda and Zambia;
2. Americas: Canada, Chile, Guatemala, Mexico, Panama, Paraguay and Peru;
3. Eastern Mediterranean: Cyprus, Egypt, Iran, Saudi Arabia and Tunisia;
4. Europe: Bulgaria, Ireland, Kazakhstan and Russia;
5. Asia: Myanmar, Cambodia, Fiji, Japan, Kiribati, Laos, Malaysia, Philippines and Singapore;
6. Western Pacific: some Australian States, New Zealand and Vanuatu.

4.3.4 Inclusive countries

Bibliography

Andersen J. O., *Health seeking in pluralistic health care systems*, in: Johannessen H. (co-authors: Launso L., Gosvig Olesen S., Staugard F.) (I), *Studies in Alternative Therapy 1 – Contributions from the Nordic Countries*, Odense University Press, 1994, Gylling: 114–25; Fulder S., *The handbook of alternative medicine*, 2nd edition, Oxford University Press, 1988, Oxford/New York: 111ss; Stepan J., *Traditional and alternative systems of medicine: A comparative review of legislation*, in: International Digest of Health Legislation, 1985, vol. 36, n° 2, Genève: 304ss; WHO (V), *Legal status of traditional medicine and complementary/alternative medicine – A World overview*, WHO, 2001, Geneva.

4.3.4.1 *Presentation of the Inclusive System*

The principal characteristic of countries having an inclusive system is the coexistence of two or more systems of general health care. This is the position, in law and practice, in large parts of Southern Asia. In several countries, alternative or traditional systems of medicine are not merely tolerated, but recognised, in addition to biomedicine, as being a part of the State structure of health care, and are supported as such by their respective governments. However, as Stepan stresses, "the two systems in that category are not yet integrated in the sense that professionals trained in the different systems of medicine do not work together as members of a single national health care network".[417] But in any case, alternative practitioners are recognised and their work is fully legalised and regulated by law. For example, they may be employed in public health institutions and perform some official medical functions.

Today, those countries having an inclusive system share a long history of use of traditional medicine, based on Ayurveda (including Siddha) and Unani, evolving respectively in Thailand and Burma.[418] During the 19th century, Western medicine was introduced into these countries and was considered by the various colonial administrations to be the only acceptable system of proper health care. Nevertheless, the overwhelming majority of the population continued to be treated by traditional practitioners. During the last century, after several attempts to achieve recognition of traditional medicines, other systems including both traditional and biomedicine have emerged.[419]

4.3.4.2 *India*

In this country, traditional medicine forms an integral part of the health care delivery system. All of the Indian States have enacted acts to regulate the teaching and practice of, as well as research in, Ayurveda and other systems. These include the Madras Registration of Practitioners of Integrated Medicine Act of 1956, the Mysore Ayurvedic and Unani Practitioners Registration Act of 1962, and the Mysore Homoeopathic Practitioners

417 Stepan J., *op.cit.*: 312.

418 Stepan stresses that "in order for the systems to operate effectively together, it seems advantageous that the particular traditional system should be formalized to a considerable degree, i.e. have medical traditions, literature, and teaching systems that can be studied and continued" (Stepan J., *op.cit.*: 304).

419 For more information on these developments, see Fulder S., *op.cit.*: 111–12; Stepan J., *op.cit.*: 304–05.

Act of 1961. The Indian States, responsible for the strengthening of traditional colleges, hospitals, dispensaries, and pharmacies, have also established Directorates of Indian Medicine for the development of traditional systems.[420]

In 1969, a Central Council for Research in Indian Medicine and Homoeopathy was created. By 1976, it supervised 15 research institutions and 130 research units. A Central Council of Indian Medicine, established in 1970, is responsible for regulating the teaching and supervising the practice of Ayurvedic, Siddha, and Unani medicines and appears to have been an effective regulator.[421]

In order to lawfully practise Indian medicine, all persons holding a diploma must be listed in a register. Since 1970, the practice of Indian medicine by a person who is not registered constitutes an offence.[422, 423]

Only those who are registered can undertake court proceedings to recover fees for treatment, hold appointments as physicians in public or semi-public institutions, issue medical certificates, appear as expert witnesses before the courts, and produce and sell medicines. Fulder notes that, even so, incompetent practitioners continue to practise, as there are no real measures in the law to prevent the unregistered from practising.[424]

More specifically, homeopathy is regulated by the Homoeopathy Central Council Act of 1973[425] provides for the registration of homoeopaths in State registers, and which has established a Central Council for Homoeopathy. Medical institutions, including universities that possess a faculty of homoeopathy or provide teaching in homoeopathy, may grant degrees, diplomas, or licences. The Central Council is empowered to prescribe standards of professional conduct and a code of ethics for homeopaths. It may also prescribe minimum educational standards for the granting of qualifications by medical institutions.[426]

420 WHO (V), *op. cit.*: 131–32; FULDER S., *op. cit.*: 112ss; STEPAN J., *op. cit.*: 305–06.

421 WHO (V), *op. cit.*: 132–34; FULDER S., *op. cit.*: 112ss; STEPAN J., *op. cit.*: 305–06.

422 A "grandfather clause" allows persons who have practised for at least five years prior to 1970 to continue their practice without further conditions.

423 WHO (V), *op. cit.*: 132–33; FULDER S., *op. cit.*: 112ss; STEPAN J., *op. cit.*: 305–06.

424 STEPAN J., *op. cit.*: 305–06.

425 27(3) *International Digest of Health Legislation* 902 (1966).

426 WHO (V), *op. cit.*: 132–34; FULDER S., *op. cit.*: 113–14; STEPAN J., *op. cit.*: 305–06.

4.3.4.3 *Other Countries*

Other countries that have an inclusive system, or tend towards such a system, are, by continent:

1. Africa: Benin, Cameroon, Lesotho and Zimbabwe;
2. Americas: none;
3. Eastern Mediterranean: none;
4. Europe: none;
5. Asia: Burma, Bangladesh, Cambodia, India, Pakistan, Sri Lanka and Thailand;
6. Western Pacific: Indonesia.

4.3.5 Integrated countries

Bibliography

AKERELE O. (co-editor: STOTT G., WEIBO L.), *The role of traditional medicine in primary health care in China*, WHO, 1985, Geneva; FULDER S., *The handbook of alternative medicine*, 2nd edition, Oxford University Press, 1988, Oxford/New York: China: 107ss; JINGFENG C., *Integration of traditional Chinese medicine with Western medicine – Right or wrong?*, Social Science & Medicine, vol. 27 (5), 1988, n° 521; COMMITTEE ON TRADITIONAL CHINESE MEDICINE, *Traditional Chinese Medicine*, Ministry of Health, 1995, Singapore: 35; JINGFU T., *Traditional Chinese Medicine: Past, present and future*, in: AKERELE O. (co-editor: STOTT G., WEIBO L.), *The role of traditional medicine in primary health care in China*, WHO, 1985, Geneva: 11–18; STEPAN J., *Traditional and alternative systems of medicine: A comparative review of legislation*, in: International Digest of Health Legislation, 1985, vol. 36, n° 2, Genève: 312ss; WHO (II), *Report of the third meeting of directors of WHO collaborating centres for traditional medicine*, WHO, 1995, Geneva: 7–11; WHO (V), *Legal status of traditional medicine and complementary/alternative medicine – A World overview*, WHO, 2001, Geneva.

4.3.5.1 *Presentation of the Integrated System*

Only in a few countries is medicine considered as a whole, in that several systems of medicine are integrated. In these countries, there is official promotion of the integration of traditional medicine into the national health care system. Furthermore, integrated training of health practitioners is the official policy.[427] In contrast to inclusive countries, the several categories

427 For more details regarding training in China, see chap. 3.3.1.4 and 3.3.2.16.

of health care providers work together, and not in two separate parallel systems.[428]

4.3.5.2 *China*

In China, traditional medicine forms an integral part of the health care delivery system.[429] The Constitution of the People's Republic of China clearly states that both modern and traditional Chinese medicine should be developed. In 1997, the government reiterated its commitment to equality of treatment for traditional Chinese medicine and modern medicine as one of its guiding principles of health.[430] Traditional medicine and modern medicine are practised in tandem at every level of the health care system.[431]

Practitioners of Chinese medicine are employed in modern hospitals; Western-style and traditional Chinese doctors work together at the township center in accordance with the policy of integrating the two systems of medicine. Patients may see either type of doctor. Brigade-based services

428 STEPAN J., *op. cit.*: 304.

429 Regarding the evolution of the regulation of alternative traditional medicine in China, Fulder writes, "The communist party was originally committed to the final eradication of traditional medicine. It was seen as superstitious and feudalism, standing in the way of progress into the modern world. During the Civil war both sides relied heavily on traditional medicine, the Nationalists willingly, the Communists grudgingly. Subsequently, the Communists had to admit that traditional medicine had proved itself in the ultimate test: the epidemics, injuries, and chaos of the war. As early as 1944, Mao stated, 'to surrender to the old style is wrong; to abolish or discard is wrong. Our responsibility is to unite those of the old style that can be used, and to help, stimulate and reform them'" (FULDER S., *op. cit.*: 107–08).

430 A 1988 statement by the Central Secretariat of the Chinese Communist Party leaves no doubt as to the importance of traditional medicine and suggests a symbiotic relationship between the traditional and modern traditions: "Both traditional Chinese medicine and Western medicine should be placed on an equally important position. On the one hand, in our causes of public health and hygiene, the aspects of our predominance and unique peculiarity is traditional Chinese medicine. Hence, traditional medicine should not be abandoned, instead, it is to be well preserved and developed further. On the other hand, Chinese medicine must actively make full use of advanced science and technology and modern measures as well so that further development can be ensured. The policy of integration of traditional Chinese medicine and Western medicine should persist. Both systems should cooperate in each other, learn from each other's merit to make up its shortcomings. Both should strive for the full play of its own predominance" (JINGFENG C., *op. cit.*: 528).

431 WHO (V), *op. cit.*: 148–49.

carry out preventive public health measures, although some curative services provided by traditional doctors are also available.[432]

The criteria for qualification as a Chinese physician or assistant are set out in the 1985 management stipulations for physicians and assistants of traditional Chinese medicine.[433] Qualification as a physician can be achieved by a number of routes, typically combining post-secondary academic studies with either treatment, teaching or research in traditional Chinese medicine in medical institutions for between one and two years.[434, 435]

A similar, but less demanding, combination of academic studies and practical involvement in traditional Chinese medicine for one year is typically needed for qualification as a Chinese medical assistant (article 7).[436] Under a 1985 Circular[437] issued by the Department of Traditional Chinese Medicine, which forms part of the Chinese Ministry of Public Health, those who studied under the former apprenticeship system are encouraged to take formal examinations leading to qualification as a Chinese medical physician or assistant. The examinations are administered by private institutions with government recognition and can be taken by correspondence course, night school or workers' university.[438]

Candidates who fail these exams, or persons who decide not to take them, must pass a "unified examination" offered by the Health Department, before their qualifications to practise as traditional Chinese medicine assistants will be recognized. The examination is based on the secondary school level. A more demanding unified exam, based on a three-year

432 Stepan J., *op. cit.*: 312ss; WHO (V), *op. cit.*: 149–51.
433 Issued by the State Administration of Traditional Chinese Medicine, Jan. 14, 1989.
434 The academic component can be undertaken either at a university or college devoted to traditional Chinese medicine, within a department of Chinese medicine in a Western medical school, or by completion of a state-approved diploma or certificate (article 5).
435 WHO (V), *op. cit.*: 150.
436 A further mechanism for qualification as a physician or assistant is available only to those traditional Chinese medicine personnel who studied under the apprenticeship system in place before the 1960s, which did not require formal examinations.
437 Circular from the Department of Traditional Chinese Medicine, Ministry of Public Health and Personnel Department for the unified examination given to personnel without official education employed as physicians (assistants) of traditional Chinese medicine, Dec. 31, 1985.
438 WHO (V), *op. cit.*: 150–51.

post-secondary education, exists for those who wish to convert their existing status under the apprenticeship system to pharmacists or physicians of traditional Chinese medicine.[439]

In addition to physicians and assistants, a third tier of health professionals exists in the Chinese model of traditional medicine. A number of individuals proficient in a particular branch of Chinese medicine are also examined and officially recognized. However, according to a recent circular issued by the State Administration of Traditional Chinese Medicine, the absence of a uniform method of assessment has led to some unqualified individuals being able to obtain official recognition. Motivated by a desire to protect the integrity of traditional medicine, and to safeguard patients' interests, the response of the State Administration has been to introduce annual testing of the members of this third tier by an assessment group of senior Chinese medical practitioners. The annual testing involves both a theoretical component, and a clinical examination. Successful completion of the annual testing results in the issuance of a certificate, which details the specific skills of the practitioner and the range of diseases that can be treated.[440] A failure of the annual test results in a cancellation of the candidate's certificate and right to practise, pending re-examination.[441]

A series of provisional stipulations,[442] released in 1988, regulates the operation of private health care offered by physicians of Chinese medicine within the State-sponsored socialist health-care system. The stipulations endorse the official policy favouring preventative care and instruct private-sector physicians to undertake primary health care assigned by the local health authority (article 4). The right to practise traditional Chinese medicine privately is restricted to those who[443]

1. have passed the unified examination and technical assessment, or met the requirements of the assessment regulation for health professional title formulated by the Ministry of Public Health and;
2. have practised medicine in State or collective-owned medical institutions for three years.

439 WHO (V), *op. cit.*: 150–51.

440 Circular regarding the re-certification of persons who are proficient in a particular branch of traditional Chinese medicine, issued by the State Administration of Traditional Chinese Medicine, Aug. 12, 1989, art. 2 and 3.

441 WHO (V), *op. cit.*: 150–51.

442 Provisional Management Stipulations for the Private Practice for Doctors of Western Medicine and Physicians of Traditional Chinese Medicine, issued by the Ministry of Public Health and State Administration of Traditional Chinese Medicine, Nov. 21, 1988.

443 WHO (V), *op. cit.*: 151.

A license must be obtained in order to open a private practice and the license holder must strictly observe the approved practice, place, range of service, and business limits to the practice.

Under the 1989 Regulations,[444] traditional Chinese medical assistants are only permitted to open their own practice in rural towns, such as townships (under the county level) and villages. They are only allowed to serve in private physicians' clinics in small towns and cities. Persons with a certified proficiency in a particular branch of traditional Chinese medicine, which is subject to annual retesting, are only permitted to open their practice within their local county or district (article 2).[445]

More specifically, in 1989, regulations were enacted for medical Qigong.[446] The impetus behind the regulations was the desire to protect patients from abuses and deception.[447] The regulations provide that practitioners of qigong must obtain approval from the local health authority before they may teach qigong in public places. Teaching must be based on "scientific approaches" (article 1). Practitioners of qigong in medical institutions must be qualified as Chinese medical physicians or assistants under the management stipulations described above and possess medical qigong skills (article 2). Those who intend to treat patients with Qi must have their methodology and the claimed curative effect approved by the city health authority. If the curative effect is shown to be "tenable", based on a study of 30 cases of the same type of illness by a designated medical institution, a licence will be issued (article 4). Non-medical institutions, including the army, are prohibited from rendering medical treatment (article 6).[448]

444 Additional Regulations to the Management Stipulations for the Privately Practised Personnel of Traditional Chinese Medicine, issued by the State Administration of Traditional Chinese Medicine, May 3, 1989.

445 WHO (V), *op. cit.*: 151.

446 Qigong is described in the preamble to the Regulations as "a self cultivation approach to keep fit through dredging meridians, adjusting the mind, balancing yin, yang, qi and blood to get rid of diseases".

447 Regulations for Strengthening the Management of Medical Qigong Treatment (Trial Implementation), issued by the State Administration of Traditional Chinese Medicine, Oct. 19, 1989.

448 WHO (V), *op. cit.*: 151.

4.3.5.3 Other Countries[449]

Other countries having an integrated system, or tending towards such a system, are, by continent:

1. Africa: none;
2. Americas: none;
3. Eastern Mediterranean: none;
4. Europe: none;
5. South East Asia: Nepal;
6. Western Pacific: Republic of Korea and Vietnam.

4.3.6 Countries with Multiple Systems

In some federal States such as Switzerland or the United States, the states have wide discretionary powers[450] in the regulation of public health.[451] Thus, each state has its own regulation on the licensing of medical professions. As a result, two different systems, tolerant and monopolistic in these examples, may exist within the same country. For this reason it was decided to address these countries separately.

4.3.6.1 Switzerland[452]

Bibliography

See AUER A. (co-authors: MALINVERNI G., HOTTELIER M.), *Droit constitutionnel suisse – Volume II: Les droits fondamentaux*, Staempfli, 2000, Bern: 307ss; BERNER D., *L'exercice illégal de la médecine ou les problèmes juridiques posés par les médecines parallèles*, in: *Aspects du droit médical*, Editions universitaires, 1988, Fribourg; CONFÉRENCE DES DIRECTEURS CANTONAUX DES AFFAIRES

449 For a world-wide overview of countries having an integrated system, see WHO (V), *op. cit.*

450 Although there are some relevant federal regulations on the topic.

451 Germany is also a federal state. However, as the regulation dealing with the licensing to practise alternative medicines is similar throughout Germany, it was included in the precedent section.

452 For a presentation of the evolution of the licensing to practise medical activities in Switzerland, see CONFÉRENCE DES DIRECTEURS CANTONAUX DES AFFAIRES SANITAIRES(II), *op. cit.*: 5–6 (the author describes the trend, over the past 100 years, towards the professionalisation of medical activities).

SANITAIRES (I), *Rapport du groupe de travail "Autorisations de pratiquer les professions du domaine de la santé"*, CDS, 2000, Bern, available at: http://www.sdk-cds.ch/fr/berufsbildung-f.html; CONFÉRENCE DES DIRECTEURS CANTONAUX DES AFFAIRES SANITAIRES (II), *Rapport du groupe de travail "Critères pour déterminer l'aptitude d'une formation à être reconnue ou réglementée"*, CDS, 1997, Bern, available at: http://www.sdk-cds.ch/fr/berufsbildung-f.html; CONFÉRENCE DES DIRECTEURS CANTONAUX DES AFFAIRES SANITAIRES (III), *Rapport annuel 1998*, CDS, 1998, Bern; COTTIER T. (co-author: MERKT B.) (I), *La fonction fédérative de la liberté du commerce et de l'industrie et la loi sur le marché intérieur suisse: L'influence du droit européen et du droit international économique*, in: *De la Constitution – Etudes en l'honneur de Jean-François Aubert*, Helbing & Lichtenhahn, 1996, Basel: 449–71; COTTIER T. (co-author: WAGNER M.) (II), *Das neue Bundesgesetz über den Binnenmarkt (BGBM) – Übersicht und kurzer Kommentar*, in: AJP, 1995, n° 12: 1582ss; DE REYNIER V. (co-author: RIVA E.), *Les effets de la loi fédérale sur le marché intérieur (LMI) sur les professionnels de la santé détenteurs d'une autorisation de pratiquer délivrée par un canton*, Conférence des directeurs cantonaux des Affaires Sanitaires, 1998, Bern; DUMOULIN J.-F. (co-authors: GUILLOD O., MÉROZ J.-C.), *L'impact d'une adhésion suisse à l'Union Européenne sur le droit de la santé*, in: COTTIER T. (co-editor: KOPSE A. R.), *L'adhésion de la Suisse à l'Union Européenne – Enjeux et conséquences*, Schulthess, 1998, Zürich: 925–48; FISCHER S., *Commission de surveillance des professions de la-santé: La situation en Suisse romande,* in: Médecine et Hygiène, 1999, vol. 57: 979; GUILLOD O. (I), *Rebouteux, naturopathes et guérisseurs: Pour un traitement légal alternatif*, Recueil de Jurisprudence Neuchâtelois, 1989, Neuchâtel: 9–45; GUILLOD O. (II), *Market integration in a small federal State (Switzerland): The role of public health*, in: COTTIER T., MAVROIDIS P. C. (editors), *Regulatory barriers and the principle of non-discrimination in world trade law*, The University of Michigan Press, 1999: 211–30; GUILLOD O. (co-author: ZENGER C., RUCKSTUHL N.) (IV), *Structure et organisation de la santé publique en Suisse,* in: GUTZWILLER F. (co-editor: JEANNERET O.), *Médecine sociale et préventive – Santé publique*, Hans Huber, 1999, Bern: 233–35; GUGGENHEIM S., *Naturopathes et guérisseurs – Autoriser ou interdire?*, in: Argus, Feb. 7, 1997; HÄFELIN U. (co-author: HALLER W.), *Schweizerisches Bundesstaatrecht*, 3. Auflage, 1993; KAHIL-WOLFF B., *L'accord sur la libre circulation des personnes Suisse-CE et le droit des assurances sociales,* in: Semaine Judiciaire, 2001, vol. 123, n° 4: 81–135; KUHN H. P., *Autorisation de pratiquer: Deux fois non, une fois oui*, in: BMS, 1999, vol. 80, n° 40: 2399–401; KÜNZI M. (I), *Komplementärmedizin und Gesundheitsrecht*, Helbing & Lichtenhahn Verlag AG, 1996, Basel: 14–75; KÜNZI M. (III), *Naturheilerinnen und Naturheiler: Zulassen dulden oder verbieten? Inventar, Kritik, Empfehlungen*, in: Schweizerische Zeitschrift für Ganzheitsmedizin, vol. 2, 1997; ANONYMOUS (VIII), *Meinungsumfrage zur Alternativmedizin*, in: Das Beste, 1997, n° 7; MARTENET V. (co-author: RAPIN C.), *Le marché intérieur suisse – Les mesures restrictives du droit suisse à la lumière du droit européen*, Staempfli (Cahiers Suisse de l'Intégration Européenne), 1999, Bern; METTLER H., *Particularités appenzelloises*, in: Hôpital Suisse, 1989, vol. 7: 14–15; POLEDNA T. (co-author: BERGER B.) (II), *Öffentliches Gesundheitsrecht*, Stämpfli, 2002, Bern (To be published); ROBARD I., *La santé hors la loi: Les hors la loi de la santé*, 4th ed., Ed. de l'Ancre, 1994, Suresnes:

255–59; Rösch B., *Die Stellung der Erfahrungsheilkundigen aus verfassungs- und verwaltungsrechtlicher Sicht, dargestellt am Beispiel der geistig Heilenden*, Helbing & Lichtenhahn Verlag AG, 1994, Basel; Vallender K. A., *Grundzüge der "neuen" Wirtschaftsverfassung*, in: AJP, 1999: n° 6; Waldburger N. (co-author: Marcer N.), *Définition d'un niveau de formation adéquat – Exigences d'un examen final pour l'obtention d'un diplôme reconnu par le Service de la Santé Publique*, 2001, Lausanne; Wicki M., *Komplementärmedizin im Rahmen des Rechtes*, Dissertation, Stämpfli, 1998, Bern; Zenger C., *Geschichte und Bedeutung des eidgenössischen Greizügigkeitsgesetzes*, in: Schweitzerische Ärztezeitung, 1986: 2039ss. Interesting and updated information may also be found at http://www.naturaerzte.ch/franzoesisch/index.asp.

A. Introduction

The regulation of Swiss health policy reflects the country's federal structure. Indeed, there are rules at the federal, cantonal,[453] and the intercantonal level.[454]

In order to understand the legal status of alternative practitioners in Switzerland, the (three-level) legal framework of licensing health professions will first be briefly presented. Then, an analysis will be made of the conditions necessary to fulfil in order to practise in the health field, and more specifically to practise alternative medicines.

B. The legal framework of licensing health professions

Constitutional principles

As a result of the federal system, legislative powers are split between the Confederation and the cantons under art. 3 of the Swiss Federal Constitution (CH-Cst). The overriding principle is that cantons are sovereign, as long as the Federal Constitution does not limit their sovereignty. The public health field and, in particular, the regulation of medical activities is mainly a cantonal competence.[455] There has also been a shift of competences from

453 Cantons are Swiss states.

454 Conférence des Directeurs Cantonaux des Affaires Sanitaires (I), *op. cit.*: 8; Dumoulin J.-F., *op. cit.*: 927.

455 The Confederation has the power to recognise health professions taught at the university level, health insurance (illness and accident), the fight against communicable diseases, food products and drugs.
Cantons are responsible for regulating hospitals, the promotion of health, the prevention of disease and regulation regarding patients' rights. Although cantons are competent in these fields, they must respect the Federal Constitution and, in particular, constitutional rights.
It is noticeable that private organisations have also had an impact on health regulation. For example, the postgraduate training of physicians and the delivering of

cantons to the Confederation, which should favour an increasing harmonisation of health law within Switzerland generally.[456]

The right to choose a profession, to have access to an independent, private and lucrative activity, and to practise such activity are guaranteed by the economic freedom enshrined in art. 27 CH-Cst. This freedom may be restricted under specific conditions (art. 36 CH-Cst).[457] In particular, every restriction must:

1. have a legal basis;[458]
2. be justified by being in the public interest;[459]
3. be proportionate to the goals pursued;[460]
4. preserve the essence of fundamental rights.[461]

Federal rules[462]

Although health is mainly within the competence of the cantons, the Confederation is responsible for the regulation of specific fields in this area. It is proposed to focus on the five federal acts set forth below:

related diplomas is undertaken by the Federation of Swiss physicians. The Swiss Academy of Medical Sciences also issues ethical Directives on relevant topics.

456 CONFÉRENCE DES DIRECTEURS CANTONAUX DES AFFAIRES SANITAIRES (I), *op. cit.*: 8; DUMOULIN J.-F., *op. cit.*: 927–29; GUILLOD O. (IV), *op. cit.*: 233–35; HÄFELIN U., *op. cit.*: 87; WICKI M., *op. cit.*: 69.

457 See, for example, the following decisions of the Federal Court: ATF 124 I 310 E.: 313; ATF 123 I 212 E 3a: 217.

458 Such as a law adopted by the lawmaker during a democratic procedure.

459 Public health protection has long been recognised as a legitimate public interest allowing a canton to restrict economic freedom. The health professions, social policy interests (ATF 97 I 504ss) or other public goods may be considered as sufficient to justify a restriction of the economic freedom. For a development on this point, see ATF 119 Ia 382; AUER A., *op. cit.*: 307ss; GUILLOD O. (II), *op. cit.*: 216ss.

460 The cantonal measure must not go beyond what is necessary to reach its protective aim, must be the appropriate means to achieve it, and must be reasonably related to such aim.

461 In practice, the analysis of these conditions consists in a weighing of interests, at different levels, between contradictory individual rights (protected by various constitutional right) and public interests (justifying a restriction).

462 Swiss federal laws may be accessed at http://www.admin.ch/ch/f/rs/rs.html, and http://www.europa.admin.ch/ba/expl/factsheets/f/fs_personen/index.htm, accessed June 27, 2001.

1. the Federal Act regulating the Exercise of the Professions of Physicians, Pharmacists and Veterinarians;[463]
2. the Federal Act on Professional Training;[464]
3. the Federal Act on Health Insurance;[465]
4. the Federal Act on the Internal Market;[466]
5. and the Sectorial Agreements with the EU.[467]

The Federal Act regulating the Exercise of the Professions of Physicians, Pharmacists and Veterinarians

The Federal Act regulating the Exercise of the Professions of Physicians, Pharmacists and Veterinarians is based on art. 33 CH-aCst, which gives cantons the competence to ensure that the exercise of the liberal professions depends upon a proof of capacity. The purpose of the Act, which is now under revision, was to guarantee the validity of diplomas[468] in the entire country.[469, 470]

Currently, there is an ongoing project for a new Federal Act on the University Training for Health Professions (the Act on Medical Professions),[471] that will ultimately regulate the basic, post-graduate, and continuous education of physicians, dentists, veterinarians, pharmacists and chiropractors. The new Act, that will not come into force before 2005, aims at the encouragement of high quality health care through an optimal training, and on the establishment of freedom of movement at both the intercantonal and international level, particularly in light of the implementation of the agreements between Switzerland and the EU.

463 RS 811.11.
464 RS 412.10.
465 RS 832.10.
466 RS 943.02.
467 FF 1999 VI, pp. 6319ss (RO 2002 I 701) (in French: "Accord entre la Communauté européenne et ses Etats membres, d'une part, et la Confédération Suisse, d'autre part, sur la libre circulation des personnes du 21 juin 1999").
468 For physicians, dentists, veterinarians, and pharmacists.
For an overview of the physician's profession in Switzerland, see KÜNZI M. (I), *op. cit.*: 14–26.
469 The requirements for obtaining a licence to practise are similar between cantons. Usually the cantons require: 1. the holding of a recognised diploma (possibly a practical experience); 2. a good mental and physical health (in order to be able to practise); 3. no previous administrative or criminal sanction in relation to professional practice; 4. to have both civil capacity and civil liability insurance.
470 CONFÉRENCE DES DIRECTEURS CANTONAUX DES AFFAIRES SANITAIRES (I), *op. cit.*: 11; ZENGER C., *op. cit.*: 2042.
471 In French: "Loi sur les professions médicales universitaires".

The Act on Medical Professions will be modified in compliance with the Federal Act on the Agreement between the Confederation and the European Community and its Member States on Freedom of Movement, which came into force on June 1, 2002.[472] Since then, in order to be allowed to practise medicine in an independent way, practitioners must hold a post-graduate diploma.[473] Practitioners holding only a federal diploma will be allowed to practise under the supervision of a MD holding a post-graduate diploma. Foreign diplomas will be recognised, as long as there is an agreement on the mutual recognition of diplomas with the foreign country concerned. The Act will also introduce the rules governing the recognition of diplomas issued by private schools.[474]

Although cantons must recognise federal diplomas, they are still free to create their own certificates to regulate specific activities, which may require less training than federal diplomas.[475]

The Federal Act on Professional Training

Since January 1, 2000, with the implementation of the new Federal Constitution, the Confederation has been responsible for the regulation of the health, social, and arts professions. In particular, art. 63 CH-Cst states that the Confederation regulates professional training. A new Act on Professional Training, in force since 2004[476], regulates those professions that are not taught in high schools.[477] The objectives of the new Act are the development of new training programs,[478] the establishment of a clearly defined non-academic professional training, the development of more responsibility for participants, the creation of bridges between training programs

472 For more details, see below.

473 Until June 2002, holders of federal diplomas are allowed to practise everywhere in Switzerland, without holding a post-graduate diploma.

474 CONFÉRENCE DES DIRECTEURS CANTONAUX DES AFFAIRES SANITAIRES (I), *op. cit.*: 11–12; DUMOULIN J.-F., *op. cit.*: 931–32.

475 CONFÉRENCE DES DIRECTEURS CANTONAUX DES AFFAIRES SANITAIRES (I), *op. cit.*: 11; KÜNZI M. (I), *op. cit.*: 19; ZENGER C., *op. cit.*: 2043. For a development regarding professions regulated by cantons, see below, same chap.

476 FF 2000 5256. Draft available at www.bbt.admin.ch/dossiers/nbb/f/main.htm, accessed on Sept. 1, 2001.

477 The following professions were already regulated by the Federal Office of Professional Training and Technology, according to the Act on Professional Training: pharmacist-assistant, optician, acoustician, dentist-technician, drugstore dealer, dietician, medical assistant and beautician.

478 Such as apprenticeships or shorter training programs.

and the provision of greater financing based on benefits.[479] However, no alternative professions are regulated by this Act.[480]

The Federal Act on Health Insurance

The Federal Act on Health Insurance (FAHI)[481] recognises several professions as being health care providers (art. 35 FAHI),[482] namely physicians, pharmacists, chiropractors, midwifes and including those persons providing care on a physician's referral, in particular, nurses, ergotherapists, physiotherapists, logopedists and dieticians.[483]

Only the Federal Council, being the Swiss government, and the Parliament may decide the conditions to determine which health care practices will be covered by the FAHI.[484] Cantons do not have this competence.[485]

The Sectorial Agreements with the European Union[486]

The Federal Act on the Agreement between the Confederation and the European Community and its States Member on the Freedom of Movement,[487] establishes the right to freedom of movement, including the freedom to take residence, and the freedom to provide services, between Switzerland and the EU. As part of the implementation process, Switzerland and the EU will take measures to mutually recognise diplomas and other professional qualifications. In this respect, the regulation regarding medical

479 For more details, see www.bbt.admin.ch/dossiers/nbb/f/main.htm, accessed on Sept. 1, 2001.
480 Conférence des Directeurs Cantonaux des Affaires Sanitaires (I), *op. cit.*: 12; de Reynier V., *op. cit.*: 10.
481 In French, "Loi sur l'Assurance Maladie" (LAMal).
482 Health care providers holding foreign diplomas are recognized if their diploma is equivalent to a federal one. The recognition of foreign diplomas may also be submitted on the basis of reciprocity, namely the diploma will be recognized if the foreign country recognizes the Swiss equivalent.
483 Conférence des Directeurs Cantonaux des Affaires Sanitaires (I), *op. cit.*: 12–13.
484 FF 1992 I 165.
485 Conférence des Directeurs Cantonaux des Affaires Sanitaires (I), *op. cit.*: 13.
486 For a development regarding EU regulation, see chap. 4.3.1.
487 The agreements were accepted on May 20, 2000. This Act implements the sectorial agreements between Switzerland and the EU.

professional training would already appear to be EU compatible. Therefore, an adhesion to the Community should not involve serious problems.[488]

Freedom of movement between Switzerland and the EU will be progressively implemented.[489] The health field is the focus of special Directives concerning physicians, dentists, veterinarians, midwifes and nurses.[490] These Directives stipulate that service providers are allowed to provide their services for 90 days each year.[491] It must be stressed that this rule regards only the freedom to provide services and not the freedom to take up residence.[492]

Some commentators have pointed out that the implementation of the European "Cassis-de-Dijon" principle could lead to discrimination among national residents.[493] Indeed, according to this principle, as long as those service providers are allowed to practise in their own EU country, service providers who have not taken up residence in Switzerland will be permitted to provide their services anywhere in Switzerland, while Swiss residents will have to satisfy, the perhaps potentially higher, requirements of the canton of residence.[494]

This principle of EU law does not protect service providers from existing national rules that restrict the providing of goods or services. The new Act on the Internal Market (AIM) does not change the situation.[495]

488 CONFÉRENCE DES DIRECTEURS CANTONAUX DES AFFAIRES SANITAIRES (I), *op. cit.*: 14, 15; DUMOULIN J.-F., *op. cit.*: 932; HÄFELIN U., *op. cit.*: 16; KAHIL-WOLFF B., *op. cit.*: 81–86, 99–107.

489 For a development, see CONFÉRENCE DES DIRECTEURS CANTONAUX DES AFFAIRES SANITAIRES (I), *op. cit.*: 15.

490 Pharmacists are not allowed to provide services outside their own country (see Directive 85/433/CEE).

491 During a transition period, national residents will, however, have priority over foreigners, and controls will be implemented regarding conditions of salary and work.

492 CONFÉRENCE DES DIRECTEURS CANTONAUX DES AFFAIRES SANITAIRES (I), *op. cit.*: 15; KAHIL-WOLFF B., *op. cit.*: 82, 103–04.

493 According to the decision of the Court of Justice of the European Communities (Feb. 20 1979, 649, ch. 8), in the absence of imperative requirements of the member State (e.g., in order to protect public health), any goods put on the market in a member State may be introduced without further restrictions in another member State. This rule is based on the principle of mutal recognition.

494 CONFÉRENCE DES DIRECTEURS CANTONAUX DES AFFAIRES SANITAIRES (I), *op. cit.*: 14–15; DE REYNIER V., *op. cit.*: 7–8.

495 For a development regarding the implementation of the "Cassis-de-Dijon" principle, see CONFÉRENCE DES DIRECTEURS CANTONAUX DES AFFAIRES SANITAIRES (I), *op. cit.*: 15 (the Swiss government considers that this principle could not be implemented in Switzerland).

Indeed, art. 6 AIM only guarantees the equality, in an international context, between Swiss residents of canton and foreigners, but does not guarantee non-discrimination between residents of different cantons within Switzerland itself. Therefore, the Confederation and cantons must adapt their legislation to the EU Directives regarding the recognition of professional diplomas in order to avoid possible discrimination between national residents.[496]

The Federal Act on the Internal Market[497]

According to art. 95 (2) CH-Cst, the Confederation is responsible for creating a single Swiss economic space, where people may freely have access to, and practise a private lucrative activity in any part of the country.[498] From this perspective, the (AIM) aims to suppress cantonal protectionist rules.[499] Although the AIM concerns all professions regulated by cantons, precedence is given to intercantonal agreements existing between cantons that regulate a specific profession (art. 4. (4) AIM).[500]

The AIM does not aim to harmonise the law, as this would violate the constitutional power of the cantons according to art. 3 and 31 (2a) CH-Cst. Instead, it only establishes certain principles in order to avoid cantonal protectionism. One of these principles is the non-discrimination of

496 CONFÉRENCE DES DIRECTEURS CANTONAUX DES AFFAIRES SANITAIRES (I), *op. cit.*: 15.

497 For a development on the subject, see COTTIER T. (I), *op. cit.*: 449–71; COTTIER T. (II), *op. cit.*: 1582ss; DE REYNIER V., *op. cit.*; GUILLOD O. (II), *op. cit.*: 211–30; MARTENET V., *op. cit.*

498 In this respect, Guillod reminds us that art. 31 aCst regarding the freedom of trade and industry has three main functions: 1. guaranteeing the right of an individual to choose any lucrative economic activity; 2. ensuring an economic system based on competition and a free market; 3. achieving a Swiss single market (GUILLOD O. (II), *op. cit.*: 212–13).

499 On the subject, Guillod states that "cantons and municipalities alike had actually erected all kind of local walls and hurdles (technical barriers, non-recognition of cantonal diplomas, etc.) that had hindered access to the market by outsiders" (GUILLOD O. (II), *op. cit.*: 213).
For an historical approach on the development of the regulation of the internal market, see COTTIER T. (I), *op. cit.*: 450–58.

500 CONFÉRENCE DES DIRECTEURS CANTONAUX DES AFFAIRES SANITAIRES (I), *op. cit.*: 13, 17; COTTIER T. (I), *op. cit.*: 450–60; DE REYNIER V., *op. cit.*: 3, 6–7, 23–24; GUILLOD O. (II), *op. cit.*: 213; MARTENET V., *op. cit.*: 7–9; VALLENDER K. A., *op. cit.*

external providers,[501] as well as the "Cassis-de-Dijon" principle, developed in EU law, and translated into Swiss law.[502] Thus, the conditions required in order to obtain cantonal authorisations are intended to be equivalent, particularly personal requirements.[503] However, the Federal Court has stated that cantons are allowed to establish higher requirements than the original canton of residence.[504]

Restrictions to the access to the market are allowed only when three conditions are fulfilled (art. 3 (2) (a), (b), (c) AIM), namely that:[505]

1. the restriction is the same for both local and external providers;[506]
2. the restriction is indispensable in order to preserve predominant public interests. Public health, which includes the protection of the life and the health of people, and a sufficient level of training for those professions whose exercise needs a licence to practise, is considered a predominant public interest;[507]
3. the restriction is proportional to the targeted objective.

501 According to art. 1 (1) AIM, every person having his or her administrative headquarters or residence in Switzerland must have a free and non discriminatory access to the whole Swiss market in order to have a lucrative activity.
Art. 2 AIM provides that every person has a right to propose or provide goods and services in the whole country, as long as the exercise of the lucrative activity is legal in the canton where the person has his or her administrative headquarters or residence.
The AIM also avoids a possible discrimination between Swiss and foreign residents. Indeed, according to international agreements, foreigners could (with regard to the access to the Swiss market) have a better position than Swiss residents. Art. 6 (1) AIM states that the rights regarding access to the market are the same for both Swiss residents and foreigners (whose access to the Swiss market is regulated by international agreements).

502 For a development regarding the influence of EU and international economical law, see COTTIER T. (I), *op. cit.*: 465–71.

503 ATF 125 II 56 E. 4a, and b: 61ss.

504 CONFÉRENCE DES DIRECTEURS CANTONAUX DES AFFAIRES SANITAIRES (I), *op. cit.*: 17–18; COTTIER T. (I), *op. cit.*: 459–71; DE REYNIER V., *op. cit.*: 3, 6–9, 12–13; MARTENET V., *op. cit.*: 7–20.

505 CONFÉRENCE DES DIRECTEURS CANTONAUX DES AFFAIRES SANITAIRES (I), *op. cit.*: 18; COTTIER T. (I), *op. cit.*: 461–63; DE REYNIER V., *op. cit.*: 3–4, 6–10; MARTENET V., *op. cit.*: 21–24, 59–63.

506 This principle is based on the rules set up by the World Trade Organisation.

507 In this respect, the definition of "sufficient level of training" varies. When the profession is widespread throughout the country, then this level must be understood as being equivalent to several diplomas in the cantons. If the training is less widespread, this means a specific standard of quality that it is possible to compare the training with.

When the restriction has a material form such as the requirement of holding a diploma (proof of capacity),[508] art. 4 AIM states that such a diploma is valid throughout Switzerland. When a canton considers that such a diploma insufficient and refuses to authorise the holder of such a diploma to practise, then it must justify such restriction. The Federal Court has made several decisions on this subject:[509]

1. The Federal Court (FC) ruled (on June 4, 1999), in the case of a dental prosthesis maker holding a federal certificate of capacity delivered by canton Zürich and wishing to take residence in canton Graubünden,[510] that the AIM concerns only the providing of services, and not the right to take up residence. The FC also stated that the AIM does not provide any protection against possible market restrictions set up by cantonal regulation, as long as such regulation respects the Federal Constitution. Therefore, even if the canton does not regulate a profession, such profession may not be authorised in the canton under art. 4 AIM. Indeed, the AIM preserves the right of cantons to require a licence to practise, and even to establish more severe requirements.
2. A further decision of the FC on May 4, 1999, regarded the refusal of canton Graubünden to allow a German dentist to practise. The dentist held a German diploma, and was resident in the canton. In the ruling, the FC stated that the requirement of a federal diploma did not violate freedom of commerce. Indeed, such a diploma provided a guarantee of a solid training. Although the German training could also satisfy such a requirement, it was difficult for Swiss authorities to evaluate the foreign diploma. Therefore, such a restriction was not disproportionate.

   Furthermore, the FC considered that the AIM was not applicable, for two reasons; first, it was an intracantonal case, and second, the freedom of movement guaranteed by art. 4 AIM concerns only Swiss

508 For a development regarding the notion of proof of capacity, see DE REYNIER V., *op. cit.*: 22–23 (the author stresses the distinction between proof of capacity, for which the AIM guarantees the validity throughout the whole country, and the licence to practise delivered by a canton. The first one is usually one of the conditions necessary to fulfil in order to obtain the second).

509 CONFÉRENCE DES DIRECTEURS CANTONAUX DES AFFAIRES SANITAIRES (I), *op. cit.*: 18–20; COTTIER T. (I), *op. cit.*: 462; DE REYNIER V., *op. cit.*: 4–5, 12–13, 22–25; GUILLOD O. (II), *op. cit.*: 215–16; KUHN H. P., *op. cit.*: 2399–401.

510 ATF 122 I 49.

certificates of capacity, and not foreign ones, even if they are recognised by some cantons as being equivalent to Swiss diplomas.[511]

3. A third case concerned a naturopath holding a diploma obtained in canton Appenzell External Rhodes, who unsuccessfully attempted to acquire a licence to practise in canton Zürich. The FC[512] ruled that a practitioner holding a cantonal diploma attesting training to practise a specific profession could not use the argument of right to freedom of movement under the AIM in order to practise in another canton that did not itself regulate the specific profession.[513] Furthermore, as the constitutional freedom of trade (art. 31 CH-Cst) does not provide the right to an authorisation, one could not rely on it under the AIM. Finally, the FC stated that the level of training leading to the diploma of naturopath was not equivalent to a physician's training.[514]

According to the Conference of Cantonal Directors of Health Affairs (CCDHA), the decisions of the CF demonstrate that the principle of freedom of movement contained in the AIM must not be overestimated, at least in regard to health professions. Some minor differences have been eradicated and it is assumed that equivalence exists. However, after taking into consideration art. 3 (2) (a), (b) and (c) AIM, this supposition becomes virtual, allowing cantons enough freedom of action to restrict, and possibly forbid, a professional activity in order to protect patients health.[515]

511 In this respect, one may mention the decision of the Supreme Court of canton Luzern on Dec. 2, 1998, that also addressed the refusal to provide a licence to practise in an independent way to a physician. The Court left the question open as to whether the above-mentioned decision of the FC was sustainable, with regard to EU law. For a development on this area, see CONFÉRENCE DES DIRECTEURS CANTONAUX DES AFFAIRES SANITAIRES (I), *op. cit.*: 19.

512 ATF 125 I 322, cited in San News, May 2000, n° 12: 18. Also in Semaine Judiciaire, 2000, vol. 122, n° 4: 49.

513 Cantons are free to have a stricter notion of public health protection. This is a question of cantonal policy, which is allowed, as long as it does not constitute a disguised cantonal protectionism (art. 3 (4) AIM).

514 In a former ruling, the FC stated that, for a question of proportionality, partial authorisations are possible where one may clearly define specific fields of a professional activity, and when a specific profile, alongside an adapted training exist in order to practise this "partial" activity. For a development on the subject, see KUHN H. P., *op. cit.*: 2399–401. For further development on this area, see below.

515 CONFÉRENCE DES DIRECTEURS CANTONAUX DES AFFAIRES SANITAIRES (I), *op. cit.*: 20.

Inter-cantonal rules

Since January 1, 2000, the Confederation has regulated professional medical training (art. 63 CH-Cst), and therefore also non-academic health professions.[516] Until the new Federal Act on Professional Training comes into force, in 2005, the regulation of professional training remains mainly a cantonal competence.[517]

According to the Intercantonal Agreement on the Recognition of Diplomas of February 18, 1993, (art. 5 (2)), the CCDHA is responsible for the recognition of Swiss and foreign diplomas in the health field. According to this agreement,[518] the CCDHA may delegate the task to others.[519] The CCDHA has the power to decide whether a specific training must be recognised and therefore regulated.[520] First, only chiropractic[521] was directly

516 The regulation of professional training in industry, the arts and craft professions, commerce, agriculture and house keeping was already the competence of the Confederation.

517 CONFÉRENCE DES DIRECTEURS CANTONAUX DES AFFAIRES SANITAIRES (I), *op. cit.*: 16; DE REYNIER V., *op. cit.*: 24–25.

518 Order of the CCDHA of Nov. 20, 1997, regarding the recognition of foreign diplomas; Order of the CCDHA of Nov. 20, 1997, regarding the recognition of cantonal diplomas of public health training.

519 E.g., the Swiss Red Cross has been in charge of regulating specific professions such as podologists or orthoptists (Convention between cantons and the Swiss Red Cross of Apr. 28/May 20, 1976). The Swiss Red Cross also regulates the training of nurses. For further information on the subject, see DE REYNIER V., *op. cit.*: 18–21.

520 For a development regarding the criteria necessary for determining whether a profession must be recognised, see CONFÉRENCE DES DIRECTEURS CANTONAUX DES AFFAIRES SANITAIRES(II), *op. cit.*

521 Several requirements must be fulfilled before being allowed to practise as a chiropractor, namely;
1. holding Swiss citizenship;
2. holding a diploma giving access to a university;
3. studying at least four years at a chiropractic college recognised by the American Council on Chiropractic Education;
4. passing the exam before an American State commission;
5. passing the Swiss intercantonal exam;
6. passing the Swiss federal exam to be allowed to X-ray;
7. completing at least one year of internship by a Swiss authorised chiropractor.

For more details regarding the exams of chiropractors, go to http://www.sdk-cds.ch/fr/berufsbildung-f.html, accessed Sept. 1, 2001. See also KÜNZI M. (I), *op. cit.*: 66–68.

regulated by the CCDHA. On November 2002, the CCDHA decided to regulate also osteopathy. Currently, a task force is working on the conditions regarding the training of osteopaths.[522] The Conference of Health and Social Affairs of French Swiss speaking cantons (hereafter CHSAFS[523]) is currently also working on an inter-cantonal agreement regarding the training and licensing of osteopathy.[524] Music therapy should also be regulated by the CCDHA in the near future.[525]

Cantonal rules[526]

When a profession is not regulated at the federal or inter-cantonal level, then cantons retain competence. Cantons have exploited their competence in this area by regulating both allopathic and non-allopathic professions.

522 For more details, see http://www.gdk-cds.ch/120+M52087573ab0.0.html, accessed Feb. 1, 2005.

523 In French: "Conférence Romande des Affaires Sanitaires et Sociales" (CRASS). The CHSAFS is the equivalent of the CCDHA for only the Latin cantons. The CCDHA is represented at the CHSAFS. Where principles regarding the training and licensing of osteopathy are adopted by the CHSAFS, such adoption will probably constitute the basis for a later extension at the Swiss level, through the CCDHA.

524 The CHSAFS noted that the profession of osteopath has already been (or will be) introduced in several cantons (Fribourg, Vaud, Geneva, Berne, Jura). The CHSAFS aims to establish suitable regulation for osteopathy or, at the very least, to propose specific rules that may be accepted by cantons. In this perspective, an Intercantonal Commission for the Recognition for the Practice of Osteopathy (hereafter ICRPO) was created (in French: "Commission Intercantonale de Reconnaissance pour l'Exercice de l'Ostéopathie (CIREO)"). The ICRPO must: 1. establish scientific criteria regarding the required training to practise in a dependent or independent way (on the basis of the Waldburger report (WALDBURGER N., *op. cit.*)); 2. provide the authorities relevant information about the training of practitioners wishing to obtain a licence to practise; 3. evaluate whether training at Swiss schools is compatible with scientific and international requirements; 4. if necessary, define the content of complementary training. To have access to the final report regarding the ICRPO, go to http://www.gdk-cds.ch/fileadmin/pdf/Ausbildung/Osteopathie/B-CIREO-2002-f.pdf, accessed Feb. 1 2005.

525 CONFÉRENCE DES DIRECTEURS CANTONAUX DES AFFAIRES SANITAIRES (I), *op. cit.*: 16; DE REYNIER V., *op. cit.*: 24–25; KÜNZI M. (III), *op. cit.*; ROBARD I., *op. cit.*: 255–56.

526 For a criticism and evaluation of cantonal regulation on alternative medicines, see CONFÉRENCE DES DIRECTEURS CANTONAUX DES AFFAIRES SANITAIRES (I), *op. cit.*: 31ss; GUGGENHEIM S., *op. cit.*; KÜNZI M. (I), *op. cit.*: 74–75. For updates regarding the regulation on the subject, go to http://www.naturaerzte.ch/franzoesisch/index.asp, accessed Feb. 1, 2005.

Recently, certain types of health professions, which are neither allopathic nor alternative, have acquired a status equal or similar to classic allopathic professions. These professions are recognised, either through the setting up of cantonal licensing schemes, or through coverage of the activities provided by these practitioners. For example, art. 50 of the Order of the Federal Act on Health Insurance,[527] considers logopedists as health care providers. Furthermore, this profession is or shall be recognised by several cantons.[528, 529]

C. Conditions to practise in the health field

In general

In order to prevent abstract dangers, cantonal lawmakers have several means at their disposal. According to the principle of proportionality, they may either:[530]

1. strictly forbid an activity linked with intolerable risks such as the dealing of illegal drugs; or
2. create a monopoly of dangerous but necessary activities, for example, providing nuclear energy, or burials; or
3. ban an activity, but leave open the possibility of obtaining a licence to practise; or
4. authorise an activity, where the State does not consider repressive measures to be necessary, such as psychotherapy in canton Zürich, but leading open the possibility of banning it.

527 In French: "Ordonnance de la loi sur l'assurance maladie" (RS 832.102).

528 Currently, in cantons Aargau, Basel-Stadt, Graubünden, Jura, Solothurn, St-Gallen, Thurgau, Ticino and Valais.
In the future, in cantons Appenzell Internal Rhodes, Fribourg, Glaris, Schwyz, and Zürich.
In this respect, the Swiss Conference of the Directors of Public Education is currently preparing a regulation regarding recognition based on the inter-cantonal agreement on the recognition of diplomas.
Of interest is also the position of non-physician psychotherapists. This profession will not be regulated in the new Act on Medical Professions. However, the Swiss government has decided to legislate for it separately. Currently, this profession is regulated in 21 cantons. In order to be allowed to practise, a university postgraduate training in a recognised therapeutic method is required.

529 CONFÉRENCE DES DIRECTEURS CANTONAUX DES AFFAIRES SANITAIRES (I), *op. cit.*: 21.

530 CONFÉRENCE DES DIRECTEURS CANTONAUX DES AFFAIRES SANITAIRES (I), *op. cit.*: 23; DE REYNIER V., *op. cit.*: 15–22. For an analysis of the effectiveness of these modalities of regulation, see the same author at 31ss.

The third option is the police authorisation system, which is the classic way in which health professions are regulated. As soon as candidates have fulfilled the requisite conditions, they have a right to obtain a licence to practise. A few cantons use a less restricting method by obliging practitioners to give notice to health authorities when they start their practice.[531, 532]

The professions regulated by the cantons are usually listed in the statute or decree of the respective canton.[533] Other cantons prefer to describe the type of activities requiring an authorisation, namely Sankt-Gallen and Valais.[534, 535]

The licence to practise allows both the exercise of a human activity, the setting up of an establishment and the use of facilities associated with a particular permitted profession. It confirms that the holder has, at that point in time, satisfied all the necessary legal conditions. In this respect, the CCDHA makes a distinction between the conditions to get the authorisation,[536] and the conditions linked to the practice of the activity.[537, 538]

The most important condition is the requirement of education. According to this criterion, it is possible to justify the proportionality of requiring an authorisation. The Federal Court has developed case law stating that cantons may condition the licence to practise an activity upon the holding of a certificate of capacity. However, they may do so only when the risks linked with the activity can be reduced because of an appropriate training.[539, 540]

531 E.g., in canton Zug, for people practising non-scientific treatments.

532 CONFÉRENCE DES DIRECTEURS CANTONAUX DES AFFAIRES SANITAIRES (I), *op. cit.*: 23.

533 Basel Stadt, Basel Land, Bern, Geneva, Schwyz and Zürich.

534 According to the new Act, alternative professions do not need a licence to practise in Valais, as long as they do not perform dangerous acts, and receive consent from their patients.

535 DE REYNIER V., *op. cit.*: 17.

536 Such as 1. an adequate training; 2. the capacity to practise (good reputation, good mental and physical conditions, the absence of criminal sentences); 3. knowledge of the topic; 4. civil liability insurance; 5. Swiss residency; 6. practical experience.

537 Such as 1. the maximal age to practise; 2. the uninterrupted the professional practice or continuing training; 3. the obligation to be registered; 4. having an appropriate office.

538 CONFÉRENCE DES DIRECTEURS CANTONAUX DES AFFAIRES SANITAIRES (I), *op. cit.*: 24; DE REYNIER V., *op. cit.*: 21–22; DUMOULIN J.-F., *op. cit.*: 931. See also ATF 119 Ia 35 E. 5: 40.

539 ATF 112 Ia 322 E 4b: 325.

540 CONFÉRENCE DES DIRECTEURS CANTONAUX DES AFFAIRES SANITAIRES (I), *op. cit.*: 23–24.

The Federal Court considered the following restrictions and requirements as being proportionate:[541]

1. the banning of independent practice as a dental prosthesis maker. Indeed, a dentist with several years of experience provides a better guarantee than a dental prosthesis maker with only 400 hours of additional training;[542]
2. the requirement of a certificate of capacity for practice as a beautician;[543]
3. the requirement of a certificate of capacity to adjust contact lenses;[544]
4. the requirement of a training in psychology, and a three years internship in order to practise psychotherapy in an independent way;[545]
5. the regulation of the practice of reflexology, with the setting up of an authorisation system;[546]
6. the baning of the practice of homeopathy for non-physicians;[547]

In contrast, the Federal Court considered the following as being disproportionate:[548]

1. holding that a master's degree was necessary for the independent practice of an optician shop;[549]
2. requiring a pathological exam in order to be able to provide a prescription for adjusting contact lenses;[550]
3. forbidding a dentist to have more than 2 consulting rooms;[551]
4. holding a Swiss certificate of capacity for independent practice as a physiotherapist. Indeed, the question of whether a foreign certificate is equivalent or not has to be examined by the Swiss Red Cross (on mandate of cantons);[552]

541 CONFÉRENCE DES DIRECTEURS CANTONAUX DES AFFAIRES SANITAIRES (I), *op.cit.*: 25–26; KUHN H. P., *op.cit.*: 2399.
542 Decision of Nov. 18, 1988.
543 ATF 103 Ia 259.
544 ATF 103 Ia 272.
545 ATF of Dec. 3, 1993.
546 ATF 109 Ia 180 E. 3.
547 ATF of May 12, 1989.
548 CONFÉRENCE DES DIRECTEURS CANTONAUX DES AFFAIRES SANITAIRES (I), *op.cit.*: 25; KUHN H. P., *op.cit.*: 2400–01.
549 ATF 112 Ia 322.
550 ATF 110 Ia 99.
551 ATF 113 Ia 38.
552 Decision of June 9, 1995, in RSJ 1995, 713 E. 3.

5. the refusal to deliver a licence to practise to a medical massage provider as one may not restrict the practice of a defined field of medicine to physiotherapists only;[553]
6. the refusal to authorise an independent acupuncturist (not holding a diploma as physician) to practise, who had been trained as well as or better than a physician in the field.[554] The practitioner held a foreign diploma on acupuncture and was licensed to practise in canton Graubünden. The FC noted that acupuncture was covered by the FAHI, and that this technique was sufficiently defined to allow its practice also to non-physicians being correctly trained.[555]

In addition to these decisions of the Supreme Court, the following cantonal rulings are also of interest:

1. the Supreme Court of canton Zürich stated that the practice of magnetotherapy may not be regulated under an authorisation system. The court noted that the concept of "medical act" includes only those techniques that may be provided on the basis of a medical training, and does not include therapies such as touch therapy, faith healing, hypnosis, or spiritualism. The court considered that these techniques, using para- and supernatural forces, could not be considered as natural sciences, and therefore could not be taught;[556]
2. In contrast, the Supreme Court of canton Bern[557] confirmed that it was necessary to hold a licence to practise in order to practice touch therapy as this technique gave the impression of being a serious treatment;
3. The district court of Meilen[558] stated that the practice of melotherapy and reflexology required an authorisation. It also accepted that this type of therapy has been scientifically recognised.[559]

553 ATF 117 Ia 440.
554 ATF 125 I 335, cited in San News, Jan. 2000, n° 11: 16.
555 For a criticism of the decision of the Federal Court, see KUHN H. P., *op. cit.*: 2399–401.
556 Revue Suisse de Jurisprudence, 1983: 87.
557 This decision was confirmed by the Swiss Federal Court on June 2, 1989.
558 Schweizerisches Jurisprudenz Zeitung, 1984: 168ss.
559 This is not the opinion of Wicki (WICKI M., *op. cit.*: 129).

The situation of alternative medicines (at the cantonal level)

General trends

Several Swiss cantons have decided to regulate the practise of alternative medicines, particularly as they are not regulated at either the federal or inter-cantonal level. Both monopolistic and tolerant regulations have been adopted with the tolerant approach being traditionally more used in the Eastern Cantons, and the monopolistic approach being more typical of the Western cantons. However, the situation has evolved greatly over the past decade.

In some cantons the reality of practice does not meet the theory behind it. In other words, interdictions to practise (alternative) medicine are often not enforced, or are enforced only after the intervention of interested persons.[560]

In several cantons, the practice of medicine remains an activity restricted to allopathic professions and the exercise of unregulated professions is prohibited.[561] On occasion, some exceptions are made, such as the promotion of well-being. However, the main condition to obtain a licence to practise is still the holding of a diploma attesting the successful completion of training.[562]

There is a growing trend[563] of a more tolerant approach towards alternative medicines with many hostile attitudes being slowly left aside. In 1992, canton Bern even introduced into its new Constitution (art. 41 (4)) specific encouragement of natural therapeutic methods. Many more cantons are modifying their legislation in order to regulate alternative medicines. In Swiss canton Appenzell External Rhodes, which has a typical tolerant system, non-allopathic practitioners have traditionally been allowed to practise and it was only in 1986 that an authorisation to practise was introduced. Obwalden (1991), Ticino (1989), and Zug have a similar regulation. In these cantons practitioners are required only to give notice to the authorities that they intend to practice. Basel-Land (1982), Graubünden (1984), Thurgau (1987), Shaffhausen (1993), and St-Gallen (1994) regulate

560 E.g., in cantons Aargau, Vaud and formerly in Geneva.
According to the CCDHA, the reverse is also true. Indeed, in cantons having no interdiction, authorities are very strict in practice. See also GUILLOD O. (I), *op. cit.*: 23, 26, and 29.

561 E.g., in canton Appenzell Internal Rhodes or Nidwalden.

562 CONFÉRENCE DES DIRECTEURS CANTONAUX DES AFFAIRES SANITAIRES (I), *op. cit.*: 27.

563 Created by new health regulations, case law and doctrine.

the practise of naturopathy, but have stricter requirements, in particular regarding exams. Also, between St-Gallen and Shaffhausen, Thurgau and St-Gallen, Graubünden and Thurgau, there are agreements in place regarding the mutual recognition of training in naturopathy.[564]

Basel-Land, Basel-Stadt, and St-Gallen have a relatively difficult examination for the training of alternative practitioners, including some elements of biomedicine. In addition, St-Gallen requires three years of health training combined with an internship. The purpose of the Appenzell External Rhodes examination is to detect charlatans. In canton Graubünden it is possible to pass an examination set up by a recognised centre of naturopathy.[565]

In recent years, lawmakers have used general criteria to define those practices requiring a licence to practise. For example, in canton Bern, Fribourg and Geneva, authorisation is required in order to practise dangerous activities. Similarly, in Zürich, authorisation is required in order to provide scientifically recognised treatments. Generally, details of the regulation are specified in a decree, which may be easily modified if necessary.

Overview of the cantonal regulation on alternative medicines

Among those cantons having a monopolistic system, it is possible to distinguish between those having a very strict policy on the subject, namely Appenzell Internal Rhodes, Nidwalden and Uri, and those cantons having a less restrictive approach. In this second category, cantons such as Jura and Vaud regulate the practice of osteopathy while in cantons such as Glaris, Schwyz and Zug, various alternative practices are regulated such as acupuncture, reflexology and advise on health. Finally, in canton Aargau, a licence to practise is not necessary to provide specific health care to healthy persons.

Those cantons with a monopolistic system are the following:[566]

1. Aargau.[567] In this canton, non-allopathic practitioners are not allowed to practise medicine. However, a licence is not compulsory in order to

564 Reciprocity declarations of Aug. 4, 1997, (SG-SH), Aug. 8, 1997, (TG-SG), Aug. 12, 1997, (GR-TG).

565 CONFÉRENCE DES DIRECTEURS CANTONAUX DES AFFAIRES SANITAIRES (I), *op. cit.*: 26–28; DE REYNIER V., *op. cit.*: 15.

566 Sometimes, even if the law is monopolistic, the authorities are relatively tolerant with regard to non-allopathic practitioners. Unfortunately, we do not have recent data for all cantons.

567 Gesundheitgesetz vom 10. Nov. 1987; Verordnung über die medizinischen Hilfsberufe, vom 24. Oktober 1968.

provide care to healthy people, for example, when treating nervousness, stress or sleeplessness due to fear of exams;[568]

2. Appenzell internal Rhodes.[569] In this canton, non-allopathic practitioners are not allowed to practise medicine;
3. Glarus.[570] In this canton, non-allopathic practitioners are not allowed to practise medicine. However, reflexology, acupressure and other similar massages may be freely provided;
4. Jura.[571] In this canton, non-allopathic practitioners are not allowed to practise medicine. Recently a motion has been made by the cantonal parliament in order to regulate the practise of osteopathy;
5. Nidwalden.[572] In this canton, non-allopathic practitioners are not allowed to practise medicine;
6. Schwyz.[573] In this canton, non-allopathic practitioners are not allowed to practise medicine. However, it is possible to obtain a licence to practise acupuncture.

   The Act on Public Health is currently under revision. The purpose of the revision is to adapt the current regulation regime to the recent developments in the FAHI. The revision also attempts to find a solution to the increasing number of (alternative) health professions;[574]
7. Uri.[575] In this canton, non-allopathic practitioners are not allowed to practise medicine;
8. Vaud.[576] In this canton, there have been recent changes to the Act on Public Health. Non-allopathic practitioners are, in principle, not allowed to practise medicine. However, authorities have been relatively

568 In order to be compatible with the FAHI, the canton introduced an authorisation for the independent practice of dental hygienist, ergotherapist, dietician, and logopedist.

569 Gesundheitgesetz vom 28. Apr. 1974.

570 Gesetz über das Gesundheitswesen vom 5. Mai 1963.

571 Loi sanitaire du 14 décembre 1990.

572 Gesetz über das Gesundheitswesen vom 29. Apr. 1973.

573 Verordnung über das Gesundheitswesen im Kanton Schwyz, vom 9. Sept. 1971.

574 Conférence des Directeurs Cantonaux des Affaires Sanitaires (I), *op. cit.*: 31.

575 Gesetz über das Gesundheitswesen, vom 27. Sept. 1970.

576 Loi sur la santé publique, du 19 mars 2002. The new Act modifies the Act on Public Health of May 29, 1985; Règlement du 22 novembre 1969 concernant les exigences minimales de l'examen de chiropraticien; Règlement du 10 janvier 2000 sur les professions de la santé pour lesquelles il n'est pas exigé d'autorisation de pratiquer.

tolerant over the past few years with non-allopathic practitioners and intervene only when a patient lodges a complaint against a practitioner. Furthermore, the practice of osteopathy is now regulated;[577]

9. Zug.[578] In this canton, non-allopathic practitioners are not allowed to practise medicine, with the exception of acupuncturists.[579] However, the practice of reflexology, sport massages, acupressure, and health advising may be freely provided under the surveillance of the direction of health.

Those cantons with a tolerant system are the following:

1. Appenzell external Rhodes.[580] Non-allopathic practitioners are allowed to practise medicine as self-employed practitioners. However, they must first pass an exam and obtain a licence from the Health Department. Furthermore, non-allopathic practitioners are not allowed to advertise, to use an allopathic recognised title, to provide specific medical acts for the treatment of communicable diseases, to perform surgical acts, or to provide some injections;[581]
2. Basel Landschaft.[582] Non-allopathic practitioners are allowed to practise medicine as self-employed practitioners. However, they must first pass an exam and obtain a licence from the Health Department. The cantonal regulation encloses a list of medical activities that non-allopathic practitioners are permitted to undertake.[583] However, they

577 Art. 77ss, in particular art. 122e, 122f, and 122g.

578 Gesetz über das Gesundheitswesen, vom 21. Mai 1970/30. Apr. 1981; Verordnung I zum Gesundheitsgesetz (medizinische und pharmazeutische Berufe, Hilfsberufe sowie wissenschaftlich nicht anerkannte Behandlungen), vom 22. Dezember 1981/3. Apr. 1990.

579 The minimal requirements in order to be allowed to practise acupuncture are the following:
1. to have a three year training including both theoretical and practical teaching;
2. to pass a cantonal exam.

580 Gesetz über das Gesundheitswesen, vom 25. Apr. 1965/27. Apr. 1986; Verordnung zum Gesundheitsgesetz, vom 8. Dezember 1986; Prüfungsreglement für Heilpraktiker, vom 7. Apr. 1987.

581 For a development of the position in this canton, see WICKI M., *op. cit.*: 96–99.

582 Gesundheitsgesetz vom 10. Dezember 1973; Verordnung zum Gesetz über das Gesundheitswesen, vom 17. Nov. 1975; Regierungsratsverordnung über Heilberufe, vom 14. Dezember 1976; Regierungsratsverordnung über die Naturärzteprüfung, vom 14. Dezember 1982.

583 E.g., phytotherapy, homeopathy, use of natural forces, and dietetic advising.

are not allowed to treat communicable diseases, to practise surgery, to prescribe drugs, or to provide care in obstetrics;[584]

3. Basel Stadt.[585] In this canton, the Act on Public Health is currently under revision. The objective is to change the regulation already existing for the medical professions. Before the enforcement of the new Act, the canton had already decided to put an end to the ban on the practise of specific alternative medicines. Since July 1, 1999,[586] authorisation is necessary for those persons practising *"curative medicine"* (naturopathy and phytotherapy, homeopathy, traditional Chinese medicine, acupuncture, and ayurveda).[587] In addition, authorised physiotherapists and masseurs are allowed to use reflexology. To provide other techniques, practitioners have only to inform the relevant public authorities when they commence their activities;[588]
4. Bern.[589] In this canton, non-allopathic practitioners were originally not allowed to practise medicine. However, acupuncture provided by non-allopathic practitioners was tolerated when provided under the surveillance of a physician.

   Recently, the Act on Public Health was modified. A licence to practise is necessary for those activities requiring special measures in order to protect a patient's health. The list of activities to be regulated under the new statute will be included in a decree instead of in the Act. This will allow health authorities to quickly react to changes in the field. A

584 For a development of the position in this canton, see WICKI M., *op. cit.*: 100–01.

585 Gesetz betreffend Ausübung des Berufs der Medizinalpersonen, vom 26. Mai 1879/16. März 1945; Verordnung über die Ausübung nicht-ärtzlicher Medizinalberufe vom 5. Januar 1999; Verordnung über die Ausübung nicht-ärtzlicher Komplementärmedizin vom 22. Juni 1999; Reglement über die Prüfungen in Berufend (Medizinsystemen) der nicht-ärtzlichen Komplementärmedizin vom 3. März 2000; Verordnungbetreffend Chiropraktik vom 29. Juli 1975.

586 Verordnung über die Ausübung der Nicht-Ärtzlichen Komplementärmedizin vom 29. Juni 1999.

587 The requirements in order to acquire a licence to practise are the following: 1. holding a recognised diploma from a Swiss or foreign school; 2. having a good reputation; 3. having at least 200 hours of practice; 4. being mentally and physically fit for practise; 5. eventually acquiring the appropriate authorisation for the implementation and use of specific material.

588 CONFÉRENCE DES DIRECTEURS CANTONAUX DES AFFAIRES SANITAIRES (I), *op. cit.*: 28.

589 Loi du 2 décembre 1984 sur la santé publique; Ordonnance du 5 septembre 1990 sur les chiropraticiens et les chiropraticiennes.

licence to practise will be necessary in order to practise homeopathy, acupuncture, traditional Chinese medicine, and osteopathy. The providing of any remaining activities not requiring a licence to practise will be free of any licence requirements;[590]

5. Fribourg.[591] This canton adopted a new Act on November 16, 1999 (the Act). Although the statute does not contain a list of health professions, it does, however, provide a clear definition of the rights and duties of health professionals.[592] The main criterion in order to include a profession within the new legislation is whether it has been included in the FAHI.[593] Health professionals that do not practise in an independent way do not require a licence to practise. They may provide any alternative technique they wish to, as long as they have been trained in that technique (art. 76 of the Act). Furthermore, non-professionals may use alternative techniques, as long as they are not dangerous, and do not interfere with the activities provided by a regulated profession;[594, 595]
6. Geneva.[596] Until recently non-allopathic practitioners were not allowed to practise medicine but, in practice, authorities were already relatively tolerant over the past years towards non-allopathic practitioners.

590 Conférence des Directeurs Cantonaux des Affaires Sanitaires (I), *op. cit.*: 30; Wicki M., *op. cit.*: 85ss.

591 Loi du 16 novembre 1999 sur la santé; Réglement du 21 novembre 2000 concernant les fournisseurs de soins et la Commission de Surveillance.

592 The lawmaker considered that this area was changing at such a speed that it was more sensible to let the cantonal government decide which professions must be regulated.

593 The purpose is to create coordination between the licensing to practise and the coverage of medical activities. Of note is the fact that other professions such as osteopathy have been recognised in the law.

594 Furthermore, the law stipulates that health professionals must regularly attend continuous education (art. 87).

595 Conférence des Directeurs Cantonaux des Affaires Sanitaires (I), *op. cit.*: 29.

596 Loi sur l'exercice des professions de la santé, les établissements médicaux et diverses entreprises du domaine médical du 11 mai 2001; Règlement d'exécution de la loi sur l'exercice des professions de la santé, les établissements médicaux et diverses entreprises du domaine medical du 25 juillet 2001, Accessible at http://www.geneve.ch/legislation, accessed Nov. 30, 2001
Rapport de la Commission de la santé concernant PL 7948-A, PL 7588-A, PL 8000-A, PL 8099-A, PL 8222-A, P 1242-A, Secrétariat du Grand Conseil, date de dépôt: 20 mars 2001.

A new tolerant Act has been adopted which permits the practice of alternative medicines. Chiropractic and osteopathy are regulated as allopathic professions, while the remaining alternative activities are regulated by specific rules. These latter activities are permitted as long as they are not dangerous, and if non-allopathic practitioners clearly inform patients about the nature of their practices;[597]

7. Graubünden.[598] Non-allopathic practitioners are allowed to practise medicine as self-employed practitioners. However, they must first pass an exam and obtain a licence from the Department of Health. The cantonal regulation encloses a list of medical activities that non-allopathic practitioners are permitted to perform.[599] In addition, non-allopathic practitioners are not allowed to treat communicable diseases, to practise surgery, to prescribe drugs and medications, to provide care in obstetrics, or to provide specific injections;[600]
8. Luzern.[601] Non-allopathic practitioners are allowed to practise medicine as self-employed persons. However, they first have to obtain a licence from the department of health. When practitioners use supernatural forces, they must first to be registered. Furthermore, they are not allowed to advertise, to provide treatments requiring specific knowledge relating to allopathic recognised practitioners, to prescribe drugs, or to damage body integrity, namely to practise surgery or to provide injections, among others;
9. Neuchâtel.[602] Since the introduction of the new Act in 1995, non-allopathic practitioners are tolerated and may provide non-dangerous alternative medicines. A licence is not required, but they may not advertise;

597 In order to be allowed to practise, non-allopathic practitioners must be registered at the register of the cantonal physician.

598 Gesetz über das Gesundheitswesen, vom 2. Dezember 1984; Verordnung über die Ausübung von anderen Berufen des Gesundheitswesen (Nichtmedizinalberufe), vom 26. Februar 1986; Reglement für Naturheilpraktiker, vom 19. Dezember 1990; Verordnung über die medizinischen Vorträge, vom 4. Nov. 1974.

599 E.g., phytotherapy, homeopathy, use of natural forces and dietetic advising.

600 For a development of the current situation in this canton, see WICKI M., *op. cit.*: 101–03.

601 Gesetz über das Gesundheitswesen, vom 29. Juni 1981; Verordnung über die Berufe des Gesundheitspflege, vom 17. Dezember 1985.

602 Loi de santé, du 6 février 1995; Règlement provisoire d'exécution de la loi de santé, du 31 janvier 1996; Réglement concernant l'exercice des professions médicales et des autres professions de la santé du 2 mars 1998; Arrêté interdisant les séances et représentations publiques de magnétisme ou d'hypnotisme, du 28 décembre 1886.

10. Obwalden.[603] Non-allopathic practitioners are allowed to practise medicine as self-employed persons. However, they must first obtain a licence.[604] Furthermore, they are not allowed to advertise, to provide acupuncture without a licence, to practise in surgery and obstetrics, to provide injections, to treat communicable and sexual diseases, to prescribe drugs and medications or to provide treatments requiring the specific knowledge of allopathic recognised practitioners;
11. St-Gallen.[605] Non-allopathic practitioners are allowed to practise medicine as self-employed persons. However, they must first pass an exam and obtain a licence from the department of health;
12. Shaffhausen.[606] Non-allopathic practitioners are allowed to practise medicine as self-employed persons. However, they must first pass an exam and obtain a licence from the department of internal affairs;
13. Solothurn.[607] In the past, non-allopathic practitioners were not allowed to practise medicine. Since January 2000, when the new Act on Public Health was passed, a licence to practise has been introduced for the practice of phytotherapy, homeopathy, traditional Chinese medicine, acupuncture, and ayurveda (art. 27 of the new Act). In order to obtain a licence to practise, candidates must hold a diploma attesting that they have completed a full training. For the remaining professional activities linked with mental or physical problems, practitioners must provide advice concerning their practice (art. 11 of the new Act). Practitioners of non-dangerous activities and professions, such as beautician, sport massage practitioners, do not have to give notice health authorities of their practice (art. 13 (3) of the decree). Also included is the giving of advice to healthy persons;[608]

603 Gesundheitsgesetz vom 20. Oktober 1991; Verordnung über Berufe des Gesundheitspflege, vom 20. Oktober 1991.
604 It is possible to obtain a licence to practise acupuncture and reflexology.
605 Gesundheitsgesetz vom 28. Juni 1979; Verordnung über die Ausübung der medizinischen Berufe, vom 10. Nov. 1981; Verordnung über die Ausübung von Berufen der Gesundheitspflege, vom 2. Februar 1982.
606 Gesundheitsgesetz vom 19. Oktober 1970; Verordnung über die Medizinalpersonen und medizinischen Hilfspersonen, vom 30. Nov. 1976.
607 Gesundheitsgesetz vom 27. Januar 1999; Vollzugverordnung zum Gesundheitsgesetz vom 28. Juni 1999.
608 CONFÉRENCE DES DIRECTEURS CANTONAUX DES AFFAIRES SANITAIRES (I), *op. cit.*: 29.

14. Thurgau.[609] Non-allopathic practitioners are allowed to practise medicine as self-employed persons. However, they must first pass an exam and obtain a licence from the Department of Social and Financial Affairs. The cantonal regulation encloses a list of medical activities that non-allopathic practitioners are permitted to practise.[610] In addition, they are not allowed to advertise, to provide specific medical acts in the treatment of communicable diseases, to practise in surgery or to provide care in obstetrics;
15. Ticino.[611] Non-allopathic practitioners may freely practise medicine without a public licence. However, they must clearly inform their patients that they do not have an allopathic education. Furthermore, they are not allowed to advertise, to use optical, mechanic, electric or ionising equipment or to prescribe medications and drugs;
16. Valais.[612] Non-allopathic practitioners were allowed to practise medicine only when providing care to healthy persons. Since the introduction of the new Act on Public Health in 1996, they are allowed to provide non-dangerous alternative medicines. However, they have to clearly inform their patients that they do not have any allopathic education. In addition, they must first obtain a licence from the Health Department and cannot advertise their services;[613]
17. Zürich.[614] In this canton, non-allopathic practitioners are not allowed to practise medicine. Magnetism is, however, not considered medicine and, as such, its practice does not require a State authorisation. According to a recent decree, the providing of cares to healthy persons

609 Gesetz über das Gesundheitswesen, vom 5. Juni 1985; Verordnung über Berufe des Gesundheitswesens, vom 16. Juni 1987; Reglement über die Prüfung für Naturheilpraktiker, vom 14. Sept. 1987.

610 E.g., phytotherapy, homeopathy, use of natural forces and dietetic advising.

611 Legge sulla promozione della salute e il coordinamento sanitario (Legge sanitaria), del 18 aprile 1989; Regolamento concernante l'esercizio delle arti sanitarie maggiori, del 31 ottobre 1958.

612 Loi sur la santé du 9 février 1996; Ordonnance sur l'exercice des professions de la santé et leur surveillance du 20 novembre 1996.

613 In this canton, health care professionals are defined legally in an abstract way, as persons who, in a professional way, are in direct contact with patients, to provide them with health care, which involve such risks that the control of the State is required. Furthermore, the health care professions are defined in a decree. The law also specifies that such practitioners must obtain a licence to practise (art. 55 of the law).

614 Gesetz über das Gesundheitswesen vom 4. Nov. 1962/6. Sept. 1987; Verordnung über die Berufe der Gesundheitspflege, vom 8. Januar 1992.

in order to improve their well-being is considered to be medical and is not subject to a licence to practise.

The Act on Public Health is currently under revision. According to the draft, a licence to practise will be required only for those professions based on scientifically recognised methods or for professions covered by the health insurance, and for potentially dangerous methods. In exceptional cases, the state will be permitted to forbid a practitioner to practise. Any licences to practise will be delivered for a limited period only.[615] Non-allopathic practitioners will not have to inform health authorities when they commence practising.[616, 617]

The Conference of Directors of Health Affairs and the Conference of Health Directors of Central Switzerland

The Conference of Directors of Health Affairs has made several comments and proposals concerning the licensing to practise 'alternative' medicine, namely:[618]

1. Swiss cantons are free to enact different regulations, so long as they respect the Federal Constitution. The new Federal Constitution and the AIM do not modify the legal situation. As a result, there is a need for coordination between cantons, particularly in regard to the regulation of alternative medicines;
2. the traditional-monopolistic- system, which excludes alternative medicines does not support the making of any effort regarding coordination. Such a system must be abandoned as it does not respect the Federal Constitution;
3. the obligation to require a licence to practise should be limited to;
   a. those activities based on evidence-based-medicine;
   b. those professions whose activities are covered by the basic health insurance;
   c. other dangerous medical acts;

615 The conditions for the admission will be included in the law in order to facilitate the work of the administration when implementing it. The purpose is also to avoid an extensive interpretation of the conditions by courts.
616 The lawmaker did not want to give the impression that these professions were regulated.
617 CONFÉRENCE DES DIRECTEURS CANTONAUX DES AFFAIRES SANITAIRES (I), *op. cit.*: 30–31.
618 CONFÉRENCE DES DIRECTEURS CANTONAUX DES AFFAIRES SANITAIRES (I), *op. cit.*: 35ss.

4. the conditions leading to the obligation to obtain a licence to practise must be:
   a. set up in the act;
   b. listed in a positive and exhaustive way;
   c. put into effect in a decree;
5. all health care activities outside the domain controlled by the State must be provided without authorisation;
6. the system based on the necessity to require an authorisation for specific activities must be favoured. However, the system based on the risks of practise (a licence being necessary to practise all dangerous activities) is also valuable, particularly because it guarantees the fundamental liberalisation of medical activities;
7. cantons should ensure that both the training and the scope of practice of 'alternative' medicines be in accordance;
8. cantons should apply the rules concerning the licensing to practise of nationals, also to those foreign health care providers who provide their services during short-term periods, i.e. 90 days per year.

The Conference of Directors of Health of Central Switzerland does not endorse the banning of alternative medicines no their liberalisation. It has instead proposed that the Confederation or the CCDHA should regulate the training of two to five widely used alternative techniques, in particular those that may be considered as a whole system (complete diagnosis and treatment), and those benefiting from a recognised training.[619]

Furthermore, the Conference also recognised that the demand from physicians to include some alternative medicines within the basic social insurance, the uneven practice of cantons regarding the training and licensing of alternative medicines, the threat of a slowing of therapeutic progress, the trend to professionalism in this field, and an excellent cost-effectiveness ratio were serious arguments supporting the recognition and regulation of alternative medicines.[620]

619 Conférence des Directeurs Cantonaux des Affaires Sanitaires (I), *op. cit.*: 36.

620 Conférence des Directeurs Cantonaux des Affaires Sanitaires (I), *op. cit.*: 36.

4.3.6.2 United States

Bibliography

See: ABBOTT A., *The system of professions: An essay on the division of expert labor*, University of Chicago Press, 1988, Chicago: 20–23; AMERICAN CHIROPRACTIC ASSOCIATION, *Alternative medicine: Hearing before the subcommittee on Labor, Health, and Human Services, and Education and Related Agencies of the Senate Committee on Appropriations*, American Chiropractic Association, 103d Congress, 1st. Sess. 153; AMERICAN MEDICAL ASSOCIATION, *Principles of medial ethics*, American Medical Association, Chicago, 1956, chap. 3.1.; ANDREWS L. B., *The shadow health care system: Regulation of alternative health care providers*, in: Houston Law Review, 1996, vol. 32: 1273–1317; BERG R., *Note, HMO exclusion of chiropractors*, in: S. Cal. L. Rev., 1993, vol. 66: 807–38; BOOZANG K. M. (I), *Western medicine opens the door to alternative medicine*, in: American Journal of Medicine, 1998, vol. 24, n° 2/3: 185–212; BOOZANG K. M. (II), *Is the alternative medicine? Managed care apparently thinks so*, in: Connecticut Law Review, Winter 2000, vol. 32: 567–69; BOOZANG K. M. (III), *National policy on CAM: The White House Commission report*, in: The Journal of Law, Medicine and Ethics, 2003, vol. 31, n° 2: 251–61; CALLENDER A., *Buckeye chiropractic: Turbulence in a limited branch of medicine, 1915–1975*, in: Chiropract. Hist., Dec. 1995., vol. 15, n° 2: 1532–34; CHAPMAN-SMITH D. A., *Legislative approaches to the regulation of the chiropractic profession*, in: Journal of the Canadian Chiropractic Association, June 1996, vol. 40, n° 2: 108–14; COHEN M. H. (I), *Complementary and alternative medicine – Legal boundaries and regulatory perspectives*, The Johns Hopkins University Press, 1998, London & Oxford; COHEN M. H. (II), *Holistic health care: Including alternative and alternative medicine in insurance and regulatory schemes*, in: Arizona Law Review, Spring 1996, vol. 38: 85–90; DANNE W. H., *Acupuncture as illegal practice of medicine*, in: A.L.R.3d, 1977–1998, vol. 72: 1257ss; DRECHSLER C. T., *Physicians, surgeons and other healers*, in: American Jurisprudence, 2nd edition, April 1996: § 4; FURROW B. R. (co-authors: GREANEY T. L., JOST T., SCHWARTZ R. L.) (I), *Health law*, West Publishing, 1995, St Paul; GILHOOLEY M., *Herbal remedies and dietary supplements: The boundaries of drug claims and freedom of choice*, in: Florida Law Review, 1997, vol. 49: 663ss; GREANEY T. L., *Public licensure, private certification, and credentialing of medical professionals: an antitrust perspective*, in: JOST T. S., *Regulation of the healthcare professions*, Health Administration Press, 1996, Chicago: 149–68; HALL M., *Institutional control of physician behaviour: Legal barriers to health care cost containment*, in: U. Pa. L. Rev., 1988, vol. 137, n° 80: 453; HOFFMEYER P., *Etats-Unis: Appel pour une réglementation plus stricte des traitements à base de plantes*, in: Médecine et Hygiène, 1998, vol. 56, n° 225: 1861; JACKSON R. B., *"Empyricism" in Kansas: Chiropractic's legal struggle, 1906–1915*, in: J. Manipulative Physiol. Ther., 1996 Feb., vol. 19, n° 2: 113–17; JOSEFEK K. J., *Alternative medicine's roadmap to mainstream*, in: American Journal of Law and Medicine, 2000, vol. 26: 295–310; JOST T. S. (II), *Introduction – Regulation of the health care professions*, in: JOST T. S., *Regulation of the healthcare professions*, Health

Administration Press, 1996, Chicago: 7ss; JOST T. S. (III), *Oversight of the competence of healthcare professionals*, in: JOST T. S., *Regulation of the healthcare professions*, Health Administration Press, 1996, Chicago: 17–44; LAMM L. C. (co-authors: WEGNER, E., COLLORD, D.), *Chiropractic scope of practice: What the law allows – update 1993*, in: J. Manipulative Physiol. Ther., Jan. 1995, vol. 18, n° 1: 16–20; LAY B. F., *Healer-patient privilege: Extending the physician-patient privilege to alternative health practitioners in California*, in: Hastings Law Journal, March 1997: 633–66; MCRAE G., *A critical overview of U.S. acupuncture regulation*, in: Journal of Health Politics, Policy and Law, 1982, vol. 7, n° 1: 163–96; MARWICK C., *Alterations are ahead at the OAM*, in: JAMA, 1998, vol. 280, n° 18: 1553–54; REHM W. S., *Kansas coconuts: Legalising chiropractic in the first State, 1910–1915*, in: Chiropractic. Hist., Dec 1995, vol. 15, n° 2: 43–50; ROSS-LEE B. (co-authors: KISS L. E., WEISER M. A.), *The application of antitrust laws to the healthcare industry*, in: Journal of the American Osteopathic Association, Aug 1995, vol. 95, n° 8: 480–86; SAGE W. M. (co-author: AIKEN L. H.), *Regulating interdisciplinary practice*, in: JOST T. S., *Regulation of the healthcare professions*, Health Administration Press, 1996, Chicago: 72–73, 79; SALE D. M., Overview of legislative developments concerning alternative health care in the United States, 1995; SHEKELLE P. G., *What role for chiropractic in health care?*, in: The New England Journal of Medicine, 1998, vol. 339: 1074–75; STARR P., *The social transformation of american medicine*, Basic Books, 1982; STEPNO E. M., *Acupuncture – Stricter standards for those performing acupuncture*, in: M. George L. Rev., 1998, vol. 29: 411–15; WARDWELL W. I., *Alternative medicine in the United States*, in: Social Science and Medicine, 1994, vol. 38, n° 8: 1061–68; WHITE HOUSE COMMISSION ON COMPLEMENTARY AND ALTERNATIVE MEDICINE POLICY, *Final report*, March 2002, available at http://www.whccamp.hhs.gov/pdfs/fr2002_document.pdf, accessed Feb. 1 2005; YESSIAN M. R. (co-author: GREENLEAF M.), *The ebb and flow of federal initiatives to regulate healthcare professionals*, in: JOST T. S., *Regulation of the healthcare professions*, Health Administration Press, 1996, Chicago: 169–98.

A. Historical evolution of the licensing to practise

Until the twentieth century, the practice of medicine in the American society was not the monopoly of physicians only. There were, in fact three spheres of practice, roughly equal in importance – the practise of domestic household medicine,[621] the practise of medicine by physicians, and the practise of medicine by lay practitioners. As physicians failed in their efforts to establish themselves as an exclusive and privileged profession due to popular resistance, lay practitioners were able to offer their services in an unregulated environment.[622, 623]

621 At that time, the family was the natural centre of most medical care. Books regarding domestic medicine were widespread and people mistrusted hospitals as well as physicians (STARR P., *op. cit.*: 32–37, 145–180).

During this period, physicians were not highly regarded.[624] To give more substance to the profession, physicians started a movement toward professionalism, which found expression in the creation of medical societies (New Jersey 1766), medical schools (Philadelphia 1765)[625] and licensure (New York 1760).[626] With the emergence of medical societies,[627] medical schools began to proliferate and to gain prestige.[628] Since independence, the legislature has extended the licensing authority to both medical schools and licensing boards, thereby creating a dual system. However, these licensing powers were ultimately ineffective.[629]

622 Starr writes that "Americans came to regard all those who practised medicine as doctors, abandoning the linguistic forms that reflected traditional class distinctions in medical practice" (STARR P., *op. cit.*: 39).

623 COHEN M. H. (I), *op. cit.*: 15; STARR P., *op. cit.*: 30–32, 39, 47, 54.

624 Concerning this period, Beck states that "many ignorant and unskilful persons presume to practise physic and surgery within the city and the county of New York to the detriment and hazard of the lives and limbs of the citizens thereof", in: COHEN M. H. (I), *op. cit.*: 16. Furthermore, at that time, conflicts between physicians who promoted their own theories and condemned those of rivals were frequent.

625 For more details regarding the development of medical schools, see STARR, *op. cit.*: 112–27.

626 New York was one of the earliest colonies to establish medical licensure. In 1760, its legislature passed an act regulating the practice of physic and surgery. The rationale for this statute was expressed in terms of consumer protection and it prohibited the practice as a physician or surgeon by any person who had not been examined, approved and admitted by certain government officials. If approved, the candidate received a licence to practise.

The statute was updated in 1792. A supplementary condition was added, which required a period of study lasting for two to three years with a "reputable physician".

In 1797, a new act was adopted, which applied to the entire state, and which required applicants to show evidence of having studied or having been apprenticed with a reputable physician or surgeon for four years.

In 1806, a law was passed to incorporate the medical societies for the purpose of regulating the practice of physic and surgery, although a practitioner could be licensed upon the filing of proof of graduation from a college of medicine. One should note that until 1844 the licensing laws were weakly enforced.

627 By 1830, nearly every state in the Union had a medical society (COHEN M. H. (I), *op. cit.*: 17).

628 There were 42 schools in 1850, and more than 400 in 1900.

629 This was the result of lobbying by the medical societies to obtain a delegation of the licensing authority from states, and by medical schools seeking the licensing of graduates without further any examination.

For further details, see COHEN M. H. (I), *op. cit.*: 15–17; STARR P., *op. cit.*: 39–46.

In this context, alternative medicines were not merely a substitute for professional medicine; they became an active rival with a coherent structure of its own and the willingness of State legislatures to vote down, at least until the 1850s, medical licensure strengthened their position.[630, 631]

The revolt against "heroic medicine",[632] which dominated American medical practice during the first half of the nineteenth century gave rise to the emergence of alternatives. The two major attacks on heroic medicine came from Thomsonism[633] and homeopathy. Thomsonism was essentially a protest against the dominant order and its therapeutic and political ideas. Samuel Thomson attacked heroic medicine and advised patients to depend more upon themselves and less upon doctors.[634] His followers organised local infirmaries and founded Thomsonian societies in an attempt to create a professional monopoly. In retaliation, regular physicians attempted to discredit Thomsonism and to sue its followers for illegal practice. Then, Thomsonism waned and eclectic physicians[635] grew in favour.[636]

The second movement, homeopathy, was imported from Germany. As the technique gained success and supporters, regular physicians and, in particular, the American Medical Association (AMA) took steps not only to purge the homeopaths from their ranks but also to turn public opinion against homeopathy.[637] In response, homeopaths created the Homeopathic Medical College of Pennsylvania. However, by the end of the nineteenth century, homeopaths were not any longer the major competitors of allopathic practitioners.[638]

630 This period was characterised by a fight against privileges and monopolies, which resulted in the decline of licensing in law and medicine (Starr P., *op. cit.*: 57).

631 Cohen M. H. (I), *op. cit.*: 15; Starr P., *op. cit.*: 47–54.

632 It relied on bloodletting, purgatives, emetics and blistering.

633 The system was based on existing American botanical tradition, and included the theory that all bodies were composed of four elements: earth, air, fire and water.

634 Thomson wrote a book in 1832, entitled *New Guide to Health*, which contained a complete system of practice, including a description of vegetables and directions for preparing and administering them.

635 Eclectics were native American doctors, herb doctors and natural bonesetters.

636 Cohen M. H. (I), *op. cit.*: 18–19; Starr P., *op. cit.*: 47–54; Wardwell W. I., *op. cit.*: 1061.

637 This included lawsuits, expulsion from medical societies and attacks in the medical literature. They also organised public campaigns promoting improved medical education, scientific rigor and protection against charlatans. The AMA even prohibited regular physicians from consulting with "irregular" practitioners.

638 Starr recalls that "the myth persists today that homeopaths and herbal doctors were suppressed by the dominant allopathic profession. Yet the sequence of events

While the homeopaths and Thomsonians began to decline, new groups emerged. Two of these groups were mechanistic in conception (osteopathy and chiropractic), while the third group was spiritual (Christian Science).[639] These movements remained independent and survived on their own. During the same period, new and more rigid licensing acts concerning the practice of medicine were adopted in several US States supported not only by the States themselves but also by the courts, including even the Supreme Court.[640, 641]

At the end of the nineteenth century, the decline of homeopathy combined with the use of licensing acts to control and restrict entry into the profession enabled regular physicians to dominate the healing arts.[642] Three additional factors consolidated the position of regular physicians. First,

---

suggests otherwise. Both the homeopaths and Eclectics won a share in the legal privileges of the profession. Only afterward did they lose their popularity. [...] Homeopathy had one foot in modern medicine, the other in pre-scientific mysticism; this became an increasingly untenable position. While regular medicine was producing important and demonstrable scientific advances, homeopathy generated no new discoveries." And further, homeopaths "disappeared only after they were licensed" (STARR P., *op. cit.*: 107–08, 229).

For further details, see COHEN M. H. (I), *op. cit.*: 17–19; FURROW B. R. (I), *op. cit.*: 65; STARR P., *op. cit.*: 47–54, 93–112; WARDWELL W. I., *op. cit.*: 1061.

639 This movement, founded by Mary Baker Eddy in Boston, denied the reality of matter, and claimed that disease was purely a function of mind and spirit.

640 A crucial test of the legitimacy of licensure was passed in 1888. In *Dent v. West Virginia* (1888), an Eclectic physician had been convicted and fined under an 1882 West Virginia statute requiring a physician to hold a degree from a reputable medical college. The court stated that reliance had to be placed on the assurance given by a license and therefore reasonable considerations might prompt a state to exclude people without licences from practising medicine. The Supreme Court upheld Dent's conviction for practising medicine unlawfully, stating that the police power includes "prescribing all such regulations as, in its judgement, will secure or tend to secure [...] (the public) against the consequences of ignorance and incapacity as well as deception and fraud". See also *Hawker v. New York* (1898).

According to Cohen, "The late nineteenth century's political and economic establishment of biomedical dominance drove the regulatory paradigm toward a monopolistic perspective on health care licensure" (COHEN M. H. (I), *op. cit.*: 21).

641 COHEN M. H. (I), *op. cit.*: 17–19; STARR P., *op. cit.*: 42, 47–54, 93–112.

642 The states enacted licensure requirements in the 1870s and 1880s. The AMA began a campaign to establish standards for medical education, and to ensure that only graduates of medical schools meeting those standards were allowed to sit for state licensing examinations (FURROW B. R. (I), *op. cit.*: 58–59).

was the rise of scientific medicine.[643] Second, was the growing power of the AMA as the prominent voice of American medicine.[644]

At the beginning of the twentieth century, the AMA undertook an intensive reorganisation, with the purpose of becoming an institution "whose power to influence public sentiment will be almost unlimited, and whose requests for desirable legislation will everywhere be met with the respect which the politician always has for organised votes".[645] In 1903, the AMA invited homeopaths to join the Association. However, in order to join, homeopaths would have had to renounce their connection with homeopathic institutions and practices.[646] The result was a division among homeopaths.[647]

The third factor was a report by Abraham Flexner. The report exposed the weakness of medical schools and urged for a reorganisation of medical faculties.[648] A consequence of the report was that university medical schools and the AMA Council on Medical Education co-operated with State licensing boards to raise standards.[649] After the report was published, foundations supported only those schools that had been approved by the AMA. In particular, the Flexner report advised denying philanthropical funds to homeopathic schools. Hence, homeopathic schools, such as existed in Boston, New York, and Philadelphia, were gradually converted into regular medical schools.[650]

643 Discoveries included the use of anaesthesia (1842) and the introduction of successful methods for disinfecting (1865–97). They also enabled physicians to systematise the diagnosis and to quantify a patient's condition.

644 ABBOTT A., *op. cit.*: 20–21; COHEN M. H. (I), *op. cit.*: 19–20; FURROW B. R. (I), *op. cit.*: 58–59; STARR P., *op. cit.*: 103–23.

645 COULTER, *Divided Legacy*, in: JAMA, vol. 36, n° 525: 430.

646 This change of attitude displayed by the AMA, i.e. to be more tolerant toward sectarism, was part of a more general effort to unify and strengthen the profession.

647 COHEN M. H. (I), *op. cit.*: 19–20; FURROW B. R. (I), *op. cit.*: 58–59; STARR P., *op. cit.*: 103–23.

648 Nursing had its own "Flexner report" in the Goldmark Report and the report of the Committee of the Grading of Nursing Schools, both produced in the 1920s. For more details regarding the evolution of licensing for nursing, see FURROW B. R. (I), *op. cit.*: 58–59.

649 Boards took into consideration the recommendations of the AMA council when deciding to recognise diplomas. The council established a three-tier rating system for schools. Schools fully approved were rated A. Class B consisted of schools that were imperfect, but redeemable. States generally denied recognition to institutions designated class C. They were considered beyond salvage and forced out of existence.

650 COHEN M. H. (I), *op. cit.*: 19–20; FURROW B. R. (I), *op. cit.*: 58–59; STARR P., *op. cit.*: 103–23.

The new system shaped by the AMA greatly increased the homogeneity and cohesiveness of the classic medical profession.[651] However, physicians could not prevent rival practitioners from winning legal protection and staying in business. Osteopaths and chiropractors obtained licensing acts in nearly every State and chiropractors practised openly even in those states where they had not gained statutory approval. However, although successful in winning licensing privileges,[652] they were usually unable to win access to hospitals or the right to prescribe drugs.[653] Furthermore, where alternative practitioners could not obtain a special status on their own, courts interpreted broadly and inclusively the notion of medical practice. For example, in *Smith v. People*, an individual who cured disease by the laying on of hands was convicted for practising medicine without a licence because the medical practice act, "as a protection to public health", should be construed liberally, including "the practice of the healing arts commercially, regardless of the curative agency employed".[654] Unlike the homeopaths in the mid-nineteenth century, they did not represent a serious challenge to the regular medical profession, which by the end of the 1920s, had succeeded in resolving the most difficult problems confronting it.[655, 656]

651 The period of training was extended, hospitals internships helped to instil common values, to standardise the education and to discourage sectarian divisions. Slowly, physicians succeeded in controlling their own numbers, the cost of education increased, increasing requirements limited the entry into universities, and policies of discrimination against Jews, women and blacks appeared.

652 For a historical study regarding the legalisation of chiropractic, see Callender A., *op. cit.*: 1532–34; Jackson, *op. cit.*: 113–17; Rehm W. S., *op. cit.*: 43–50.

653 For further details regarding the coverage of alternative medicines within the US, see chap. 5.3.5.15.

654 The court added that "one form of examination is required of all sorts of healers. All applicants must be examined in anatomy, physiology, chemistry, symptomatology, toxicology, pathology, surgery and obstetrics" (*Smith v. People*, 117 P. 612, 615 (Colo. 1911)).

655 Indeed, it had put aside sectarian divisions; won stronger licensing laws; transformed hospitals, drug manufacturers, and public health into support; and checked the entry of corporations and mutual societies into the health services. Furthermore, it succeeded in controlling the development of technology, organisational forms, and the division of labour.

656 Cohen M. H. (I), *op. cit.*: 22; Starr P., *op. cit.*: 123–27, 223, 232.

Following World War II, various acts set forth the rights and privileges of health professionals. Federal and State acts governing healthcare professions started to emerge,[657] regulating all the practice of medicine.[658]

Later court rulings reinforced the states' broad legal definition of the practice of medicine,[659] illustrated by decisions regarding naturopaths,[660] practitioners of mental suggestion,[661] hypnotism,[662] massage, nutritional service, and even ear piercing.[663] For its part, the AMA continued to denounce competing modalities,[664] such as osteopathy or chiropractic.[665]

During the 1970s, alternative medicines, in a revival of a therapeutic counterculture with political issues, gained clientele and respectability primarily because they were part of a broader cultural and political movement. In this respect, Starr points out that

657 This included state licensure, certification, and registration laws that determined the scope of practice; unauthorised practice statutes enforced by criminal penalties or professional discipline; laws determining the structure and control of professional disciplinary authority; antitrust statutes and government enforcement policies; professional liability and judicial decisions; health education funding laws; etc.

658 Sage W. M., *op. cit.*: 72–73.

659 According to Cohen "such broad enforcement and interpretation of medical practice acts reflects a biomedically oriented perspective. This also finds expression in judicial interpretation of scope-of-practice rules, which blur the line between services appropriate to the holistic profession and unlicensed medical diagnosis and treatment." (Cohen M. H. (I), *op. cit.*: 22).

660 In states where they have not been licensed, naturopaths have been prosecuted for the unlicensed practice of medicine (see *Hitchcock v. State*, 131 A.2d 714 (Md. 1957)).

661 See State *ex rel. Bierring v. Robinson*, 19 N.W.2d 214 (Iowa 1945) (faith healer's conviction for practising medicine illegally).

662 See *People v. Cantor*, 18 Cal. Rptr. 363 (Col. Aool Dep'r Super. Ct. 1961) (unlawful practice of medicine when defendant used hypnosis and laid hands).

663 Certain authors consider that these prosecutions suggest "how far courts are willing to go in supporting the medical profession's desire to protect its domain" (Hall M., *op. cit.*: 453).

664 In 1955, the AMA declared osteopathy to be a "cultist healing" and the AMA's 1956 Principles of Medical Ethics stated that "all voluntarily associated activities with cultists are unethical". The AMA even admonished physicians to adhere to medical doctrine, warning that "the physician who maintains professional relations with cult practitioners would seem to exhibit a lack of faith in the correctness and efficacy of scientific medicine" (American Medical Association, *op. cit.*).

665 Andrews L. B., *op. cit.*: 1291–94; Cohen M. H. (I), *op. cit.*: 21–22.

> much of the new counterculture went under the rubric "holistic medicine" and presented itself as a human alternative to an overly technical, disease-oriented, impersonal medical system. Just as nineteenth-century heroic medicine had given rise to therapeutic dissent, so did twentieth-century technological medicine. And just as nineteenth-century critics called for a democratisation of medical knowledge, so did the new advocates of self-care.[666]

Until the 1980's, the AMA attempted many times to eliminate alternative practitioners. The willingness of the AMA to continue to preserve a professional monopoly is illustrated in the case, *Wilk v. American Medical Association.*[667] Here, chiropractors brought an antitrust action[668] against the AMA alleging a conspiracy to eliminate the chiropractic profession.[669] The court decided in favour of the chiropractors and stated that the AMA had failed to establish that its alleged concern for scientific methods in patient care was objectively reasonable or that it had justified its "nationwide conspiracy to eliminate a licensed profession". Following the decision, the AMA changed its position, and held that it was ethical for a physician to associate professionally with a chiropractor. As a result, chiropractors now have the right to consult professionally with MDs, to use hospital diagnostic facilities, to apply for appointment to hospital staffs for the purpose of co-admitting patients, to administer chiropractic treatments, and to order tests, diets and physical therapy. Today, at least 60 hospitals or ambulatory surgical centres now collaborate with chiropractic colleges in research on problems related to spinal pathology and spinal manipulative techniques. However, as Andrews notes "despite this visible victory of alternative providers against the AMA, the more common variety of

666 BOOZANG K. M. (I), *op. cit.*: 199; STARR P., *op. cit.*: 392. For an historical study regarding the emergence of acupuncture in the United States, see MCRAE G., *op. cit.*: 163–96.

667 *Wilk v. American Medical Ass'n*, 719 F.2d 207 (7th Cir. 1983), *cert. denied*, 467 U.S. 1210 (1984), *on remand*, 671 F. Supp. 1465 (N.D: Ill. 1987) *aff'd*, 895 F.2d 352 (7th Cir. 1990).

668 For a presentation of antitrust laws, see FURROW B. R. (I), *op. cit.*: 364–497; GREANEY T. L., *op. cit.*: 149–68.

669 The appellate court noted that the AMA had tried to "destroy a competitor, namely chiropractic" by actions designed "to prevent medical physicians from teaching at chiropractic colleges or engaging in any joint research and to prevent any cooperation between the two groups in the delivery of heath care services" (idem at 356).

antitrust suits against physicians and hospitals are often difficult for alternative providers to win".[670, 671]

B. General remarks

Introduction

Hence, as in Switzerland, there have been several approaches towards alternative medicines ranging from tolerance to hostility and equally the US shares Switzerland's lack of federal regulation for alternative professions. The solutions vary from almost unlimited freedom to practice as in Minnesota to a regulated environment like in Washington which provides licensure, registration, or exemption for several categories of alternative practitioners, based on their education.[672, 673]

Practical and legal barriers remain an obstacle in the US[674] to the widespread practice of alternative medicines despite the gains made by some alternative professions in attaining licensing privileges over the past century. These barriers have often been erected as a result of lobbying from physicians.[675, 676]

670 Andrews L. B., *op. cit.*: 1293. The author adds that "Hospitals that deny admitting privileges to nurses anaesthetists, midwifes, or other allied health professionals can often fend off an antitrust action based on S1 of the Sherman Act by claiming that they do not have sufficient market power to restrain trade or that the exclusion is pro-competitive because it allows them to attract consumers with a claim of high quality service due to all-physician staff" (idem).

671 Andrews L. B., *op. cit.*: 1291–96; Boozang K. M. (I), *op. cit.*: 196–97; Cohen M. H. (I), *op. cit.*: 20; Ross-Lee B., *op. cit.*: 480–86; Sage W. M., *op. cit.*: 79; Wardwell W. I., *op. cit.*: 1066.

672 White House Commission on Complementary and Alternative Medicine Policy, *op. cit.*: 91.

673 For recent developments regarding the difficulities of setting up federal regulation in the US, see Yessian M. R. (co-author: Greenleaf M.), *op. cit.* 169–98. See also Jost T. S. (II), *op. cit.*: 7ss.

674 Such as laws regulating the unauthorised practice of medicine or regulations that limit the alternative practitioners' power to prescribe.
Other barriers are limitations on direct reimbursement to alternative practitioners, practices excluding them from admitting privileges at health care institutions, or the inability to obtain malpractice insurance.

675 According to Andrews, "In many instances, the barriers to the use of alternative providers have been erected due to the pressures from their main competitors, physicians. Physicians convince legislatures to restrict the scopes of practice of other providers and pressure prosecutors to bring criminal actions against non physician providers. Physician groups have tried to eliminate the practice of various

This chapter shall briefly present the various licensing practices for alternative medicines in the US,[677] outlining first some general elements followed by a consideration of specific alternative modalities. Finally, some topical areas currently of interest in this area shall be addressed including the treatment of unprofessional and unauthorised practice, medical freedom acts and general federal developments.

Police power rationale

States are authorised to decide who may practise medicine and to establish licensing boards that admit or exclude persons from practice under their police power to protect citizen's health, safety and welfare.[678] Licensing statutes regulate entry into the licensed professions, disciplinary actions and the delivery of health care services by unlicensed persons.[679] Boards dominated by the regulated professions implement the statutes.[680] Other private quasi-regulatory processes of quality control by the professions are

---

alternative health care providers including acupuncturists, chiropractors, homeopaths, midwives, and naturopaths." (ANDREWS L. B., *op. cit.*: 1288–89).

676 ANDREWS L. B., *op. cit.*: 1287–99; BOOZANG K. M. (I), *op. cit.*: 186; JOSEFEK K. J., *op. cit.*: 301–02, 304ss.

677 As it was not possible to present the current position in all 50 US states, it was decided to focus on the regulation of specific alternative techniques in the US generally.

678 The states' regulation of health care practitioners finds authority in the Tenth Amendment to the United States Constitution. The Amendment provides that powers not delegated to the federal government by the Constitution, nor prohibited by it to the states, are reserved to the states. Among these is the "police power", i.e. the power to protect the health, safety and welfare of citizens, which includes the power to require a licence for the practice of healing arts, and to control practitioners through regulatory and disciplinary schemes.

679 The aim of such regulation is to prevent the indiscriminate practice of the healing arts by "unskilled and unlicensed practitioners" and to protect the public from "the menace of the ignorant, the unprepared, the quacks and the fakers" (*People v. Amber*, 349 N.Y.S.2d 604. 612 (Sup. Ct. 1973); *People v. Steinberg*, 73 N.Y.S.2d 475 (Mag. Ct. 1947)).

680 The licensing of health professions in the United States is often described as a system of professional self-regulation. For a criticism of the licensure authorities, see JOST T. S. (III), *op. cit.*: 17–44.

certification by voluntary professional boards and the credentialing system for clinical staff privileges within hospitals and other institutions.[681, 682]

Courts have upheld the state's use of the police power to regulate health care providers against free exercise, due process and patients. In *Dent v. West Virginia*, a physician challenged a state statute requiring him to obtain a diploma from the State Board of Health. The Board refused Dent a certificate, claiming that the medical college he had attended was not reputable.[683] In a further case *(State v. Hinze)*, the court sentenced a pharmacist using the title "doctor" (he held a degree in naturopathy from a Canadian college), for giving seminars on naturopathy and homeopathy, and for suggesting specific remedies. The court rejected the claim that the First Amendment right to freedom of speech protected him.[684, 685]

Entry requirements

Licensure statutes usually set minimum requirements and qualifications for each of the licensed health professions. Typical conditions include graduation from an approved educational program, acceptable performance on a standardised examination, and a review of personal history.[686]

681 According to Cohen "today, the practice of medicine is tightly controlled by state medical practice acts, licensing boards and disciplinary committees. State medical boards have extensive authority over physician activity, including, in many states, the authority to punish 'any departure from, or the failure to conform to, the standards of acceptable and prevailing medical practice... irrespective of whether or not a patient is injured thereby'. Similarly, state medical practice acts authorize prosecution of the unlicensed practice of 'medicine', including such acts as 'diagnosis', 'prescription', 'operation' and 'treatment' within the purview of medical practice. Non-medical health care professionals, such as nurses, physical therapists, and chiropractors, have limited licensure, authorising them to perform specific functions such as supportive or restorative care under physician supervision, or detecting and correcting structural imbalances in the spine." (COHEN M. H. (II), *op. cit.*: 85).

682 COHEN M. H. (I), *op. cit.*: 24; COHEN M. H. (II), *op. cit.*: 87; FURROW B. R. (I), *op. cit.*: 56–58.

683 *Dent v. West Virginia*, 129 U.S. 114 (1888).
See also *Jacobson v. Massachusetts*, 197 U.S. 11 (1905) (state's right to order compulsory vaccination for public school children); *Washington v. Harper*, 194 U.S. 210 (1990) (state's interest in maintaining the safety and security of its prisons justified forced medication of inmates). See also *Reynolds v. McNichols*, 488 F.2d 1378, 1382 (10th Cir. 1979)).

684 *State v. Hinze*, 441 N.W.2d 593, (Neb. 1989).

685 COHEN M. H. (I), *op. cit.*: 25.

686 For a criticism of entry requirements, see FURROW B. R. (I), *op. cit.*: 57.

In order to practise chiropractic, for example, regulations will usually require graduation from an accredited educational program as a prerequisite for licensure.[687]

C. The position of specific alternative medicines

Introduction

This section presents an overview of state legislation for four well-known alternative medicines, which are regulated by provider practice acts in several jurisdictions. These alternative medicines are acupuncture, chiropractic, homeopathy and naturopathy.[688]

There are several trends to be noted in the licensing of alternative therapies:[689]

1. many states have chosen mandatory licensing schemes for alternative practitioners along the lines of the medical practice acts;[690]

687 CHAPMAN-SMITH D. A., *op. cit.*: 113.

688 Osteopathy has not been included in this overview. As chiropractic, this technique has gained a certain acknowledgement and is incorporated into the mainstream health care. The American Osteopathy Association reports that osteopathy is currently allowed in all 50 states and in the District of Columbia. One of the significant legislative issues in the osteopathic field regards the removal of barriers to membership by osteopaths on the medical staff of hospitals and other health care facilities and programs. See Iowa Code Ann. § 135B.7 (Supp. 1994), which forbids a hospital from denying clinical privileges to an osteopath or an osteopathic surgeon solely by reason of the license held by the osteopath or the school or institution in which the practitioner received training, whether the medical schooling or postgraduate training is accredited by an organisation recognised by the Council on Postsecondary Education or an accrediting group recognized by the U.S. Department of Education. See also Calif. Bus. & Prof. Code § 2453 (Supp. 1994); Colo. Rev. Stat. § 12-36-129(5) (1991); and Ohio Rev. Code Ann. § 3701.351(B) (1992) (SALE D. M., *op. cit.*: iii, 53–54).
For an overview of the regulation of other alternative techniques in the US such as acupressure, Alexander technique, aromatherapy, art therapy, bioenergetics, biofeedback, bodywork, chelation, dance therapy, drugless healing, Feldenkrais, Hellerwork, herbology, holistic healing, hydrotherapy, hypnotherapy, music therapy, naprapathy, oriental medicine, polarity therapy, reflexology, reiki, rolfing, shiatsu, spiritual healing, touch therapy and Trager, see COHEN M. H. (I), *op. cit.*: 41–46; SALE D. M., *op. cit.*: 15–33.

689 COHEN M. H. (I), *op. cit.*: 36–38; FURROW B. R. (I), *op. cit.*: 63–64.

690 E.g., the Alaska acupuncture licensing statute provides that a licence is compulsory to provide acupuncture (Alaska Stat. Ann. § 08.06.101); Rhode Island and Washington provide that only licensed massage therapists are allow to practise massage therapy (R.I. Gen. Laws § 23-20.8-3 (a); Wash. Rev. Code § 18.108.030 (1));

2. State acts frequently establish a professional board to approve educational institutions, clinical programs and examinations as a basis for licensure;[691]
3. professional accreditation as a basis for licensure has developed in widespread professions such as acupuncture, chiropractic, massage therapy, and naturopathy;[692]
4. internal accreditation or certification may become the basis for upgrading professional status within an existing licensed profession;[693]
5. in a few instances, the state legitimises the nonconforming practice but requires that patients sign standard disclosure and consent forms.[694]

Acupuncture

Introduction

The Chinese art of acupuncture is regulated by practice acts at least in 26 States and in the District of Columbia. Even though the technique was already well-known, its use exploded during the 1970's. As a consequence, most states enacted acupuncture acts in the 1970's and 1980's.[695]

Texas has a mandatory registration scheme, which provides that practitioners of massage therapy must register with the state (registration requires the presentation before a regulatory board of satisfactory evidence of training) (Tex. Rev. Civ. Stat. Ann. art. 4512k, § 2).

691 See Ariz. Rev. Stat. §§ 32-1522 through 32-1525 (naturopathy).

692 E.g., Alaska's naturopathic licensing statute requires that the applicant (1) has graduated from a four-year naturopathic school accredited by the Council on Naturopathic Medical Education; and (2) has passed the Naturopathic Physicians Licensing Examination (Alaska Stat. Ann. § 08.06.030 (a) (3)–(4)).

693 E.g., the National Commission for the Certification of Acupuncturists has proposed licensed acupuncturists additional certification in Chinese herbology; the American Massage Therapy Association and other massage therapy organisations has created the National Certification Board for Therapeutic massage and Bodywork which has established a national certification examination. Several states have adopted the examination as a requirement for licensure.
Cohen notes that "alternative practitioners seeking licensure often create state-accredited educational institutions, professional organisations, and national professional accrediting bodies and examination (e.g. acupuncture schools are accredited by the National Accreditation Commission for Schools and Colleges of Acupuncture and Oriental Medicine, etc.), which then offer convenient an inexpensive bases for state licensure." (COHEN M. H. (I), *op. cit.*: 36–37).

694 See *Clark v. Department of Professional Regulation*, 463 So.2d 328 (Fla. App. 1985).

695 For more information regarding early acupuncture legislation in the United States, see MCRAE G., *op. cit.*: 163–96.

However, there has also been legislative activity in recent years with the adoption of practice acts in several States such as Iowa, Texas and North Carolina in 1993. In states where such practice of acupuncture acts have not been enacted, the use of this technique is deemed to be the practice of medicine and rights to practise the technique are limited to designated medical providers or granted to non-physician acupuncturists under medical supervision.[696]

Scope of practice

The statutory definition of acupuncture varies. However, the technique is frequently described as the stimulation of precise points on or near the surface of the human body by the insertion of needles to treat some diseases or dysfunctions of the body, to normalize physiological functions, or to prevent or modify the perception of pain.[697] Several statutes define acupuncture on the basis of the traditional Chinese or Oriental medicine system of health care providing. Esoteric concepts are sometimes added.[698, 699]

State legislations usually permit acupuncturists to use a wide variety of adjunctive therapies during the acupuncture treatment.[700]

696 Cohen M. H. (I), *op. cit.*: 43; Danne W., *op. cit.*: 1257–58; Sale D. M., *op. cit.*: 1.
For recent developments regarding the use of acupuncture constituting the unlawful practice of medicine, see Danne W., *op. cit.*: 1257ss.

697 See Alaska Stat. Ann. § 08.06.190(1) (1991); Cal. Bus. and Prof. § 1937 (b) (West 1990); D.C. Code Ann. § 2.3301.2(1) (1994); Pa. Stat. Ann. tit. 63, § 1802 (Purdon Supp. 1993); Utah Code Ann. § 58-2-58 (1) (Supp. 1993).

698 E.g. the energetic quality of acupuncture and its utility in "controlling and regulating the flow and balance of energy in the body" or "normalizing energetic physiological function" (see Hawaii Rev. Stat. § 436 E-2 (1985); Md. Health Occ. Code Ann. § 1A-101 (1) (Supp 1994); Nev. Rev. Stat. § 634A 020 (1) (1991); N.M. Stat. Ann. § 61-14A-3A (1993).

699 Cohen M. H. (I), *op. cit.*: 43–44; Sale D. M., *op. cit.*: 1.

700 The permitted therapies vary from state to state. The following techniques are an illustration of the broad range of supplementary techniques authorized under current law: moxibustion; cupping; mechanical, thermal, electrical, and electromagnetic treatment; dietary guidelines; therapeutic exercise; Oriental or therapeutic massage; acupressure; breathing techniques; herbs, vitamins, minerals, and drugless substances; Oriental medical therapies; dermal friction technique; infra-red; sono-acupuncture; laser-puncture; point injection therapy or lifestyle counselling.

Administrative structure

States with an acupuncture practice act may have different administrative structures. Some have established acupuncture boards composed principally of non-physician acupuncturists who are charged with exercising independent regulatory authority over the profession.[701] Other jurisdictions have a medical board exercising administrative control over acupuncture, often with the assistance of an acupuncture board or committee.[702] Finally, states regulate the profession above the board level within a state agency, generally with the assistance of an acupuncture unit whose authority varies from state to state.[703, 704]

There are three types of authorisation for the practice of medicine. Licensure is the most common form and is granted in most of the states.[705] Other states issue certifications[706] or states have mandatory registration for acupuncturists.[707] The structure of these three types of legislation is similar: practice acts usually utilise two forms of authorization either by

701 At least six states adopted such approach. See Hawaii Rev. Stat. §§ 436E-1 to 436E-14 (1985), (Supp. 1992), and (Comp. 1993); Me. Rev. Stat. Ann. tit. 32, §§ 12401–12413 (1988) and (Supp. 1994); Md. Health Occ. Code Ann. §§ 1A-101 to 1A-502 (Supp. 1994); Nev. Rev. Stat. §§ 634A.010–634A.240 (1991); N.M. Stat. Ann. §§ 61-14A-1 to 61-14A-22 (1993); and N.C. Gen. Stat. §§ 90-450 to 90-459 (1993).

702 At least thirteen states adopted such approach, such as California, Florida, Iowa, Louisiana, Massachusetts, Montana, New Jersey, Oregon, Pennsylvania, South Carolina, Texas, Virginia and the District of Columbia. In the states of California, Florida, Massachusetts, New Jersey, Pennsylvania, Texas and Virginia, there is a collateral existence of an acupuncture board or committee.
E.g., see Calif. Bus. & Prof. Code §§ 4925–4979 (West 1990) and (West Supp. 1994); Fla. Stat. Ann. §§ 457.101–457.118 (1991) and (Supp. 1994); N.J. Stat. Ann. §§ 45:2C-1 to 45:2C-18 (West 1991); S.C. Code Ann. §§ 40-47-70 and 40-47-75 (Law. Co.-op. 1986).

703 At least 8 jurisdictions adopted such approach, such as Alaska, Colorado, New York, Rhode Island, Utah, Vermont, Washington and Wisconsin. Concurrent existence of an acupuncture unit or body of advisors exist in some states (New York, Rhode Island, Utah, Vermont and Washington).
E.g., see Alaska Stat. Ann. §§ 08.06.010–08.06.190 (1991) and (Supp. 1993); N.Y. Educ. Law §§ 8210–8216; Vt. Stat. Ann. tit. 26, §§ 3401–3411 (Supp. 1994).

704 SALE D. M., *op. cit.*: 2.

705 At least sixteen of them, such as Alaska, California, Hawaii, Maine, Maryland, Montana, Nevada, New Mexico, New York, North Carolina, Oregon, Rhode Island, Texas, Utah, Virginia and the District of Columbia.
See Alaska Stat. Ann. §§ 08.06.010–08.06.190 (1991) and (Supp. 1993); Hawaii Rev. Stat. §§ 436E-1 to 436E-14 (1985), (Supp. 1992), and (Comp. 1993); N.Y. Educ. Law §§ 8210–8216 (McKinney Supp. 1994).

requiring both licensure and registration or by mandating a choice between registration and certification.[708] An exception to this regime is the legislation of South Carolina, which requires only an "approval" from the state medical board to practise acupuncture, and which makes no reference to licensure, certification or registration.[709, 710]

Medical supervision

Acupuncture legislations in some states require non-physician acupuncturists to be supervised by a licensed physician or by another specific provider. This requirement may necessitate a referral from a physician before the beginning of the treatment, prior evaluation of the patient by a physician, direct employment or supervision of acupuncturists by a physician or physician acupuncturist, or formal notification to a patient at the time of the acupuncture treatment of the importance of consulting a physician regarding a patient's condition.[711] Sometimes, the degree of physician supervision is linked to the nature of a patient's condition.[712, 713]

706 At least five States, such as Florida, Louisiana, New Jersey, Washington, and Wisconsin.
See Fla. Stat. Ann. §§ 457.101–457.118 (1991) and (Supp. 1994); N.J. Stat. Ann. §§ 45:2C-1 to 45:2C-18 (West 1991); and Wis. Stat. Ann. §§ 451.01–451.16 (West Supp. 1993).

707 At least three statues, such as Iowa, Pennsylvania and Colorado.
See Iowa Code Ann. §§ 148E.1–148E.10 (West Supp. 1994); Pa. Stat. Ann. §§ 1801–1806 (Purdon Supp. 1994).

708 See Mass. Gen. Laws Ann. ch. 112, §§ 148–162 (West Supp. 1994) (both licensure and registration required); Vt. Stat. Ann. tit. 26, §§ 3401–3411 (Supp. 1994) (either registration or certification required).

709 See S.C. Code Ann. §§ 40-47-70 and 40-47-75 (Law Co-op. 1986).

710 SALE D. M., *op. cit.*: 2–3.

711 D.C. Code Ann. § 2.3301.2(1) (1994) (general collaboration with physician required); Iowa Code Ann. § 148E.10 (West Supp. 1994) (prior evaluation and referral by medical doctor, osteopath, chiropractor, podiatrist or dentist required); Pa. Stat. Ann. tit. 63, § 1803 (Purdon Supp. 1993) (general supervision by a physician required).

712 See Texas Rev. Civ. Stat. Ann. art. 4495b, § 6.11 (g) (Vernon Supp. 1994) (no prior referral from physician, dentist, or chiropractor is required if acupuncture treatment is for smoking addiction, weight loss, or as permitted by administrative rules substance abuse); and Wash. Rev. Code Ann. § 18.06.140 (Supp. 1994) (in absence of consultation with or recent written diagnosis from a physician, continuation of acupuncture treatment is precluded if patient has a potentially serious disorder, such as a cardiac condition, acute abdominal symptoms or other similar conditions).

713 COHEN M. H. (I), *op. cit.*: 43; SALE D. M., *op. cit.*: 3; STEPNO E. M., *op. cit.*: 411–15.

Practice rights of other providers

The acupuncture practice rights of other health care providers exist both in states where there is an acupuncture practice act, and where such a statute is not present.[714] The categories of practitioners permitted to practise acupuncture varies widely from state to state. Thus, practice rights may be extended to medical doctors, osteopaths, chiropractors, physician assistants, naturopaths, homeopaths, podiatrists, nurses, veterinarians and dentists. Training requirements are also diverse and in many jurisdictions are non-existent.[715]

Legislative developments

Legislative developments during 1993–1994 illustrate the lack of uniformity in this field, in particular regarding the administrative structure and the medical supervision. For example, the new Act in Iowa requires that acupuncturists register with the state medical board as well as meeting examination and training standards established by the board. Furthermore, prior to receiving a treatment, patients must have a medical evaluation by and a referral from a medical doctor, osteopath, chiropractor, podiatrist, or dentist.[716]

Under the new Texan Act, an evaluation by a physician prior to treatment is also mandatory. However, this requirement is not necessary if the patient has been referred by a chiropractor or if the treatment is for smoking addiction, weight loss, or if allowed by administrative rules for treating substance abuse. Moreover, in Texas there is a State board of acupuncture examiners.[717, 718]

In contrast to the Texas and Iowa statutes, the new North Carolina Act has established an acupuncture licensing board with independent

714 This right may be conferred through legislation or through an interpretation recognizing acupuncture as within the scope of practice of another therapy.

715 Cohen M. H. (I), *op. cit.*: 43; Sale D. M., *op. cit.*: 3; Stepno E. M., *op. cit.*: 411–15.

716 Moreover, acupuncturists are held to the same standard of care as a licensed medical doctor or homeopath (Iowa Code Ann. §§ 148E.10 (West Supp. 1994).

717 The board is composed of four non-physician acupuncturists, two physicians experienced in the practice of acupuncture, and three members of the general public. The powers of the board, such as the establishment of educational and training qualifications, of a procedure for complaints, recommendation of rules, or of the enforcement of the law, are subject to the advice and approval of the State medical board (Tex. Rev. Civ. Stat. Ann. art. 4495b, §§ 6.01–6.14 (Vernon Supp. 1994)).

718 Sale D. M., *op. cit.*: 3–4.

regulatory authority over the profession. Licensure is compulsory for all acupuncturists, excepting physicians, chiropractors, and students practising under the direct supervision of a licensed acupuncturist. The board consists of four physician acupuncturists and one layperson. The board is responsible for disciplinary authority over licensees, for establishing requirements for and approval of schools of acupuncture within the State, and to formulate practice parameters for acupuncture.[719, 720]

Substance abuse legislation

Drug court programs throughout the country recognise the utility of acupuncture in treating substance abuse. Authorization for the use of acupuncture in such cases is also formally recognised in the statutory law of a number of States.[721]

Federal developments

In 1973, the Federal Food and Drug Administration (FDA) deemed acupuncture needles to be "experimental devices", and therefore subject to cautionary labelling requirements and restrictive classification under the Food, Drug and Cosmetic Act. As a result, the practice of acupuncture could be provided only under the supervision of licensed medical or dental practitioners.[722, 723]

In 1987, the FDA changed its position. Since then, non-allopathic practitioners who were legally qualified as health professionals were allowed to conduct acupuncture investigations.[724, 725]

Finally, in 1996, after multiple citizen petitions were filed with the FDA, acupuncture was reclassified from experimental devices (class III) to devices for which performance standards exist to provide reasonable assurance of their safety and effectiveness (class II). This reclassification would enhances the prospect of coverage for acupuncture treatment under federal Medicare and Medicaid programs.[726]

719 N.C. Gen. Stat. §§ 90-450 to 90-459 (1993).
720 SALE D. M., *op. cit.*: 4.
721 For recent developments, see SALE D. M., *op. cit.*: 4–5.
722 38 Fed. Reg. 6419 (Mar. 9. 1973).
723 SALE D. M., *op. cit.*: 6.
724 Food and Drug Administration, *Compliance Policy Guide* § 7124.11 (Sept. 24, 1987).
725 SALE D. M., *op. cit.*: 6.
726 SALE D. M., *op. cit.*: 6.

Chiropractic

Introduction

While, at the turn of the century, chiropractors lacked licensure and were often jailed for violating medical practice acts,[727] they are today part of the dominating health care system.[728] Indeed, chiropractors are currently licensed in all fifty States and the District of Columbia, and covered under most commercial health insurance policies and federal health care programs.[729, 730]

Scope of practice

Definitions of chiropractic vary in breadth and focus. Some definitions, such as that of the State of Iowa, emphasize the provider's use of spinal manipulation and adjustment.[731] Other statutes, such as that of Delaware, make reference to concepts such as the location and the removal of interference with "the transmission of nerve energy".[732, 733]

727 For a historical study regarding the licensing of chiropractic, see Callender A., *op. cit.*: 1532–34; Jackson R. B., *op. cit.*: 113–17; Rehm W. S., *op. cit.*: 43–50.

728 Chiropractors have become the third largest group of health professional in the US (after physicians and dentists) who have primary contact with patients. Even more recent attempts to eliminate chiropractic did not succeed.

729 The American Chiropractic Association points out that chiropractic should be distinguished from alternative medicines that are studied by the Office of Alternative Medicine at the National Institute of Health and stated that "We do not wish to belittle any other professions that will come under study at the OAM. While some have and others will doubtlessly make significant contributions to human health, as a group they have not yet reached the level of broad acceptance achieved by the chiropractic profession. Considering the fact that 19 million patients visit DCs yearly, that 85% of major employers cover chiropractic services under their employee health plans and that most major federal, state and commercial health care programs cover chiropractic services, it becomes clear that chiropractic does not belong to the same category as these other professions" (American Chiropractic Association, *op. cit.*).
Today, more than 45,000 chiropractors are licensed in the US.

730 Boozang K. M. (I), *op. cit.*: 196–97; Cohen M. H. (I), *op. cit.*: 40; Sale D. M., *op. cit.*: iii; Shekelle P. G., *op. cit.*: 1074; Wardwell W. I., *op. cit.*: 1066.

731 In Delaware, chiropractors "treat human ailments by adjustment of the neuromusculoskeletal structures, primarily, by hand or instrument, through spinal care" (Iowa Code Ann. § 151.1 (2). See also Kan. Stat. Ann. § 65-2871; Mo. Ann. Stat. § 331.010 (1)).

732 The North Carolina statute defines chiropractic as "the science of adjusting the cause of disease by realigning the spine, releasing pressure on nerves radiating from the spine to all parts of the body, and allowing the nerves to carry their full quota of health current (nerve energy) from the brain to all parts of the body"

The licensing statutes allow non-allopathic practitioners to provide services within a specific scope of practice. Usually, these statutes provide a general definition of professional practice, specify some acts within the scope of practice, and/or delegate further definition of the scope to professional regulatory boards.[734, 735]

Recently, a survey determined on a state-by-state basis showed that diagnostic and treatment procedures were allowed by statute in the various practice acts. All the state licensing boards were questioned. The results were as follows:[736]

1. More than 50% of state boards allow clinical lab procedures, the conducting of components of routine physical exams, the examination of a woman pelvis, the performance of rectal exams, and the conducting of electromyographic electrocardiographic and nerve conduction studies;
2. More than 80% allow a variety of X-ray procedures, the use of thermography, and the administration of a vascularzer;
3. More than 90% permit chiropractors to employ some form of physiotherapy, to adjust soft tissue or extremities, to supplement with vitamins and to conduct impairment ratings.

The right to provide other techniques has sometimes been controversial, for example, when chiropractors attempted to incorporate nutritional care into professional practice.[737, 738]

(N.C. Gen. Stat. § 90-143 (a). See also Del. Code Ann. tit. 24, § 701; Alaska Code Ann. § 34-24-120(a)).

733 For more details, see BERG R., *op. cit.*: 817–18; CHAPMAN-SMITH D. A., *op. cit.*: 110–11; COHEN M. H. (I), *op. cit.*: 39–40, 47–49; DRECHSLER C. T., *op. cit.*: § 4.

734 In this jurisdiction, chiropractors are prohibited from "the practice of medicine, surgery, osteopathy, dentistry or optometry" (Cal. Bus. & Prof. Code §§ 1000–1007). See also Miss. Code Ann. § 73-6-1.

735 For more details, see BERG R., *op. cit.*: 817–18; COHEN M. H. (I), *op. cit.*: 39, 47–49; DRECHSLER C. T., *op. cit.*: § 4.

736 LAMM L., *op. cit.*: 16–20.

737 Some statutes allow chiropractors to provide nutritional care, usually with some restrictions (prohibition to make a "profit from the sale of nutritional products coinciding with the nutritional advice rendered" (Iowa Code Ann. § 151.1)). However, some court rulings forbid the providing of nutritional care. E.g., in *Foster v. Board of Chiropractor Examiners*, the court stated that the prescribing, or dispensing of vitamins, minerals, or nutritional substances constitutes the unauthorized practice of medicine (*Foster v. Board of Chiropractic Examiners*, 359 S.E.2d 877 (Ga.1987)).

738 For more details, see COHEN M. H. (I), *op. cit.*: 39, 47–49; DRECHSLER C. T., *op. cit.*: § 4; LAMM L., *op. cit.*: 16–20.

Statutes also vary in prohibiting or permitting chiropractors to use colonic irrigation. Some jurisdictions require additional certification for chiropractors desiring to include "counselling about hygienic and other non-invasive ancillary procedures".[739] Many acts are silent on this point and judicial interpretations vary.[740, 741]

There are several approaches concerning the inclusion of acupuncture within the scope of practice of chiropractic. While some statutes expressly allow it,[742] others prohibit it.[743] In many states, courts have had to interpret the practice of medicine as legislative guidance is lacking. Hence, while some courts consider constituting acupuncture as a surgical act,[744] others do not.[745, 746]

With regard to physical examinations and other procedures, the view of chiropractic as being limited to spinal manipulation has dominated judicial interpretation of the licensing statutes. For example, in *State v. Beno*,[747] the court stated that the scope of chiropractic does not include a general physical examination of a patient complaining of a sore elbow and a low back pain. The court further interpreted the policy goal of protecting patients' health as a mandate to limit, rather than support, the alternative provider's practice authority.[748] However in some states, such as Alaska,[749] chiropractors are authorised to use ancillary methods such as

739 Such as Washington, D.C. (D.C. Code Ann. § 2-33-1.2(3) (A)).

740 E.g., in *Ohio State Board of Chiropractic Examiners v. Fulk*, the court held that colonic irrigation was within the scope of chiropractic practice, because it has not been expressly excluded.

741 Cohen M. H. (I), *op. cit.*: 49.

742 Such as Arizona or Colorado (Ariz. Rev. Stat. Ann. § 32-925; Colo. Rev. Stat. § 12-33-102(1) ("when performed by an appropriately trained chiropractor as determined by the Colorado state board of chiropractic examiners").

743 Such as Louisiana or Ohio (La. Rev. Stat. Ann. tit. 37, § 2801(3); Ohio Rev. Code Ann. § 4734.09).

744 See *Stockwell v. Washington State Chiropractic Disciplinary Board*, 622 P.2d at 910.

745 See *Acupuncture Soc'y v. Kansas State Bd. of Healing Arts*, 602 P.2d 1311 (Kan. 1979).

746 Cohen M. H. (I), *op. cit.*: 50–51; Drechsler C. T., *op. cit.*: § 4.

747 *State v. Beno*, 373 N.W.2d 544 (Mich. 1985).

748 See also *Zabrecky v. Connecticut Board of Chiropractors*, n° 0702118, 1991 Conn. Super. Ct. LEXIS 2682, at *7 (Nov. 15, 1991) (authorization to treat human body by the oral administration of foods, food concentrate, food extracts or vitamins does not authorize to inject a substance into the body).

749 Alaska Stat. Ann. § 08.20.900 (1) (B).

"counselling on dietary regimen, sanitary measures, physical and mental attitudes affecting health, personal hygiene, occupational safety, lifestyle habits, posture, rest and work habits that enhance the effects of chiropractic adjustment".[750, 751]

Administrative structure

There are several models of regulation in chiropractic legislation. The first and most common is self-regulation, under a chiropractic council or board. The board generally has a majority composed of practising chiropractors but some lay representation exists as well. State chiropractic boards are usually composed of four to eight members with only one or two lay persons. In Florida and in California, the government appoints all members of the board.[752]

The second type of regulation is a modified self-regulation under an interdisciplinary board, with a variety of arrangements. For example, in the State of Illinois, there is a Medial Licensing Board that coordinates the regulation of the three professions of health care providers defined as physicians in that state. These consist of medical doctors, doctors of chiropractic (DC) and doctors of osteopathy (DO). The Board has seven members: five MDs, one DC, and one DO. Nevertheless, separate subsidiary boards on which professional members have a majority handle day-to-day licensing and disciplinary functions for each profession.[753]

Medical supervision

Chiropractors may usually work as independent practitioners, without the need for the supervision by a physician.

750 See also *State Board of Chiropractic Examiners v. Clark*, 713 S.W.2d 621 (Mo. Ct. App. 1986) (chiropractic is extended to the techniques taught in chiropractic schools and for which practitioners are trained, such as physical therapy and cosmetology).
751 BERG R., *op. cit.*: 817–18; COHEN M. H. (I), *op. cit.*: 51–53.
752 CHAPMAN-SMITH D. A., *op. cit.*: 111–12.
753 CHAPMAN-SMITH D. A., *op. cit.*: 112.

Homeopathy[754]

Homeopathy practice acts exist at least in three states, namely Arizona, Connecticut and Nevada. The Connecticut Act dates from 1902, while the Arizona and Nevada statutes were enacted in 1980 and 1983 respectively. Practice rights for this technique may also be recognised within the scope of practice provided for other health care providers in those states, not possessing such practice acts.[755]

Scope of practice

The Arizona statute defines homeopathy as a "system of medicine employing substances of animal, vegetable or mineral origin which are given in micro dosage and prepared according to homeopathic pharmacology, in accordance with the principle that a substance which produces symptoms in a healthy person can cure those symptoms in an ill person".[756] The statute permits homeopaths to use as adjunctive therapies: acupuncture, neuromuscular integration, orthomolecular therapy, nutrition, chelation therapy, pharmaceutical medicine and minor surgery.[757, 758]

The Nevada Homeopathic Practice Act similarly defines homeopathy, adds more details regarding the specificities of the technique.[759] In contrast, the Connecticut statute provides no definition of homeopathy nor does it specifies which adjunctive therapies a homeopath may use.[760, 761]

754 For a development regarding the situation of homeopathic products, see chap. 7.2.4.

755 See Ariz. Rev. Stat. Ann. §§ 32-2901 to 32-2951 (1992); Nev. Rev. Stat. §§ 630A.010–630A.600 (1991); and Conn. Gen. Stat. Ann. §§ 20-8, 20-10, 20-11, and 20-13 (Supp. 1994).

756 Ariz. Rev. Stat. Ann. §§ 32-2901A(4) (1992).

757 Idem.

758 COHEN M. H. (I), *op. cit.*: 42–43; SALE D. M., *op. cit.*: 6.

759 For more details, see SALE D. M., *op. cit.*: 7 and Nev. Rev. Stat. §§ 630A.040 (1991).

760 However, applicable administrative guidelines provide that the compulsory licensing examination must be based upon the principles of classical homeopathy. See Department of Public Health and Addiction Services, Division of Medical Quality Assurance, *Physicians Application for Homeopathic Licensure-Instructions* 3 (Aug. 1993).

761 COHEN M. H. (I), *op. cit.*: 43; SALE D. M., *op. cit.*: 7.

Administrative structure

Both Nevada and Arizona have independent homeopathic boards.[762] In Connecticut, the Homeopathic Medical Examining Board is principally an advisory unit to the State Department of Public Health and Addiction Services. However, it has independent authority to hear and decide matters concerning the suspension or revocation of licenses, to adjudicate complaints against practitioners, and to impose related sanctions.[763]

Licensure is utilised in all three states to authorise the practice of homeopathy. The current statutes in both in Nevada and Arizona specify the powers and duties of the independent homeopathy boards, the disciplinary measures that may be taken against licensees, the qualifications required for licensure, and the prohibitions and penalties for violations of the statutes.[764] In contrast, the Connecticut statute consists of only a few references intermingled with the statutory provisions concerning the practice of medicine and the general regulatory authority of the Department of Public Health and Addiction Services over other health professions.[765, 766]

Practice rights of other providers

In Arizona, the Homeopathy Practice Act indirectly acknowledges the right of physicians and osteopaths to practise homeopathy.[767] This right is also granted in those states, which do not have homeopathic acts as part of the scope of practice for such alternative modalities as oriental medicine, naturopathy and chiropractic.[768] Furthermore, physicians seem able to

762 Ariz. Rev. Stat. Ann. §§ 32-2902 and 32-2904 (1992) and Nev. Rev. Stat. §§ 630A.200 (1991).

763 Conn. Gen. Stat. Ann. §§ 20-8 (Supp. 1994). See also, id. §§ 19a-14(a) and (b) (7) and 19a-17 (Supp. 1994).

764 See Ariz. Rev. Stat. Ann. §§ 32-2904, 32-2912, 32-2913, 32-2931, 32-2933, 32-2934, and 32-2938 (1992); and Nev. Rev. Stat. §§ 630A.200, 630A.230, 630A.240, 630A.340, 630A.380, 630A.2560 to 630A.600 (1991).

765 Conn. Gen. Stat. Ann. §§ 20-8, 20-10, 20-11, and 20-13 (Supp. 1994). In respect of the authority of the Department of Public Health and Addiction Services over the Homeopathic Medical Examining Board, see id. §§ 19a-14 (a) and (b) (7) (Supp. 1994).

766 SALE D. M., *op. cit.*: 7.

767 Ariz. Rev. Stat. Ann. § 32 2907 (1992).

768 Concerning the right of a naturopath to use homeopathy, see Alaska Stat. § 08.45.200(3) (1991); Hawaii Rev. Stat. § 455-1 (Supp. 1992).

administer homeopathic preparations in jurisdictions that either tolerate or formally authorize the use of alternative therapies under a state medical practice act.[769]

Naturopathy

More than a dozen jurisdictions have adopted naturopathy practice acts. Both Montana (1991) and New Hampshire (1994) have adopted regulations in this field.[770] States that do not have naturopathy practice acts may allow use of this technique to providers holding a medical licence. They may also require licensure in another health profession that has a scope of practice allowing the use of naturopathic methods.[771]

Scope of practice

Definitions of naturopathy usually emphasise the use of "natural" forms of health care treatment.[772] Several acts also define this technique in terms of an understanding regarding a natural human capacity for self-healing. A recent example is the Act adopted in New Hampshire, which defines naturopathy as "a system of primary health care practice, by doctors of naturopathic conditions, injuries, and diseases that uses education, natural medicines and therapies to support and stimulate the individual's intrinsic self-healing processes".[773, 774]

769 E.g., the recent North Carolina Act allowing physicians to use alternative modalities was enacted in the wake of disciplinary action by the State Medical Board against a medical doctor who employed homeopathic remedies without any harm to his patients.
For more details, see SALE D. M., *op. cit.*: 7–8, 33–37.

770 See Mont. Code Ann. §§ 37-26-101 to 37-26-414 (1993) and N.H. Rev. Stat. Ann. §§ 328-E: 17 (Supp. 1994).

771 COHEN M. H. (I), *op. cit.*: 41–42; SALE D. M., *op. cit.*: 12–13.

772 See Mont. Code Ann. §§ 37-26-103 (7) (1993).

773 N.H. Rev. Stat. Ann. §§ 328-E:2 (IX) (Supp. 1994).

774 COHEN M. H. (I), *op. cit.*: 41–42; FURROW B. R. (I), *op. cit.*: 64–65; SALE D. M., *op. cit.*: 13.

Practice acts usually allow naturopaths to utilise an extensive array of adjunctive therapies.[775] Furthermore, in some States, the scope of practice that naturopathy encompasses such well-known alternative modalities as acupuncture, homeopathy, biofeedback, hypnotherapy or massage.[776] A few statutes allow naturopaths to perform minor surgery,[777] and naturopathic or natural childbirth.[778, 779]

Administrative structure

Five states have established independent boards to regulate naturopathy.[780] Three other jurisdictions regulate naturopathy at the departmental level, with two jurisdictions receiving assistance from of a naturopathy board

775 E.g., the New Hampshire Act provides that naturopaths may use the following techniques: physical agents (air, water, heat, cold, sound, light, and electromagnetic non-ionising radiation); physical modalities (electrotherapy, diathermy, ultraviolet light, ultrasound, hydrotherapy, naturopathic manipulative therapy and therapeutic exercise); natural medicines and therapies for preventive and therapeutic purposes (food, food extracts, vitamins, minerals); diagnostic procedures (physical and orifice examinations, X-rays, ultrasounds); non-prescription medications and therapeutic devices; diagnostic procedures commonly used by medical practitioners in general practice; naturopathic childbirth; and acupuncture (N.H. Rev. Stat. Ann. §§ 328-E: 2(x), 328-E: 4(I)–(III), and 328-E: 12(I) (Supp. 1994)).

776 In the states of Hawaii, Montana, New Hampshire, and Washington. See N.H. Rev. Stat. Ann. §§ 328-E:4 (I) and 328-E: 12 (I) and (III) (Supp. 1994) (homeopathic preparations, hypnotherapy, biofeedback and acupuncture).

777 See Mont. Code Ann. §§ 37-26-103 (5) (a) and (6) and 37-26-301 (1) (c) and (2) (c) (1993) (the alternative health care board, which regulates naturopathy, has discretion to adopt rules excluding minor surgery from the scope of practice for naturopathy); N.H. Rev. Stat. Ann. §§ 328-E:4 (I) and 328-E: 12 (I) and (III) (Supp. 1994) (authorising minor surgery in connection with "naturopathic childbirth").

778 See Mont. Code Ann. §§ 37-26-103 (6) and 37-26-301 (2) (c) (1993); N.H. Rev. Stat. Ann. §§ 328-E:2 (VII) and 328-E: 12 (I) and (II) (Supp. 1994).

779 SALE D. M., *op. cit.*: 13–14.

780 The states of Arizona, Hawaii, Montana, New Hampshire and Oregon. See Mont. Code Ann. §§ 2-15-1840, 37-26-103 (2) and 37-26-201 (1993) (the alternative health care board regulates both naturopaths and direct-entry midwives).

or advisory committee.[781] In the District of Columbia, naturopaths must register with the office of the Mayor.[782, 783]

Practice acts generally specify licensure as the required form of practice authorisation. An exception is the District of Columbia that has a registration system.[784] In several jurisdictions, naturopathy licensees must also have a special certificate to practise natural childbirth or acupuncture or to dispense a natural substance or device.[785] Licensing acts usually define the scope of practice of the technique and in specify the qualifications leading to the application of practice disciplinary grounds, and the imposition of prohibitions, penalties, and related matters.[786]

Practice rights of other providers

The right to practise "naturopathy" as such does not appear to be conferred in the practice acts of other providers. However, the multiplicities of modalities that typically comprises the legislative definition of naturopathy will often fall within the scope of practice for other professions.[787] Accordingly, naturopathic statutes often provide that these acts are not applicable to persons authorized to practice other health care professions under other state acts (with the condition that these procedures are also within the scope of practice of these providers).[788] States sometimes limit

781 The states of Alaska, Connecticut, and Washington. See Wash. Rev. Code Ann. § 18.36A.010–18.36A.901 (1989) and (Supp. 1994).

782 D.C. Code Ann. § 2-3309-1(a) (1994).

783 Cohen M. H. (I), *op. cit.*: 42; Sale D. M., *op. cit.*: 14.

784 In the states of Alaska, Arizona, Connecticut, Hawaii, Montana, New Hampshire, Oregon and Washington. See Wash. Rev. Code Ann. § 18.36A.030 (Supp. 1994).

785 In the states of Arizona, Montana, New Hampshire and Oregon. See Mont. Code Ann. § 37-26-304 (certificate of speciality practice required to practice naturopathic childbirth attendance) (1993).

786 Cohen M. H. (I), *op. cit.*: 42; Sale D. M., *op. cit.*: 14.

787 E.g., the Montana Naturopathic Practice Act "recognizes that many of the therapies used by naturopathic physicians, such as the use of nutritional supplements, herbs, foods, homeopathic preparations, and such physical forces as heat, cold, water, touch, and light, are not the exclusive privilege of naturopathic physicians, and their use, practice, prescription, or administration by persons not licensed to practice naturopathic medicine is not prohibited" (Mont. Code Ann. § 37-26-302 (1) (1993)).

788 In the states of Arizona, Montana and New Hampshire. See Mont. Code Ann. § 37-26-302 (1) (1993).

the categories of providers, typically to physicians, osteopaths, chiropractors, Christian scientists, providers of Oriental medicine, Oriental herbology, or of other dietary or nutritional advice, who may provide naturopathy.[789, 790]

D. Unauthorised and unprofessional practice

Medical and professional practice acts place two categories of practitioners at risk of prosecution for unlawfully and unprofessional practising medicine. The first category encompasses those providers lacking licensure who may violate medical practice acts, and/or professional practice acts. Licensed practitioners constitutes the second category who may be prosecuted for violating their legally authorised scope of practice by engaging in the diagnosis and treatment of disease either by departing from conventionally accepted standards of medicine or by employing or referring patients to providers practising medicine unlawfully.

Non-licensed providers

When non-licensed providers diagnose or treat patients, as defined under the medical licensing statutes, they risk prosecution under the unlawful medical practice acts. In some States, modalities,[791] which are not specifically addressed by medical acts, may in principle not be provided by unlicensed medical professionals. For example, in *People v Amber*,[792] an acupuncturist was indicted for practising medicine without a licence (at the time, New York had no acupuncture licensure). It was argued for the defence that the prohibition (regarding the unlicensed practice of medicine) referred to "Western allopathic medicine" and did not encompass alternative systems of medicine such as Chinese medicine, which differs in its "philosophy, practice and technique".[793] The court disagreed stating that "whether certain actions constitutes the practice of medicine depends on facts, and not on the name of the procedure, its origins or the legislative

789 In the States of Connecticut (licensed physicians), Oregon (physicians and surgeons, osteopaths, chiropractors, and Christian Scientists), South Carolina, Tennessee and Washington (provider of Oriental medicine, Oriental herbology, or other dietary or nutritional advice). See Wash. Rev. Code Ann. § 18.36A.030 (Supp. 1994).

790 SALE D. M., *op. cit.*: 14–15.

791 Such as naturopathy, massage therapy, hypnosis or therapeutic touch.

792 *People v. Amber*, 349 N.Y.S.2d 604 (Sup. Ct. 1973).

793 *People v. Amber*, 349 N.Y.S.2d 604, 611 (Sup. Ct. 1973).

lack of clairvoyance", and further that "a statute intended to regulate, limit or control the diagnosis and treatment must necessarily be broad enough to include the gamut of those known, whether or not recognised and even those not yet conjured".[794, 795]

Cohen observes that "although providers such as acupuncturists now are licensed in many States, cases such as Amber and Stetina retain precedential value and express a judicial view of certain non licensed practitioners. In jurisdiction where (alternative practices) are neither specifically licensed nor specifically prohibited, their providers risk prosecution under state medical practice acts. In fact, courts have interpreted the medical practice acts broadly against providers in situations in which state legislatures have failed to create separate licensure".[796] In addition, under the broad justification of protection and preservation of public health,

794 *People v. Amber*, 349 N.Y.S.2d 604, 611 (Sup. Ct. 1973).
The Court added that even determining "the existence of a disharmony brought about by the disequilibria of Yin and Yang" constituted a diagnosis under the statute which included nutritional, psychological, spiritual, and other non-medical assessments of health (Amber, 349 N.Y.S.2d 604, 612 (Sup. Ct. 1973)).
Another case, *Stetina v. State*, involved a nutritionist practising iridology without licence. The court observed that the medical practice act was not solely designed to protect patients from their own gullibility and from fraudulent practitioners; the act was also intended to protect against "the well-intentioned but unskilled practices of health care professionals, as well as against those well-intentioned and skilled practices which simply exceed the scope of acceptable health care". However, the appellate court agreed that Stetina could "disseminate information concerning the value of good nutrition" (*Stetina v. State*, 513 N.E.2d 1234, 1238, 1239 (Ind. Ct. App. 1987)).
See also *State v. Rich*, 44 Ohio St. 2d, 195, 73 Ohio Ops 2d 487, 339, N.E.2d 630 (1975) (a licensed chiropractor who had employed acupuncture was held to have been convicted violated a statute making it unlawful to practise medicine without a certificate from the state medical board); *State v. Won*, 528 P.2d 594, 72 A.L.R.3d 1253 (1974) (chiropractor providing acupuncture); *State v. Wilson*, 111 Wash. App. 916, 528 Pd 279 (1974) (statute precluding chiropractor from performing surgery, including acupuncture).
For a study regarding acupuncture as the illegal practice of medicine, see DANNE W., *op. cit.*: 1257ss.

795 COHEN M., *op. cit.*: 29–30; DANNE W., *op. cit.*: 1257ss; FURROW B. R. (I), *op. cit.*: 60–63; JOSEFEK K. J., *op. cit.*: 301–02.

796 COHEN M., *op. cit.*: 31. E.g. *State v. MountJoy* et al., 891 P.2d 376, 384 (Kan. 1995) (midwives); *State v. Howard*, 337 S.E.2d 598 (N.C. Ct. App. 1985) (naturopaths); *Sabastier v. State*, 504 So.2d 45 (Fla. Dist. Ct. App. 1987) (homeopaths); *Williams v. State of Alabama* ex rel, medical Licensure Comm'n, 453 So.2d 1051, 1053 (Ala. Civ. App. 1984) (colonic irrigation practitioners).

piercing, tattooing, and massage have been indicted for unlawfully practice of medicine.[797]

Often, the states themselves license various alternative practitioners. Thus, non-licensed practitioners risk prosecution not only under the Medical Practice Act but also under professional practice acts, which usually prohibit the unlicensed practice of psychology, massage and other fields.[798] Therefore, alternative practitioners must be careful not to cross over the line into a State regulated profession. For example, in *Feingold v. Commonwealth of Pennsylvania, State Board of Chiropractic*,[799] an unlicensed provider practising in the field of chiropractic was convicted for the unlicensed practice of chiropractic.[800] In other jurisdictions, alternative practitioners such as massage therapists and chiropractor who provide emotional material that seeks to address the underlying dysfunction should be careful not to interfere with counselling or psychology.[801, 802]

In those states having statutes drafted in an exclusive or monopolistic fashion, the risk of prosecution that alternative practitioners face for unauthorised practice is greater. For example, in Texas, a statute provides that the practice of psychology includes "hypnosis for health purposes, hypnotherapy, and biofeedback".[803] Thus, those providers practising hypnotherapy, where their legislatively defined scope of practice does not expressly include it, would have to obtain licensure in psychology, in order to avoid risk of prosecution.[804]

797 COHEN M., *op. cit.*: 31.

798 California, e.g., has enacted a statute setting up stricter standards for those providing acupuncture. It makes it a misdemeanour for any person, other than licensed dentists, podiatrists, or physicians, to practice acupuncture. In addition, it makes it unprofessional conduct for a physician, osteopathic physician, dentist, or podiatrist to direct or supervise the administering of acupuncture on a patient by a healing arts practitioner that is not licensed under the Acupuncture Licensure Act. It is also unprofessional conduct under this statute for one licensed as a healing arts practitioner, but not as an acupuncturist, to perform acupuncture at the direction of or under the supervision of a physician, osteopathic physician, dentist, or podiatrist. For more details, see STEPNO E. M., *op. cit.*: 411–15.

799 *Feingold v. Commonwealth of Pennsylvania, State Board of Chiropractic*, 568 A.2d 1365 (Pa. Commw. Ct. 1980).

800 See also *Andrews v. Ballard*, 498 F. Supp. 1038, 1039 (S.D. Tex. 1980) (challenging a Texas statute prohibiting non-physicians from administering acupuncture).

801 See *Makris v. Bureau of Professional and Occupational Affairs, State Board of Psychology*, 599 A.2d 279 (Comm. Ct. Pa. 1991).

802 ANDREWS L. B., *op. cit.*: 1288–89; COHEN M. H. (I), *op. cit.*: 45.

803 Tex. Rev. Civ. Stat. Ann. art. 4512c, § 2(c), § 20.

804 COHEN M. H. (I), *op. cit.*: 45.

In contrast, as we have seen, some statutes include, within the practitioner's scope of practice, ancillary techniques on a nonexclusive basis.[805, 806]

Even though alternative practitioners are usually not recognised as regular health care providers,[807] medical practice acts may create a space of coexistence within which these providers and regular providers may work. For example, Massachusetts's Medical Practice Act specifies that the prohibition on unlicensed medical practice does not apply to "clairvoyants or persons practising hypnotism, magnetic healing, mind cure, massage, Christian science or cosmopathic method of healing".[808] Other recent licensing statutes acknowledge that providers ranging from chiropractors to acupuncturists do engage in the "sizing up" of conditions, namely diagnosis and treatment.

Another current trend that can be observed in the interpretation of medical practice acts consists of the creation of a differentiated terminology which aims to regulate the unlawful practice of medicine without restricting independent holistic practice.[809, 810]

805 E.g., several States expressly authorize acupuncturists, chiropractors or naturopaths to offer homeopathy (e.g. Alaska Stat. § 08.45.200 (3); Haw. Rev. Stat. § 455-1; N.H. Rev. Stat. Ann. § 328-E:4.1.
Cohen adds that "In this case, authorizing the licensed provider to offer the modality (such as hypnotherapy) does not prohibit either unlicensed providers or other types of licensed providers from offering that healing modality" (COHEN M. H. (I), *op. cit.*: 46).

806 Josefek notes that "In the past, non-allopathic providers were referred to the board for sanction any time that a 'condition' had been 'diagnosed' that ran contrary to allopathic standards. [...] Hearing board decisions are only subject to judicial review on an arbitrary and capricious standard or rational basis review standard. [...] Therefore many board decisions, although professionally biased in their evaluation, have been upheld because of limited judicial review. To rectify this situation, states should pass individualised enabling acts that define the scope of practice for each alternative modality. [...] This would correct erroneous decisions predicated on inhibiting language found in current medical practice acts" (JOSEFEK K. J., *op. cit.*: 302).

807 With the exception of chiropractors (who are recognised in all the states) and osteopaths (recognised in most of the states).

808 Mass. Gen. Laws Ann. ch. 112, § 7. States also usually exempt healers, practising in a religious context as part of a recognised spiritual tradition and practice (e.g., D.C. Code Ann. § 2-3301.4 (d) (1)).

809 See *Sermchief v. Gonzalez*, 660 S.W.2d 683, 689–90 (Mo. 1983) (nursing diagnosis, as opposed to a medical diagnosis); *Parma v. Wolff*, 635 N.E.2d, 76, 78–79 (Ohio Mun. Ct. 1993) (non-licensed provider's use of a machine to determinate imbalances of shoulders and hips does not constitute a chiropractic diagnosis, particularly since the provider informed patient: "this is only a preliminary

Furthermore, a broad range of alternative providers can, in general, practise freely,[811] without being prosecuted in those states lacking a professional licensure of their own.[812]

Licensed providers

Licensed providers may also violate medical practice and professional acts.

First, licensed providers (physicians and non-physicians) employing or referring patients to providers practising medicine unlawfully may be liable for "aiding and abetting" unlicensed medical practice.[813]

Second, non-physician licensed practitioners may be prosecuted if they violate the legal scope of practice. For example, the Michigan Court of Appeals held that chiropractors violated the medical llicensing statute when they performed physical exams and ultrasound or prescribed vitamins and food supplements.[814, 815]

Finally, when health care providers depart from conventionally accepted medical standards (in particular physicians) in order to provide alternative medicines, they risk professional discipline for "unprofessional conduct" or "professional misconduct". Unprofessional conduct includes a variety of acts.[816, 817]

Because medical boards decisions are generally confidential, relatively few medical board decisions result in published judicial opinions that

---

screening, this is not an examination, and […] any examination must be done by a licensed chiropractor").

810 COHEN M., *op. cit.*: 32.

811 E.g., lay homeopaths, nutritionists, iridologists, reflexologists, yoga and meditation teachers, energy healers, Feldenkrais and Alexander instructors, purveyors of nutritional supplements, etc. But see *State v. Kellogg*, 568 P.2d 514 (Idaho 1977) (the exemption from the prohibition on dispensing prescription drugs includes physicians but not naturopaths).

812 COHEN M., *op. cit.*: 32–33.

813 COHEN M., *op. cit.*: 29.

814 *State v. Beno*, 373 N.W.2d 544, 559, 562–63 (Mich. 1985). Other cases even include nurse practitioners providing breast and pelvic examinations.

815 ANDREWS L. B., *op. cit.*: 1291–92, 1306; DRECHSLER C. T., *op. cit.*: § 4; FURROW B. R. (I), *op. cit.*: 60–63.

816 Such as obtaining the licence fraudulently; practising the profession fraudulently, beyond its allowed scope, with incompetence, or with negligence; practising while impaired by alcohol or drugs or while convicted of a crime; or failing to comply with relevant rules and regulations. See N.Y. Educ. Law § 6509.

817 COHEN M. H. (I), *op. cit.*: 87; FURROW B. R. (I), *op. cit.*: 63–66.

discuss, for example, the use of homeopathy, ozone therapy, and chelation therapy by MDs. According to Cohen, "these cases, [...], arose not because of demonstrated injury to patients or even complaints by patients, but because the treatments challenged medical boards' view of safety or effectiveness within the practice of medicine".[818]

A few cases regarding the unprofessional conduct of licensed providers are presented below:

1. In *re Guess*,[819] after a long trial, decisions and reversals, a physician who provided homeopathic remedies when conventional treatments had failed was charged with "unprofessional conduct". The North Carolina Supreme Court held that the medical board was allowed to revoke a physician's licence for "any departure from, or the failure to conform to, the standards of acceptable and prevailing medical practice, [...] irrespective of whether or not a patient is injured thereby".[820] Furthermore, the court specified that a revocation did not require that the board to find an actual threat of harm to patients and rejected the argument that the board's decision invaded the patient's constitutional privacy interests in his choice of treatment;[821]
2. In the applicable Florida statute, the definition of unprofessional conduct is similar to the statute in Guess.[822] However, unlike the Guess court, the appellate court in *Rogers v. State Board of Medical Examiners*, a case involving a physician providing chelation therapy instead of a classic cure for arteriosclerosis,[823] held that absent evidence of fraud, deception, harm, or quackery, and because sanctions were imposed solely because the board did not recognise chelation therapy,

818 COHEN M. H. (I), *op.cit.*: 87.
819 *State v. Guess*, 393 S.E.2d at 833 (N.C. Ct. App. 1989).
820 Ibid. at 836.
821 COHEN M. H. (I), *op.cit.*: 88–90.
822 Here, unprofessional conduct is defined as "any departure from, or the failure to conform to, the standards of acceptable and prevailing medical practice in [...] [the physician's] area of expertise as determined by the [State Medical Board], in which proceeding actual injury to a patient need not be established". Fla. Stat. Ann. § 458.1201 (1) (m) (West 1975) According to Cohen "the broad language in the statute analysed in Guess [...], suggests that practitioners can become targets of bias on the part of state medical boards hostile to a particular therapy" (COHEN M. H. (I), *op.cit.*: 88).
823 *State Board of Medical Examiners v. Rogers*, 387 So. 2d 937 (Fla. 1980).

the board's limitation on chelation therapy lacked a reasonable relationship to the protection of public health and welfare;[824, 825]

3. In *Atkins v. Guest*,[826] a woman diagnosed with breast cancer consulted Atkins, a physician providing ozone therapy and nutritional program. After the second week of treatment, the patient felt weak and was sent to a hospital. The Board of Professional Medical Conduct issued a subpoena and Atkins was held to be incompetent and as engaging in negligent behaviour, solely on the basis of his practice of ozone therapy.[827]

E. State medical freedom practice acts

As we have seen above, physicians providing alternative medicines risk disciplinary sanctions. Some legislatures have enacted medical freedom acts in order to protect physicians who provide alternative medicines and innovative or experimental treatments,[828] as well as to protect a patient's freedom of choice. These acts conditionally limit the authority of a state medical board to discipline physicians providing alternative modalities and protect patients from harm.[829]

Statutes usually address health care freedom in a general manner. The first such statute was enacted in Alaska in 1990 and was followed by Washington (1991), North Carolina (1993), South Dakota (1993),[830] Oklahoma (1994),[831] New York (1994) and Oregon (1995).[832]

These statues have different approaches, for example:[833]

824 *State Board of Medical Examiners v. Rogers*, 387 So. 2d 939–40 (Fla. 1980). The decision departs from *United States v. Dent*, 129 U.S.114 (1888).

825 COHEN M. H. (I), *op. cit.*: 90–91.

826 *Atkins v. Guest*, 601 N.Y.S.2d 234 (Sup. Ct. 1993), aff'd, 607 N.Y.S.2d 655 (App. Div. 1994).

827 COHEN M. H. (I), *op. cit.*: 91–92.

828 For a development on the subject, see COHEN M. H. (I), *op. cit.*: 57–59.

829 BOOZANG K. M. (II), *op. cit.*: 567–69; COHEN M. H. (I), *op. cit.*: 92–93; SALE D. M., *op. cit.*: 33.

830 The South Dakota statute is a limited version of the medical freedom acts. Indeed, it only prohibits the Board of Medical and Osteopathic Examiners from basing a finding of unprofessional conduct solely on the basis that a licensee practises "chelation therapy" (S.D. Codified Laws § 36-4-29 (Supp. 1994)).

831 Oklahoma's legislation provides that nothing "shall prohibit services rendered by any person practising any non-allopathic healing practice". Okla. Stat. Ann. tit. 59, § 480 (West Supp. 1995).

832 COHEN M. H. (I), *op. cit.*: 92–93; SALE D. M., *op. cit.*: 33–36.

833 On the subject, see JOSEFEK K. J., *op. cit.*: 302–304.

1. The requirement of harm and injury.
   Both Washington and Alaska have revised their practicing medicine statutes to require "demonstrable physical harm" to a patient, even if the technique is "unconventional or experimental" before finding a practitioner incompetent to practice. The purpose of these amendments was to protect alternative practitioners from historically discriminatory legislation favouring allopathic caregivers.[834] According to Josefek, such statutes are "a step forward towards alternative medicine's total independence from conventional providers".[835]
2. The requirement of safety or efficacy.
   In response to Guess,[836] North Carolina enacted a new legislation providing that "the board shall not revoke the license of or deny a license to a person solely because of that person's practice of a therapy that is experimental, non-traditional, or that departs from acceptable and prevailing medical practices unless, by competent evidence, the Board can establish that the treatment has a safety risk greater that the prevailing treatment or that the treatment is generally not effective".[837] Thus, the new statute not only requires proof that a patient was harmed, but places the burden on the state medical board to establish by competent evidence a lack of effectiveness or a safety risk.[838]

   Similarly, Oregon's statute provides that "the use of an alternative medical treatment shall not by itself constitute unprofessional conduct".[839] Alternative medical treatments are defined as treatments "that the treating physician, based on the physician's professional experience, has an objective basis to believe that has a reasonable probability for effectiveness in its intended use even if the treatment is outside recognised scientific guidelines, is unproven, is no longer used as a generally recognised or standard treatment or lacks the approval

834 Alaska's legislation provides that the medical board "may not base a finding of professional incompetence solely on the basis that a licensee's practice is unconventional or experimental in the absence of demonstrably physical harm to patient" (Alaska Stat. § 08.64.326.).
Washington's legislation provides that "the use of non-traditional treatment by itself does not result in injury to a patient or create an unreasonable risk that a patient may be harmed" (Wash. Rev. Code Ann. § 18.130.180 (4)).

835 JOSEFEK K. J., *op. cit.*: 303.

836 The case involved a physician who provided chelation therapy when regular treatments had failed. See above.

837 N.C. Gen. Stat. § 90-14 (a) (6).

838 COHEN M. H. (I), *op. cit.*: 93–94; SALE D. M., *op. cit.*: 33–34.

839 Or. Rev. Stat. § 677.190 (1)(b).

of the United States Food and Drug Administration; [as long as that therapy] [...] is supported for specific usages or outcomes by at least one other physician licensed by the Board of medical Examiners; and poses a greater risk to a patient than the generally recognised or standard treatment".[840, 841]

3. Anti-discrimination practice statutes
New York's Medical Practice Statute provides that nothing in the Medical Practice Act shall be construed to affect or prevent a licensed physician from using "whatever medical care, conventional or non conventional, [...] effectively treats human disease, pain, injury, deformity, or physical condition".[842] The legislation also creates a board for professional medical conduct, consisting of at least two physicians "who dedicate a significant portion of their practice to the use of non-conventional medical treatments".[843, 844]
Similarly, Oklahoma's Medical Practice Statute states that nothing within the statutes "shall prohibit services rendered by any person [...] practising any non-allopathic healing practice".[845]

F. General federal developments

Although the regulation of alternative medicines occurs primarily at the state level, the federal government has also been active in the field, establishing an Office of Alternative Medicine, and engaging in regulatory actions through the FDA concerning dietary supplements and acupuncture. Congress has, however, failed to enact comprehensive health care reforms[846] and, with limited exceptions, to include alternative medicines as an integral part of any proposed reform legislation. At the same time, legislative consideration of the Access to Medical Treatment Act reflects public and practitioners' interest regarding the right to provide alternative treatments, and to receive treatments that may be subject to excessive regulation by the FDA.[847]

840 Or. Rev. Stat. § 677.190 (1)(b)(A).
841 Cohen M. H. (I), *op. cit.*: 94.
842 N.Y. Educ. Law § 6527 (4) (e). For a criticism, see Sale D. M., *op. cit.*: 34–35.
843 N.Y. Pub. Health Law § 230.
844 Cohen M. H. (I), *op. cit.*: 94; Sale D. M., *op. cit.*: 35–36.
845 Okla. Stat. Ann. tit. 59, § 480 (West Supp. 1995).
846 For a study see Sale D. M., *op. cit.*: 44–46; Congressional Quartely 2797–2801 (Oct. 1, 1994).
847 Sale D. M., *op. cit.*: 38.

National Center for Complementary and Alternative Medicines

In 1991, pursuant to a congressional Directive,[848] the Office of Alternative Medicine (OAM) of the National Institutes of Health was established.[849]

The objectives of the OAM are to facilitate the evaluation of alternative medicines (including acupuncture and Oriental medicine, homeopathic medicine, and physical manipulation therapies) and to establish an information clearinghouse to exchange information with the public about alternative medicine and support research training in the field. Furthermore, the Secretary of the National Institutes of Health (NIH) has been directed to establish an advisory council to advise the Director of the Office.[850, 851]

Regarding the efforts of the OAM to develop a plan for research activities at NIH in the field of alternative medicines, Congress also requires the OAM coordinate its work with ongoing work in other nations and to pay particular attention to activities that emphasize ethnomedicine. Moreover, Congress has asked the OAM to develop databases in functional support of both research and information transfer.[852] By the end of 1994, the

848 National Institutes of Health Revitalization Act of 1993, Pub. L. n° 103–43, 197 Stat. 122 (1993) (codified at scattered sections of 42 U.S.C.); National Center for Complementary and Alternative Medicine homepage, available at: http://nccam.nih.gov, accessed June 1, 2002.
In explaining the need for the Office, the committee indicated that "the Committee is not satisfied that the conventional medical community as symbolised by NIH has fully explored the potential that exists in unconventional medical practices. Many routine and effective medical procedures now considered commonplace were once considered unconventional and counter indicated. Cancer radiation therapy is such a procedure that is now commonplace but once was considered to be a quackery. In order to more adequately explore these unconventional medical practices the Committee requests that NIH establish within the Office of the Director an office to fully investigate and validate these practices. The Committee further directs that the NIH convene and establish an advisory panel to screen and select the procedures for investigation and to recommend a research program to fully test the most promising unconventional medical practices." (S. Rep. n° 104, 102d Cong., 1st Sess. 147 (1991)).

849 BOOZANG K. M. (III), *op. cit.*: 252; LAY B. F., *op. cit.*: 640; SALE D. M., *op. cit.*: 38–39.

850 42 U.S.C.A. § 283g(b) and (c) (Supp. 1994).

851 LAY B. F., *op. cit.*: 640; SALE D. M., *op. cit.*: 39.

852 H. Rep. n° 100, 103d Cong., 1st Sess. 117 (1993), reprinted in 1993 U.S. Code Cong. & Ad. News 299.
According to the Senate Committee "the purpose of the data is to bring together all the existing data and literature on alternative medicine and to develop organised,

OAM had made available grants for forty-two research projects regarding specific alternative medicines and two additional grants for exploratory centers in alternative medical research.[853, 854]

In 1998, Congress gave the OAM increased status and authority by renaming it the National Centre for Complementary and Alternative Medicine (NCCAM) and by increasing its budget from the current $20 million to $50 million. The NCCAM is now in a position to fund its research grants and other projects directly.[855] Meanwhile, research supported by the NCCAM is currently moving from the exploratory phases towards the establishment evidence-producing studies.[856]

In March 2000, a White House Commission on Complementary and Alternative Medicine was established, to develop public policy proposals geared toward maximizing "the benefits to Americans of complementary and alternative medicine".[857]

White House Commission on Complementary and Alternative Medicine Policy

In March 2000, the President and Congress created the White House Commission on Complementary and Alternative Medicine Policy (herafter WHCCAMP).[858] The mandate of the Commission was to develop legislative and administrative recommendations in order to help public policy

systematic, and up-to-date reviews of the relevant scientific data. The data base should prepare and maintain a register of randomised controlled trials and other research efforts in this area, and should also contain a compilation of basic and clinical research relevant to alternative and alternative medicine. This review of the literature should also be made available to health care providers and consumers" (S. Rep. N. 318, 103d Cong., 2d Sess. 112 (1994)).

853 From an initial budget of $2 million in 1992, funding for the OAM has increased to $5.4 million in 1995. For a development regarding the opportunity to continue granting research in this field, see BOOZANG K. M. (III), *op. cit.*: 251–61.

854 SALE D. M., *op. cit.*: 39.

855 According to Harlan, the greatest change since the OAM began is in the medical professions attitude towards alternative medicine. The author writes "those in conventional research and medical practitioners have become very interested in alternative medicine and in doing research in it. It is now recognised that there are a lot of promising therapies that need to be tested in the most appropriate manner" (cited in MARWICK C., *op. cit.*: 1553).

856 MARWICK C., *op. cit.*: 1553–54.

857 For a summary of the national policy on alternative medicine, see BOOZANG K. M. (III), *op. cit.*: 251–61.

858 The Commission was established by Executive Order n° 13147 in March 2000.

maximize potential benefits, to consumers and American health care, of alternative medicines. The final report of the Commission was published in March 2002.[859]

The WHCCAMP has made several recommendation in order to better integrate alternative medicines in the American health care system. This involves also measures regarding the licensing to practise alternative medicines. In particular, the WHCCAMP is of the opinion that:[860]

1. The Department of Health and Human Services should evaluate current barriers to consumer access to safe and effecxtive CAM practices and to qualified practitioners and should develop strategies for removing those barriers in order to increase access and to ensure accountability;
2. The Federal Government should offer assistance to states and professional organisations in 1) developing and evaluating guidelines for practitioner accountability and competence in CAM delivery, including regulation of practice, and 2) periodic review and assessment of the effects of regulations on consumer protection;
3. States should evaluate and review their regulation of CAM practitioners and ensure their accountability to the public. States should, as appropriate, implement provisions for licensure, registration, and exemption consistent with the pracittioners' education, training, and scope of practice;
4. Nationally recognised accrediting bodies should evaluate how health care organisations under their oversight are using CAM practices and should develop strategies for the safe and appropriate use of qualified CAM practitioners and safe and effective products in these organisations.

Access to the Medical Treatment Act

On May 19, 1994, Senator Thomas Daschle presented the Access to Medical Treatment Act to the United States Senate.[861] The purpose of the Act,

859 WHITE HOUSE COMMISSION ON COMPLEMENTARY AND ALTERNATIVE MEDICINE POLICY, *op. cit.*

860 WHITE HOUSE COMMISSION ON COMPLEMENTARY AND ALTERNATIVE MEDICINE POLICY, *op. cit.*: 153–54.

861 S. 2140, 103d Cong., 2d Sess. (1994).
An identical act was introduced in the House of Representatives on May 25, 1994, by Delegate Eleanor Norton of the District of Columbia and referred to the House Committee on Energy and Commerce (H. R. 4696, 103d Cong., 2d Sess. (1994)).

not yet enacted, was to provide health care consumers with increased access to alternative medicines and to allow greater opportunity for the trial of alternative treatments that may prove to be effective.[862] In particular, the bill aimed at facilitating conditional access for health care consumers to food, drugs, devices, and procedures that might otherwise be delayed from authorised use by the (long) FDA approval process.[863]

The Act generally authorises the right of individuals to be treated by a category of health care providers such as physicians, osteopaths, chiropractors or naturopaths using any technique the patient desires.[864, 865] However, the right to treatment is subject to the following conditions:[866]

1. the health provider must agree to treat the individual;
2. the administration of the treatment must be within the scope of practice of the practitioner;
3. there must be no evidence that the treatment, when taken as prescribed, is a danger to the individual;[867]
4. if the treatment involves a food, drug, or device that has not been approved by the FDA, then the individual must be informed of this fact and the food, drug, or device (or accompanying information) must contain a warning concerning the absence of FDA approval and assumption of risk by the individual;
5. the individual must be informed regarding the nature of the treatment (i.e., its contents, reasonably foreseeable side effects and results of past applications);
6. no claim may be made regarding the efficacy of the treatment, except that the practitioner may report the results of treatments in recognised journals or at seminars, conventions, or similar meetings as long as the practitioner will not gain financially as a result of the claim apart from any reimbursement received from the patient; and

862 140 Cong. Rec. S6130 (daily ed. May 19, 1994) (statement of Senator Dachsle).

863 COHEN M. H. (I), *op. cit.*: 79–81; SALE D. M., *op. cit.*: 46–47.

864 S. 2140, §§ 2 (6) and 3 (a) 103d Cong., 2d Sess. (1994).

865 "Treatment" is defined in the act as the use of any food, drug, device, or procedure (Id. § 2(9)).

866 SALE D. M., *op. cit.*: 47.

867 "Danger" means a serious negative reaction that occurred as a result of the method of treatment, would not otherwise have occurred, and is more serious than reactions frequently experienced with accepted treatments for the same or similar health problems. Furthermore, if the practitioner discovers that a treatment is a danger to the individual, the practitioner has to report this fact to the Secretary of Health and Human Services Id. §§ 2(2) and (4).

7. the individual must sign an informed consent form indicating his or her permission to be treated.

The Act also authorised the interstate delivery of medication or equipment for use in treatments allowed by the legislation and forbade state licensing boards from suspending, denying, or revoking the licence of a covered practitioner solely because the practitioner provided treatment permitted by the Act.[868] However, if a provider violated the Act the practitioner would lose the benefits of the protection accorded by the bill and be subject to any other applicable statute or regulation.[869, 870]

Opponents of the legislation argued that the absence in the Act of any requirement for scientific testing of treatments for safety before use could expose patients to dangerous products and undermine the Act's requirement that a patient give informed consent prior to treatment. They added that the Act failed to preserve the FDA's enforcement authority in this area, would undermine efforts by the OAM to assess the effectiveness and safety of alternative medicines, and potentially expose patients to quackery.[871]

In rebuttal, supporters of the Act alleged that there is already a substantial risk in many conventional treatments, that a firm basis for many approved medical procedures does not exist, and that treatments allowed by the bill would be provided by licensed practitioners who would, in any case, remain subject to malpractice liability. Furthermore, the Act would enhance the health interests of consumers by guaranteeing their right to choose the desired treatment.[872]

G. Conclusion

A number of significant patterns are apparent within the US. First, legislative activity relating to alternative treatments appears to be intensifying, probably in relation to the increasing consumer usage of alternative medicines and the interest of alternative practitioners in obtaining professional practice rights. In particular, the recent adoption of medical freedom

868 Id. §§ 5 and 6.

869 Id. § 7.

870 SALE D. M., *op. cit.*: 48.

871 *Access to Medical Treatments Act: Heating on S. 2140 before the Senate labour and human resources committee*, 103d Cong., 2d Sess. 68–93 (1994) (Statement of Mary K. Pendergast, Deputy Commissioner, Food and Drug Administration) and id. at 103–08 (Statement of Robert J. Corolla, Legislative Counsel, Consumers Union).

872 SALE D. M., *op. cit.*: 48.

practice acts have allowed physicians to move beyond the provision of conventional medicine. There has also been recent adoptions of provider practice statutes not only for such well-known alternative medicines as acupuncture and massage, but also for less familiar techniques such as art therapy, naprapthy, reflexology and the Alexander technique. Thus, there has been a considerable evolution from the turn of the last century when professional acts allowing alternative practitioners to practise medicine were few in number. This indicates that the practice and access interests of a growing number of alternative practitioners and their patients are forming part of many States legislative and regulatory agenda.

Second, the cross-practice rights allowing alternative practitioners to make from the practice of one technique to another is not only widespread but formally recognised in several statutes. This suggests the existence of a multidisciplinary orientation and fluidity in the providing of alternative medicines and practice boundaries for many alternative practitioners.

Third, there is a lack of uniformity among the various State regulations in this field. The statutory requirements differ substantially from State to State, even with respect to the same technique.

Fourth, the federal legislative activity in this field including the evolution of the status of dietary supplements and acupuncture at the FDA, the creation of the OAM and propositions to enhance an access to medical treatment act, highlights the significance of alternative medicines for the nation as a whole. Furthermore, as Sale notes "greater legislative interest may well develop as a result of increasing demand by American consumers for access to these relatively safe therapies and the desire of insurers to control the spiralling costs of conventional health care".[873]

Fifth, many alternative practitioners still risk prosecutions under the various State medical practice acts, and even licensed practitioners may be viewed as having crossed the line into the medical diagnosis and treatment areas associated with other professions.[874]

Finally, as Sale states "legislative developments are particularly significant as formal expressions of public policy in any subject area. Given the synergistic momentum that arises from a high level of consumer usage of alternative therapies, the continuing interest of alternative providers in securing professional practice rights, and other patterns of activity in this

873 SALE D. M., *op. cit.*: 50–51.

874 According to Furrow "whether the deferential posture of the courts toward the very restrictive regulation of nonconforming medical practices will change as a result of new research on such practices remains to be seen" (FURROW B. R. (I), *op. cit.*: 64).

field, it seems likely that the legislative area will experience intense pressure in the coming years to accommodate alternative modes of care. In new enactment's are predicated on a patient-centred ideal that accords the individual substantial freedom to select a mode of personal care, the interests of health care in the United States would indeed seem well-served".[875]

4.3.7 Comparative Charts

Two maps are provided below, which provide a schematic overview of the licensing to practise alternative medicines in Switzerland and in Europe.

Map 1 – Licensing to practise in Switzerland

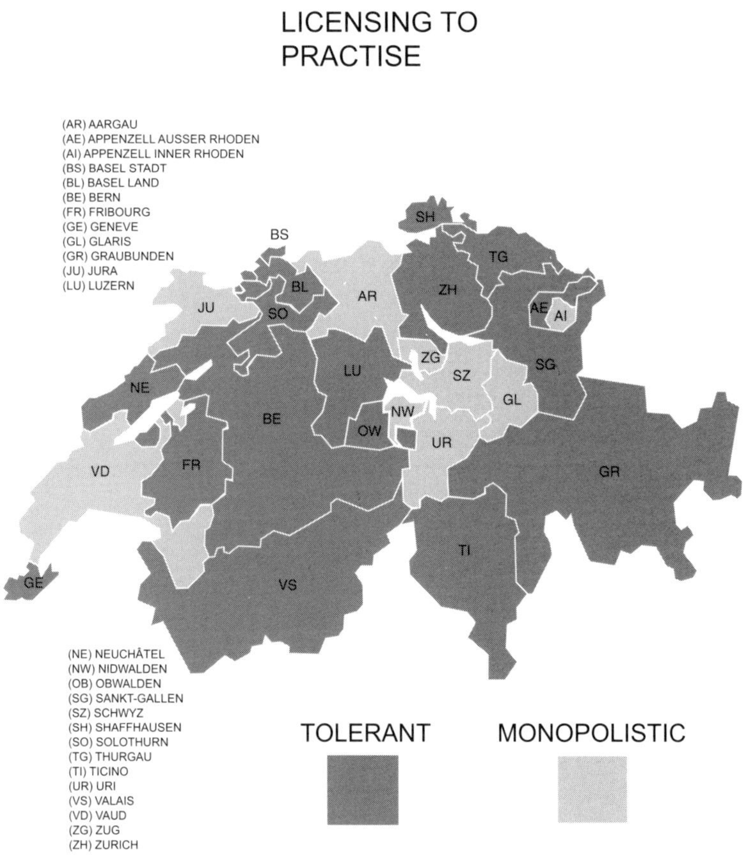

875 SALE D. M., *op. cit.*: 51.

Map 2 – Licensing to practise in Europe

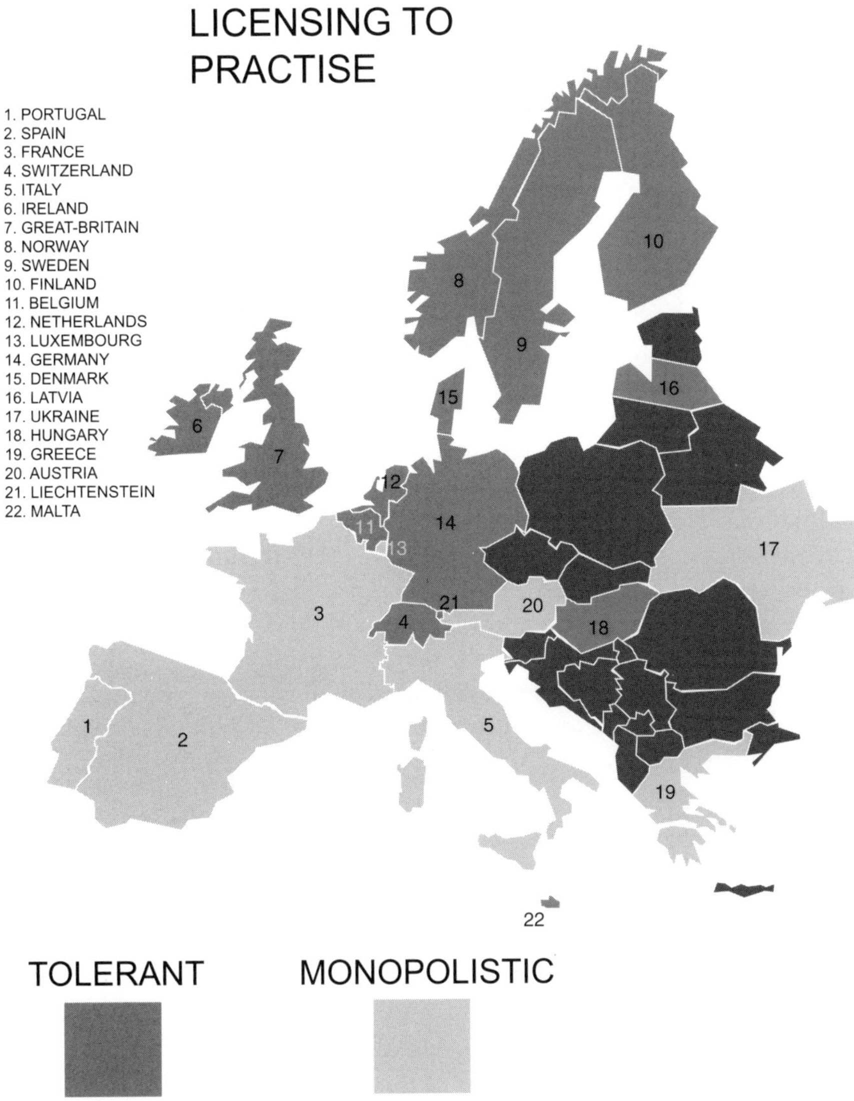

4.4 Conclusion

For the past two decades, there has been a clear trend towards tolerance and a more effective integration of alternative practitioners in Western countries. This has been the result of a gradual change of policy. The importance of the cultural context must be stressed. Indeed, countries adopt regulations on alternative medicines and tolerate various practices according to their medical history and their traditions.

Alternative medicines have had to operate within a legal framework which was not originally designed for them and following a period of strict repression. Authorities have come to realise that continuing to utilise repressive policies is not only ineffective but also inadapted for the regulation of alternative medicines. As a result, although in theory most regulations continue to have a monopolistic bent, public authorities and courts have in practice been more tolerant towards alternative practitioners. Recently, this change of attitude has resulted in the setting up of new regulations that not only tolerate alternative practitioners but also regulate the practices of these practitioners in order to ensure a certain level of quality and security. Thus, systems have appeared that on the one hand regulate specific alternative techniques in a similar way to allopathic techniques, and on the other allow (with fewer conditions) the practice of non-dangerous or non-scientific medical acts. Medical acts involving substantial risks remain the exclusive competence of allopathic practitioners. It is also noteworthy that no country has moved from a tolerant policy to a monopolistic policy.

However, although regulations of alternative medicines have evolved, there still remains a lack of uniformity among such regulations. In particular, licences to practise and diplomas are not widely recognised between the various states. This situation impedes the development of an area allowing the free movement of practitioners based on the mutual recognition of diplomas and licences to practise.

In a more technical sense, it has been possible to observe the increasing use of criteria in various legislative initiatives where the scientific character of the risks has been linked to the practice of the technique in order to define which professions require an authorisation to practice. Lawmakers have also recently favoured policies that have as their aim the protection of restricted titles. This change of approach has resulted in a shift from the unqualified practice of medicine to the unqualified use of title.

5. The Coverage of Alternative Medicines

5.1 Introduction

The second main topic analyzed in this research shall be the coverage of alternative medicines by both public and private insurance funds.

After a presentation of several approaches relating to the coverage of alternative medicines, the situation in several Western countries shall be presented. Our attempt is to describe both the theoretical framework of the coverage provided and the actual practice of insurance funds. The charts at the end of this chapter provide a schematic view of the situation.

As one shall see, this field is in constant evolution. Private and public insurance funds are introducing some forms of coverage for alternative therapies, and are developing criteria in order to better evaluate their medical necessity.

5.2 Classification

A classification of the existing systems that provide coverage for alternative medicines does not exist. The coverage of alternative medicines varies widely; it may be provided by social security and/or private insurance companies, it can be complete or restricted by the number or type of treatment and sometimes a co-payment is required. When coverage for alternative medicines is available, it may be either official or unofficial. In some countries, case law has determined the criteria dealing with the coverage of these techniques.

If one takes as a criterion the access of patients to alternative medicines, then the following approaches can be identified:

1. the closed system, where there is no coverage of alternative medicines, neither public nor private;[1]

1 E.g., Ukraine.

2. the private system, where alternative medicines are covered only by private insurance funds to the exclusion of the social insurance. Such coverage requires the insured to have an additional private insurance policy. One cannot exclude the fact that unofficial coverage also exists in such countries. However, based on current information available it is not widespread;[2]
3. The public system. In this system, some alternative medicines are covered by social insurance in addition to possible private coverage. There are two types of coverage:
   3.1 unofficial coverage is when allopathic practitioners provide alternative medicines under an allopathic appellation or as a general consultation. Sometimes this is the only type of coverage available from social insurance;[3]
   3.2 official coverage is when in addition to possible unofficial coverage, some alternative medicines are officially reimbursed, either through a catalogue of benefits enclosed in a decree[4] or when case law has set up specific criteria.[5]

5.3 Overview

5.3.1 European Union[6]

Bibliography

BAEYENS A., *Free movement of good and services in health care: A comment on the court cases Decker and Kohll from a Belgian point of view*, in: European Journal of Health Law, 1999, n° 6: 373–83; BRITISH MEDICAL ASSOCIATION (LAMONT T.), *Alternative medicine – New approaches to good practice*, Oxford University Press, 1993, Oxford/New York; DOMMERS J., *An introduction to European Union health law*, in: European Journal of Health Law, vol. 4,

2 E.g., Spain, Liechtenstein.
3 E.g., Belgium, Ireland.
4 E.g., Austria, Denmark, Finland, France, Germany, Great Britain, Latvia, Italy, Luxemburg, Malta, Norway, Netherlands and Switzerland.
5 E.g., Austria and Germany.
6 For a brief presentation of the several insurance systems available in Europe, see FRÉCHELIN K. (I), *op. cit.*: 134–36; HAMILTON G. J., *op. cit.*: 323–29.
For an overview of the general principles of EU regulation, see chap. 4.3.1.1.

n° 1, 1997: 19–41; FRÉCHELIN K. (I), *Couverture en cas de maladie et d'accidents dans les Etats de l'UE*, in: Sécurité Sociale, 1999, n° 3: 134–36; HAMILTON G. J., *Competition and solidarity in European health care systems*, in: European Journal of Health Law, 1996, n° 3: 323–29; KAHIL-WOLFF B., *L'accord sur la libre circulation des personnes Suisse-CE et le droit des assurances sociales*, in: Semaine Judiciaire, 2001, vol. 123, n° 4: 108–134; LANNOYE P., *Is there a future for complementary medicine in Europe? – European report on the status of non-conventionnal medicine*, The Natural Medicines Society, 1996, Heanor; PROCOMED, *Lettre d'information de l'Association pour la reconnaissance et la promotion des médecines complémentaires en Europe*, Bulletin n° 2, December 1997, Bruxelles.

5.3.1.1 General Principles

Public health is almost exclusively the competence of member States and not of the European Union (EU). However, in order to ensure the free movement of persons, the Council adopted certain measures in the field of social security. EC Regulations 1408/71[7] and 574/72 were adopted to ensure that migrant workers and migrant self-employed persons,[8] with their family-members, could rely upon social insurance.[9] The first regulation provides for the coverage of treatment for patients needing immediate care,[10] while the second one comprises of arrangements for medical treatment during a temporary stay[11] in another Member State.[12] However, these regulations do not govern private health insurance, the free movement of private

7 This regulation coordinates legislation of the Member States concerning branches of social security such as sickness and maternity benefits, invalidity benefits in respect of accidents at work and occupational diseases, and unemployment benefits.

8 And also EU citizens travelling in the EU.

9 The basic principle of Regulation 1408/71 is that people shall be subject to the social security legislation of the Member State in which they work, even when they reside in another Member State (DOMMERS J., *op. cit.*: 27).

10 According to article 22 of Regulation 1408/71, as amended by regulation 2793/81, a national social or health insurance authority may not refuse a patient to seek medical treatment in another Member State if, with regard to the current health status of the patient, the necessary treatment cannot be delivered in time in the patient's own country and there is an immediate need for treatment (Official Journal EC n° L275, 1981).

11 E.g., a business trip, temporary employment, studies and vacations.

12 It is, however, better to take private health insurance rather than depend solely on Regulation 574/72 and its many bureaucratic E-Forms. In addition, national health insurance schemes differ from one country to another (DOMMERS J., *op. cit.*: 30).

insurance services being ruled by specific EC Directives.[13] In the future, it seems unlikely that there will be any developments in relation to free movement for patients, as social security schemes for the benefit of public interest shall remain a primary competence of the Member States.[14, 15]

The European Court of Justice has stated that the provisions concerning the free movement of goods and services also apply to health care.[16] In particular, it has pointed out that every insured person is free to buy glasses and to receive medical treatments in another Member States.[17]

13 DOMMERS J., *op. cit.*: 28.

14 However, as Baeyens notes, "Community law does not detract from the powers of Member States to organise their social security themselves. But this does not mean that the social security sector would be like an island outside the influence of Community law, and that therefore no national or similar regulation would be covered by the law. [...] Furthermore, the fact, that under the current state of European law Member States are competent in the field of social security, is not such that it would enable Member States to legislate contrary to Community law" (BAEYENS A., *op. cit.*: 375).

15 BRITISH MEDICAL ASSOCIATION, *op. cit.*: 15–16; DOMMERS J., *op. cit.*: 30; KAHIL-WOLFF B., *op. cit.*: 108–22.

16 See Decker (Case 120/95 *Decker v. Caisse de Maladie des Employés Privés* [1998] ECR), and Kohll (Case 158/96 *Kohll v. Union des Caisses de Maladie* [1998] ECR).
These two cases caused much controversy in the Member States of the European Union. While in Decker, the principle of free movement of goods was at stake, in Kohll the free movement of services was discussed in relation to medical treatment.

17 In Decker, the Court considered that the national law prevented an insured person from purchasing medical products in another Member State. Consequently, it was hindering the import of medical devices and goods and therefore was incompatible with article 28 of the EC treaty.
In Kohll, the Court estimated that national rules did not prevent an insured person from receiving medical treatment in another Member State, but sufficiently discouraged an insured person from doing so, and so constituted a barrier to the freedom to provide services.
The control of health expenditure, and protection of public health were not accepted by the Court as sufficient arguments to make an exception to the principle of free movement of goods and services.
Baeyens notes that the effects of the two above-mentioned cases is that "several Member States refuse to recognise the general scope of the recent jurisprudence and therefore interpret it very strictly. Other Member States, like Belgium, are occupied adapting their legislation, even if they prefer to review their policy gradually on a step by step basis" (BAEYENS A., *op. cit.*: 382).

5.3.1.2 Situation of Alternative Medicines

At the end of 1995, the Conference of Presidents of the European Parliament proposed that a report on alternative medicines be undertaken. The objective of the report, which enclosed a proposition regarding the coverage of alternative medicines, was to involve the Commission in the process of recognizing alternative medicines.[18]

The Conference noted that two systems had emerged in relation to the coverage of alternative medicines. On one hand, some alternative disciplines had been partially integrated into health care systems and, on the other hand, private insurance companies had agreed to set up a parallel reimbursement system. According to Lannoye "neither of these approaches can be used for the long term: the first one because it is inconsistent, and the second one because if it is generalized, it would become a trend towards privatizing social security, which would threaten the whole way in which our society is developing".[19] Consequently, as soon as a given therapy is approved, it should be reimbursed by the social security. Furthermore, governments should be attentive to the fact that alternative medicines play a role in the prevention of illnesses.

On February 27, 1997 the Commission on Welfare, Public Health and Consumers' Protection adopted a project rejecting the proposition regarding coverage of alternative medicines by national health care systems.[20]

In brief, it appears very difficult to envisage the adoption of a European Directive on the subject. Indeed, although recent decisions of the European Court of Justice have enlarged the scope of free movement of persons and goods, the field of social insurance remains mainly a national and not an European competence.[21]

5.3.2 Country with a Closed System[22]

The Ukraine is the only country, among the countries reviewed, that has a closed system in relation to the coverage of alternative medicines. These treatments are not reimbursed by social insurance or private companies.

18 LANNOYE P., *op. cit.*: 6–7; PROCOMED, *op. cit.*: 2.
19 LANNOYE P., *op. cit.*: 6–7.
20 PROCOMED, *op. cit.*: 2–3.
21 For more details, see chap. 4.3.3.1.
22 Dr. Hmelewskaja A., Mar. 1998, Kiew. To the best of our knowledge, the situation has not changed since then.

There are no hospitals providing alternative medicines nor do private insurance companies reimburse alternative medicines.

5.3.3 Countries with a Private Coverage System

5.3.3.1 Liechtenstein[23]

Liechtenstein has a private coverage system for alternative medicines. Alternative techniques are not covered by the compulsory social insurance and it does not appear that these therapies are provided under an allopathic appellation. However, it is possible to be covered by private insurance.[24] The limit of such coverage is between CHF 500 and 1,500 per year.[25]

5.3.3.2 Spain[26]

Bibliography

Alonso Olea M., *Las prestaciones sanitarias de la seguridad social*, Editorial civitas, 1994, Madrid; Guzman L. (co-author: Casero J. V.), *Aproximación a la regulación juridica de la homeopatia*, Revista general de derecho, 1992, vol. 48: 3947–48; McCarthy M. (co-author: Rees S.), *Health systems and health medicine in the European Community*, Royal College of Physicians of London, 1992, London: 49–54; Schneider M. (co-authors: Biene-Dietrich P., Gebanyi M., Hofmann U., Huber M., Köse A., Sommer J. H.), *Gesundheitssysteme im internationalen Vergleich*, ed. 1994, BASYS, 1995, Augsburg: 459–72.

Spain has a private coverage system for alternative medicines. These alternative techniques are not covered, officially or unofficially, by social insurance. However, in some rare instances private insurance companies provide coverage for a few alternative medicines.

23 For an overview of the health care system in Liechtenstein, see Hoch H., *Geschichte des Liechtenstein Sozialversicherungrechts*, Inaug.-Dissert., 1991, Schaan: 36–56.

24 Unfortunately, we did not obtain precise information regarding the types of alternative medicines and the extent of the cover provided by private insurance companies, but they seem to be quite extensive.

25 Cornelia Marxer-Broder, collaborator at the Liechtenstein Government, Vaduz, Sept. 2001.

26 Dr. Juan R. Villaverde, Mar. 2001, Spain, also provided the information regarding the country.
For an overview of the Spanish health care system, see e.g., Alonso Olea M., *op. cit.*; McCarthy M., *op. cit.*; Schneider M., *op. cit.*

To the best of our knowledge, there are two public hospitals providing outpatients with homeopathy but patients appear to pay the cost of the treatments themselves.[27]

For more specifically homeopathic products, coming under art. 94 of the Law 26/1990 of December 20 on Medicine, there is no justification for these medicines to be financed through state funds (INSALUD).[28]

5.3.4 Country with a Public Unofficial Coverage System[29]

Bibliography

Aldridge D., *Unconventional medicine in Europe*, Advances, 10 (2): 52–60, 1994; Fisher P. (co-author: Ward A.), *Alternative medicine in Europe*, in: BMJ, vol. 309, July 9, 1994: 107–11; Frost and Sullivan Ltd, *Alternative medical practices in Europe*, Report n° E874, Sullivan House, Grosvenor Gardens, 1987, London SW1: 187–92; Lüschen G., and co-authors, *Health systems in the European Union*, Oldenburg Verlag, 1995, München: 38–39; McCarthy M. (co-author: Rees S.), *Health systems and health medicine in the European Community*, Royal College of Physicians of London, 1992, London: 10–13; Miralles J., *Homéopathie et ostéopathie – Pour la 1ère fois, une mutualité rembourse!*, in: La Dernière Heure, 13 mars 1997; Robard I., *La santé hors la loi: Les hors la loi de la santé*, 4th ed., Ed. de l'Ancre, 1994, Suresnes: 214–15; Sermeus G., *Alternative health care in Belgium: An explanation of various social aspects*, in: Lewith G. (co-editors: Aldridge D.), *Alternative medicine and the European Community*, CW Daniel, 1991, Saffron Walden: 61–74; Weber A. (co-authors: Leienbach V., Dohle A., Strunk S., Teyukov A., Schulte-Mimberg U., Angele S.), *Soziale Sicherung in West-, Mittel-, und Osteuropa*, Nomos Verlagsgesellschaft, 1994, Baden-Baden: 14–24.

Belgium has an unofficial public coverage system with regard to alternative medicines. In this country, both public and private insurance funds cover alternative medicines.

27 Hospital del Nen Deu, Barcelona and Hospital Homeopatico de San Jose, Madrid.

28 The Homeopathic Physicians Charter of the Spanish State has solicited for the inclusion of homeopathic medications within the social security system, but without success (Guzman L., *op. cit.*: 3955).

29 For an overview of the Belgian health care system, see, Lüschen G., *op. cit.*; McCarthy M., *op. cit.*; Weber A., *op. cit.*

Where public coverage is concerned, the social security system does not officially reimburse alternative medicines,[30] regardless of whether such treatments are provided by physicians or non-allopathic practitioners. Indeed, the current nomenclature does not contain dispositions about them. However, practically speaking, doctors using alternative medicines may guarantee their patients that part of their fees will be reimbursed.[31] Similarly, in order to obtain reimbursement for osteopathic treatments, physiotherapists prescribe treatments under a classic designation.[32]

In March 1997, a mutual insurance company[33] was the first to decide to partially reimburse homeopathic medicine and osteopathic treatments.[34] In order to ensure certain guarantees, the list of reimbursed homeopathic remedies is based on the EU Directive on homeopathic products.[35] The treatments are covered only if provided by physicians, nurses and physiotherapists.[36]

Besides mutual insurance, there are also private insurance companies that partially reimburse chiropractic and acupuncture.[37]

30 Health insurance is compulsory for most of the population.

31 ALDRIDGE D., *op. cit.*: 55; FROST AND SULLIVAN LTD, *op. cit.*: 192; SERMEUS G., *op. cit.*: 61, 68.

32 ROBARD I., *op. cit.*: 215.

33 The socialist mutual insurance of Tournai-Ath.
There are six main health insurance organizations, which are federations of regional alliances or composed of local mutual health insurance societies. Five of them are aligned along religious and ideological lines and the sixth, the auxiliary fund, is managed by the Government (FROST AND SULLIVAN, *op. cit.*: 187–88; LÜSCHEN G., *op. cit.*: 38; MCCARTHY M., *op. cit.*: 11).

34 These techniques are not recognized in Belgium as medical specialties.
The insurance reimburses 25% of homeopathic remedies up to a maximum cost of 320 Euros per year and per beneficiary. For osteopathy, the insurance reimburses 20 Euros for each treatment with a maximum of six treatments. In December 2001, discussions between the professional unions of physicians, dentists and veterinarians, and social security institutions were still ongoing regarding extending the coverage of homeopathic drugs.
However, in Belgium, co-payments are required for approximately 25% of physicians' costs, but some expensive treatments are completely and directly reimbursed by insurance funds (LÜSCHEN G., *op. cit.*: 39).

35 Insurance companies have considered extending the reimbursement to other techniques, such as acupuncture and phytotherapy, among others. In this respect, one physician out of four wants reimbursement for such therapies while 59% of users and 36% of non-users expressed their willingness to pay higher premiums to cover such reimbursement (SERMEUS G., *op. cit.*: 68–70).

36 MIRALLES J., *op. cit.*

37 FISHER P., *op. cit.*: 108; ROBARD I., *op. cit.*: 214.

5.3.5 Countries with a Public Official Coverage System

5.3.5.1 Austria[38]

Bibliography

Binder M., *Zur Kostendeckung alternativmedizinischer Behandlungsmethoden durch die Krankenversicherung*, in: Recht der Medizin, vol. 4, n° 2, April 1997: 39–44; Frost and Sullivan Ltd, *Alternative medical practices in Europe*, Report n° E874, Sullivan House, Grosvenor Gardens, 1987, London SW1: 248; Schneider M. (co-authors: Biene-Dietrich P., Gebanyi M., Hofmann U., Huber M., Köse A., Sommer J. H.), *Gesundheitssysteme im internationalen Vergleich*, ed. 1994, BASYS, 1995, Augsburg: 385–404; Schwartz W., *Von Exorzisten und Heilpraktkern: Geistheilungen rechtlich betrachtet*, in: Recht der Medizin, 1999, n° 1: 18; Vogel G., *Medikation mit Aussenseitermethoden-eine Kostenfrage?*, in: RdM, 1994, n° 4: 108–11.

Austria has a public coverage system in respect of alternative medicines. In this country, some techniques are, officially or not, reimbursed both by social and private insurance. Case law has also played a role in the development of criteria dealing with the coverage of alternative medicines.

Several public insurance funds cover some alternative medicines.[39] For example, the OOGKK provides full coverage for chiropractic, acupuncture, homeopathy and neuraltherapy, when two conditions are satisfied; first, physicians must have a contract with the OOGKK. Second, physicians must hold a diploma from the Austrian Chamber of Medicine.[40] When doctors providing the alternative techniques do not have a contract with the fund, only 80% of the costs that would be covered with a contract physician

38 The information provided for Austria regarding the country was made available by the Ministry of Work, Health and Social of Austrian Republic, July 1997, Vienna; Schmadlbauer H., oberösterreichische Gebietskrankenkasse, Linz, Aug. 2001.
For an overview of the Austrian health care system, see Schneider M., *op. cit.*: 385–404.

39 In Austria, there are eight main insurance funds, one for each federal state, ruled by the Code of Social Insurance (in German: "Allgemeines Sozialversicherungsgesetz"). For example, the "oberösterreichische Gebietskrankenkasse" (OOGKK) provides health insurance for all employed persons (and their relatives) in Upper Austria (about 1 million people). It is a public, non-governmental and non-profit institution, ruled by law.

40 For more details, see chap. 4.3.2.1.

are reimbursed.[41] The OOGKK published a "black list" of 20 alternative techniques,[42] which physicians having a contract with the OOGKK may not use with the insured patients any more. This action affects only those methods that are proven to be absolutely ineffective, cost-ineffective or even dangerous.[43]

Furthermore, social insurance may decide to cover alternative techniques in some specific cases. The reimbursement criteria are the usual ones, namely, scientific proof of effectiveness, cost-effectiveness and appropriateness. A strict interpretation of these principles would seem to indicate that alternative medicines should not be covered. Nevertheless, the courts and current literature have been open-minded in their responses to coverage of alternative medicines.[44] For example, the Social Supreme Court has allowed coverage for homeopathy.[45] Furthermore, massages, balneotherapy[46] and electrotherapy are now included as pain relief treatments.[47]

Moreover, when allopathic treatments are unsuccessful, and alternative treatments are the ultima ratio, social insurance will provide coverage so long as the alternative technique demonstrates that it has some chance of success. Some authors consider that alternative medicines should be reimbursed not only in these cases, but whenever doctors and patients decide to use them.[48]

Several authors consider that alternative medicines should be reimbursed according to the same principles governing general services. They argue that, in addition to the above-mentioned criteria, consideration must also be paid to whether a treatment could, in specific cases, result in a positive effect in specific cases. They further state that as long as physicians diligently provide alternative medicines, they should be allowed to provide them. Furthermore, as soon as alternative medicines are taught in the

41 The other public health insurance funds have a similar system. Often, a co-payment of 20% is required from patients.

42 Namely, Aromatherapy, Aura-Healing, Blood Bach therapy, "Baunscheitieren", "Biologische Terrain-Analyse", Bio-resonance therapy, Colon hydrotherapy, "Edelsteinmedizin", "Eigenurintherapie", Hair analysis, Honey therapy, Iridology, "Klangmassage", Magical healing techniques, Magnetotherapy, Pendulum, Rei-Ki, Schamanism, "Wünschelrute" and Cell therapy.

43 H. Schmadlbauer, oberösterreichische Gebietskrankenkasse, Linz, Aug. 2001.

44 BINDER M., *op. cit.*: 40–43; VOGEL G., *op. cit.*: 108–10.

45 Homeopathy has been covered since the end of the 19th century.

46 Co-payments are required for massages and balneotherapy (SCHNEIDER M., *op. cit.*: 390).

47 BINDER M., *op. cit.*: 40–44; FROST AND SULLIVAN, *op. cit.*: 248; SCHWARTZ W., *op. cit.*: 18; VOGEL G., *op. cit.*: 108–10.

48 BINDER M., *op. cit.*: 43; VOGEL G., *op. cit.*: 108–10.

universities, they should be covered by social insurance. From this perspective, the principle of freedom of choice for patients seems to be paramount for these commentators.[49]

One should note that some private insurance companies cover alternative medicines as well.[50]

5.3.5.2 Denmark[51]

Bibliography

Fisher P. (co-author: Ward A.), *Alternative medicine in Europe*, in: BMJ, vol. 309, July 9, 1994: 107–11; Frost and Sullivan Ltd, *Alternative medical practices in Europe*, Report n° E874, Sullivan House, Grosvenor Gardens, 1987, London SW1: 249; McCarthy M. (co-author: Rees S.), *Health systems and health medicine in the European Community*, Royal College of Physicians of London, 1992, London: 14–17; Robard I., *La santé hors la loi: Les hors la loi de la santé*, 4th ed., Ed. de l'Ancre, 1994, Suresnes: 232; Stepan J., *Traditional and alternative systems of medicine: A comparative review of legislation*, in: International Digest of Health Legislation, 1985, vol. 36, n° 2, Genève: 323; Weber A. (co-authors: Leienbach V., Dohle A., Strunk S., Teyukov A., Schulte-Mimberg U., Angele S.), *Soziale Sicherung in West-, Mittel-, und Osteuropa*, Nomos Verlagsgesellschaft, 1994, Baden-Baden: 44–55.

Denmark has a public coverage system in respect of alternative medicines.[52] Generally, there is no reimbursement for alternative medicines. Only those allopathic practitioners who are qualified to practise medicine are entitled to reimbursement through social security. Since 1975, however, a special agreement between the public insurance schemes and the chiropractors provides partial cover, being one third of the cost, for up to five consultations in chiropractic and one X-ray examination per year. Further, these treatments must be provided by chiropractors recognized by the Danish Chiropractic Association.[53]

In addition, there is some reimbursement provided by insurance funds for acupuncture. Osteopathic treatments are also covered by these funds when registered physicians refer patients.[54]

49 Binder M., *op. cit.*: 43; Vogel G., *op. cit.*: 108–10.
50 Unfortunately, sufficient information on the subject is not available.
51 For an overview of the Danish health care system, see McCarthy M., *op. cit.*; Weber A., *op. cit.*
52 No information was obtained in respect of private reimbursement.
53 McCarthy M., *op. cit.*: 15; Robard I., *op. cit.*: 232; Stepan J., *op. cit.*: 323.
54 Fisher P., *op. cit.*: 108; Frost and Sullivan, *op. cit.*: 249.

5.3.5.3 *Finland*[55]

Bibliography

Aldridge D., *Unconventional medicine in Europe*, Advances, 1994, vol. 10, n° 2: 55; Frost and Sullivan Ltd, *Alternative medical practices in Europe*, Report n° E874, Sullivan House, Grosvenor Gardens, 1987, London SW1: 250; Preusker U. K., *Gesundheitssysteme in Scandinavien – Eine Aktuelle Darstellung des schwedischen, norwegischen und finnischen Gesundheitswesens*, Bergisch Gladbach, 1996, Heider; Vaskilampi T., *The role of alternative medicine: The Finnish experience*, in: Lewith G. (co-author: Aldridge D.), *Alternative medicine and the European Community*, CW Daniel, 1991, Saffron Walden: 101–12.

Finland has a public coverage system in respect of alternative medicines. Indeed, some alternative medicines are officially and unofficially reimbursed both by social insurance and by private insurance companies.

Generally, alternative medicines are not reimbursed from private insurance or public funds.[56] However, some forms of alternative medicines are reimbursed by social security when provided by physicians who do not specify which treatment they provide.[57] Also, acupuncture sessions given in health centers[58] are now covered by the SII, as long as physicians carry them out.[59, 60]

Moreover, treatment given by recognised chiropractors, naprapath practitioners and osteopaths is reimbursed when:[61]

55 Information regarding Finland was also provided by Vaskilampi T., Professor in sociology, Finland, Sept. 2001; Tiina Telakivi, M.D. expert physician at the Social Insurance Institution, Sept. 1997, Helsinki.
For an overview of the Finnish health care system, see Preusker U. K., *op. cit.*

56 Aldridge D., *op. cit.*: 55; Vaskilampi T., *op. cit.*: 101.

57 The Social Insurance Institution (SII) does not make further enquiries about a doctor's fee. In particular, it does not ask about the making of the diagnosis or what prescriptions were given during the session. Consequently, doctors are not expected to provide information as to the types of treatment they give.

58 Already in 1987, approximately 200 local health centres were providing acupuncture treatment (Frost and Sullivan, *op. cit.*: 250).

59 Although social insurance considers lymphatic draining as an alternative therapy, this technique is reimbursed when: 1. a medical doctor has referred patients to the therapist and; 2. the condition treated was caused by surgery for breast cancer, radiation treatment to lower abdomen and genital region, erysipelas in the lower extremities or congenital illness of the lymphatic system.

60 Vaskilampi T., Professor in sociology, Finland, Sept. 2001; Tiina Telakivi, M.D. expert physician at the Social Insurance Institution, Sept. 1997, Helsinki.

61 Tiina Telakivi, M.D. expert physician at the Social Insurance Institution, Sept. 1997, Helsinki. To the best of our knowledge, the situation has not changed since then.

1. a physician made the first diagnosis; and
2. the patient was referred to the therapist by a licensed physician; and
3. the therapist works in an institution led by a physiotherapist or a physician.

Alternative medication (drugs) is not reimbursed by the SII.[62]

In respect to private reimbursement, there is still, to the best of our knowledge, no private insurance company reimbursing alternative medicines. However, in some cases, treatments are reimbursed by private insurance companies according to the same principles followed by the SII.[63, 64]

5.3.5.4 France[65]

Bibliography

ALBER J. (co-author: BERNARDI-SCHENKLUHN B.), *Westeuropäische Gesundheitssysteme im Vergleich, Bundesrepublik Deutschland, Schweiz, Frankreich, Italien, Grossbritanien*, Campus Verlag, 1992, Frankfurt: 323–413; ALDRIDGE D., *Unconventional medicine in Europe*, Advances, 1994, vol. 10, n° 2: 55; BEDEE H. (co-authors: D'HAESE W., PETRY V., ROMPELMAN A. J.), *The international guide to social security*, Kluwer Law International, 1995, The Hague/London/Boston; BOUCHAYER F., *Alternative medicines: A general approach to the French situation*, in: LEWITH G. (co-editor: ALDRIDGE D.), *Alternative medicine and the European Community*, CW Daniel, 1991, Saffron Walden: 45–60; CHAUCHARD, *Droit de la sécurité sociale*, LGDJ, 1994, Paris; FROST AND SULLIVAN LTD, *Alternative medical practices in Europe*, Report n° E874, Sullivan House, Grosvenor Gardens, 1987, London SW1: 213–24; HARICHAUX M., *Réformes de l'assurance maladie et protection des assurés*, in: Revue de droit sanitaire et social, Oct.-Dec. 1996, vol. 43, n° 4,: 842–52; LANNOYE P., *Is there a future for alternative medicine in Europe? – European report on the status of non-conventionnal medicine*, The Natural Medicines Society, 1996, Heanor: 2; MOREAU J. (co-author: TRUCHET D.), *Droit de la santé publique*, Mémento Dalloz, 1997, Paris; ROBARD I., *La santé hors la loi: Les hors la loi de la santé*, 4th ed., Ed. de l'Ancre, 1994, Suresnes: 55–57, 143–44; SCHNEIDER M. (co-authors: HOFMANN U., VASIKJEVIC S.) (II),

62 Tiina Telakivi, M.D. expert physician at the Social Insurance Institution, Sept. 1997, Helsinki. To the best of our knowledge, the situation has not changed since then.

63 Treatments have to be given in an authorised private institute headed by a medical doctor or a physiotherapist.

64 Antti Marttila, Director at the National Board of Medico-legal Affairs, Mar. 1998, Helsinki; Tarja Holi, Director at the National Authority for Medico legal Affairs, Sept. 2001.

Die Honorierung naturheikundlicher Verfahren – Untersuchung für den Bundesminister für Arbeit und Sozialordnung, Basys, 1989, Augsburg; SCHNEIDER M. (co-authors: BIENE-DIETRICH P., GEBANYI M., HOFMANN U., HUBER M., KÖSE A., SOMMER J. H.) (II), *Gesundheitssysteme im internationalen Vergleich*, ed. 1994, BASYS, 1995, Augsburg: 245–64.

France has a public coverage system in respect of alternative medicines. Some alternative medicines are officially and unofficially covered, either by social security or by private insurance companies. In particular, social security reimburses acupuncture sessions and homeopathic prescriptions when provided by certified physicians. Furthermore, specific medical activities and products are covered.[66] Treatments provided by non-allopathic practitioners are not covered by social security or private insurance companies.

In France, there is a trend toward integrating some alternative medicines into the official coverage system provided by social security. A good example of this increasing integration is the treatment of acupuncture. In the past, MEP physicians[67] were fined because they reported acupuncture treatments as classic consultations. After discussions between those physicians using acupuncture and social security, an agreement was reached. The social security now officially reimburses acupuncture treatment provided by MEP physicians, as they do for consultations in general practice.[68] Homeopathic prescriptions are covered by social security as well when provided by authorized physicians. Also covered are medical activities and products, such as medical phytotherapy consultations or alternative technical sessions by an approved kinesitherapist.[69, 70]

65 For an overview of the French health care system, see ALBER J., *op. cit.*: 323–413; BEDEE H., *op. cit.*; CHAUCHARD, *op. cit.*; HARICHAUX M., *op. cit.*: 842–52; MOREAU J., *op. cit.*; SCHNEIDER M. (II), *op. cit.*: 245–64.

66 Between 3.5% and 7% of health care expenditure in France is linked to alternative medicines, excluding alternative treatments provided in hospitals (BOUCHAYER F., *op. cit.*: 45, 55).

67 Doctors using alternative medicines are designated as "doctors with a particular type of practice" (in French: "Médecin à mode d'Exercice Particulier (MEP)"). The MEP is neither a specialty nor a qualification. It only indicates a physicians' orientation, without guarantee of the quality of care. There are 9 types of MEP: in acupuncture, homeopathy, thermalism, allergology, angelology, medicine and sport, biology, phoniatry, and echotomography. In order to be registered as MEP, physicians must hold an academic degree (PORTELLI N., *op. cit.*: 34; Caisse Nationale de l'Assurance Maladie, Jan. 1998, Paris).

68 ROBARD I., *op. cit.*: 143–44.

In addition to treatments officially covered by social insurance, MEP physicians and kinesitherapists continue to provide alternative treatments, which they report as allopathic treatments, amounting to fraudulent use of the social security system.[71]

Usually, private insurance companies do not cover alternative medicines. They merely reimburse the part not covered by social security for alternative treatments included in the nomenclature of the social security system. In other words, private insurance companies[72] only partially reimburse costs linked to the providing of homeopathic and acupuncture treatments. There is no reimbursement for other alternative treatments, such as chiropractic or osteopathy.

5.3.5.5 Germany[73]

Bibliography

Alber J. (co-author: Bernardi-Schenkluhn B.), *Westeuropäische Gesundheitssysteme im Vergleich, Bundesrepublik Deutschland, Schweiz, Frankreich, Italien, Grossbritanien*, Campus Verlag, 1992, Frankfurt: 31–176; Anonymous (III), *Zur Leistungspflicht der Krankenkassen für alternative Heilmethoden*, in: MedR, 1998, n° 5: 230ss; Anonymous (II), *Zur Leistungspflicht der Krankenkassen bei Heilbehandlung durch Heilpraktiker*, in: MedR, 1998, n° 6: 269; Berthod-Wurmser M., *La santé en Europe*, La documentation française, 1994, Paris: 72–77; Cramer R., *Strafrechtliche Grenzen der Therapiefreiheit und*

69 Regarding kinesitherapy, according to Bouchayer, "because of the bad compatibility between operations conducted by alternative kinesitherapists – osteopathy for instance – demanding much time, and 'conventional' price rates established for the profession, an increasing number of kinesitherapists treat their patients on a 'non-conventionalised' basis" (Bouchayer F., *op. cit.*: 56–57).

70 Bouchayer F., *op. cit.*: 55–56; Frost and Sullivan, *op. cit.*: 222; Portelli N., *op. cit.*: 36–37.

71 It is very difficult to assess the actual prevalence of this kind of behaviour. Indeed, there is currently no way to evaluate the respective proportion of shared costs assumed by users and social security with regard to alternative pharmaceuticals and alternative health care. However, co-payment from patients using these techniques must be substantially higher than co-payment connected with the use of classic allopathic medical acts (Bouchayer F., *op. cit.*: 56).

72 This is the case for the following private insurance companies: GAN, UAP, FNMS, AXA, Lloyd Continental and UNIM.

73 For an overview of the German health care system, see Alber J., *op. cit.*: 31–176; Berthod-Wurmser M., *op. cit.*: 72–77; McCarthy M., *op. cit.*: 23–26; Schneider M. (I), *op. cit.*: 193–225.

der Heilbehandlung durch den Heilpraktiker, Dissertation, 1995, Köln: 42–45; Ehlers A. P. F., *Medizin in den Händen von Heilpraktikern – "Nicht-Heilkundigen"*, Springer Verlag, 1995, Berlin/Heidelberg: 169–77; Freudenberg U., *Der Leistungsanspruch bei alternativen Heilmethoden gegenüber der gesetzlichen Krankenversicherung, der privaten Krankenversicherung und der Beihilfe*, Dissertation, 1994, Bonn; Grupp K., *Rechtliche Probleme alternativer Behandlungsmethoden*, in: MedR, 1992, vol. 5: 256–63; Hauff M. (co-author: Prätorius R.), *Leistungsstruktur alternativer Arztpraxen*, in: Soziale Hygiene; Jost T. S., *Health care rationing in the courts: A comparative study*, in: Hasting International and Comparative Law Review, 1998, vol. 21, n° 3: 639–714; Jung H. (co-author: Neumann J. N.), *Alternative Behandlungsmethoden* in: Eser (co-authors: Lutterotti, Sporken), *Lexikon Medizin – Ethik – Recht*, Freiburg, 1989; Lanz, *Erstattung einer Heilpraktikertherapie bei Aids-Erkrankten*, in: NJW, 1996, n° 37: 2434–35; McCarthy M. (co-author: Rees S.), *Health systems and health medicine in the European Community*, Royal College of Physicians of London, 1992, London: 23–26; Nüchtern E., *Die Begutachtung unkonventioneller Heilmethoden im Rahmen der gesetzlichen Krankenversicherung – Probleme vor dem Hintergrung der derzeitigen Rechtsprechung*, in: Gesundh.-Wes., vol. 57, 1995: 437–42; Anonymous (I), *Gerichtsurteil gegen die deutschen Krankenkassen – Indirekte Anerkennung von Naturheilverfahren*, in: NZZ, July 8 1988; Oepen I. (I), *Zur Leistungspflicht der Krankenkasse sowie zur Behilfefähigkeit bei unkonventionnellen medizinischen Verfahren*, in: Med Sach 82: 46; Oepen I. (II), *Unkonventionelle medizinische Verfahren – ein Beitrag zur Kostendämpfung?*, in: Versicherungsmedizin, 1989, 41: 53; Ostendorf G.-M., *Probleme der Alternativmedizin in der privaten Personenversicherung*, in: Versicherungsmedizin 47, 1995, n° 6: 224–31; Péntek M., *Die Leistungspflicht der Gesetzlichen Krankenversicherung bei der Anwendung von Aussenseitermethoden in der Medizin*, Dissertation, 1996, Konstanz; Schmidt-Rögnitz A., *Die Gewährung von alternativen sowie neueren Behandlungs- und Heilmethoden durch die gesetzliche Krankenversicherung*, Duncker & Humblot, 1996, Berlin; Schneider M. (I) (co-authors: Biene-Dietrich P., Gebanyi M., Hofmann U., Huber M., Köse A., Sommer J. H.), *Gesundheitssysteme im internationalen Vergleich*, ed. 1994, BASYS, 1995, Augsburg: 193–225; Schneider M. (II) (co-authors: Hofmann U., Vasikjevic S.), *Die Honorierung naturheikundlicher Verfahren – Untersuchung für den Bundesminister für Arbeit und Sozialordnung*, Basys, 1989, Augsburg: 193–225; Schulin B., *Alternative Medizin in der gesetzlichen Krankenversicherung*, in: Zeitschrift für Sozialreform, 1994, vol. 40, n° 8: 546–65; Wiesendanger H., *Das grosse Buch vom geistigen Heilen*, Scherz Verlag, 1994, Bern/München/Wien: 338–40.

A. Introduction

Germany has a public coverage system in respect of alternative medicines. The public insurance and private insurance companies officially reimburse some alternative medicines. Here the courts have been active in developing criteria and conditions to regulate the reimbursement of alternative medicines.[74]

Some private health insurance companies have even proposed coverage for treatments provided by "Heilpraktikers" and for treatments that do not benefit from a general scientific recognition.

B. Criteria conditioning the coverage of alternative medicines

Given that the conditions determining the right to alternative benefits from social insurance and private insurance companies are generally the same,[75] they will be presented together.

In Germany, the basic principle of health insurance is that when an insured person is ill, he/she has the right to obtain the care necessary to treat the affection or to reduce the pain.[76] According to Section 2 of the German Social Code (GSC),[77] services must be provided effectively and economically, and only to the necessary extent (appropriateness). In this respect, efficiency and quality of services must comply with the general state of medical knowledge.[78, 79]

74 The literature concerning the coverage of alternative medicines by social insurance and private insurance companies is quite impressive. Indeed, there are several dissertations, articles and courts rulings on the subject. As it is not possible in the frame of this study to examine in detail this entire set of problems, we only present the general rules regulating the coverage of alternative medicines. Readers interested in the subject may refer to the bibliography, in particular FREUDENBERG U., *op. cit.*; JOST T. S., *op. cit.*: 639–714; PÉNTEK M., *op. cit.*; SCHMIDT-RÖGNITZ A., *op. cit.*

75 FREUDENBERG U., *op. cit.*: 228; GRUPP K., *op. cit.*: 262.

76 For a brief analysis of the right to obtain medical benefits in the field of alternative medicines, see SCHULIN B., *op. cit.*: 548–56.

77 In German: "Sozial Gesetz Buch" (SGB).

78 Art. 2, 12, 70 and 72 GSC (social insurance) and art. 5 MB/KK (private insurance). Specific sections (12, 28, and 35) state that health care practitioners must provide services according to the standards of medical practice. In particular, they may not provide unnecessary or non-economically justified treatments.
Furthermore, recommendations from public institutions determine when new diagnostic treatment methods must be covered. Currently, these recommendations are issued on the basis of the medical necessity and efficiency of the procedure as well as its effectiveness.
For more details, see JOST T. S., *op. cit.*: 664; SCHMIDT-RÖGNITZ A., *op. cit.*: 92–93, 96–97.
For a brief analysis of the criteria leading to the coverage of medical treatments, as well as the appreciation of the placebo effect and side effects when using alternative medicines, see NÜCHTERN E., *op. cit.*: 438–41. See also, e.g., JOST T. S., *op. cit.*: 663ss.

79 GRUPP K., *op. cit.*: 260; SCHULIN B., *op. cit.*: 548.

However, other legal provisions are more open toward alternative medicines. For example, section 2 GSC V states that, in principle, alternative medicines can not be excluded from coverage. A provision adopted during the 1997 health reform goes further, providing that new procedures are supposed to be reviewed according to the state of knowledge "in the particular school of therapy".[80] In this respect, Jost notes that "this provision was clearly added to encourage the extension of coverage to non-traditional medicine".[81]

The decisions of the Supreme Court interpreting the coverage of alternative therapies have been complex and contradictory.[82] In the end, even though the Supreme Court has ruled that there is no constitutional right to obtain a reimbursement for a specific alternative treatment,[83] relatively precise criteria have been established which determine the coverage of alternative medicines by social insurance and private insurance companies. These are the following:[84]

1. if no allopathic treatment is available to treat a specific illness or to reduce the pain or if the aetiology is unknown, the use of alternative medicines is reimbursed, on condition that the treatment has a minimum chance of success.[85] For example, in respect of the treatment of

80 "Zweites Gesetz zur Neuordnung von Selbstverwaltung und Eigenverantwortung in der gesetzlichen Krankenversicherung" (2.GKV-NOG), section 50, to be codified at section 135(a)(1) 1 GSC V. Alternative medical procedures must be evaluated in terms of their effectiveness, efficiency, and necessity.

81 JOST T. S., *op. cit.*: 665.

82 Reimbursement of treatments by social insurance and private insurance companies has led to several disputes, particularly concerning the scientific proof of a treatment's effectiveness and appropriateness. On the subject, see CRAMER R., *op. cit.*: 42–43; EHLERS A. P. F., *op. cit.*: 169; FREUDENBERG U., *op. cit.*: 229; HAUFF M., *op. cit.*; GRUPP K., *op. cit.*: 260–62; JUNG H., *op. cit.*: 61–62; PÉNTEK M., *op. cit.*: 187; SCHULIN B., *op. cit.*: 549–50; WIESENDANGER H., *op. cit.*: 339–40.

83 MedR 1998, H. 6: 269: BVerfG, Beschl. v. Dec. 15 1997 – 1 BvR 1953/97. See on the subject, e.g., ANONYMOUS (II), *op. cit.*: 269.

84 For a whole study on the subject, see FREUDENBERG U., *op. cit.* See also, e.g., JOST T. S., *op. cit.*: 665ss.

85 This was the position first taken by private insurance companies.
The rulings of the courts have evolved in respect of coverage by public insurance funds. While they first refused to admit that the above-mentioned criteria (appropriateness, etc.) were fulfilled for alternative medicines, they admit today coverage in some cases. In particular, the Supreme Court stated on June 23, 1993 that the objective of the health insurance law is not reached if the coverage of

multiple sclerosis or certain forms of cancer, it is irrelevant that the method of treatment is generally scientifically recognised;[86, 87]

2. if the aetiology is known but no allopathic treatment is available,[88] then recourse to alternative medicines is allowed, on the condition that, according to the aetiology, the treatment has a minimum chance of success.[89] The same principle applies when a previous allopathic treatment was unsuccessful;[90]
3. when an allopathic treatment and an alternative treatment are both available, but side effects are related to the allopathic treatment or there are risks, in general or in particular, for the patient, the use of alternative medicines is reimbursed.[91] However, in this scenario, it is necessary to balance the existing risks against the cost-effectiveness of the treatment;[92]

---

alternative medicines is not guaranteed when no allopathic treatment is available and that the alternative treatment has a minimum chance of success.
For a further development on the subject, see EHLERS A. P. F., *op. cit.*: 170–172; FREUDENBERG U., *op. cit.*: 228; GRUPP K., *op. cit.*: 260–63; NÜCHTERN E., *op. cit.*: 438.

86 A court has stated that, in relation to treatment provided by a "Heilpraktiker", even if a treatment is not recognised by the classic allopathic school of medicine, this does not mean that the treatment may not be generally scientifically recognised. Therefore, it may be reimbursed. In this respect, one must note that all medical methods recognised by the predominant opinion in every specific field are considered as generally scientifically recognised methods and constitute scientific proof of a treatment's effectiveness.

87 ANONYMOUS (III), *op. cit.*: 230ss; CRAMER R., *op. cit.*: 42–43; EHLERS A. P. F., *op. cit.*: 169–73; FREUDENBERG U., *op. cit.*: 8–9, 229; GRUPP K., *op. cit.*: 260–63; HAUFF M., op.cit.; JUNG H., *op. cit.*: 61–62; NÜCHTERN E., *op. cit.*: 438–39; OSTENDORF G.-M., *op. cit.*: 228–29; PÉNTEK M., *op. cit.*: 187; SCHULIN B., *op. cit.*: 549–50; WIESENDANGER H., *op. cit.*: 339–40.

88 E.g., AIDS, or some allergies.

89 E.g., ozontherapy was covered for the treatment of AIDS, or more specifically of side effects related to AIDS. Similarly, the treatment of allergies with homeopathy, neuraltherapy and acupuncture has been covered.

90 EHLERS A. P. F., *op. cit.*: 173; FREUDENBERG U., *op. cit.*: 9–10, 228; GRUPP K., *op. cit.*: 261–63; NÜCHTERN E., *op. cit.*: 437; NZZ, *op. cit.*; OSTENDORF G.-M., *op. cit.*: 228–29.

91 E.g., the providing of Ney-Tumorin to treat side effects of chemotherapies has been covered.

92 FREUDENBERG U., *op. cit.*: 10–11, 228; GRUPP K., *op. cit.*: 261–63; NÜCHTERN E., *op. cit.*: 437, 440.

4. if there are safe allopathic and non-allopathic treatments at a patient's disposal, he/she may choose the less expensive method, irrespective of whether the treatment is allopathic or alternative.[93]

Some private insurance companies reimburse treatments as long as their effectiveness is not completely rejected.[94] According to a Stuttgart court decision, if a private insurance policy includes coverage of medical activities provided by "Heilpraktikers" as part of its benefits, it has to reimburse prescribed medications even if they are not scientifically proven.[95]

Certain authors advise the legislature to allow reimbursement, in certain cases not mentioned above, where the treatment has been successful.[96] Others who are opposed to alternative medicines consider that supporters of alternative medicines assert excessive claims.[97]

C. The coverage of treatments provided by "Heilpraktikers"

While private insurance companies are beginning to reimburse alternative treatments provided by "Heilpraktikers", social insurance has remained less open in its coverage of them. The exclusion of "Heilpraktikers" from the social insurance is in accordance with the practice of the courts. The courts consider that, in order to ensure public interests, only treatments provided by physicians must be reimbursed by social insurance. Indeed, it is important for the insured community that the type of provided treatment as well as the training of health care providers be good enough to guarantee a high standard of health care.[98]

Both Parliament and social insurance have rejected the argument of discrimination between "Heilpraktikers" and approved physicians. They consider that as long as "Heilpraktikers" do not have the same type of education as physicians, there is no infringement of the principle of equality when the treatments they provide are not covered by social insurance.[99]

93 FREUDENBERG U., *op. cit.*: 229.
94 E.g., vitamin products, ozontherapy or acupuncture (CRAMER R., *op. cit.*: 43).
95 EHLERS A. P. F., *op. cit.*: 174. This decision was affirmed in 1996, concerning a treatment provided by a "Heilpraktiker" treating an AIDS patient (LANZ, *op. cit.*: 2434).
96 FREUDENBERG U., *op. cit.*: 229.
97 OEPEN I. (II), *op. cit.*: 55–57.
98 CRAMER R., *op. cit.*: 42–45; EHLERS A. P. F., *op. cit.*: 175; NÜCHTERN E., *op. cit.*: 437.
99 CRAMER R., *op. cit.*: 42–45; EHLERS A. P. F., *op. cit.*: 175–76.
A recent decision from the Supreme Court affirmed this view (*Zur Leistungspflicht…, op. cit.*: 269).

5.3.5.6 *Great Britain*[100]

Bibliography

ALBER J. (co-author: BERNARDI-SCHENKLUHN B.), *Westeuropäische Gesundheitssysteme im Vergleich, Bundesrepublik Deutschland, Schweiz, Frankreich, Italien, Grossbritanien*, Campus Verlag, 1992, Frankfurt: 533–621; ALDRIDGE D., *Unconventional medicine in Europe*, Advances, 1994, vol. 10, n° 2: 56; BRITISH MEDICAL ASSOCIATION (LAMONT T.), *Alternative medicine – New approaches to good practice*, Oxford University Press, 1993, Oxford/New York; FISHER P. (co-author: WARD A.), *Complementary medicine in Europe*, in: BMJ, vol. 309, July 9, 1994: 107–11; FROST AND SULLIVAN LTD, *Alternative medical practices in Europe*, Report n° E874, Sullivan House, Grosvenor Gardens, 1987, London SW1: 235–47; MCCARTHY M. (co-author: REES S.), *Health systems and health medicine in the European Community*, Royal College of Physicians of London, 1992, London: 54–58; ROBARD I., *La santé hors la loi: Les hors la loi de la santé*, 4th ed., Ed. de l'Ancre, 1994, Suresnes: 221; SELECT COMMITTEE ON SCIENCE AND TECHNOLOGY, *Complementary and alternative medicine*, House of Lords – Session 1999–2000 6th Report, The Stationary Office, 2000, London: 94ss; SCHNEIDER M. (co-authors: BIENE-DIETRICH P., GEBANYI M., HOFMANN U., HUBER M., KÖSE A., SOMMER J. H.), *Gesundheitssysteme im internationalen Vergleich*, ed. 1994, BASYS, 1995, Augsburg: 495–514; WEBER A. (co-authors: LEIENBACH V., DOHLE A., STRUNK S., TEYUKOV A., SCHULTE-MIMBERG U., ANGELE S.), *Soziale Sicherung in West-, Mittel-, und Osteuropa*, Nomos Verlagsgesellschaft, 1994, Baden-Baden: 80–92.

Great Britain has a public coverage system in respect of alternative medicines. In this country, some alternative medicines are reimbursed both by public insurance and private insurance companies.

Fees for alternative practices are generally not reimbursed by the State[101] through the social security system.[102] However, several alternative medicines are available at five specific government hospitals,[103] such

100 For an overview of the health care system, see ALBER J., *op. cit.*; MCCARTHY M., *op. cit.*; SCHNEIDER M., *op. cit.*; WEBER A., *op. cit.*

101 The new National Health Service, which was introduced in 1990 with the Community Care Act, provides health care in Great Britain. The whole population is covered and health care is free (FROST AND SULLIVAN, *op. cit.*: 237–38; MCCARTHY M., *op. cit.*: 54).

102 The British Select Committee on Science and Technology notes that the majority of alternative medicines is practised in the private sector. It is often accessed without referral from a GP (SELECT COMMITTEE ON SCIENCE AND TECHNOLOGY, *op. cit.*: 104).

103 Namely, the NHS hospitals in London, Glasgow, Liverpool, Bristol and Tunbridge Wells. Furthermore, at Saint Mary's Hospital where relaxation treatments,

as homeopathy, yoga, massage and aromatherapy. Acupuncture, osteopathy and chiropractic are occasionally available. When these treatments are available within NHS government hospitals they are free of charge and there are also referrals from GPs or other members of primary care team to alternative practitioners.[104, 105] Chiropractors' and osteopaths' services are equally reimbursed by trade bodies and by several associations, such as industrial and veterans associations.[106]

Furthermore, some of the private insurance programs will generally integrally reimburse some alternative medicines, namely homeopathy, osteopathy, herbalism, acupuncture and naturopathy, on the condition that they are provided by medically qualified practitioners.[107] Otherwise, patients directly pay alternative medicines to private practitioners.[108]

The new agreement of April 1, 1990 between general practitioners and the Family Health Services Authorities, does not contain a definition of "qualifying staff". Thus, a GP may claim payments for a wider range of staff including, for example, physiotherapists, chiropractors and dieticians. However, the authorities have the freedom to pay all, part, or none of these costs, and this deters GPs' from employing "additional" alternative staff, but it is likely that this situation will change in the future.[109]

---

dietetic advising, yoga and meditation are dispensed, physicians work closely with non-physicians. This type of cooperation, which exists also outside hospitals, is increasing (British Medical Association, *op. cit.*: 28–29; Fisher P., *op. cit.*: 108; Robard I., *op. cit.*: 221; Thomas K. J., *op. cit.*: 125, 129).

104 According to the British Select Committee on Science and Technology "in conclusion, it seems that there are already several successful models of integration, although current levels of provision are patchy" (Select Committee on Science and Technology, *op. cit.*: 107). For a presentation of the several ways patients access alternative medicines within and outside the NHS and for proposals, see the same author at 104ss.

105 Aldridge D., *op. cit.*: 56; McCarthy M., *op. cit.*: 55; Robard I., *op. cit.*: 221; Select Committee on Science and Technology, *op. cit.*: 104ss; Monckton J., European Depute and director of the COST B4 program, Aug. 2000, London.

106 Robard I., *op. cit.*: 221.

107 Aldridge D., *op. cit.*: 56; McCarthy M., *op. cit.*: 55; Robard I., *op. cit.*: 221; Monckton J., director of the EU COST B4 program, Aug. 2000, London.

108 Frost and Sullivan, *op. cit.*: 245.

109 British Medical Association, *op. cit.*: 44–45.

5.3.5.7 Italy[110]

Bibliography

ALBER J. (co-author: BERNARDI-SCHENKLUHN B.), *Westeuropäische Gesundheitssysteme im Vergleich, Bundesrepublik Deutschland, Schweiz, Frankreich, Italien, Grossbritanien*, Campus Verlag, 1992, Frankfurt: 415–532; FROST AND SULLIVAN LTD, *Alternative medical practices in Europe*, Report n° E874, Sullivan House, Grosvenor Gardens, 1987, London SW1: 225–33; MCCARTHY M. (co-author: REES S.), *Health systems and health medicine in the European Community*, Royal College of Physicians of London, 1992, London: 34–38; SCHNEIDER M. (co-authors: BIENE-DIETRICH P., GEBANYI M., HOFMANN U., HUBER M., KÖSE A., SOMMER J. H.), *Gesundheitssysteme im internationalen Vergleich*, ed. 1994, BASYS, 1995, Augsburg: 295–312.

Italy has a public coverage system in respect of alternative medicines. Some alternative medicines are officially and unofficially reimbursed by both public insurance and private insurance companies.

With regard to public coverage, each Italian region has its own regulation on the reimbursement of medical acts. In Lombardy, for example, a patient's co-payment of approximately 100 Euros is required to obtain coverage for alternative medicines, while social insurance pays the surplus.[111] Only treatments provided by doctors holding a medical university degree are reimbursed. Furthermore, physicians sometimes provide alternative medicines under an allopathic appellation.

There are also some private insurance companies reimbursing alternative treatments. The reimbursement varies according to specific agreements. In general, treatments have to be provided by a physician, with the exception of articulation manipulations, which can be provided by non-physicians. The reimbursement may be partial or complete. The insurance's premiums vary according to the age, sex, and health status of the patient.[112]

110 Information regarding this country was also provided by Gilberto Colussi, Insurance Agent at the Riunione Adriatica di Sicurtà, Sept. 2001, Milano. For an overview of the Italian health care system, see ALBER J., *op. cit.*: 415–532; MCCARTHY M., *op. cit.*: 34–38; SCHNEIDER M., *op. cit.*: 295–312.

111 The covered alternative medicines are the following: acupuncture; hypnosis; antalgic lasertherapy; acupressure; lymphatic drainage; reflexology; vertebral manipulation and other articulation massage; bio feedback.

112 Generally premiums are of approx. 740 Euros to 2,220 Euros for an adult per year.

5.3.5.8 Latvia[113]

Latvia has a public coverage system in respect of alternative medicines. In fact, some alternative medicines are officially reimbursed both by public insurance and private insurance companies.

As far public coverage is concerned, alternative medicine activities are generally not covered by compulsory health insurance, the expenses being usually covered by patients. However, since 1994, when acupuncture and homeopathy were included in the list of medical specialties, social insurance has reimbursed all expenses in connection with those treatments.

The current trend is towards the extension of private coverage for alternative medicines. From September 1998, two insurance companies (Balta and Parex)[114] now cover alternative medicines, providing reimbursement for all alternative medicines recognised by local statutes. Initially starting with acupuncture and homeopathy, these companies are also going to partially cover the rest of the consultations and treatments given by authorized doctors.[115] The reimbursement will be partial, covering 2/3 of expenses, but only when physicians provide the treatments.

5.3.5.9 Luxembourg[116]

Bibliography

FROST AND SULLIVAN LTD, *Alternative medical practices in Europe*, Report n° E874, Sullivan House, Grosvenor Gardens, 1987, London SW1: 192–93; MCCARTHY M. (co-author: REES S.), *Health systems and health medicine in the European Community*, Royal College of Physicians of London, 1992, London:

113 The information regarding Latvia was provided by Nickolay A. Nickolaev, Traditional Chinese Medicine and Acupuncture Department in Ministry of Social Welfare, Sept. 2001; WHO liaison Officer, Riga, 2000.
For an overview of the health care system of Latvia, see WEBER A. (co-authors: LEIENBACH V., DOHLE A., STRUNK S., TEYUKOV A., SCHULTE-MIMBERG U., ANGELE S.), *Soziale Sicherung in West-, Mittel-, und Osteuropa*, Nomos Verlagsgesellschaft, 1994, Baden-Baden: 232–37.

114 The Balta insurance is a half private insurance and Parex is a private insurance.

115 Such as Dr. R. Voll electropuncture therapy, iridodiagnosis, or bioresonance.

116 The information regarding Luxembourg was also provided by Schleder-Leuck A., at the Ministry of Health, Sept. 2001, Luxembourg.
For an overview of the health care system in Luxembourg, see MCCARTHY M., *op. cit.*: 39–41; SCHNEIDER M., *op. cit.*: 349–64.

39–41; ROBARD I., *La santé hors la loi: Les hors la loi de la santé*, 4th ed., Ed. de l'Ancre, 1994, Suresnes: 217; SCHNEIDER M. (co-authors: BIENE-DIETRICH P., GEBANYI M., HOFMANN U., HUBER M., KÖSE A., SOMMER J. H.), *Gesundheitssysteme im internationalen Vergleich*, ed. 1994, BASYS, 1995, Augsburg: 349–64.

Luxembourg has a public coverage system in respect of alternative medicines. To the best of our knowledge, only public insurance reimburses some of the alternative medicines.

Alternative techniques are theoretically not covered by the health insurance. However, alternative medicines are unofficially reimbursed as long as they are provided by a recognised health care professional. Indeed, approved physicians are free to choose the treatment they want to apply. As a result, treatments using alternative medicines are reimbursed as a normal consultation.[117] Furthermore, homeopathic treatments are officially partially (80%) covered.[118]

While it appears that private insurance companies do not offer coverage for alternative medicines.

5.3.5.10 Malta[119]

Malta has a public system in respect of the coverage of alternative medicines. To the best of our knowledge, only public insurance officially reimburses some alternative medicines.[120]

While there is no reimbursement for traditional medical services obtained privately, the State does run acupuncture clinics within the national health services, which are free to the general public.

Private acupuncture clinics also provide services, but against payment by patients and such costs are not reimbursed.

117 Schleder-Leuck A., at the Ministry of Health, Sept. 2001, Luxembourg.

118 ROBARD I., *op. cit.*: 217; Jomé L. at the MINISTRY OF HEALTH, Mar. 1998, Luxembourg; Schleder-Leuck A., at the Ministry of Health, Sept. 2001, Luxembourg.

119 The information on Malta was provided by Dr. D. Falzon, Principal Medical Officer at the Department of Public Health, Mar. 1998, Valletta, and by De. Gafa, Legal Office, Department of Health, Mar. 1998, Valletta. To the best of our knowledge, the situation in this country remains unchanged.

120 In Malta, there is a national health service that is free at the point of delivery, covering Maltese citizens and foreigners benefiting from bilateral agreements. This includes primary, secondary and tertiary health care.

5.3.5.11 *Netherlands*[121]

Bibliography

BOS M., *Health and health care in the Netherlands*, Zorgverzekeraars, 1998, Zeist; CARTER J. P., *Racketeering in medicine – The suppression of alternatives*, Hampton Roads Publishing Co., 1993, Norfolk: 237–42; DUTCH HEALTH COUNCIL, *Report on alternative therapies and research*, Dutch Health Care Council, 1993, The Hague; FISHER P. (co-author: WARD A.), *Alternative medicine in Europe*, in: BMJ, vol. 309, July 9, 1994: 107–11; MINISTRY OF HEALTH (I), WELFARE AND SPORT, *Medical Treatment Contracts Act*, Ministry of Health, Welfare, and Sport, 1995, Rijswijk; MINISTRY OF HEALTH (II), WELFARE AND SPORT, *Health insurance in the Netherlands*, Ministry of Health, Welfare, and Sport, 1995, Rijswijk; MINISTRY OF HEALTH, WELFARE AND SPORT (III), *The Care Institutions Quality Act*, Ministry of Health, Welfare, and Sport, 1996, Rijswijk; MINISTRY OF HEALTH, WELFARE AND SPORT (IV), *Preventive health policy in the Netherlands*, Ministry of Health, Welfare, and Sport, 1997, Rijswijk; ROBARD I., *La santé hors la loi: Les hors la loi de la santé*, 4th ed., Ed. de l'Ancre, 1994, Suresnes: 239–50; SCHNEIDER M. (co-authors: BIENE-DIETRICH P., GEBANYI M., HOFMANN U., HUBER M., KÖSE A. AND SOMMER J. H.), *Gesundheitssysteme im internationalen Vergleich*, ed. 1994, BASYS, 1995, Augsburg: 365–83; SLOTTE T., *Meeste maatschappijen vergoeden alternatieve geneeswijzen*, in: Consumentengids, February 1997; VISSER G. J. (co-author: PETERS C.) (I), *Alternative medicine and general practitioners in the Netherlands: Towards acceptance and integration*, in: Family Practice, 1990, vol. 7, n° 3, 227–32; VISSER G. J. (II), *Alternative medicine in the Netherlands*, in: LEWITH G. (co-editor: ALDRIDGE D.), *Alternative medicine and the European Community*, CW Daniel, 1991, Saffron Walden.

The Netherlands have a public coverage system in respect of alternative medicines. Social insurance as well as private insurance companies cover the most important types of alternative medicines. However, in order to qualify for reimbursement, treatments must be provided by allopathic professionals, in particular, physicians and physiotherapists. The recent trend in the Netherlands has been to extend the coverage for alternative medicines from both private and public insurance.[122]

121 For an overview of the Dutch health care system, see BOS M., *op. cit.*; MINISTRY OF HEALTH (I), *op. cit.*; MINISTRY OF HEALTH (II), *op. cit.*; MINISTRY OF HEALTH (III), *op. cit.*; MINISTRY OF HEALTH (IV), *op. cit.*; SCHNEIDER M., *op. cit.*: 365–83.

122 Homeopathy, anthroposophical medicine, acupuncture, manual therapies, chiropractic, naturopathy and neuraltherapy are generally covered.

Officially, only homeopathic and anthroposophic medicines are reimbursed by the social insurance. However, health insurance funds, which two-thirds of the population are registered under, unofficially reimburse alternative care given by GPs (and only by them) during general consultations.[123]

In addition to the legally defined "standard package", which is the same for all 45 sickness funds in the country, the sickness funds also offer a supplementary package to which their clients can voluntarily subscribe. Although the scope of the package varies from one fund to another, most of them cover some forms of alternative medicines, when given by a medical doctor or a physiotherapist. Generally, the alternative medicines covered are mainly homeopathy, acupuncture and anthroposophic medicine.[124]

Some government officials have proposed that alternative medicines be included, because they are convinced that the integration of alternative medicines save money, in the various insurance schemes. Others argue that the reverse is true and that the inclusion of alternative medicines would increase medical costs.[125]

123 ROBARD I., *op. cit.*: 240; VISSER G. J. (I), *op. cit.*: 227; VISSER G. J. (II), *op. cit.*: 120.

124 ROBARD I., *op. cit.*: 240; VISSER G. J. (I), *op. cit.*: 227; VISSER G. J. (II), *op. cit.*: 120.

125 According to the Commission on Alternative Medicines, an important consideration in determining whether a specific alternative medicine has to be included in the health-insurance scheme is whether research findings show that such inclusion will raise or lower medical costs. Calculating the debit and credit aspects of a therapy would entail establishing: 1. the direct cost of treatment; 2. the indirect cost (production losses) and; 3. the gain in health (CARTER J. P., *op. cit.*: 241–42; ROBARD I., *op. cit.*: 245–46).

The Dutch Health Council noted that "with respect to the 'recognition' of alternative modes of treatment, a number of closely related social and insurance considerations and quality-related and legislative aspects may be distinguished. In practice, evidence of quality – as might be supplied by means of scientific research – has not proved necessary for recognition by patients or insurers. On the other hand, 'recognition' by the government requiring compliance with the quality standards for practitioners and leading to inclusion in the social insurance package of medical services does need to be based on 'quality'. This means that if repeated scientific studies, carried out in accordance with the guidelines as laid down by the committee, show effectiveness of a particular mode of treatment, that treatment should be recognized. On the other hand it means that if such research repeatedly indicates that no effectiveness can be attributed to a particular form of treatment, recognition must be withheld. The committee takes the same views with respect to orthodox methods of treatment" (DUTCH HEALTH COUNCIL, *op. cit.*).

Private health insurance companies have responded to public demand[126] by providing for the reimbursement of alternative medicines. Since 1988, all large private insurance companies include at least homeopathy, acupuncture and manipulative therapy, either in their standard package or in a supplementary package. In many cases, reimbursement is given only when the practitioners concerned are medical doctors or physical therapists, and members of their respective professional organizations. Later, in 1991, an insurance scheme was developed covering a broad range of alternative and additional therapies, including those practised by non-allopathic practitioners. Finally, in 1998, 47 private insurance companies proposed complete or partial coverage[127] for alternative treatments provided by physicians or members of professional organisations. The package generally includes homeopathy, anthroposophy, acupuncture, manual therapies, chiropractic, naturopathy and neuraltherapy.[128]

5.3.5.12 Norway[129]

Bibliography

FROST AND SULLIVAN LTD, *Alternative medical practices in Europe*, Report n° E874, Sullivan House, Grosvenor Gardens, 1987, London SW1: 251; MINISTRY OF HEALTH AND SOCIAL AFFAIRS (I), *Report on alternative medicine – English summary*, Norges Offentliche Utredniger NOU 1998: 21, 1998, Oslo: 273–74; PREUSKER U. K., *Gesundheitssysteme in Scandinavien – Eine Aktuelle Darstellung des schwedischen, norwegischen und finnischen Gesundheitswesens*, Bergisch Gladbach, 1996, Heider: 169ss; ROBARD I., *La santé hors la loi: Les hors la loi de la santé*, 4th ed., Ed. de l'Ancre, 1994, Suresnes: 227.

126 According to a consumer survey, about 80% of the Dutch population would like to have complete freedom of choice over the medical treatments they want and favour the recognition of alternative medicines by the Health Insurance. In addition, 60% of the Dutch population are even willing to pay extra-health insurance premiums in order to have access to alternative medicines (FISHER P., *op. cit.*: 107).

127 From 25 to 100%, with a maximum limit from 150 to 1,250 Euros per year.

128 ROBARD I., *op. cit.*: 240; SLOTTE T., *op. cit.*: 40–41; VISSER G. J. (I), *op. cit.*: 227; VISSER G. J. (II), *op. cit.*: 121.

129 The information regarding Norway was also provided by Kirsten Been, Secretary for the Alternative Medicine Commission, Jan. 1998, Oslo; Vegar Nore, Norwegian Ministry of Health and Social Affairs, Sept. 2001, Oslo.
For an overview of the Norwegian health care system, see PREUSKER U. K., *op. cit.*: 97, 169–172.

Norway has a public coverage system in respect to alternative medicines. Some alternative medicines are reimbursed both by official public insurance and private insurance companies.

Public reimbursement is generally not available for alternative medicines. However, a partial reimbursement from the national insurance scheme is available for treatments by chiropractors when they are authorized as health care professionals. Reimbursement is only given if a physician has referred patients to the chiropractor. Furthermore, the cover is limited to 10 and up to a maximum of 14 consultations per year.[130]

Regarding private coverage, some companies[131] offer coverage for certain alternative medicines. They cover acupuncture performed by licensed medical doctors, and chiropractic. The reimbursement of related costs is only partial.

With respect to refunding alternative medicines from national insurance, the majority of the Committee on Alternative Medicine considered that no such scheme should be introduced. The main arguments against its introduction were the low levels of documented efficacy, and increased public expenditure on the health sector. The Committee also pointed out that there were other treatments provided by recognised professionals that were not covered, such as ordinary dental treatment. As a consequence, patients wanting access to these techniques must pay for them out of their own private resources. The Committee, however, does serve the purpose of enhancing co-operation between conventional health care services and alternative practitioners.[132]

A minority of the Committee has taken the opposite view in proposing the introduction of a refund scheme for treatments provided by registered alternative practitioners.[133] Possible criteria proposed for coverage were first, establishing co-operation between a doctor and the alternative practitioner, and second, that the alternative treatment shows a demonstrably positive effect on the patient's health and welfare. Finally, the treatment must be of considerable significance for the patient's functional capacity.[134]

130 ROBARD I., *op. cit.*: 227.

131 Such as Norsk Helseforsikring, which has connections to an international company called International Health Insurance Denmark AS.

132 MINISTRY OF HEALTH AND SOCIAL AFFAIRS (I), *op. cit.*: 273–74.

133 In the register proposed by the Committee. For more details, see chap. 4.3.3.8.

134 MINISTRY OF HEALTH AND SOCIAL AFFAIRS (I), *op. cit.*: 274.

5.3.5.13 *Sweden*[135]

Bibliography

Frost and Sullivan Ltd, *Alternative medical practices in Europe*, Report n° E874, Sullivan House, Grosvenor Gardens, 1987, London SW1: 253–54; Preusker U. K., *Gesundheitssysteme in Scandinavien – Eine Aktuelle Darstellung des schwedischen, norwegischen und finnischen Gesundheitswesens*, Bergisch Gladbach, 1996, Heider: 163ss; Schneider M. (co-authors: Biene-Dietrich P., Gebanyi M., Hofmann U., Huber M., Köse A., Sommer J. H.), *Gesundheitssysteme im internationalen Vergleich*, ed. 1994, BASYS, 1995, Augsburg: 419–38; Swedish Commission on Alternative Medicine, *Report on alternative medicine*, Regeringskansliet, 1989, Stockholm.

It appears that Sweden has a public coverage system in regard to alternative medicines.[136] Only acupuncture, which may be provided by physicians, seems to be partially reimbursed.[137]

Non-allopathic practitioners are permitted to offer their services in Sweden, but there is no general reimbursement from the health care system. However, some county councils who have responsibility for health care have negotiated agreements concerning reimbursement with some licensed chiropractors and naprapaths, and with the anthroposophical hospital Vidarkliniken, in Stockholm.[138]

The Swedish Committee on Alternative Medicine noted in its report that

> the Committee discussed the question of whether sickness benefit should be payable from national insurance funds for some types of alternative treatment. Since, at the present time, some types of treatment provided by health services are already accepted, but no sickness benefit are payable from national insurance funds, the Committee does not propose that sickness benefit be payable for treatment obtained from practitioners of alternative medicines.[139]

135 The information drawn up for this section was also provided by Dr. Motzi Eklöf, at the Department of Physical Education and Health, Örebro University, Örebro, Sept. 2001. To the best of our knowledge, the situation has not changed since then.
For an overview of the Swedish health care system, see Preusker U. K., *op. cit.*: 163ss; Schneider M., *op. cit.*: 419–38.

136 Unfortunately, no information was obtained regarding private reimbursement.

137 Frost and Sullivan Ltd, *op. cit.*: 253–54.

138 Dr. Motzi Eklöf, at the Department of Physical Education and Health, Örebro University, Örebro, Sept. 2001.

139 Swedish Commission on Alternative Medicine, *op. cit.*: 35.

5.3.5.14 Switzerland

Bibliography

CONFÉRENCE DES DIRECTEURS CANTONAUX DES AFFAIRES SANITAIRES (I), *Rapport du groupe de travail "Autorisations de pratiquer les professions du domaine de la santé"*, CDS, 2000, Bern, available at: http://www.sdk-cds.ch/fr/berufsbildung-f.html, accessed Aug. 1 2001; DUC J.-L., *Médecines parallèles et assurances sociales (plus spécialement au regard de la nouvelle LAMal)*, CMS, 1996, vol. 40, n° 1: 41–51; FRÉCHELIN K. (II), *Conséquences de l'accord sur la libre circulation des personnes en matière d'assurance-maladie, d'assurance-accidents et d'allocations familiales*, in: Sécurité Sociale, 1999, n° 3: 134–36; GASSMANN J., *Therapiewahlfreiheit in der stationären Psychiatrie – auch für komplementäre Methoden!*, in: BORGHI M. (co-editor: GASSMAN J.), *Thérapies complémentaires ou alternatives en psychiatrie: Un défi? Un droit?*, Schriftenreihe der Schweizerischen Stiftung Pro Mente Sana n° 20, 1999, Zürich: 309–13; GUILLOD O. (II), *Legislation: A new Federal Act on Health Insurance*, in: European Journal of Health Law, 1995: 271–79; GUILLOD O. (co-author: ZENGER C., RUCKSTUHL N.) (IV), *Structure et organisation de la santé publique en Suisse*, in: GUTZWILLER F., *op. cit.*: 229–35; GUTZWILLER F. (co-editor: JEANNERET O.), *Médecine sociale et préventive – Santé publique*, Hans Huber, 1999, Bern: 221–55; HÄNGGELI C., *Une étape décisive pour la FMH*, in: BMS, 1998, vol. 79, n° 48: 2447–48; HEUSSER P., *Kriterien zur Beurteilung des Nutzens von komplementärmedizinischen Methoden*, Bundesamt für Sozialversicherung, Mar. 1998, Bern; KAHIL-WOLFF B., *L'accord sur la libre circulation des personnes Suisse-CE et le droit des assurances sociales*, in: Semaine Judiciaire, 2001, vol. 123, n° 4: 81–135; KOCH-WULKAN P. W., *Evaluation de l'utilité des méthodes de médecines "parallèles": On touche au but!*, in: Sécurité Sociale, 1998, n° 1: 21; KÜNZI M. (I), *Komplementärmedizin und Gesundheitsrecht*, Helbing & Lichtenhahn Verlag AG, 1996, Basel: 76–94; OFFICE FÉDÉRAL DES ASSURANCES SOCIALES, *Manuel de standardisation pour l'évaluation médicale et économique des prestations médicales*, Office Fédéral des Assurances Sociales, 1998, Bern; PACCAUD F. (co-author: GUTZWILLER F.), Structure *et organisation de la santé publique en Suisse,* in: GUTZWILLER F., *op. cit.*: 223–28; PETIT-PIERRE M.-C. (I), *Les médecines alternatives ont six ans pour prouver leur efficacité*, in: Le Temps, July 14 1998; PETIT-PIERRE M.-C. (II), *L'homéopathie et la médecine chinoise décrochent le titre envié de spécialité*, in: Le Temps, Oct. 24 1998; POLEDNA T. (co-author: NÜESCH S.) (I), *Komplementärmedizin in der sozialen Krankenversicherung*, in: AJP, 2001: 638–44; POLEDNA T. (co-author: BERGER B.) (II), *Öffentliches Gesundheitsrecht*, Stämpfli, 2002, Bern (to be published); REETZ C., *Komplementärmedizin in der Grundversicherung – auch für stationäre PsychiatriepatientInnen?*, in: BORGHI M. (co-editor: GASSMAN J.), *Thérapies complémentaires ou alternatives en psychiatrie: Un défi? Un droit?*, Schriftenreihe der Schweizerischen Stiftung Pro Mente Sana n° 20, 1999, Zürich: 259–64; RICHLI P., *Hoheitliche Leistungspflichten und Leistungsbeschränkungen im Gesundheitswesen als Grundrechtsproblem*, in: Revue Suisse d'Assurances, 1998, n° 9–10: 243–58; SOCIÉTÉ NEUCHÂTELOISE DE MÉDECINE, *Les médecines dites "parallèles"*, in: SNM News, Dec. 1998, n°20: 7, 9; SOMMER J. H. (co-author: BÜRGI M.), *Gesundheitsökonomische Analyse der Wirkungen des Angebotes komplementärmedizinischer Leistungen der Krankenkassen*, in: FREY F. (co-editor: BAUMANN P. H.), *Supplementum 62, FNRS-PNR 34: Médecines complémentaires*, Schwabe, 1994, Basel: 13–17; SPAHNI M., *Le tri des prestataires de médecine alternative est un terrible casse-tête*, in: Le Temps, Jan. 10, 2000; WICKI M., *Komplementärmedizin im Rahmen des Rechtes*, Dissertation, Stämpfli, 1998, Bern: 34, 185–86.

A. Introduction

Switzerland has a public coverage system regarding alternative medicines. Here, alternative medicines are officially and unofficially covered by both public and private funds.[140]

Set forth below, a brief overview of the Swiss health care system (in particular the health insurance context) shall first be presented. Then, the social insurance of coverage of alternative medicines shall be analysed.

B. Overview of the health care system[141]

The powers of regulation in the health field are divided between the Confederation and the cantons. While the cantons are primarly responsible for public health, the Confederation is in charge of several fields,[142] in particular health insurance. The Federal Office of Public Health and the Federal Office of Social Insurance are in charge of the implementation of the decisions taken at the Federal level.[143] The Swiss Conference of Health Directors was created, in order to co-ordinate the action of the cantons in public health, but it may only issue recommendations.[144]

140 In 1993, approximately 14 billion Swiss Francs were spent on alternative medicines (WICKI M., *op. cit.*: 34).

141 For a development regarding the free movement of patients between Switzerland and Europe, see, e.g. FRÉCHELIN K. (II), *op. cit.*: 134–36; KAHIL-WOLFF B., *op. cit.*: 81–135.

142 Namely: exercise and training of medical professions, making and marketing of drugs, control of narcotics, environmental protection, marketing of poisons, marketing of food products, fight against epidemics, fight against accidents (technical protection), health insurance, accident insurance, prevention of diseases and accidents, assisted conception and genetics, as well as transplantation.

143 I.e., by the parliament and the Federal Council (Swiss federal government).

144 PACCAUD F., *op. cit.*: 224–27; GUILLOD O. (IV), *op. cit.*: 232–35. For a brief overview of the historical evolution of the Swiss health system, see PACCAUD F., *op. cit.*: 223–24; GUILLOD O. (IV), *op. cit.*: 229–30; KÜNZI M. (I), *op. cit.*: 76–77.

There is no national health service in Switzerland. The only compulsory insurance is the basic health care insurance,[145] introduced by the Federal Act on Health Insurance on January 1, 1996 (FAHI).[146]

The new Act may be viewed as promoting three main goals: the strengthening of solidarity, the extension of basic coverage and the containment of health costs.[147]

In order to achieve the first goal of increasing solidarity between younger and older people, both men and women as well as rich and poor, several rules have been created, namely that:[148]

1. any Swiss resident must have health insurance covering basic medical needs (art. 3 (1) FAHI);[149]
2. every insured person can move freely from one health fund to another, without suffering any disadvantage (art. 7 FAHI);[150]
3. state subsidies must be used only to reduce the premiums of low-income people (art. 65 FAHI).

The basic compulsory health insurance package includes a wider range of benefits that extends the basic coverage. The new legal regime does not, however, leave any room for health funds to modify the basic insurance package.[151] The general rules dealing with the coverage of benefits are the following:

1. art. 24 FAHI states that the basic social insurance covers the costs of benefits, which is defined according to art. 25–31, taking into consideration the conditions of art. 32 to 34. In this respect, art. 25 provides

145 In French: "Loi sur l'Assurance Maladie" (LAMal) RS 832.10.

146 GUILLOD O. (IV), *op. cit.*: 230.

147 GUILLOD O. (II), *op. cit.*: 272–74.

148 GUILLOD O. (II), *op. cit.*: 272–73; GUILLOD O. (IV), *op. cit.*: 230–31.

149 The cantons are responsible for implementing this rule. Complementary insurance policies are optional and are regulated by private law. Therefore, insurance companies may refuse candidates or set up restrictions.

150 Sex or age may not influence premiums.

151 Under the FAHI, the wider range of benefits covered in the basic coverage are: medical services provided in a hospital or another medical institution, on an outpatient basis or at the patient's home, unlimited hospitalisation, drugs, medical analysis and devices, various measures of preventive medicine, transportation for medical reasons, maternity care, abortion, some dental care and finally, accidental injuries suffered by people without professional activity.
It is noteworthy that maternity remains regulated as an illness (art. 1 par. 2 let. C, art. 29 LAMal).

that the insurance covers the costs of those benefits whose purpose is to diagnose or treat an illness and its side-effects. This being provided by physicians, chiropractors and practitioners providing benefits on the referral of a physician;[152]

2. art. 32 FAHI stipulates that, in order to be covered, medical acts must be effective, appropriate and cost-effective. The Federal Council (the Swiss government) and the Federal Office of Social Insurance (FOSI), when deciding to whether or not to cover medical acts, are advised by several commissions, in particular the Federal Commission on Benefits (CFP)[153] (art. 33 (4) FAHI);[154]
3. art. 33 FAHI states that the Federal Council may decide which benefits will not be covered, or will not be entirely covered, or that will be covered under certain conditions laid down in the compulsory health insurance;[155]
4. in relation to new or controversial benefits, whose effectiveness, appropriateness or cost-effectiveness are currently under evaluation, the Federal Council may decide to include them in the compulsory health insurance (art. 33 (3) FAHI).

The third feature of the new law is its attempt to contain health costs through several provisions in the FAHI, namely that:

1. insured people must pay a fixed annual fee (between 300 and 1,500 CHF) and a contribution of 10% of all costs paid by the

152 According to art. 46ss of the Decree of the Federal Act on Health Insurance (DFAHI) (in French: "Ordonnance sur l'Assurance Maladie" (OAMal) RS 832.102), these practitioners are the following: physiotherapist, ergotherapist, nurse and logopedist-speech therapist.

153 In French: "Commission Fédérale des Prestations". According to art. 37 d DFAHI, the Commission is composed of 7 members representing physicians (2 of them representing alternative medicines), 2 members representing hospitals, one pharmacist, one representing the Commission of Drugs, 6 members representing sickness funds (2 of them must be physicians), 2 members representing of insured people, one member representing cantons, and one member representing the Federal Office of Public Health.
The recent introduction of members representing alternative medicines and patients will probably influence future decisions taken by the Commission.

154 DUC J.-L., *op. cit.*: 45ss; GUILLOD O. (II), *op. cit.*: 272–73; KÜNZI M. (I), *op. cit.*: 83–86; POLEDNA T. (I), *op. cit.*: 638–39; WICKI M., *op. cit.*: 185–86.

155 According to art. 25 par. 2, 26 (prevention measures), 29 par. 2, a and c (maternity), and art. 31 par. 1 (dental care) FAHI. On the subject, see POLEDNA T. (I), *op. cit.*: 639.

insurer (with a ceiling of 700 CHF for adults and 300 CHF for children) (art. 74 FAHI);
2. alternative forms of insurance are allowed. This includes HMO, PPO, insurance that charges the patient a higher annual fee, insurance with a system of bonus and other forms (art. 62 FAHI);
3. cantons have to establish a plan for hospitals and other health institutions that will be decisive in order for hospitals to be allowed to charge their services to health funds (art. 39 FAHI);
4. in addition, various provisions have been devised with the intent of enhancing competition between various health funds as well as between health-care providers (art. 54ss, art 62 FAHI).

Sickness funds are organised as private organisations at both the cantonal and federal level. Most of these organisations provide complementary health insurance including coverage of private inpatient care, alternative medicines, new drugs, and dental care.

At least 80% of physicians are also members of cantonal and federal associations within the FMH structure. Until June 1 2002, the FMH was in charge of post-graduate education for physicians.[156] It will remain in charge of establishing a Code of Professional Ethics and for negotiating physicians' fees.

There are three types of hospitals: public hospitals, hospitals subsidised by public funds and private clinics. Hospitals are also members of cantonal and regional associations.

Patients may freely choose their practitioners, unless they chose a sickness fund providing health care through an HMO structure.

C. The coverage of alternative medicines by the social insurance[157]

Under the old Federal Act on Health Insurance, alternative medicines were not reimbursed. The legislature considered that only scientifically recognized treatments provided by physicians had to be reimbursed.[158] The

156 For a development, see chap. 3.3.1.14 and 4.3.6.1.

157 For a recent development regarding the coverage of alternative techniques in psychiatry, see REETZ C., *op. cit.*: 259–64; GASSMANN J., *op. cit.*: 309–13. For an interesting article dealing with constitutional rights and the right to have access to alternative medicines, see RICHLI P., *op. cit.*: 243–58. For a development regarding alternative medicines and hospital planning, see POLEDNA T. (I), *op. cit.*: 640ss.

158 According to the Decree III of Health Insurance, when the scientific character, therapeutic value or cost-effectiveness of a technique was questioned, the Federal Department of Interior had to decide if the technique was to be covered under

objective was to guarantee patients a high level of quality for health care and to protect patients against unlicensed and potentially unsafe practitioners.[159]

Unofficially, physiotherapists and physicians were providing alternative medicines as a general consultation. This situation still persists today.

---

the basic social insurance. A technique was considered as established when it was largely recognised by researchers and practitioners.

The FCB, which advises the government when deciding to cover or not a medical act, has made the following decisions:

1. acupuncture. In 1969, the FCB did not recognise acupuncture, stating that the technique was not scientifically recognised. In 1980, the FCB admitted that acupuncture could be covered when provided by physicians. However, it did not consider the technique as being scientifically recognised and recommended a reasonable use of the technique;
2. dietetic advice. In 1984, the FCB considered that practitioners giving dietetic advice must not be considered as ancillary staff working under the referral of a physician and under the coverage of the basic health insurance;
3. reflexology. In 1980, the FCB considered that reflexology was not scientifically recognised, and therefore recommended that it not be included in the package of covered benefits;
4. curative eurythmy. In 1969, the FCB considered that curative eurhythmy was not scientifically recognised;
5. hippotherapy. This technique was not been recognised as scientific by the FCB in 1973, and 1984. In 1995, it was recognised as a physical therapeutic measure that may be provided by physiotherapist when treating multiple sclerosis;
6. iscadortherapy. In 1968, the FCB considered that this technique was not scientifically recognised for the treatment of cancer;
7. lymphatic drainage. In 1973, the FCB considered that lymphatic drainage was a particular form of massage. However, it could not yet be considered as scientific, even though it was already practised in hospitals and university clinics. According to a 1976 decision, the technique was admitted in the basic benefits package;
8. neuraltherapy. Although the results of neural therapy as a mean to alleviate suffering has been recognised, this technique is not recognised as scientific yet. Künzi criticises the fact that, in the past, the Commission included only representatives of allopathic practitioners and advocated the inclusion of some scientific researchers in order to provide another view on the subject (Künzi M. (I), *op. cit.*: 92). Recently, representatives of alternative medicines and patients have been included in the Commission (see above).

159 DUC J.-L., *op. cit.*: 42, 44–46; KÜNZI M. (I), *op. cit.*: 79–80; WICKI M., *op. cit.*: 185.

Since the introduction of the FAHI in 1996,[160] but before the introduction of several alternative medicines into the basic health insurance in 1999, courts made various decisions concerning alternative medicines. Several of these cases concerned acupuncture,[161] two concerned homeopathy,[162] one concerned manual therapy[163] and two cases concerned the same treatment, but one was as a treatment covered by the compulsory insurance, and one was as a treatment covered by an alternative insurance.[164] Acupuncture was considered as being covered under the compulsory health insurance to the extent of the consultations necessary to the treatment but not to the cost linked to the acupuncture itself. Similarly, homeopathic treatments were not considered as being covered under the compulsory health insurance. Manual therapy was not covered because a foreign practitioner had provided it and because it was not scientifically recognised in Switzerland, despite the good results observed in the specific case. The last two decisions concerned the providing of alternative medicines by a physician who was not allowed to practise in Switzerland. As such, coverage was refused by both the public and private insurance because the provider did not hold a Swiss licence to practise.

Until July 1 1999, only chiropractic, one acupuncture session lasting 20 minutes,[165] and, in specific circumstances, lymphatic draining and reflexology were reimbursed from the health insurance.[166] However, in July 1998, the Swiss government approved the new benefits catalogue, which came into force in 1999.[167, 168] Since July 1999, five among the most used

160 According to the federal government, one of the objectives of the FAHI was to give patients free choice over the kind of treatment they wanted and, in particular, the introduction of coverage for the most important alternative medicines. In this respect, it is noteworthy that insurance companies were already proposing coverage of alternative medicines. For more details, see DUC J.-L., *op. cit.*: 42–43.

161 Decision 525/97 TA BE, 78/98 TA SZ, 467/98 TA GE, 535/98 TA TG, 663/98 Sozialversicherungsgericht ZH, 63/99 TAss VD, 187/99 Sozialversicherungsgericht ZH, 321/99 Versicherungsdreiergericht BS, 437/99 Versicherungsgericht AG, 666/99 Versicherungsgericht AG.

162 Decision 1/99 Versicherungsgericht SO et 479/98 TA ZG.

163 Decision 540/99 TAss VD.

164 Decision 742/99 et 743/99 TAss VD.

165 Acupuncture has been recognised since 1981.

166 DUC J.-L., *op. cit.*: 47–49; KÜNZI M. (I), *op. cit.*: 81–89.

167 RS 832.112.31.

168 According to the Conference of Directors of Health Affairs, the decision to include alternative medicines within the health insurance is dictated more by market and politic arguments than by a conviction of efficacy (CONFÉRENCE DES DIRECTEURS

alternative medicines are reimbursed on an experimental basis from the compulsory social insurance when provided by physicians holding a post-graduate recognised education (FMH).[169] These five therapies are the following:[170]

1. homeopathy;
2. Chinese medicine;
3. anthroposophical medicine;
4. neuraltherapy;
5. phytotherapy.

In order to maintain reimbursement for these therapies, excepting acupuncture, beyond 2005, their efficacy, appropriateness, and cost-effectiveness must be demonstrated until 2005. Currently, the Federal Commission on Benefits (FCB) is conducting the evaluation.[171] The FCB had to develop specific criteria for alternative medicines in order to evaluate these techniques. As the FCB did not have any criteria regarding the evaluation of alternative medicines, the Federal Office of Social Insurance required reports by specialists and set up specific guidelines. These guidelines may be summarised as follows:[172]

CANTONAUX DES AFFAIRES SANITAIRES (I), *op. cit.*: 23). In this respect, one may note that the practice or private insurance companies regarding the coverage of alternative medicines influenced the decision of the Swiss government to allow reimbursement for the most used therapies.

169 The FMH set up a post-graduate training for homeopathy, Chinese therapy (including acupuncture), anthroposophic medicine and neural therapy. The FMH considered that a post-graduate training was not necessary to provide phytotherapy. Therefore, phytotherapy is covered even though the physician does not hold a post-graduate title.
Treatments provided by non-physicians are not reimbursed.

170 HÄNGGELI C., *op. cit.*: 2447; POLEDNA T. (I), *op. cit.*: 638–39; REETZ C., *op. cit.*: 260–61.

171 HÄNGGELI C., *op. cit.*: 2447–48; KOCH-WULKAN P. W., *op. cit.*: 21; PETIT-PIERRE M.-C. (I), *op. cit.*; PETIT-PIERRE M.-C. (II), *op. cit.*; POLEDNA T. (I), *op. cit.*: 638ss; REETZ C., *op. cit.*: 260, 262; SOCIÉTÉ NEUCHÂTELOISE DE MÉDECINE, *op. cit.*: 7, 9; SPAHNI M., *op. cit.*; WICKI M., *op. cit.*: 185–86.
The reports regarding the evaluation of alternative medicines by the FCB will be available at http://www.pekswiss.ch/, accessed on Oct. 1 2001. A final report should be available during summer 2005.

172 For a recent development regarding the guidelines and criteria adopted by the Federal Office of Social Insurance, see HEUSSER P., *op. cit.*; OFFICE FÉDÉRAL DES ASSURANCES SOCIALES, *op. cit.*

1. *hypothesis for the evaluation of alternative medicines:*

1.1 the evaluation of alternative and allopathic medicines must be done with the same (evidence-based-medicine) methods;

1.2 the evaluation of alternative medicines is limited for two reasons:
1.2.1 the particularities of alternative medicines whose fundamentals are different from those of allopathic medicine such as, for example, the holistic vision of the human being or the importance of the health care provider-patient relationship;
1.2.2 the limits of experimental methods, for example, the differences between real practice and clinical experience, the impossibility of taking into consideration subjective and relationship aspects and the impossibility of demonstrating the mechanism of action of both biomedical and alternative methods;

2. *criteria for the evaluation methods:*

1.1 methods must take into consideration the specificities of techniques. They must also evaluate the technique as a whole and not only some parameters of the technique. Furthermore, methods must take into consideration not only the experience of physicians, but also historical and cultural practice;

1.2 methods without experimental variation must be used in priority;

1.3 personal and multi-factorial aspects must be taken into account such as, for example, the health care provider-patient relationship and other subjective elements;

1.4 observational studies may be adequate to evaluate the security and quality of techniques;

3. *the following evaluation methods may be employed:*

3.1 methods without experimental variation including retrospective use of medical experiences, study of cases, non-controlled studies and inquiries among patients;

3.2 methods with experimental variation including controlled trials and double-blind testing;

3.3 qualitative methods of evaluation;

4. *the implementation of classic criteria:*

4.1 the criterion of appropriateness is fulfilled when:
4.1.1 the patient has chosen the alternative technique after having been informed about all allopathic and non-allopathic therapeutic possibilities;

4.1.2 the expected result is the same as the targeted objective;
4.1.3 the targeted objective may not be more effectively reached with another technique;

4.2 the evaluation of the security and quality of the technique must focus on:
4.2.1 the training of the practitioner for the providing of health care;
4.2.2 the use of the same processes for the evaluation of biomedical and alternative drugs;
4.2.3 the use of good practice methods for the evaluation of the other techniques;

4.3 the evaluation of the cost-effectiveness of the technique must focus on:
4.3.1 the cost-effectiveness analysis;
4.3.2 the evaluation of indirect and intangible cost such as, for example, the feeling of well-being, the impact on social life, or the loss of earnings.

D. The coverage by private insurance companies

In addition to the above-mentioned techniques, other alternative techniques are covered only when patients have a complementary private insurance policy covering the specific technique.[173] For example, the supplementary health care policy of the Caisse Vaudoise partially reimburses[174] many alternative treatments.[175] The supplementary monthly payment for the alternative policy varies between 10 and 20 CHF per month.[176]

The Register of Empirical Medicines (RME)[177] has been created,[178] for the purpose of registering the therapists who provide alternative medicines.

173 According to Duc, this situation will create a two-speed medicine where only those having the opportunity to have additional policies will benefit from alternative care (DUC J.-L., *op. cit.*: 43–44).
174 The reimbursement varies between 30 and 100 CHF per consultation and between 3 and 10 consultations are covered per year.
175 E.g., acupuncture, acupressure, Alexander technique, anthroposophical medicine (when provided by a physician), audiopsychophonology, auriculotherapy, lymphatic drainage, etiopathy, curative eurythmy, eutony, homeopathy, postural integration, iridology, columnic irrigation, Kneipp therapy, kinesiology, mesotherapy, naturopathy, osteopathy, polarity, energetic balancing, reflexology, relaxation, respiration, shiatsu, sophrology, and sympathicotherapy.
176 See also, e.g., DUC J.-L., *op. cit.*: 47.
177 In French: "Registre des Médecines Empiriques".
178 Available at http://www.rme.ch/rme.htm, accessed July 19, 2001.

The RME performs the function, on behalf of private insurance companies[179], of ensuring that alternative practitioners[180] have had sufficient training before they may provide specific alternative medicines.[181] The RME also indicates the number of hours of allopathic and/or alternative training that is required in order for practitioners to be allowed to provide the techniques, as well as regulating which practitioners may provide it.[182] Some alternative practitioners associations registered a complaint by the Swiss Competition Commission against the RME.[183] On April 26 2004, the Commission decided to close the investigation regarding the RME, as the RME changed its practice regarding the way it registers therapists.[184]

5.3.5.15 US

Bibliography

Andrews L. B.(I), *The shadow health care system: Regulation of alternative health care providers*, in: Houston Law Review, 1996, vol. 32: 1273–1317; Berg R., *Note, HMO exclusion of chiropractors*, in: S. Cal. L. Rev., 1993, vol. 66: 807–38; Bissel T., *United States*, in: Bedee H. (co-authors: D'haese W., Petry V., Rompelman A. J.), *The international guide to social security*, Kluwer Law International, 1995, The Hague/London/Boston: 401–12; Boozang K. M. (I), *Western medicine opens the door to alternative medicine*, in: American Journal of Medicine, 1998, vol. 24, n° 2/3: 187; Boozang K. M. (II), *Is the alternative medicine? Managed care apparently thinks so*, in: Connecticut Law Review,

179 More than 30 are members of the RME.
180 More than 120 techniques are registered.
181 In order to be registered, the following conditions must be fulfilled: 1. the method must be recognised (i.e., at least one insurance covers it); 2. the method cannot be a group therapy; 3. the provider must hold a diploma attesting a training including both allopathic and alternative aspects; 4. the provider must have practical experience; 5. the provider must practise in a professional way (at least 30% of his/her activities); 6. the provider must have an office; 7. the provider must have no criminal record; 8. the provider must have civil liability insurance; 9. the provider must provide the information that the customer requires; 10. the provider must provide information regarding the patient, similar to physicians' medical records; 11. the provider must have a licence to work in Switzerland; 12. the provider must attend continuing training.
182 The RME only verifies the training of, but not the personal qualities of therapists. It does not test practitioners on their knowledge.
For more information, go to http://www.rme.ch/rme.htm. See also Spahni M., *op. cit.*
183 In French: "Commission de la concurrence" (Comco).
184 For more information go to www.comco.ch, accessed Feb. 1 2005.

Winter 2000, vol. 32: 567–613; Cline J. S. (co-author: Rosten K. A.), *The effect of policy language on the containment of health care cost*, in: Tort and Insurance Law Journal, 1985, vol. 21: 120ss; Cohen M. H. (I), *Alternative medicine – Legal boundaries and regulatory perspectives*, The Johns Hopkins University Press, 1998, London & Oxford: 96–104; Colgate M. A., *Gaining insurance coverage for alternative therapies*, in: Journal of Health Care Marketing, 1995, vol. 15, n° 1: 24ss; Eisenberg D. M. and co-authors, *Trends in alternative medicine use in the United States, 1990–1997*, in: JAMA, 1998, vol. 280, n° 18: 1569–75; Furrow B. R. (co-authors: Greaney T. L., Jost T., Schwartz R. L.) (I), *Health law*, West Publishing, 1995, St Paul; Goodwin J., *A health insurance revolution*, in: New Age Journal's Guide to Holistic Medicine, 1997–1998: 66–69; Griffin K., *Alternative care: Finally some insurance coverage*, in: Health, Oct. 1995; Hartley J. E., *Refusal to cover alternative providers or new technology*, in: *Antitrust in the healthcare field*, National Health Lawyers Association, 1992, Washington; Hooper (co-authors: Lundy & Bookman), *ERISA does not preempt state plan requiring alternative medicine offerings*, in: Cal. Health L. Monitor, 1998, vol. 6, n° 19: 2ss; Japsen B., *Cost-conscious providers take to holistic medicine: Once scorned or banned, alternative treatments have gone mainstream as less expensive but effective cures*, in: Mos. Healthcare, Aug. 21, 1995: 140; Josefek K. J., *Alternative medicine's roadmap to mainstream*, in: American Journal of Law and Medicine, 2000, vol. 26: 295–310; Jost T. S., *Health care rationing in the courts: A comparative study*, in: Hasting International and Comparative Law Review, 1998, vol. 21, n° 3: 639–714; Kilgore C., *Expanding coverage signals growing demand, acceptance for alternative care*, in: Medicine & Health Perspectives, May 4 1998: 1–4; Lay B. F., *Healer-patient privilege: Extending the physician-patient privilege to alternative health practitioners in California*, in: Hastings Law Journal, Mar. 1997: 633–66; Mitchell Weitzman S., *Insurance coverage for complementary and alternative medicine – Access, challenges, and policy*, in: Humber J. M. (co-editor: Almeder R.), *Alternative medicine and ethics*, Humana Press, 1998, Totowa: 127–61; Patel V., *Understanding the integration of alternative modalities into an emerging healthcare model in the United States*, in: Humber J. M. (co-editor: Almeder R.), *Alternative medicine and ethics*, Humana Press, 1998, Totowa: 68–71; Pelletier K. R. (co-authors: Krasner M. A), *Current trends in the integration and reimbursement of complementary and alternative medicine by managed care, insurance carriers, and hospital providers*, in: Am. J. Health Promot., 1997, n° 12: 112–122; Powers Monaco G. (co-author: Smith G.), *Healthcare plans as gatekeepers*, in: Humber J. M. (co-editor: Almeder R.), *Alternative medicine and ethics*, Humana Press, 1998, Totowa: 97–124; Russel S., *HMOs try dose of alternative medicine*, in: S. F. Chron., Jan. 22, 1996: A1, A4; Safriet B. J., *Health care dollars and regulatory sense: The role of advanced practice nursing*, in: Yale Journal on Regulation, 1992, vol. 9; Sage W. M. (co-author: Aiken L. H.), *Regulating interdisciplinary practice*, in: Jost T. S., *Regulation of the healthcare professions*, Health Administration Press, 1996, Chicago: 80–81; Schneider M. (co-authors: Biene-Dietrich P., Gebanyi M., Hofmann U., Huber M., Köse A., Sommer J. H.), *Gesundheitssysteme im internationalen Vergleich*, ed. 1994, BASYS, 1995, Augsburg: 473–94; Senn D., *Insurance commissioner, every category of provider*, in: Washington Office of Insurance Commissioner Bulletin, Dec. 19, 1995, n° 95–99;

Shekelle P. G., *What role for chiropractic in health care?*, in: The New England Journal of Medicine, 1998, vol. 339: 1074–75; Starr P., *The social transformation of American medicine*, Basic Books, 1982: 333; Stepno E. M., *Acupuncture – Stricter standards for those performing acupuncture*, in: M. George L. Rev., 1998, vol. 29: 411–15; Thomson B., *The medical revolution*, in: Natural Health, Mar.–Apr. 1996: 98ss; Vincler L. A. (co-author: Nicol M. F.), *When ignorance isn't bliss: What healthcare practitioners and facilities should know about complementary and alternative medicine*, in: J. Health & Hosp. L., 1997, vol. 30: 160ss; Weiss R., *Acupuncture gets a clean bill of health by US panel*, in: International Herald Tribune, November 7 1997; White House Commission on Complementary and Alternative Medicine Policy, *Final report*, March 2002, available at http://www.whccamp.hhs.gov/pdfs/fr2002_document.pdf, accessed Feb. 1 2005: 21–22, 88–89, 105–23.

A. Overview of the health care system

Introduction

Unlike other industrialised nations, the United States have not yet developed a program for making health care comprehensively available to its citizens. Instead, it has depended for its financing of health care by relying mainly on employment-related group health insurance, supplemented by individual insurance policies and a variety of federal, state and local programs aimed at special populations.[185, 186]

The two largest single health care programs are Medicare[187] and Medicaid. While Medicare is generally perceived to be a social insurance program similar to the national health insurance programs of Western Europe, Medicaid, by contrast, is clearly a welfare program.[188]

In 1991, 178 million Americans were covered by some form of private health insurance, including Blue Cross and Blue Shield plans, self-funded employer plans, commercial insurance or prepaid plans such as HMOs. The private health insurance sector accounts for approximately one third of national health expenditures.[189]

185 Today, the government finances several health care institutions and programs. In 1990, the government accounted for 42% of health care cost. Health care expenditures constituted 15.3% of federal expenditure and 11% of state and local expenditures.
In 1992, 14.7% of the population was not covered by any type of insurance.

186 Furrow B. R. (I), *op. cit.*: 561; Schneider M., *op. cit.*: 473, 477–79.

187 This program accounts for 17% of the nation's health care spending.

188 Bissel T., *op. cit.*: 401–02; Furrow B. R. (I), *op. cit.*: 561–62, 604–05; Schneider M., *op. cit.*: 477–78.

189 Furrow B. R. (I), *op. cit.*: 498–99; Schneider M., *op. cit.*: 477.

Finance and organisation

Medicare is a program limited both in eligibility and scope but which pays for a significant share of health care in the country. It covers that part of the population most in need of medical care and also the most expensive types of care required by that population.[190]

The Medicare program is essentially made up of two programs. The first program, Part A, the Hospital Insurance program, covers inpatient hospital, skilled nursing, home health and hospice services.[191] This part of the program is funded by payroll taxes assessed against employers, employees, and the self-employed and by interest income on this trust fund.[192] Usually patients must pay a deductible that varies according to the medical acts provided.[193]

The second program, Part B (Supplemental Medical Insurance), helps pay for physician services, outpatient hospital services, speech and physical therapy, renal dialysis, ambulatory surgery, home health services, durable medical equipment, rural health clinic services, comprehensive outpatient rehabilitation facility services and some diagnostic tests.[194] This program is voluntary and therefore, only those persons who pay the part B premium and are eligible may receive its benefits. Part B was originally designed as a premium-financed insurance program, however, the Part B trust fund has increasingly been financed by general revenue funds, which now cover 75% of the costs of the Part B program. A significant share of Part B premium revenues also comes from State revenues because State Medicaid programs pay Part B premiums for persons eligible for both Medicare and Medicaid. Under this program, patients must usually pay a deductible of $100, as well as a copayment of 20%.[195]

The Health Care Financing Administration of the Department of Health and Human Services is responsible for the administration of Medicare. A number of other public and quasi-public entities also play key roles in the Medicare program.[196]

190 BISSEL T., *op. cit.*: 401–02; FURROW B. R. (I), *op. cit.*: 562.

191 42 U.S.C.A. § 1395d.

192 General revenues may not be used to fund the Part A program, if this part may borrow from other federal social insurance trust funds.

193 BISSEL T., *op. cit.*: 401, 405; FURROW B. R. (I), *op. cit.*: 562, 565–66; SCHNEIDER M., *op. cit.*: 473, 479–80.

194 42 U.S.C.A. § 1395k; 42 F.C.R. § 410.3.

195 BISSEL T., *op. cit.*: 407–08; FURROW B. R. (I), *op. cit.*: 562, 581–89; SCHNEIDER M., *op. cit.*: 479–80.

196 FURROW B. R. (I), *op. cit.*: 562.

The Medicaid program is a co-operative federal and state program that finances health care for the poor. Medicaid has come to serve three main different functions. First, it is a program to finance health care for the worthy poor who receive cash assistance through federal assistance programs.[197] Second, the program is a catastrophic insurance program for those having to pay extraordinary medical bills, particularly bills for care in nursing facilities or facilities that care for mentally retarded. Finally, Medicaid has expanded its coverage to include low-income children and pregnant women, regardless of their eligibility for cash assistance. Approximately 52% of persons nation-wide with income levels below the federal poverty limit[198] are covered by Medicaid, however coverage varies from State to State.[199]

Although federal statutes and regulations establish basic requirements for eligibility, benefits, payment and administration, there are significant differences between the States in all aspects of Medicaid. The federal government contributes from 50% to 83% of Medicaid program expenditures with States taking responsibility for the remaining part.[200]

The nature of private health insurance has changed withing the US. First, the Blue Cross and the Blue Shield, which had dominated health insurance, now covers only about 73 millions insured people and has become more commercial. Then, the domination by the Blue Cross and the Blue Shield of hospitals and physicians has ended. Another major change has been the growth of employer self-insurance and, finally, there has been a major change in the growth of managed care.[201, 202]

Health insurance is generally subject to some form of cost sharing, whereby the insured pays some share of medical costs.[203] Employees commonly pay some part of the premium for employment-related health insurance. Insurance is also often subject to a deductible that the insured must pay each year before expenses begin to be covered. After the deductible is met, most insurance plans impose either a percentage coinsurance or

197 People with minimal income and assets and those who are aged, blind, disabled, as well as the families of dependent children fall into this category.

198 From 32% in Florida and Texas to 68% in New England.

199 FURROW B. R. (I), *op. cit.*: 604.

200 FURROW B. R. (I), *op. cit.*: 604.

201 Managed care encompasses a variety of private approaches to health care cost containment ranging from Preferred Provider Organizations, Health Maintenance Organizations and various hybrid health care delivery organizations to simple utilization review.

202 FURROW B. R. (I), *op. cit.*: 499–500.

203 E.g., the first $400 of covered expenses must be paid by the insured.

a flat per-service copayment on the insured.[204] Cost-sharing obligations are commonly subject to an annual out-of-pocket maximum obligation of the insured,[205] but the insurance is also commonly limited to a maximum obligation over the lifetime of the insured.[206, 207]

Health insurers are subject to extensive regulation by the states. The purpose of the regulation is to ensure the solvency of the insurers and review insurance policies to ensure that they are not unfair or deceptive in their terms. States also regulate Blue Cross and Blue Shield, HMOs, PPOs and utilization review.[208] During the last years, states have also mandated the terms of insurance contracts, in particular, requiring that insurance contracts cover certain benefits (mandate benefit laws), providers (mandate provider laws), or insured people (mandate coverage laws).[209] They also tend to adopt regulations extending insurance to the uninsured.[210]

Providers of care

Outpatient care

Only one sixth of the physicians are GPs, while most of the outpatient physicians are specialists. Patients must usually pay for the treatment, which is then reimbursed by the insurance. Furthermore, there is usually a co-payment from patients. Most of the medical doctors practise privately.[211]

Physicians working with Medicare often have an agreement with Program Medicare allowing them to directly receive a payment for the provided treatment.[212]

204 E.g., 20% of covered expenses.
205 Commonly between $1,000 and $2,000.
206 Usually $1 million or more.
207 FURROW B. R. (I), *op. cit.*: 500–01; SCHNEIDER M., *op. cit.*: 480.
208 For more details regarding regulation of managed care, see FURROW B. R. (I), *op. cit.*: 525–35.
209 For more details, see FURROW B. R. (I), *op. cit.*: 509–11.
210 The Consolidated Omnibus Budget Reconciliation Act, which mandates a continuing opportunity for coverage for certain persons who otherwise would have been terminated from coverage under group health insurance plans, and the Employee Retirement Income Security Act, which pre-empts state regulation of self-insured benefits plans, are two significant federal acts affecting health insurance.
For more details, see FURROW B. R. (I), *op. cit.*: 513–24.
211 SCHNEIDER M., *op. cit.*: 484.
212 SCHNEIDER M., *op. cit.*: 485.

Access to specialist physicians varies according to the type of health coverage. Some insurance programs allow a patient to directly see a specialist. However, in other health care plans (in particular in managed care) patients must first see a gatekeeper, usually a physician, who makes the referral.

Hospitals

The coverage of inpatient health care costs varies according to the type of insurance and hospital. A few States have tried to introduce fixed prices.[213]

B. The situation of alternative medicines

Introduction

The US has a public coverage system for alternative medicines; some alternative medicines are covered both by federal programs and private insurance companies.

If, during the past, alternative medicines were not included in insurance schemes, an increasing number of insurers and managed care organisations now offer alternative medicine programs and benefits.[214] As Goodwin notes

> these days, more and more health insurers are covering therapies that were once considered alternative but are now accepted as mainstream. And increasingly, states are not waiting for insurance companies and health organisations (HMOs) to offer such coverage but are mandating that they provide it.[215]

However, out-of-pocket payments continue to represent a considerable part of payment for receiving alternative care.

It is noticeable that the provision of alternative medicines currently represents a considerable part of the market share of health care in the country. Indeed, expenditures for alternative services increased 45.2 % between 1990 ($14.6 billion.) and 1997 ($21.2 billion), with at least $12.2 billion

213 SCHNEIDER M., *op. cit.*: 488–90.
214 EISENBERG D. M., *op. cit.*: 1569; PELLETIER K. R., *op. cit.*; WHITE HOUSE COMMISSION ON COMPLEMENTARY AND ALTERNATIVE MEDICINE POLICY, *op. cit.*: 105.
215 GOODWIN J., *op. cit.*: 66.

paid out-of-pocket.[216] This amount exceeds the 1997 out-of-pocket expenditures for all US hospitalisations.[217]

The total 1997 out-of-pocket expenses in relation to alternative medicines, including professional services, herbal products, high-dose vitamins, books, classes, and diet products, was estimated at $27.0 billion, which is comparable with the out-of-pocket expenditures for all US physician services. The majority of people who saw alternative practitioners paid all of the out-of-pocket costs in 1997 (58.3 % as compared to 64.0 % in 1990).[218, 219]

216 The percentage of users paying entirely out-of-pocket for services provided by alternative practitioners decreased from 64% in 1990 to 58% in 1997.
The Food and Drug Administration estimated that more than 1 million Americans were spending a total of about $500 million a year solely on acupuncture. It has also been estimated that up to 15 million Americans have tried acupuncture at least once.

217 EISENBERG D. M., *op. cit.*: 1569, 1573–74; WEISS R., *op. cit.*

218 The percentage of insurance coverage of some alternative medicines in the country in 1997 and in 1990 are as follows:

	Complete (in %)		Partial (in %)		None (in %)	
	1990	1997	1990	1997	1990	1997
Relaxation techniques	5.3	28.8	25.9	6.6	68.7	64.7
Herbal medicine	30.7	8.6	15.5	11.2	53.8	80.2
Massage	19.1	11.8	18.3	16.7	62.6	71.5
Chiropractic	11.5	17.6	32.8	38.1	55.9	44.3
Imagery	16.1	51.5	0.0	3.5	83.9	45.0
Lifestyle diet	62.3	0.0	0.0	44.9	37.7	55.1
Homeopathy	0.0	0.0	19.1	0.0	80.9	100.0
Biofeedback	14.1	30.5	19.9	43.7	66.0	26.0
Acupuncture	21.6	0.0	23.0	40.7	55.4	59.3

219 EISENBERG D. M., *op. cit.*: 1569, 1573–74.

Refusal of coverage

Historically, insurers have refused coverage for alternative health care.[220] The two main reasons were first, that the biomedical view of what constitutes health care dominated reimbursement, namely that only those therapies that were based on the results of randomised controlled trials published in generally accepted journals could be covered.[221] Second, those physicians that were generally hostile to the spreading of alternative practitioners became the gatekeepers to benefits for insurances.[222] For example, the AMA[223] House of Delegates adopted a resolution "opposing any attempt at empowering nonphysicians to become unsupervised primary medical care providers and be directly reimbursed for case management activities".[224, 225]

220 Eisenberg writes that "the magnitude of the demand for alternative therapy is noteworthy, in light of the relatively low rates of insurance coverage for these services. Unlike hospitalisations and physician services, alternative therapies are only infrequently included in insurance benefits. Even when alternative therapies are covered, they tend to have high deductibles and co-payments and tend to be subject to stringent limits on the number of visits or total dollar coverage. Because the demand for health care (and presumably alternative therapies) is sensitive to how patients must pay out-of-pocket, current use is likely to under represent utilisation of patterns if insurance coverage for alternative therapies increases in the future" (EISENBERG D. M., *op. cit.*: 1575). On the subject, see also, e.g., MITCHELL WEITZMAN S., *op. cit.*: 133ss.

221 See POWERS MONACO G., *op. cit.*: 103ss.

222 Starr points out that during the 1950s, the market for private insurance increased and that the classical medical profession and physicians became the gatekeepers to benefits for insurances. The eligibility for reimbursement became the chief obstacle for any competing group of practitioners. Thus, for example, even though chiropractic could circumvent the licensing laws, they usually could not get reimbursed from Blue Shield, nor could patients be reimbursed under indemnity plans (STARR P., *op. cit.*: 333).
Andrews notes that, "since physicians are the main breadwinners for hospitals, health maintenance organizations, and other health care institutions, they exert a large amount of power over the fashioning of policies to govern these institutions. Physician groups have bullied hospitals into adopting policies that favour physicians and disadvantage or even eliminate alternative health care providers, even when there is no evidence that such policies are necessary to protect patients" (ANDREWS L. B., *op. cit.*: 1289).

223 American Medical Association, the most important association of American physicians.

224 SAFRIET B. J., *op. cit.*: 437.

225 ANDREWS L. B., *op. cit.*: 1291–92; BOOZANG K. M. (I), *op. cit.*: 567–69; COHEN M. H. (I), *op. cit.*: 96; SAFRIET B. J., *op. cit.*: 437; STARR P., *op. cit.*: 333.

Thus, non-physicians alternative practitioners must face various legal barriers when providing alternative medicines, such as limitations on direct reimbursement, practices excluding them from privileges at health care institutions, and the inability to obtain malpractice insurance. For example, in *Hahn v. Oregon Physicians' Service* (OPS),[226] several podiatrists contended that OPS, a physician-controlled health plan, violated the Sherman (antitrust) Act by excluding podiatrists from membership and by reimbursing non-members at a lower rate than members. The court held that the exclusion of podiatrists from the health plan and the partial reimbursement schedule constituted a boycott and an unreasonable restraint of trade.[227]

Antitrust actions have also been brought against insurers that have refused to reimburse alternative practitioners practising independently. In *Virginia Academy of Clinical Psychologists v. Blue Shield of Virginia*,[228] a physician-controlled plan (Blue Shield) refused to pay psychotherapist fees unless the services were billed through a physician. The court rejected the argument of Blue Shield that the restriction prevented needless psychotherapy when the health problems had a physical basis. In a related case *(Blue Shield of Virginia v. McCready)*,[229] the Supreme Court held that consumers have a right to bring suit against the insurer when they are forced by the insurance plan to consult a physician before getting access to a psychotherapist.[230]

Voluntary and mandated coverage

Today, many insurers, and in particular HMOs, are experimenting with coverage of various types of alternative medicines. A 1995 survey of the nation's largest HMOs found that as many as 86% of HMOs covered some types of alternative medicines.[231, 232] Lay notes that

226 *Hahn v. Oregon Physicians' Service*, civil n° 78-0887-MA, 1990 U.S. Dist. Lexis 16899 (D. Or. Oct. 26, 1990).

227 ANDREWS L. B., *op. cit.*: 1296–97.

228 *Virginia Academy of Clinical Psychologists v. Blue Shield of Virginia*, 624 F.2d 476 (4th Cir. 1980), cert. denied, 450 U.S. 916 (1981).

229 *Blue Shield of Virginia v. McCready*, 457 U.S. 465 (1982).

230 ANDREWS L. B., *op. cit.*: 1297–98.

231 However, some HMOs exclude, for example, chiropractors from their plans, which are usually dominated by physicians. For an interesting study on this question see BERG R., *op. cit.*: 807–38.

232 According to a study carried out by Stanford's Centre for Research in Disease Prevention in 1996, 18 large insurance and managed care companies had or were developing policies to cover unconventional therapies. A year later, 30 major

> as part of this shift in American healthcare towards alternative therapies, full-services primary healthcare facilities are springing up across the nation, offering both standard and alternative treatments, including bodywork, botanical medicine, biofeedback, guided imagery, acupuncture, and nutritional counselling. [...] These new clinics, called "integrated centers", [...] allow a patient to see an alternative practitioner only after a licensed physician has examined the patient for serious illnesses that require conventional treatment.[233]

For example, new alternative medicine clinics and programs at Stanford,[234] Robert Wood Johnson University Hospital in New Brunswick (N.J.), Columbia-Presbyterian Complementary Care Center (NY), and Cedars Sinai Medical Center in Los Angeles are offering therapies ranging from acupuncture and massage therapy to biofeedback, herbal medicine and homeopathy.[235]

The main reasons explaining the increase in alternative medicines' coverage are the potential cost saving for insurers, consumer demand, a "wellness approach"[236] that is attractive to employers.[237] Some examples of recent developments in the coverage of alternative medicines are presented below:[238]

---

insurers were covering more than one alternative medicine, half of them being Blue Cross or Blue Shield. In 1998, at least 39 important health insurance companies were covering alternative treatments.

233 LAY B. F., *op. cit.*: 638–39.

234 Stanford also houses one of 10 speciality research centers funded by the Office of Alternative Medicine to study alternative medicines for specific health conditions. Researchers are also studying nutrition and mind-body interventions.

235 GOODWIN J., *op. cit.*: 66–69; KILGORE C., *op. cit.*: 1, 3; LAY B. F., *op. cit.*: 638–39; WHITE HOUSE COMMISSION ON COMPLEMENTARY AND ALTERNATIVE MEDICINE POLICY, *op. cit.*: 21, 106–08.

236 COHEN M. H. (I), *op. cit.*: 97.

237 BOOZANG K. M. (I), *op. cit.*: 192, 202–04; COHEN M. H. (I), *op. cit.*: 97; WHITE HOUSE COMMISSION ON COMPLEMENTARY AND ALTERNATIVE MEDICINE POLICY, *op. cit.*: 107.
Sage notes that "state legislature and insurance regulators have imposed additional coverage requirements on private insurers in response to lobbying by non-physician health professionals and their patients" (SAGE W. M., *op. cit.*: 80).

238 ANDREWS L. B., *op. cit.*: 1279; BOOZANG K. M. (I), *op. cit.*: 192, 202–04; BOOZANG K. M. (II), *op. cit.*: 576–80; COHEN M. H. (I), *op. cit.*: 97; GOODWIN J., *op. cit.*: 66–69; GRIFFIN K., *op. cit.*; KILGORE C., *op. cit.*: 1–3; LAY B. F., *op. cit.*: 638–39; MITCHELL WEITZMAN S., *op. cit.*: 133ss; PATEL V., *op. cit.*: 68–71; PELLETIER K. R., *op. cit.*: 112–122; RUSSEL S., *op. cit.*: A1, A4; THOMSON B., *op. cit.*: 98ss; VINCLER L. A., *op. cit.*: 160ss.
For a chart including 39 insurance companies and HMOs and the covered therapies, covering, see GOODWIN J., *op. cit.*: 67–68.

1. American Western Life Insurance now offers Prevention Plus, an integrated health insurance plan offering up to twelve annual visits to alternative practitioners alongside a conventional medical network of over 650 hospitals;
2. The Mutual of Omaha Companies offers the Reversal Program, which is a prevention and behaviour modification program to reduce the risk of heart disease through yoga, diet, meditation, and support behavioural medicine, including mind-body relaxation, as preventive care;[239]
3. Health Net Plan offers coverage for acupuncture through a benefit rider. Pending state approval, those members whose employers purchase the rider will have direct access to a network of acupuncturists and coverage for musculoskeletal pain, post-stroke recovery, and nausea from chemotherapy and pregnancy;[240]
4. Health Partners, which is an HMO, has a different approach. Members must pay $ 18 per year for the right to access providers in a network run. Members who pay the fees get 15% discounts for 50 alternative medicine services;[241]
5. Additionally, several Health Plans such as Alternative Health Insurance Services;[242] Alternare Group;[243] the Harvard Community Health Plan;[244] the Oxford Health Plan;[245] Kaiser Permanente;[246]

For a criticism regarding the inclusion of alternative modalities within the HMOs programs, see, e.g. BOOZANG K. M. (II), *op.cit.*: 567–613.

239 The Reversal Program costs $4.000 per individual.

240 Homeopathy, yoga, and naturopathy may be considered next.

241 E.g., massage therapy, structural bodywork, homeopathy or naturopathy. Fees for services are paid directly to providers.

242 The insurance is available in all the states. It covers acupuncture, alternative birthing centers/midwifery, ayurvedic medicine, biofeedback, bodywork/massage therapy, chelation therapy, chiropractic, colon therapy, herbal medicine, homeopathy, naturopathy, nutrition counselling, oriental medicine, osteopathy, and transcendental meditation.

243 The group established in Seattle has created one of the largest alternative care networks in Alaska, Washington, and Chicago, and provides access to a host of alternative specialists as well as a variety of food and herbal supplements.

244 In Massachusetts. There are discounts on the Personal Health Improvement Program for stress-related illness, chronic disease, and mood disorders.

245 In Connecticut, New Jersey and New York. Following a survey that showed that 75% of its members wanted alternative treatments, the fledgling Connecticut-based Oxford Health Plans, which is already a $3 billion HMO with 1.5 million members, introduced some alternative medicines in the plan. This plan permits access to alternative practitioners, divided between core providers (chiropractors, acupuncturists, and naturopathic physicians) and supplemental providers (yoga teachers, massage therapists, nutritional counsellors and others).

and American Medical Security's,[247] propose some form of coverage for alternative modalities.[248]

Some insurers provide coverage only when treatments, such as acupuncture,[249] are administered, prescribed or supervised by a licensed physician, while others cover treatments irrespective of physician involvement. Some health plans have opted for a direct access to alternative practitioners. Indeed, many health plan officials say that they truly want more integrated care but are stymied by the conventional physician's beliefs.[250] For that reason Health Net provides direct access to patients wishing to receive services from alternative practitioners. Health Net officials say they will stay with this approach until there is greater acceptance from the conventional medical fraternity.[251]

States have also imposed several insurance mandates that affect the provision of alternative medicines[252] through various types of laws:[253]

Since it launched its pioneering alternative medicine network, an estimated 40–50% of plan members have seen at least one of the 3,000 alternative practitioners the company contract with.

246 In California. It is one of the nations' largest non-profit HMO and was a pioneering company in the field of alternative medicines. It has provided acupuncture to its members for over a decade. Now, its broad-based wellness program includes nutrition counselling, meditation, massage, acupressure, and behavioural medicine as well.

247 In Arizona. The HealthCareChoice plan includes acupuncture, acupressure, biofeedback, chiropractic, Dean Ornish program, herbal medicine, hypnotherapy, homeopathy (if practised by a M.D.), massage, naturopathy and nutrition counselling.

248 In Arizona, Wisconsin, Texas, North Carolina and Colorado.

249 According to Stepno, over 100 insurance plans nationwide now cover some aspect of alternative care (STEPNO E. M., *op. cit.*: 413).

250 These plans tried to promote integration by proposing that patients' alternative treatment plans be routinely sent to their primary care physicians. The idea was scrapped after officials recognised that many patients do not want their doctors to know about their use of alternative care. As they are afraid of being humiliated or scolded. Furthermore, Health Net has experienced problems in that, even if they cover acupuncture where it is medically indicated, most physicians do not provide referrals for it.

251 COHEN M. H. (II), *op. cit.*: 155; KILGORE C., *op. cit.*: 2–3.

252 A report estimates that "at least 41 state governments now require chiropractic coverage in some form; six require acupuncture coverage; and nine licensed naturopaths." (*Managed care organisations begin covering alternative treatment*, 12 Med. Malpractice L. & Strategy 3, 3 (1996), cited in BOOZANG K. M. (I), *op. cit.*: 187).

253 BOOZANG K. M. (II), *op. cit.*: 580–86; COHEN M. H. (I), *op. cit.*: 98–99; SAGE W. M., *op. cit.*: 80.

1. mandate benefit laws that require insurers to cover certain benefits. For example, forty-six states require insurers to reimburse patients for chiropractic care, and at least six states require reimbursement for acupuncture;[254]
2. mandate provider laws that require insurers to provide reimbursement for services offered by various alternative practitioners when the insurer would cover the service when provided by a physician (for example chiropractors and acupuncturists);
3. any willing provider laws that require that insurance proposing preferred provider policies establish the conditions governing providers' eligibility to be preferred, that such conditions may not discriminate against or among health care practitioners, and that such policies may not exclude any preferred provider willing to meet the terms and conditions to set forth.[255] In other words, these laws require insurers to contract with, and therefore reimburse the services of any practitioner willing to meet their basic terms and conditions. Some states extend or vary the rule to plans other than preferred provider policies. In Florida, for example, the insurance may not discriminate against chiropractors who, within their scope of practice, offer the same service or benefit as does a biomedical physician.[256, 257] Furthermore, Florida's statute provides that any policy of individual health insurance covering acupuncture must cover the services of a certified acupuncturist "under

254 Although the provisions of ERISA usually pre-empts state law relating to employee benefit plans, some courts have held that state laws mandating coverage constitute insurance regulation that is saved from ERISA pre-emption. See also Furrow B. R. (I), *op. cit.*: 510, 519 and accompanying text (citing cases).

255 E.g., Virginia's statute provides that "no hospital, physician, or type of provider listed [...] willing to meet the terms and conditions offered to it or him shall be excluded" (Va. Code Ann. § 38.2-3407.B.). This means that, whether a hospital sets contract terms and conditions for providers offering rehabilitative care, and such care is offered by licensed physicians, physical therapists, and chiropractors, each within their scope of practice, then the hospital has to make the contract available to any of the three practitioners and may not discriminate among them.

256 Fla. Stat. § 627.419 (4).

257 Louisiana has adopted similar rules. Louisiana's statute provides that when an insurance policy offers reimbursement of any service that may be performed by chiropractors within their scope of practice, the insurer has to reimburse the chiropractor's treatment (La. Rev. Stat. Ann. § 22:668 (quoted in *Chiropractic Ass'n of Louisiana v. State*, 595 So. 2d 316, 317)).

the same condition that apply to services of a licensed physician";[258]
4. freedom-of-choice laws that allow insured people to obtain care from any licensed professional and to claim reimbursement regardless of the existence of a contract between the professional and the plan.[259]

In addition to these new types of laws that facilitate the provision of alternative medicines, the State of Washington has a particularly expansive statute enacted as part of its health care reform. The statute requires that state health plans allow "every category of health care provider to provide health services or care for conditions included in the basic health plan services to the extent that:

a) the provision of such health services or care is within the health care provider's permitted scope of practice; and
b) the providers agree to abide by standards related to:
    i) provision, utilisation review, and cost containment of health services;
    ii) management and administrative procedures;
    iii) provisions of cost-effective and clinically efficacious health services."[260]

Thus, for example, if coverage for rehabilitation therapy is part of the State's plan, then every insurance company has to cover that service, whether the treatment was given by a licensed osteopathic physician, physical therapist, chiropractor, or massage therapist (even if such practitioners were not originally included in the insurance contract), provided the practitioner is duly licensed, certified, or registered, is providing the service within the authorized scope of practice, and complies with utilisation review and other standards indicated in the statute. Similarly, insurers must cover claims for treatments by acupuncturists (even if acupuncturists were excluded from coverage by the specific health plan), if the condition treated is included in the basic health plan and the practitioner is providing service within his or her scope of practice.[261]

258 Fla. Stat. § 627.6403. See also Mont. Code Ann. § 33-22-111 (1) where the insured "has full freedom of choice in the selection" of any licensed physician, chiropractor, acupuncturist, or other provider.
259 Sage notes that, "although these laws are now being backed by physicians concerned about managed care, they traditionally protected politically powerful groups of non-physician professionals such as independent pharmacists, podiatrists, and chiropractors" (SAGE W. M., *op. cit.*: 80).
260 Wash. Rev. Code 48.43.045 (1996).
261 BOOZANG K. M. (I), *op. cit.*: 187; BOOZANG K. M. (II), *op. cit.*: 584–86; COHEN M. H. (I), *op. cit.*: 99–100; KILGORE C., *op. cit.*: 4.

In regard to enforcement of the law and following a narrow interpretation of the Washington statute by some insurers,[262] the State Insurance Commissioner has, in response, made it clear in several bulletins that insurers were attempting to evade statutory requirements and affirmed its willingness "to take all enforcement actions to prevent any other practices that circumvent the statute".[263] A coalition of HMOs, insurers, and HCSCs have also sued the State of Washington, claiming that the statute was pre-empted by ERISA. However, the appellate court disagreed.[264]

It is important to note that that, even though various mandates to cover alternative medicine have been passed, there are fewer people benefiting than might be supposed. As Coorsh[265] states

> State-mandated benefits apply only to plans regulated by the State. A little more than half of consumers who have employer-sponsored coverage are in programs that are not regulated by the state but rather by the federal government. This means that many people may not get state-mandated benefits.[266]

Sage has put into perspective the extent of these laws, noticing that ERISA pre-empts State efforts to regulate the payment practices of employer-sponsored health plans. For example, States may not enforce mandate-benefit laws against the increasing number of employers who self-insure their employees.[267]

Some authors have criticized the mandatory inclusion of alternative modalities within HMOs programs. Boozang, for example, states that

262 They attempted to exclude plans or practitioners, added several hurdles for specific practitioners and limited the number of visits or maximum benefit amount depending on the provider.

263 The Commissioner stated that services within the practitioner's authorized scope of practice must be covered "without discrimination on the basis of provider type". Furthermore, he added that insurance may not exclude a category of provider by asserting that the category fails to meet the insurance's standards for provision of "cost-effective and clinically efficacious health services".

264 COHEN M. H. (I), *op. cit.*: 100; HOOPER, *op. cit.*: 2ss; KILGORE C., *op. cit.*: 4; SENN D., *op. cit.*

265 Spokesman for the Health Insurance Association of America.

266 Coorsh adds, "The decision to cover is made by the purchaser, not the seller. [...] If an employer insists on reimbursement for acupuncture, for example, then it is incumbent upon the employer to insert that in its contracts. And it is happening. After all, insurers are in the business of selling coverage, and they respond to market demand. The message is clear. Consumers should demand it" (cited in GOODWIN J., *op. cit.*: 69).

267 SAGE W. M., *op. cit.*: 80–81.

> no doubt, many alternative offerings will prove to be not only safe and effective, but superior to conventional offerings. Unfortunately, we have no idea which of the thousands of treatment choices advanced by CAM proponents these will be. Consequently, it is premature for legislatures to even consider forcing health plans to pay for alternative treatments. If and when we can be more certain CAM therapies improve patient care, both providers and payors will presumably adopt those treatments, without government intervention. Until then, the State should be more attentive to its consumer protection role, ensuring that payors are not dedicating scarce resources to methods that are no health care, or that will do patients no good.[268]

Besides mandatory coverage, it is interesting to note that, in 1997, a comprehensive initiative to codify patients' freedom of choice in healthcare was introduced in Congress: the Patient Access to Responsible Care Act (PARCA).[269] If PARCA had been enacted, it would have expanded patient access to alternative medicines in two ways. First, PARCA would have given enrolees the option, during the enrolment period, of selecting an insurance coverage that provided for services that were not furnished through health professionals who were members of the plan.[270] Second, PARCA would have provided enrolees with the option to select a coverage that permitted them to visit alternative practitioners, with the existing health plan covering such costs.[271, 272]

Thus, PARCA would have had the effect of protecting alternative practitioners from discrimination by the various health plans that were reluctant to reimburse them. Indeed, it would have eradicated the bias that alternative practitioners had faced in the past and that would have created parity of payment between conventional and alternative providers within the healthcare industry.[273, 274]

268 BOOZANG K. M. (II), *op. cit.*: 613. For further information on this subject, see the same author at 567–613.
269 See Patient Access to Responsible Care Act (PARCA), H.R.: 1415, 105th Cong. (1997).
270 H.R. 1415 § 2772 (b)(1).
271 H.R. 1415 § 2773 (c).
272 JOSEFEK K. J., *op. cit.*: 306.
273 When PARCA was introduced in Congress, a study was cited in which 90% of the respondents where in favour of patients in HMOs having access to a full range of healthcare professionals.
274 JOSEFEK K. J., *op. cit.*: 306.

Medicare and Medicaid coverage

Non-physician health care providers have successfully lobbied for Medicare reimbursement. In fact, the statute's definition of "physician" now includes dentists, podiatrists, optometrists, and chiropractors.[275] Other provisions mandate coverage for the services of psychologists, many advanced practice nurses, and selected allied health practitioners.[276, 277]

Under Medicaid regulation, services provided by optometrists and chiropractors receive federal funding if the States elect to cover them.[278, 279]

Following the reclassification of acupuncture needles in 1996,[280] a federal panel concluded, for the first time, that acupuncture was an effective treatment for certain kinds of pain and nausea, and that it also showed promise for a variety of other conditions. However, the panel, which was convened by the National Institute of Health, had and has no binding power over doctors or insurers.[281] But, as Weiss notes, "experts said it would almost certainly increase the number of patients opting for treatment by America's 10,000 acupuncturists, and could eventually lead to greater coverage of acupuncture by insurance companies and government programs such as Medicare and Medicaid".[282]

Experimental treatments

Insurers may exclude experimental treatments from coverage in order to avoid paying for expensive medical treatments of unknown efficacy.[283] The definition of "experimental treatments" varies with some courts interpreting the term broadly to include treatments that are not generally accepted

275 42 U.S.C. § 1395x(r)(1996).
276 See 42 U.S.C. §§ 1395k(a), 1395x(s) (1996).
277 FURROW B. R. (I), *op. cit.*: 566, 618; SAGE W. M., *op. cit.*: 81; SHEKELLE P. G., *op. cit.*: 1074–75.
278 42 U.S.C. §§ 1396d(e),(g) (1996).
279 SAGE W. M., *op. cit.*: 81.
280 See below.
281 The panel concluded that there was "clear evidence" that acupuncture was an effective treatment for vomiting and nausea caused by chemotherapy, surgical anaesthesia or pregnancy, and for pain following dental surgery. In contrast, the group said that there was weaker evidence that acupuncture might be effective against other conditions such as menstrual cramps, tennis elbow, the generalised muscle pain, drug addiction, stroke, and headache. Furthermore, it was reported that acupuncture has fewer side effects and is less invasive than many other procedures that doctors perform.
282 WEISS R., *op. cit.*
283 See CLINE J. S., *op. cit.*: 120.

or supported by satisfactory documentation. A narrow definition involves procedures designed to test a hypothesis or contribute to generalised knowledge as part of a defined research protocol.[284]

In 1996, the FDA reclassified acupuncture needles from Class III, investigational devices limited to research, to Class II devices, or medical devices for general use, by acupuncturists.[285, 286] The new policy of the FDA could prompt insurers to reclassify treatments such as acupuncture as reimbursable, rather than to exclude them as investigational or experimental.[287]

Medical Necessity, Exclusion and Fraud[288]

Health insurance policies may limit coverage to "medically necessary" treatments, being those treatments that are "reasonably intended, in the exercise of good medical practice, for the treatment of illness or injury".[289] Medicare, for example, excludes items and services that are of questionable medical value, considering that they are "not reasonably necessary for the diagnosis or treatment of illness or injury or to improve the functioning of a malformed body part".[290] Under Medicare, the following criteria are considered when determining whether or not to cover a technology, namely whether the technology is medically necessary or not:[291]

1. whether the service is safe and effective;
2. whether the service is still no longer experimental or investigational;
3. whether the service is cost-effective; and
4. whether the service is appropriate.

Sometimes, the provision of alternative medicines and the submission of appropriate claims for reimbursement, which are not considered to be medically necessary, can be deemed to be fraudulent per se. For example, in relation to the controversial cancer treatment provided by the Stanislav

284 For a criticism of the interpretation of alternative treatments as experimental treatments, see COHEN M. H. (I), *op. cit.*: 101–02.

285 According to the FDA decision, acupuncture needles have to be labelled "For single use only", their sale must be clearly limited to qualified acupuncturists, and regulations on "device material biocompatibility" and "device sterility" must be followed.

286 21 C.F.R. § 880.5580. See also chap. 4.3.6.2.C.

287 COHEN M. H. (I), *op. cit.*: 102.

288 For a study regarding health care rationing, see JOST T. S., *op. cit.*: 639–714.

289 *Sarchett v. Blue Shield*, 729 P.2d 267, 270 (Cal. 1987).

290 42 U.S.C.A § 1395y(a)(1).

291 FURROW B. R. (I), *op. cit.*: 568–69.

Burzynski's Research Institute,[292] the FDA obtained a prohibition banning interstate commerce of the antineoplaston treatment and several tribunals considered the treatment to be fraudulent.[293, 294]

Insurance companies sometimes have argued that alternative medicines are not medically necessary because they do not enjoy the same level of scientific support as corresponding biomedical treatments.[295] However, during the past decade, various court decisions have suggested some acceptance of reimbursement for therapies outside biomedicine. For example, courts have accepted treatments such as chiropractic and massage therapy, as well as non-standard medical treatments, within the definition of medical necessity.[296] In *Day v. Aetna Employees Benefit Divison*,[297] an Ohio court considered that chelation therapy, which a patient had decided to undergo instead of bypass surgery, was "broadly accepted professionally as essential to the treatment of the disease" and was, therefore, "*necessary*" treatment, according to the meaning of the patient's insurance policy, for reimbursement purposes. The Northern District of Georgia, in *Dallis v. Aetna*, held that immunoaugmentative therapy for cancer was not medically unnecessary within the meaning of the insurance policy.[298, 299] In *McLauglin v. Connecticut General Life Insurance*

292 See *United States v. Burzynski Cancer Research Inst.*, n° H-83-2069 (S. D. Tex., May 24, 1983) (order granting permanent injunction); *Trustees of the Northwest Laundry and Dry Cleaners Health and Welfare Fund v. Burzinsky*, 27 F.3d 153–55 (5th Cir. 1994), *reh'g, en banc, denied*, 38 F.3d 571 (5th Cir. 1994), *cert. denied*, 115 S. Ct. 1110 (1995); Burzynski, 819 F.2d at 1313–14 (quoting *United States v. Hoxsey Cancer Clinic*, 198 F.2d 273, 280 (5th Cir. 1952), *cert. denied*, 346 U.S. 897 (1953)).

293 See e.g., *Burzynski v. Aetna Life Ins. Co., Inc.*, n° H-89-3976, 1992 U.S. Dist. LEXIS 21300 (S.D. Tex., Mar. 31, 1992) (the insurance companies usually consider that specific alternative treatments are worthless, and hence not only medically unnecessary but also fraudulent). See also *Burzyinski v. Aetna Life Ins. Co.*, 967 F.2d 1063 (5th Cir. 1992), remaded, 989 F.2d 733 (5th Cir. 1993); Prudential Ins. Co. of Am. v. Brown, n° B14-89-00695-CV (Tex. Ct. App. 1990).

294 COHEN M. H. (I), *op. cit.*: 105–08, 112–14.

295 CLINE J. S., *op. cit.*: 120ss; COHEN M. H. (I), *op. cit.*: 103.

296 See *Scalia v. Liberrty Mut. Ins. Co.*, n° 9308, 1995 WL 296772, at *3 (Mass. App. Div., May 10, 1995) (chiropractic); *Wait v. Metropolitan Life Ins. Co.*, 564 N.Y.S.2d 535 (App. Div. 1990).

297 *Day v. Aetna Employees Benefit Div.*, No 88CA00463, 1989 Ohio App. LEXIS 2458 (Ohio Ct. App. June 21, 1989).

298 The court relied on the fact that the patient had previously received conventional cancer treatment, which did not have any effect, and on the ambiguity inherent in the notion of necessity.

Company, the court held that lack of FDA approval of immunoaugmentative therapy did not necessarily exclude the treatment from coverage as being non medically necessary. The court pointed out that "the fact that the FDA has not approved a treatment does not automatically mean that a treatment is worthless".[300, 301]

In *Tudor v. Metropolitan Life Insurance Company*,[302] the court held that a treatment based on nutritional deficiencies and food allergies was medically necessary. The court stated that the treatment was not so deviant from generally accepted medical practices as to be nonmedical.[303, 304]

Finally, a Michigan court held in *Shumake v. Travelers Insurance Company* that laetrile and nutritional therapies were medically necessary because medicine continually evolves and the physician had recommended theses therapies as necessary before the medical community had discredited laetrile.[305, 306]

299 Similarly, in *Taulbee v. the Travelers Company*, an Ohio appellate court stated that immuno-augmentative therapy was medically necessary because chemotherapy failed (*Taulbee v. Travelers Company Co.*, 537 N.E.2d 670 (Ohio Ct. App. 1987)).

300 *McLauglin v. Connecticut Gen. Life Ins. Co.*, 565 F. Supp. 434, 451 (N.D. Cal. 1983). According to Cohen "McLauglin suggests a departure not only from reliance on the biomedical model for interpretation of medical necessity, but also from insurer dependence on FDA approval to legitimise alternative therapies" (COHEN M. H. (I), *op. cit.*: 104).

301 CLINE J. S., *op. cit.*: 120ss; COHEN M. H. (I), *op. cit.*: 103–04.

302 *Tudor v. Metropolitan Life insurance Company*, 539 N.Y.S.2d 690 (Dist. Ct. 1989).

303 See also *Harvey v. Travelers Insurance Company*, 339 F. Supp. 262 (N. D. Ga. 1971) (goals of an environmental therapy to treat brain injury).

304 COHEN M. H. (I), *op. cit.*: 104.

305 *Shumake v. Travelers Ins. Co.*, 383 N.W.2d 259 (Mich. App. 1985), *appeal denied*, 425 Mich. 859 (1986). But *see Zuckerberg v. Blue Cross & Blue Shield*, 490 N.E.2d 839 (N.Y. 1986) (the insured failed to present evidence to controvert the conclusion of the insurance, and the medical literature on which his opinion was based, that a nutritionally based treatment known as Gerson therapy was not a generally accepted cancer therapy and hence was properly excludable from coverage as experimental or unnecessary treatment).

306 COHEN M. H. (I), *op. cit.*: 104.

The White House Commission on Complementary and Alternative Medicine Policy

Regarding the evolution of the health delivery care for alternative medicines, the WHCCAMP notes

> some people believe that existing practice structures have worked well for those who use CAM and that no further action is required. But market demand for CAM is already reshaping the dynamics of health care delivery, requiring that some issues be addressed. For example, insurers and managed care plans are offering CAM options more frequently, and integrated medical clinics and private practices are spreading. As more evidence is published on the safety and effectiveness of CAM practices, they are more likely to be incorporated into health care treatment protocols.
>
> Now is the time to look at policy options for the future and to design strategies for addressing potential issues of access and safety. Beyond these basic concerns, protecting the public, maintaining free competition in the provision of CAM services, and maintaing the consumer's freedom to choose appropriate health professionals are issues to be considered when developing strategies and policies. Moreover, the need to maintain CAM styles of practice, rather than allowing them to be subsumed into the conventional medical model, aslo must be considered when addressing the issues.[307]

The recommendations of the WHCCAMP regarding coverage of alternative are the following:

1. Evidence should be developed and disseminated regarding the safety, benefits, and cost-effectiveness of CAM interventions, as well as the optimum models for complementary and integrated care;
2. Insurers and managed care organizsations should offer purchasers the option of health benefit plans that incorporate coverage of safe and effective CAM interventions provided by qualified practitioners;
3. Purchasers, including federal agencies and employers, should evaluate the possiblity of covering benefits or adding health benefit plans that incorporate safe and effective CAM interventions.

Conclusion

In the United States, expenditures on alternative services have increased considerably during the past two decades. While in the past, alternative medicines were not included in insurance schemes, an increasing number

307 WHITE HOUSE COMMISSION ON COMPLEMENTARY AND ALTERNATIVE MEDICINE POLICY, *op. cit.*: 89.

of insurers have now begun to offer coverage for alternative medicines, in particular HMOs.[308]

The crucial debate centering on the correct criteria to employ when determining whether an alternative medicine is a "*medical necessity*" or not is still evolving. Courts have extended the relevant criteria to be employed when determining the medical necessity of various alternative medicines in order to allow the coverage of some alternative medicines. One may anticipate that there will be other evolutions on the topic.

With regard to both Medicare and Medicaid, chiropractors are already part of professions whose treatments are covered by these two programs. Other alternative professions will be able in the future to obtain the same status as chiropractic in the government programs coverage schemes.

A particularly interesting development is the setting up of mandates that are imposed by the various States on insurers and that directly affect provision of alternative medicines.[309] It opens a way for new forms of reimbursement that could influence other Western countries.

Despite these recent and promising developments in the coverage of alternative medicines, alternative practitioners still have to face strong legal and internal barriers when providing alternative medicines, for example, an internal barrier faced by alternative practitioners is the reality of practice within managed structures dominated by physicians.[310]

308 As Kilgore notes, "together new services at hospitals and academic medical centers and a growing number of courses at medical schools, coverage changes are propelling alternative medicine to a higher plateau of acceptance and legitimacy" (Kilgore C., *op. cit.*: 1).

309 E.g., mandated benefit laws, mandate provider laws, any willing provider laws, and freedom-of-choice laws.

310 Pelletier notes that "although the popular media report an increasing number of insurers are offering coverage of CAM, the current status of CAM coverage is quite-limited. [...] It's not full integration – what you don't see is a well integrated benefits structure... but it's quite an increase." (Pelletier K. R., *op. cit.*: 112–122).

5.4 Comparative Charts

Set forth below is a map, providing a schematic overview of the coverage of alternative medicines in Europe.[311]

Map 3 Coverage

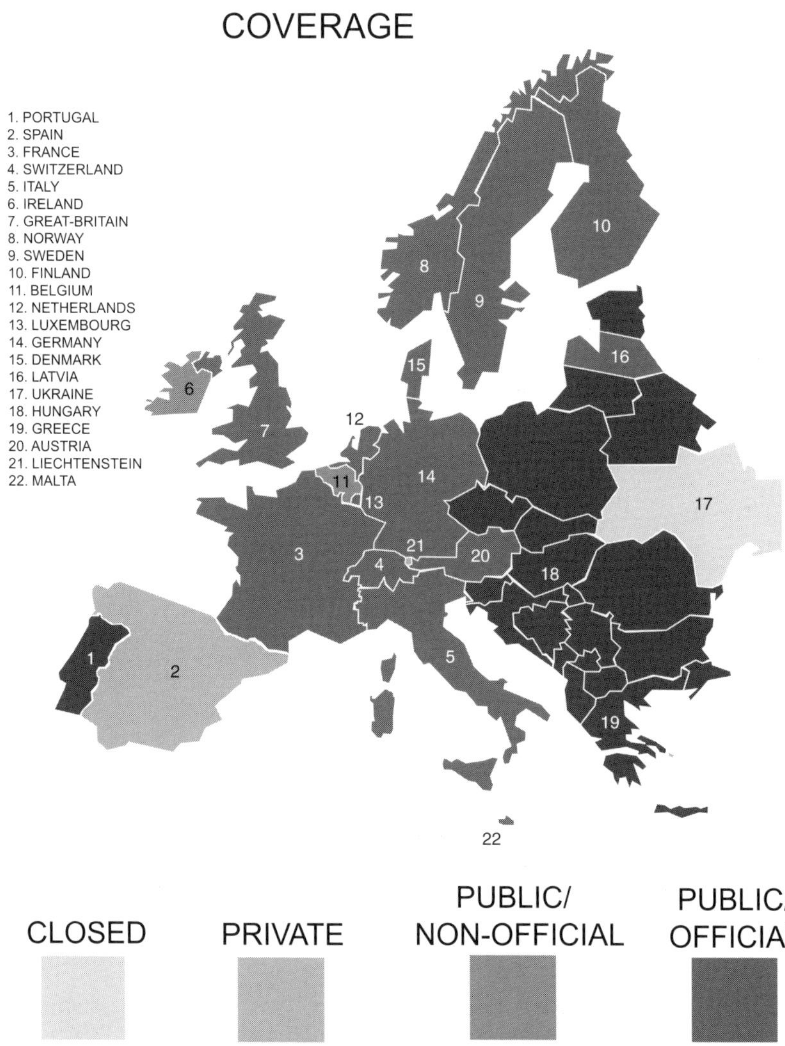

311 For a classification of the several approaches towards the coverage of alternative medicines, see chap. 5.2.

5.5 Conclusion

The coverage of alternative medicines by social insurance and private insurance companies follows a pattern of extension similar to the licence to practise alternative medicines. Indeed, almost all of the countries addressed in this chapter have proposed in a private or public way some form of coverage for various types of alternative medicines.

The coverage of alternative medicines can take several forms. Usually, the coverage is only partial and a deductible is often required. Education is always a decisive criterion in order to obtain coverage by social insurance, for both allopathic (e.g., in Italy) or non-allopathic practitioners (e.g., in Scandinavian countries). There have been interesting developments in the area of access to alternative medicines. For example, in the US some networks (HMO and PPO) have set up a system where the gatekeeper (usually a physician) may refer patients to either allopathic or non-allopathic practitioners or both, according to the wishes of patients and the opinion of gatekeepers.

Similar to the licensing to practise alternative medicines, the coverage of alternative medicines has had to evolve within a legal framework that was not designed or developed for it. The coverage of alternative medicines was, at first, unofficial but the effect of pressure placed by both patients and alternative providers on various authorities has led to the official coverage of some alternative techniques in various countries. For example, in France, coverage is usually ensured through the establishment of a positive list in a catalogue of benefits. In Germany, various decisions by the courts have led to the creation of a body of case law that defines the specific criteria necessary in order for a person to have the right to obtain public coverage for some alternative techniques. In this respect, it is interesting to observe some recent US laws, such as mandate benefit or provider laws, that have extended the rights of patients to have access to alternative practitioners. In addition, some authors have advocated the introduction of coverage as soon as a particular alternative technique becomes part of the curriculum at a university or, alternatively, a posteriori, when the treatment has proven to be medically effective in a specific case. More generally, the implementation of criteria to assess the medical necessity of medical techniques has become less rigid.

It is important to emphasize that there is not necessarily a correlation between being allowed a licence to practice alternative medicines and being given coverage for these techniques. For example, some countries (such as France or Italy) while adopting a restrictive attitude towards licensing to practice medicine have also proposed some form of coverage by the social insurance for some techniques.

There have also been some initiatives taken in the evaluation of alternative medicines, such as proof of effectiveness, appropriateness and cost-effectiveness, in order to assess whether such medicines should be entitled to coverage. In Switzerland, for example, there has been a proposal to use evidence-based-medical methods, while still taking into account the specificities of alternative medicines. This proposal involves the use of both quantitative and qualitative methods.

Part II

Analysis of the Current Position of Alternative Medicines in Western Countries

6. Scientific Background for Regulating Alternative Medicines

6.1 Introduction

In any analysis concerning the regulation of alternative medicines, it is critical to realise the importance of scientific arguments put forward by opponents and supporters of alternative medicines.

Defenders of evidence-based-medicine consider that only scientifically demonstrated therapies or drugs must be provided for and covered. Western health care systems have usually adopted that view, by making coverage generally depend upon the assessment of effectiveness, appropriateness, and cost-effectiveness of the technique. Similarly, only practices having a serious biomedical background, which are recognised by the scientific community, have usually been allowed and regulated in medical practice acts.

However, supporters of alternative medicine question the scientific character of classic methods. These methods are viewed as limited because they take into consideration only some aspects of the illness and curative phenomenon. Therefore, they are not adapted to evaluate alternative techniques. The use of other criteria and/or the setting up of a different clinical testing framework, better adapted to alternative medicines, is often proposed.

The safety and quality of treatments are also a major concern of the legislator who attempts to give patients access to treatment but at the same time must protect them from incompetent practice.

It appears that scientific elements play a crucial role and also provide solid validation for regulation. As scientific issues are recurrent when analysing several aspects of alternative medicines, the focus of this introductory chapter shall be on the particular set of problems that such scientific issues present.

A closer look shall be taken to the notion of "scientific method" in both its restrictive and broad sense (i.e. limited or not to natural and physical science). It is hoped that it will allow the reader to become more informed and critical about the scientific debate surrounding alternative medicines. Finally, the current situation concerning the safety of alternative treatments shall be presented.

6.2 Relativism of Scientific Method

Bibliography

BATTERMAN R. C., *Appraisal of new drugs*, in: JAMA, 1955, n° 158: 1547; BULL J. P., *The historical development of clinical therapeutic trials*, in Journal of Chronic Diseases, 1959, vol. 10: 218–48; CAROLL K. M. (co-authors: ROUNSAVILLE B. J., NICH C.), *Blind man's bluff: Effectiveness and significance of psychotherapy and pharmacotherapy, blinding procedures in clinical trials*, in: Journal of Consulting and Clinical Psychology, 1994, vol. 62: 276–80; CHARLTON B. G. (co-author: MILES A.), *The rise and fall of EBM*, in: QJM, 1998, vol. 91: 371–74; COHEN M. H. (I), *Complementary and alternative medicine – Legal boundaries and regulatory perspectives*, The Johns Hopkins University Press, 1998, London & Oxford: 2–3; DAGUET R., *Per una cura integrata: Riflessioni su medicina moderna e terapie alternative*, in: BORGHI M., *op. cit.*: 17–20; DESCARTES R., *Discourse on method and the meditations*, Pinguin Classics, 1987; DOMENIGHETTI G. (co-authors: GRILLI R., GUILLOD O., GUTZWILLER F., QUAGLIA J.), *Usage personnel de pratiques relevant des médecines douces ou alternatives parmi les médecins suisses*, in: Médecine et Hygiène, 2000, vol. 58, n° 2291: 570–72; ESKINAZI D. P., *Factors that shape alternative medicine*, in: JAMA, 1998, vol. 280, n° 18: 1621–22; GOLD H. (co-auhors: KWIT N. T., OTTO H.), *The xanthines (theobromine and aminophylline) in the treatment of cardiac pain*, in: JAMA, 1996, vol. 108: 2173–79; FEARS T. R. (co-author: SCHNEIDERMAN M. A.), *Pathologic evaluation and the blind technique*, in: Science, 1974, n° 183: 21–22; GREINER T. H. (co-authors: GOLD H., CATTELL M. et al.), *A method for the evaluation of effects of drugs on cardiac pain in patients with angina of effort: A study of khellin (visamin)*, in: American Journal of Medicine, 1950, vol. 9: 143–55; GRMEK M. D. and co-authors, *Histoire de la pensée médicale en Occident*, Editions du Seuil, 1999, Paris; HEUSSER P., *Kriterien zur Beurteilung des Nutzens von komplementärmedizinischen Methoden*, Bundesamt für Sozialversicherung, Mar. 1998, Bern: 6–7; HILL A. B., *The clinical trial*, in: New England Journal of Medicine, 1952, n° 247: 113–19; HOFFER A., *A theoretical examination of double-blind design*, in: Canadian Medical Association Journal, 1967, n° 97: 123–27; JOST T. S., *Health care rationing in the courts: A comparative study*, in: Hasting International and Comparative Law Review, 1998, vol. 21, n° 3: 646; JUNOD A.-F. (I), *Analyse décisionnelle et/ou "evidence-based medicine"?*, in: Médecine et Hygiène, 1997, vol. 55: 2027–29; KING L. S., *The road to scientific therapy*, in JAMA, 1966, vol. 197: 92–98; KISSEL P. (co-author: BARRUCAND D.), *Placebo and placebo effect in medicine*, Masson, 1964, Paris; KUHN T. S., *La structure des révolutions scientifiques*, Flammarion, 1983, Manchecourt; MINISTRY OF HEALTH AND SOCIAL AFFAIRS (I), *Report on alternative medicine – English summary*, Norges Offentliche Utredniger NOU 1998: 21, 1998, Oslo: 265; KING L. S., *The road to scientific therapy*, in JAMA, 1966, vol. 197: 92–98; MODELL W., *Origins and development of pharmacology*, in: MODELL W. (co-editors: SCHILD H. O., WILSON H. O.), *Applied pharmacology*, W. B. Saunders, 1976, Philadelphia: 10; MORREIM E. H., *A dose of our own medicine:*

Alternative medicine, conventional medicine, and the standards of science, in: The Journal of Law, Medicine and Ethics, 2003, vol. 31, n° 2: 222–35; NASH H., *The double-blind procedure: Rationale and empirical evaluation*, in: Journal of Nervous and Mental Disease, 1962, n° 134: 34–37; *The Oxford English Dictionary*, 2nd ed., Clarendon Press, 1989, Oxford; PFEIFFER C. C., *Critical discussion of research designs for determining the effect of therapy which may increase or decrease the schizophrenic state*, in: Modern Hospital, 1957, n° 88: 104–10; RIVERS W. H. R. (I), *The influence of alcohol and other drugs*, Arnold, 1908, London: 137; RIVERS W. H. R. (II), *Medicine, magic, and religion*, Macmillan, 1927, London; SELECT COMMITTEE ON SCIENCE AND TECHNOLOGY, *Complementary and alternative medicine*, House of Lords – Session 1999–2000 6th Report, The Stationary Office, 2000, London: 10; SANDIFER M. G. (co-author: HAWKINGS D. R.), *A double-blind study of the effects of drugs on mood, mentation, and sedation*, Paper presented at the convention of the American psychiatric association, 1958, San Francisco; SHAPIRO A. K. (co-author: SHAPIRO E.) (I), *The powerful placebo – From ancient priest to modern physician*, The Johns Hopkins University Press, 1997, Baltimore/London; SHAPIRO A. K. (co-authors: SHAPIRO E., STRUENING E. L.) (II), *Reliability and validity of placebo test*, in: Journal of Psychiatric Research, 1980, vol. 15: 253–90; SHAPIRO A. K. (co-authors: SHAPIRO E., STRUENING E. L.) (III), *Diazepam: How much better than placebo?*, in: Journal of Psychiatric Research, 1980, vol. 17: 51–73; SILVERMAN W. A., *The myth of informed consent: In daily practice and in clinical trials*, in: Journal of Medical Ethics, 1989, vol. 15: 6–11; SLEISENGER M. H., *Reply to Dr. Tomenius*, in: Amercian Journal of Digestive Diseases, 1958, n° 3: 415–16; STANLEY B., *An integration of ethical and clinical considerations in the use of placebos*, in: Psychopharmacology Bulletin, 1988, vol. 24: 18–20; TETREAULT L. (co-author: BORDELEAU J. M.), *On the usefulness of the placebo and of the double-blind technique in the evaluation of psychotropic drugs*, in: Psychopharmacology Bulletin, 1971, n° 7: 44–54; WICKI M., *Komplementärmedizin im Rahmen des Rechtes*, Dissertation, Stämpfli, 1998, Bern: 195–222, 204–07, 212–15; YOUNG J. H. (I), *The medical messiah*, Princeton University Press, 1967, Princeton: 2 47; YOUNG J. H. (II), *American health quackery*, Princeton University Press, 1992, Princeton.

6.2.1 Rise of Scientific Methodology

Historically, medicine did not place any reliance on a serious scientific background. As Shapiro stresses, "the history of medical treatment, was essentially the history of the placebo effect".[1] In fact, among the various treatments that had traditionally been used for centuries there were not only placebos,[2] but also several dangerous and possibly life-threatening methods.[3] Although useful drugs did exist,[4] they were often used inappropriately, and healers lacked the capacity to evaluate their specific usefulness.[5]

Formal experimentation did not exist before the nineteenth century.[6] Until then, treatment was determined by theories, mysticism, tradition, and superstition.[7] The development of mathematical methods (then called statistics) by British physicians in the second half of the eighteenth century led to the improvement of methods based on observation, recording, and systematic interpretation by means of simple arithmetic. Later, Claude Bernard's exposition of scientific method "based on observation and proved by

1 SHAPIRO A. K. (I), *op. cit.*: 228. The author has given an overview of the evolution of medical treatments and placebos from prehistoric times until today. The study is focused on the evolution of methods to assess the effectiveness of medical treatments.
For a definition of "placebo" and "placebo effect", see the glossary. See also, e.g., SELECT COMMITTEE ON SCIENCE AND TECHNOLOGY, *op. cit.*: 27ss.

2 The effectiveness of most procedures was due to non-specific factors: the placebo effect.

3 Until the nineteenth century, sick patients continued to submit to puking, purging, poisoning, cutting, blistering, cupping, bleeding, freezing, heating, etc. Most of these techniques resulted in the dehydration of patients, while modern medicine has recognised that it is necessary to do the exact opposite. As King notes, fortunately, humans managed to survive not only the diseases but also the remedies (KING L. S., *op. cit.*). For further analysis, see SHAPIRO A. K. (I), *op. cit.*: 1–27.

4 E.g., opium was used for centuries, quinine was discovered in the seventeenth century.

5 However, historians continue to exaggerate the effectiveness of these preparations. For further analysis, see SHAPIRO A. K. (I), *op. cit.*: 60–73. For a development regarding the evolution of medicine in Western countries, see GRMEK M. D., *op. cit.*

6 The dissemination of scientific methods during the seventeenth century in physics, chemistry, and biology, did not affect medicine, and experimentation was still a rarity in the eighteenth century.

7 As medical knowledge and vocabulary were limited, psychological problems were expressed in somatic complaints. E.g., depressive symptoms were considered as exhaustion, insomnia symptoms, etc.

experience"[8] and his ideas about experimental medicine strongly influenced clinical testing and contributed to the development of allopathic medicine. During the second half of the nineteenth century, rapid progress was made and came from many sources,[9] including new knowledge about chemistry, new sciences such as pharmacology, bacteriology, or genetics, the study of evolution, the use of antisepsis, anaesthesia in surgery, the discovery of viruses, microscopy, and X-rays, among others.[10]

By the turn of the twentieth century, although clinicians recognised how important it was to carefully observe patients and record cases with a description of treatments, controlled trials were still rare.[11] Then, the medical community began to institute changes. In the US, the creation of the Food and Drug Administration (FDA) had a decisive impact. The Food and Drug Act, which was passed in 1906, placed drugs under federal control. Later, amendments to the Act were enacted which required, among others, that drug manufacturers conduct tests to ensure safety before marketing (1938) and that sponsors of a new drug submit substantial evidence of efficacy (1960). Several campaigns were also held against nostrums and quackery,[12] while deep changes affected medical education and practice,[13] as well as pharmacology.[14, 15]

8 MODELL W., *op. cit.*: 10.
9 Major pioneers in this evolution were, e.g., Francis Bacon, Claude Bernard, Louis Pasteur, Robert Koch or Rudolph Virchow.
10 SHAPIRO A. K. (I), *op. cit.*: 25, 123–30.
11 John E. Coover was the first to use the terms "controlled", "control experiments", and "randomisation", in 1917.
12 However, Young, as late as in the mid-1960s, concluded that "quackery is not only not vanquished; never in previous history has medical quackery been such a big business as it is now" (YOUNG J. H. (I), *op. cit.*: 247). See also YOUNG J. H. (II), *op. cit.*
13 At the end of the nineteenth century, the Flexner report advocated changing medical training by giving medical students a postgraduate education centred in a university hospital taught by a full-time faculty. It also emphasised a research and scientific orientation. For more details, see chap. 4.3.6.2.A.
14 In 1912, the American Medical Association (AMA) established a Committee on Therapeutic Research, and provided funds to focus attention of experimental and clinical investigators in pharmacology.
15 SHAPIRO A. K. (I), *op. cit.*: 131–36. The author notes that "the inclusion of the terms placebo effect and double-blind method as references in the computer files of the National Library of Medicine in 1990 is perhaps a symbolic indication of a belated triumph over the several-thousand-year hegemony of the placebo effect" (idem at 136).

6.2.2 Development of Controlled Trials

The use of placebo controls and double-blind testing have been the most important developments in the history of clinical trials. In early experiments held at the end of the nineteenth century, control groups were generally passive comparison groups. Individual patients were alternately given an active agent and no treatment, or an active drug and a placebo at different times. It is possible that historical controls were used when experimental groups were compared with previously treated or untreated ones. The next step was the use of control substances. The first technique used was the single-blind procedure. In this experimental framework, the investigator knows that control substances (usually an inert placebo) are being used and knows which patients are receiving them, but the patient does not.[16] In the 1920s and 1930s, researchers slowly began to use controls but not blinding ones.[17] During these years, investigators became aware that the influence of physicians administering the drugs could actually be biasing the results.[18, 19]

Kwit and Gold conducted a crucial testing from 1932 to 1937.[20] The experiment was aimed at assessing the effectiveness of xanthine for the relief of *angina pectoris* by comparing it with an inert placebo.[21] The study

16 Rivers was among the first to use an inert material as a control. During studies of the influence of alcohol and other drugs on fatigue, he realised the importance of controls to account for the sensory stimulations caused by the experiment. Therefore, he advocated using an inert substance as a control for the active agent. The inert material was designed to taste and appear indistinguishable from the experimental drug. The subjects had no knowledge of the substances they received (RIVERS W. H. R. (I), *op. cit.*).

17 At that time, the reputation of placebo was so poor that doctors in general had no use for it.

18 Rivers, who undertook one of the first published blind testing, wrote in 1927 that "the action of suggestion can never be excluded in any form of medical treatment, whether it be explicitly designed to act upon the mind or whether ostensibly, it is of purely physical character" (RIVERS W. H. R. (II), *op. cit.*: 137), and further that "if we confine our attention to our own culture, it is only within the last fifty or sixty years that there has been any clear recognition of the vast importance of the mental factor in the production and treatment of disease, and even now this knowledge is far from being fully recognised either by the medical profession or the laity" (idem, at 123). These observations of Rivers seem equally valid today.

19 SHAPIRO A. K. (I), *op. cit.*: 137–46.

20 GOLD H., *op. cit.*: 2173–79.

21 The placebo was indistinguishable from the active medication having the same size, shape, colour and taste.

began as a single blind study. As the study progressed, Kwit and Gold discovered that the physicians administering the drug were asking the patients leading questions about its effect on the severity of pain and, thus, could be biasing the results. Kwit observes that,

> toward the end of the study we realised that the doctor must not know what he gives, the patient must not know what he receives, and the questioner must not know what was given. The study started out single blind, it then became partially, and finally fully blind [...] by the time we finished the paper, we had already established what we meant by the double-blind testing, and that the only proper way of evaluating anything was with a double-blind.[22]

After the combination of the two methods (placebo control and double-blind procedure) the use of xanthine for cardiac pain decreased. The study of Kwit and Gold generated little interest in the following years. By the 1950s, the controlled trials were still accepted by only a few researchers.[23] In the late 1950s, the American Medical Association (AMA) approved the use of double-blind method, controlled comparisons, randomisations, statistics, and other procedures recommended in clinical trials. Since then, controlled trials have slowly become the standard in the US.[24] In Europe, however, double-blind methods and placebo controls have evolved independently and more slowly than in the US.[25] In France, for example, there were very few controlled studies until the 1970s and placebos were rarely used until 1978. That same year, a set of guidelines was published by the FDA,[26] which called for controlled studies and mandated the use of placebo controls in order for psychotropic drugs to gain registration in the US. Since 1980, applications for FDA approval of new drugs, with rare exceptions, have required studies using the double-blind method as well

22 Shapiro is reporting an interview he had with Kwit in 1969 (SHAPIRO A. K. (I), *op. cit.*: 142–43).

23 Under the direction of Gold (GREINER T. H., *op. cit.*), a paper was published in 1950, containing recommendations and a comprehensive explanation about the necessity of using double-blind studies in clinical trials. It has had an important influence on the history of clinical studies.

24 This evolution has also affected psychiatry and psychology, and particularly psychopharmacology. The first studies using double-blind methods were published as early as 1954, and such studies strongly increased since the 1960s.

25 See BULL J. P., *op. cit.* with a review of therapies testing from ancient times until 1951.
In Great Britain, of interest is the work done by Sir Austin Bradford Hill in the development of controlled trials since the 1950s.

26 Namely, "Guidelines for the clinical evaluation of psychotropic drugs: Antidepressants and anti-anxiety drugs".

as randomisation and other methodological safeguards. Since then, it has become a requirement for scientific publication.[27]

6.2.3 Limits of Controlled Trials

As controlled trials became more popular among the medical community, methodological and ethical critics began a critical assault on double-blind studies. Clinicians attacked the new methods as inhumane, in that they replaced humanism with mathematical formulas, thus shrinking the physicians' responsibility to return the patient to health. Some observed that the results demonstrated during clinical testing were rarely confirmed when tested by the general practitioner. Psychiatrists noted that the double-blind method did not make allowance for the heterogeneity of the psychiatric population, and that an essential element of the physician-patient relationship was violated by the double-blind, namely the physician's and patient's faith and trust in each other.[28, 29] Some objected that the method deprived them of the necessary information required to make an informed judgment and further that it was an intrusion in medical practice.[30] Still others cited the possible influence of patient participation on the outcome of the

27 SHAPIRO A. K. (I), *op. cit.*: 141–68.

28 Testing conducted outside the psychiatric field was also criticised, with some critics considering that not only was the studied population heterogeneous, but that the detailed observation, and duration of the observation were insufficient. See ANONYMOUS (IV), *op. cit.*; HILL A. B., *op. cit.*: 113–19; HOFFER A., *op. cit.*: 123–27.
Recent studies in genetics have placed this argument under a new light. Indeed, it now seems that the particular genetic structure of individuals plays a substantial role in the response of the organism to pharmaceutical substances. In other words, it is impossible to have a perfect homogeneous group, which is a requirement for a solid randomised testing.

29 These arguments were refuted by investigators considering that, without the double-blind method, results may be attributed to the effects of experimenter bias and subject expectation. See FEARS T. R., *op. cit.*: 21–22.
It is noticeable that psychiatrists were particularly hostile to controlled trials. They were strongly against the use of placebos which they regarded as poor medicine, inexcusable and unethical. They also asserted that psychotherapy could not be a placebo. See BATTERMAN R. C., *op. cit.*: 1547; PFEIFFER C. C., *op. cit.*: 104–10; SHAPIRO A. K. (I), *op. cit.*: 176.

30 NASH H., *op. cit.*: 34–37.

study,[31] or that the use of double-blind technique could not validate otherwise poorly designed experiments that might lead to wrong interpretation. Some critics noted that the side effects of the active drug broke the double-blind code, or that the patient's faith in drug healing was such that it was likely to influence all results.[32] Other critics stated that, although controlled trials were useful, the policy of using a placebo at all costs was an exaggerated policy.[33] Investigators also raised various ethical problems related to the double-blind methodology, such as the administration of inert material to seriously ill patients, and the need for obtaining informed consent from patients.[34] With the growing acceptance of controlled trials, increasing importance was attached to principles governing the avoidance of deception, the obtaining of informed consent, and the protection of patient autonomy.[35, 36]

Once controlled trials became widely accepted,[37] critics shifted their stance from outright rejection to seeking ways of improving the double-

31 E.g., in a study on multiple risk factor intervention, investigators suspected patients in the no-intervention group to have altered their behaviour to lower their risks for cardiovascular mortality. See Sleisenger M. H., *op. cit.*: 415–16.

32 Sleisenger M. H., *op. cit.*: 415–16.

33 See Tetreault L., *op. cit.*: 44–54.

34 See Auerbach A., *op. cit.*: 1480–82.

35 Suggestions have been made to guarantee an ethical providing of drugs when carrying out clinical testing. For example, the American College of Gastroenterology emphasises three factors: 1. it becomes more difficult to justify a placebo if the illness is life threatening; 2. it becomes less important to use placebo controls in conditions that have a predictable and stable course than in those that are plagued by remissions and exacerbations; and 3. the efficacy of the standard treatment must be taken into account (leading to a greater use of placebo if the treatment is of low efficacy) (Stanley B., *op. cit.*: 18–20).
Silverman states that, "a way must be found […] to experiment with various discretionary approaches that would strike a realistic balance among the competing interests. We need an approach that would conserve the spirit of informed consent without snuffing out the flame of responsible clinical duty" (Silverman W. A., *op. cit.*: 10).

36 Junod A. F. (I), *op. cit.*: 2027–29; Shapiro A. K. (I), *op. cit.*: 168–89.

37 Often, health care providers have serious difficulty admitting that the placebo effect may be a component of the treatments they provide. They usually consider that other health care providers have more recourse to the placebo effect than themselves (Shapiro A. K. (I), *op. cit.*: 133, 177–78).

blind procedure.[38] Two issues of endless controversy remain the break of the blind,[39] and the failure of most studies to match active and placebo agents adequately.[40] Various methods have been developed to improve and control the variables that may result in the unblinding of a study, such as making identical matching placebos,[41] making identical units of active drug and placebo, having similar length of treatment, ensuring compliance,[42] doing an appropriate selection of physicians administering treatments, and not informing patients about the design of studies.[43] But, despite these methodological improvements, entirely satisfactory solutions have not yet

38 As controlled trials become more sophisticated and well accepted, research has become more focused on changes in efficacy, which has resulted in the setting up of more accurate diagnostic and research criteria for disorders, as well as sophisticated statistical methods for data analysis, and multiple rating scales and checklists to ensure the reliability of variables reflecting improvement (SHAPIRO A. K. (I), *op. cit.*: 172).

39 Several studies have been conducted on drug guessing. See SHAPIRO A. K. (II), *op. cit.*: 253–90; SHAPIRO A. K. (III), *op. cit.*: 51–73. These studies show that physicians correctly guessed whether patients were on a drug or a placebo. Similar studies showed patients guessing. The factors influencing guessing are the type of drug (weak or potent), the severity and pattern of adverse effect, the pattern of improvement, or drug dosage. Physicians guessed also on the basis of the responses of patients on drugs and those of patients on placebos.
Successful guessing has also been evaluated in psychotherapy. A study showed that 76% of the guesses correctly identified active and placebo treatment, and 75% of the guesses correctly identified drug and placebo treatment (CAROLL K. M., *op. cit.*: 276–80).

40 An essential requirement of the controlled trial using placebos is that the placebo and active medications must be identical in all respects. They must have the same size, colour, texture, taste, etching, dissolvability, the same pattern of administration, and the same pattern of adverse effects. Now, studies have shown that it is particularly difficult to perfectly match the placebo, and that patients may guess the nature of the administrated substance through variables such as the dosage units of the active drug and placebo, differences among raters, the length of the study, etc.

41 In particular, through the setting up of active placebos that have the same side effects of drugs, without the therapeutic effect. However, it is difficult to formulate them, and may involve ethical problems.

42 Some patients do not follow the indications of physicians as to the administration of the treatment.

43 However, this may deprive participators of motivation in the treatment. Furthermore, the lack of informed consent from patients would render the design of studies unethical.

been found and the placebo effect continues to play a role in double-blind studies.[44] As a result, modern medicine is often speculative and not as soundly based on evidence as one might ingenuously think.[45] Several studies have demonstrated the lack of scientific background of several drugs[46]

44 Current estimates of the prevalence of placebo response rates range from 21 to 58%. In psychopharmacology, placebo response rates vary from 30% to 50% in depression cases. Placebos have been found 59% as effective as tricyclic antidepressant, 65% as effective as lithium, 58% as effective as non-pharmacological treatment of insomnia, and 55% as effective as injected morphine and common analgesics. For more details, see SHAPIRO A. K. (I), *op. cit.*: 206–07. Shapiro notes that "there is little doubt that unblinding a double-blind study compromises the method. The extent of the unblinding determines the validity of the results. [...] Studies [...] indicate that subtle and multiple features of controlled trials may allow clinicians, patients, and staff members to discern drug allocation, thus unmasking the double-blind. Because small significant differences between an active drug and placebo are frequent, compromising the design could influence the results and lead to the finding of spurious significant differences between active drug and placebo." (SHAPIRO A. K. (I), *op. cit.*: 212).

45 Shapiro also notes that "despite the proliferation of nonplacebo drugs and procedures, placebo remedies are destined to fill the gap in knowledge as long as there are illnesses that cannot be treated adequately and the causes of illnesses are unknown" (SHAPIRO A. K. (I), *op. cit.*: 77).
Charlton stresses the lack of self-criticism, and avoidance of debate regarding the basic principles of evidence-based medicine by supporters of EBM (CHARLTON B. G., *op. cit.*).

46 A study revealed that patients were reacting in a manner opposite to the classical effects described for amphetamine and morphine (SANDIFER M. G., *op. cit.*).

and treatments,[47] such as psychotherapies[48] or surgery.[49] One may also stress the inability of modern science to explain the placebo effect.[50, 51]

47 Heusser notices that the effectiveness of allopathic treatments is demonstrated only for 10–20% of them (HEUSSER P., *op. cit.*: 6–7).
Kiessel and Barrucand have summarised the placebo effects seen in studies of various medical illnesses before 1960: 28.5% placebo effects in twenty-five studies of analgesics, 32.3% in five studies of migraine, 58% in a study of seasickness, 41% in two studies of cough relief, 49% in eighteen studies of rheumatism, and 24% in four studies of dysmenorrhoea and menopausal complaints (KISSEL P., *op. cit.*).
One may also be surprised that, in Germany, prescriptions for cardiac troubles are six times higher than in France or in England, while there is neither a higher rate of mortality nor a reduction of this rate for coronary illnesses (DAGUET R., *op. cit.*: 18–20).
See also JOST T. S., *op. cit.*: 646; SHAPIRO A. K. (I), *op. cit.*: 77–84; WICKI M., *op. cit.*: 212–15.

48 Psychotherapy has been reported to be more effective than placebos. However, its efficacy has yet to be proven, as studies in psychotherapy often fail, in particular when attempting to use controls. Actually, the psychotherapeutic surrounding is so complex, that it is difficult to take into account all the factors, and to estimate their respective effect. There are, in fact, more than 250 different schools of psychotherapy, and data supporting the theories of efficacy of any particular school do not exist.
Regarding treatments for manic-depressive disorder and schizophrenia, studies often violate basic methodological principles and fail to specify and test stated hypotheses, to clearly report and identify retrospective analyses and results, and so on, thus contributing to erroneous conclusions. Furthermore, reports contradict each other or are not replicated by other studies.

49 Because controlled trials in surgery are technically more difficult to devise and ethically more difficult to justify, surgery is not subject to controlled studies. As a result, surgery is more prone to placebo than other medical fields may be. The same observation is valid for mechanical procedures, tests to aid diagnosis, and for the monitoring of therapeutic progress that can be marketed without supporting evidence of efficacy and safety. This policy is responsible for the excessive use of many unsafe and expensive procedures, tests, and surgery, as tonsillectomies, colostomies, junostomies, sympathectomies, hysterectomies, caesarean sections, appendectomies, and cardiac bypass surgery. One may also mention the case of prefrontal lobotomy. This monstrous treatment, theoretically grounded, and used by intelligent and reasonable practitioners, lacked controlled studies, which would have easily demonstrated the ineffectiveness of the treatment.

50 Shapiro states that "the placebo effect is a compelling explanation for many zealous conclusions about the purported effectiveness of therapies which are unsupported by experimental evidence. The placebo effect helps to explain many arcane clinical phenomena that otherwise cannot be easily understood. That it escaped scientific notice for so long is surprising. Its potency, widespread use, and therapeutic potential have not been acknowledged until recently.

Currently, there is no definitive evidence demonstrating that techniques based on placebo effect[52] are clinically useful or effective. However, Shapiro stresses that

> we do know that non-specific factors involved in the art of medicine, the doctor-patient relationship, and the placebo effect on treatment can be used to improve therapy in largely unknown, non-specific, and unpredictable ways. As our research demonstrated, certain factors in the doctor-patient relationship augment placebo effects: belief in the effectiveness of the treatment, and the patient's perception of the physician as empathic, physically attractive, likable, and competent. Physicians who are sensitive to these factors, who like their patients, respond positively to them, and use of this factor, knowingly or unknowingly, may thereby contribute to a positive therapeutic outcome.[53]

Psychotherapy and other psychological procedures are not exempt from the placebo effect either.[54] It is noticeable that successful therapies, such as the placebo itself, have become associated with placebo effects. However, if placebo has become respectable, and its power to heal is more recognised, its therapeutic power has been exaggerated. The increasing role of patients in today's healer-patient relationship may induce some positive attitudes that are likely to result in the placebo effect.[55, 56]

Study of the underlying mechanism and dynamics of the placebo effect is a relatively recent area of research" (SHAPIRO A. K. (I), *op. cit.*: 74).

51 JUNOD A. F. (I), *op. cit.*: 2027–29; MORREIM E. H., *op. cit.*: 222–35; SHAPIRO A. K. (I), *op. cit.*: 170–72, 190–216, 230.

52 In this regard, one may note the use of megavitamins, nutrition, organic foods, stress reduction and alternative medicines (including behavioural medicine).

53 SHAPIRO A. K. (I), *op. cit.*: 232–36. Regarding the placebo effect itself, there is a lack of systematic approach. Thus, the findings vary from one study to the other, which makes it difficult to compare the results and derive general conclusions. However, studies have highlighted interesting features. For example, patients seem to respond in different ways to placebos. Some patients have the capacity to be optimistic, but while positive attitudes may have an influence on positiveissues, negative attitudes may result in demoralisation and increase the probability of chronic disease or even death.

54 Other techniques speculate on the effects of stress, depression, social isolation, personality or other psychological factors on the body.

55 As Shapiro writes "Implicit in the placebo effect is the recognition that patients bring to the healing process their own attitudes and belief systems, which can be stronger than the specific action of a drug" (SHAPIRO A. K. (I), *op. cit.*: 237). Although there is no substantive evidence yet that these methods can influence health, favourable preliminary reports about self-methods, holistic medicine, and behavioural medicine warrant further investigation.

56 SELECT COMMITTEE ON SCIENCE AND TECHNOLOGY, *op. cit.*: 27ss; SHAPIRO A. K. (I), *op. cit.*: 233–37.

Thus, although medicine has made tremendous progresses during the last century, potential improvements are still considerable. Even though biomedicine may explain some pathogenic mechanism, and be particularly effective in treating a great number of illnesses, it still cannot completely understand the experience of health and illness, which are complex phenomena.[57] As a result, biomedicine is not able to establish effective solutions for the treatment of many illnesses and health problems.[58] For these reasons, the biomedical paradigm is challenged and could be disrupted, through a change of paradigm.[59]

57 According to the World Health Organisation (WHO), health is "a state of physical, mental and social well-being" (The WHO constitution is published at Swiss RS 0.810.1).
The Norwegian Committee on alternative medicine states that "there exists no generally accepted definition of illness. The views of what constitutes illness vary from one culture and social stratification to another" (MINISTRY OF HEALTH AND SOCIAL AFFAIRS (I), *op. cit.*: 265).
A Swiss study showed that between 40% and 68% of physicians consider medicine to not be an exact science (40% for physicians not using alternative medicines, and 68% for those using them) (DOMENIGHETTI G., *op. cit.*: 571).

58 Cohen notes that "the biomedical model provides a clearly articulated scientific framework for understanding the disease process and mechanisms of remedy, and it succeeds at treating infectious diseases and acute traumatic injuries. Biomedicine excels in emergency care: a patient who suddenly experiences heart failure, needs a cardiac specialist, not an acupuncturist. The model also cures many conditions that have single specific causes. The model is less successful with chronic, multifaceted, and terminal illnesses, such as chronic fatigue, AIDS, and cancer [...] Biomedicine rarely cures chronic, debilitating conditions such as arthritis, allergies, pain, hypertension, depression, and cardiovascular and digestive problems, which account for 70 percent of the health care budget in the United States and affect almost 33 million Americans" (COHEN M. H. (I), *op. cit.*: 2–3). See also SELECT COMMITTEE ON SCIENCE AND TECHNOLOGY, *op. cit.*: 10.

59 For developments regarding the notion of paradigm and change of paradigm, see chap. 8.3.2.
In relation to controlled trials Shapiro writes that "These procedures are likely to be controversial until new and better techniques can be developed" (SHAPIRO A. K. (I), *op. cit.*: 189). In the conclusion, he states that "The relationship between the placebo and the underlying mechanisms of the body that control and maintain health still eludes us. We hope that our studies, and those of other investigators, will contribute understanding about the laws governing the non-specific, as yet mystifying but very powerful therapeutic potential of the placebo effect. If the no specificity of the placebo effect can be rendered specific and its strength can be unleashed, the terms placebo and placebo effect can appropriately disappear into medical history" (SHAPIRO A. K. (I), *op. cit.*: 237).

6.2.4 Summary

Clinical trials using the double-blind method and placebos as control are currently the best means we have at our disposal. However, they are limited and any improvement in the future is likely to encounter several legal, ethical and economic obstacles. Moreover, even if the impact of several factors, such as the psychological components, the placebo effect, and other non-specific (alternative) therapies on physical and mental health have been demonstrated, current scientific methods and knowledge still does not allow to understand the mechanisms underlying these phenomena.

In the future, these mechanisms may potentially be explained by the tremendous progress being made by research in the medical and related sciences. Until then, the reliability of scientific methods employed to assess the effectiveness of medical treatments must be viewed with caution.

As a result, the validation that modern scientific methods may provide to medical techniques is crucial. However, one should be open minded, considering that the lack of scientific demonstration of the effectiveness of some techniques does not deprive them from their value. As one shall see later, other ways may be used to justify the regulation of a technique.

6.3 Scientific Validation in a Restrictive Sense

Bibliography

American Cancer Society, *Questionable methods of cancer management: The committee for freedom of choice in medicine, Inc.*, in: a Cancer Journal for Clinicians, 1993, vol. 43, n° 2: 117–23; Angell M. (co-author: Kassirer J. P.), *Alternative medicine – The risks of untested and unregulated medicine*, in: New England Journal of Medicine, 1998, vol. 339, n° 12: 839–41; Anonymous (IV), *Integrated healthcare – A way forward for the next five years?*, Foundation for Integrated Medicine, 1997: 10–12, 57–59; Balon J. and co-authors, *A comparison of active and simulated chiropractic manipulations as adjunctive treatment for childhood asthma*, in: New England Journal of Medicine, 1998, vol. 338, n° 15: 1013–27; Beck A., *La chaire de médecine complémentaire à l'Université de Berne: Une création récente*, in: CMS, 1996, vol. 40: 56–57; Bettschart R. (co-authors: Glaeske G., Langbein K., Saller R., Skalnik C.), *Bittere Naturmedizin – Wirkung und Bewertung der alternativen Behandlungsmethoden, Diagnoseverfahren und Artzneimittelrecht*, Kieper & Witsch, 1995, Köln; Binder M., *Zur Kostendeckung alternativmedizinischer Behandlungsmethoden durch die Krankenversicherung*, in: Recht der Medizin, 1997, vol. 4, n° 2: 40–42; Black N., *Why we need observational studies to evaluate the effectiveness of health care*, in: British Medical Journal, 1996, n° 312: 12215–8; BOOZANG K. M. (I), *Western medicine opens the door to alternative medicine*, in: American Journal of Medicine, 1998, vol. 24, n° 2/3: 189–90; BOOZANG K. M. (II), *Is the alternative medicine? Managed care apparently thinks so*, in: Connecticut Law Review, Winter 2000, vol. 32: 586–604; BOOZANG K. M. (III), *National policy on CAM: The White House Commission report*, in: The Journal of Law, Medicine and Ethics, 2003, vol. 31, n° 2: 251–61; BORGHI M. (co-editor: GASSMAN J.), *Thérapies complémentaires ou alternatives en psychiatrie: Un défi? Un droit?*, Schriftenreihe der Schweizerischen Stiftung Pro Mente Sana n° 20, 1999, Zürich; BRADFORD G. E., *The "respectable minority" doctrine in Missouri medical negligence law*, in: Journal of the Missouri Bar, Dec. 2000, vol. 56: 326–34; BRUSET S., *Holism and individualism – The Yin and Yang in complementary medicines*, in: JOHANNESSEN H. (co-authors: LAUNSO L., OLESEN S. G., STAUGARD F.) (I), *Studies in alternative therapy 1 – Contributions from the Nordic countries*, Odense University Press, 1994, Gylling: 186–96; COHEN M. H. (I), *Complementary and alternative medicine – Legal boundaries and regulatory perspectives*, The Johns Hopkins University Press, 1998, London & Oxford: 58–59, 102, 150–51; COMMISSIE ALTERNATIEVE GENEESWIJZEN, *Alternative geneeswijzen in Nederland*, Staatsuitgeverij, 1981, Den Haag; COST ACTION B4, *COST action B4 unconventional medicine – Final report of the management committee, 1993–1998*, European Communities, 1998, Luxembourg; CUCHERAT M. (co-author: DÜRR F.), *Contexte de la médecine factuelle*, in: Médecine et Hygiène, 2000, vol. 58: 850–55; DAGUET R., *Per una cura integrata: Riflessioni su medicina moderna e terapie alternative*, in: BORGHI M., *op. cit.*: 17–20; DUC J.-L., *Médecines parallèles et assurances sociales (plus spécialement au regard de la nouvelle LAMal)*, in: CMS, 1996, vol. 40, n° 1: 45; ESKINAZI D. P., *Factors that shape alternative medicine*, in: JAMA, 1998, vol. 280, n° 18: 1622; FREUDENBERG U., *Der Leistungsanspruch bei alternativen Heilmethoden gegenüber der gesetzlichen Krankenversicherung, der privaten Krankenversicherung und der Beihilfe*, Dissertation, 1994, Bonn: 154–61, 184–98; GAIER H. C. (I), *Evolving problems for natural medicines within the European Community – And the biocentric practitioners who use them*, in: Complementary Medical Research, 1991, vol. 5, n° 1: 37; GRUNWALD D., *Pratiques médicales non éprouvées*, Session de l'Ordre des médecins, Sept. 1997, Paris; GYSIN T. (co-author: ZIEGLER C.), *Klinische Hypnotherapie/Selbsthypnose für unspezifische chronische und episodische Kopfschmerzen ohne Migräne und andere definierte Kopfweharten bei Kindern und Jugenlichen*, in: FREY F., *op. cit.*: 64–66; HÄNGGELI C., *Une étape décisive pour la FMH*, in: BMS: 1998, vol. 79, n° 48: 2447–48; HEUSSER P., *Kriterien zur Beurteilung des Nutzens von komplementärmedizinischen Methoden*, Bundesamt für Sozialversicherung, Mar. 1998, Bern: 5ss, 136ss; HOCHSTRASSER B. (co-author: MATTMANN P.), *Homöopathie und Schulmedizin in der Schwangerschafts- und Geburtsbetreuung*, in: FREY F., *op. cit.*: 28–35; HUFFORD D. J., *Evaluating complementary and alternative medicines: The limits of science and scientists*, in: The Journal of Law, Medicine and Ethics, 2003, vol. 31, n° 2: 198–212; HÜRNY C. and co-authors, *Verbessern nicht-konventionelle Zusatztherapien die Lebensqualität von Krebspatienten?*, in: FREY F., *op. cit.*: 55–63; JOSEFEK K. J., *Alternative medicine's roadmap to mainstream*, in: American Journal of Law and Medicine, 2000, vol. 26: 305–06; JUNOD A. F. (I), *Analyse décisionnelle et/ou "evidence-based medicine"?*, in Médecine et Hygiène, 1997, vol. 55: 2027–29; KILGORE C., *Expanding coverage signals growing demand, acceptance for alternative care*, in: Medicine & Health Perspectives, May 4 1998: 1–4; KÜNZI M. (I), *Komplementärmedizin und Gesundheitsrecht*, Helbing & Lichtenhahn Verlag AG, 1996, Basel: 83–91, 96; LANNOYE P., *Is there a future for complementary medicine in Europe? – European report on the status of non-conventionnal medicine*, The Natural Medicines Society, 1996, Heanor: 4; LAPLANTINE F. (co-author: RABEYRON P.-L.), *Les médecines parallèles*, PUF, collection Que sais-je, 1987, Paris: 81–108; LAUNSO L. (co-author: BRENDSTRUP E.) (II), *Description of a holistic integrated treatment model used by cancer patients and research evaluated part I and II*, in: Townsend for Doctors, Dec. 1994 and Jan. 1995; LEMOINE P., *La mystérieuse efficacité des placebos et autre poudres de perlimpinpin*, in: Le Temps Stratégique, 1999, n° 89: 84–91; MARGOLIN A., *Investigating alternative medicine therapies in randomized controlled trials*, in: JAMA, 1998, vol. 280, n° 18: 1626–28; MARWICK C., *Alterations are ahead at the OAM*, in: JAMA, 1998, vol. 280, n° 18: 1553–54; MATTHIESSEN P. F., *Unkonventionelle Behandlungsmethoden im Kontext medizinischer Versorgung*, in: Zeitschrift für Sozialreform, 1994, vol. 40, n° 8: 522–36; MEDICIS T. C., *Akupunktur und Bronchialasthma*, in: FREY F., *op. cit.*: 39–48; MINISTRY OF HEALTH AND SOCIAL AFFAIRS (I), *Report on alternative medicine – English summary*, Norges Offentliche Utredniger NOU 1998: 21, 1998, Oslo: 269–70, 273–74; MITCHELL WEITZMAN S., *Insurance coverage for complementary and alternative medicine – Access, challenges, and policy*, in: HUMBER J. M. (co-ed.: ALMEDER R.), *Alternative medicine and ethics*, Humana Press, 1998, Totowa: 141–44; MONTAKAB H. (co-author: LANGEL G.), *L'effet de l'acupuncture dans le traitement de l'insomnie*, in: FREY F., *op. cit.*: 39–48; MORREIM E. H., *A dose of our own medicine: Alternative medicine, conventional medicine, and the standards of science*, in: The Journal of Law, Medicine and Ethics, 2003, vol. 31, n° 2: 222–35; OEPEN I. (III), *Pseudo-Naturheilverfahren und Aussenseitermethoden in der Rheumatologie*, in: Zeitschrift für Rheumatologie, 1993, vol. 52: 264–74; *The Oxford English Dictionary*, 2nd ed., Clarendon Press, 1989, Oxford; OFFICE FÉDÉRAL DES ASSURANCES SOCIALES, *Manuel de standardisation pour l'évaluation médicale et économique des prestations médicales*, Office Fédéral des Assurances Sociales, 1998, Berne: 136; PERREZ M., *Möglichkeiten und Grenzen der Evaluation von alternativen Behandlungsmethoden*, in: BORGHI M., *op. cit.*: 252–53; REETZ C., *Komplementärmedizin in der Grundversicherung – Auch für stationäre PsychiatriepatientInnen?*, in: BORGHI M., *op. cit.*: 262; RICHLI P., *Hoheitliche Leistungspflichten und Leistungsbeschränkungen im Gesundheitswesen als Grundrechtsproblem*, in: Revue Suisse d'Assurances, 1998, n° 9–10: 243, 253–58; ROBARD I., *La santé hors la loi: Les hors la loi de la santé*, 4th ed., Ed. de l'Ancre, 1994, Suresnes: 178; SARNER L. (co-author: ROSA L.), *Using daubert to aid the injured: A case of therapeutic touch?*, in: Quinnipiac Health Law Journal, 1999–2000, vol. 3: 25–35; SELECT COMMITTEE ON SCIENCE AND TECHNOLOGY, *Complementary and alternative medicine*, House of Lords – Session 1999–2000 6th Report, The Stationary Office, 2000, London; SHAPIRO A. K. (co-author: SHAPIRO E.) (I), *The powerful placebo – From ancient priest to modern physician*, The Johns Hopkins University Press, 1997, Baltimore/London: 86ss; SCHULIN B., *Alternative Medizin in der gesetzlichen Krankenversicherung*, in: Zeitschrift für Sozialreform, 1994, vol. 40, n° 8: 546–65; SOMMER J. H. (co-author: BÜRGI M.), *Gesundheitsökonomische Analyse der Wirkungen des Angebotes komplementärmedizinischer Leistungen der Krankenkassen*, in: FREY F., *op. cit.*: 13–17; STONE J. (co-author: MATTHEWS J.), *Complementary medicine and the law*, Oxford University Press, 1996, Oxford: 92–93, 95; SUTER B. (co-author: KISTLER A.), *Beeinflusst Akupuntur die Hautdurchblutung über das autonome Nervensystem?*, in: FREY F., *op. cit.*: 36–38; VAUTRAVERS P. (co-author: LECOQ J.), *Lombalgies communes et manipulations vertébrales – Etat des lieux*, in: Revue du Rhumatisme, 1993, n° 7–8: 518–23; WHITE HOUSE COMMISSION ON COMPLEMENTARY AND ALTERNATIVE MEDICINE POLICY, *Final report*, March 2002, available at http://www.whccamp.hhs.gov/pdfs/fr2002_document.pdf, accessed Feb. 1 2005: 30ss; WICKI M., *Komplementärmedizin im Rahmen des Rechtes*, Dissertation, Stämpfli, 1998, Bern: 205–07, 215–22; WÖLK W., *Paramedizinische Therapie und Rechtsprechung*, in: MedR, 1995, vol. 13, n° 12: 492–96; WOOLF S. H. and co-authors, *Clinical practice guidelines in complementary and alternative medicines*, in: Arch. Fam. Med., 1997, n° 6: 149–54.

6.3.1 General Remarks

In Western countries, scientific validation in a restrictive sense provides a basis to regulate the medical field.[60] Indeed, as soon as a technique has been proven, according to evidence based medical standards, to be safe and effective, and when its mechanism of action is known, including the possible recognition by the scientific community,[61] then it offers sufficient guarantees to be licensed and covered.[62]

60 According to Stone, "certainly, the argument that therapies should be able to provide scientific validation of their efficacy before winning the right to statutory protection is very prominent within the medical establishment". And further "the argument for scientific validation is likely to remain very strong, especially for the discrete clinical disciplines. Unless such therapies can eventually substantiate their claims through scientific research in some form or other, they are likely to lose some of their therapeutic and political credibility" (STONE J., *op. cit.*: 92, 95).

61 Other criteria are also possibly employed, such as sociological, ethical, or political elements and will be explored later, in chap. 6.4. Cost-effectiveness also plays a role in deciding whether or not to cover a specific technique. However, as it is linked only to the coverage of alternative medicines, it will be developed further in chap. 7.4.3.2.C.

62 In Germany, for example, a method is recognised as scientific when it is accepted and taught in numerous universities and confirmed by numerous statistical, reproducible, and successful cases (in German: "Anerkennung [...], wenn die Methode mindestens von zahlreichen und namhaften Universitätslehrern gelehrt werde und nach statistischer Wahrscheinlichkeit ein beliebig reproduzierbarer

The interpretation and implementation of these criteria deeply influence the content of a regulation. For example, when regulating the licensing to practice, if these criteria are interpreted in a strict sense (i.e. according to classical evidence-based-medicine criteria), the regulation will have a monopolistic orientation. Alternatively, if these criteria are interpreted in a more open way, then the regulation will be more tolerant. Similarly, the coverage for alternative medicines will be limited if these criteria are strictly interpreted.

The major problem that supporters of alternative medicines are facing is the effective demonstration of the mechanism of action as well as the effectiveness of alternative medicines. As long as a solution is not found to these problems, supporters of alternative medicines will continue to be confronted by the scepticism and antagonism of biomedicine supporters.[63]

Some authors, including Stone, undermine the power of scientific validation, arguing that

> governments do not necessarily give this argument (i.e., that therapies should be able to provide scientific validation) the weight that some in the medical profession would like to see. It is being increasingly accepted that when usage levels of complementary therapies are reaching 25 percent of the population, an insistence on sci-

therapeutischer Erfolg in der weitaus überwiegenden Zahl der Fälle erreicht werden könne" (Künzi M. (I), *op. cit.*: 83)).
For a definition and the meaning of the concept of scientific recognition, see e.g., Freudenberg U., *op. cit.*: 154–61, 184–98; Künzi M. (I), *op. cit.*: 83–91, 96; White House Commission on Complementary and Alternative Medicine Policy, *op. cit.*: 30.

63 Margolin contends that there is a fundamental antagonism between supporters of alternative medicines and supporters of evidence-based-medicine; where "the validity and credibility of alternative medicine investigations will be enhanced by using research designs that embody the highest standards for demonstration of efficacy: the randomised clinical trial. However, controlled evaluation of alternative medicine therapies may require its practitioners to undertake a fundamental conceptual shift from a view of patients as requiring individualised treatment that may vary at each session to one in which trial participants are regarded as members of an equivalence class, defined by the diagnosis, who all will be given a standard prescribed treatment. [...] We recognise that this approach may be viewed by others as irremediably distorting the content of those treatments. This complex issue, comprising a wide range of opinions concerning the cultural relativity of methodological principles, has yet to be resolved" (Margolin A., *op. cit.*: 1627–28). See also, e.g., American Cancer Society, *op. cit.*: 117–23; Angell M., *op. cit.*: 839–41; Grunwald D., *op. cit.*; Matthiessen P. F., *op. cit.*: 522–36; Ministry of Health and Social Affairs (I), *op. cit.*: 273–74; Oepen I. (III), *op. cit.*: 264–74; Sarner L., *op. cit.*: 25–35.
For further details regarding research in alternative medicine, see chap. 3.2.

> entific validation is at worst a "red herring" and at best a detraction from the need to focus on higher priorities such as establishing higher training standards.[64]

In this respect, the opinion of the Dutch Commission for Alternative Medicines should be stressed, which

> believes that the division between alternative and orthodox medicine is not – or not principally – of a scientific nature, but owes its origins and its continued existence to both politico-social and scientific factors. This implies that simply making scientific recommendations cannot close the gap. The demand that alternative practitioners must demonstrate the effectiveness of their treatment before they can be granted any form of recognition thus seems to the Commission to be indefensible.[65]

After taking into consideration the argument put forward by Stone, it still remains, however, important to understand the ongoing debate about which criteria and methods should or should not be used when evaluating alternative medicines, in order to establish their scientific validation. Indeed, evidence-based-medicine will remain the gold standard in Western countries given the lack of another paradigm that exerts the same domination in medicine. Therefore, a pure and simple rejection of evidence-based-medicine is not conceivable,[66] a more constructive attitude consists first, in seeing which are the main problems that arise when evaluating alternative medicines, and second how to solve them constructively.

The first section of this chapter consists of defining the general background to clinical trials. The classical parameters employed to establish scientific validation of alternative medicines shall be presented, namely the mechanism of action, its effectiveness, and the corresponding acknowledgement from the medical community.[67]

64 STONE J., *op. cit.*: 92–93.

65 COMMISSIE ALTERNATIEVE GENEESWIJZEN, *op. cit.*
In the same perspective, the Swiss government decided to include (under social pressure) the most widespread alternative medicines in the compulsory basic insurance. Biomedical criteria are adapted according to the specificities of alternative medicines to demonstrate their medical necessity. For further developments, see chap. 5.3.5.14.C.

66 As Angell reports, defenders of alternative medicines sometimes argue that scientific methods do not apply to alternative techniques. According to the author, "what most sets alternative medicine apart, in our view, is that it has not been scientifically tested and its advocates largely deny the need for such testing. [...] Many advocates of alternative medicine, in contrast, believe the scientific method is simply not applicable to their remedies. They rely instead on anecdotes and theories" (ANGELL M., *op. cit.*: 839). See also, e.g., WICKI M., *op. cit*: 215–22.

67 The conclusions reached from research into the scientific validation (mainly proof of efficacy) of the various alternative medicines are outside the remit of

6.3.2 Mechanism of Action

Biology, chemistry and physics are usually employed to demonstrate the mechanism of action of a technique, essentially how it interferes with the organism.

This mechanism is usually not well understood in relation to alternative medicines.[68] The necessity to demonstrate the mechanism of action of a technique is subject to controversy. Some authors consider that without effective demonstration, therapies cannot then be validated as scientific.[69] However, in response, there are several treatments and drugs employed in biomedicine that lack this scientific explanation as well,[70] and in any case, the proof of the effectiveness of the treatment in and of itself is sufficient.[71]

Therefore, even if the demonstration of the mechanism of action remains of importance,[72] it is not decisive when evaluating a medical technique.

---

this research. However, it is necessary to understand the general state of the evidence base, in order to examine what type of evidence needs to be collected and to understand the controversy over alternative medicines.

68 Margolin A., *op. cit.*: 1626; Shapiro A. K. (I), *op. cit.*

69 See Angell M., *op. cit.*: 839–40; Grunwald D., *op. cit.*; Ministry of Health and Social Affairs (I), *op. cit.*: 273–74; Wölk W.: *op. cit.*: 492–96.

70 A famous example is aspirin, whose mechanism has long been a mystery and even now is not entirely resolved. However, aspirin has been administered for more than 70 years. The mechanism of action of psychotherapies is not well understood either. Similarly, on the basis of knowledge about the physiopathology of the illness and the pharmacological effects of the treatment, it is possible to elaborate a theoretical mechanical theory presupposing a beneficial effect. In practice, this type of theory has demonstrated its limits. For further discussion, see Cucherat M., *op. cit.*: 850–55, Robard I., *op. cit.*: 178; Shapiro A. K. (I), *op. cit.*: 86ss.

71 The British Select Committee on Science and Technology stresses "many of our witnesses have argued that if there is evidence for efficacy, then it is not necessary to understand exactly how the effect is achieved, and we agree. This is, indeed, the position with several conventional therapies" (Select Committee on Science and Technology, *op. cit.*: 34). For further discussion on the subject, see the same author at 34–35.
When private insurance companies or social securities decide to cover a medical act, the decisive criterion is not the demonstration of the mechanism of action, but the proof of effectiveness. On this subject, see, e.g. Richli P., *op. cit.*: 243.

72 Indeed, it is fundamental to continue to undertake basic research (for both biomedical and alternative techniques) in this field, in order to establish a solid scientific basis. See Suter B., *op. cit.*: 36–38 (acupuncture sessions affecting the cardiovascular system via the autonomic nervous system); Lemoine P., *op. cit.*: 84–91 (placebo effect); Wicki M., *op. cit.*: 220–22.

6.3.3 Effectiveness[73]

Today, the proof of the effectiveness of a medical technique seems to be a decisive criterion with which to valuate it.[74] The question then arises as to which methods must be employed to assess the effectiveness. The answer to this question is not obvious. Indeed, as the Swiss Federal Office of Social Insurance (FOSI) stresses, several procedures may be used to evaluate the effectiveness of medical techniques, from the individual experience of physicians to the most complex randomised controlled trials. The latter are the reference in clinical research. As such, these complex trials will first be analysed in their application to alternative medicines. However, given that they are not applicable to all technologies, our attention will also focus on other ways to evaluate the effectiveness of alternative medicines.

The common methods used in "evidence-based-medicine" (typically double-blind testing or randomised controlled trials (hereafter RCT)[75] are not easily applicable to alternative treatments. In fact, research conducted under classical biomedical criteria often does not demonstrate any effectiveness of alternative medicine.[76] In this respect, Margolin notes,

73 For an analysis regarding the criterion of cost-effectiveness when covering medical treatments, see chap. 7.3.4.2.C.

74 Some reports have put into perspective the evidence of effectiveness. For example, the British Select Committee on Science and Technology has reported the opinion of the Royal Society of Edinburgh that "makes the point that evidence of the validity of diagnostic procedures is as important as evidence supporting efficacy of treatment. Diagnostic procedures must be reliable and reproducible and more attention must be paid to whether CAM diagnostic procedures as well as CAM therapies have been scientifically validated. We agree that this is an issue that should always be kept in mind when doing research in this area" (SELECT COMMITTEE ON SCIENCE AND TECHNOLOGY, *op. cit.*: 32).

75 According to Angell "By testing, we mean the marshalling of rigorous evidence of safety and efficacy, as required by the Food and Drug Administration (FDA) for the approval of drugs and by the best peer-reviewed medical journals for the publication of research reports" (ANGELL M., *op. cit.*: 839).

76 The Norwegian Committee on Alternative Medicine has made an interesting categorisation regarding effectiveness of alternative medicines (MINISTRY OF HEALTH AND SOCIAL AFFAIRS (I), *op. cit.*: 270). It distinguishes treatments which are:

1. documented effective: extensive positive research results combined with good clinical experience exist, providing a basis for considering the method's efficacy to be duly documented. Only acupuncture treatment for post-operative and chemotherapy induced nausea in adults was listed in this category;
2. possibly effective: some positive scientific research results and good clinical experience exist. However, the method's efficacy cannot be deemed to be documented until confirmed by further clinical studies. Acupuncture for nausea in

alternative medicine comprises a large and heterogeneous group of treatments, [...] many of which are procedures that are not readily testable under blinded conditions and for which the choice of appropriate control conditions is by no

---

pregnancy, pain following dental surgery, as an aid in detoxification regimes for drug and alcohol rehabilitation, and as an aid for stroke rehabilitation; transcendental meditation in relation to dependency issues; and homeopathy in general were listed in this category;

3. conceivably effective: a few positive scientific research results and some good clinical experience exist, which provide a basis for further research into the method. Acupuncture treatment of pain following general surgery, chronic pain conditions, asthma, and in connection with nicotine withdrawal; ayurvedic medicine; and healing were listed in this category;
4. treatments for which there is inadequate data: the sparse documentation makes it impossible to draw a conclusion. Acupuncture for pulmonary problems; kinesiology; osteopathy for systemic illnesses; zone therapy; transcendental meditation for cardiovascular illness were listed in this category.

In general, the Norwegian Committee on Science and Technology concluded that alternative medicines seem to have potential in the treatment of a range of illnesses apart from acute medicine, but research has not developed sufficiently or perhaps is headed in a direction that is unhelpful. Furthermore, the Norwegian Committee stated that for long-term, but not life-threatening, illnesses and complaints, it is appropriate to take a holistic approach that may consist of several components. For another categorisation of alternative medicines as to their effectiveness, see SELECT COMMITTEE ON SCIENCE AND TECHNOLOGY, *op. cit.*: 17ss.

Effectiveness has been reported for some alternative medicines. See HOCHSTRASSER B., *op. cit.*: 28–35 (homeopathy and pre-natal measures for treatment of certain obstetrical conditions); MEDICIS T. C., *op. cit.*: 39–48 (acupuncture for treatment of both allergic inflammation of the bronchial mucosa and asthmatics' clinical symptoms, bronchial hyperactivity); MONTAKAB H., *op. cit.*: 39–48 (acupuncture for treatment of insomnia); GYSIN T., *op. cit.*: 64–66 (hypnotherapy for treatment of insomnia); COST ACTION B4, *op. cit.*: 47–62 (overview of clinical trial evidence as assessed in actually available systematic reviews on acupuncture, homeopathy, phytomedicine and manipulative therapies).

Regarding the non-effectiveness of alternative treatments, see AMERICAN CANCER SOCIETY, *op. cit.*: 117–23 (no evidence that specific alternative techniques result in objective benefit in the treatment of cancer in humans); ANGELL M., *op. cit.*: 839–41 (regarding the work done by the American Office of Alternative Medicine at the National Institute of Health); BALON J., *op. cit.*: 1013–27 (the addition of chiropractic care provided no benefit for children with mild or moderate asthma); BOOZANG K. M. (II), *op. cit.*: 586–604; OEPEN I. (III), *op. cit.*: 264–74 (rheumatology and biological medicine).

See also HÜRNY C. and co-authors, *op. cit.*: 55–63 (controversy regarding the proof of effectiveness of alternative treatments to improve the life quality of cancer patients); COST ACTION B4, *op. cit.*: 48–49 (contradictory results regarding acupuncture); SELECT COMMITTEE ON SCIENCE AND TECHNOLOGY, *op. cit.*: 30–31 (presentation of several studies); SOMMER J. H., *op. cit.*: 13–17; VAUTRAVERS P.

> means straightforward. Furthermore, alternative medicine therapies may also possess a theoretical basis, may stem from a cultural tradition that is seemingly anti-ethical to a quantitative biomedical framework, or may possess little foundational research on which to base a controlled evaluation.[77]

Some authors, representing a large section of the medical community consider, however, that alternative medicines should be acknowledged only when they have satisfied conventional criteria.[78]

Although RCT is the common reference method in clinical research, one must accept that such medical evidence in medicine may be questionable, that several accepted biomedical drugs or treatments have not been demonstrated to be effective, and that RCT is not applicable to all technologies.[79] In this perspective, an author writes, that

---

op. cit.: 518–23 (promising but not conclusive results regarding spinal manipulations).
For a development regarding the limitation of clinical trials, see above chap. 6.2.3.

77 Margolin A., *op. cit.*: 1626–28.
Robard notices that it would be particularly difficult for alternative medicines to satisfy evidence-based-medicine criteria, because in doing so, some factors contributing to their efficacy would be suppressed (Robard I., *op. cit.*: 178).
See also Boozang K. M. (I), *op. cit.*: 189–90; Bruset S., *op. cit.*: 186–96; Cohen M. H. (I), *op. cit.*: 102; Eskinazi D. P., *op. cit.*: 1622; Cost Action B4, *op. cit.*: 46–47; Heusser P., *op. cit.*: 5–6; Lemoine P., *op. cit.*: 84–91; Mitchell Weitzman S., *op.cit.*: 141–44; Select Committee on Science and Technology, *op. cit.*: 8–9, 30ss, 76ss; Wicki M., *op. cit.*: 215–22.

78 E.g., Angell writes, "it is time for the scientific community to stop giving alternative medicine a free ride. There cannot be two kinds of medicine – conventional and alternative. There is only medicine that has been adequately tested and medicine that has not, medicine that works and medicine that may or may not work. Once a treatment has been tested rigorously, it no longer matters whether it was considered alternative at the outset. If it is found to be reasonably safe and effective, it will be accepted. But assertions, speculations, and testimonials treatments do not substitute for evidence. Alternative treatments should be subjected to scientific testing no less rigorous than that required for conventional treatments" (Angell M., *op. cit.*: 840). See also, e.g., Boozang K. M. (II), *op. cit.*: 593ss; Oepen I. (III), *op. cit.*: 264–74 (the author considers that since the alleged benefit of alternative methods has never been proved, they must without any exception be considered as totally unnecessary); Select Committee on Science and Technology, *op. cit.*: 32.

79 E.g., the 1948 Nobel Prize in medicine was awarded to the discoverer of the powerful insecticide called DDT, when there were already fears about the possible damages to the eco-system. A few years later, DDT was forbidden, or at least in advanced countries (Daguet R., *op. cit.*: 18–19).

> although the advantages of using randomised controlled trials are clear, other research methods are also valuable and, for some research questions and situations, more appropriate. This is not specific to the field of complementary medicine.[80]

The author adds that there are

> circumstances in which observational studies would be the methodology of choice for evaluating the effectiveness of healthcare situations in which experimentation is unnecessary, in which it is inappropriate, in which it may be impossible, and in which it may be inadequate. In such situations, a considerable, repertoire of methods are available, many deriving from research by clinical professionals other than doctors (e.g. nursing and psychology) or from social science research.[81]

Some authors today have noticed a lack of uniform guidelines and methodologies in alternative medicines.[82] Researchers have attempted to develop

---

For further comments on this subject, see chap. 6.2.3. See also, e.g., BLACK N., *op. cit.*: 12215–18; BOOZANG K. M. (II), *op. cit.*: 593ss; COST ACTION B4, *op. cit.*: 46; FREUDENBERG U., *op. cit.*: 154–61, 184–98; HEUSSER P., *op. cit.*: 5ss, 136ss (including a list of the several types of procedures (quantitative and qualitative) that exist to evaluate medical techniques); HUFFORD D. J., *op. cit.*: 198–212; KÜNZI M. (I), *op. cit.*: 83–91, 96; MORREIM E. H., *op. cit.*: 222–35; OFFICE FÉDÉRAL DES ASSURANCES SOCIALES, *op. cit.*: 136.
The Norwegian Committee on Alternative Medicine considers that it is "impossible to establish general, exhaustive criteria for what constitute effective treatments and what outcomes are necessary for a treatment to be used beyond the trial stage" (MINISTRY OF HEALTH AND SOCIAL AFFAIRS (I), *op. cit.*: 269).

80 ANONYMOUS (IV), *op. cit.*: 57–58.

81 ANONYMOUS (IV), *op. cit.*: 57–58. Similarly, Gaier notes that "although the Directive of May 1975 (75/319 EC) defined clinical trials as randomised therapeutic comparisons, it goes on to state expressly that non-randomised medical investigations may likewise be presented. Happily, some of the investigative models proposed [...] by various authors [...] would [...] be perfectly acceptable in law." (GAIER H. C. (I), *op. cit.*: 37). See also BLACK N., *op. cit.*: 12215–18; SELECT COMMITTEE ON SCIENCE AND TECHNOLOGY, *op. cit.*: 77–79.
The COST B4 commission reported that acupuncture has claimed positive results from clinical experience *and* observational studies (COST ACTION B4, *op. cit.*: 49).

82 According to Margolin, "because alternative therapies do not possess well-established clinical practice guidelines, wide variations may exist in the treatment provided for a given disorder. This raises the question of whether the experimental treatment is regarded as representative of common practice in the field, and, if so, whether the treatment has been standardised for the trial's diagnostic category" (MARGOLIN A., *op. cit.*: 1626). See also WOOLF S. H., *op. cit.*: 149–54.
Similarly, the American Office of Alternative Medicine at the National Institute of Health notes that disciplines like acupuncture and naturopathy and modalities

new criteria and new procedures to fill this gap,[83] by taking into consideration the specificities of alternative medicines, in particular, their holistic orientation.[84] Thus, psychological elements as well as the relationship

---

like mind-body therapies are backed by an increasing amount of literature including randomised, controlled trials. It adds, however, that this work is largely ignored by mainstream medicine because journal boards, researchers, and clinicians arbitrarily vary the criteria for scientific validation (KILGORE C., *op. cit.*: 3). However, the Select Committee on Science and Technology states that "there are two notable weaknesses of the evidence base for CAM that at present exists. One is that in most of these areas little research is being done, and the second is that the few studies which have been completed are given disproportionate weight [...] Another problem [...] is that many old studies are recycled again and again through reviews and meta-analyses" (SELECT COMMITTEE ON SCIENCE AND TECHNOLOGY, *op. cit.*: 30–31).
See also, e.g., ANONYMOUS (IV), *op. cit.*: 10–12; BETTSCHART R., *op. cit.*; COST ACTION B4, *op. cit.*: 47; SELECT COMMITTEE ON SCIENCE AND TECHNOLOGY, *op. cit.*: 30ss, 76ss. For a development regarding research in alternative medicines, see also chap. 3.2.

83 E.g., the Complementary Medicine Field of the Cochrane Collaboration – a world wide network of medical researchers aiming to perform, update and disseminate systematic reviews of clinical trials in all health care – is now trying to collect all available clinical trials in a central database (located at the Research Council for Complementary Medicine in London) and to summarise the existing evidence in systematic reviews (www.rccm.org.uk, accessed Dec. 11 1999; COST ACTION B4, *op. cit.*: 47). Several research programs at the University of Bobigny in Paris are also currently in progress. See also MARGOLIN A., *op. cit.*: 1626–28 (noting that the National Acupuncture Detoxification Association has a protocol which may be applied to patients meeting diagnostic mental disorders criteria for cocaine abuse or dependence by practitioners trained by the acupuncture association); MARWICK C., *op. cit.*: 1553–54 (the author stresses that the US National Center for Complementary and Alternative Medicine is developing research programs including experts in both allopathic and alternative medicine on topics such as evaluation of efficacy related to therapies for cancer).
For more information regarding which research method to use and when, see the SELECT COMMITTEE ON SCIENCE AND TECHNOLOGY, *op. cit.*: 82–85.

84 According to Kilgore, "research in alternative medicine is complicated by numerous factors: some therapies are mainly used as preventive medicine and are hard to evaluate in a diagnosis-based system, for example. There's also often a need for a very long-term follow-up. And many alternative practitioners use individualized treatments that often consist of multiple, concurrent therapies. Unlike most conventional practitioners, they also tend to give more weight to patient's perceptions than to physiological endpoints in judging outcomes" (KILGORE C., *op. cit.*: 3).
Margolin also analyses the various criteria of RCTs when applied to alternative medicines and makes some suggestions regarding the basis for undertaking

between the patient and the practitioner are taken into account.[85] Some researchers have attempted to demonstrate that a medical treatment may be considered as being effective not only according to prevailing general standards but also when considered in relation to specific cases.[86] Various authors have also stressed the necessity of undertaking not only a quantitative but also a qualitative evaluation,[87] taking into account such

---

controlled trials, clinical practice guidelines, the identification of objective outcomes, control conditions, blinding procedures, and the problem of checking bias (MARGOLIN A., *op. cit.*: 1626–28). See also SELECT COMMITTEE ON SCIENCE AND TECHNOLOGY, *op. cit.*: 8–9, 78–79 (including issues to consider when designing RCTs for alternative therapies, such as alternative theoretical framework, different diagnostic systems, single-blind or double-blind trials, individual differences in treatment and responses to treatment, and the contributions for the patient and the practitioner).

See also, e.g., ANONYMOUS (IV), *op. cit.*: 57–59; BECK A., *op. cit.*: 56–57; BINDER M., *op. cit.*: 40–42; BOOZANG K. M. (I), *op. cit.*: 189–90; COST ACTION B4, *op. cit.*: 70, 76–78; KILGORE C., *op. cit.*: 3; LAPLANTINE F., *op. cit.*: 81–108; LAUNSO L. (II), *op. cit.*; ROBARD I., *op. cit.*: 178.

85 According to Bruset, "research in complementary medicine must be based on the agreement that if an effect of a therapy does exist, there must be a way of measuring this effect. This can be done by using methods developed by modern science after modifying them to meet the individual characteristics of each treatment method. This implies a more holistic view of the patients when treating diseases – and perhaps, when the methods and their use in society are compared" (BRUSET S., *op. cit.*: 196).

The Foundation for Integrated Health Care adds that "there is a need for further work in the development of suitable outcome measures by which to evaluate the full benefit experienced by users of complementary therapies. They should include outcome measures reflecting symptomatic as well as curative treatments and their development should involve close consultation with practitioners, researchers and users" (ANONYMOUS (IV), *op. cit.*: 12).

See also, e.g., BETTSCHART R., *op. cit.*: 20ss; DAGUET R., *op. cit.*: 19–20 (regarding experimentation in the psychiatric field); FREUDENBERG U., *op. cit.*: 154–61, 184–98; KÜNZI M. (I), *op. cit.*: 84–85; LANNOYE P., *op. cit.*: 4; OFFICE FÉDÉRAL DES ASSURANCES SOCIALES, *op. cit.*: 136; PERREZ M., *op. cit.*: 152–53; WICKI M., *op. cit.*: 205–07.

86 This principle has been applied in Germany where courts take into consideration (when dealing with the coverage of medical acts) the degree of chance of success of medical treatment (see chap. 5.3.5.5.B). See also, e.g., SCHULIN B., *op. cit.*: 546–65.

87 For a recent development regarding the advantages and disadvantages of qualitative research to evaluate alternative medicines, see SELECT COMMITTEE ON SCIENCE AND TECHNOLOGY, *op. cit.*: 81.

sociological elements as the satisfaction of patients,[88] their personal experience, as well as the experience and good practices developed by alternative practitioners. In addition, the cost-effectiveness analysis may also be taken into account.[89] Recently, the US White Commission on Complementary and Alternative Medicines has argued for the development of an open-minded research framework to investigate this field.[90]

In brief, it is possible to observe that first, the effectiveness of alternative medicines is difficult to demonstrate through randomised controlled trials and that these trials may not easily be applicable to alternative techniques. Second, that the guidelines and methodologies based on a multidisciplinary approach are improving, which take into account objective (i.e. biomedical) and subjective elements.

6.3.4 Acknowledgement from the Medical Community

A treatment may achieve scientific validation when it is recognised on a large scale by the medical community effectively by researchers and practitioners.[91] The problem, of course, consists in determining what a large

88 Indeed, when patients are satisfied with a treatment, this may indicate that the treatment has been effective, because it has improved the patient's health, i.e. the feeling of well being (mental, physical, or social). On this subject, the British Select Committee on Science and Technology points out that "patient satisfaction has its place as part of the evidence base for CAM but its position is complicated. [...] Therefore, ideally studies should include patient satisfaction as one of a number of measures in evaluating a treatment, but it alone cannot be taken as a proof or otherwise of a treatment's efficacy or as evidence to justify provision" (SELECT COMMITTEE ON SCIENCE AND TECHNOLOGY, *op. cit.*: 33).

89 Warren argues that alternative therapies have a "soft" variable that makes them less amenable to clinical trials. These techniques rely on a "greater degree of patient participation and self-responsibility [...] (which make them) more individualised and subjective in their application". Therefore, in some instances it would be virtually impossible to test treatment that varies so widely in scope and practice depending on each individual specialised care (cited in JOSEFEK K. J., *op. cit.*: 305–06).
See also HEUSSER P., *op. cit.*: 7ss; JUNOD A. F. (I), *op. cit.*: 2027–29.

90 WHITE HOUSE COMMISSION ON COMPLEMENTARY AND ALTERNATIVE MEDICINE POLICY, *op. cit.*: 33ss.

91 E.g., in Switzerland, a technique was considered as established when it was generally recognised by researchers and practitioners (DUC J.-L., *op. cit.*: 45; KÜNZI M. (I), *op. cit.*: 83; RKUV Kranken- und Unfallversicherung, Rechtsprechung und Verwaltungspraxis, 1992, n° 3: 108).

or sufficient basis is. In the US, courts may take into consideration, when dealing with medical malpractice liability,[92] the "respectable minority", or "two schools of thought". However, courts differ as to what constitutes a respectable minority; some accept it where there is one physician following a particular approach, others require that the minority view be "reasonable and prudent".[93]

As a consequence, the notion of "recognition by the medical community" is difficult to define. In our view, this criterion may be taken into account when deciding to recognise a technique, as it allows for the development of techniques that could benefit patients. However, other parameters defining the environment of the technique may also be considered. In this respect, Cohen notes that, as soon as medical schools incorporate alternative therapies into their curriculum and physicians increase their use of alternative medicines, or refer patients to providers for such therapies, standards of care in medical communities begin to incorporate alternative medicines, and therefore provide validation to regulate.[94]

6.3.5 Summary

Scientific validation, in the restrictive sense, remains an indispensable tool for regulating the medical field, because it offers undeniable guarantees.[95] It is important not to consider the requirement of scientific validation as an obstacle, or as an obstacle to simply ignore. A better approach consists first, in retaining a critical approach toward scientific methods, in being aware of their advantages and limits. Second, while remaining open-minded, one should consider whether other tools, potentially applicable to alternative medicines, exist or whether such tools could be developed in order to

---

Similarly, Angell, when determining the notion of scientific testing, includes "the best peer-reviewed medical journals for the publication of research reports" (Angell M., *op. cit.*: 839). See also, e.g., Hänggeli C., *op. cit.*: 2447–48; Künzi M. (I), *op. cit.*: 83ss.

92 See chap. 7.2.3.2.

93 *Chumbler v. McClure*, 505 F.2d 489, 491–92 (6th Cir. 1974) (permitting defence where there was "a division in the medical profession" regarding the use of a specific drug for the treatment of a cerebral vascular insufficiency, and the minority view was "supported by responsible medical authority", even though only one neurosurgeon followed it). See also Bradford G. E., *op. cit.*: 326–34; Cohen M. H. (I), *op. cit.*: 58, 150–51.

94 Cohen M. H. (I), *op. cit.*: 58–59. See also, e.g., Künzi M. (I), *op. cit.*: 83ss.

95 Therefore, as soon as it is established, a technique could expect to be licensed and covered.

establish scientific support. In this respect, it is important not to polarise the discussion, which has been a constant trend between defenders of and opponents to alternative medicines.

With respect to the criteria commonly employed to establish scientific validation, the mechanism of action, that is difficult in any case to demonstrate for alternative medicines, is not decisive. The attention should be focused on actual evidence of effectiveness. In this respect, even if alternative medicines have usually had problems meeting conventional standards, the effectiveness of certain techniques have been demonstrated for specific conditions. Attempts and proposals have been made to adapt existing methods of assessing effectiveness to alternative medicines. Furthermore, there is a growing trend towards the use of a multidisciplinary approach, which could prove more appropriate to these – holistic – techniques. This would include, for example, observational studies and the social sciences. Thus, scientific validation is becoming less restrictive in its ambit.

In brief, when scientifically evaluating alternative medicines, evidence-based-medicine may be prioritised, but it is important that other methods and other fields of knowledge are not denied or underestimated, as they may also be valuable, in providing useful information and validation.

6.4 Scientific Validation in a Broad Sense

Bibliography

Andersen J. O., *Health seeking in pluralistic health care systems*, in: Johannessen H. (co-authors: Launso L., Olesen S. G., Staugard F.) (I), *Studies in alternative therapy 1 – Contributions from the Nordic countries*, Odense University Press, 1994, Gylling: 114–25; Boozang K. M. (II), *Is the alternative medicine? Managed care apparently thinks so*, in: Connecticut Law Review, Winter 2000, vol. 32: 567–69; Cost Action B4, *COST action B4 unconventional medicine – Final report of the management committee, 1993–1998*, European Communities, 1998, Luxembourg 32–33; Domenighetti G. (co-authors: Grilli R., Guillod O., Gutzwiller F., Quaglia J.), *Usage personnel de pratiques relevant des médecines douces ou alternatives parmi les médecins suisses*, in: Médecine et Hygiène, 2000, vol. 58, n° 2291: 570–72; Select Committee on Science and Technology, *Complementary and alternative medicine*, House of Lords – Session 1999–2000 6th Report, The Stationary Office, 2000, London: 33; Shapiro A. K. (I) (co-author: Shapiro E.), *The powerful placebo – From ancient priest to modern physician*, The Johns Hopkins University Press, 1997, Baltimore/London: 228; Sprumont D. (II), *La protection des sujets de recherche: Notamment dans le domaine biomédical*, Disertation, Stämpfli, Berne, 1993; Stone J. (co-author:

Matthews J.), *Complementary medicine and the law*, Oxford University Press, 1996, Oxford: 93–95.

6.4.1 General Remarks

Although scientific validation in the restrictive sense, may be particularly adapted for some fields of medicine, it is possible to speculate as to whether regulation could be based on different elements. For example, political or ethical issues play a decisive role when regulating the medical applications of new technologies, such as *in vitro* fertilisation, genetic analysis and gene therapy. In respect of alternative medicines, other scientific factors, in the broad sense, such as historical or sociological elements may also be viewed as relevant when deciding to regulate.

The components of socio-historical validation are analysed below, including how their interpretation has impacted on the regulatory framework.

6.4.2 Socio-historical Validation: Concept and Impact

The integration of alternative medicines into the conventional medical tradition,[96] given that they do not benefit from scientific validation in the restrictive sense, may be a decisive element in any approach seeking to regulate these techniques. Two key factors have historically determined the degree of integration a practice has in any medical tradition; first, is the length of time that a practice has been used (historical component). Second, is the extent of use of the technique by the population (sociological component).[97] These two elements are considered as a whole, as they

96 As shown, (see chap. 1.2) and as some authors recall (see Robard I., *op. cit.*: 178; Stone J., *op. cit.*: 93–94) the degree of integration in the medical tradition varies from one country to another and from one technique to another. Some alternative medicines are already well integrated in Western countries. For example, some therapies such as Chinese medicine (including acupuncture) have been practised in their country of origin for thousands of years. However, they are still relatively new in Western countries. Moreover, there is a large number of less utilised techniques that have originated within the past 60 years.

97 According to some authors (see below, chap. 6.4.4), when the rate of use of alternative medicines by the population reaches a certain percentage, regulation should be undertaken, irrespective of their scientific acknowledgement (sociological validation in a restrictive sense). Other sociological observations may also be taken into consideration when justifying a regulation on a socio-historical basis, such as the reasons to seek alternative medicines, or the willingness of the population to have a regulation in a specific field (sociological validation in a broad sense).

influence each other. Indeed, a practice must be used by a significant part of the population before it can be considered as a part of medical history. Similarly, a practice will require some time before it reaches a sociological acceptable level. Therefore this kind of validation will be considered as "socio-historical".

The main argument supporting socio-historical validation is that, if therapies have survived, and/or are used by a substantial part of the population, then it is because they have provided some benefit to patients. Although studies concerning the effectiveness of alternative medicines have shown this argument to be often irrelevant,[98] socio-historical elements continue to be taken into consideration when regulating alternative medicines. For example, States that have decided to regulate or, at least, tolerate long-established indigenous alternative practices and their practitioners have long been sensitive to these socio-historical arguments.[99] In Switzerland, the widespread use of some alternative therapies, as well as the willingness of a significant part of the population to have some alternative medicines covered played a significant role in the introduction of coverage for some alternative practices in the Swiss compulsory illness insurance.[100] The importance of socio-historical and political elements is even more important for countries having an inclusive or integrated system such as, respectively, India and China.[101]

98 SHAPIRO A. K. (I), *op. cit.*: 1–27, 60–73, 228.

99 E.g., in the Swiss canton of Ticino or in the state of New Mexico, indigenous practitioners may practise, under relatively few conditions.

100 See chap. 5.3.5.14.B. Similarly, in Belgium, the fact that many patients were using alternative medicines and wished these techniques to be covered influenced the adoption of the new act on the licensing of alternative practitioners.
Private insurance, when deciding to propose coverage for specific alternative medicines, takes these criteria into consideration. Indeed, they illustrate the potential market in the field. For a reflection on this subject in relation with the problems to assess scientific validation, see, e.g. BOOZANG K. M. (II), *op. cit.*: 567–69.
Today, a justification for regulation based only on historical elements seems increasingly difficult to support. Stones notes that alternative medicines "will find it increasingly difficult to rely on the argument that their therapy has been used safely for hundred of years" (STONE J., *op. cit.*: 95). See also the COST ACTION B4, *op. cit.*: 32–33.

101 In these countries, the tradition of using indigenous medicine deeply influenced the setting up of modern regulation including alternative medicines in the public health care system. For further discussion, see chap. 4.3.4.2 (India), and 4.3.5.2 (China). For a comparison between the Danish and the Sri-lankan health care systems and ways to integrate other health care approaches, see ANDERSEN J. O., *op. cit.*: 114–25.

6.4.3 Scope of Socio-historical Validation

If sociological and historical elements are a serious indication that a regulation is needed, should a regulation be justified solely on a socio-historical basis? To answer this question, we shall assume that the level of use is considered as being sufficient.[102]

The answer is affirmative when regulating the licensing to practice. Ultimately, if alternative medicines satisfy patients' needs and their security is guaranteed, we do not see any valid reason for justifying a restriction.[103] Biomedical arguments against this justification may be given. However, as we have seen, the scientific methods used to establish evidence-based-medicine validation are questionable. As these are limited, it is possible to take other elements into account.[104]

With respect to the actual coverage of alternative medicines, the answer is subtler. Insurance may take socio-historical elements into consideration when deciding to cover a technique. Indeed, they show that patients use and/or want to have access to specific types of treatments. However, because the objective of private insurance is to make at least some profit, or at least not to lose money, and given that social insurance involves the whole community who finances it, the technique must further be effective, appropriate, and cost-effective.[105] However, these additional evidences may be required in a second phase, not when first introducing the coverage, but later, as a confirmation of the validation to cover the technique. In this respect, the solution adopted in Switzerland is interesting; the coverage of the most widely used alternative medicines has been introduced mainly on the basis of socio-historical elements. The coverage is then

102 This chapter regards only the validation to regulate. In order to grant a licence to practise or to be covered, a therapy will have to satisfy other requirements. See below, chap. 7.3.5.
The level of use of the technique should reach the "sufficient" or "reasonable" rate to justify the regulation (see below chap. 6.4.4).

103 According to Domenighetti, on the basis of a sociological study of the use of alternative medicines by the Swiss population, a restrictive policy towards alternative medicines, as well as their (non-)coverage by insurance seems unacceptable not only by consumers, but also by a great proportion of the medical corpus (DOMENIGHETTI G., *op. cit.*: 570). See also SELECT COMMITTEE ON SCIENCE AND TECHNOLOGY, *op. cit.*: 33.

104 However, it is obvious that the validation to regulate will be stronger when a specific technique is justified on scientific and non-scientific elements. Actually, each technique should be able to gain this double validation.

105 For more developments see 7.4.3.2.

confirmed only if these techniques prove to be effective, appropriate and cost-effective.[106]

Therefore, it is possible to consider that regulation is justified when a scientific *or* a socio-historical validation is demonstrated. The cost-effectiveness must also be demonstrated at a later stage to confirm the validation to cover a technique.

6.4.4 Minimal Rate of Use to Regulate

If socio-historical elements may justify a regulation, one may wonder what the bottom-line is to envisage a regulation. A predominant component of socio-historical validation is that part of the population has recourse to the technique. If this criterion is taken as the benchmark, what should be the minimal level of use to justify a regulation. Stone sets this rate at 25%,[107] however, the justification for this rate is not known. Furthermore, there is no mention whether this rate corresponds to that part of the population who have used alternative medicines at least once, or to those who have used them at least once during the previous year. Nor does the author specify whether such a rate is necessary for each therapy or for all therapies evaluated together.[108] One may go further and ask what if the level of use

106 When establishing the medical necessity of alternative treatments, an open approach, involving biomedical and non-biomedical parameters has been favoured. For more details regarding Switzerland, see chap. 5.3.5.14.C. See also Domenighetti who notes that consumers and providers of alternative medicines, in particular alternative physicians, strongly criticise the use of evidence-based medicine when deciding to cover or not alternative medicines (DOMENIGHETTI G., *op. cit.*: 570–72).

107 STONE J., *op. cit.*: 93.

108 This distinction is important. Indeed, the percentage of the population who used a specific alternative medicine during the prior year varies widely from the percentage of the population who have used at least once one type of alternative medicines.
As we have seen before, the percentage of the population using alternative medicines varies from one country to another, and it is not higher in tolerant countries than in monopolistic ones. For example, during the year of study, the following rates of use (of all alternative medicines taken together) were reported: Belgium: 24%; Denmark: 10–37%; Finland: 15–20%; France: 16%; Germany: 5–12%; Great Britain 8–10%; Netherlands: 6–7%; Norway: 10%; Switzerland: 45–80%; USA: 46%. One should be aware that the methods employed to establish this rate vary from one study to another. For more details, see chap. 2.2 and 2.3.
If one takes as the criterion that percentage of the population who employed a specific technique during the prior year, a percentage of 25% would be unreasonable.

of a practice is near zero? In other words what happens when a specific practice does not have any or almost no[109] socio-historical validation? In such a case, would a regulation remain legitimised?

To answer this question amounts to, in essence, finding a solution to the regulation of alternative "experimental" treatments. Indeed, by definition, experimental treatments have almost no validation.[110]

When a technique is developed according to biomedical principles in a biomedical environment, rules – on the licensing and the coverage – regarding experimental treatments will apply.[111] However, when a technique has a holistic orientation, the situation becomes more difficult. One solution would be to extend the scope of experimental regulation, but as we have seen, this type of regulation is evidence-based-medicine oriented. Thus, a new alternative technique may try to adapt itself to the classical experimental framework, but ultimately be unsuccessful. Nevertheless, several techniques have a potential to heal. Defenders of biomedicine would argue that such experimental framework is not conceivable, that research and development in medicine may be envisaged only when biomedical criteria are satisfied. One should remember that, at one time, leading experts in medicine refused to acknowledge the reality of X-rays.[112] The discoveries of Pasteur and of Freud were also rejected initially. Furthermore, such practices will exist in any case.[113] In our view, a more sensible approach consists in admitting the existence of such practices and building a framework to control them rather than seeking to ignore or forbid them.[114] For the above mentioned reasons, the creation of a regulated experimental framework should, in our view, be envisaged.[115]

Indeed, no therapy – biomedical or alternative – is used by at least 25% of the population during one year.

109 This distinction must be made. If not made, it would be impossible to justify a hypothesis admitting that such a hypothesis does not exist.

110 This is not the case for "traditional practitioners" using long-established indigenous practices, because they rightly have a socio-historical validation.

111 For more information regarding the legal framework of experimental treatments, see SPRUMONT D. (II), *op. cit.*

112 For a development on this subject, see chap. 6.2.

113 Monopolistic systems have been shown to be ineffective in eliminating alternative practices.

114 Moreover, "experimental" alternative treatments may prove to be useful for patients. Therefore, the refusal to allow experimentation is likely to impede the spreading out of potential useful techniques.

115 Regarding the implementation of the proposed regulatory framework, there are several problems to solve. In particular, as these techniques have little validation, some safeguards should be set up. The most important would be the complete

When addressing the coverage of such a technique, an estimation of the mininal rate is difficult to establish.[116] In order to have an idea of this rate, one may look at the situation in Switzerland, where the five most used alternative therapies are covered under the basic social compulsory coverage.[117] In 1993, the percentage of the population who used once a particular alternative medicine during the prior twelve months was estimated at 44%.[118, 119] The percentage of the population who used at least once one of the following alternative therapies is as follows:[120]

1. homeopathy: 11%;
2. phytotherapy: 6%;
3. Chinese medicine: 1.76%;
4. anthroposophic medicine: 1.3%;
5. neural therapy: 0,2%.

It is noticeable that the rate of use varies between 11% and 0.2% of the population.[121] Whereas these figures may give some indication of the rate, it

satisfaction of the education requirement, i.e. that such "experiments" should be permitted only for those practitioners holding a high or medium level of education including an allopathic background. Furthermore, the practitioner wishing to develop such practice should obtain the approval of a research protocol. This would consist in demonstrating sufficient preliminary research, as well as research procedures or guidelines regarding the providing and the evaluation of the effectiveness and safety of the therapy. Finally, implementation rules should be set up, such as the length of the period of testing, criteria to determine when a practice is not experimental anymore, etc. This framework would allow an alternative practice to develop itself until it either reaches a sufficient level of socio-historical validation to be acknowledged, or not and therefore disappears.

116 We do not consider here the question of coverage of experimental alternative treatments, as it involves several elements that are not addressed here due to the constraints of space.

117 The covered alternative medicines do not have a definitive established scientific validation, in the restrictive sense. Their reimbursement was decided on the basis of socio-historical elements.

118 For more details, see chap. 2.2.

119 At that time, the basic compulsory social insurance did not cover the five most used alternative therapies. For more details, see chap. 5.3.5.14.

120 The following rates are an estimate. For more details, see chap. 2.2 and 2.3.

121 The rate varies widely between those people having or not having complementary insurance (see chap. 2.2 and 5.3.5.14). Among those people possessing such insurance, the rate varies between 3% and 49%, and among those not possessing such insurance between 0.2% and 11%.

is still difficult to propose a minimal rate as in the Swiss example, other elements based on political grounds have been taken into consideration.[122] Thus, alternative techniques should always (if the level of the use is assumed to be not as equal to zero) have a chance to develop within an open environment regarding their experimentation and practice. However, they should not be reimbursed until they demonstrate having sufficient socio-historical validation, mainly based on the use of the population (private coverage). Other criteria, such as appropriateness and cost-effectiveness, are also necessary to legitimise the coverage of the technique. However, they may be brought in within a second phase, to serve as a confirmation of the validation based on socio-historical elements. Other elements including the desire of the population to have specific techniques covered, the percentage of allopathic practitioners using alternative medicines, and the level of scientific (in its restrictive sense) recognition of an alternative technique must also be taken into consideration.

6.4.5 Summary

To regulate alternative medicines, there are sound reasons for the choice of socio-historical validation.

When licensing the practice of a specific technique, as soon as the level of use is not equal to zero, the regulation is legitimised. Therefore, a regulation on the licensing to practise should always be a consideration.

Concerning the coverage of a specific technique, it may be considered as justified as soon as the level of use reaches a reasonable rate. Additional parameters, in particular the proof of its (cost-) effectiveness, may be necessary at a later stage to confirm the validation based on socio-historical elements.

122 E.g., the number of physicians using such techniques, the historical background of the technique in the country, the existence of practice guidelines, the level of scientific acceptance, etc.

6.5 Safety

Bibliography

ANGELL M. (co-author: KASSIRER J. P.), *Alternative medicine – The risks of untested and unregulated medicine*, in: New England Journal of Medicine, 1998, vol. 339, n° 12: 840–41; BRITISH MEDICAL ASSOCIATION (LAMONT T.), *Complementary medicine – New approaches to good practice*, Oxford University Press, 1993, Oxford/New York: 60; BOOZANG K. M. (II), *Is the alternative medicine? Managed care apparently thinks so*, in: Connecticut Law Review, Winter 2000, vol. 32: 586–604; COHEN M. H. (I), *Complementary and alternative medicine – Legal boundaries and regulatory perspectives*, The Johns Hopkins University Press, 1998, London & Oxford: 62–64, 66; COST ACTION B4, *COST action B4 unconventional medicine – Final report of the management committee, 1993–1998*, European Communities, 1998, Luxembourg: 30–33; EHLERS A. P. F., *Medizin in den Händen von Heilpraktikern – "Nicht-Heilkundigen"*, Springer Verlag, 1995, Berlin/Heidelberg: 84–87; FURROW B. R. (co-authors: GREANEY T. L., JOST T., SCHWARTZ R. L.) (II), *Health law: Cases, materials and problems*, West Publishing, 1997, St Paul: 39–47; GUILLOD O. (I), *Rebouteux, naturopathes et guérisseurs: Pour un traitement légal alternatif*, Recueil de Jurisprudence Neuchâtelois, 1989, Neuchâtel: 31–32; HEUSSER P., *Kriterien zur Beurteilung des Nutzens von komplementärmedizinischen Methoden*, Bundesamt für Sozialversicherung, Mar. 1998, Bern: 12–13; HOFFMEYER P., *Etats-Unis: Appel pour une réglementation plus stricte des traitements à base de plantes*, in: Médecine et Hygiène, 1998, vol. 56, n° 225: 1861; JOSEFEK K. J., *Alternative medicine's roadmap to mainstream*, in: American Journal of Law and Medicine, 2000, vol. 26: 305; KOHN L. T. (co-editors: CORRIGAN J. M., DONALDSON M. S.), *To err is human: Building a safer health system*, National Academy Press, 2000, Washington D. C.; MAGNER G., *Chiropractic – The victim's perspective*, Prometheus Book, 1995, New York; MANAÏ D., *Les droits du patient face à la médecine contemporaine*, Helbing & Lichtenhahn, 1999, Basel/Genève/München: 118; New England Journal of Medicine, 1998, n° 339: 785–906, 827, 846; OEPEN I. (III), *Pseudo-Naturheilverfahren und Aussenseitermethoden in der Rheumatologie*, in: Zeitschrift für Rheumatologie, 1993, vol. 52: 264–74; OFFICE FÉDÉRAL DES ASSURANCES SOCIALES, *Manuel de standardisation pour l'évaluation médicale et économique des prestations médicales*, Office Fédéral des Assurances Sociales, 1998, Berne: 132; SELECT COMMITTEE ON SCIENCE AND TECHNOLOGY, *Complementary and alternative medicine*, House of Lords – Session 1999–2000 6th Report, The Stationary Office, 2000, London: 9, 32–33; STONE J. (co-author: MATTHEWS J.), *Complementary medicine and the law*, Oxford University Press, 1996, Oxford: 90–91, 95; STUDDERT D. M. and co-authors, *Medical malpractice implications of alternative medicine*, in: JAMA, 1998, vol. 280, n° 18: 1610–15; WHITE HOUSE COMMISSION ON COMPLEMENTARY AND ALTERNATIVE MEDICINE POLICY, *Final report*, Mar. 2002, available at http://www.whccamp.hhs.gov/pdfs/fr2002_document.pdf, accessed Feb. 1 2005: 20–21, 90–91; WHO (IV), *Guidelines on basic training and safety in acupuncture*, WHO, 1999, Geneva;

WICKI M., *Komplementärmedizin im Rahmen des Rechtes*, Dissertation, Stämpfli, 1998, Bern: 66ss.

When examining 'alternative' medical practice, safety is a key priority for the legislator. The rationale is primarily the need to protect patients from being harmed by the treatments they receive.[123] Indeed, while the purpose of medical practices and drugs is to maintain or to improve health, they also have the potential for harm.[124] However, nearly everyone is subject to risks,[125] and alternative medicines are not an exception.[126]

When regulating 'alternative' medical practice, the lawmaker has to weigh the benefits against the risks and find ways to limit the risks.[127] In other words, first, it has to assess the potential that an alternative medical practice has for harming people, second, to establish whether it is justifiable and finally, to build a framework to regulate it.[128] As the British Medical Association stresses, "the value of any treatment depends on the balance between the likely benefits and harms, since it cannot be assumed that any given therapy or method of medical practice is completely harmless".[129]

Thus, the implementation of the safety requirement is variable.[130] As a result, in order to be accepted, a treatment must be "reasonably safe".[131]

123 Many definitions can be given for safety. However, in its essence, it is always related to proper diagnosis and appropriate treatment.
For an analysis of the definitions of "side effects" "adverse reactions", "toxicity", and "complications", see COST ACTION B4, *op. cit.*: 31–32.

124 As Manaï stresses, one must weigh up the gravity of risks and their frequency, and the necessity to obtain medical intervention (MANAÏ D., *op. cit.*: 118).

125 For a development regarding the error rate in the practice of allopathic medicine, see FURROW B. R. (II), *op. cit.*: 39–41.

126 COST ACTION B4, *op. cit.*: 30; WHO (IV), *op. cit.*: 17ss; WICKI M., *op. cit.*: 72ss.

127 For a development regarding the cause of medical errors, and the ways to limit them, see FURROW B. R. (II), *op. cit.*: 39–47 (means to reduce medical error include a system for the discovery of errors, prevention of errors (i.e., reduced reliance on memory, improved information access, error proofing, standardisation, and training), absorption of errors, psychological precursors, and the institutionalisation of safety). See also KOHN L. T., *op. cit.*; WICKI M., *op. cit.*: 74ss.

128 In this perspective, standards of practice, rules concerning liabilities (including informed consent), or the production and marketing of drugs are set up.

129 BRITISH MEDICAL ASSOCIATION, *op. cit.*: 60. See also SELECT COMMITTEE ON SCIENCE AND TECHNOLOGY, *op. cit.*: 32.

130 In this respect, the Swiss Federal Office of Social Insurance considers that the frequency and importance of side effects must be in relation to the risks of the illness (HEUSSER P., *op. cit.*: 12).

131 ANGELL M., *op. cit.*: 841.

Furthermore, as the Swiss Federal Office of Social Insurance states, the evaluation of the quality of a medical technique, whether alternative or not, must be made taking into consideration the specificities of the technique.[132, 133]

There are three main risks associated with alternative medicines. First, an alternative drug or product can have side effects on the organism. Although alternative products, such as homeopathic products or herbal remedies, are relatively non-toxic and lacking in side effects, their potential to cause harm is real and should not be under-valued.[134] Here, some authors have noted that safety measures determined by adverse effects or side effects should be accepted with caution. In certain therapies, such as traditional Chinese medicine and homeopathy, side effects, often perceived by biomedicine as a part of "safety" issues, are a specific and vital part

132 E.g., regarding acupuncture, controls should be particularly focused on the sterilisation of needles (HEUSSER P., *op. cit.*: 12–13; WHO (IV), *op. cit.*: 17ss).

133 For a development regarding the appropriateness of medical treatments and the relation between safety and efficacy, see chap. 7.4.3. See also, e.g., OFFICE FÉDÉRAL DES ASSURANCES SOCIALES, *op. cit.*: 132.

134 Angell says that "fortunately, most untested herbal remedies are probably harmless". However, the author adds "there are risks of alternative medicine in addition to that of failing to receive effective treatment" (e.g., digitalis toxicity in a person who had ingested a contaminated herbal concoction; another person suffered central nervous system depression after ingesting a substance sold as a growth hormone stimulator; another patient developed lead poisoning after taking an Indian herbal remedy for his diabetes) (ANGELL M., *op. cit.*: 840).
Authors have reported risks and harmful effects such as kidney destruction by interstitial fibrosis by herbs of the Aristolochia group; hypertension crises through ephedrine like effect stimulating herbs (Ephedra); hepatitis of liver failure, caused by several herbal medications, including Valerian; carcinogenic effects by direct effect on DNA by the Aristolochia group; allergic reactions linked to many herbal medications and with low dilution homeopathy; hepatitis and blood poisoning transmitted by non-sterilised acupuncture needles; heart rhythm disturbance due to potassium loss after coffee enema treatment; etc. (COST ACTION B4, *op. cit.*: 32–33). See also BOOZANG K. M. (II), *op. cit.*: 587–89 (homeopathic remedies can contain toxic concentrations of dangerous substances, or sufficient amount of natural substances to induce allergic reactions); HOFFMEYER P., *op. cit.*: 1861 (stating that the condition of patients being treated with herbal treatments worsened); New England Journal of Medicine, 1998, n° 339: 785–906, 827, 846. The British Select Committee on Science and Technology also points out that a potential risk arising from the use of alternative medicines is that patients may not tell their GPs that they are receiving other treatment, and thus risk complications from drug interactions (SELECT COMMITTEE ON SCIENCE AND TECHNOLOGY, *op. cit.*: 9).

of the treatment. Thus, the significant point should be whether the side effects that manifest themselves are desired.[135]

Second, when an untrained or incompetent practitioner provides an alternative product or therapy, patients may be directly harmed.[136] To prevent such a risk, the establishment of appropriate training and guidelines is crucial. It would then be possible to restrict potentially dangerous acts to those practitioners who can demonstrate that they have acquired a certain level of skills.[137]

Finally, a patient may be prevented from seeking appropriate biomedical care, which could ultimately provide a more effective cure. The implication being that harm may result as a consequence of serious medical problems being ignored or undetected.[138] Stone minimises this risk,[139] arguing that people who consult alternative practitioners are among those who place a high priority on their own health, and therefore are "more likely to have their serious health problems detected at an early stage".[140] The author considers that "the only situation in which taking the advice of a complementary health practitioner might conceivably be harmful is where the therapist takes advantage of a vulnerable patient and persuades him not to seek medical advice".[141] Similarly, other authors argue that the holistic approach of alternative practitioners reduces the risks related to

135 BOOZANG K. M. (II), *op. cit.*: 587–89; COST ACTION B4, *op. cit.*: 30.

136 E.g., a patient takes too many medicines, or a physical therapist performs a wrong movement causing muscular damage (e.g., when practising chiropractic or osteopathy). See also, e.g., MAGNER G., *op. cit.*; OEPEN I. (III), *op. cit.*: 264–74; WHO (IV), *op. cit.*: 17.

137 For a development on this subject, see chap. 7.3.2.

138 This risk is particularly important during the treatment of serious diseases which include all degenerative illnesses, particularly those for which no treatment is available, such as cancer, diabetes, multiple sclerosis, acute forms of psychiatric diseases, etc. In this case, the risks result less from the providing of the technique, than from the situation of the patient.
See BOOZANG K. M. (II), *op. cit.*: 588; BRITISH MEDICAL ASSOCIATION, *op. cit.*: 60.

139 The author assumes that it will be almost impossible to base a cause of action (in English common law) on this situation.

140 Stone says that "additionally, as it is now known, they are likely to use complementary medicines as a supplement to, and not a substitute for, orthodox treatment" and further that alternative medicines usually emphasise the preventative nature of their approach and that "most therapists are well aware of their ethical obligation to recommend medical attention" (STONE J., *op. cit.*: 90–91).

141 STONE J., *op. cit.*: 91.

the practice of alternative medicines.[142] These arguments should be taken into consideration, however, one may not, on the basis of philosophical or sociological observations, minimise a risk which is real. Indeed, there have been reported cases holding that all medical practices, including alternative techniques, are linked with risks.[143] Furthermore, it is important to stress that patients seeking health care, even when they are particularly concerned about their health, may very easily be in a vulnerable

142 E.g., Cohen writes, in relation to the situation in the US, that "there is little case law on malpractice claims against complementary and alternative health care providers, not only because standards of care are so diffuse, [...] but also because patients have different expectations of complementary and alternative providers that they do of biomedical physicians. Naturopaths, chiropractors, acupuncturists, massage therapists, and other providers on the whole render individualized and personalized health services, leading to a lower incidence of malpractice litigation". And further, that "[alternative providers] reduce malpractice exposure by structuring the provider-patient relationship as a collaborative venture to health" (COHEN M. H. (I), *op. cit.*: 66).
Similarly, Guillod stresses that the risk of taking patients away from allopathic medicine has not been demonstrated in Switzerland. Indeed, it seems that patients, in general do not consult non-allopathic practitioners for all health problems, but only for specific ones (muscular and joint problems, insomnia, headaches, anxiety, etc.). Furthermore, when they have the choice, they generally consult first an allopathic practitioner. However the author reminds us that the risk still exists for some type of illnesses (e.g., degenerative ones) (GUILLOD O. (I), *op. cit.*: 31–32).
Regarding the criticism that the diversion of care may delay diagnosis and treatment of many serious diseases, Josefek points out that "this criticism largely originates from allopathic practitioners who refuse to see the benefits individuals enjoy from alternative modalities and thus, refuse to refer their patients for care" (JOSEFEK K. J., *op. cit.*: 305).

143 E.g., a famous Austrian case involved parents who refused to seek conventional treatment to treat their child, based on the advice of a physician rejecting biomedicine (see chap. 4.3.2.1). A similar case happened in the US where a 15-year-old boy had Hodgkin's disease and chose to forgo the recommendations for radiation and chemotherapy treatments in favour of a compound of herbs and dietary extracts. Five months later, the boy's condition had deteriorated and he required intensive chemotherapy (JOSEFEK K. J., *op. cit.*: 305).
Cases were also reported of diabetics having serious complications after stopping insulin on advice of alternative practitioners; malnutrition following irresponsible diets; loss of valuable time for cancer patients by undergoing ineffective treatments; poliomyelitis and measles by refusing vaccination on advice of alternative practitioners (COST ACTION B4, *op. cit.*: 33). Complementary treatments may also be contra-indicated for patients pursuing conventional treatments (BOOZANG K. M. (II), *op. cit.*: 589).

position.[144] The problem, however, without underestimating the potential risk, is more a question of adequate training for alternative practitioners, co-operation between allopathic and non-allopathic practitioners,[145] and education of patients.[146]

In order to assess effectively the potential risks linked to alternative medicines, Germany is an example of country where there has been a long tradition of tolerant practice, and where incidents would theoretically have more chance to happen. However, Ehlers[147] notes, in relation to criminal prosecution, that even though Wimmer and Oepen have emphasised incidents due to "Heilpraktikers" and/or diagnostic or therapeutic mistakes, these incidents are quite rare.[148] The situation seems to be similar in other Western countries such as Great Britain,[149] Finland,[150] Switzerland[151] and the US.[152]

144 For a presentation of the problem of "assumption of risks" in the United States, see COHEN M. H. (I), *op. cit.*: 62–64.

145 Josefek stresses that "Unfortunately, many patients become isolated from their primary care physicians because of the belief that they will not work cooperatively with alternative practitioners to give patients complete integrated care" (JOSEFEK K. J., *op. cit.*: 305).

146 Boozang notes, "little information exists about the safety of CAM, and much concern exists about patients' complacency towards potential risks, frequently in the belief that alternative treatments are natural, and therefore not harmful" (BOOZANG K. M. (II), *op. cit.*: 587). For a development on the subject, see the same author at 586–604.

147 EHLERS A. P. F., *op. cit.*: 84–87.

148 The following cases have been reported: death and complications cases caused by acupuncture, ozone therapy, cell-therapy, neuraltherapy, unconventional cancer therapy, biologic substances, serum and extract organic substances, and homeopathy treatments.
In Germany, the Department of Health issued, in 1980, a report listing all such cases since 1976. It counted only 65 cases. There are no reliable empirical data regarding civil and criminal procedures involving alternative practitioners. Indeed, publications concerning this set of problems are rare and only published rulings are available. It seems that this set of problems is not (yet?) to main concern of governments.
Guillod also stresses that it is striking to observe the absence of civil actions against "Heilpraktikers" in Germany (GUILLOD O. (I), *op. cit.*: 31).

149 See chap. 4.3.3.3. See also STONE J., *op. cit.*: 189.

150 See chap. 4.3.3.8.

151 Guillod notes the absence of penal prosecutions in some Swiss cantons (Vaud, Neuchâtel), and the opinion of some health authorities that non-allopathic practitioners (in particular healers) do not constitute a substantial risk for public health (GUILLOD O. (I), *op. cit.*: 31). See also chap. 4.3.6.1.

152 See STUDDERT D. M., *op. cit.*: 1610–15 (the author found that claims against alternative practitioners occurred less frequently and typically involved injury

Another indicator of risks found to be linked with the providing of alternative medicines are sociological studies on the satisfaction of patients when using alternative treatments. Such studies show that only a few patients have had a bad experience such as a worsening health condition.[153]

Thus, it is possible to observe that, while risks linked with alternative medicines exist, they are usually less important than those linked to biomedical treatments.[154] As a result, the risk linked to the providing of alternative medicines may almost certainly be qualified as reasonable. However, such risk should never be underestimated and, as such, should always be carefully verified by appropriate clinical testing.[155]

6.6 Conclusion

Scientific validation is a crucial element in the regulation of 'alternative' medical techniques. Although scientific methods, in the restrictive sense, appear to be the best means at our disposal, and the most widely used in Western countries, they are not entirely satisfactory. As a result, one should be open minded, understanding that any scientific validation must be considered in a broad sense, and includes not only methods from the natural and physical sciences, but also from other sciences, which could be valuable, such as sociology or history. Moreover, one must also consider those elements that could lead to the future evolution of medicine.

---

that was less severe than claims against physicians during the same period). See also, e.g., COHEN M. H. (I), *op. cit.*: 66.

153 See chap. 2.5 for more details.

154 HEUSSER P., *op. cit.*: 12; SELECT COMMITTEE ON SCIENCE AND TECHNOLOGY, *op. cit.*: 33 ("there is no doubt that many CAM therapies are very safe, as compared to many new powerful conventional remedies").

155 The Swiss Federal Office of Social Insurance considers that the quality and security of alternative medicines are guaranteed through (HEUSSER P., *op. cit.*: 13):
1. a control of the training of practitioners providing alternative medicines (in Switzerland, only the treatments provided by physicians holding an FMH diploma in alternative medicines are covered by the social insurance);
2. the fulfilment of quality conditions for alternative drugs, as for allopathic drugs;
3. the setting up of strict practice guidelines regarding the advices that are given and products that are proposed to patients.

Scientific validation in the restrictive sense is the classical justification. As soon as such validation is established, it justifies the licensing and the coverage of a technique. In this respect, three parameters must be considered: the mechanism of action, the effectiveness of the technique and its safety. While the mechanism of action, in any case difficult to demonstrate for alternative medicines, is not indispensable, evidence of effectiveness is a decisive criterion. Although alternative medicines are usually unable to comply with evidence-based-medicine requisites, research guidelines are evolving, to more effectively address the specificities of alternative medicines.

Socio-historical validation is also valuable, and may justify both the licensing to practise and the coverage of alternative techniques. Its main component is the level of use of a technique. In principle, regulation on the licensing to practise should be envisaged as soon as the technique is safe, irrespective of whether the technique has been proven to be effective or not.

The coverage of alternative medicines requires that use of the technique must reach a reasonable level before regulation may be justified. Moreover, any evidence supporting the appropriateness and cost-effectiveness of the technique must first be demonstrated. However, it may also be brought in later, in order to validate the decision to regulate.

Finally, it seems that the risks associated with alternative medicines are generally of less importance than those risks linked to biomedical treatments. These risks may certainly be qualified as reasonable, but even if so qualified, they should not be underestimated and should always be carefully verified by clinical testing in order to ensure that alternative medicines are safely provided to the public.

7. Building a Regulatory Framework

7.1 Introduction

This chapter presents and analyses several possibilities for regulating the licensing and coverage of alternative medicines. In this respect, attention is focused on the principal choices that the lawmaker must make and how the selection of those choices gives the regulation its general form.

As will be seen, there has been much activity in recent years within Western countries. These evolutions and initiatives shall be analysed from a comparative perspective, in order to highlight the main features of current trends in the regulation of alternative medicines.

The regulatory fields influencing the licensing and coverage of alternative medicines are first presented in order that the reader may better understand the complete framework.

Education and standards of practice are crucial elements when setting up the regulatory framework. These two topics will close this chapter.

7.2 Influential Fields

7.2.1 Introduction

The licensing to practise and the coverage of alternative medicines are the two principal regulatory fields. However, other areas of importance such as patients' rights, criminal and civil liability, or drug regulation must also be taken into consideration when deciding to regulate alternative medicines.

Unfortunately, the scope of this study does not permit further development of these areas. However, it is important that the reader is provided with a brief overview of the legal framework surrounding alternative medicines. The purpose is to show the complexity of this set of problems and the interrelationship that exists between various regulatory fields. Similarly, a few international developments are presented in order to provide a comparison between various countries and to highlight some current trends among Western countries.

7.2.2 Patients' Rights

Bibliography

ANDREWS L. B., *The shadow health care system: Regulation of alternative health care providers*, in: Houston Law Review, 1996, vol. 32: 1273–1317; ANNAS G. J., *The right of patients*, 2nd edition, Humana Press, 1992, Totawa; BACKES O., *Die Rechtslage beim Einsatz wissenschaftlich nicht gesichter Therapieverfahren*, in: MELCHART D. (co-author: WAGNER H.), *Naturheilverfahren – Grundlagen einer autoregulativen Medizin*, K. F. Schattauer Verlagsges, Stuttgart, 1993: 550–69; BINDER M., *Zur Kostendeckung alternativmedizinischer Behandlungsmethoden durch die Krankenversicherung*, in: Recht der Medizin, 1997, vol. 4, n° 2: 39–44; BOOZANG K. M., *Western medicine opens the door to alternative medicine*, in: American Journal of Medicine, 1998, vol. 24, n° 2/3: 208–12; BORGHI M., *Droit fondamental à des thérapies alternatives ou complémentaires en psychiatrie?*, in: BORGHI M. (co-editor: GASSMAN J.), *Thérapies complémentaires ou alternatives en psychiatrie: Un défi? Un droit?*, Schriftenreihe der Schweizerischen Stiftung Pro Mente Sana n° 20, 1999, Zürich: 265–81; BRETT A. S. (co-author: MCCULLOUGH L. B.), *When patients request specific interventions*, in: New England Journal of Medicine, 1986, vol. 315: 1347ss; BRITISH MEDICAL ASSOCIATION (LAMONT T.), *Complementary medicine – New approaches to good practice*, Oxford University Press, 1993, Oxford/New York: 49–50; COHEN M. H. (I), *Complementary and alternative medicine – Legal boundaries and regulatory perspectives*, The Johns Hopkins University Press, 1998, London & Oxford; COMMISSIE ALTERNATIEVE GENEESWIJZEN, *Alternative geneeswijzen in Nederland*, Staatsuitgeverij, 1981, Den Haag; DE BIJL N. (co-author: NEDERVEEN-VAN DE KRAGT I.), *Legal safeguards against medical practice by not suitably qualified persons: A comparative study in seven EU-countries*, 1997, in: European Journal of Health Law, vol. 4: 15; FREUDENBERG U., *Der Leistungsanspruch bei alternativen Heilmethoden gegenüber der gesetzlichen Krankenversicherung, der privaten Krankenversicherung und der Beihilfe*, Dissertation, 1994, Bonn; FURROW B. R. (co-authors: GREANEY T. L., JOST T., SCHWARTZ R. L.) (I), *Health law*, West Publishing, 1995, St Paul: 67, 268–88; GASSMANN J., *Therapiewahlfreiheit in der stationären Psychiatrie – Auch für komplementäre Methoden!*, in: BORGHI M. (co-editor: GASSMAN J.), *Thérapies complémentaires ou alternatives en psychiatrie: Un défi? Un droit?*, Schriftenreihe der Schweizerischen Stiftung Pro Mente Sana n° 20, 1999, Zürich: 309–11; GRUNWALD D., *Pratiques médicales non éprouvées*, Session de l'Ordre des médecins, September 1997, Paris; GRUPP K., *Rechtliche Probleme alternativer Behandlungsmethoden*, in: MedR, 1992, vol. 5: 258–60; GUILLOD O. (VI), *Le consentement éclairé du patient*, Dissertation, Editions Ides et Calendes, 1986, Neuchâtel; JOST T. S., *Health care rationing in the courts: A comparative study*, in: Hasting International and Comparative Law Review, 1998, vol. 21, n° 3: 639–714; KARPMAN A., *Informed consent: Does the first amendment protect a patient's right to choose alternative treatment*, in: New York School of Human rights, Summer 2000: 667; MANAÏ D., *Les droits du patient face à la médecine contemporaine*, Helbing & Lichtenhahn, 1999, Basel/Genève/München; MILES S. H., *Informed demand for "non-benefi-*

cial" medical treatment, in: New England Journal of Medicine, 1991, vol. 325: 512ss; Paradis N., *Making a living off the dying*, in: New York Times, April 25, 1992; Patterson E. G., *Health care choice and the Constitution: Reconciling privacy and public health*, in: Rutgers Law Review, Fall 1989, vol. 42: 1–91; Péntek M., *Die Leistungspflicht der Gesetzlichen Krankenversicherung bei der Anwendung von Aussenseitermethoden in der Medizin*, Dissertation, 1996, Konstanz: 50–70; Robard I., *La santé hors la loi: Les hors la loi de la santé*, 4th ed., Ed. de l'Ancre, 1994, Suresnes: 88–92; Sage W. M. (co-author: Aiken L. H.), *Regulating interdisciplinary practice*, in: Jost T. S., *Regulation of the Healthcare Professions*, Health Administration Press, 1996, Chicago: 80–81, 87–88; Select Committee on Science and Technology, *Complementary and alternative medicine*, House of Lords – Session 1999–2000 6th Report, The Stationary Office, 2000, London: 9, 94ss; Shapiro A. K. (co-author: Shapiro E.) (I), *The powerful placebo – From ancient priest to modern physician*, The Johns Hopkins University Press, 1997, Baltimore/London: 237; Shultz M., *From informed consent to patient choice: A new protected interest*, in: Yale Law Journal, 1985, vol. 95: 229–33; Siebert A., *Strafrecthliche Grenzen ärtzlicher Therapiefreiheit*, Springer Verlag, 1983, Berlin/Heidelberg/New York: 133; Sprumont D., *Droit des patients: Survol de la législation*, in: Plaidoyer, 1998, n ° 4: 41–46; Steffen G., *Droit aux soins et rationnement: Approche d'une définition des soins nécessaires*, Stämpfli, 2002, Bern; Stone J. (co-author: Matthews J.), *Complementary medicine and the law*, Oxford University Press, 1996, Oxford: 179–80; Sugarman J. (II), *Informed consent, shared decision-making, and complementary and alternative medicine*, in: The Journal of Law, Medicine and Ethics, 2003, vol. 31, n° 2: 247–50; Swedish Commission on Alternative Medicine, *Report on alternative medicine*, Regeringskansliet, 1989, Stockholm: 26, 28; Wicki M., *Komplementärmedizin im Rahmen des Rechtes*, Dissertation, Stämpfli, 1998, Bern: 356–94; Wiegand W., *3. Kapitel – Die Aufklärungspflicht und die Folgen ihrer Verletzung*, in: Honsell H. (co-editor: Bär W.), *Handbuch des Artzrechtes*, Schulthess, 1994, Zürich: 139–41.

7.2.2.1 *General Remarks*

Human rights encompass patients' rights. While human rights express a set of principles that are strictly related to human dignity, patients' rights relate to the experience of a patient during a therapeutic relationship and to its legal consequences.[1]

Essentially, patients' rights are made of a whole series of rights, such as the right to have access to health care, to choose a health care provider, to obtain information, to accept or refuse a medical act, to self-determination, to access medical records, to preserve privacy and confidentiality or to make a decision about death and dying. In addition, the rights of relatives, the rights of patients during psychiatric treatments, or the rights of people undertaking clinical testing are also directly relevant.[2]

Although the nature and extent of these rights may vary from one country to another, they remain similar throughout the Western countries.[3] The purpose of this section is to provide the reader with some basic information regarding patients' rights that may have a role to play in the field of alternative medicines, such as the right to have access to health care, to choose a health care provider, to obtain information and to make a decision freely that is materialised through the principle of informed consent.[4]

7.2.2.2 *Right to Access to Health Care*

The right to (have access to) health care may be partial or complete. The right is complete when patients, in addition to being able to choose the treatment they want (partial right), may also obtain reimbursement for the treatment they receive (as a benefit).

1 MANAÏ D., *op. cit.*: 16. According to the author, the concept of patient's rights includes as well, in its broad meaning, the legal and ethical thinking about the status of the ill person, as a free and autonomous individual, who nevertheless is dependent and fragile because of the illness (idem). See also SPRUMONT D., *op. cit.*: 41–42.

2 MANAÏ D., *op. cit.*: 16–17. For a development of these rights, see the same author, at 115–260. See also ANNAS G. J., *op. cit.*; SPRUMONT D., *op. cit.*: 41–46. In Switzerland, several cantonal statutes now include some of these rights, such as the statutes of cantons Fribourg, Geneva, Vaud or Valais.

3 For a comparative study on the subject, see GUILLOD O. (VI), *op. cit.*

4 Some patients' rights require duties from health care providers, such as the provision of information regarding the health of the patient and available treatments.

Recently, this right has been incorporated legislatively in various statutes.[5] However, the extent of such right is relative, and its implementation depends upon the organisation and financing of the health care system.[6] In Switzerland, for example, art. 3 of the Federal Act on Health Insurance (FAHI) provides that all Swiss residents must have health insurance. However, the benefit is limited as only medical acts that have been recognised as effective, appropriate and economic are covered (art. 32 of FAHI). Thus, by covering medical acts deemed necessary, the FAHI guarantees a certain level of access to health care. As far as alternative medicines are concerned, the Swiss government has decided to include some alternative medicines in the benefits catalogue,[7] which is covered under the compulsory social insurance.

In Germany and in the United States, a right to access to alternative medicines has been permitted, to some extent, to those benefiting from the coverage of insurance funds.

The right to have access to alternative medicines is guaranteed by German law under specific conditions.[8] The property and equal protection rights of persons required by law to be insured would be violated if there were major gaps in their coverage, because supplemental commercial

5 E.g., in the relevant statutes of Swiss cantons Berne, Jura, Neuchâtel, Ticino and Valais. For an international perspective, see BORGHI M., *op. cit.*: 266–68 (the author stresses that rules adopted at the international level do not create any obligation for states, merely a moral commitment).

6 The Swiss Federal Court has admitted the principle that every person has a fundamental right to have minimal conditions for a decent life. Given that health care is a minimal condition necessary to reach such standard of life, one may consider that the right to have access to health care is a fundamental right. See ATF 121 I 367; ATF 122 I 101; ATF 126 III 353; ATF 127 III 68; ATF 127 III 289. For a development regarding the implementation of this right at the Swiss level, see BORGHI M., *op. cit.*: 268ss; STEFFEN G., *op. cit.*

7 Namely, homeopathy, Chinese medicine, anthroposophic medicine, neural therapy and phytotherapy.

8 E.g., when an allopathic treatment and an alternative treatment are both available, but that side effects are related to the allopathic treatment, or there are risks, in general or specifically for the patient, the use of alternative medicines is reimbursed.
In Germany, a total ban on coverage for services not listed in the evidence-based-medicine would also violate various constitutional rights, such as the right of doctors to professional freedom, the right of self-determination and personal integrity of persons who are required by law to be insured.
On this subject, see GRUPP K., *op. cit.*: 258–60. For further development, see FREUDENBERG U, *op. cit.*, PÉNTEK M., *op. cit.*: 50–70.

insurance is neither affordable, nor available to fill the gaps.[9] In the same perspective, some Austrian commentators consider that, as soon as an alternative medicine is taught in a medical faculty, physicians should have the opportunity to recommend it, and patients to choose it, under the coverage of social insurance.[10]

In the United States, there are various Mandate Benefit Acts that require insurers to cover certain benefits. For example, forty-six states require insurers to reimburse for chiropractic care, and at least six states require reimbursement for acupuncture. Similarly, Mandate Provider Acts require insurers to reimburse services offered by various alternative practitioners whether or not the insurer would cover the service when provided by a physician.[11] Andrews writes "several commentators have suggested that the constitutional right to privacy might encompass an individual's right to choose a treatment not currently accessible under the law".[12]

7.2.2.3 Right to Choose the Health Care Provider

The right to choose the health care provider is guaranteed by several regulations.[13] For example, art. 41 of the Swiss FAHI states that an insured person may choose among those recognised health care providers who are able to treat their illness. The right to choose is an important pre-condition to create a relationship of trust between a patient and the selected health care practitioner. However, the right may be limited as health care

9 Art. 1 and 2 Grundgesetz. For more details, see JOST T. S., *op. cit.*: 667.

10 BINDER M., *op. cit.*: 43–44.

11 Sage undelines the extent of these statutes, noting that the Employee Retirement Income Security Act of 1974 preempts state efforts to regulate the payment practices of employer-sponsored health plans. For example, States may not enforce Mandate Benefit Acts against the growing number of employers who self-insure (SAGE W. M., *op. cit.*: 80–81).
Also of note is the initiative of Senator Thomas Daschle who introduced, in 1994, the Access to Medical Treatment Act to the US Senate. The purpose of the Act, still to be enacted, was to provide health care consumers with increased access to alternative medicines and to allow greater opportunity for the trial of alternative treatments.

12 ANDREWS L. B., *op. cit.*: 1312. For further development, see the same author at 1312ss.

13 The right to access to health care and the right to choose a health care provider have two dimensions. First, the licensing framework must be such as to allow patients to seek help from authorised health care providers. Second, the coverage framework must be designed in such a way as to cover the treatments provided by the practitioner.

practitioners may refuse to take care of a patient[14] and as they may not have the competence to treat the patient.[15]

With respect to alternative medicines, some insurance companies have introduced a direct access to alternative practitioners allowing patients access to the type of treatment they want. In the US, for example, Freedom of Choice Acts guarantee patients an easier access to alternative medicines. These Acts allow insured persons to obtain care from any licensed professional and to claim reimbursement regardless of whether there is a contract between the professional and the insurance plan. In the same perspective, the Any Willing Provider Acts require insurers to contract with, and reimburse the services of any practitioner willing to meet their basic terms and conditions.[16]

7.2.2.4 *Informed Consent*

A patient visits a physician because the recovery of his or her health requires competences he or she does not possess. The patient must give the physician sufficient information to establish a diagnosis. On this basis, the physician will propose a treatment or procedure. However, the physician will not be allowed to treat the patient until the patient has been provided with information as to what the physician intends to do and the patient has agreed to the proposed treatment or procedure.[17] The information

14 However, in an emergency case, health care practitioners may not refuse to take care of a patient.

15 In Switzerland, the FAHI put some limits to this right, in particular for in-patient care outside the canton. Furthermore, this right is restricted when the patient chooses to be part of a managed care structure.
For further development regarding the situation in the US, see PATTERSON E. G., *op. cit.*: 1–91.

16 Similarly, a statute that the State of Washington enacted as part of its health care reform, requires that state health plans allow every category of health care provider to provide health care services for conditions included in the basic health plan services, subject to certain conditions. See also ANDREWS L. B., *op. cit.*: 1308ss, in particular 1312–13; BINDER M., *op. cit.*: 43–44 (regarding the situation in Austria).

17 Annas stresses that the consent must be "competent, voluntary, informed, and understanding" (ANNAS G. J., *op. cit.*: 89). The author writes "information is power, and because information sharing inevitably results in decision sharing, the doctrine of informed consent has helped transform the doctor–patient relationship. [...] Informed consent is the most important legal doctrine in both the doctor–patient relationship and treatment in health care facilities. [...] Not only is it important because of its implications for power and accountability, but it is also important because many of the other rights patients have are either derived from or enhanced by the doctrine of informed consent" (idem, at 83).

that the patient receives must include all those aspects that may influence his or her decision.[18]

In practice, the information provided to the patient includes the following, which must be presented in such a way as to be easily understood:[19, 20]

1. a description of the diagnosis and the recommended treatment or procedure, including information regarding modalities and length. The major problems anticipated in recuperation, and the time period during which the patient will not be able to resume his or her normal activities;
2. a description of the risks and benefits of the recommended procedure, with special emphasis on risks leading to death or serious bodily disability. Information regarding the result if no treatment is undertaken, the probability of success, and what the physician means by success, must also be provided;
3. a description of the alternatives, including other treatments or procedures, together with the risks and benefits of these alternatives;
4. any other information generally provided to patients in this situation by other qualified physicians, such as the cost of the treatment, or the correct way the patient must behave.

After taking into consideration the information provided by the physician, the patient may decide to undergo the treatment recommended by the physician, to accept an alternative treatment, or to refuse the treatment altogether.[21]

Although physicians must provide patients with information concerning alternative forms of treatment such information does not usually encompass non-biomedical treatments. Cohen points out that, in the US, "the informed consent doctrine, as presently conceived, insufficiently protects

18 ANNAS G. J., *op. cit.*: 83–85; COHEN M. H. (I), *op. cit.*: 60; MANAÏ D., *op. cit.*: 115–17.

19 The principles listed below apply to both allopathic and alternative practitioners. For a development, see SUGARMAN J. (II), *op. cit.*: 247–50.

20 ANNAS G. J., *op. cit.*: 86–87; BACKES O., *op. cit.*: 554–62; COHEN M. H. (I), *op. cit.*: 60; FURROW B. R. (I), *op. cit.*: 268–79; GUILLOD O. (VI), *op. cit.*; MANAÏ D., *op. cit.*: 118–20; WICKI M., *op. cit.*: 356–94.

21 Paradis has reported a true story that illustrates the total disregard shown by an impersonal healthcare system towards the principle of free and informed consent, where a patient diagnosed with terminal pancreatic cancer had to endure medical procedures against his will (PARADIS N., *op. cit.*).

patients' interests in therapies outside biomedicine".[22] For example, a Louisiana appellate court held that disclosure of alternatives to chemotherapy was not required, since "in conventional medical wisdom, the alternative to chemotherapy in this situation would simply be to not undergo chemotherapy".[23] Similarly, in Great Britain, Stone states, "until now, a very narrow view has been taken of the duty that a conventional practitioner owes a patient to give information about alternatives to the treatment proposed. Invariably, this has been seen as options (including no treatment at all) within orthodox medicine".[24]

Although physicians usually do not provide information about alternative treatments, there is a trend towards favouring an expansion in the information provided in both biomedical and alternative treatments, which results in a right to possibly choose between these two types of treatment. In the US, Schultz maintains that vindicating patients' autonomy by requiring disclosure of certain information should not depend on whether the information is the kind that physicians usually disclose. Rather, the information should incorporate the full spectrum of available treatments, in order to fill the patient's need for information.[25] There are also some court

22 COHEN M. H. (I), *op. cit.*: 60.

23 *Plumber v. Dep't of Health and Human Resources*, 634 So.2d 1347 (La. Ct. App. 1994), *cert. denied*, 637 So. 2d 1056 (La. 1994). On this subject, FURROW states that "patients have attempted to claim a constitutional right to choose a particular form of health care treatment in the face of statutory prohibitions against the provision of health care services they desire. These claims have singularly been unsuccessful [...], except in the cases of access to abortion or contraceptives which implicate the heightened constitutional status of reproductive decision making" (FURROW B. R. (I), *op. cit.*: 67).
An important reason for not expanding the information provided to patients on alternative medicines is that the physician proposing such alternatives may face civil lawsuits and disciplinary risks in the US. On this subject, see KARPMAN A., *op. cit.*: 943–44.

24 STONE J., *op. cit.*: 179. In France, physicians are also hindered if they wish to provide information on alternative medicines to patients. See ROBARD I., *op. cit.*: 88–92 (citing the case of a physician who was prosecuted for providing to his patients a booklet about iridology). See also GRUPP K., *op. cit.*: 258–60 (situation in Germany).

25 SHULTZ M., *op. cit.*: 229–33. For a development regarding health care freedom, see COHEN M. H. (I), *op. cit.*: 81–86, 112–14.
See also the opinion of Miles regarding terminally ill patients. The author notes that a patient's entitlement to treatment can be more important than a patient's choice in using the entitlement, especially in cases where treatment is futile (MILES S. H., *op. cit.*: 514). According to Boozang "until safety and efficacy data become available, physicians should not offer or accede to patient demands for

rulings moving in this direction. For example, a Connecticut appellate court upheld the patient's informed consent claim in a case where a physician had failed to inform the patient that corrective surgery was elective and that a more conservative treatment plan was an option.[26] The court considered that the physician had breached the duty to obtain informed consent by failing to disclose a viable alternative that might have produced a less perfect result but that may have represented a safer or less invasive procedure.[27] Also of note are various court rulings regarding the doctrine of assumption of risks, which shifts the focus from the physician's decision making to the patient's choice of treatment.[28] This expanded view of the informed consent doctrine may lead physicians to propose alternative treatments if they are required to disclose safe and efficacious treatments outside biomedicine.[29]

---

unproven treatments. [...] Once an alternative therapy is shown to be curative, or important to patient wellness, physicians become obliged to include such options among those they offer to their patients" (BOOZANG K. M., *op. cit.*: 210). The author leaves open the possibility for the physician to propose "experimental" treatments to patients, which could also be non-biomedical (idem at 210–12). See also BRETT A. S., *op. cit.*: 1347ss.

26 *Gemme v. Goldberg*, 626 A.2d 318 (Conn. App. Ct. 1993).

27 See also *Andrews v. Ballard*, 498 F. Supp. 1038 (S.D. Tex. 1980) (regarding the constitutional right to obtain acupuncture treatment).

28 In *Schneider v. Revici* the court concluded that the evidence that Schneider had assumed the risk of refusing conventional treatment to undergo the Revici method (to treat breast cancer) was sufficient to allow the jury to consider the assumption-of-risk defence. This conclusion was supported by evidence mainly constituted by the signed detailed consent form acknowledging that Revici's treatment lacked FDA approval, and that no guarantees were made as the results. Actually, the Revici treatment did not result in positive effects, and Schneider who refused at first a biopsy had eventually to undergo a mastectomy as well as sixteen months of chemotherapy (*Schneider v. Revici*, 817 F.2d 987 (2d Cir. 1987)). See also *Boyle v. Revici*, 961 F.2d 1060 (2d Cir. 1992).

29 In this respect, Cohen states that "the doctrine of informed consent could [...] evolve to under-gird a right of access to complementary and alternative medicine. Whereas the respectable minority and clinical innovation doctrines serve as shields to liability, expanded informed consent rules, like more inclusive standards of care, serve to stimulate greater physician use of complementary and alternative therapies" (COHEN M. H. (I), *op. cit.*: 61).
Similarly, Karpman notes that "certain state courts and legislative bodies have demonstrated a positive trend in enhancing the medical freedom of the physicians to counsel, and implementing alternative treatments, as well as promoting the patient's right to receive all of the necessary information to make a medical decision" (KARPMAN A., *op. cit.*: 956–57). See also ANDREWS L. B., *op. cit.*: 1308ss.

Various commentators have taken different approaches as to whether physicians must inform patients about alternative medicines or not. Siebert writes that physicians must inform patients only about those techniques that are taught within medical faculties, which do not include alternative medicines,[30] and that patients should be informed about these possibilities only if the patient requests such information.[31] Wiegand differs in his approach in that he considers that information about alternative medicines should be provided when the alternative technique has reached a certain level of scientific recognition.[32, 33] Wicki is of the opinion that the information must be provided only when the effectiveness of alternative techniques has been clearly demonstrated.[34] In our view, however, the criterion of effectiveness must be put into its perspective. Indeed, as demonstrated above, several biomedical treatments or drugs are advised and provided to patients, even though their effectiveness has not been rigorously demonstrated.[35] Therefore, care must be taken with any use of such treatments or drugs. The criterion of education, namely that information on a technique should be provided as soon as the technique is taught in medical schools, is more likely to be implemented. Indeed, it demonstrates that a technique has a substantial potential to heal that may be of interest to patients, irrespective of whether its effectiveness has been demonstrated or not. The Swedish Commission on Alternative Medicine has gone further considering "it is important that the value of different alternative therapies be tested scientifically. However, the right of people to choose between therapies available must be respected, regardless of the scientific value a therapy may be considered to have".[36]

30 SIEBERT A., *op. cit.*: 133.
31 This criterion may be difficult to implement. Indeed, there are a growing number of courses on alternative medicines within medical faculties. Therefore, one may wonder which information should be communicated to patients.
32 E.g., the use of acupuncture to treat some rheumatism illnesses.
33 WIEGAND W., *3. op. cit.*: 139–41.
34 WICKI M., *op. cit.*: 366.
35 E.g., there is no scientific proof concerning the effectiveness of psychotherapy. For a development on this area, see chap. 6.
36 SWEDISH COMMISSION ON ALTERNATIVE MEDICINE, *op. cit.*: 26. The author adds that "in the health services, it should be permissible to use alternative forms of treatment if the patient has expressed a desire for such treatment, if the type of treatment is not dangerous and if it is only given after generally accepted methods have been used or is given in conjunction with such methods" (idem, at 28).
In the Netherlands, part of the medical profession was opposed to ending to the monopoly. It attempted to retain the legal monopoly by arguing the effectiveness of these therapies was not scientifically proven. However, the Minister of Health stated that the argument was not convincing enough, because the public

In order to guarantee the right to choose alternative treatments, it is necessary that physicians have the knowledge to provide accurate information to patients on alternative forms of treatment. This requirement implies that physicians must have been trained in alternative medicines, or that they have, at least, sufficient knowledge to properly advise patients.[37]

7.2.2.5 Summary

Patients' rights have evolved in recent years leading to their integration within recent regulations dealing with access to medical treatment, health care providing and health insurance.

The right to access alternative health care has been taken into account in some regulations. While the majority of Western countries allow for the licensing of alternative practitioners to practise (under some conditions), some countries have gone further by covering the treatments provided by alternative practitioners. For example, in the US, Mandate Benefit Acts require insurers to cover certain benefits such as chiropractic or acupuncture sessions.

The right of a patient to choose the health care provider follows the same pattern of extension. For example, some insurance companies have introduced direct access to alternative practitioners to allow patients to have access to the type of treatment they want.

Similarly, although physicians do not usually have to provide information about alternative treatments, there is a growing trend favouring an expansion of the information made available to patients, including both biomedical and alternative treatments. This is in accordance with

---

demand for freedom of choice in medicine is more important than generating new laws than scientific verification (COMMISSIE ALTERNATIEVE GENEESWIJZEN, *op. cit.*).

Stone states that "the more that is known about alternative therapies, the more plausible it is to make a case establishing a legal duty on the part of an orthodox practitioner to recommend an alternative therapy, if this is the most appropriate form of treatment for the patient. [...] The more evidence becomes available as to the efficacy of certain complementary therapies, the less justifiable it will be for GPs not to consider referring patients to an appropriately trained complementary therapist" (STONE J. *op. cit.*: 179–80).

For recent developments regarding the right to choose an alternative treatment in psychiatry, see GASSMANN J., *op. cit.*: 309–11.

37 The set of problems that arises when considering the training of alternative practitioners will not be explored here. For an overview of the education in alternative medicines for physicians, see chap. 3. For proposals regarding specifically education, see chap. 7.5.2.2.

the current view of health care in the Western world, where patients have become more aware and informed about medical possibilities, are more responsible, and thus ask for greater freedom of choice.[38]

Finally, it is possible to envisage that the development of patients' rights related to alternative medicines will contribute to the setting up of a more favourable legal framework for non-biomedical health care.

7.2.3 Malpractice and criminal liability

Bibliography

ANDREWS L. B., *The shadow health care system: Regulation of alternative health care providers*, in: Houston Law Review, 1996, vol. 32: 1285; COHEN M. H. (I), *Complementary and alternative medicine – Legal boundaries and regulatory perspectives*, The Johns Hopkins University Press, 1998, London & Oxford: 56–72, 110–11; CORBOZ B., *Les principales infractions – Volume II*, Stämpfli, 1999, Bern: 63ss; CRAMER R., *Strafrechtliche Grenzen der Therapiefreiheit und der Heilbehandlung durch den Heilpraktiker*, Dissertion, 1995, Köln: 183–84, 189; DRECHSLER C. T., *Physicians, surgeons and other healers*, in: American Jurisprudence, 2nd edition, April 1996: § 213; EHLERS A. P. F., *Medizin in den Händen von Heilpraktikern – "Nicht-Heilkundigen"*, Springer Verlag, 1995, Berlin/Heidelberg: 199–268; EISENBERG D. M. (III), *Advising patients who seek alternative medical therapies*, in: Ann. Intern. Med., 1997; n° 127: 61–69; FURROW B. R. (co-authors: GREANEY T. L., JOST T., SCHWARTZ R. L.) (I), *Health law*, West Publishing, 1995, St Paul: 237; GOLDBERG B. D., *As alternative increases, so malpractice claims*, in: Med. Malpractice l. & Strategy, 1999, vol. 16, n° 7: 1ss; GRUPP K., *Rechtliche Probleme alternativer Behandlungsmethoden*, in: MedR, 1992, vol. 5: 258–60; JOSEFEK K. J., *Alternative medicine's roadmap to mainstream*, in: American Journal of Law and Medicine, 2000, vol. 26: 304–05; JUNG H. (co-author: NEUMANN J. N.), *Alternative Behandlungsmethoden*, in: ESER (co-authors: LUTTEROTTI, SPORKEN), *Lexikon Medizin – Ethik – Recht*, Freiburg, 1989: 59–61; KILGORE C., *Expanding coverage signals growing demand, acceptance for alternative care*, in: Medicine & Health Perspectives, May 4 1998: 1–4; LAUFS A., *Sorgfaltspflichten des Heilpraktikers*, in: MedR, 1991, n° 4: 195–98; LAWLOR J. D., *Chiropractor's liability for failure to refer patient to medical practitioner*, in: A.L.R. 3d, 1975–1998, vol. 58: 590ss; MANAÏ D., *Les droits du patient face à la médecine contemporaine*, Helbing & Lichtenhahn, 1999, Basel/Genève/München: 115–16; ROBARD I., *La santé hors la loi: Les hors la loi de la santé*, 4th ed., Ed. de l'Ancre, 1994, Suresnes: 88ss; SAGE W. M. (co-author: AIKEN L. H.), *Regulating interdisciplinary practice*, in: JOST T. S., *Regulation*

38 Shapiro notes that "today more patients are taking a more active role in their treatment. Patients seek greater individual responsibility and an active, independent role" (SHAPIRO A. K. (I), *op. cit.*: 237). See also SAGE W. M., *op. cit.*: 87–88.

of the Healthcare Professions, Health Administration Press, 1996, Chicago: 71–101; STONE J. (co-author: MATTHEWS J.), *Complementary medicine and the law*, Oxford University Press, 1996, Oxford: 161–82; STRATENWERTH G., *Schweizerisches Strafrecht – Besonderer Teil I: Straftaten gegen Individualinteressen*, 5th ed., Stämpfli, 1995, Bern: 58ss; STUDDERT D. M. and co-authors, *Medical malpractice implications of alternative medicine*, in: JAMA, 1998, vol. 280, n° 18: 1610–15; WICKI M., *Komplementärmedizin im Rahmen des Rechtes*, Dissertation, Stämpfli, 1998, Bern: 259–309.

7.2.3.1 General Remarks

In the field of alternative medicines, regulations dealing with malpractice and criminal liability play an important role. Although these rules may differ from one jurisdiction to another, the underlying principles are similar. When an injury occurs, a court will apply malpractice liability principles to establish whether a practitioner breached the requisite standard of care and if so, to potentially award damages for such injury. A practitioner may also be held criminally liable if the injury or death occurred during the actual treatment of a patient.

These liability principles are applied instead of, or in addition to any existing rules dealing with alternative medicines and become particularly important where no regulation specific to alternative medicines has been enacted.[39] A brief overview of these liabilities is outlined below.[40]

7.2.3.2 Malpractice Liability

A. General remarks

A practitioner is usually subject to malpractice liability as a result of unskillful practice that fails to conform to the required standard of care[41] in the

39 Lawmakers take into consideration malpractice liability, education and standards of practice issues when deciding to set up licensing regulations. This is a clear demonstration of the interaction that exists among these fields. For example, prosecutors take into account the level of knowledge that a diligent practitioner should have in order to provide the best possible care. On the other hand, because there is a potential risk of prosecution, there is an impetus for educational standards to be developed and improved.

40 For a discussion on the criminal liability that may apply when a practitioner infringes a defined scope of practice, or helps a non-licensed practitioner to provide health care, see chap. 7.3.4.

41 Defined in the US as a failure to exercise "the required degree of care, skill and diligence" under the circumstances (*Baderbessono v. Michels*, 91 Cal. Rptr. 760, 764, 478 P.2d 480, 484 (Cal.1970)).
For further discussion of existing standards of care, see chap. 7.5.3.

profession, resulting in injury or death to the patient.[42] Both physicians and non-physician alternative practitioners may face potential liability under a malpractice claim.

B. Situation of allopathic practitioners

When physicians provide alternative techniques, they depart (by definition) from biomedical norms of practice. For this reason, they may already risk liability for malpractice.[43]

When patients have been injured, several questions may arise. The behaviour of the physician when engaged in alternative medical practice is usually compared either with the biomedical standard he or she should have applied or with an existing standard of practice of the specific alternative technique.[44] An interesting example of this in the US is the use of chelation therapy[45] to treat arteriosclerosis.[46] Although the use of chelation therapy is not prohibited by the rules of the Federal and Drug Administration (FDA), physicians using it risk liability under state medical practice rules. Indeed, in a malpractice action, the patient will claim that bypass surgery is the standard procedure for the specific condition, and that chelation therapy falls below the accepted standard of care.[47] In Italy, courts and the Physician Code of Professional Ethics allow physicians to use alternative medicines. However, they also state that physicians using these techniques have to assume the consequences of taking patients away from allopathic medicine, which presupposes that if an injury occurs, the behaviour of alternative physicians will be judged according to biomedical standards.

42 COHEN M. H. (I), *op. cit.*: 56; FURROW B. R. (I), *op. cit.*: 237.

43 In this case, the physician is also likely to face a disciplinary, professional or criminal sanction. This will depend upon state regulations. See, for example, the case of a French physician who was sentenced for having advised patients and practitioners to employ non-biomedical therapies in order to treat some forms of cancer (ROBARD I., *op. cit.*: 88ss).

44 For a development regarding the situation in Great Britain, see STONE J., *op. cit.*: 161ss.

45 For a description of this therapy, see Glossary.

46 For further discussion on this area, see COHEN M. H. (I), *op. cit.*: 56–59.

47 The use of chelation therapy for the treatment of arteriosclerosis is not a generally accepted treatment in medical literature and lacks FDA approval.
A statute even provides that using chelation therapy to treat medical conditions, excepting heavy metal poisoning, without FDA approval, constitutes unprofessional conduct (Ariz. Rev. Stat. § 32–1401 (gg) (iii)).
See *Ireland v. Eckerly*, 1989 Minn. App. LEXIS 13, at 3 (Minn. Ct. App., Jan. 10, 1989).

In France, Luxembourg and Spain, codes of professional ethics state that physicians are not allowed to suggest to their patients the use of non-scientifically proven techniques. A breach of these duties is an element that civil courts may take into account when considering a malpractice action.

The doctrine of informed consent usually does not encompass therapies outside biomedicine.[48] However, in the future, the duty to inform could evolve so as to include information about alternative techniques. As a result, alternative physicians could become less likely to face a malpractice action if they advise an alternative treatment.[49] It is conceivable that even physicians could face such action if they refused to advise their patients of an alternative treatment.[50]

Physicians may potentially defend their actions by arguing that such treatment constitutes the "respectable minority" (or "two schools of thought"),[51] or a clinical innovation. However, these defences are limited. A better argument may be made by utilising the doctrine of assumption of risks in order to avoid an action.[52]

The best defense for physicians against a malpractice action remains the existence of biomedical research and established medical education demonstrating that the alternative treatment is an appropriate choice for the condition. In this scenario, an alternative treatment may become the standard to treat a health care condition.[53]

48 See chap. 7.2.2.4. See also COHEN M. H. (I), *op. cit.*: 60–62.

49 E.g., in Austria, physicians are allowed to use alternative medicines, provided they have the agreement of their patients. Similarly, the Spanish Code of Medical Professional Ethics in Catalonia provides that physicians using alternative medicines must inform their patients about the necessity to continue a medical treatment and about the non-conventional character of the treatment.

50 For further discussion, see chap. 7.2.2.4.

51 For further discussion, see chap. 6.3.4.

52 For further discussion, see chap. 7.2.2.4.

53 Cohen writes that "as medical schools further incorporate complementary and alternative therapies into the curricula, and conventional physicians increase their use of complementary and alternative therapies or their referral of patients to providers of such therapies, standards of care in medical communities and in medical practice will begin to incorporate these modalities" (COHEN M. H. (I), *op. cit.*: 58–59). For a development on the subject, see the same author at 56–59, 111. See also GOLDBERG B. D., *op. cit.*: 1ss.

Physicians may also face a malpractice action by referring patients to non-allopathic practitioners.[54] Usually, when physicians decide to do so, they retain clinical responsibility for their patients.[55]

C. Situation of non-allopathic practitioners

Non-allopathic practitioners are also likely to face malpractice liability action.[56] Some US states hold this category of practitioners to a professional standard of care and thus provide a statutory definition for the standard of care to be applied.[57] It is difficult to determine precisely which procedures are within the standard of care for alternative medicine, since outside biomedicine, standards are more fluid. However, some professions have established guidelines for practice that may become a basis for standards of care in malpractice actions.[58]

When there is an overlap in an area of knowledge or treatment between allopathic and alternative medicines, non-allopathic practitioners may be held to a heightened, biomedical standard of care. Thus, US courts will judge the non-allopathic practitioner against that of a reasonable physician under similar circumstances.[59] In Germany, principles guiding "Heilpraktikers" malpractice liability are the same as those applying to a physician's liability. Thus, "Heilpraktikers" are judged as if they were physicians, in the same situation.[60]

54 EISENBERG D. M. (III), *op. cit.*: 61–69; JOSEFEK K. J., *op. cit.*: 304–05; SAGE W. M., *op. cit.*: 89; STUDDERT D. M., *op. cit.*: 1610–15.

55 See STONE J., *op. cit.*: 161–82 (Great Britain). In the US, Kilgore states that the fear of physicians to refer patients to acupuncturists is irrational as there is no case law to support it. Furthermore, their legal exposure in sending a patient suffering from back pain to a spine surgeon is hundreds of times higher (KILGORE C., *op. cit.*: 2–3).

56 A US court held in a case concerning chiropractic that the plaintiff had the burden of proving "the degree of knowledge and skill possessed or the degree of care ordinarily exercised" by practicing chiropractors in similar circumstances (*Piazza v. Behrman* Chiropractic Clinic, 601 So. 2d 1378, 1379 (La. 1992)).

57 In Nevada, e.g., homeopathic malpractice is defined as "failure on the part of a homeopathic physician to exercise the degree of care, diligence and skill ordinarily exercised by homeopathic physicians in good standing in the community in which he practices" (Nev. Rev. Stat. § 630A.060).

58 COHEN M. H. (I), *op. cit.*: 64ss; DRECHSLER C. T., *op. cit.*: § 213. For a further discussion on this subject, see chap. 7.6.3.

59 See *Wengel*, 473 N.W.2d at 744. For a development on the subject, see COHEN M. H. (I), *op. cit.*: 66–67.

60 EHLERS A. P. F., *op. cit.*: 199–236; LAUFS A., *op. cit.*: 195–98.

Non-allopathic practitioners may also be obliged to provide clear information to their patients about their training and skills. Thus, in Germany, "Heilpraktikers" must also provide clear information to their patients about their knowledge, skills and the risks of treatments in order to obtain an informed consent from their patients.[61] In Swiss canton Geneva, non-allopathic practitioners are allowed to practise if the treatments they provide are non-dangerous and if they clearly inform their patients about the nature of their practice. In Swiss canton Ticino and Valais, non-allopathic practitioners must also clearly inform their patients that they do not have an allopathic education.[62]

Non-allopathic practitioners may also face malpractice litigation if they fail to refer the patient to a biomedical professional.[63] In the US, for example, courts and State statutes have set up guidelines regarding the duty to refer.[64] Various other countries have also enacted rules to ensure a good relationship between allopathic and alternative practitioners. For example, in Belgium, registered alternative practitioners must take precautions to avoid patients being deprived of biomedical treatments. Prior to any treatment, they must obtain from their patients a recent diagnosis from a

61 CRAMER R., *op. cit.*: 183–84, 189; GRUPP K., *op. cit.*: 258–60; JUNG H., *op. cit.*: 59–61; LAUFS A. (II), *op. cit.*: 195–98.

62 Similarly, in Swiss Canton Fribourg, the Public Health Act states that non-allopathic practitioners may provide any alternative technique they want, as long as they have been trained for it. Such a legal rule could constitute an element for a possible malpractice action.

63 For a development regarding the limits of scope of practices, see chap. 7.3.3 and 7.3.4.

64 E.g., courts impose a duty of reasonable care when treating patients with chiropractic. Further duties include the duty to determine if the patient presents a problem treatable through chiropractic, to refrain from further chiropractic treatment when the patient's condition will not be responsive to further treatment, and if the problem is outside the chiropractor's skills, to inform the patient that the condition is not treatable through chiropractic (*Kerman v. Hintz*, 418 N.W.2d 795, 802–03 (Wis. 1988)).
See also, e.g., Minn. Stat. § 147B.06.I (a) (before treating a patient, the acupuncturist must ask whether the patient has been examined by a licensed physician and must review the diagnosis).
Andrews observes that, "the fact that the patients of physician assistants and advanced practice nurses fare as well as those of physicians indicates that these alternative providers accurately perceive the limits of their abilities and refer complicated patients to physicians" (ANDREWS L. B., *op. cit.*: 1285).
For further development on the subject, see COHEN M. H. (I), *op. cit.*: 68–69; LAWLOR J. D., *op. cit.*: 590ss.

physician.[65] In the same perspective, the British and Hungarian regulations provide that non-allopathic practitioners cannot contradict instructions or prescriptions given by physicians. In Malta, patients diagnosed as suffering from an infectious disease must be referred to a registered medical practitioner for treatment.[66] Some commentators have also stressed the importance of referring patients to physicians when it is necessary, and of informing patients that the treatment will not be covered by insurance.[67] Non-allopathic practitioners are also vulnerable to misrepresentation when they make claims exceeding the boundaries of their own professional training and skill.[68] In Finland, non-allopathic practitioners are allowed to provide health care as long as they do not pretend to be health care professionals.[69] In Switzerland, non-allopathic practitioners are not allowed to use an allopathic recognised title.

7.2.3.3 Criminal Liability

Alternative practitioners may face criminal liability in several cases. Typically, they may be prosecuted for injuring, or killing a patient, when providing health care.[70] They may also infringe a defined scope of practice, or help non-licensed practitioners to do so.[71]

Health and bodily integrity are usually viewed as fundamental rights.[72] Every infringement on health or bodily integrity is an offence, even when provided by health care providers. However, health care providers are not prosecuted if, prior to the treatment, they received the informed consent of the patient.[73]

65 The situation is similar in Hungary.
66 The Spanish Code of Medical Professional Ethics in Catalonia provides that physicians using alternative medicines have to co-ordinate their action with the physician in charge of the basic treatment.
67 BRITISH MEDICAL ASSOCIATION, *op.cit.*: 46–48; GUILLOD O. (I), *op.cit.*: 39; SWEDISH COMMISSION ON ALTERNATIVE MEDICINE, *op.cit.*: 27.
68 E.g., in claiming that osteopathy may cure cancer or diabetes.
69 They may not provide medical acts restricted to physicians, or practise in the public services.
70 Health care insurance fund fraud may also be prosecuted, as well as infringing professional secrecy. Formerly, non-licensed practitioners were also sentenced for charlatanism. These problems will not be developed in this research.
71 This topic is presented in chap. 7.3.4.
72 See the decision of the Swiss Federal Court ATF 104 Ia 486.
73 E.g., the new Dutch Act on Health Care Professionals considers any injury to any person's health an offence. The purpose is to make health care providers aware of their responsibility when providing health care. The Dutch perspective is sensible. Indeed, when the law guarantees freedom of practice, the corollary of such

In Germany, "Heilpraktikers" may commit two types of offences while conducting their professional activities: voluntary offences and offences due to negligence. The following acts are punished:[74]

1. to cause a physical injury (art. 223 of the German Penal Code (GPC)). "*Heilpraktikers*" are rarely sentenced for voluntary physical injury because they obtain the consent of their patients beforehand. However, they may be sentenced according to rules regarding physical injury through carelessness;
2. to cause a dangerous physical injury (art. 223 a GPC);
3. to cause a physical injury by omission (art. 223, 13 GPC);
4. to cause a physical injury through carelessness (art. 230 GPC). "Heilpraktikers" may be sentenced for physical injury through carelessness when they start a treatment, when they know that their knowledge and abilities are not insufficient to provide a proper treatment;
5. to cause a homicide through carelessness (art. 222 GPC).

The Swiss Penal Code[75] (SPC) provides for similar offences that may be committed by health care providers. Art. 123 SPC deals with basic physical injury, art. 122 SPC with serious physical injury, and art. 125 SPC with physical injury through carelessness. Homicide through carelessness is punished by art. 117 SPC.[76]

It is apparent that criminal regulation regarding injuries caused to patients has a preventive and punitive role. Its purpose is to ensure good protection of patients. Furthermore, rules applying to health care professionals may, in our view, similarly be applied to non-allopathic practitioners.[77]

---

freedom is the setting up of strict rules regarding the liability of health care providers.

For a development regarding Swiss law, see CORBOZ B., *op. cit.*: 71; STRATENWERTH G., *op. cit.*: 62ss; WICKI M., *op. cit.*: 259–309.

74 CRAMER R., *op. cit.*; EHLERS A. P. F., *op. cit.*: 237–68.

75 RS 311.0.

76 CORBOZ B., *op. cit.*: 63ss; STRATENWERTH G., *op. cit.*: 58ss.

77 Some American authors consider that attention should be more focused on tort liability, rather than criminal liability. E.g., Cohen writes that "Tort law provides appropriate protection because it serves to compensate an injured party for the harm suffered, whereas in criminal actions there is an implication of 'bad mind [or] immorality' […] Even if the provider is acting with intent to deceive or with malice, civil liability for malpractice, fraud, and misrepresentation (including, where appropriate, punitive damages) provides appropriate deterrent and punitive functions" (COHEN M. H. (I), *op. cit.*: 110–11).

7.2.3.4 *Summary*

Regulation dealing with malpractice and criminal liability plays an important role in alternative medical practice. It works as a preventive and compensatory tool. Alternative practitioners, whether physicians or not, are aware that if the health care they provide results in an injury, they will face a malpractice action and possibly a criminal action. As a consequence, education and standards of practice are likely to be influenced, given that the best way to avoid prosecution is to possess a serious educational background.

In Western countries, there is little case law on malpractice suits and criminal sanctions against alternative practitioners, in particular non-allopathic practitioners. The fact that professional standards of care for alternative techniques are not well established certainly plays a role. But the differing expectations of patients[78] as to the services provided by alternative practitioners and the low risks involved in the provision of alternative medicines are also important.[79]

7.2.4 Drug Regulation[80]

Bibliography

ABBOTT A., *Europe tightens rules that govern homeopathic products*, in: Nature, vol. 359, Oct. 8, 1992; ALBER J. (co-author: BERNARDI-SCHENKLUHN B.), *Westeuropäische Gesundheitssysteme im Vergleich, Bundesrepublik Deutschland, Schweiz, Frankreich, Italien, Grossbritanien*, Campus Verlag, 1992, Frankfurt: 92–94, 134–49; BAEYENS A., *Free movement of good and services in health care: A comment on the court cases Decker and Kohll from a Belgian point of view*, in: European Journal of Health Law, 1999, n° 6: 375; COHEN M. H. (I), *Complementary and alternative medicine – Legal boundaries and regulatory perspectives*, The Johns Hopkins University Press, 1998, London & Oxford; 79–81; DOMMERS J., *An introduction to European Union health law*, in: European Journal of Health Law, vol. 4, n° 1, 1997: 31; DUMOULIN J.-F. (co-authors: GUILLOD O., MÉROZ J.-C.), *L'impact d'une adhésion suisse à l'Union Européenne sur le droit de la santé*, in: COTTIER T. (co-editor: KOPSE A. R.), *L'adhésion de la Suisse à l'Union Européenne – Enjeux et conséquences*, Schulthess, 1998, Zürich: 934ss;

78 See chap. 1.1 and 2.5 for more information on this area.
79 For a development on this area, see chap. 6.5.
80 For a world overview concerning the regulation of herbal medicines, see STEINHOFF B., *op. cit.*; WHO REGIONAL OFFICE FOR WESTERN PACIFIC, *op. cit.*; WHO REGIONAL OFFICE FOR WESTERN PACIFIC (III), *op. cit.*

FISHER P. (co-author: WARD A.), *Complementary medicine in Europe*, in: BMJ, vol. 309, July 9, 1994: 109; FRIEDEL E. (co-author: FREUNDLICH M.), *European community harmonisation of the licensing and manufacturing of medicinal products*, in: Food and Drug Law Journal, 1994, vol. 49: 141–70; GAIER H. C. (I), *Evolving problems for natural medicines within the European Community – And the biocentric practitioners who use them*, in: Complementary Medical Research, 1991, vol. 5, n° 1: 36–41; GILHOOLEY M., *Herbal remedies and dietary supplements: The boundaries of drug claims and freedom of choice*, in: Florida Law Review, 1997, vol. 49: 663ss; GRUPP K., *Rechtliche Probleme alternativer Behandlungsmethoden*, in: MedR, 1992, vol. 5: 261; GUZMAN L. (co-author CASERO J. V.), *Aproximación a la regulación juridica de la homeopatia*, Revista general de derecho, 1992, vol. 48: 3943–56; KELLER K. (I), *Herbal medicinal products in Germany and Europe: Experiences with national and European Assessment*, in: Drug Information Journal, 1996, vol. 30: 933–48; KELLER K. (II), *Homeopathic medicinal products in Germany and Europe: Legal requirements for registration and marketing authorisation*, in: Drug Information Journal, 1998, vol. 32: 803–11; LANNOYE P., *Is there a future for complementary medicine in Europe? – European report on the status of non-conventional medicine*, The Natural Medicines Society, 1996, Heanor: 7–8; MATTOLI P., *La legislazione omeopatica in Italia*, in: AUSSER O., *Handbuch zu den natürlichen Heilweisen und besonderen Therapierichtungen*, Alfred & Söhne, 1992, Meran; MONTANDON J.-B., *Remèdes homéopathiques et aspects réglementaires*, in: SOCIÉTÉ NEUCHÂTELOISE DE MÉDECINE, *Les médecines dites "parallèles"*, in: SNM News, Dec. 1998, n° 20: 27–31; ROBARD I., *La santé hors la loi: Les hors la loi de la santé*, 4th ed., Ed. de l'Ancre, 1994, Suresnes: 212; SALE D. M., *Overview of legislative developments concerning alternative health care in the United States*, 1995: 8, 40–44; SCHNEIDER M. (co-authors: BIENE-DIETRICH P., GEBANYI M., HOFMANN U., HUBER M., KÖSE A., SOMMER J. H.), *Gesundheitssysteme im internationalen Vergleich*, ed. 1994, BASYS, 1995, Augsburg: 204–05, 212–16; SCHROEDER-PRINTZER G., *"Aussenseitermethoden"*, in: MedR, 1996, n° 8: 373–79; SCHULIN B., *Alternative Medizin in der gesetzlichen Krankenversicherung*, in: Zeitschrift für Sozialreform, 1994, vol. 40, n° 8: 546–65; SELECT COMMITTEE ON SCIENCE AND TECHNOLOGY, *Complementary and alternative medicine*, House of Lords – Session 1999–2000 6th Report, The Stationary Office, 2000, London: 40, 55–57; STEINHOFF B., *Regulatory situation of herbal medicines – A world Review*, World Health Organisation, WHO/TRM/98.1, Geneva 1998; TREECE S. J., *An evaluation of medicines regulation*, in: Medical Law International, 1997, vol. 2: 315–36; WHO REGIONAL OFFICE FOR WESTERN PACIFIC, *Research guidelines for evaluating the safety and efficacy of herbal remedies*, WHO, 1993, Manila; WHO REGIONAL OFFICE FOR WESTERN PACIFIC (III), *Report – Working group on herbal remedies*, WHO, 1998, Manila; WICKI M., *Komplementärmedizin im Rahmen des Rechtes*, Dissertation, Stämpfli, 1998, Bern: 137–72.

7.2.4.1 *General remarks*

Several alternative therapies involve the providing of substances and preparations, some of these having the same status as regular drugs. Apart from prescriptions provided by health care providers, patients may also want direct recourse to some substances, outside of possible therapeutic relationship.[81] Thus, a consistent regulation of alternative medicines implies a proper marketing of alternative preparations.[82]

All the various western countries analysed during this research have been active in the field of alternative drug regulation.

7.2.4.2 *European Union*

Within the European Union, the free movement of goods is ensured by art. 28 and 30 of the Treaty of the European Community. Member States are normally not allowed to take measures, which could hinder intra-Community trade. The concept of goods covers medical goods as well. Various Directives have been adopted in order to harmonise the legislation of the Member States in the areas of pharmaceuticals, blood products, medical devices, foodstuffs, dangerous substances and preparations, cosmetics, safety of products, precursors, tobacco products, personal protective equipment and personal (medical) data protection. Since 1985, the Community has attempted to remove the technical barriers by adopting very detailed directives concerning the harmonisation of national technical product manufacturing specifications.[83, 84]

81 The market for alternative products has become impressive. In Great Britain, according to the Pharmaceutical Society of Great Britain, and the Proprietary Association of Great Britain, while the total size of the market of alternative products is difficult to estimate, it must be between £93 million and up to £240 million per annum (SELECT COMMITTEE ON SCIENCE AND TECHNOLOGY, *op. cit.*: 55).

82 E.g., the Hungarian regulation on alternative provides that all drugs may be used when providing alternative medicines. A homeopathic product that is not registered in Hungary may be used if a procedure of registration is in process.

83 See, Standard EN 27740 concerning instruments for surgery for the purpose of Directive 93/42/EEC (on the approximation of statutes of the Member States relating to medical devices) (Official Journal EC n° L. 169, 12.07.1993), which aims to harmonise the conditions for marketing and operating medical devices. The purpose is to create the same basis for protection of health and safety of patients and users throughout the EU. See also Directive 89/381/EEC on medicinal products derived from human blood or plasma.

84 BAEYENS A., *op. cit.*: 375; DOMMERS J., *op. cit.*: 31.

The first phase for European harmonisation in the field of homeopathic products was the adoption of two European Directives – one on Homeopathic medicinal products and on homeopathic veterinary medicinal products, which both came into force on January 1, 1994.[85] The purpose of these Directives was to ensure a unique European Market for these products by regulating the manufacture, inspection, marketing and labelling. The most important rule was the establishment of a simplified registration procedure applying to medicines containing less than one part per 10,000 of the undiluted tincture, or less than 1/100th of the smallest dose used in allopathy.[86] The European Commission sent a report to the Parliament and the Council on the application of the Directives 92/73 and 92/74. The report stated that the existing level of harmonisation was not sufficient as countries had not appropriately implemented the Directives as directed.[87]

Following a decision of the European court of Justice,[88] a marketing authorisation granted by the competent authority is required (art. 4 of the Council Directive 65/65 EEC) if herbal remedies are sold as finished medicinal products.[89] The applicant must document the quality, safety and efficacy of its product.[90] The EC Directive on proprietary medicinal

85 Official Journal EC n° L. 297, Oct. 13 1992/8–11, 12–15.

86 Keller considers the safety of Homeopathic medicinal products needs strict control, because of the risks they may present. "Therefore", he adds, "homeopathic products should be included in pharmacovigilance systems". Further, "However, safety requirements should not be applied in a way that might discriminate against this particular therapy. The requirements should be adequate and in proportion" (KELLER K. (II), *op. cit.*: 811).
Lannoye considers that the European Pharmacopoeia should be opened up to other pharmacopoeia. Directives 65/65/EEC, 75/319/EEC and Regulation 2309/93 need to be revised in order to allow the free movement of all medicinal products (LANNOYE P., *op. cit.*: 7–8).

87 ABBOTT A., *op. cit.*; FISHER P., *op. cit.*: 109; GAIER H. C., *op. cit.*; KELLER K. (II), *op. cit.*: 803–11.

88 Decision of Jan. 14, 1993; Case C-177/91 (see Official J. n° C 310/2, Nov. 27 1992). The case involved German law.

89 The term "herbal remedies" includes medicinal products containing exclusively plant material or vegetable drug preparations as active ingredients. These do not include homeopathic preparations.

90 The criteria for the evaluation of safety and efficacy apply to herbal remedies in the same way as they apply to other medicinal products with comparable indications.
For further development of this area, see KELLER K. (I), *op. cit.*: 933–48.
For further development of concepts of safety and efficacy, see chap. 6.

products considerably restricted product licensing for herbal medicines[91] while the disturbing possible carcinogenic effects of pyrolizidine alkaloids, which occur in a number of medicinal herbs, prompted both the German and British governments to restrict the availability of these herbs. A working group was set up by the Pharmaceutical Committee of the European Commission to respond to the growing unease within the EU concerning the inadequate regulation of herbal products. The Committee is currently working on a draft of a Directive for the regulation of herbal medicinal products, that would allow for the licensing of herbal medicines if evidence of traditional use was provided, instead of new clinical or other evidence of efficacy, provided that normal medicinal quality and safety controls were applied.[92]

As a result of the Directives adopted at the EU level, Member States have set up regulations for the production and marketing of homeopathic drugs, as well as other alternative preparations.[93]

7.2.4.3 *Italy*

In Italy, homeopathy has a long tradition. Since 1841, there have been several attempts to regulate this field through initiatives such as requiring a license to practise, training in homeopathy and the pharmacopoeia.[94] Finally, on March 17, 1995, the legislative Decree n° 185 of Directive 92/73/CEE[95] regarding homeopathic products was adopted.[96]

7.2.4.4 *Germany*

In Germany, section 34 SGB dealing with covered drugs, refers to "alternative therapeutic modalities such as homeopathy, phytotherapy, and anthroposophy". This section requires that drugs linked to the providing of these modalities be evaluated following the standards of these

91 Official Journal EC n° L. 102, Apr. 22, 1992/23–24; 92/C 102–55.
92 FISHER P., *op. cit.*: 109; KELLER K. (II), *op. cit.*: 803–11; SELECT COMMITTEE ON SCIENCE AND TECHNOLOGY, *op. cit.*: 57.
93 For further development on this area, see FRIEDEL E., *op. cit.*: 141–70; GUZMAN L., *op. cit.*: 3943–56; KELLER K. (II), *op. cit.*: 803–11; TREECE S. J., *op. cit.*: 315–36.
94 For a historical development of homeopathy in Italy, see MATTOLI P., *op. cit.*
95 The Directive regulates the marketing and the registration of homeopathic and anthroposophic products.
96 MATTOLI P., *op. cit.*; ROBARD I., *op. cit.*: 212.

modalities.[97, 98] In order for experimental treatments, to be reimbursed they must first be recognized, in broad terms, as being useful and certain in their application.[99]

7.2.4.5 *Great Britain*

In Great Britain, the Food and Safety Act 1990 controls the sale and supply of non-medical products for human consumption, which includes some products associated with alternative medicines.[100] The Department of Health states that,

> the present regulatory arrangements for herbal medicines have significant weaknesses. The regime for unlicensed herbal remedies does not provide sufficient protection or information for the public. At the same time, some of the regulatory hurdles for licensed medicines may be unnecessarily demanding for relatively benign herbal remedies.[101]

The British Select Committee on Science and Technology has recommended finding a mechanism that would allow members of the public to identify those health products that had met the stringent requirements of licensing in order to differentiate them from unregulated competitors. This should be accompanied by a strong enforcement of the law in regard to those products that might confuse the public with claims and labelling resembling those permitted by marketing authorisations.[102]

7.2.4.6 *Norway*

Homeopathic remedies are considered as drugs in Norway. With some exceptions, these products may only be sold from pharmacies. An authorisation is necessary to market homeopathic products when the degree of dilution of the homeopathic product is less than one million.[103]

97 See also section 92 (2) SGB V (requiring that drug guidelines be set up by experts from these modalities).
98 This section does not explicitly limit alternative therapeutic modalities to these three schools, however, and other schools of treatment may be covered by sections 2 and 34 SGB.
99 Art. 92 (1) and 135 (1) SGB.
For more details, also with regard to the criteria dealing with the reimbursement of new medications, see GRUPP K., *op. cit.*: 261; SCHROEDER-PRINTZER G., *op. cit.*: 373; SCHULIN B., *op. cit.*: 546, 553–56.
100 SELECT COMMITTEE ON SCIENCE AND TECHNOLOGY, *op. cit.*: 40.
101 Cited in SELECT COMMITTEE ON SCIENCE AND TECHNOLOGY, *op. cit.*: 56.
102 SELECT COMMITTEE ON SCIENCE AND TECHNOLOGY, *op. cit.*: 56–57.
103 GUZMAN L., *op. cit.*: 3948.

7.2.4.7 *Switzerland*

Although Switzerland is not part of the European Union, rules have been established between Switzerland and the EU that guarantee uniformity in the field of drug regulation. On January 1, 2002, the new Federal Act of December 15, 2000 on Drugs and Medical Devices (FADMD) came into force.[104] Under the FADMD, homeopathic and anthroposophic preparations are considered as regular drugs and must therefore be registered. However, the registering is made easier for these substances (art. 15).[105]

7.2.4.8 *US*

In the US, drugs listed in the Homeopathic Pharmacopeia of the United States (HPUS) are considered by the Federal Food, Drug, and Cosmetic Act (FFDCA) as "drugs". Moreover, the HPUS is recognised as the official compendium of standards of source, composition and preparation of homeopathic products.[106] Homeopathic drugs must meet the standards specified in the HPUS for strength, purity and quality and comply with the manufacturing, labelling and packaging requirements specified in the FFDCA and applicable regulations.[107] Furthermore, the FFDCA exempts these products from requirements of laboratory testing to determine the identity and strength of each active ingredient before distribution of the product,[108] as well as other rules concerning expiration dating.[109] The FDA has been asked to hold homeopathic remedies to the same standard of efficacy and safety that apply to over-the-counter drugs.[110, 111]

104 RS 812.21. In French "Loi sur les agents thérapeutiques". For more details, see Dumoulin J.-F., *op. cit.*: 935ss.

105 Dumoulin J.-F., *op. cit.*: 934ss; Montandon J.-B., *op. cit.*: 27–31; Wicki M., *op. cit.*: 137–72.

106 21 U.S.C.A. § 321 (g) (1) (A) (Supp. 1994). See also Food and Drug Administration, *Compliance Policy Guide*, § 7132.15 (May 31, 1998).

107 21 U.S.C.A. § 352 (b) and 352 (Supp. 1994).
Food and Drug Administration, *Compliance Policy Guide*, § 7132.15 (May 31, 1998) at 3–7. 21 U.S.C.A. §§ 352 and 353 (b) and 21 C.F.R. § 201 (1994) (labelling requirements) and 21 C.F.R. § 211 (1994) (good manufacturing requirements, including packaging).

108 Food and Drug Administration, *Compliance Policy Guide*, § 7132.15 (May 31, 1998) at 7. For current laboratory testing, see 21 C.F.R. § 211.165 (1994).

109 21 C.F.R. § 211.137 (e) (1994).

110 Petition regarding Homeopathic Drugs, n° 94P-0316 (Aug. 21, 1994).

111 Sale D. M., *op. cit.*: 8.

In 1994, the FDA promulgated new regulations under the Nutrition Labelling and Education Act, which concerned dietary supplements such as vitamins, minerals, herbs, and other similar substances.[112] The regulations contain, in particular, standards to govern nutritional labelling and nutrient content and health claims made by manufacturers on the labels or in the labelling of dietary supplements. An important feature of the new regulations is that the FDA will hold any health claims made by manufacturers of dietary supplements to the same statutory standard that applies to food in its conventional form. The essential element of that standard is the need for "significant agreement" to support the claim while the provisions regarding health claims for dietary supplements remain controversial.[113]

An independent Commission on Dietary Supplement Labels appointed by the President, was also established whose objective was to study dietary supplements and make recommendations to the President and the Congress. An Office of Dietary Supplements at the National Institutes of Health[114] was also created to explore the potential role of supplements in maintaining health and to promote its scientific study.[115]

7.2.4.9 Summary

It is apparent that several initiatives have been undertaken in Western countries to establish a regulatory structure for alternative preparations and drugs. It is the area where harmonisation in the regulation of alternative medicines has reached its highest degree, although there is still no uniformity among countries yet. This indicates that harmonisation in other regulatory fields is possible, and may provide a basis to develop and strengthen cooperation between countries. Pharmaceutical companies will probably play a decisive role in the development of a free market for alternative preparations, given its potential as a future key player in this area.

112 Nutrition Labelling and Education Act of 1990, Pub. L. n° 101–535, 194 Stat. 2353 (codified as amended in scattered sections of 21 U.S.C.).

113 For an analysis see COHEN M. H. (I), *op. cit.*: 79–81; GILHOOLEY M., *op. cit.*: 663ss; SALE D. M., *op. cit.*: 40–44.

114 Dietary Supplement Health and Education Act of 1994, Pub. L. N. 103–417, 108 Stat. 4325 (1994).

115 COHEN M. H. (I), *op. cit.*: 79–81; GILHOOLEY M., *op. cit.*: 663ss; SALE D. M., *op. cit.*: 44.

7.2.5 International Developments

Bibliography

Abbing R., *Quality of medical practice and professional misconduct in the European Union*, in: European Journal of Health Law, 1997, n° 4: 273–78; Bonnamour M.-C. (co-author: Granturco T.), *The Lannoye report on non-conventional medicines was adopted by the European Parliament*, CP Info, June 1997, Bruxelles: 2; British Medical Association (Lamont T.), *Complementary medicine – New approaches to good practice*, Oxford University Press, 1993, Oxford/New York: 10–12, 15–17, 27; Conférence des Directeurs Cantonaux des Affaires Sanitaires, *Rapport annuel 1998*, CDS, 1998, Bern; Cohen M. H. (I), *Complementary and alternative medicine – Legal boundaries and regulatory perspectives*, The Johns Hopkins University Press, 1998, London & Oxford: 114; Dumoulin J.-F. (co-authors: Guillod O., Méroz J.-C.), *L'impact d'une adhésion suisse à l'Union Européenne sur le droit de la santé*, in: Cottier T. (co-editor: Kopse A. R.), *L'adhésion de la Suisse à l'Union Européenne – Enjeux et conséquences*, Schulthess, 1998, Zürich: 929–34; Grunwald D., *Pratiques médicales non éprouvées*, Session de l'Ordre des médecins, Sept. 1997, Paris; Hoff W. (I), *Guidelines for training traditional health practitioners in primary health care*, Divison of Strengthening of Health Services and Traditional Medicine Programme, Geneva 1995; Künzi M. (I), *Komplementärmedizin und Gesundheitsrecht*, Helbing & Lichtenhahn Verlag AG, 1996, Basel: 74–75, 98; Lannoye P., *Is there a future for complementary medicine in Europe? – European report on the status of non-conventionnal medicine*, The Natural Medicines Society, 1996, Heanor: 3; Pew Health Professions Commission (co-authors: Finocchio L. J., Dower C. M., McMahon T., Gragnola C. M., and the Taskforce on Health Care Workforce Regulation), *Reforming health care workforce regulation: Policy considerations for the 21st Century*, Pew Health Professions Commission, 1995, San Francisco; PROCOMED, *Lettre d'information de l'Association pour la reconnaissance et la promotion des médecines complémentaires en Europe*, Bulletin n° 2, Dec. 1997, Bruxelles: 2–3; Richli P. (co-author: Wunder K.), *Über die Möglichkeiten zur Beschrännkung des freien Warenverkehrs nach dem Binnenmarktgesetz*, in: AJP, 1996, n° 6: 908–17; Robard I., *La santé hors la loi: Les hors la loi de la santé*, 4th ed., Ed. de l'Ancre, 1994, Suresnes: 271–72; Sage W. M. (co-author: Aiken L. H.), *Regulating interdisciplinary practice*, in: Jost T. S., *Regulation of the healthcare professions*, Health Administration Press, 1996, Chicago: 83–84; Sale D. M., *Overview of legislative developments concerning alternative health care in the United States*, 1995; Schneider H., *Die Annerkennung von Diplomen in der Europäischen Gemeinschaft*, Maklu, 1995, Uitgevers Antwerpen; Segest E., *Consumer protection and the free movement of medical practitioners in the European Union*, in: European Journal of Health Law, 1997, n° 4: 267–72; Stone J. (co-author: Matthews J.), *Complementary medicine and the law*, Oxford University Press, 1996, Oxford: 102–03; Vyborny K. M., *Legal and political issues facing telemedicine*, in: Annals of Health Law, 1996, vol. 5: 61–119; White House Commission on Complementary and Alternative

MEDICINE POLICY, *Final report*, March 2002, available at http://www.whccamp.hhs.gov/pdfs/fr2002_document.pdf, accessed Feb. 1 2005: 90–91; WHO (IV), *Guidelines on basic training and safety in acupuncture*, WHO, 1999, Geneva; YESSIAN M. R. (co-author: GREENLEAF M.), *The ebb and flow of federal initiatives to regulate healthcare professionals*, in: JOST T. S., *Regulation of the healthcare professions*, Health Administration Press, 1996, Chicago: 169–98.

7.2.5.1 General Remarks

Today, (alternative) medical practitioners have the opportunity to move easily from one place to another. If such practitioners are allowed to practise within a specific jurisdiction, the question arises as to whether they may provide health care in other jurisdictions as well.

The position in certain jurisdictions is presented below. As will become apparent, the status of alternative practitioners varies from one profession and from one region to another.

7.2.5.2 European Union

At the European Union level, "specific" Directives have been enacted to regulate the free movement of classic allopathic professions.[116] These Directives contain precise rules about the training necessary and the coordination required between Member States for a mutual recognition of diplomas. As these specific Directives are difficult to set up and implement, the EU decided to adopt "general" Directives based on the principle of mutual trust. Thus, these Directives assume that training in the field of allopathic professions is considered as equivalent among States.[117] Interestingly, chiropractic could be the first alternative technique to be regulated by a general Directive at the EU level. Although this technique is not regulated in all EU States,[118] the setting up of a general EU Directive could guarantee practitioners, under some conditions, to practise freely within the EU area. Also of note is the Resolution on May 29, 1997, taken by the European Parliament with the stated aim of establishing a better integration of alternative medicines within the EU.

116 Such as physicians, nurses, dentists, midwife, veterinarians and pharmacists.

117 For an opinion regarding the establishment of quality of care standards within the EU as a result of the EU Directives, see SEGEST E., *op. cit.*: 267–72.

118 E.g., in Spain, Italy, or Luxembourg. In France, the situation is different. A Decree of 1953 states that chiropractic would be taught within medical schools. However, this Decree has never been implemented.

The diversity of national systems at the EU level is such that it will be difficult to adopt a Directive regulating free movement for all categories of practitioners.[119] Lannoye, in his response to the adoption of the 1997 resolution considered the final vote to be a disappointment.[120] However, he believed that the adoption of the resolution was an important step, which could open the way for the exploration of new perspectives.[121] Currently, it appears likely that any adoption of Directives concerning alternative medicines will need to be undertaken separately for each profession.[122] The adoption of a general Directive regarding the practice of chiropractic could, perhaps, provide an impetus for the regulation of other alternative professions.

7.2.5.3 Federal States

A. Switzerland

In Switzerland, cantons are competent to regulate those health care professions that are not subject to federal or inter-cantonal regulation. As a result, there is a great diversity of regulations among cantons. There are,

119 Stone argues, regarding the principle of free movement within the EU, that "currently, such movement would be impossible for complementary health practitioners, given the diversity in training standards and the widely differing legal requirements operating in different European countries. [...] Whilst European initiatives are unlikely to affect domestic policy in the short term, the prospect of European harmonisation is likely to act as a spur to those interested in promoting higher, uniform standards of training" (STONE J., *op. cit.*: 102–03). See also ABBING R., *op. cit.*: 273–78. For a development regarding the recognition of diplomas within the EU, see SCHNEIDER H., *op. cit.*

120 Although the resolution is not a binding act, but rather a declaration of policy, it has had some effect. E.g., some countries such as France, Italy or Austria have considered the position more carefully and other countries such as Belgium have decided to modify their legislation as a result.

121 Bonnamour considers that "although the perspective of recognition of complementary medical practices is postponed until the results of an 'in-depth study on the harmlessness, timeliness, scope of application and the complementary or alternative nature of each discipline' are given, the objective of a recognition nevertheless remains" (BONNAMOUR M.-C., *op. cit.*: 2). That is also the opinion of PROCOMED (PROCOMED, *op. cit.*: 2–3) and of the French National Order of Physicians (GRUNWALD D., *op. cit.*: 28).

122 Considering the case of a non-medically qualified acupuncturist practising in France (Case n° 61/89), the European Court of Justice confirmed the right for Member States to reserve or not the practice of the healing art to doctors, in accordance with their own legislation.

however, several initiatives tending toward a better recognition of (alternative) professions within Switzerland as a whole.

For example, the Federal Act regulating the Exercise of the Professions of Physicians, Pharmacists and Veterinarians,[123] allows holders of federal diplomas for these professions to practise everywhere in Switzerland.[124] This Act, which was revised, will also regulate the practice of chiropractic.[125]

Also of interest was the adoption of the Act on the Internal Market (AIM). The objective of this Act was to create a unique Swiss economic space, where people could freely have access to, and practise a private lucrative activity throughout the entire country. In furtherance of this objective, the AIM aims to suppress cantonal protectionist rules. The Federal Court has stated, in relation to non-allopathic practitioners, that a practitioner holding a cantonal diploma attesting training to practise a specific profession could not rely on the freedom of movement provided for in the AIM, in order to practise in another canton that has no regulation of the specific profession.

The Federal Act on Professional Training will regulate the training of all remaining professions.[126] The Act does not include as of (yet) non-allopathic professions. For instance, only chiropractic is directly regulated at the intercantonal level, which guarantees recognised chiropractors the right to freely practise throughout the entire country.

Osteopathy has not been admitted into the Federal Act on Medical Professions, nor is it regulated at the intercantonal level. However, the Conference of Health and Social Affairs of French speaking cantons is currently working on an inter-cantonal agreement regarding the training and licensing of osteopathy in cantons Geneva, Fribourg, Vaud, and Jura, that will allow osteopaths to practise within these cantons. Similarly, there are agreements, between St-Gallen and Shaffhausen, Thurgau and St-Gallen,

123 Also called Federal Act on Medical Professions.

124 The Act aims to establish freedom of movement at the intercantonal and international level, particularly in light of the implementation of the agreements between Switzerland and the European Union.

125 This profession is currently regulated at the intercantonal level, which allows practitioners to practise throughout Switzerland as a whole.

126 Regulated professions will be allowed to practise throughout Switzerland as a whole.
Until the enforcement of the new Federal Act on Professional Training, the Conference of Cantonal Directors of Health Affairs (CCDHA) is in charge of recognising Swiss and foreign diplomas in the health field, through the intercantonal agreement on the recognition of diplomas of Feb. 18, 1993.

Graubünden and Thurgau, regarding the mutual recognition of training in naturopathy.

In Switzerland the situation is slowly moving towards an improved harmonisation, although there is still no regulation allowing all categories of non-allopathic practitioners to practise in the country as a whole.[127] However, as the Swiss Conference of Directors of Health Affairs has observed, there is still a need for better coordination between cantons.[128]

B. US

In the US, there is still no regulation giving the right to alternative practitioners to provide health care throughout the US as a whole. Practitioners who have gained a licence to practise in a particular State may practise in other States, as long as the profession is regulated, and the practitioners comply with the requirements of the State where permission to practise has been granted. Proposals have been made to supersede those State acts that define the scope of practice with federal regulation, however no such regulation has been adopted.[129] Nevertheless, some authors are of the opinion that "uniformity is possible without federal intervention".[130] The Pew Commission has proposed the setting up of consistent regulatory terminology[131] and uniform standards for entry to practise by directly measuring knowledge and skills, with interstate reciprocal licensure by endorsement.[132] Indeed, there is a marked lack of uniformity among State

127 In particular, non-allopathic practitioners will not be able to claim the principle of freedom of movement contained in the AIM in order to practise in another canton.

128 CONFÉRENCE DES DIRECTEURS CANTONAUX DES AFFAIRES SANITAIRES, *op. cit.*: 36. See also KÜNZI M. (I), *op. cit.*: 98.
For further reading regarding the relationship between Switzerland and the EU, see DUMOULIN J.-F., *op. cit.*: 929–34.

129 Of note is the initiative in Montana to adopt a Uniform Licensing Act that would regulate all professional and technical occupations (Mont. Uniform Professional Licensing and Regulatory Procedures, § 37–1: 301–19 (1995)).

130 SAGE W. M., *op. cit.*: 83.

131 Robard notices the same problem at the EU level, namely the lack of unified terminology (ROBARD I., *op. cit.*: 271).

132 PEW HEALTH PROFESSIONS COMMISSION, *op. cit.*: 1–8.
For further reading on this area, see SAGE W. M., *op. cit.*: 83–84.
For further discussion concerning standards of practice, see chap. 7.5.3.

regulations in this field. Even with respect to the same technique, the statutory requirements differ substantially from one state to another.[133]

Sage states, concerning the opportunity to set up an area of free movement of practise, that

> Inconsistent state laws may make it difficult for many health professional to relocate to another state. Unlike professions such as law, where knowledge is state specific, training in the health professions is science based and universal. State laws also constitute a barrier to cost-effective, collaborative methods of services such as telemedicine, because health professionals rendering care by electronic means must nonetheless be licensed in the state in which the patient is located [...]. In addition, [...] lack of regulatory coordination may result in substandard professionals being admitted to practice when providers relocate.[134]

Even though the position from one Western country to another may vary more deeply than in the US, these arguments remain valid in a wider Western and international context. Actually, standards of training and practice of several alternative medicines have reached such a level in certain jurisdictions that restrictions to the right to practise seem to be less a mean to ensure public protection than a disguised form of protectionism.[135] Thus, the lack of uniform regulation, in particular, of mechanisms for the recognition of foreign diploma and/or licences to practise, has the effect of preventing competent health care providers from practising in those countries where patients desire access to alternative forms of health care.

133 In this respect, Sale notes that "a greater degree of standardization would undoubtedly be helpful in securing interstate reciprocity for alternative practitioners and in rendering access to these modalities by consumers less subject to the circumstance of geographic residence" (SALE D. M., *op. cit.*: 50). See also WHITE HOUSE COMMISSION ON COMPLEMENTARY AND ALTERNATIVE MEDICINE POLICY, *op. cit.*: 90.

134 SAGE W. M., *op. cit.*: 84.
On the subject, see also COHEN M. H. (I), *op. cit.*: 114; SEGEST E., *op. cit.*: 267–72 (the author stresses the benefits of international exchanges as well as ways of ensuring proper and equivalent quality of care among countries); VYBORNY K. M., *op. cit.*: 61–119 (regarding the emergence of telemedicine that challenges the state-restricted vision of licensing to practise medicine); YESSIAN M. R., *op. cit.*: 169–98 (difficulties to implement federal regulation for health care providers).

135 See chap. 7.3.2.2.

7.2.5.4 *Education*

Several countries recognise foreign education. For example, Swiss chiropractors must at least have studied four years at a chiropractic college recognised by the American Council on Chiropractic Education, in order to obtain a licence to practise.[136]

The recognition of foreign education opens up some interesting perspectives as such recognition demonstrates that it is possible to license the practice of non-allopathic practitioners, even if the training itself has not reached a sufficient level of expertise in the country (as yet).[137] It is, in fact, entirely possible that the recognition of foreign diplomas may be the foundation stone upon which a cross-border space could be established within which alternative practitioners could freely move and practice. In any case, the mutual recognition of diplomas is usually the primary condition to be satisfied and the main problem that countries face when setting up a cross-border space within which alternative practitioners may freely move and work. This is particularly interesting at the EU level where the free movement of health care providers is based upon such mutual recognition.[138]

Initiatives aiming to recognise or adopt foreign training curriculum, standards of practise, or terminology should be enhanced[139] as such initiatives will build a network and set up common standards, and thus constitute the basis to set up regulations on the free movement of alternative

136 Norwegian candidates wanting to become members of the Norwegian Association of Chiropractors must fulfill the same requirement.

137 See also the situation in Spain and in Swiss canton Zürich. Both States do not have any legal rules in place ensuring the recognition of external authorisations to practise or diplomas. However, courts have recognised the right to practise of some alternative practitioners holding a foreign diploma. For further developments regarding these rulings, see chap. 4.3.2.6 (Spain), and 4.3.6.1 (Switzerland).
Regarding the debate about recognition of diplomas within the EU, Schneider stresses that Member States are required to consider any education and training received by the migrant. The Member State must in case of equivalence recognise the qualification obtained in another Member State (Schneider H., *op. cit.*: 464).

138 Authors such as Künzi are of the opinion that harmonisation at the EU level may be created only through the setting up of training standards EU wide (Künzi M. (I), *op. cit.*: 74–75). See also Robard I., *op. cit.*: 271–72.

139 The World Health Organisation has developed standards for training and research for alternative (traditional) medicines. See Hoff W. (I), *op. cit.*; WHO (IV), *op. cit.*

practitioners. In this respect, it seems difficult to set up regulation regulating all types of alternative practitioners. Indeed, there are such differences among techniques that it seems illusory to set up a unique standard for all of them. Therefore, the development in the mid-term must focus on specific techniques.

7.2.5.5 Summary

There have been some recent developments regarding the free movement of practitioners. However, serious obstacles still exist to the establishment of a free area of practice for non-allopathic practitioners. More specifically, the EU is becoming more open in its approach to the regulation of non-allopathic professions. The establishment of a General Directive concerning the practice of chiropractic within the EU may be the first step towards a uniform regulation of alternative practitioners within the EU.

In Switzerland, there is a trend towards better harmonisation regarding the practice of alternative medicines. However, improved coordination between cantons is required. In the US, there is still a lack of interstate or federal statutes to regulate the practice of alternative medicines within the US as a whole.

Education is currently developing within an international framework. Some countries already recognise foreign diplomas and such acknowledgement could provide the foundation for the setting up of a cross-border space where alternative practitioners could freely move and practice. The creation of such a space may also be helped through the development of uniform training and standards of practise, which presupposes terminology uniformity. However, although recent developments have shown improvements in the educational field,[140] the general position is far from being satisfactory.

7.2.6 Conclusion

The regulation of alternative medicines is a complex area to conceive and to implement. In order to achieve a coherent system, it is crucial to take into consideration other regulatory fields such as patients' rights, criminal and civil liability, drug regulation and international development.

140 For a development regarding standards of practice, see chap. 7.6.3.

There have been some developments giving more rights to patients wishing greater access to alternative health care, as well as to a patient's right to choose an alternative practitioner. There are also more incentives encouraging physicians to provide information to patients about alternative medicines. Of note is that in the current world of health care, patients have become more aware of medical possibilities, are more responsible, and thus ask for more freedom of choice over both allopathic and alternative medicines.

Regulation dealing with malpractice and criminal liability works as a preventive and compensatory tool. It also plays an important role when regulating alternative medicines. Even though there is still little case law on malpractice claims and criminal sanctions against alternative practitioners, liability rules are likely to influence, for example, education and standards of practice. Furthermore, lawmakers will take into consideration malpractice liability, education and standards of practice issues when deciding to set up licensing regulations.

The provision of several therapies implies the administration of specific preparations and various initiatives have been taken in Western countries to set up regulation regarding alternative products and drugs. There is already a certain harmonisation among countries in this field.

When lawmakers set up a regulation, they should take into account the regulatory position in other countries and consider the wish or necessity of patients and practitioners to freely move from one country to another. Although there have been recent developments that have been more encouraging towards the free movement of practitioners, serious obstacles still exist to the setting up of a free area of practice for non-allopathic practitioners.

In brief, the legal framework surrounding alternative medicines and techniques is slowly developing towards a better integration of these therapies within western regulatory health care systems.

7.3 Licensing Framework

7.3.1 Introduction

The regulation of 'alternative' medical practice requires the making of a choice over several alternatives. For example, various licensure modalities are at the disposal of the lawmaker who may decide or not to permit both allopathic and non-allopathic practitioners to provide alternative medicines.

Once this initial choice has been made, the scope of practice for each category of practitioner may be defined, with the aid of several criteria. There is also a need to redefine institutions in charge of implementing regulations on the practice of medicine.

The main issues that arise at each step of the regulatory process are presented below.

7.3.2 Licensure modalities

Bibliography

ABBOTT A., *The system of professions: An essay on the division of expert labour*, University of Chicago Press, 1988, Chicago; ANONYMOUS (IV), *Integrated healthcare – A way forward for the next five years?*, Foundation for Integrated Medicine, 1997: 31–34; BOOZANG K. M. (I), *Western medicine opens the door to alternative medicine*, in: American Journal of Medicine, 1998, vol. 24, n° 2/3: 211; BRITISH MEDICAL ASSOCIATION (LAMONT T.), *Complementary medicine – New approaches to good practice*, Oxford University Press, 1993, Oxford/New York: 21, 62–63, 67; CHAPMAN-SMITH D. A., *Legislative approaches to the regulation of the chiropractic profession*, in: J. Can. Chiropractic Assoc, June 1996, vol. 40, n° 2: 111–13; COBURN D., *State authority, medical dominance, and trends in the regulation of the health professions: The Ontario case*, in: Social-Science-and-Medicine Oct. 1993, vol. 37, n° 7: 841–50; COHEN M. H. (I), *Complementary and alternative medicine – Legal boundaries and regulatory perspectives*, The Johns Hopkins University Press, 1998, London & Oxford: 35–38, 45–46; COHEN M. H. (II), *Holistic health care: Including alternative and complementary medicine in insurance and regulatory schemes*, in: Arizona Law Review, Spring 1996, vol. 38: 86; CONFÉRENCE DES DIRECTEURS CANTONAUX DES AFFAIRES SANITAIRES (I), *Rapport du groupe de travail "Autorisations de pratiquer les professions du domaine de la santé"*, CDS, 2000, Bern, available at: http://www.sdk-cds.ch/fr/berufsbildung-f.html, accessed July 30 2001: 27ss; DE BIJL N. (co-author: NEDERVEEN-VAN DE KRAGT I.), *Legal safeguards against medical practice by not suitably qualified persons: A comparative study in seven EU-countries*, 1997, in: European Journal of Health Law, vol. 4: 14–15; DE REYNIER V. (co-author: RIVA E.), *Les effets de la loi fédérale sur le marché intérieur (LMI) sur les professionnels de la santé détenteurs d'une autorisation de pratiquer délivrée par un canton*, Conférence des directeurs cantonaux des affaires sanitaires, 1998, Bern: 15ss; DOMENIGHETTI G. (co-authors: GRILLI R., GUILLOD O., GUTZWILLER F., QUAGLIA J.), *Usage personnel de pratiques relevant des médecines douces ou alternatives parmi les médecins suisses*, in: Médecine et Hygiène, 2000, vol. 58, n° 2291: 572; EHLERS A. P. F., *Medizin in den Händen von Heilpraktikern – "Nicht-Heilkundigen"*, Springer Verlag, 1995, Berlin/Heidelberg: 275–78; FEASBY C., *Determining standard of care in alternative contexts*, in: Health Law Journal, 1997, vol. 5: 54–55; FURROW B. R. (co-authors: GREANEY T. L., JOST T., SCHWARTZ R. L.) (I), *Health law*, West Publishing, 1995, St Paul: 56–58, GRUNWALD D., *Pratiques médicales non éprouvées*, Session de l'Ordre des médecins, Sept. 1997, Paris; GUILLOD O. (I), *Rebouteux, naturopathes et guérisseurs: Pour un traitement légal alternatif*, Recueil de Jurisprudence Neuchâtelois, 1989, Neuchâtel: 30–32, 38; JOSEFEK K. J., *Alternative medicine's roadmap to mainstream*, in: American Journal of Law and Medicine, 2000, vol. 26: 304–06; HOLCOMBE R. G., *Eliminating scope of practice and licensing laws to improve health care*, in: The Journal of Law, Medicine and Ethics, 2003, vol. 31, n° 2: 236–46; JOST T. S. (II), *Introduction – Regulation of the health care professions*, in: JOST T. S., *Regulation of the healthcare professions*, Health Administration Press, 1996, Chicago: 1–16; LANNOYE P., *Is there a future for complementary medicine in Europe? – European report on the status of non-conventionnal medicine*, The Natural Medicines Society, 1996, Heanor: 4; LIANG B. A., *Health law and policy – A survival guide to medicolegal issues for practitioners*, Butterworth-Heinemann, 2000, Woburn: 149; MINISTRY OF HEALTH AND SOCIAL AFFAIRS (I), *Report on alternative medicine – English summary*, Norges Offentliche Utredniger NOU 1998: 21, 1998, Oslo: 272–73; MINISTRY OF HEALTH, WELFARE AND SPORT, *The individual health care professional act*, Ministry of Health, Welfare, and Sport, 1997, Rijswijk: 2; OEPEN I. (III), *Pseudo-Naturheilverfahren und Aussenseitermethoden in der Rheumatologie*, in: Zeitschrift für Rheumatologie, 1993, vol. 52: 264–74; ORENTLICHER D., *The role of professional self-regulation*, in: JOST T. S., *Regulation of the healthcare professions*, Health Administration Press, 1996, Chicago: 129–48; ROBARD I., *La santé hors la loi: Les hors la loi de la santé*, 4th ed., Ed. de l'Ancre, 1994, Suresnes: 66ss, 203; RÖSCH B., *Die Stellung der Erfahrungsheilkundigen aus verfassungs- und verwaltungsrechtlicher Sicht, dargestellt am Beispiel der geistig Heilenden*, Dissertation, Helbing & Lichtenhahn Verlag, 1994, Basel: 118–22, 263–65, 348; SELECT COMMITTEE ON SCIENCE AND TECHNOLOGY, *Complementary and alternative medicine*, House of Lords – Session 1999–2000 6th Report, The Stationary Office, 2000, London; STONE J. (co-author: MATTHEWS J.), *Complementary medicine and the law*, Oxford University Press, 1996, Oxford; SWEDISH COMMISSION ON ALTERNATIVE MEDICINE, *Report on alternative medicine*, Regeringskansliet, 1989, Stockholm: 27, 33–34; WARDWELL W. I., *Alternative medicine in the United States*, in: Social-Science-and-Medicine, 1994, vol. 38, n° 8: 1062; WHITE HOUSE COMMISSION ON COMPLEMENTARY AND ALTERNATIVE MEDICINE POLICY, *Final report*, March 2002, available at http://www.whccamp.hhs.gov/pdfs/fr2002_document.pdf, accessed Feb. 1 2005: 91, 93; WICKI M., *Komplementärmedizin im Rahmen des Rechtes*, Dissertation, Stämpfli, 1998, Bern: 66ss, 74ss.

7.3.2.1 General Remarks

It is usually a state's task to decide who will be allowed to practise medicine, and under which conditions.[141] Indeed, an individual state will have the power to regulate health care professionals under the state police power which is for the protection of the health, safety and general welfare[142] of the community.[143] In so doing, a state will usually take into account the right to have access to 'alternative' medical treatment.[144]

Presented below are the several licensure modalities and the criteria at the disposal of the lawmaker to regulate the practice of (alternative) medicine.

This is followed by an evaluation of these modalities and also some proposals as to the most appropriate way to regulate the practice of alternative providers, in particular, by non-allopathic practitioners.

7.3.2.2 Licensure Modalities

There are various possibilities available to the lawmaker in order to regulate the practice of medicine, from the total exclusion of non-allopathic practitioners and alternative medicines to the free practice of medicine. Four main licensure modalities have been identified when regulating the practice of alternative practitioners, namely:[145]

141 Sometimes, this competence is delegated to local authorities or professional orders. For a study on the relationship between the State and the professions, see COBURN D., *op. cit.*: 841–50.

142 In medicine, there is a risk of damage to the health of individuals, and by extension to public health. For a development, see chap. 6.5.

143 The British Select Committee on Science and Technology notes that "the principal purpose of regulation of any healthcare profession is to protect the public from unqualified or inadequately trained practitioners. The effective regulation of a therapy thus allows the public to understand where to look in order to get safe treatment from well-trained practitioners in an environment where their rights are protected. It also underpins the healthcare profession' confidence in a therapy's practitioners and is therefore fundamental in the development of all healthcare professions" (SELECT COMMITTEE ON SCIENCE AND TECHNOLOGY, *op. cit.*: 36).

144 ABBOTT A., *op. cit.*: 62–63; DE BIJL N., *op. cit.*: 5–16; FURROW B. R. (I), *op. cit.*: 56; LIANG B. A., *op. cit.*: 149; SELECT COMMITTEE ON SCIENCE AND TECHNOLOGY, *op. cit.*: 36–37; SWEDISH COMMISSION ON COMPETENCE, *op. cit.*: 34.

145 These licensure modalities are the solutions adopted by countries defined as monopolistic, tolerant, inclusive and integrated. For more details, see chap. 4.2. Regarding the presentation of licensure modalities, see CHAPMAN-SMITH D. A., *op. cit.*: 111–13 (chiropractic); COHEN M. H. (I), *op. cit.*: 36–37 (US); DE REYNIER V., *op. cit.*: 15ss (Switzerland); RÖSCH B., *op. cit.*: 118ss (Switzerland, with

1. Mandatory licensure. Unlicensed practitioners are prohibited from providing licensed services. The holding of a diploma attesting that the practitioner successfully attended a training program is usually required. Although this system is typical of monopolistic countries,[146] some tolerant states also employ such a system in order to regulate the practice of specific alternative medicines.[147]
2. Registration. Providers must register their name, address and practice with a body, which may be public or semi-public, to receive a registration certificate or licence to practise. The same body receives and investigates complaints against those registered and provides appropriate disciplinary measures. The registration may be mandatory. In this case, non-registered practitioners are prohibited from practising. States may require practitioners to provide a diploma attesting that they successfully attended a training program before they can be registered.[148]
3. Title licensure. This requirement makes a demonstrable level of skill or training mandatory for those who claim a particular title. Uncertified providers may continue to offer services without risking prosecution

criticism at 263ss); WICKI M., *op. cit.*: 74ss (Switzerland); WHITE HOUSE COMMISSION ON COMPLEMENTARY AND ALTERNATIVE MEDICINE POLICY, *op. cit.*: 93 (US).

146 E.g., in France, Italy, Spain and formerly in Belgium. In these countries a licence to practise is compulsory for the providing of all medical acts. Furthermore, only the practice of allopathic medicine is allowed. E.g., in Spain, the providing of non-scientifically proven techniques as well as the simulation of the making of a diagnosis, or the application of therapeutic treatments are prohibited.

147 E.g., in Hungary or in Belgium. This is also the case in several US states. In Alaska, only those licensed as acupuncturists (a diploma is required) are allowed to provide acupuncture. Similarly, Rhode Island and Washington provide that only licensed massage therapists may practise massage therapy. Swiss canton Schwyz also has a similar system regarding the practice of acupuncture. In Germany, "Heilpraktikers" must pass the "Heilpraktiker" exam to be allowed to practise. See also the situation in Swiss cantons Aargau, Basel Land, Graubünden, Obwalden, Solothurn, Sankt-Gallen and Shaffhausen.
Liechtenstein is a special case. In this country, "natural medicine" is not considered as being medicine. Therefore, a commercial authorisation (and not a licence to practise medical acts) is sufficient to practise.

148 E.g., several US States mandate registration for specific practices such as acupuncture in the states of Iowa, Pennsylvania and Colorado, or massage in Arkansas, North Dakota and Texas. The practice of chiropractic is similarly regulated in Norway and Sweden.

for illegal or unauthorised practice, provided they do not use the statutorily defined title.[149]

4. Free practice. Non-allopathic practitioners are allowed to provide alternative treatments without any licence or registration. They may freely develop self-regulation.[150]

For all the countries analysed in this research, specific medical procedures are strictly reserved to physicians through a mandatory licensure system although some combinations are possible. For example, in Great Britain any person is, in principle, free to practise medicine excepting those medical acts reserved specifically for physicians.[151] However, some titles are protected and in order to be allowed to claim the title, a competent body must register those practitioners who wish to obtain such title. In Swiss canton Basel Stadt, an authorisation is necessary for the independent practice of "curative medicine" (naturopathy and phytotherapy), homeopathy, traditional Chinese medicine, acupuncture and ayurveda. For other techniques a person is only required to advise the competent body concerned that he or she is starting to practice, which implies entering a register.

Another element is that protection of titles may also be ensured in mandatory licensure[152] or registration systems.

149 E.g., in Great Britain the titles of osteopath and chiropractor are protected, as are the titles of chiropractor, naprapath, and osteopath in Finland, and chiropractor in Norway. To be allowed to provide treatments under the protected title, the holding of a diploma is necessary.
In the Netherlands, the new legislation is oriented in the same direction. Unregulated professions have the possibility to organise themselves, and to gain a protected title, when some conditions are satisfied.
In the US, psychology licensing statutes often use this approach: any person may practice psychology, but only licensed psychologists may use the title or describe their services by using the words psychologist, psychology or psychological.

150 E.g., in Denmark or in the Netherlands. States allowing lay or traditional practice have usually also adopted such a system (e.g., Swiss cantons Neuchâtel and Ticino, or the US state of New Mexico). Self-regulation is the model generally employed to regulate the practice of chiropractic (for further discussion on this area, see CHAPMAN-SMITH D. A., *op. cit.*: 111–13).
Holcombe proposes to suppress state regulation to regulate the practice of medicine, leaving private initiatives, in other words the market, to auto-control the providing of alternative medicines (HOLCOMBE R. G., *op. cit.*: 236–46).

151 Through a compulsory licensure scheme.

152 In this system, the protection of titles is implicit. Indeed, only those licensed are allowed to practise and therefore to use the title.

Although some licensure modalities are typical to a regulation orientation,[153] none of these excludes the providing of alternative medicines.[154]

7.3.2.3 *Evaluation*

A. Protection of patients vs. Access to treatment

The lawmaker has three main objectives to focus upon when it decides to regulate 'alternative' medical practice. First, the regulation must protect patients. Second, the regulation must guarantee the quality of care. Finally, the regulation must allow patients access to the treatments they want. The several licensure modalities will be evaluated according to these objectives in the section below.[155]

The protection of public health and the requirement of good faith has driven many countries to reserve to the allopathic professions the provision of all therapeutic methods, in particular, to physicians. The first argument justifying such regulation is the concern that the health of citizens could be endangered if a person lacking the requisite attempts to. Second, there is the risk that non-allopathic practitioners will be unable to make a correct diagnosis or will take the patient away from allopathic medicine. Finally, legislators feared that non-allopathic practitioners would prey on uneducated and economically disadvantaged individuals by proposing services at lower costs and thus making remedies more appealing to them than those of primary care physicians. It is noticeable that the protection of public health and quality of care are viewed as being inseparable. Indeed, as the practice of medicine is considered a dangerous activity, only those having sufficient training may safely and appropriately deliver health care, that

153 E.g., mandatory licensure is typical to monopolistic countries and free practice typical of tolerant countries.

154 E.g., some US states regulate several alternative professions in a mandatory way, such as osteopaths or acupuncturists. In these states, the providing of health care is restricted to licensed professionals.

155 See, e.g. ANONYMOUS (IV), *op. cit.*: 31; LANNOYE P., *op. cit.*: 4; WICKI M., *op. cit.*: 66ss; WHITE HOUSE COMMISSION ON COMPLEMENTARY AND ALTERNATIVE MEDICINE POLICY, *op. cit.*: 91.

is according to the standards of practice and quality. In other words, the quality of care is part of the protection of patients.[156, 157]

This approach, however, seems less sustainable today. The first two arguments are refuted by the fact that, as we demonstrated earlier,[158] the risks are low, and may be contained within other licensure modalities.[159] In response to the final argument, Josefek states that, in a world of medical care where patients require access to alternative techniques and are always more informed about medical acts in general, this reason sounds more like a protectionist measure in favour of the allopathic professions. He adds "abuses exists in all areas of medicine; therefore, it is up to the legislature to appoint foot soldiers to police all the halls of medicine, not just those that run outside the mainstream".[160] In this respect De Bijl also observes that

156 Liang observes that "licensing [...] is based on overlapping concerns that unqualified practice could pose a serious risk to an individual patient's health, safety, or economic well-being; this risk would be likely to occur without a licensing system; the public could not adequately assess a practitioner's qualifications without guidance; and the benefits of licensure would be greater than the potential harmful effects of licensing" (LIANG B. A., *op. cit.*: 149).
Similarly Furrow states that "Licensing statutes regulate entry into the licensed professions, disciplinary actions and the delivery of health care services by unlicensed persons" (FURROW B. R. (I), *op. cit.*: 56). And then "The general justification for licensure entry requirements is the same as that used for licensure in general: entry requirements contribute to the quality of health care; and the expertise of the regulatory system, rather than consumer choice in the market, is required for effective quality control" (idem, at 58). See also WICKI M., *op. cit.*: 66ss.
In the US, Josefek notes that "opponents [to alternative medicines] maintain that alternative care providers represent a wider ethnic cross-section of the American public; therefore, disadvantaged or under-represented classes feel more comfortable visiting these practitioners and may be seduced by their attentiveness. [...] Without safeguards in place, these opponents maintain, uneducated individuals may be inclined to seek alternative treatment rather than visit their primary care physician and be misled by these practitioners simply because of the emotional satisfaction that they derive from these practitioners" (JOSEFEK K. J., *op. cit.*: 304).

157 BOOZANG K. M. (I), *op. cit.*: 211; EHLERS A. P. F., *op. cit.*: 275–78; GUILLOD O. (I), *op. cit.*: 31; JOSEFEK K. J., *op. cit.*: 304–06; RÖSCH B., *op. cit.*: 119–20.

158 See chap. 6.5.

159 For further developments, see below.

160 JOSEFEK K. J., *op. cit.*: 304. Similarly, Stone notes "We shall argue that the present 'medical model' of regulation is too heavily centred on the maintenance of professional self-interest at the expense of the interests of the consumer" (STONE J., *op. cit.*: 3).

> in principle, the monopolistic system can offer patients much protection, but with a view to the factual freedom of patients to choose either a doctor or someone who is not, a prohibition system seems to represent a too massive method to do justice to both protection and freedom of choice of patients.[161]

There is no doubt today that exclusive policies aiming to forbid the use of alternative medicines to all medical practitioners are questionable.[162] As previously shown, the use of alternative medicines and the role they play in Western society is already important and will probably increase.[163] Alternative medicines often fulfil the needs of certain patients in a way that biomedicine cannot[164] and may be as valuable an approach to a specific medical problem as biomedicine.[165] Thus, policies based on simple ignorance, outright rejection or banning of alternative medicines are no longer appropriate.[166] There is, in fact, a trend toward either an increasing tolerance of alternative medicines and practitioners, whether allopathic or not,[167] or an increasingly tolerant perspective taken of any regulation controlling the licensing to practise alternative medicines.[168] It is also noteworthy that in

161 De Bijl N., *op. cit.*: 14–15.
Similarly the Swiss Conference of Directors of Health Affairs states that the traditional system of licensing, based on mandatory licensure restricted to allopathic professions, is in general, considered to be excessively strict and ineffective. Furthermore, it is not compatible with the recent rulings of the Swiss Federal Court regarding economical freedom (Conférence des Directeurs Cantonaux des Affaires Sanitaires (I), *op. cit.*: 32).
Furrow notes, in relation to the situation in the US, that "entry requirements for licensed health care practitioners have been criticised as discriminating against minorities; as raising the price of services; [...] as inappropriately restricting access of individuals to the occupational market; [...] and as slowing innovation in health care by mandating uniformity in education" (Furrow B. R. (I), *op. cit.*: 58). See also Jost T. S. (II), *op. cit.*: 2ss.
See also Holcombe R. G., *op. cit.*: 243ss, as well as chap. 7.2.2.3.

162 See Conférence des Directeurs Cantonaux des Affaires Sanitaires (I), *op. cit.*: 36 ; Holcombe R. G., *op. cit.*: 236–46.

163 See chap. 2.

164 See chap. 2.

165 See chap. 2 and 6.

166 See Domenighetti G., *op. cit.*: 570. The author states that, on the basis of a sociological study of the use of alternative medicines by the Swiss population, a restrictive policy towards alternative medicines seems unacceptable not only to consumers, but also by a great proportion of the medical corpus.

167 E.g., countries (more specifically their courts) such as Spain, Italy or the Swiss canton Vaud have become more tolerant toward alternative practitioners.

168 E.g., some states in the US, where physicians were still risking prosecution for providing treatments whose efficiency had not yet proven, Freedom Practice Acts were enacted, to formally allow physicians to provide alternative treatments.

all the monopolistic countries studied, both allopathic and non-allopathic practitioners provide alternative medicines and further, that no country has changed its tolerant approach to that of a monopolistic one.[169]

The protection of patients in monopolistic countries is supposedly guaranteed through a strict access to medical professions and while this vision may have made sense in the past, it is no longer in accordance with the needs and wishes of the modern informed patient. Therefore, it should in our view be left aside.[170]

Some countries still have a monopolistic system in theory, but no longer implement it in practice. As non-allopathic practitioners still face the risk of prosecution given the lack of security provided by the legal structure, it is evident that such a situation should be only transitional. The definitive position should be to inject some certainty into the law, by allowing non-allopathic practitioners to practise a specific alternative technique when they satisfy certain requirements.

In Belgium and in the Netherlands, the system used to be monopolistic, however, today, the practice of alternative medicines by non-allopathic practitioners is allowed. Regarding the former situation in Netherlands, De Bijl notes that "in the monopolistic system it is possible to offer the patient a high level of protection. However, the experience in the Netherlands under the 1865 Act learns that it is very difficult to enforce the prohibition on unauthorised practice. It is contravened so often that in practice only unauthorised practitioners who have caused serious harm to their patients have been prosecuted. So the monopoly system in the Netherlands does not succeed in protecting the patient completely from untrained and unqualified people" (DE BIJL N., *op. cit.*: 14–15).
In Switzerland, new health regulations, case law, and theory are moving towards a more open approach regarding alternative medicines while hostile attitudes are being slowly left aside. In 1992, canton Berne even introduced in its new Constitution (art. 41 (4)) encouragement of natural therapeutic methods. All of the recent regulations (Basel Stadt, Solothurn, Bern, Valais, Neuchâtel, Fribourg, Geneva and Zürich) allow for the providing of alternative medicines by both allopathic and non-allopathic practitioners.

169 However, in some monopolistic countries, physicians still risk prosecution when providing alternative medicines, such as France.

170 According to Cohen "By separating medical from nonmedical practitioners, and granting state medical boards bread authority to punish deviation from medical orthodoxy, irrespective of patient injury, the existing regulatory environment favours a health care system dominated by orthodox medicine, based on technological approaches to disease and healing, and modelled on the assumption that patients lack the requisite sophistication to choose who may minister to the diseased body. This regulatory approach is not well suited to a health care system in which chiropractors, naturopaths, acupuncturists, nutritionists, massage therapists and the patient share responsibility for the task of healing, in which patients value freedom of access to treatment, and in which patient autonomy supersedes paternalistic approaches to well-being." (COHEN M. H. (II), *op. cit.*, 86).

B. A controlled liberalisation

Free practice and title protection

As we have seen, the risk criterion should not be applied from a monopolistic perspective. That is to say that the Western traditional way of licensing health care practitioners should be reversed. Indeed, it seems a more sensible approach today to commence with the guaranteeing of access to treatment, and then to set up a framework in order to ensure the protection of patients and the quality of care. In other words, the providing of health care must be liberalised, but in a controlled way.[171]

The most appropriate modality licensure is, in our view, free practice without any requirement of authorisation, as it provides the best guarantee of freedom of choice[172] for both allopathic and non-allopathic health care.[173] However, the state should still have the possibility to intervene in exceptional circumstances in order to forbid the practice of a specific technique or to prohibit a particular individual from practising.[174]

Once freedom of choice is guaranteed, the focus should be on the encouragement of high quality treatment. In this respect, the title licensure modality is a good solution. Indeed, the creation of protected titles provides a guarantee as to the seriousness of the practitioners, and therefore as to the high standard and safety of the provided care. The creation of protected and recognised titles is particularly indicated in the field of alternative medicines where patients are often unable to separate the wheat from the chaff. The protection of patients will finally result from the information they receive rather than from restrictive licensing policies. In addition to title protection, general information concerning alternative medicines should not only be made available upon request from a patient but publicised generally.[175]

171 The Swiss Conference of Directors of Health Affairs is in favour of such a system, namely a fundamentally liberal system, but with the possibility to implement interdictions as a preventive tool (CONFÉRENCE DES DIRECTEURS CANTONAUX DES AFFAIRES SANITAIRES (I), *op. cit.*: 33, 37).

172 Of course, to take advantage of this freedom, coverage of alternative medicines should also be guaranteed. This question will be analysed later (chap. 7.4).

173 For a comparison of the advantages and disadvantages of a statutory and self-regulation, see SELECT COMMITTEE ON SCIENCE AND TECHNOLOGY, *op. cit.*: 42ss.

174 The revised Swiss canton Zürich Act on Public Health (art. 9) should provide such a possibility.

175 The British Select Committee on Science and Technology notes that, "the popularity of CAM raises important questions in terms of information provision and validation. For a patient or a doctor wishing to find out more about a CAM therapy,

A profession[176] should be regulated and thereby benefit from a protected title when some conditions are fulfilled. Of interest are the sound criteria established by the British government that must be fulfilled in order to gain a statutory regulation:[177]

1. "The therapy has been long established and has an established and credible system of voluntary regulation;

information will be required to answer the following questions: What is involved in the treatment? What conditions do its advocates claim it can treat? What is the evidence to support these claims? What might be the side effects? Whose views can I trust? Whose views can I trust? For patients, two furthers questions are likely to be: What does my doctor think about it? And what conventional medical treatment should I compare it to? Doctors are likely to ask: What is the consensus medical view?". Possibly, patients will ask "Is the treatment available on the NHS? How much does it cost privately? Where are the local practitioners? Which one is well-qualified and proficient?" (SELECT COMMITTEE ON SCIENCE AND TECHNOLOGY, *op. cit.*: 94). For proposals regarding the situation in Great Britain, see the same author at 97 where the Department of Health should make information on CAM directly available through NHS. For further developments in this area, see the same author at 94ss. See also BRITISH MEDICAL ASSOCIATION, *op. cit.*: 46; HOLCOMBE R. G., *op. cit.*: 241ss, and chap. 7.3.5.8.

176 Feasby identifies three indicia of health professions, namely; 1. a statutory recognition; 2. a specialised education; and 3. a substantially different treatment. The author considers that when the three markers, or at least the last two are demonstrated, one may consider a practice as a profession (FEASBY C., *op. cit.*: 54–55).
The last index (substantially different treatment) requires that the school of alternative medicine in question have some degree of uniformity of treatment. See also SELECT COMMITTEE ON SCIENCE AND TECHNOLOGY, *op. cit.*: 49 (criteria for a profession); ABBOTT A., *op. cit.* (analysis of the professionalism phenomenon).

177 BRITISH MEDICAL ASSOCIATION, *op. cit.*: 62–63.
Also of note are the Dutch criteria developed for the implementation of the new Health Practitioners Act. The criteria for registering a profession are: 1. the need for disciplinary procedures and; 2. the need for direct authorisation to carry out reserved procedures. The criteria applicable to a profession are: 1. the need for public information (protected title); 2. the need to regulate the independent providing of reserved procedures, and; 3. the need to regulate a specific training (MINISTRY OF HEALTH, *op. cit.*: 2). For the British Select Committee on Science and Technology, the criterion for determining the need for statutory regulation is whether the therapy poses significant risk to the public from its practice (SELECT COMMITTEE ON SCIENCE AND TECHNOLOGY, *op. cit.*: 50).
For further developments concerning the ways to achieve statutory regulation in Great Britain, see SELECT COMMITTEE ON SCIENCE AND TECHNOLOGY, *op. cit.*: 44ss.

2. there are recognised courses of training, including a structured system of assessment with external examiners;
3. there is a consensus upon the way forward amongst all the different organisations within the therapy;
4. the medical profession is broadly supportive of the move towards statutory regulation."

Enhancement of self-regulation

Professions that do not benefit from a protected title should have the opportunity to evolve within the regulatory framework. Indeed, it could result in the inclusion of valuable new standardised treatments within existing framework.[178] In the same perspective, these professions could set up self-regulations, which could form the basis for first a complete training program, and then a protected title.[179] As Stone observes,

> more important than the length of establishment is the degree of organisation of the therapy. A credible system of voluntary regulation will be a vital pre-requisite of statutory regulation. The osteopaths and chiropractors were well established and well organised as professional groups for decades before achieving statutory recognition.[180]

She adds that as far as Great Britain is concerned,

> the current professionalisation taking place within CAM is to be encouraged. Effective voluntary regulation and the existence of single professional registers can provide many of the safeguards of statutory regulation. Voluntary self-regulation is less expensive to administer and for that reason alone carries the support of many practitioners. Since incidence of serious harm appears to be low, and is equally capable or arising in a statutory context, there would seem to be

178 Such phenomenon in the US has been highlighted by Cohen (COHEN M. H. (I), *op. cit.*: 37).

179 Budd has developed the features of an effective voluntary self-regulatory body, which are the following: 1. to maintain a register of individual members or member organisations; 2. to set educational standards and to run an accreditation system for training establishments; 3. to maintain professional competence among its members with an adequate program of continuing professional development; 4. to provide codes of conduct, ethics and practice; 5. to have in place a complaints mechanism for members of the public; 6. to have in place a disciplinary procedure that is accessible to the public; 7. to require members to have adequate professional indemnity insurance; 8. to have the capacity to represent the whole profession; 9. to include external representation on executive councils to represent patients or clients and the wider public interest. See BUDD S., *op. cit.*

180 STONE J., *op. cit.*: 94.

> no justification at the present time for introducing mandatory licensing or statutory regulation for all practitioners.[181]

The Individual Health Care Professionals Act enacted recently in the Netherlands also enhances self-regulation. Similarly, the Norwegian Committee on alternative medicine suggests the establishment of a register for alternative practitioners, which should be open to all those persons wishing to employ alternative medicines. The purpose of such a register would be to distinguish between various practitioners based on a set of criteria.[182]

181 Stone J., *op. cit.*: 287.
A study showed that self-regulation is the model usually employed to regulate chiropractic (Chapman-Smith D. A., *op. cit.*: 111–13). Cohen notes that "holistic professions seeking licensure frequently create state-accredited educational institutions, professional organisations, and national professional accrediting bodies and examinations, [...] which then offer convenient and inexpensive bases for state licensure. [...] States look to professional organisations to accredit specific educational institutions within the profession or use these institutions or professionally developed examinations or certifying programmes as bases for licensure." (Cohen M. H. (I), *op. cit.*: 37). Further, that "internal accreditation or certification can become the basis not only for initial licensure but also for upgrading professional status within an existing licensed profession" (idem, at 38).
For recent development concerning the setting up and implementation of self-regulation, see Orentlicher D., *op. cit.*: 129–48. The author argues that professional societies (in particular physician societies) are more successful in setting up standards that they are at ensuring acceptance and implementation of such standards. The will of alternative practitioners to be fully recognised (particulary at the coverage level), and the threat of losing title protection, may be strong incentives to comply with self-regulation. The violation of professional standards should result in proper sanctions in order to ensure the implementation of such standards.
For propositions regarding the establishment of statutory self-regulatory body, see Anonymous (IV), *op. cit.*: 33–34; Select Committee on Science and Technology, *op. cit.*: 43–44, 50.
For a study regarding the evolution of professions, see Abbott A., *op. cit.* (the author shows that professionalisation may imply several steps, which may occur through non-predefined sequence).

182 The criteria for registering would be the following:
1. membership of a professional organisation for alternative practitioners. The Ministry of Health and Social Affairs should accredit organisations where membership provides grounds for registration. These organisations must make qualification requirements for membership, have professional ethical rules and a disciplinary system for considering complaints about members' professional conduct, with the option of exclusion, and have a minimum of 30 members (the committee rejected the enforcement of a requirement for a minimum competency level in basic medical subjects, and/or of a competency level in the relevant alternative medical treatment);

Registration and professional structure

To have an efficient system, a title licensure scheme may be reinforced with some features of the registration system.[183] In this respect, the recent Dutch and British regulations are particularly interesting. The Dutch regulation provides that the performance of medical procedures is no longer restricted to specific medical practitioners. However, the Individual Health Care Professions Act has introduced a system that protects the titles of a limited number of professional groups.[184] When a medical profession is regulated by law, their providers are entitled to enter their names in legal public registers. This registration gives them the right to practise under a protected title,[185] with the aim of ensuring they are qualified in a specific field of health care.[186] In order to be registered, professional practitioners have to meet some legal requirements, the most important being that the practitioner has successfully completed the appropriate training. In order to develop additional registers, the Dutch government encourages and stimulates practitioners using alternative medicines and their professional organisations, both non-allopathic and allopathic, to meet certain

2. the taking out of a liability insurance to ensure that injured patients receive economic settlement if the injury triggers compensation;
3. documentation of the business for the past year in the annual report, or general business report, or declaration from employer.

The revocation or non-award of registration or of a licence will represent a sanction. For more details, see Ministry of Health and Social Affairs, *op. cit.*: 273.

183 Such a system may offer a certain level of consumer protection, which varies according to the requirements conditioning the registration, and whether the registration is mandatory or not. As one commentator notes "while voluntary self-regulation cannot protect a professional title, such a system can, if properly structured and administered, provide patients with real safeguards. Indeed, if a voluntary regulatory scheme can establish a single, high profile, lead registering body which inspires the confidence of the public as well as practitioners, then the threat of removing a practitioner from the register can provide a significant deterrent to unethical conduct" (Anonymous (IV), *op. cit.*: 32).

184 Namely, medical doctor, dentist, pharmaceutical chemist, health care psychologist, psychotherapist, physiotherapist, midwife and nurse.

185 The registration is valid only for a limited period. Applications for re-registration will be assessed primarly on the basis of individual competence. If this requirement is not met, the applicant will not be re-registered thus losing the right to use a legally protected title.

186 The purpose is to make it clear to the public and to the insurance companies in which field they are experts.

standards of quality, to develop training courses and to set up professional codes of practice and procedures for peer review.[187]

Similarly, the British Osteopath and Chiropractor Acts are based upon registration as allopathic professions.[188] The right to use a protected title is restricted to registered practitioners and the registration depends, among other conditions, upon a recognised qualification.[189]

However, the registration system seems less appropriate when it is set up alone, without requiring serious guarantees as to the skills of practitioners if the purpose is to encourage the creation of registers in conjunction with title licensure. For example, some Swiss cantons oblige their non-allopathic practitioners to inform the authorities when they start to practise, which implies the creation of a register,[190] but without requiring any diplomas or proof of an adequate personal profile. The Swiss Conference of Directors of Health Affairs considers this solution as unsatisfactory. Indeed, such a solution gives the impression that the state controls the activity, when in fact it is not responsible for verifying the professional competences of the practitioner, nor the techniques that are provided.[191]

187 According to the British Medical Association "clearly, the Dutch legislation will have profound implications for the practice of non-conventional medicine in the Netherlands. In order to register, professional groups such as acupuncturists, osteopaths, chiropractors, and homeopaths will have to provide a clear professional profile of their scope of practice and skills" (BRITISH MEDICAL ASSOCIATION, *op. cit.*: 21).
Cohen writes of the US that "title licensure suggests that a broader class of professionals than those governmentally approved should be permitted to join the healing enterprise" (COHEN M. H. (I), *op. cit.*: 36).

188 A council is in charge of allowing candidates to practise under a protected title and of disciplinary jurisdiction. For more developments regarding the situation in Great Britain, see SELECT COMMITTEE ON SCIENCE AND TECHNOLOGY, *op. cit.*: 42ss; STONE J., *op. cit.*

189 There was also a Swiss initiative to create official diplomas for physicians in alternative medicines. Also a Finnish initiative to create protected titles for chiropractors, naprapaths and osteopaths. The European Committee for Homeopathy is also in favour of creating registers on a national level (EUROPEAN COMMITTEE FOR HOMEOPATHY, *op. cit.*: 29).

190 E.g., the Swiss cantons of Basel Stadt and Solothurn.

191 In Germany, the same effect has been noted.

Furthermore, in practice, such a system is ineffective, expensive and time consuming to implement.[192]

It is also apparent that the setting up of either statutory or self- regulation creates the need for bodies that may effectively implement these regulations.[193]

Restricted medical acts

A proposed solution would seek to avoid the creation of monopolistic situations, as the providing of health care would remain open to those professions able to fulfil the appropriate requirements. Nor would such a solution ignore the fact that dangerous activities have to be restricted to practitioners providing serious guarantee. In order to ensure good protection of patients and good quality of care, the most appropriate licensure modality seems to be the mandatory system.[194] As it sets high requirements for training and skills that practitioners must comply with in order to be authorised to provide care.[195] However, a title licensure system as

192 CONFÉRENCE DES DIRECTEURS CANTONAUX DES AFFAIRES SANITAIRES (I), *op. cit.*: 32, 34; MINISTRY OF HEALTH AND SOCIAL AFFAIRS (I), *op. cit.*: 273. Some authors have, however, proposed the division of alternative practitioners into two categories, namely those who attended a basic medical training, and those who did not undergo such training. In this system, practitioners of both categories could be registered (SWEDISH COMMISSION ON ALTERNATIVE MEDICINE, *op. cit.*: 27, 33–34). We do not agree with such a proposal, for the above-mentioned reasons.

193 For other developments on the subject, see chap. 7.3.6.
The British Select Committee on Science and Technology notes that, "in many circumstances, voluntary self-regulation may, when administered by a single professional body, be as effective as statutory regulation", although "statutory regulation does offer greater power of control than voluntary regulation" (SELECT COMMITTEE ON SCIENCE AND TECHNOLOGY, *op. cit.*: 42, 43).

194 Holcombe goes further. He proposes to suppress all state regulations regarding the practise of medicine. The market and private initiatives should, in the author's view, regulate the field. See HOLCOMBE R. G., *op. cit.*: 236–46.

195 As Cohen writes, "because mandatory licensing often sets the highest requirements for training and skill, it offers holistic providers the greatest rigor, status, and prestige" (COHEN M. H. (I), *op. cit.*: 36). The author adds "licensure offers nonlicensed holistic providers several benefits in addition to protection from medical acts. First, licensure creates a minimum level of professional competence, elevates the image of a profession, and assuages public and legislative concern over quality control. [...] Second, independent licensure prevents other professionals from gaining control over the licensed profession [...]. Third, licensure furnishes a recognised basis for hospital privileges, insurance reimbursement, and other professional opportunities" (idem at 35).

described above, particularly if serious guarantees are provided as to the training and survey of practitioners, could provide the same guarantees as a mandatory system. Typically, only practitioners holding a specific title would be allowed to provide specific medical acts whether allopathic or not, or possibly an entire technique,[196] if such activity is linked to substantial risks.[197]

The question then arises as to how to determine which activity is dangerous, and how to make such activity safe. To avoid the introduction of an indirect form of monopoly, these activities must be clearly defined.[198] In this respect, the use of criteria[199] may be particularly useful.[200]

Even regulation for alternative medicines

An advantage of the suggested system would be the creation of an even regulation for all medical practices, and thus to provide clear guidelines to the various participants in the field. As the Norwegian Ministry of Health and Social Affairs states, it is

196 For more developments regarding the limits of competence, see STONE J., *op. cit.*: 245ss.

197 Currently, in the Netherlands, allopathic professions are regulated through a title licensure system.
One may add that allopathic practitioners (and more slowly some non-allopathic professions as well) need affiliation with those institutions (hospitals, health insurance companies, malpractice liability insurers), which can play an oversight role. In this example, the title provides some interesting advantages for those holding it.
Guillod opts for an authorisation system where non-allopathic practitioners could obtain a licence to practise upon compliance with several basic conditions (GUILLOD O. (I), *op. cit.*: 38). Nevertheless, his proposal meets the same objective, namely limiting first the right to practise dangerous activities solely to those practitioners providing some guarantees, and then giving the right to practise in a preferential way to those having serious training.

198 On this subject, Andrews states that "Legislators should take several steps to gain the benefit of alternative providers while protecting against risks. First, they should limit the definitions of the practice of medicine so that they cover not all of health care, but only particularly hazardous interventions and so that they do not apply to mere 'conditions'." (ANDREWS L. B., *op. cit.*: 1315). See also EHLERS A. P. F., *op. cit.*: 279ss (Germany); SWEDISH COMMISSION ON COMPETENCE, *op. cit.*: 40 (Sweden).

199 For further developments on this subject, see chap. 7.3.3.2.

200 For further developments regarding the relationship between the control of risks and the training of practitioners, see chap. 7.3.5.2.
For further developments regarding the notion of risk and safety, see chap. 6.5.

> unnecessary and rather unfruitful to suggest a special licensing scheme for alternative medicine practitioners. A special scheme would create uncertainty and confusion, and help sustain the perception that there is a sharp distinction between such practitioners and health personnel.[201]

Nevertheless, some authors have proposed different way to regulate alternative medicines. For example, Stone is of the opinion that

> existing complementary therapies are at such disparate stages of therapeutic and professional organisations that it would be absurd to attempt to unite them under a single statutory scheme, even if they uniformly wanted to pursue statutory regulation, which clearly many therapies do not.[202]

The particularity of the system we propose is precisely to provide a regulatory framework for practices already in a position to be regulated, while offering the possibility to others to develop and gain statutory recognition. The opinion of many commentators who are against an even regulatory scheme is based on their concerns about adequate protection for the patient.[203] However, the system proposed takes into account the importance of safety and quality in health care, and at the same time inserts solid safeguards to guarantee them.

Certain authors have argued that some categories of alternative practitioners, especially non-allopathic practitioners, should be permitted to provide alternative medicines without any authorisation. In particular, some supporters of alternative medicines fear that the philosophy behind the field will be lost through the licensure process.[204]

201 MINISTRY OF HEALTH AND SOCIAL AFFAIRS (I), *op. cit.*: 273.

202 STONE J., *op. cit.*: 285.
We do not agree with the opinion of Cohen who argues for a differentiated regulation of medical techniques. In particular, he considers that registration may be more appropriate for some techniques, such as massage therapy, because they require fewer hours of training and mastery of a more streamlined corpus of information and skills (COHEN M. H. (I), *op. cit.*: 36). Similarly, others consider that "not all non-conventional therapies require regulation by statute. For the majority of therapies, adoption of a code of practice, training structures, and voluntary registration would be sufficient" (BRITISH MEDICAL ASSOCIATION, *op. cit.*: 67). See also, e.g., ANONYMOUS (IV), *op. cit.*: 31.

203 The British Medical Association is of the opinion that "no single method of control will be suitable for all forms of non-conventional therapy. Those therapies posing greater potential risks to patients require legal regulation by statute to protect consumers from unskilled or incompetent practitioners" (BRITISH MEDICAL ASSOCIATION, *op. cit.*: 62). See also, e.g., ANONYMOUS (IV), *op. cit.*: 31.

204 COHEN M. H. (I), *op. cit.*: 35–36.

It is not a sustainable argument to state that non-allopathic practitioners must be allowed to freely practise because alternative medicines have a holistic orientation, which is not in accordance with Western concepts. Indeed, the biomedical model still remains the prevailing standard in Western countries, and practices must be so regulated as to be in accordance with it, particularly in the providing of serious guarantees regarding the safety and quality of care. This does not mean that alternative techniques must be modified, but rather that the provision of alternative medicines must satisfy specific requirements, especially when there are potential risks. In this respect, we are convinced that the system we have proposed here, which is inspired by recent regulatory solutions, may be implemented for such practices,[205] without killing "the heart and art" of the technique.[206]

Finally, the above-proposed system allows reluctant practitioners to develop the provision of non-dangerous activities outside a restricting framework without the requirements of statutory recognition if not desired.

Quality of care

In this proposed regulatory perspective, the concept of quality of care is dissociated from the strict concept of patient protection. Indeed, quality of care is guaranteed for dangerous activities by reserving such activities solely to those practitioners who can provide serious guarantees. The same guarantee applies to non-dangerous activities, through the incentives given to alternative practitioners to practise under a protected title.

Medical supervision

Another recurrent question concerns the right to practise alternative medicines without being under the supervision of a physician or another health care provider. The solution adopted by some countries which is to allow non-allopathic practitioners to practise only under the surveillance of a physician may be viewed as excessive. In reality, this limitation is seldom respected in practice.[207] In our view, such a right is mainly a question of

205 See the various regulations in the US, as well as the new laws in Belgium and Hungary.

206 Even inclusive and integrated systems, such as exist in China or India, have set up strict conditions that must be met before the practise of alternative medicines is allowed.

207 In France and in Spain, where ancillary professionals provide alternative medicine without the supervision of a physician, even if they are not authorised to do so.

training. If ancillary practitioners or non-allopathic practitioners are correctly trained, they should be able to directly provide care to patients in an independent way. This means that even if practitioners have not been sufficiently trained, they should still be allowed, under certain circumstances, to practise under the supervision of a qualified practitioner.[208] More generally, medical referral and supervision is acceptable when patients are seriously ill,[209] in order to ensure their safety.[210] In this hypothesis, the practitioner making the referral should remain responsible for any subsequent care provided to the patient if such care is given as a result of the referral.[211]

7.3.2.4 Summary and Proposals[212]

In short, a system regulating the provision of medical practices must provide good protection for patients, ensure a high quality of care, and guarantee access to both allopathic and non-allopathic treatments.

208 The new Dutch regulation provides that two groups of medical practitioners may provide reserved procedures: those with direct authorization (namely doctors, dentists and midwives) and those performing the procedure under the instructions of the former category (and thereby authorised).

209 E.g., a physician in charge of a patient undertaking chemotherapy to treat cancer could propose acupuncture sessions to relieve the patient from side effects related to the chemotherapy.

210 The British Select Committee on Science and Technology recommends that all NHS provision of alternative medicines should continue to be through a GP or other healthcare professional working in the NHS in primary, secondary or tertiary care (SELECT COMMITTEE ON SCIENCE AND TECHNOLOGY, *op. cit.*: 9).

211 Great Britain has established some rules in this area. Even if physicians decide to refer patients to non-allopathic practitioners during the period of treatment, they still retain clinical responsibility for their patients. Thus, when employing auxiliary staff, doctors have to ensure that they work with practitioners having the appropriate academic and vocational qualifications. Furthermore, alternative practitioners must not contradict instructions or prescriptions given by physicians. For more details, see ANDREWS L. B., *op. cit.*: 1305; BRITISH MEDICAL ASSOCIATION, *op. cit.*: 46–48; STONE J., *op. cit.*: 276–77.

212 The following proposals are based on observations made during our research. Of course, these proposals must be considered as forming a basic model that must be adapted to the particularities of each country. In this respect, it is important to stress that other licensure modalities may be chosen. However, the functions of these modalities should be similar, in order to reach the same objectives namely, access to, quality of, and security of treatments.

In the current world of health care, where patients are more aware of medical possibilities, are more responsible, and ask therefore for more freedom of choice, the monopolistic approaches are out of date.

However, in order to ensure the protection of patients and the quality of care, a properly structured and administered title licensure (including some registration specificities) should be established. Indeed, it would offer the same guarantees as a mandatory licensure scheme, particularly as regards the skills of practitioners. In addition, general information about alternative medicines should be enhanced and controlled.

The right to deliver health care under a protected title should be made conditional upon registration in a legal public register. The main requirement for obtaining a registration should be the holding of a diploma attesting the skills of the candidate. Obviously, practitioners should also satisfy classic entry requirements prior to the delivering of a licence.

Only those holding a protected title should be permitted to provide health care that involves specific dangerous acts. Therefore, practitioners who do not benefit from a protected title could be allowed to practise only non-dangerous activities. Indeed, such a title could be misinterpreted and give patients the impression that these practitioners have received serious training and are therefore fully competent.

Professions without a protected title should have the opportunity to develop further within the regulatory framework, with the possibility eventually of gaining statutory recognition.

Practitioners working under the medical supervision of an authorised health care provider should be allowed to provide restricted activities.

We are also aware that licensure is not always feasible, generally for political reasons.[213] For this reason, the cost involved in the establishment and administration of a regulatory system, whether self-regulated or administered by public authorities, should also be taken into account.[214]

213 E.g., in the US, where political mobilisation for licensure may be counterproductive, resulting in more restrictive regulation (typically for massage techniques) (COHEN M. H. (I), *op. cit.*: 35).

214 See ANONYMOUS (IV), *op. cit.*: 32; CONFÉRENCE DES DIRECTEURS CANTONAUX DES AFFAIRES SANITAIRES (I), *op. cit.*: 32–33.

7.3.3 Scope of Practice

Bibliography

ANDREWS L. B., *The shadow health care system: Regulation of alternative health care providers*, in: Houston Law Review, 1996, vol. 32: 1305, 1315; BERNER D., *L'exercice illégal de la médecine ou les problèmes juridiques posés par les médecines parallèles*, in *Aspects du droit médical*, Editions universitaires, 1988, Fribourg: 155–58; BRITISH MEDICAL ASSOCIATION (LAMONT T.), *Complementary medicine – New approaches to good practice*, Oxford University Press, 1993, Oxford/New York: 46–48; CHAPMAN-SMITH D. A., *Legislative approaches to the regulation of the chiropractic profession*, in: J. Can. Chiropractic Assoc, June 1996, vol. 40, n° 2: 108–14; COHEN M. H. (I), *Complementary and alternative medicine – Legal boundaries and regulatory perspectives*, The Johns Hopkins University Press, 1998, London & Oxford; CONFÉRENCE DES DIRECTEURS CANTONAUX DES AFFAIRES SANITAIRES (I), *Rapport du groupe de travail "Autorisations de pratiquer les professions du domaine de la santé"*, CDS, 2000, Bern, available at: http://www.sdk-cds.ch/fr/berufsbildung-f.html, accessed July 30 2001; DE BIJL N. (co-author: NEDERVEEN-VAN DE KRAGT I.), *Legal safeguards against medical practice by not suitably qualified persons: A comparative study in seven EU-countries*, 1997, in: European Journal of Health Law, vol. 4: 14; EHLERS A. P. F., *Medizin in den Händen von Heilpraktikern – "Nicht-Heilkundigen"*, Springer Verlag, 1995, Berlin/Heidelberg: 279ss; FURROW B. R. (co-authors: GREANEY T. L., JOST T., SCHWARTZ R. L.) (I), *Health law*, West Publishing, 1995, St Paul: 67; GUILLOD O. (I), *Rebouteux, naturopathes et guérisseurs: Pour un traitement légal alternatif*, Recueil de Jurisprudence Neuchâtelois, 1989, Neuchâtel: 38; JOSEFEK K. J., *Alternative medicine's roadmap to mainstream*, in: American Journal of Law and Medicine, 2000, vol. 26: 301; LAMM L.C. (co-authors: WEGNER E. COLLORD D.), *Chiropractic scope of practice: What the law allows – update 1993*, in: J. Manipulative Physiol. Ther., Jan. 1995, vol. 18, n° 1: 16–20; LAY B. F., *Healer-patient privilege: extending the physician-patient privilege to alternative health practitioners in California*, in: Hastings Law Journal, Mar. 1997: 646–47; ROBARD I., *La santé hors la loi: Les hors la loi de la santé*, 4th ed., Ed. de l'Ancre, 1994, Suresnes: 95ss; RÖSCH B., *Die Stellung der Erfahrungsheilkundigen aus verfassungs- und verwaltungsrechtlicher Sicht, dargestellt am Beispiel der geistig Heilenden*, Dissertation, Helbing & Lichtenhahn Verlag AG, 1994, Basel: 66ss, 107ss, 123–24; STEPAN J., *Traditional and alternative systems of medicine: A comparative review of legislation*, in: International Digest of Health Legislation, 1985, vol. 36, n° 2, Genève: 329ss; STONE J. (co-author: MATTHEWS J.), *Complementary medicine and the law*, Oxford University Press, 1996, Oxford: 245–250, 276–77; SWEDISH COMMISSION ON ALTERNATIVE MEDICINE, *Report on alternative medicine*, Regeringskansliet, 1989, Stockholm: 27; SWEDISH COMMISSION ON COMPETENCE, *Report on the new legislation on competence to pursue a profession within the health and medical services*, in: Statens offentliga utredningar 1996: 138, Socialdepartementet, 1996, Stockholm: 40; WARDWELL W. I. (I), *Alternative medicine in the United States*, in: Social-Science-and-Medicine, 1994, vol. 38, n° 8: 1065; WHITE HOUSE

COMMISSION ON COMPLEMENTARY AND ALTERNATIVE MEDICINE POLICY, *Final report*, March 2002, available at http://www.whccamp.hhs.gov/pdfs/fr2002_document.pdf, accessed Feb. 1 2005: 93–95; WICKI M., *Komplementärmedizin im Rahmen des Rechtes*, Dissertation, Stämpfli, 1998, Bern: 87.

7.3.3.1 General Remarks

Once a licensure modality has been chosen to regulate medical practice, the next step consists of delimiting the field of practice of each category of health care providers. Usually, the objective of delimiting such scope of practice is to forbid unlicensed practitioners to practise within it. This regulatory approach is usually justified by concern for patients' safety.[215] The way in which scopes of practice and any infringements are shaped reflects the policy with regard to the licensing to practise allopathic and alternative medicines. As we have observed, the regulation of alternative medicines moves between imposing a total ban and permitting free practice. Defining an appropriate scope of practice is a challenge that face regulation of alternative medicines.[216]

Various criteria are employed to define the scope of practice of a regulated activity directly conditioning the obligation to get a licence to practise, to be registered, or to practise under a protected title.[217] These criteria, namely the activity concerned, the risk of such activity, and medical supervision, are presented and evaluated in this chapter.

215 As Furrow states "a licensed non-physician health care provider may be prosecuted for violation of the prohibition against unauthorised practice of medicine. The licensed professional, in contrast to the unlicensed practitioner, will have a defence against prosecution to the extent that the actions identified as the unauthorised practice of medicine fall within the legitimate scope of practice allowed under his or her license" (FURROW B. R. (I), *op. cit.*: 67).
The unauthorised practice of medicine will be addressed later (see chap. 7.3.4). Several requirements condition the right to be allowed to practise in a specific scope of practice. For further discussion of this area, see below, chap. 7.3.5.

216 E.g. disagrement may surround the nature and scope of practice of alternative professions. There is also a concern involving confusion and potential legal consequences that arise from the overlap of approaches and techniques used by alternative practitioners. On the subject, see WHITE HOUSE COMMISSION ON COMPLEMENTARY AND ALTERNATIVE MEDICINE POLICY, *op. cit.*: 93–95.

217 In order to make the text more readable and in the interests of consistency, we will summarise these criteria as the condition to get a licence to practise.

7.3.3.2 *Criteria Defining the Scope of Practice*

A. The activity

In Western countries, the practice of medicine has traditionally been precisely and positively defined. Cohen has listed the elements included in the definition of the practice of medicine in the US medical practice acts, which are generally the same elements found in European regulations. Although definitions vary from state to state all such definitions include at least some of the following elements:[218]

1. diagnosing, preventing, treating, and curing disease. These words are generally used in conjunction with disease, deformity, injury and mental or physical condition;[219]
2. holding oneself out to the public as being able to perform the above mentioned acts. Some statutes describe this as publicly professing to assume duties incident to the practice of medicine,[220] while others include advertising.[221] Courts have included holding oneself out to the public as a physician as falling within the definition of the practice of medicine;[222]
3. intending to receive a gift, fee, or compensation for the above. Some courts have incorporated the requirement of a fee within the definition of the practice of medicine[223] while others state that one can be held to practice medicine irrespective of compensation;[224]

218 COHEN M. (I), *op.cit.*: 26–29. See also LAY B. F., *op.cit.*: 646–47 (difference between practice of medicine and "healing arts").

219 E.g., New York defines the practice of medicine as "diagnosing, treating, operating, or prescribing for any human disease, pain injury, deformity or physical condition" (N.Y. Educ. Law § 6521). See also the regulation of medical practice in Austria, former regulation in Belgium, in Germany, or the French regulation of illegal practice of medicine, which all include these elements.

220 See Ill. Ann. Stat. Ch. 111, para. 4459: Neb. Rev. Stat. § 71-1, 102: Tenn. Code Ann. § 63-6-204. See also the Finnish and Swedish regulation.

221 Haw. Rev. Stat. § 453-2; Or. Rev. Stat. § 677.085; Wyo. Stat. § 33-26-102 (a) (x) (A).

222 *Reams v. State*, 279 so. 2d 839 (Fla 1973) (holding that a person was deemed to be practising medicine if he or she held him/herself out as being able to diagnose). See also *People v. Mastromarino*, 265 N.Y.S. 864 (Sup. Ct. 1933); *State v. Nelson*, 317 S.E.2d 711, 714 (N.C. Ct. App. 1984).

223 *State v. Ghadili*, 175 A. 315, 318 (Del. 1933), *cert. dismissed*, 292 U.S. 653 (1934); *State v. Nelson*, 317 S.E.2d 711, 714 (N.C. Ct. App. 1984). See also the Finnish regulation.

224 Haw. Rev. Stat. § 453-2 ("either gratuitously or for compensation"); La Rev. Stat. Ann. § 1262; Utah Code Ann. § 58-12-28.

4. attaching such titles as M.D. to one's name. In several states, there is a legal assumption that practitioners practise medicine as soon as they attach their name to one or more of the following titles: *doctor, doctor of medicine, doctor of osteopathy, physician, surgeon, Dr., M.D., D.O.*, or other words or abbreviations intended to indicate or induce others to believe that one is licensed to practise medicine. The State of Delaware has included the word "healer";[225]
5. maintaining an office for reception, examination and treatment;[226]
6. performing surgery. Half the states surveyed have included performance of surgical operations as falling within the definition of the practice of medicine;[227]
7. using, administering, or prescribing drugs or medicinal preparations. More than half the states include such terms in the definition of the practice of medicine[228] but only a few define the term drug;[229]
8. miscellaneous definitional provisions. Other terms may be included in the definition of the practice of medicine such as: ending a human pregnancy,[230] diagnosing of any person including dead persons,[231] treatments such as manipulations,[232] or hypnotism and the use of any means or method either tangible or intangible.[233]

225 Del. Code Ann. Tit. 24, § 1703; Ohio Rev. Code Ann. § 4731.4. See also the regulation in Belgium, Finland or in the Netherlands.
226 In Texas, maintaining an office to treat people was held to constitute the practice of medicine, whether or not the defendant claimed to be a physician or a medical practitioner (*Black v. State*, 216 S. W. 181 (Tex. Crim. App. 1919)).
227 Sometimes, as in Massachusetts, medical practice acts do not mention surgery, but courts have held that "the practice of medicine in any of its branches" includes the practice of surgery and the art of setting fractured bones (*Commonwealth v. Dragon*, 132 N.E. 356, 357 (Mass. 1921)).
228 See N.C. Gen. Stat. § 90-18; Utah Code Ann. § 58-12-28.
229 Indiana has adopted a broad definition: "any medicine, compound, or chemical or biological preparation intended for internal or external use of humans, and all substances intended to be used for the diagnosis, cure, mitigation, or prevention of diseases or abnormalities of humans, which are recognised in the latest editions published of the United States pharmacopoeia or national formulary, or otherwise established as a drug or medicine". Ind. Code Ann. § 25-22.5-I-I.I. See also Okla. Stat. Ann. Tit. 59, § 353.I.
According to Cohen "such a broad definition of drug in the definition of medicine may pose problems for nonmedical providers who offer herbal and nutritional therapies as part of professional practice" (COHEN M. (I), *op. cit.*: 28).
230 Md. Code Ann., Health Occ. § 14-101 (k) (2) (ii).
231 Del. Code Ann. tit. 24, § 1703 (b) (2).
232 Ark. Code Ann. § 17-93-202; Me. Rev. Stat. Ann. tit. 32, § 3270.
233 Haw. Rev. Stat. § 453-1.

The scope of practice as defined above has generally been reserved for physicians. This is due to the principle of "universality" of the physician's diploma, which allows medical doctors to perform all medical acts[234] with only very few restrictions.[235]

In some countries, in particular, those who have adopted a mandatory licensure scheme to regulate the practice of alternative medicines, the scope of practice of alternative practitioners has been defined in the same way. For example, in the US, practices such as acupuncture,[236] chiropractic,[237] or homeopathy.[238] have been defined. However, the approach remains exclusive. As a result, non-allopathic practitioners are allowed to practise only within their own defined scope of practice. For this reason, in some states, the lawmaker has extended the scope of practice, in order to allow

Cohen points out that "although it is relatively unusual for medical practice acts to expressly include within the definition of medicine such modalities as manipulative therapy and hypnosis, such broad language reflects the late-nineteenth-century view of regular physicians that healing must come from legislatively authorised biomedical practice" (COHEN M., *op. cit.*: 29).

234 This is typical of French regulation. Similarly, in the US states, where practice of acupuncture acts have not been enacted, the use of this technique is deemed the practice of medicine with rights reserved to designated medical providers.
Austria has the opposite approach. Here, medical acts that are not provided by authorised medical professionals, such as midwifes, medical-technical services or nurses, are reserved for physicians.

235 E.g., in France, some acts are restricted to the sole pharmacists.

236 Acupuncture has frequently been described as the stimulation of precise points on or near the surface of the human body by the insertion of needles to treat some diseases of dysfunctions of the body, to normalize physiological functions, or to prevent or modify the perception of pain.

237 Definitions of chiropractic vary in breadth and focus. Some definitions emphasize the provider's use of spinal manipulation and adjustment, other make reference to concepts such as the location and the removal of interference with the transmission of nerve energy. The North Carolina statute defines chiropractic as "the science of adjusting the cause of disease by realigning the spine, releasing pressure on nerves radiating from the spine to all parts of the body, and allowing the nerves to carry their full quota of health current (nerve energy) from the brain to all parts of the body" (Del. Code Ann. tit. 24, § 701. See also Ala. Code § 34-24-120(a)).

238 The Arizona statute defines homeopathy as a "system of medicine employing substances of animal, vegetable or mineral origin which are given in microdosage and prepared according to homeopathic pharmacology, in accordance with the principle that a substance which produces symptoms in a healthy person can cure those symptoms in an ill person" (Ariz. Rev. Stat. Ann. § 32-2901).

alternative practitioners to provide those medical acts, which are usually not part of the range of activities linked with their technique.[239]

The scope of practice may also consist of a general description of the type of activities engaged in. For example, in Swiss canton Zürich, the practice of medicine is, in principle, free. However, the provision of evidence-based medical activities is conditioned upon the holding of a diploma.[240] In Swiss cantons Luzern and Obwalden, non-allopathic practitioners are not allowed to provide any treatments that require knowledge specific to recognised allopathic practitioners. Similarly, in Malta and Spain, non-allopathic practitioners are not allowed to perform procedures which fall within the remit of listed professions, such as physiotherapists, physicians or pharmacists.

The scope of practice may also be defined in a negative way. In the Swiss canton Aargau, for example, a licence is not compulsory to provide care to healthy people, for example when treating nervousness, stress, sleeplessness or fear of exams. The situation is similar in Liechtenstein where the practice of medicine does not include natural medicine, namely health care that does not consist of bodily intrusions, of delivery acts, of the treatment of infectious diseases, and of the prescription of medication.[241]

239 E.g., in the US, the right to practise acupuncture may be extended to medical doctors, osteopaths, chiropractors, physician assistants, naturopaths, homeopaths, podiatrists, nurses, veterinarians and dentists. In Arizona, the Homeopathy Practice Act indirectly acknowledges the right of physicians and osteopaths to practise homeopathy. On the other side, some acts allow homeopaths to use as adjunctive therapies: acupuncture, neuromuscular integration, orthomolecular therapy, nutrition, chelation therapy, pharmaceutical medicine and minor surgery. The right for chiropractors to practise other modalities has sometimes been controversial, as chiropractors' attempt to incorporate nutritional care into professional practice. For more details, see LAMM L. C., *op. cit.*: 16–20.

240 In the same perspective, the Austrian regulation states that the practice of medicine is restricted solely to physicians, the term "medicine" including all activities based on medico-scientific knowledge carried out directly or indirectly on human beings. In Luxembourg, France and Spain, the scope of practice of physicians is limited by various ethical codes to medical techniques that have been scientifically proven.

241 See also the position in Swiss canton Glarus where non-allopathic practitioners are not allowed to practice medicine. However, the practice of reflexology, acupressure and other similar massages may be freely provided. Similarly, in canton Basel Landschaft, Graubünden, and Thurgau, cantonal regulations enclose a list of medical activities that non-allopathic practitioners may practise, namely phytotherapy, homeopathy, use of natural forces and dietetic advising.

B. The risk

The risk criterion is employed in relation to two contrasting perspectives. For example, the risk criterion underpins monopolistic regulations where the practice of medicine is generally considered a dangerous activity.[242] Therefore, in principle, the practice of medicine is banned to unqualified practitioners, and only those practitioners providing sufficient guarantees may provide medical care.

In contrast, some tolerant States view the practise of medicine as free. However, this freedom is often restricted for those medical acts which involve substantial risks, and which require a licence to practise (usually as a physician).[243] In addition, a list of those specific dangerous medical acts restricted to physicians is usually established.[244]

Even though there are variations among tolerant countries, restrictions usually include some of the following:[245]

242 E.g., in Austria, the infringement of illegal practice of medicine results in the creation of an abstract, dangerous situation.

243 E.g., the regulations in Swiss cantons Fribourg, Neuchâtel, Ticino and Valais specifically mention that non-allopathic practitioners are not allowed to provide dangerous medical acts.

244 However, some tolerant states did not set up such a list, such as Swiss canton Neuchâtel.
Although the listing of medical acts restricted to physicians is typical of tolerant countries, some monopolistic states have also set up such a list. However, in these cases, it must not be viewed as a means of highlighting those activities whose provision may endanger public health, but rather as a way to reinforce the general interdiction already existing against the practise of medicine by non-allopathic practitioners. For example, in France, all manipulations of joints, enclosing slipped disc, osteopathy, vertebrotherapy and chiropractic, as well as prosthetic and gynaecologic massages, or specific physiotherapeutic acts are restricted to the sole physicians.

245 On the subject, see RÖSCH B., *op. cit.*: 123–24 (presentation of restricted activities in Switzerland); STEPAN J., *op. cit.*: 329ss (presentation of restricted activities in the World).

1. to treat specific diseases such as communicable and epidemic diseases,[246] the treatment of cancer, diabetes, epilepsy, glaucoma, dangerous anaemia, struma/goitre with sticky forms, and tuberculosis;[247]
2. to practise in specific fields of medicine,[248] such as dentistry, obstetrics, gynaecology, or surgery.[249] Some tolerant countries also restrict some alternative techniques to the sole physicians;[250]
3. to provide specific acts such as to give or provide anaesthetics and narcotics in Scandinavian countries,[251] to practise autopsies, to deliver death certificates in Germany, to perform am abortion in Great Britain, to perform catheterisations, endoscopies, cardioversion, defibrillation, electroconvulsive therapy, lithotripsy, artificial insemination, punctures or injections in the Netherlands,[252] or to test or supply contact lenses in Sweden;
4. to treat a child under a certain age;[253]
5. to deliver certain drugs;[254]

246 E.g., in Denmark, Germany, Great Britain, Norway, Sweden, and Swiss cantons Appenzell external Rhodes, Basel Landschaft, Graubünden, Obwalden, and Thurgau, part or all of the following activities is restricted solely to physicians: the treatment of venereal diseases, infectious hepatitis, HIV infection, poliomyelitis and infectious meningitis.

247 E.g., in Great Britain, Norway and Sweden, some or all of these acts are restricted solely to physicians.

248 The list of restricted acts may include the description of some activities. As such descriptions are related to the risks involved with such activities, these descriptions are discussed in this sub-chapter, and not in the one regarding the "activity" criterion.

249 All or parts of these acts are forbidden to non-physicians in Denmark, Germany, Netherlands, Norway, Sweden and in Swiss cantons Appenzell external Rhodes, Basel Landschaft, Graubünden, Luzern, Obwalden and Thurgau.

250 E.g., in Hungary, the practice of homeopathy, manual therapies, Chinese and Tibetan medicine (in particular acupuncture), biologic dentistry, therapies using oxygenation, neuraltherapy, anthroposophy and magnetic bio resonance are restricted solely to physicians. In Sweden, the practice of acupuncture is forbidden to non-physicians.

251 Also in Germany.

252 However, in the Netherlands, the practice of acupuncture is not restricted to physicians. In Norway, and in the Swiss cantons Graubünden, Luzern and Obwalden, only physicians may give an injection.

253 E.g., in Sweden, the treatment of a child who is less than eight years old is forbidden to non-physicians.

254 E.g., in Denmark, Germany, Great Britain, Norway, and in the Swiss cantons Basel Landschaft, Graubünden, Luzern and Obwalden.

6. to undertake procedures involving the use of radioactive substances such as ionising radiation requiring specific medical equipment.[255]

The regulation in some countries provides that the list of reserved medical acts is not exhaustive and that further additions are possible when specific criteria are satisfied. In the Netherlands, for example, there must first be a risk of considerable damage in the case of unqualified treatment, and then a real likelihood that unqualified persons would be practising in that area before further additions are considered.

C. Medical supervision

Although the scope of practice for a specific profession may not include certain activities, the right to practise them may be, either officially, or unofficially, granted to some practitioners if they work under the supervision of a practitioner, usually a physician. In this way, the scope of practice of the health care provider working under the supervision of another practitioner is extended. In Belgium, for example, ancillary professionals may provide alternative medicines as long as they work under the supervision of a physician. Thus, Belgian physiotherapists may provide osteopathy. Similarly, in Denmark, the insertion of a needle that breaks the patient's skin, was declared in 1981 by the Supreme Court as being a surgical operation. As a result, acupuncture can be performed either by physicians, or by ancillary practitioners and non-allopathic practitioners working under the supervision of a physician.[256] Another recent trend is to give ancillary practitioners and non-allopathic practitioners more independence. For example, Belgian regulation states that patients may decide to visit a physician or not before seeking a non-allopathic practitioner.

Medical supervision may even legitimise the practice of activities that are not permitted legally. For example, in Italy, the practice of chiropractic by non-physicians is tolerated when chiropractors work under the supervision

255 E.g., in Denmark, Germany, the Netherlands and Sweden.

256 In Hungary also, non-physicians or "natural doctors" are allowed to practise independently if such intervention occurs after a physician's diagnosis.
In Spain, authorised ancillary professionals are allowed to perform medical acts only if supervised by a physician. However, some of them provide alternative medicines in an independent and therefore illegal way. The situation is similar in Norway.

of a doctor. Similarly, in some US states, non-allopathic practitioners are allowed to practise, but only under the supervision of a physician.[257]

7.3.3.3 *Evaluation*

A. Avoidance of wide monopolies

Many Western countries define the physician's scope of practice so broadly that it effectively creates a monopoly in favour of such physicians. As a result, it is theoretically impossible for other practitioners to practise in this field. For example, in France, the scientific value, efficacy and innocuousness of the medical technique is irrelevant. As soon as an act is performed in the course of a diagnosis or treatment, it is deemed to be part of the scope of practice reserved solely to physicians.[258] This assessment has also caused some problems for states attempting to regulate the licensing to practise of non-allopathic professions. For example, some US states which have a mandatory licensure scheme must define the scope of practice of alternative practitioners. In so doing, the scope of practice pertaining to alternative practitioners often overlaps with that of physicians, which may create conflicts. Similarly, in other US states, the lawmaker has licensed so many varieties of non-allopathic professions, that non-licensed practitioners risk prosecution not only under medical practice acts but also under professional practice acts of related ancillary or non-allopathic professions.[259]

Once again, it is noticeable that the monopolistic vision is not conclusive. Apart from the above-mentioned reasons that may lead a state to abandon its exclusive system in favour of a more open approach towards the licensing to practise alternative medicine,[260] there are two additional arguments regarding the definition of the scope of practice.[261] First, medical practice

257 E.g., in states where Acupuncture Practice Acts have not been enacted, the use of this technique is deemed the practice of medicine, with rights to practise limited to designated medical providers or granted to non-physician acupuncturists who are working under medical supervision.

258 Similarly, the practice of medicine in the State of Alaska means "to diagnose, treat, operate on, prescribe for, or administer to, any [...] mental of physical condition" (Alaska Stat. § 08.64.380(6)(A) (1998).
See also BERNER D., *op. cit.*: 156ss (Switzerland); COHEN M. H. (I), *op. cit.* 28, 31, 45ss (US); ROBARD I., *op. cit.*: 95ss (France).

259 See ANDREWS L. B., *op. cit.*: 1305; COHEN M. H. (I), *op. cit.*: 45; JOSEFEK K. J., *op. cit.*: 301.

260 For more details, see chap. 7.3.2.3.

261 See the opinion of the Swiss Conference of Directors of Health Affairs (CONFÉRENCE DES DIRECTEURS CANTONAUX DES AFFAIRES SANITAIRES (I), *op. cit.*: 28).

becomes more specialised every day.[262] As a result, a monopoly over the complete practice of medicine is neither justified nor realistic. Indeed, no practitioner may pretend to be a specialist in all medical fields.[263] Also, there already exist some intrusions into the reserved field of physicians. For example, the scope of practice of some allopathic professions is part of the field reserved to physicians.[264] Therefore, in principle, other specialists, allopathic and non-allopathic, could practise in specific medical fields.[265] In this respect, the opinions of the Swiss Federal Court and Spanish Supreme Court are directly relevant:[266]

1. On June 19, 1989, the Spanish Supreme Court found a non-allopathic practitioner who practised acupuncture-moxibustion not guilty of the infraction of illegal practice of medicine. The Court held that as alternative medicines were not taught within Spanish medical schools and as there were no official certificates authorising and legitimating these professions, it was difficult to argue that these practices were the object of intrusion, since they did not legally exist, and consequently did not correspond to specific professions;[267]

262 Even practice as a general practitioner has become a speciality.

263 According to De Bijl "such an extensive competence [i.e. to have doctors authorised for the whole domain of medicine] does not seem very realistic. It is impossible for a medical doctor to be competent for the range of the medical area. It appears that in practice this extensive competence is being limited by disciplinary courts, which assess the competency, or through accreditation of medical specialists to a sub-field of medicine." (DE BIJL N., *op.cit.*: 14). See also ROBARD I., *op.cit.*: 66ss, 107ss; WICKI M., *op.cit.*: 87 (situation of physicians in Swiss canton Bern).

264 E.g., in France, dentistry covers the diagnosis and treatment of mouth-related ailments, while the profession of midwife encompasses deliveries and providing a strictly defined number of medical acts.

265 The monopolistic position of certain professions in other fields has already been questioned. For example, the giving of legal advice was formerly restricted solely to lawyers. Today, other professions are also providing advices in some specific legal areas.

266 In Ukraine, the practice is similar. Courts are tolerant towards non-allopathic practitioners, when they hold a diploma attesting a successful training provided by the Academy of Physicians Postgraduate Education or by the Ukrainian National Medical Association.

267 The Supreme Court confirmed its decision in Jan., 1993, when it released a non-physician acupuncturist. The argument behind the decision was the same, i.e. that alternative medicines were not included within medical specialities. For more details regarding this decision see chap. 4.3.2.6.

2. In 1999, the Swiss Federal Court stated in a case where an acupuncturist held a foreign diploma in acupuncture and held a licence to practise in canton Graubünden, that the practitioner had a right to obtain a licence to practise in canton Zürich. Indeed, the technique was sufficiently delimited in order to allow its practice by those non-physicians who had been correctly trained.[268]

Both courts have undermined the principle of "universality" of the physician's diploma. The Spanish Supreme Court has refused to extend the scope of practice of the allopathic professions to alternative medicines that are not taught within the country.[269] The Swiss Federal Court had taken a different approach. It has admitted that scopes of practice may lead to inference, particularly given the possibility of intrusions into the reserved field of physicians and when a profession differs from another clearly defined profession and when training specific to the profession exists.[270]

In our view, the traditional views that consists of defining a scope of practice and then forbidding any intrusion within the scope of practice as so defined is ineffective. The attempts, as did the Swiss and Spanish courts to interpret the scope of practice of physicians in order to allow the practice of alternative medicines are interesting. However, such a solution

268 The Swiss Federal Court considered that there was no reason to forbid the practice of acupuncture to a practitioner as good as, or even better trained than a physician already practising in the field (ATF 125 I 335, cited in San News, Jan. 2000, n° 11: 16). See also KUHN H. P., *op. cit.*: 2399–2401. For more details, see chap. 4.3.6.1.

269 This view differs from the French view, which considers that every medical act, recognised or not by the French Academy of Medicine, is part of the physician's scope of practice.

270 This is the same approach taken by some US regulations when they allow alternative practitioners to provide medical acts, which are usually not part of the range of activities linked with the technique. Of note is the US ruling *Ohio State Board of Chiropractic Examiners v. Fulk*, where the court held that colonic irrigation was within the scope of chiropractic practice, because it has not been expressly excluded. For more details, see COHEN M. H. (I), *op. cit.*: 28, 31ss, 49.
More generally, Wardwell notices an expansion of areas of practice in the medical field (WARDWELL W. I., *op. cit.*: 1065), and Andrews is of the opinion that legislators "should provide expansive statutory definition for other types of practice such as homeopathy, chiropractic, nurse midwifery, advanced practice nursing, lay midwifery and so forth. They should provide that, while acting within their own scope of practice, alternative providers should not be considered to be practicing medicine without a licence" (ANDREWS L. B., *op. cit.*: 1315).

may be only temporary or transitory, until a formal tolerant regulation is enacted.[271]

B. Use of criteria and restricted monopoly

A more sensible approach consists first, in defining the criteria conditioning the requirement of holding a licence to practise (or a protected title) instead of defining the scope of practice. Second, a restricted monopoly of dangerous activities could be established with the requirement that such activities are reserved solely to those practitioners possessing a serious level of training.[272] The setting up of such a limited monopoly provides clear guidelines and, therefore, safeguards for health care providers and patients. In particular, they make practitioners aware of the limits of their competences.

Some states have combined the criteria of risk and activity within a perspective of liberalisation of health care practices.[273] The risk criterion appears to be particularly adapted to be mentioned within a statute, as it demonstrates clearly the policy chosen by the legislator. In this respect, the open approach chosen by some states seems a sensible choice. For example, the regulation in Swiss canton Neuchâtel states that practice is free, but that non-allopathic practitioners are not allowed to perform dangerous activities.[274]

271 Meanwhile, practitioners still risk prosecution. On the subject, see the opinion of the Swiss Conference of Directors of Health Affairs (CONFÉRENCE DES DIRECTEURS CANTONAUX DES AFFAIRES SANITAIRES (I), *op. cit.*: 28).

272 This must be understood within the frame of the licensure modality suggested in chap. 7.3.2.3 and 7.3.2.4 as a way forward in the regulation of the practice of alternative medicines.

273 E.g., in Swiss canton Fribourg, non-professionals may use alternative techniques, as long as they are non-dangerous, and do not interfere with the activities provided by a regulated profession. The draft regulation in Swiss canton Zürich is also a good example of how to combine these criteria. A licence to practise is required only for those professions based on scientifically recognised methods, for professions recognised by health insurance, and for dangerous activities. In canton Solothurn, practitioners of non-dangerous activities and professions, such as beauticians, sport massage therapies, and advisers to healthy people do not have to notify the health authorities of their practice.

274 Similarly, in Swiss canton Valais, health care professionals are defined in an abstract way, as being those persons who, in a professional way, are in direct contact with patients, and who provide health care that involves such risks that the control of the state is required. See also the recent regulations in the Swiss cantons of Bern and Fribourg, and the draft regulation of Zürich.

Furthermore, it is appropriate to state which activities require a licence to practise, and such activities may then be put in a statute in conjunction with the risk criterion. For example, the draft statute in the Swiss canton Zürich mentions that the practice of evidence-based medicine requires an authorisation to practise as a physician.

However, one must be careful when using such a criterion. Indeed, it should not result in introducing through another door a monopoly in favour of specific categories of practitioners. The sole objective must be to provide indications to the authorities, practitioners and public as to the scope of the field of practice of the various categories of practitioners.[275] As the Swiss Conference of Directors of Health Affairs observes, such a model stresses the right to self-determination of patients and reinforces their responsibility, as they will choose whether or not they wish to be treated with non-allopathic techniques.[276]

C. Implementation

The initiative of some Swiss cantons such as Bern, Fribourg, Geneva and Zürich is interesting in relation to the implementation of the regulations. In these cantons, the lawmaker has decided to put into the statute only those criteria conditioning the necessity to hold a license to practise, and to regulate the implementation more precisely in a decree.[277] As the regulatory field is evolving rapidly, such an approach allows authorities the time to quickly react to possible changes.[278] The lawmaker in Zürich has also stated that by mentioning the criteria leading to the necessity of setting up a licence to practise it will be possible to avoid the extension of the

275 The definition of the scope of practice of alternative medicines will not be developed here. However, as the above-mentioned US examples show, it is possible to define them. On this subject, see CHAPMAN-SMITH D. A.: 108–14.

276 The author notes that patients are able to make this choice as the level of training of non-allopathic practitioners has increased, and that the information provided is more serious and accessible (CONFÉRENCE DES DIRECTEURS CANTONAUX DES AFFAIRES SANITAIRES (I), *op. cit.*: 30).

277 For other developments, see CONFÉRENCE DES DIRECTEURS CANTONAUX DES AFFAIRES SANITAIRES (I), *op. cit.*: 25ss.

278 According to the CCDHA, the conditions leading to the necessity to obtain a licence to practise must; a. be laid down in the act; b. be listed in a positive and exhaustive way; and c. put into effect in a decree (CONFÉRENCE DES DIRECTEURS CANTONAUX DES AFFAIRES SANITAIRES (I), *op. cit.*: 37). The CCDHA states that the advantage of this criterion is its particular flexibility, which allows the lawmaker to follow the rapid changes of the health market. However, the security of law may become more fragile (idem, at 33).

interpretative power.[279] Thus, the statute may, for example, specifically mention that the providing of medical activities involving substantial risks is restricted to practitioners benefiting from a protected title. A decree following the statute may then list in a positive and exhaustive way, which acts involve substantial risks, both allopathic and non-allopathic, and to which category of practitioners such acts are reserved to.

D. Medical supervision

Medical supervision should be avoided as much as possible. Indeed, it creates a blurred boundary as to the scope of practice and actual limits of a practitioner's competence. However, such supervision may be admitted in special circumstances, for example, when treating a seriously ill patient. In this scenario, the alternative practitioner could work on referral and under the supervision of the practitioner which will usually be a physician, in charge of the patient. The practitioner who supervises the activities of the alternative practitioner should remain accountable for the health of the patient throughout the course of treatment.[280]

7.3.3.4 Summary and Proposals

Western regulations usually define the scope of practice of each category of practitioner, from the perspective of forbidding unlicensed practitioners to practise within these scopes. This approach, which has been employed to regulate both allopathic and non-allopathic medical practice has been not only difficult to implement but ineffective as well.

As suggested above,[281] a better approach consists in operating a controlled liberalisation, namely, to choose a title licensure scheme where practitioners would be free to provide care. From this perspective, the scope of practice would acquire a double function. First, it would indicate to authorities, patients, and other practitioners, the actual fields of practice of various practitioners. Second, it would serve the function of defining the potentially dangerous activities that should be restricted to specific categories of health care providers.

From this perspective, it is not necessary to set up a precise scope of practice, but rather to define the criteria[282] that will condition the necessity

279 CONFÉRENCE DES DIRECTEURS CANTONAUX DES AFFAIRES SANITAIRES (I), *op. cit.*: 30, 37–38.

280 For more development in this area, see chap. 7.3.2.2 and 7.3.2.3.

281 See chap. 7.3.2.3.

282 Typically, the risk and the activity criteria.

to have acquired a certain level of competence in order to perform specific acts.

Medical supervision should be avoided as much as possible. Possibly, alternative practitioners would be allowed to provide treatments if working under the supervision of an authorised practitioner.

In order to have a durable regulation and to ensure effective implementation of the statute the most viable and sensible approach is the use of criteria within the statute followed by implementation in a decree which allows the authorities to quickly react to changes in the field.

7.3.4 Infringement on the Scope of Practice

Bibliography

ANDREWS L. B., *The shadow health care system: Regulation of alternative health care providers*, in: Houston Law Review, 1996, vol. 32: 1315; BERNER D., *L'exercice illégal de la médecine ou les problèmes juridiques posés par les médecines parallèles*, in *Aspects du droit médical*, Editions universitaires, 1988, Fribourg: 155–58; CHAPMAN-SMITH D. A., *Legislative approaches to the regulation of the chiropractic profession*, in: J. Can. Chiropractic Assoc, June 1996, vol. 40, n° 2: 113–14; COHEN M. H. (I), *Complementary and alternative medicine – Legal boundaries and regulatory perspectives*, The Johns Hopkins University Press, 1998, London & Oxford: 32, 35, 87; CRAMER R., *Strafrechtliche Grenzen der Therapiefreiheit und der Heilbehandlung durch den Heilpraktiker*, Dissertation, 1995, Köln: 20–21; DE BIJL N. (co-author: NEDERVEEN-VAN DE KRAGT I.), *Legal safeguards against medical practice by not suitably qualified persons: A comparative study in seven EU-countries*, 1997, in: European Journal of Health Law, vol. 4: 14–16; EHLERS A. P. F., *Medizin in den Händen von Heilpraktikern – "Nicht-Heilkundigen"*, Springer Verlag, 1995, Berlin/Heidelberg; FURROW B. R. (co-authors: GREANEY T. L., JOST T., SCHWARTZ R. L.) (I), *Health law*, West Publishing, 1995, St Paul: 59–66; GRUNWALD D., *Pratiques médicales non éprouvées*, Session de l'Ordre des médecins, September 1997, Paris: 12–13; LE GALLOU A., *Responsabilité pénale médicale*, in: Médecine et droit, 1997, n° 24: 26–30; MINISTRY OF HEALTH AND SOCIAL AFFAIRS, *Report on alternative medicine – English summary*, Norges Offentliche Utredniger NOU 1998: 21, 1998, Oslo: 272–73; ROBARD I., *La santé hors la loi: Les hors la loi de la santé*, 4th ed., Ed. de l'Ancre, 1994, Suresnes: 65, 68; SAGE W. M. (co-author: AIKEN L. H.), *Regulating interdisciplinary practice*, in: JOST T. S., *Regulation of the healthcare professions*, Health Administration Press, 1996, Chicago: 71–101; STEPAN J., *Traditional and alternative systems of medicine: A comparative review of legislation*, in: International Digest of Health Legislation, 1985, vol. 36, n° 2, Genève: 330–31.

7.3.4.1 *General Remarks*

The classical Western approach to regulate the practice of medicine consists in defining the scope of practice of various categories of health care providers. The right to practise within a specific scope of practice is conditioned upon several requirements, and any infringement on the scope of practice by practitioners not falling within such a definition is punished.

The various types of infringements will be presented below. Finally, an evaluation and some proposals will be made.[283]

7.3.4.2 *Types of Infringements*

A. Introduction

Both licensed and non-licensed practitioners may infringe the scope of practice if the lawmaker is willing and if the extent of the scope of practice permits. The various situation that these two categories of practitioners may face is developed below.

B. Infringement by non-licensed practitioners

General remarks

The monopolistic approach is characterised by the prosecution of those unlicensed practitioners who provide health care within the scope of practice of licensed practitioners. The extent of the prosecution varies from a complete interdiction to practise for unlicensed practitioners, usually encompassing non-allopathic practitioners, to a limited ban that they lead to prosecution in the most serious cases.

The various positions from the strictest to the most tolerant concerning the prosecution of infringement on the scope of practice is presented below.

Strict prosecution

France is the classic example of a jurisdiction which prosecutes non-licensed practitioners. Under the Code of Public Health (art. L. 372–L. 376), any person, other than licensed physicians who usually or continuously diagnose or treat illnesses, real or supposed, or who perform medical acts and procedures, commit the offence of illegal practice of medicine. Since the

283 Only infringements to the scope of practice will be addressed here. Criminal liability for mental and physical injuries is presented in chap. 7.2.3.3.

physician's scope of practice is so broad and as no alternative professions have been licensed (which would imply an interference with physicians' scope of practice), every act in relation to medical diagnosis or treatment of human beings is forbidden to any other profession other than that of physicians. As a result, the field of free practice is non-existent. Although the current trend is to impose lighter sentences, the policy of zero tolerance is still active.[284]

Luxembourg also has a restrictive attitude toward the intrusions within allopathic scope of practice.

States in the US usually have a mandatory licensure scheme to regulate the practice of medicine. In jurisdictions where alternative practices are specifically neither licensed nor prohibited, their providers risk prosecution under state medical practice acts. As in France, US courts have interpreted the medical practice acts broadly against providers in situations in which State legislatures have failed to create separate licensure schemes. In those states that have regulated some alternative practices, non licensed practitioners risk prosecution not only under the medical practice acts which regulate physician's practice but also under the professional practice acts which regulate the practice of other health care professions and which usually prohibit unlicensed practice.[285] As a result, alternative practitioners must be careful not to interfere with professional activities that are regulated by state acts. However, medical practice acts can sometimes create a space of coexistence in which these providers and regular providers may work together.[286]

284 The Medical Orders in France are usually reluctant to initiate prosecutions because in most cases the trial results in publicity for the prosecuted practitioner.

285 The legislator in California, e.g., enacted a statute setting up stricter standards for those providing acupuncture. It makes it a misdemeanour for any person, other than licensed dentists, podiatrists, or physicians, to practice acupuncture.
In Switzerland, some alternative professions are regulated together with allopathic professions. Their scope of practice is defined and the providing of health care outside such scope is prosecuted. E.g., in Swiss canton Schwyz, it is possible to obtain a licence to practise acupuncture. There is also a project to regulate the practice of osteopathy in cantons Fribourg, Vaud, Geneva, Berne and Jura. In canton Berne, a licence to practise is necessary in order to practise homeopathy, acupuncture, traditional Chinese medicine and osteopathy.

286 E.g., Massachusetts's Medical Practice Act specifies that the prohibition on unlicensed medical practice does not apply to "clairvoyants or persons practising hypnotism, magnetic healing, mind cure, massage, Christian science or cosmopathic method of healing" (Mass. Gen. Laws Ann. ch. 112, §§ 148–162).

Differentiated terminology

One current trend of medical practice acts interpretation consists in creating a differentiated terminology for the unlawful practice of medicine in order to avoid the exclusion independent holistic practice. Thus, a prohibition found within these acts applies to furnishing "disease care" within the biomedical model, not "wellness care" within the holistic healing model which focuses on the nourishing and balancing the body and on stimulating vital energy. Furthermore, a broad range of alternative providers, in general, practise freely, without prosecution in states lacking professional licensure system of their own.[287]

In Liechtenstein, the Penal Code includes the offence of illegal practice of medicine. However, the Public Health Act provides that natural medicine must not be considered as an act of health care professions, which includes health care that does not consist in bodily intrusions, in delivery acts, in the treatment of infectious diseases and in the prescription of medication. Although the link between the Penal Code and the Health Act is unclear, alternative practitioners have, until now, never been subjected to prosecution.

Similarly, in some Swiss cantons possessing a monopolistic system, some exceptions are made, where some activities are not deemed technically as being the practice of medicine, and therefore, not subject to prosecution.[288]

Tolerant interpretation

In some Western jurisdictions, courts have given a tolerant interpretation of rules dealing with the illegal practice of medicine.[289]

In Italy, despite legislation which establishes a medical monopoly, non-allopathic practitioners are seldom prosecuted. In reality, although the practice of some alternative techniques by non-physicians is theoretically not allowed, chiropractors are tolerated if they work under the supervision of a doctor. Thus, at least for now, there is peaceful cohabitation between non-physicians and physicians.

287 See the situation in some US States regarding the practice of indigenous practitioners.

288 E.g., in Swiss canton Aargau, although non-allopathic practitioners are not allowed to practise medicine, a licence is not compulsory in order to provide care to healthy people, when treating nervousness, stress, sleeplessness or fear of exams. The situation is similar in canton Glarus for the providing of reflexology, acupressure and other similar massages.

289 E.g., in Spain and in Swiss canton Zürich.

Similarly in Austria, art. 184 of the Penal Code provides that the practice of medical acts by unlicensed practitioners is an offence and may be subject to prosecution. However, courts have usually interpreted this article tolerantly and practitioners are rarely sentenced.[290]

In Switzerland several cantons still possess in their statutes the offence of illegal practice of medicine. However, in practice, interdictions against the practise of alternative medicine are generally not enforced, or enforced only after the intervention of interested people.[291]

In Finland, the offence of illegal practice of medicine also exists. However, prosecutions are rare, as courts have faced some difficulties when confronted with the task of interpreting the concept of medicine.[292] Courts intervene to protect public health only when incompetent practitioners have caused damage to health.

Limited prosecution

In Germany, the practice of medicine is illegal when practitioners provide health care without holding a licence from the relevant public authorities. This licence may be either a licence as a physician, as an ancillary professional, or as a "Heilpraktiker". This offence presupposes the infringement on the scope of practice of these professions.

The German system can be distinguished by its creation of a residual monopoly in favour of "Heilpraktikers". Indeed, these practitioners are permitted to practise any medical act, apart from those acts restricted solely for allopathic practitioners. In this respect, courts have interpreted the concept of "Heilkunde" (medicine),[293] by defining which activities must be considered as "Heilkunde" and must therefore be restricted to physicians and by allowing "Heilpraktikers" to practise all other activities.[294] In particular, the Supreme Court has ruled that only activities requiring medical knowledge are considered as "Heilkunde". Thus, activities giving

290 Courts have adopted the same approach in Latvia where non-allopathic practitioners are prosecuted only when the health of patients has been damaged.

291 E.g., in the Swiss cantons of Aargau, Vaud, and formerly in Geneva. In the Ukraine as well, authorities are tolerant with non-allopathic practitioners.

292 Indeed, for Finish courts, it is unclear whether specific acts, performed during the treatment of patients, must be considered as part of the practice of medicine or not.

293 In Germany, medicine is defined as a professional activity whose objective is to observe, cure and relieve ill persons or persons suffering from physical injuries.

294 E.g., psychotherapy practised by a psychologist without an academic degree is forbidden if such psychologist does not hold a licence to practise.

only the impression that they may contribute to recovery ("Eindruckstheorie") are not considered as "Heilkunde".

Formerly, the Netherlands had a monopoly for university-trained qualified practitioners where only the allopathic professions were allowed to perform medical procedures. Subsequent changes in the field of medicine, and in society as a whole made such a monopoly unacceptable. Slowly, the practice of public health authorities changed; even though the practice of medicine by non-recognised health care professionals was illegal, the police did not prosecute them, unless there was clear evidence of harm to patients. Today, the aim of the new legislation is that every person is allowed to provide medical care. However, in order to prevent unacceptable health risks for patients resulting from a lack of professional competence, specific procedures are restricted to authorised professional practitioners.

The situation is similar in Great Britain where non-allopathic practitioners may be prosecuted if they infringe on the scope of practice reserved to physicians.[295] Furthermore, unqualified practitioners may not claim to be, or practise as pharmacists, midwives or dentists, or imply that they are state-registered practitioners whose legal status is legally regulated.

Scandinavian countries have also opted for a limited monopoly which includes those medical acts whose provision is linked with substantial risks. In practice, non-allopathic practitioners are prosecuted only in the most serious cases. For example, in Denmark, non-allopathic practitioners are only prosecuted if death or serious deterioration of the patient's medical condition occurs, and for the sale of harmful products.[296]

The same approach has been taken by several Swiss cantons where a whole range of medical activities has been restricted solely to physicians.[297] Canton Graubünden has taken an original approach in that the cantonal regulation encloses both a list of medical activities allowed to non-allopathic practitioners and a list of activities restricted solely to physicians. In some cantons, a restricted monopoly does not exist. For example, in canton Neuchâtel, the Public Health Act provides only that non-allopathic practitioners may provide non-dangerous activities. In canton Fribourg, the Public Health Act stipulates only that non-professionals may use alternative

295 This limited monopoly includes the provision of potentially dangerous medical acts.

296 In Norway a non-medically trained person "treating" terminally ill patients by telephone at a hefty price was prosecuted.

297 E.g., in canton Appenzell external Rhodes, Basel Landschaft, Luzern, Obwalden, Thurgau and Valais.

techniques, as long as they are not dangerous, and do not interfere with the activities provided by a regulated profession.[298]

C. Infringement by licensed practitioners

Licensed practitioners may also violate medical practice and professional acts, or professional codes of ethics, by practising outside their defined scope of practice.

US

In the US, non-physician licensed practitioners may be prosecuted if they violate the legal scope of practice of another licensed category of practitioner. For example, courts have ruled that chiropractors may violate medical licensing acts when they perform specific medical acts such as using ultrasound or prescribe certain preparations such as vitamins or food supplements.

Furthermore, when health care providers, particularly physicians, depart from conventionally accepted medical standards in order to provide alternative medicines, they risk professional discipline for "unprofessional conduct", which includes a variety of specified acts.

In order to permit physicians to provide alternative medicines, some legislatures have enacted Medical Freedom Acts, which conditionally limit the authority of a state medical board to discipline those physicians who provide alternative modalities and to protect patients from harm. The consideration was that excluding licensed practitioners from providing health care outside their supposed scope of practice could impede medical progress and limit freedom of choice for patients.[299]

France

In France, when physicians use methods that are insufficiently proven, they infringe the Code of Professional Ethics, which may lead to disciplinary sanctions. Essentially, this Code establishes the principle of freedom of prescription, but at the same time forbids physicians to propose cures to their patients, which are illusory or insufficiently proved.

French disciplinary and civil jurisdictions have differing interpretations of the concept of freedom of prescription. Civil courts have extensively interpreted this concept, holding that the use of an alternative method

298 The situation is similar in canton Geneva.
299 On this subject, see COHEN M. H. (I), *op.cit.*: 32, 87.

should not be condemned merely because the medical establishment rejects it. They consider that a strict application of these rules would make it impossible to undertake new research for the purpose of discovering new treatments. However this was not the opinion of the Council of State or of the disciplinary jurisdiction of the French Order of Physicians, who have both interpreted the concept more restrictively. This has resulted in a very strict legal framework concerning the use of new medical treatments.

Apart from physicians, some French ancillary professions are also prosecuted if they provide alternative medicines. For example, kinesitherapists are regularly prosecuted for providing various medical acts restricted to physicians. These include performing any joint manipulations, providing care for slipped discs, osteopathy, vertebral therapy, chiropractic, prosthetic and gynaecologic massages.

Luxembourg

In Luxembourg, the Code of Professional Ethics provides that physicians cannot suggest to their patients the use of any salutary and harmless therapies which are based on illusory methods or which are not scientifically proven. However, the Code's rules are only intended to provide an ethical framework and as such do not constitute illegal practice of medicine.

Spain

In Spain, physicians are, in principle, legally allowed to practise in any branch of medicine. Although various statutes prohibit the use of non-scientifically proven techniques, the simulation of the making of a diagnosis, or the application of therapeutic treatments, state authorities have been relatively tolerant towards private doctors who use alternative medicines.

On June 16, 1997, Catalonia adopted a Code of Medical Professional Ethics. The Code provides that doctors using alternative medicines must inform their patients not only of the need to continue a necessary treatment but also inform them of the non-conventional character of the treatment (art. 44 of the Code). Furthermore, they must co-ordinate their treatment with the physician in charge of the basic treatment.

Other countries

Italy has a more tolerant approach. The Criminal Supreme Court of Appeal in Perugia[300] has ruled that the practice of alternative medicines

300 For more details regarding this decision, see chap. 4.3.2.3.

is allowed, but only if performed by registered physicians. However, these physicians must assume the consequences of taking patients away from allopathic medicine.

Similarly, in Austria, physicians are allowed to use all medical techniques they wish, even if not scientifically proved, providing they have the agreement of their patients. The same approach has been taken in the Ukraine, and in other tolerant countries[301] where physicians and other ancillary professionals are allowed to provide alternative medicines.

In Latvia, only those doctors certified in the field of alternative medicines may practise legally, and only after attending the special multi-step training courses. In addition, when non-licensed practitioners are helped by licensed practitioners to provide health care, the latter also run the risk of criminal prosecution.[302]

7.3.4.3 Evaluation[303]

A. General remarks

Western authorities are becoming more tolerant in their attitude towards non-allopathic practitioners. It is true to say that despite theoretical disapproval of alternative medicines, in practice alternative medicines are increasingly accepted.[304]

301 E.g., in Germany, Great Britain, Hungary, Liechtenstein, Malta, Netherlands, Scandinavian countries, Finland and in most of the Swiss cantons.

302 In France, physicians may be criminally and/or disciplinarily prosecuted for helping another person practise medicine illegally. Similarly, in Italy, the Code of Professional Ethics states that physicians may not cooperate with, or help non-allopathic practitioners practising medicine illegally, even in the field of alternative medicines. In several US states, licensed providers (physicians and non-physicians) employing or referring patients to providers practising medicine unlawfully may also be liable for "aiding and abetting" unlicensed medical practice.

303 The following evaluation takes into consideration the comments made in the precedent section on the setting up of scopes of practice. For other developments, see chap. 7.3.3.

304 See the situation in the Netherlands, Italy, France and Spain. Sage states, of the situation in the US, that "anecdotal evidence suggests that considerable unlicensed practice occurs, as does practice outside the authorised scope of a health professional license" (SAGE W. M., *op. cit.*: 78).

B. Non-allopathic practitioners

In monopolistic countries, lawmakers have taken several initiatives in order to avoid the potential possible prosecution of non-allopathic practitioners when they infringe the scope of licensed professions. For example, the provision of natural medical care is not deemed to be medicine[305] and the provision of "wellness care" is allowed without the need to hold a licence to practice.[306]

Where regulations have not been adapted to allow the practice of alternative medicines by non-allopathic practitioners, courts have stepped in and have employed various arguments to avoid sentencing alternative practitioners. For example, courts have held that as it is not possible to precisely define medicine they were unable to find unlicensed practitioners liable for its illegal practice.[307] A further tactic has been a restrictive interpretation of the concept of medicine.[308] Other courts have created a differentiated terminology in order to allow unlicensed non-allopathic practitioners to provide health care,[309] or have held that since alternative techniques are not taught within medical schools, they are not part of the scope of physicians.[310] Still others courts have avoided implementing rules dealing with the illegal practice of medicine.[311]

Thus, the monopolistic system has been unable to prevent patients from seeking help from non-licensed practitioners. As a result, in some states, the approach of public health authorities and courts has become so tolerant that it seems counter-productive to keep regulations that are, in practice, violated everyday.[312]

C. Licensed practitioners

There is a similar trend in relation to the interdictions made against licensed practitioners who provide health care outside their defined scope of practice. Indeed, courts have become more tolerant also in this area over the past few years while lawmakers have enacted freedom of practice acts that allow physicians to provide alternative medical treatments.[313]

305 E.g., in Liechtenstein.
306 In some monopolistic US states and in various Swiss cantons.
307 E.g., in Finland.
308 E.g., in Germany, which has resulted in the obligation to hold a licence to practise.
309 E.g., in the US.
310 E.g., in Spain.
311 E.g., in some Swiss cantons.
312 DE BIJL N., *op.cit.*: 14–15.
313 E.g., in the US.

Recent codes of professional ethics have also opened the door to the use of non-allopathic treatments,[314] while some regulations oblige physicians to attend specific training in alternative medicines in order to be allowed to provide them.[315]

Courts have also been tolerant towards ancillary professionals. In some monopolistic countries, ancillary professionals are tolerated as long as licensed practitioners inform their patients about the alternative character of the treatment,[316] or as being as ancillary professionals provide alternative treatments under the supervision of a physician. This constitutes an extension of the defined scope of practice.

D. Conflicting situations and paradoxes

Conflicting situations arise when allopathic practitioners are not allowed to provide alternative treatments. For example, a contradiction exists in several countries between the principle of freedom of practice (or freedom of choice), which allows physicians to use the technique they want, and standards of practice or professional rule, which prohibit the provision of insufficiently proven techniques.[317] The situation in France is typical of the lack of consistency found with regard to the regulation of alternative medicines. Here, the Code of Professional Ethics (set up by the National Order of Physicians) states that physicians are allowed to provide all the treatments they want, but they may not provide alternative medical acts. This restriction means that their scope of practice regarding medical practice is limited, while the intention of the legislator was to allow an apparently unlimited practice. Furthermore, the same National Order of Physicians has recognised the DUMENAT training in alternative medicines. Nevertheless, the Order continues to prosecute alternative physicians. Also, civil and professional courts have completely different interpretations of the concept of freedom of prescription. Similarly, while the French National Academy of Medicine does not recognise alternative medicines, the social security system within France recognises physicians providing alternative treatments,[318] and even provides coverage for some alternative treatments.

314 E.g., in Spain.
315 E.g., in Latvia.
316 E.g., in Austria.
317 See, formerly Belgium, France, Italy, Luxembourg, Spain and in the US. For more details, see STEPAN J., *op. cit.*: 331.
318 They are called MEP physicians, namely physicians with a particular mode of practice.

In Germany, the situation also remains ambiguous. German law reserves the practice of medical activities solely to licensed practitioners, including "Heilpraktikers". Thus, non-allopathic practitioners are prosecuted when they provide acts restricted to "Heilpraktikers". Even if this restriction has been justified in monopolistic countries on the basis that only allopathic practitioners have the necessary skills to correctly provide alternative medicines, "Heilpraktikers" often have only a very basic medical background. Thus, absurd situations can occur when courts sentence ancillary practitioners for providing alternative care without holding the required "Heilpraktiker" licence when they are better trained than a "Heilpraktiker".[319] These examples of inherent contradictions demonstrate just how unsatisfactory the current situation may be.

E. Updating regulation with today's needs

When Western legislators decided to penalise infringements on the scope of practice of licensed practitioners, their primary concern was the protection of public health. At the time the various acts were adopted, there still was a serious risk of charlatans providing health care to ingenuous patients. However, the severe approach taken by authorities in terms of prosecution has changed. Authorities have realised first that patients' needs have evolved and second, that prosecution was largely ineffective, as non-allopathic practitioners have still continued to practise.[320] Some countries have changed their approach towards the practice of medicine, which has resulted in the setting up of new statutes and of changes to the attitude of the courts.[321]

319 Regarding the interpretation of the notion of "Heilkunde", certain authors are of the opinion that this definition is insufficient because, according to a strict interpretation, it excludes prophylactic means, cosmetic and surgical interventions. Furthermore, medical assistants could be criminally prosecuted because they practise medicine without state authorisation. Finally, this definition does not exclude the practice of quacks. Indeed, they could pretend to not be practising in the field of medicine (Cramer R., *op. cit.*: 20–21; Ehlers A. P. F., *op. cit.*: 106–07, 240–43, 73–74).
One may add that the exam which aims to assess whether the "Heilpraktiker" candidate will or will not constitute a danger for public health varies from one State to another.

320 Furthermore, very few cases involved damage to a patient's health.

321 However, some authors continue to argue in favour of a monopoly of physicians. See Grunwald D., *op. cit.*; Le Gallou A., *op. cit.*: 26–30.

The Netherlands is a country which illustrates the shift from the traditional view that stressed the prosecution of unlicensed practitioners providing care within the scope of practice of licensed professions towards the modern view, which focuses on public information. However, if the new Dutch regulation continues to protect recognised titles, then a limited monopoly in favour of physicians is maintained.[322]

Essentially, the original purpose behind the creation of medical practice acts has evolved and has become more a tool to protect the monopoly of physicians than public health.[323] The situation in France or in Spain is striking, in that allopathic practitioners or their representatives[324] are allowed to prosecute non-allopathic practitioners if they practise within protected scopes of practice. In the US, the attitude of the medical establishment has been similar. For example, antitrust actions have been brought by chiropractors against the American Medical Association, alleging a conspiracy to eliminate the chiropractic profession.[325]

Clearly, the creation of a monopoly, unless supported by sound reasons, may lead to undesirable effects, such as impeding progress in medicine outside the reserved field, or limiting the access of patients to other forms of care.

7.3.4.4 Summary and Proposals

Generally lawmakers and courts have softened their restrictive policies when licensed and non-licensed practitioners are likely to infringe the scope of practice of licensed professions or go beyond their own scope of practice.

The monopolistic vision regarding the licensing to practise medicine has proven to be ineffective and out of date. In addition, many states are adopting regulations allowing both allopathic and non-allopathic practitioners to provide alternative health care. Similarly, courts are interpreting regulations to allow alternative practitioners to practise. In reality, the monopolistic system has resulted in the creation of an economic monopoly favouring certain categories of health care practitioners, rather than protecting the safety and freedom of choice of patients.

322 See ANDREWS L. B., *op. cit.*: 1315; BERNER D., *op. cit.*: 155–58; CHAPMAN-SMITH D. A., *op. cit.*: 113–14; DE BIJL N., *op. cit.*: 14–16; FURROW B. R. (I), *op. cit.*: 62–63; MINISTRY OF HEALTH AND SOCIAL AFFAIRS: 272–73; STEPAN J., *op. cit.*: 331.

323 On this subject, see STEPAN J., *op. cit.*: 330.

324 Such as the several orders in France.

325 See also COHEN M. H. (I), *op. cit.*: 35; FURROW B. R. (I), *op. cit.*: 59.

In our view, the monopolistic approach which consists of setting up a wide scope of practice for allopathic practitioners, and forbidding the intrusion within such scope should be abandoned as difficult to implement and ineffective to protect patients' health.

A better approach consists in limiting the monopoly solely to those dangerous activities that should, in any case, be reserved to certain categories of practitioners. Correspondingly, only those infringements that take place upon the permitted monopoly should be prosecuted. In addition, attention should be focused on public information by protecting recognised titles, and on strengthening civil and criminal liability for health care damages.

Finally, allopathic practitioners should be entitled to provide the treatments they wish, even though the effectiveness of treatments has not been demonstrated.

7.3.5 Requirements Linked with the Practice of Medicine

Bibliography

Arndt K. F., *Heilpraktikerrecht – Entstehung, Funktionswandel, Berufszulassungsregelung*, Alfred Metzner Verlag, 1985, Frankfurt am Main: 92–99; Berner D., *L'exercice illégal de la médecine ou les problèmes juridiques posés par les médecines parallèles*, in *Aspects du droit médical*, Editions universitaires, 1988, Fribourg: 157–58; British Medical Association (Lamont T.), *Complementary medicine – New approaches to good practice*, Oxford University Press, 1993, Oxford/New York: 46–48, 60–63; Budd S. (co-author: Mills S.), *Professional organisation of complementary and alternative medicine in the UK 2000: A second report to the Department of Health*, University of Exeter, 2000, London; Chapman-Smith D. A., *Legislative approaches to the regulation of the chiropractic profession*, in: J. Can. Chiropractic Assoc., June 1996, vol. 40, n° 2: 113; Conférence des Directeurs Cantonaux des Affaires Sanitaires (I), *Rapport du groupe de travail "Autorisations de pratiquer les professions du domaine de la santé"*, CDS, 2000, Bern, available at: http://www.sdk-cds.ch/fr/berufsbildung-f.html, accessed July 30 2001; Cramer R., *Strafrechtliche Grenzen der Therapiefreiheit und der Heilbehandlung durch den Heilpraktiker*; Dissertion, 1995, Köln: 45–49; De Bijl N. (co-author: Nederveen-van de Kragt I.), *Legal safeguards against medical practice by not suitably qualified persons: A comparative study in seven EU-countries*, 1997, in: European Journal of Health Law, vol. 4: 7–8, 14, 17; Ehlers A. P. F., *Medizin in den Händen von Heilpraktikern – "Nicht-Heilkundigen"*, Springer Verlag, 1995, Berlin/Heidelberg: 39, 275–78, 281–86; Fisher S., *Commission de surveillance des professions de la santé: La situation en Suisse romande*, in: Médecine et Hygiène, 1999, vol. 57: 979; Furrow B. R. (co-authors: Greaney T. L., Jost T., Schwartz R. L.) (I), *Health law*, West Publishing, 1995, St Paul: 55, 58; Furrow B. R. (co-authors:

GREANEY T. L., JOST T., SCHWARTZ R. L.) (II), *Health law: Cases, materials and problems*, West Publishing, 1997, St Paul: 42ss, 56; FURROW B. R. (co-authors: GREANEY T. L., JOHNSON S. H., JOST T. S., SCHWARTZ R. L.) (III), *The law of health care organisation and finance*, West Publishing, 1997, St Paul; GRUNWALD D., *Pratiques médicales non éprouvées*, Session de l'Ordre des médecins, Sept. 1997, Paris; GUILLOD O. (I), *Rebouteux, naturopathes et guérisseurs: Pour un traitement légal alternatif*, Recueil de Jurisprudence Neuchâtelois, 1989, Neuchâtel: 38–39; KUHN H. P., *Autorisation de pratiquer: Deux fois non, une fois oui*, in: BMS, 1999, vol. 80, n° 40: 2399–401; KÜNZI M. (I), *Komplementärmedizin und Gesundheitsrecht*, Helbing & Lichtenhahn Verlag AG, 1996, Basel: 74, 97–98; LAY B. F., *Healer-patient privilege: Extending the physician-patient privilege to alternative health practitioners in California*, in: Hastings Law Journal, Mar. 1997: 651ss; LIANG B. A., *Health law and policy – A survival guide to medicolegal issues for practitioners*, Butterworth-Heinemann, 2000, Woburn: 49–50; MINISTRY OF HEALTH AND SOCIAL AFFAIRS (I), *Report on alternative medicine – English summary*, Norges Offentliche Utredniger NOU 1998: 21, 1998, Oslo: 272–73; OEPEN I. (III), *Pseudo-Naturheilverfahren und Aussenseitermethoden in der Rheumatologie*, in: Zeitschrift für Rheumatologie, 1993, vol. 52: 264–74; ROBARD I., *La santé hors la loi: Les hors la loi de la santé*, 4th ed., Ed. de l'Ancre, 1994, Suresnes: 66ss, 107–08; RÖSCH B., *Die Stellung der Erfahrungsheilkundigen aus verfassungs- und verwaltungsrechtlicher Sicht, dargestellt am Beispiel der geistig Heilenden*, Dissertation, Helbing & Lichtenhahn Verlag, 1994, Basel: 124–125, 320ss; SCHNEIDER H., *Die Annerkennung von Diplomen in der Europäischen Gemeinschaft*, Maklu, 1995, Uitgevers Antwerpen: 463; SELECT COMMITTEE ON SCIENCE AND TECHNOLOGY, *Complementary and alternative medicine*, House of Lords – Session 1999–2000 6th Report, The Stationary Office, 2000, London; STONE J. (co-author: MATTHEWS J.), *Complementary medicine and the law*, Oxford University Press, 1996, Oxford; SUGARMAN J. (I), *Physicians' ethical obligations regarding alternative medicine*, in: JAMA, 1998, vol. 280, n° 18: 1623–25; SWEDISH COMMISSION ON ALTERNATIVE MEDICINE, *Report on alternative medicine*, Regeringskansliet, 1989, Stockholm: 27; SWEDISH COMMISSION ON COMPETENCE, *Report on the new legislation on competence to pursue a profession within the health and medical services*, in: Statens offentliga utredningar 1996: 138, Socialdepartementet, 1996, Stockholm: 31–33, 36; WHO (IV), *Guidelines on basic training and safety in acupuncture*, WHO, 1999, Geneva; WICKI M., *Komplementärmedizin im Rahmen des Rechtes*, Dissertation, Stämpfli, 1998, Bern.

7.3.5.1 General Remarks

The practice of medicine is linked inextricably to serious potential risks. In order to guarantee the quality of care,[326] and the protection of patients, various states have set up licensing schemes to control the providing of health care.

Where the practice of 'alternative' medicine is permitted both allopathic and non-allopathic practitioners are in principle licensed to deliver 'alternative' methods trough a licensing scheme, which is usually based on an authorisation[327] or registration[328] system.[329]

Several conditions must be satisfied in order to obtain such authorisation or registration.[330] The main condition is related to the education of candidates. Practitioners must either hold a diploma, or at least have successfully passed an exam. Moreover, there are additional conditions, the most important being practical experience, physical and mental abilities, morality, adhesion to professional ethics and citizenship.[331]

326 For a study regarding the concept of quality in health care, see FURROW B. R. (III), *op. cit.*: 17ss.

327 Authorisation implies permission/licensing by a competent body.

328 Registration implies entering a register.

329 For a presentation of several existing systems, see chap. 7.3.2.2.

330 Public or professional authorities provide these authorisations. For more details, see chap. 7.3.2.1 and 7.3.6.

331 The CCDHA distinguishes between the conditions necessary to fulfil in order to get the authorisation, and the conditions linked to the practice of the activity (CONFÉRENCE DES DIRECTEURS CANTONAUX DES AFFAIRES SANITAIRES (I), *op. cit.*: 24). It proposes the following conditions for first category (conditions to get the authorisation): 1. an adequate training; 2. the capacity to practise (good reputation, good mental and physical conditions, the absence of criminal sentences); 3. knowledge about the topic; 4. civil liability insurance; 5. Swiss residency; 6. non-interruption during the professional practice or the continuing training; 7. practical experience.
And for the second category (conditions linked to the practice of the activity): 1. the maximal age to practise; 2. continuing education; 3. the obligation to be registered; 4. having an appropriate office.
Sometimes a professional accreditation is also required. However, the conditions to gain a professional accreditation are the same as those linked with the providing of a licence to practice (education, practical training, etc.). Therefore, such accreditation is only a modality of licensing a profession and will not be discussed.
See also DE BIJL N., *op. cit.*: 7, 17; FURROW B. R. (I), *op. cit.*: 58.

7.3.5.2 *Education*[332]

A. Introduction

Education is the most important condition to satisfy in order to obtain a licence to practise or to be registered. First, the necessity of education when regulating the licensing to practise alternative practitioners will be discussed. Second, its real impact on licensing regulation will be presented and evaluated. Finally, some proposals will be formulated.

B. Necessity of education

There is a general consensus that the training of 'alternative' practitioners, allopathic or not, is the key element to whether or not a person should obtain a licence to practise.[333] Indeed, it is the best way to guarantee the quality of care provided, and to ensure adequate protection of patients.[334]

The requirement of education can be met either through the attainment of a diploma from a school or by passing a basic exam.[335] The diploma certifies that the trainee is competent, namely that he or she has acquired the necessary knowledge in a specific field, which consequently amounts to the guarantee that he or she masters the technique.

332 Proposals regarding the content and form of education will be made in chap. 7.5.2.2.

333 Proposals for the coverage of alternative treatments will be made in chap. 7.4.2.2.

334 The Swedish Commission on Competence states that "A modern medical sector cannot be maintained without well-trained and otherwise competent personnel discharging their duties in an expert and conscientious manner. Training questions therefore have a very important bearing on the framing of rules of authorisation for medical care and allied areas" (SWEDISH COMMISSION ON COMPETENCE, *op. cit.*: 31–33). See also, e.g., ARNDT K. F., *op. cit.*: 92–99; BERNER D., *op. cit.*: 157–58; BRITISH MEDICAL ASSOCIATION, *op. cit.*: 46–48, 60–61; CRAMER R., *op. cit.*: 45–49; EHLERS A. P. F., *op. cit*: 39, 281–86; GUILLOD O. (I), *op. cit.*: 38; KUHN H. P., *op. cit.*: 2399–401; KÜNZI M. (I), *op. cit.*: 74; SELECT COMMITTEE ON SCIENCE AND TECHNOLOGY, *op. cit.*: 32–33, 58; STONE J., *op. cit.*: 242–43, 271–73; SWEDISH COMMISSION ON COMPETENCE, *op. cit.*: 31–33.

335 The terms "diploma" and "school" must be understood in their broad sense. "Diploma" includes all types of formal recognition (e.g., degrees, speciality title, etc.) certifying that students have successfully attended a training program. "School" includes all types of institutions delivering education and training programs (e.g., universities, public and private schools, etc.).

The purpose of a basic exam is to determine whether practitioners have acquired the specific knowledge deemed necessary, irrespective of whether they attended a program course in a school or not.[336] Sometimes, these types of exam aim only to establish that practitioners do not constitute a danger to public health, as a result of the basic knowledge they acquired on their own.[337]

C. The impact of education on licensing regulations[338]

Introduction

In this section, the impact of education when licensing both allopathic, and non-allopathic practitioners to practise alternative medicines will be analysed.

Allopathic practitioners

In Western countries, where biomedicine has been considered as providing sufficient guarantees,[339] diplomas attesting knowledge in biomedicine have governed the right to practise the art of healing.[340] Thus, the biomedical model has become the standard in university faculties, and the holding of a university degree has become the indispensable condition to practise medicine.[341] The corollary effect of this development is that only the teaching of biomedicine and not alternative medicines has developed (at least in universities), because only its practice has been officially recognised as lawful.

In order to have effective statutes, lawmakers have given physicians the right to practise in any branch of medicine. Although this right was

336 E.g., for the examination of chiropractor candidates in Switzerland.

337 E.g., in Germany, or in some Swiss cantons, such as Appenzell External Rhodes.

338 For a study on the subject in Great Britain, see Budd S., *op. cit.* See also Select Committee on Science and Technology, *op. cit.*: 58ss.

339 Indeed, biomedicine based on Cartesian rationalist philosophy may explain pathogenic mechanisms, is effective to treat several illnesses, and possesses reproducible methods. For further discussion, see chap. 6.2 and 6.3.

340 In all the countries studied in this research, an allopathic diploma to practise medicine as a physician is required. In the US, e.g., physicians must show proof of postgraduate training in order to obtain a medical licence within a state (Liang B. A., *op. cit.*: 149).

341 For a historical perspective on the licensing to practise, see chap. 4.3.2.2 (France), 4.3.3.7 (the Netherlands), and 4.3.6.2 (US).

originally given from the perspective of the practice of allopathic medicine, it has generally been extended to the practice of non-allopathic medicine.[342] The consequence is that physicians are usually entitled to provide alternative treatments without having received any training or education in the field.

In monopolistic countries, although physicians should not, in theory, practice nor receive education in alternative medicine, the reality is different. Indeed, the practice of alternative medicines is usually tolerated when provided by physicians.[343] However, there is no requirement of an additional education in alternative medicines in order to practise them.

The situation is similar in tolerant countries where physicians are allowed to provide alternative treatments without holding a diploma. Even in Hungary, which adopted a statute regulating in details the training for non-allopathic practitioners, physicians are allowed to practise alternative therapies and to use the protected title "natural doctor", irrespective of whether they obtained a diploma or attended a course in natural medicine. In Switzerland, new training programs in homeopathy, Chinese medicine, anthroposophic medicine, and neural therapy have been created. Only those physicians who have successfully attended and completed the training may use the FMH title related to these techniques. While the creation of the FMH title gives undeniable credibility and guarantee of quality, any physician may call him or herself "acupuncturist" or "homeopath", as long as he or she does not use the term "FMH". In the medium- and long-term, the creation of such titles will naturally result in a system where, among physicians, only those holding such title will be able to provide alternative medicines.

The situation in both monopolistic and tolerant countries is equally unsatisfactory. Indeed, even if education in alternative medicines is improving, and even if the practice of alternative medicines is tolerated, a gap still exists between the right to practise alternative medicines and the requirement of training. Furthermore, the holding of a title in alternative

342 For more details concerning the scope of practice of practitioners, see chap. 7.3.3.2 and 7.3.3.3.

343 E.g., in Austria, or in Swiss monopolistic cantons, physicians are implicitly allowed to provide alternative treatments. In France, alternative physicians are recognised as physicians having a particular mode of practice. The situation is similar in Italy, Spain and formerly in Belgium.
In these countries, alternative training programs are available for physicians (e.g., there are courses in Italy and Spain, diploma courses have been set up in Austria and in France, as well as speciality courses in Latvia).

medicines is usually not required in order to provide them. As a result, there is no reliable guarantee as to the quality of 'alternative' services provided to patients.

There is no doubt that the development of alternative education in medical schools must be encouraged. In this respect, it is interesting that the practice of (bio-) medicine is already divided into several departments. Physicians are becoming more and more specialised in a determined field, and certain categories of practitioners are allowed to practise in precise fields of health care.[344] This demonstrates that physicians should ideally have completed additional training in a specific technique before practising it. Today, such a requirement should also be necessary for the practise of alternative medicines.

Non-allopathic practitioners

When analysing the impact of education on the licensing to practise alternative medicines by non-allopathic practitioners, a distinction must be made between monopolistic and tolerant countries.

In monopolistic countries, non-allopathic practitioners and the techniques they provide should, in theory, be non-existent.[345] As a result, these countries do not have any educational requirements regarding the practice of medicine by non-allopathic practitioners. However, in practice, these practitioners provide alternative medicines.[346] The response from public authorities to this situation has been to either prosecute these practitioners, to tolerate them, or to seek the normalisation of these practices through the recognition of alternative practitioners.[347] In the first two cases, the situation is unsatisfactory as non-allopathic practitioners will

344 E.g., physiotherapists provide physical rehabilitation care, speech therapists treat speech problems, etc.
On the subject, see ROBARD I., *op. cit.*: 107–08.

345 In monopolistic countries, the teaching of alternative medicines to non-allopathic practitioners is still at an early stage of development (for more details, see chap. 3).

346 One must underline an interesting paradox in some monopolistic regulatory structures in France, Belgium, Italy and Spain. While the practice of medicine by non-allopathic practitioners is forbidden in these countries, the fundamental right to teach protects the training of these providers. Therefore, allopathic practitioners may learn their profession but are not allowed to practise it.
In other monopolistic countries such as Austria, the situation is the opposite where a recent law forbids the creation of new schools in alternative medicines.

347 For more details, see chap. 7.3.4.2 and 7.3.4.3.

continue to 'illegally' practise, without any controls being established as to their education.

Spanish courts have adopted an interesting position regarding the necessity of education. They make a distinction between those practices implying or not implying university knowledge. If the providing of a technique requires such knowledge, then the holding of a university diploma is required. When a technique is not taught within the country, then non-allopathic practitioners may be allowed to provide the technique, as long as the practitioner holds a foreign diploma.[348]

In monopolistic countries, however, the situation is unsatisfactory. Indeed, non-allopathic practitioners still practise in all of these countries, despite the risk of prosecution. Furthermore, as these practitioners are not allowed to practise, their training remains unregulated.

A categorisation may be useful in order to understand the different approaches taken in tolerant countries regarding the requirement of education when licensing non-allopathic practitioners. One may distinguish between States on the basis of the restrictiveness of the policy used:[349]

1. where the practice of medicine is restricted to allopathic practitioners, although specific alternative techniques may be provided without possessing a diploma;[350]
2. where the practice of medicine is, in principle, free, although specific medical procedures are strictly reserved to physicians. A diploma is not necessary, but an exam must be passed, the objective of which is not to test the extended knowledge of practitioners, but to ensure that the practitioner does not constitute a danger to public health;[351]
3. where the practice of medicine is free, in principle, although specific medical procedures are strictly reserved to physicians. A diploma is

348 For more details, see chap. 4.3.2.6. and 7.3.3.3.

349 For a categorisation, see also, e.g., WICKI M., *op.cit.*: 74ss.

350 E.g., in Liechtenstein, in order to practise "natural medicine", namely health care which does not consist of bodily intrusions, deliveries, the treatment of infectious diseases, and the prescription of medication, a commercial authorisation is sufficient.
The situation is similar in some Swiss cantons. E.g., in Swiss canton Aargau, a licence is not compulsory in order to provide care to healthy persons, when treating nervousness, stress, sleeplessness or fear of exams. In canton Glarus, the practice of reflexology, acupressure and other similar massages may also be freely provided.

351 E.g. in Germany and in Swiss canton Appenzell Internal Rhodes.

not necessary to practise medicine.[352] However, a diploma may be required in order to practise under a protected title;[353]

4. where the licensing to practise allopathic and alternative medicine is regulated but not free. A licence requiring the holding of a diploma is necessary to be allowed to practise.[354]

The situation of tolerant countries is usually unsatisfactory as well. Indeed, even though a system based on free practice has been proposed above, it is important to establish standards that may help participants in the field to identify competent practitioners. This may be done, in particular, through the creation of protected titles. In the first two categories of countries, although the practice is free, there is no such guarantee. The last category, based on a mandatory system, provides guarantees as to the training of practitioners. However, it does not allow practitioners to provide health care if a standardised training is not available. The third category is satisfactory when a protected title is attached to the practice of specific activities.

Additional examination

Regulation sometimes requires that practitioners holding a diploma must pass an additional examination. This is typically the case when practition-

352 E.g., in Denmark, or in the Netherlands. States allowing lay or traditional practice also usually adopt such a system (e.g., cantons Neuchâtel and Ticino in Switzerland, or New Mexico in the US).

353 E.g. in Great Britain where the titles of chiropractors and osteopaths are protected, or in the Netherlands. For an opinion regarding the situation in this country, see BUDD S., *op. cit.*; SELECT COMMITTEE ON SCIENCE AND TECHNOLOGY, *op. cit.*: 59ss.

354 E.g., in Hungary, whenever since the introduction of a new law in 1997, non-allopathic practitioners have been allowed to carry out specific alternative medicines. The law specifies for each alternative discipline the content of the training, the required exam, and finally, the providing of the technique (within a precise legal framework).
In Belgium, a new law that was adopted in June, 1999, stipulates that only non-allopathic practitioners who have obtained an authorisation delivered by the Ministry of Public Health are allowed to practise. The conditions of training and the evaluation required in order to obtain the authorisation will be specified in a decree.
The situation is similar in several US States, where the practice of specific alternative medicines has been regulated under mandatory licensure regulations (e.g., acupuncture in Iowa or Texas). Only those licensed (the holding of a diploma is required in these States) are allowed to provide treatments.

ers have been trained in foreign schools. In Switzerland, for example, in order to obtain an authorisation to practise as a chiropractor, candidates must have studied at least four years in a chiropractic college recognised by the American Council on Chiropractic Education, have passed the exam before an American state commission, have passed the Swiss intercantonal exam, and possibly have passed the federal exam on X-ray.

From the perspective of an international space of free movement of practice, such additional requirements may seem excessive. However, until medical 'alternative' training has been standardised, additional educational requirements are likely to be employed to verify the skills of candidates.

D. Several levels of risks and education

Introduction

As demonstrated above,[355] the provision of medical acts involving substantial risks, as well as the provision of 'alternative' medicines under a protected title should be restricted to competent practitioners. As a result, education is the best means to assess this ability to practise. Therefore, the training must be in relation to the risks involved with the provision of specific techniques.[356]

Taking the risk criterion into consideration, it is possible to distinguish three categories of medical acts, namely those involving high, medium, or lesser risks, which will require a specific level of education.[357]

Public health authorities should be in charge of assessing the risks of medical techniques, on the basis of a document set up by representatives of an alternative profession, which includes information regarding the specificities of the therapy, the training of practitioners, and the results of clinical testing.

355 See chap. 7.4.2.3.

356 BRITISH MEDICAL ASSOCIATION, *op. cit.*: 62–63. For discussion on the situation in Switzerland, see WICKI M., *op. cit.*: 72ss.

357 On this subject, see STONE J., *op. cit.*: 244.
For a discussion of the risks related to alternative medicines, see chap. 6.5.
The problem is how to determine which acts or practices will be put in each category. As medicine is continuously evolving, the risks and the means available to limit them are likely to change. Although it may be difficult to list activities, the great majority of alternative medicines is likely to be listed in the second or third category. The most widespread of these (e.g., traditional Chinese medicine, anthroposophic medicine, homeopathy, manipulative techniques such as osteopathy, chiropractic and herbal therapies), would almost certainly be listed in the second group (requiring medium knowledge). Indeed, these practices are linked with non-negligible 'medium' risks.

Medical acts involving high risks

The first category of acts includes those medical acts that may result in serious injuries to the health, physical or psychological, of patients, or that may possibly endanger the life of patients. Examples include the practice of surgery, obstetrics, the treatment of venereal and contagious diseases, the provision of drugs, anaesthetics and the treatment of life-threatening illnesses.[358] Some alternative techniques are likely to be included in this category, for example, the providing of some alternative "drugs" or preparations or the treatment of serious illnesses with alternative medicines.

Only those practitioners having a high level of education, namely a university degree, and a specialisation in alternative medicine should be allowed to provide those alternative medicines, which are linked with high risks. As a result, when necessary and when possible, specialty training should be set up for alternative medicines.[359] However, alternative practitioners, in particular non-allopathic practitioners, should be able to provide health care when an allopathic treatment has been unsuccessful in curing or alleviating pain.[360] At this point, the primary health care provider, usually a physician, would remain responsible for provided treatments and the non-allopathic practitioner would work in a cooperative way with such.

Medical acts involving medium risks

The second category of medical acts includes those medical acts which involve medium risks such as certain acts of physiotherapy, osteopathy, chiropractic, herbal remedies and acupuncture, namely techniques that may result in physical or mental injury without threatening the life of patients.

To provide such acts, it is recommended that physicians hold a speciality title and that non-allopathic practitioners or ancillary professionals

358 This includes all degenerative illnesses, particularly those for which no treatment is available, such as the treatment of several forms of cancer, the treatment of diabetes, multiple sclerosis, acute forms of psychiatric diseases and the providing of chelation therapy.
These acts are those generally constituting the limited monopoly reserved to physicians who should remain the only practitioners allowed to provide a range of specific medical acts. For further discussion, see chap. 7.3.2.3.

359 For a further discussion on the content of education, see chap. 7.5.2.2.

360 E.g., the use of acupuncture to treat side effects related with chemotherapy sessions.

hold a diploma attesting that they have attended a medium training.[361] Of course, this implies the development of appropriate schools, and followed by the establishment of recognised education and standards in alternative medicines.[362]

While holding a diploma must be the main condition for entering a register[363] or receiving a licence to practise, it is unclear whether all the 'alternative' medical acts linked with medium risks must be restricted to those practitioners who have acquired a medium level of education. It is certainly acceptable for practices such as acupuncture as this practice implies a break of corporal integrity. However, the position for other techniques such as osteopathy or chiropractic is more problematic. Indeed, if one restricts the practice of osteopathy or chiropractic solely to those practitioners who have attended a recognised training, other practitioners providing manipulation techniques could find themselves in a difficult situation, not knowing if they are providing restricted care or not. Furthermore, one must be careful not to reintroduce indirectly a certain form of monopoly. As a result, the risk criterion must be strictly interpreted and the scope of restricted activities clearly defined.[364]

In this respect, one may add that if some non-allopathic practitioners are free to provide alternative medicines without having any education in the field, there are other safeguards in place, in particular, those rules dealing with civil, criminal, administrative and professional liability.[365] Thus, while non-allopathic practitioners may not be subjected to administrative or professional prosecution, they may still, however, be sued or prosecuted under various civil and criminal statutes. Moreover, although in several countries, education is not an official requirement, alternative

361 The British Select Committee on Science and Technology recommends, "that CAM training courses should become more standardised and be accredited and validated by the appropriate professional bodies. All those who deliver CAM treatments, whether conventional health professionals or CAM professionals, should have received training in that discipline independently accredited by the appropriate regulatory body" (Select Committee on Science and Technology, *op. cit.*: 62). See also, e.g., Swedish Commission on Competence, *op. cit.*: 32.

362 For more details, see chap. 7.5.2.2 (education) and 7.5.3.2–3 (standards of practice).

363 In the above-proposed system, this will guarantee the registered person the right to practise under a protected title (see chap. 7.3.2.3).

364 See chap. 7.3.3.3 and 7.3.4.3.

365 The situation is similar in both monopolistic and tolerant countries. See chap. 7.2.2 and 7.2.3.

practitioners do usually attend training, for obvious reasons.[366] Actually, incidents are very rare in those countries.[367]

Medical acts involving low risks

The last category of "medical acts" covers those "health care"[368] activities that are linked to no risks or very low, such as relaxation or prevention measures.[369] For these practices,[370] as we have seen, there is no necessity to hold a specific diploma or to pass an exam.[371] However, public authorities should still retain the power to, if required, forbid specific health care providers to practise. If necessary, the provision of specific activities could also be easily restricted to practitioners holding a protected title.

F. Proposals

The education of 'alternative' practitioners is the key element for the licensing of 'alternative' medicines. The requirement of education should vary

366 See chap. 3.
367 See chap. 6.5.
368 It is difficult to determine where the practice of medicine ends. Indeed, some acts may be considered as being both "medical" and not. These practices are on the border between medicine and life style practice. For further discussion, see chap. 1.1.
369 Also, there is always the risk that a patient may be prevented from seeking appropriate biomedical care, which could provide a more effective cure.
370 Traditional practices could be listed in the last category. Indeed, risks involved with these practices are usually relatively low. Furthermore, the practice of these techniques presupposes either an apprenticeship or a natural gift or talent. In both cases, it is difficult to organise training. Moreover, it is illusory to attempt to eliminate such practices.
For a definition of traditional practices, see chap. 1.1.
371 Some may argue that even if the risks involved with these practices are non-existent or very low, practitioners should however obtain an authorisation to practise. In order to obtain the authorisation, candidates should pass a basic exam, the purpose of which would be to establish that they do not constitute a danger to individual and public health. However, such a system may be confusing for people who consider that since these practitioners hold a licence to practise, they are competent in their own field.
On this subject, see Ministry of Health and Social Affairs (I), *op. cit.*: 273 (the Committee rejected the enforcement of a requirement for a minimum competency level in basic medical subjects, and/or of a competency level in the relevant alternative medical treatment). See also chap. 7.3.2.3.

according to the risks related to the practice of the activity. As a result, the higher the potential risks, the more serious the training must be.

Thus, only those practitioners who have completed a high level of education, at least a university degree, and a further specialisation in 'alternative' medicine should be allowed to provide 'alternative' medicines linked with high risks. This implies the creation of specialties in the field of alternative medicines.

Alternative medical acts which involve medium risks should be restricted to those practitioners who have completed a medium level of education. Under the above-proposed system, this would guarantee a registered person the right to practise under a protected title. However, the scope of practice must be clearly defined. This implies the need to set up recognised education programs in alternative medicines.

Those persons who provide health care activities linked to little or no risk should be allowed to practise without requiring a specific diploma. However, public authorities should still have the possibility to prohibit the practice of specific activities or to deny a specific health care provider the right to practise.

In order to ensure a high quality of care, practitioners holding a protected title should have the obligation to regularly update and refresh their skills and knowledge. Similarly, schools ideally should propose continuing education. Measures should also be taken to encourage alternative practitioners to follow such courses.[372]

G. Conclusion

In Western countries, after having observed that for sensible reasons the use of alternative medicines has strongly increased, public authorities are looking for solutions giving patients access to alternative medicines, but at the same time guaranteeing the quality of these techniques.

However, the situation remains unsatisfactory. Indeed, regulations usually do not require that alternative practitioners possess a diploma or attend and complete training in alternative medicines.[373]

Certainly, it is possible to argue that the development of alternative medicines in Western countries is a recent phenomenon, and that education programs, particularly in medical schools, need time to develop as

372 See SELECT COMMITTEE ON SCIENCE AND TECHNOLOGY, *op. cit.*: 63 ("we suggest that the CAM therapies, [...], should identify Continuing Professional Development in practice as a core requirement for their members").

373 See SELECT COMMITTEE ON SCIENCE AND TECHNOLOGY, *op. cit.*: 63.

well. However, several countries have demonstrated that it is possible to condition the licensing to practise (or the holding of a protected title) to a requirement of education.

When regulating the licensing to practise, the level of risks linked to the providing of a technique, being either high, medium, or low, is the method to determine which level of education, high or medium, is required from those practitioners providing them. Medical acts involving high risk must be restricted to those practitioners who have attained a high level of education. As there is no definitive criterion of risks to establish exactly when a diploma or exam should be compulsory in order to provide care, this criterion must be strictly interpreted and the scope of practice clearly defined.

Thus, while the position of alternative medicines in Western countries remains globally unsatisfactory, there are many interesting developments and ideas that open new perspectives. In brief, it is possible to say that we are still at the preliminary stages of a major shift in perspective.

7.3.5.3 Practical Experience

A. Presentation

The most important requirement after education is practical experience. This requirement is strongly linked with education as normally, any training should include some practical experiencc which is usually granted through internships. However, some countries have imposed additional practical experience or training on top of the education requirements, especially when practitioners have been trained in foreign schools. In Germany or in Great Britain for example, practical experience is required, prior to obtaining a full registration to be allowed to fully practise medicine.[374, 375] Similarly, in Norway and Switzerland, candidates must have undergone an additional practical training of one year in order to obtain a chiropractor licence to practise.[376]

374 Typically as a physician.

375 In Great Britain, one may obtain a provisional registration on graduation, and full registration after satisfactorily completing 12 months of general clinical training (De Bijl N., *op. cit.*: 7).

376 Chiropractors in both countries have generally been trained in foreign countries, usually in the US.
During this period, a preliminary authorisation is given.

B. Evaluation and proposals

In our view, if education has been correctly organised, additional practical experience should not be required. Such a requirement should be necessary when there is a lack of such education or when it is difficult to verify the practical skills of practitioners, for example when they have been trained in a foreign country.

7.3.5.4 Physical and Mental Abilities

A. Presentation

Physical and/or psychological capabilities normally play a role in the procedure to obtain access to medical practice. In Germany, for example, medical practitioners, both physicians and "*Heilpraktikers*",[377] require a declaration from a physician, confirming that there are no indications of physical or mental disability, or addiction. Similarly, in Denmark, authorisation is not granted to persons assumed to be dangerous when providing medical care, either because of physical defects or a permanently or intermittently defective state of mind. This is so whether the defective state of mind is due to illness, abuse of alcohol or drugs, or due to gross incompetence.[378] In Norway, one of the requirements to obtain an authorisation as a chiropractor is to be in such a position that there would be no withdrawal of the authorisation resulting from old age, illness, alcohol/drug abuse or other circumstances.[379]

B. Evaluation and proposals

The requirement that medical practitioners demonstrate that they have sufficient physical and mental capabilities may be a guarantee as to the quality of treatments. If such an exam must be imposed upon a practitioner when obtaining a licence to practise or when entering a register, then, in the interests of consistency, it is necessary that the capabilities of such practitioners are regularly verified. This requires an important re-certification system, aiming to establish that practitioners are still capable,

377 "Heilpraktikers" are licensed non-allopathic practitioners who are allowed to provide alternative medicines.

378 Art. 2 (3) of the Danish Order of 1970.

379 De Bijl N., *op. cit.*: 8, 17.

which could be viewed as excessive, and difficult to implement.[380] Possibly, the title protection could be withdrawn, if the practitioner does not satisfy these requirements.

7.3.5.5 *Morality*

A. Presentation

As health care providers are generally viewed as liberal professionals, their morality may be considered as important. Indeed, the practice of medicine directly concerns the health and sensitive data of patients. Therefore, it is often required that practitioners demonstrate that they possess sufficient morality to provide medical acts. Usually, at the minimum a certificate is required from public authorities attesting that the candidate has a clean criminal record.

In Belgium, for example, registration with the Order requires a certificate of good character and repute. The position in similar in both France[381] and in Liechtenstein. In Germany, "Heilpraktikers" must have a good reputation in order to obtain a licence to practise.[382] In the US, licensure assessments may also require evidence of good moral character and ethics.[383, 384]

B. Evaluation and proposals

While it may be necessary for medical providers to show that they possess sufficient morality to exercise their profession, the control should be imposed, however, only in compliance with conditions viewed as strictly

380 In this respect, De Bijl notes, "how can someone's capability or incompetence be assessed? It is legitimate that access to medical practice is subject to conditions and with a view to the protection of patients this should stay that way. Once a medical doctor has been admitted he stays in principle admitted, unless he is disqualified through penal or disciplinary rules. This should be prevented as much as possible by settling requirements to continuous professional training, refresher courses and medical audit" (DE BIJL N., *op. cit.*: 14).

381 In 1945, an administrative judge considered that a physician who administered quack treatments had not shown sufficient morality. Today, this decision would be considered out of date, as physicians providing alternative treatments are officially recognised by the social security system.

382 This condition is not satisfied if, for example, a practitioner provides health care without a "Heilpraktiker"'s licence and caused a physical injury.

383 A personal history review is usually required.

384 DE BIJL N., *op. cit.*: 8; LIANG B. A., *op. cit.*: 149–50.

related to the practice of the profession. Therefore, no controls should be imposed as to the private life of a practitioner, as such a requirement is not relevant to any assessment of his or her ability to practise.

7.3.5.6 Adhesion to Professional Ethics

A. Presentation

Professional bodies or public authorities often require that practitioners adhere to a professional code of ethics. This requirement is directly related to professional liability.[385]

Generally, a professional code of ethics will seek to provide guidance on the requirements necessary for good practice. These codes enunciate professional requirements, usually in the form of what practitioners should and should not do. In reality, they are normative instruments, which attempt to influence the behaviour of practitioners. Thus, when authorities require practitioners to adhere to a code of professional ethics, the underlying purpose is to make health care practitioners aware of their duties.[386]

The traditional way to demonstrate adherence to professional ethics is to take the Hippocratic oath, which is usually sworn by medical students during the closing ceremony at the end of medical study. In some countries such as Denmark, taking such an oath is a formal condition that must be satisfied before a student can obtain an authorisation to practise.[387] In other countries, medical practitioners must adhere to a Code of Professional Ethics. In Great Britain, for example, non-allopathic practitioners must adhere to a Code of Professional Ethics, in order to become a member of professional organisations. Similarly, in Spain, physicians must respect the Spanish Code of Professional Ethics.[388]

B. Evaluation and proposals

In order for a code of professional ethics to apply, the rules must first be established by professional bodies. They may be viewed as part of the process of professionalisation. Once a code of professional ethics is created, adhesion to the code may be formally required as a condition necessary to

385 On this subject, see STONE J., *op. cit.*: 278–81; SUGARMAN J. (I), *op. cit.*: 1623–25.

386 STONE J., *op. cit.*: 194. For further discussion, see the same author, at 194ss, 204ss, 280–81.

387 The position is similar in Liechtenstein.

388 DE BIJL N., *op. cit.*: 7; LIANG B. A., *op. cit.*: 149–50.

obtain a licence to practise. In our view, practitioners who have obtained a licence to practise should in any case be subject to these rules. Indeed, such codes not only provide standards of practice,[389] but also offer guidelines as to the appropriate behaviour of practitioners engaged in medical practice. From this perspective, the requirement of adhesion to a code of professional ethics must be viewed as serving the purpose of making practitioners aware of their duties.[390]

7.3.5.7 Citizenship

A. Presentation

Some states still require that practitioners hold the citizenship of the country from which they received a licence to practise. In France, for example, one of the conditions to obtain a licence to practise medicine (as a physician) is to be a French, Tunisian or European citizen. In the US, some statutes also include a citizenship requirement.

B. Evaluation and proposals

The condition of citizenship seems to be obsolete, especially in Europe. EU Member States enjoy the right of free movement for their citizens which means that, as soon as a profession is regulated (and the diploma recognised) in one Member State then the holding of European citizenship is sufficient for recognition of the qualification acquired in all Member States.[391] In our view, the criteria of citizenship should be abandoned in Western countries. Indeed, the contemporary world (of health care) is moving towards the increasing mobility of people generally, and where training is similar among countries. Then, the requirement of citizenship appears to be more a means by which local practitioners are protected rather than a method ensuring the quality of care.[392] Thus, a residence or

389 See chap. 7.5.3.

390 Practitioners will be subjected to other rules, particularly those dealing with civil and criminal liability. For a development, see chap. 7.2.3.

391 For more details, see SCHNEIDER H., *op. cit.*: 463. See also chap. 4.3.1.

392 FURROW notes in relation to the US, that "such requirement probably violates the US constitution" (FURROW B. R. (I), *op. cit.*: 58).
Similarly, the Supreme Swiss Court recently ruled that a foreigner with a residence permit, and married with a Swiss wife may refer to the economic freedom, and therefore be allowed to provide medical acts. In particular, in order to practise as an independent physiotherapist, it is disproportionate to require an additional permit, as well as an internship in a public institution (ATF 123 I 212, cited in SAN News, 2000, n° 11: 17).

work permit should be sufficient, particularly after taking into consideration the example (and the influence) of the EU. Attention should then be focused on the development of educational standards, and on the establishment of the appropriate regulatory mechanisms leading to the recognition of foreign diplomas.[393]

7.3.5.8 Additional Requirements

A. Generalities

Apart from the above-mentioned requirements linked to the right to practise 'alternative' medicines, regulations often have additional requirements. It is possible to distinguish two general types of dispositions; first, those rules linked with the rights and duties of practitioners, and second, the rules that practitioners must observe in order to keep their licence to practise. It is difficult to make a general evaluation as such rules are more specific to State regulations or medical techniques. Therefore, they will only be briefly presented below.

B. Rights and duties of practitioners

When the practice of alternative practitioners is specifically regulated, such practitioners are usually subject to the same duties as physicians. These include the obligation to obtain the informed consent of the patient, professional secrecy, obligation to declare communicable diseases or to practise in a diligent manner.[394] For example, in Belgium and Hungary, non-allopathic practitioners must hold a medical record for each patient. In Germany, "Heilpraktikers" are, together with allopathic practitioners, subject to the requirement of professional secrecy, and infringements of this requirement may lead to criminal prosecution.[395]

Lawmakers have also set up rules that are more specifically related to alternative medicines. For example, regarding the informed consent of

393 When one applies such a rule, an exception should, in principle, not be permitted even for small countries such as Liechtenstein, which wish to maintain a quota of practitioners having the citizenship of such country.

394 For a list of general right and duties of alternative practitioners, see RÖSCH B., *op. cit.*: 124–125, 320ss.

395 GUILLOD O. (I), *op. cit.*: 39. See also, e.g., LAY B. F., *op. cit.*: 651ss; WICKI M., *op. cit.*: 395–428.
For an analysis of the doctrine of informed consent, malpractice and criminal liability, see chap. 7.2.

patients, regulations may require that practitioners clearly inform their patients about their skills, and the training they attended.[396] Some countries also enacted rules to ensure a good relationship between allopathic and alternative practitioners.[397]

In our view, those practitioners who have a licence to practise, or who are registered, or who are practising under a protected title, should be subject to the above-mentioned complementary dispositions. For the remaining categories of practitioners, these dispositions seem more difficult to implement. Therefore, the general rules dealing with civil and criminal liability should be sufficient.

As discussed above,[398] the better protection for patients is to receive all the information necessary in order to make an informed choice. As such, information must not only be provided to the public but also publicised, and titles must be created and protected.

The main right of practitioners is to practise under a protected title, which amounts to an interdiction against other practitioners using the same title. Thus, in some jurisdictions, it is forbidden for a non-protected practitioner to use the title of doctor of medicine, or to use the title of specialist for a specific illness.[399] Similarly, in Great Britain, only registered practitioners are allowed to use the title of chiropractor and osteopath. The extent of the protection may vary. It may be the simple protection of a term associated with the profession, such as to be "registered" or "authorised", or be extended so as to protect the name of the profession (e.g., "chiropractor").[400] In this respect, Chapman-Smith states that "the

396 E.g., in Swiss canton Ticino, non-allopathic practitioners have to clearly inform their patients that they do not have any allopathic education. The position is similar in canton Valais.
For more details regarding more specifically chiropractic and informed consent, see FISHER S., *op. cit.*: 979.

397 See chap. 7.2.3.2.

398 See chap. 7.3.2.3.

399 E.g., in Norway, only those who have received a formal training are allowed to use the title of "trained" therapist, but anyone can use the plain name of a profession, such as chiropractor. Similarly, in Sweden, or in Switzerland, non-allopathic practitioners are not allowed to use an allopathic recognised title.

400 E.g., in the US, psychology licensing statutes often use this approach: any person may practice psychology, but only licensed psychologists may use the title or describe their services by using the words psychologist, psychology, or psychological. The Danish regulation forbids practitioners not holding an authorisation as chiropractors to designate themselves as such or in any terms that are likely to create the impression that they hold such authorisation.

protection should not only prevent a person from claiming to be a member of the profession, but should also prevent the claim or implication that the same methods of treatment are being used".[401]

C. Keeping the licence to practice

In addition to the conditions that practitioners must fulfil in order to obtain a licence to practise, lawmakers have also established some rules that practitioners must respect and observe in order to keep their licence. For example, a condition that often appears is a requirement to have liability insurance.[402] For licensed or registered practitioners, in particular those providing techniques linked with high or medium risks, such a requirement is indispensable.

Other regulations may sometimes provide that practitioners may not abstain from practise for more than a certain period of time. This condition is related to the re-certification requirement mentioned above. In our view, it seems more appropriate to oblige practitioners to attend continuing education and refresher training. If the practitioner fails to satisfy these requirements, then the licence to practise, or title protection could be withdrawn.

In some states, non-allopathic practitioners are not allowed to advertise their services,[403] or to practise in an itinerant way.[404] There is also sometimes the necessity to have an appropriate office. Other regulations stipulate that practitioners are not permitted to practise after reaching a certain age.

Finally, it should be remembered that obtaining a licence to practise and then practising fraudulently are usually actions subject to criminal prosecution.

401 CHAPMAN-SMITH D.A., *op. cit.*: 113.
402 E.g., in Switzerland, physicians, pharmacists and veterinarians must have such insurance, like in Belgium for authorised non-allopathic practitioners. The Norwegian Committee on Alternative Medicines has proposed such a condition.
403 E.g., in Norway (however, announcements in the press with only the indication of name, address, consultation-hours, and general information on the activities are permitted). The situation is similar in Swiss cantons Appenzell external Rhodes, Neuchâtel, Obwalden, and Thurgau.
404 E.g., in Germany, Norway or Sweden.

D. Conclusion

In addition to classical requirements concerning the right to practise, lawmakers have also established complementary dispositions to regulate the more practical aspects, such as the rights and duties of practitioners, and rules that practitioners must respect in order to keep their licence to practise or registration.

For those practitioners who are registered or who have obtained a licence to practise, it seems more appropriate that such practitioners are subject to the same rights and duties as allopathic practitioners. In addition, some rules should also be established to ensure a proper relationship between allopathic and alternative practitioners.

Finally, the right to practise under a protected title should be permitted for those practitioners who have completed serious training in the protected profession, as this would allow patients to easily identify competent practitioners.

These additional requirements should not be applied to practitioners that are not registered, or licensed, or who do not benefit from a protected title. Indeed, it would be too difficult to implement them. In our view, a better approach consists in encouraging the self-regulation of non-recognised professions and the development of appropriate rules for its members.[405] The general rules dealing with civil and criminal liability should be sufficient in addition to such self-regulation.

7.3.5.9 *Summary*

In order to be allowed to practise biomedicine, several requirements must be met. The objective of these requirements is to ensure quality of care and the protection of patients. Various countries have also demonstrated that the same requirements can be adapted in order to apply to practitioners of alternative medicines.

The most important requirement is the education of alternative practitioners. Until now, this requirement has not been given sufficient attention, however, some countries are showing the way. It is possible to distinguish the various categories of practitioners, according to their training by defining such training as high, medium or low.

The right to practice in specific areas, which is determined by the risks involved with their provision as well as the right to practise under a protected title, should be restricted to those practitioners who satisfy specific educational criteria.

405 See chap. 7.2.3.3.

Some additional requirements may be viewed as relatively important such as adherence to professional ethics, while other requirements must be put into perspective (such as physical and mental abilities, citizenship and morality). Practical experience should be required only when the educational level of the practitioners does not satisfy the standards of the country in which such practitioner wishes to practise.

The requirement of appropriate physical and mental capabilities may be imposed when obtaining a licence to practise. However, one should consider that, in principle, the practitioner is physically and mentally capable. This presumption would be reversed only when the practitioner is disqualified through penal or disciplinary rules. In addition, attention should be focused on obligating practitioners to attend continuing or refresher education.

Medical providers should also demonstrate that they have sufficient morality to exercise their profession. However, any control imposed should only be for those conditions strictly related to the profession concerned.

Once a code of professional ethics has been established, and practitioners have been licensed to practise, they should be subjected to such code, irrespective of whether they have formally adhered to the code or not.

A supplementary requirement linked to the citizenship of the practitioner should not be required with, a residence permit or work permit being sufficient.

Finally, these conditions are still not as developed for alternative medicines but may be applied to alternative professions by utilising the biomedical profession as an analogy with alternative ones.

7.3.6 Administrative/Professional Structure

Bibliography

ABBOTT A., *The system of professions: An essay on the division of expert labor*, University of Chicago Press, 1988, Chicago; ANDREWS L. B., *The shadow health care system: Regulation of alternative health care providers*, in: Houston Law Review, 1996, vol. 32: 1315; BRITISH MEDICAL ASSOCIATION (LAMONT T.), *Complementary medicine – New approaches to good practice*, Oxford University Press, 1993, Oxford/New York: 60–61; BUDD S. (co-author: MILLS S.), *Professional organisation of complementary and alternative medicine in the UK 2000: A second report to the Department of Health*, University of Exeter, 2000, London; COHEN M. H. (I), *Complementary and alternative medicine – Legal boundaries and regulatory perspectives*, The Johns Hopkins University Press, 1998, London & Oxford: 37; FISCHER S., *Commission de surveillance des professions de la santé: La situation en Suisse romande*, in: Médecine et Hygiène,

1999, vol. 57: 979; Guillod O. (I), *Rebouteux, naturopathes et guérisseurs: Pour un traitement légal alternatif*, Recueil de Jurisprudence Neuchâtelois, 1989, Neuchâtel: 23; Jost T. S. (III), *Oversight of the competence of healthcare professionals*, in: Jost T. S., *Regulation of the healthcare professions*, Health Administration Press, 1996, Chicago: 17–44; Kinney E., *Administrative law issues in professional regulation*, in: Jost T. S., *Regulation of the healthcare professions*, Health Administration Press, 1996, Chicago: 103–28; Ministry of Health and Social Affairs (I), *Report on alternative medicine – English summary*, Norges Offentliche Utredniger NOU 1998: 21, 1998, Oslo: 271–74; Pew Health Professions Commission (Finocchio L. J., Dower C. M., McMahon T., Gragnola C. M., and the Taskforce on Health Care Workforce Regulation), *Reforming health care workforce regulation: Policy considerations for the 21st Century*, Pew Health Professions Commission, 1995, San Francisco; Relman A. S., *Regulation of the medical profession: A physician's perspective*, in: Jost T. S., *Regulation of the healthcare professions*, Health Administration Press, 1996, Chicago: 199–210; Sage W. M. (co-author: Aiken L. H.), *Regulating interdisciplinary practice*, in: Jost T. S., *Regulation of the healthcare professions*, Health Administration Press, 1996, Chicago: 78; Select Committee on Science and Technology, *Complementary and alternative medicine*, House of Lords – Session 1999–2000 6th Report, The Stationary Office, 2000, London; Stone J. (co-author: Matthews J.), *Complementary medicine and the law*, Oxford University Press, 1996, Oxford: 94, 282; Swedish Commission on Alternative Medicine, *Report on alternative medicine*, Regeringskansliet, 1989, Stockholm: 33–34.

7.3.6.1 General Remarks

Professional boards or specific departments of public administrations are responsible for implementing the regulations on the practice of medicine. As the role of these structures may become crucial in the field of alternative practices, the different solutions chosen by some Western countries will be briefly presented and evaluated.[406]

406 As the British Select Committee on Science and Technology states "The type of regulation [i.e. mandatory or statutory] is probably of less importance than whether the regulation (irrespective of its type) is delivered effectively by a single competent body" (Select Committee on Science and Technology, *op. cit.*: 36).

7.3.6.2 *Role and Type of Administrative/Professional Structures*

Although the functions and powers of administrative and professional structures vary from one state and profession to another, they share a common aim, which is to ensure the safety of patients and the quality of provided care. Their role is essential to an effective regulation of medical practice, irrespective of whether the regulation is statutory of self-regulatory. In order to reach these objectives, they usually have some or all of the following functions:[407]

1. Establishment of entry requirements for practitioners with possibly the creation of a register;[408]
2. Verification of the good practice of authorised practitioners;
3. Establishment of standards of practice and a professional code of ethics;[409]
4. Prosecution of practitioners who infringe the rules of practice;[410]
5. Approval and supervision of schools;[411]
6. Information to patients and other public authorities.

407 On this subject, see BUDD S., *op. cit.*; JOST T. S. (III), *op. cit.*: 17–44; KINNEY E., *op. cit.*: 103–28; MINISTRY OF HEALTH AND SOCIAL AFFAIRS (I), *op. cit.*: 271–74; SELECT COMMITTEE ON SCIENCE AND TECHNOLOGY, *op. cit.*: 42–43, 58.

408 For further details concerning licensure modalities, see chap. 7.3.2 and chap. 7.3.5 for the conditions linked with the practice of medicine.

409 For further details concerning the establishment of standards of practice, see chap. 7.5.3.

410 For further details concerning the infringement of scope of practice, see chap. 7.3.4.

411 According to the British Select Committee on Science and Technology "there seems to be a consensus across CAM and conventional medical bodies that responsibility for training standards and the validation of training should lie with the appropriate CAM professional regulatory body. Evidence also indicates that therapies furthest down the path towards achieving a single professional regulatory body are those with the most developed educational structures" (SELECT COMMITTEE ON SCIENCE AND TECHNOLOGY, *op. cit.*: 58). Regarding the validation of training, the author considers "that it is imperative that higher educational institutions and regulatory bodies in CAM liaise in order to ensure that training is adequate for registration. If extra training is required after academic qualification to ensure fitness to practise, this should be defined by the appropriate professional body, which should then implement appropriate mechanisms in order to see what this objective is achieved" (idem, at 63).
For further discussion concerning education, see chap. 3 and 7.6.2.

The institution responsible for these tasks may take several forms.[412] The government is often directly responsible. Sometimes, professional boards are legislatively designated. Alongside these recognised institutions, other self-regulated structures have similar functions. These institutions are usually composed of representatives of the profession although, sometimes, they will also include outside representatives.

Some examples of these structures and the role they play will be presented below.

In Belgium, the Ministry of Social Affairs, Public Health and Environment is in charge of the implementation of the new Act on Medical Practice. However, a commission with parity of representation advises the government on the general conditions for the practice of alternative medicine, in particular, professional insurance, the membership of a recognised professional organisation, a system of registration, a system of advertising, and a list of acts forbidden to non-physicians.[413] The commission also advises the government on the conditions necessary in order to obtain authorisation, the modalities regulating the suspension of authorisation, the requirements regarding the training and its evaluation, as well as continuous training.

In France, professional medical orders, such as the National Medical Council, have an active role in the public health field. Furthermore, the legislature has empowered them with a number of important functions, such as the elaboration of general rules of practice,[414] the enforcement of professional rules through administrative controls, as well as the representation of medical professions before public authorities. The French

412 On this subject, see KINNEY E., *op. cit.*: 106ss.

413 The commission is composed of 5 members proposed by the medical schools and 5 members proposed by the chambers. All members must practise either biomedicine (GPs or specialists) or alternative medicine (art. 5 of the Act).
Each chamber is composed of 5 members proposed by the schools of medicine and allowed to practise medicine (with at least one GP) and 5 members practising alternative medicines proposed by a recognised professional organisation.
Each chamber proposes standards of practice. Furthermore they also advise the government on the organisation of a peer review system, and of a code of professional ethics.

414 Particularly the Professional Code of Ethics. This Code is more than a professional document, since it is published by governmental decree.

Medical Orders[415] may also introduce prosecutions against illegal practitioners of medicine.[416]

In Germany, the State Department of Health responsible for the examination of "Heilpraktiker" candidates must also verify that "Heilpraktikers" do not use the physician title, do not treat illnesses or provide treatments restricted to physicians, and do not make unauthorised advertising. With respect to professional rules, the "Heilpraktikers" association has issued a professional code of practice, which does not, however, incorporate rules setting up standards of training and skills to practise medicine diligently.

In Germany, Hungary,[417] Denmark, Norway, and in the Swiss cantons,[418] the government, through a state department of health, is responsible for the implementation of the regulation on medical practice. In addition, professional associations also play a role.

In Great Britain, the General Chiropractic and Osteopathic Councils are responsible for the maintenance of the registers. Practitioners must be registered in order to be allowed to use the protected title.[419] The Councils have also published a Code of Professional Ethics and are in charge of disciplinary jurisdiction, in particular, professional incompetence. They also re-certificate the practitioners and define training standards within Great Britain.[420]

415 The Orders are composed only of allopathic practitioners. They are in charge of the most important tasks in relation to the implementation of medical practice regulations.

416 The National Council of the Order may impose sanctions such as fines, temporary suspension or withdrawal of the licence.

417 In Hungary, the Institute of Health is in charge of the training of "natural doctors" and is authorised to examine the candidates. The Ministry of Social Welfare is the authority responsible for this institute. There is a register of "natural doctors", and a special commission is responsible for the surveillance of natural doctors.

418 For a presentation of the authorities surveying health care providers in Swiss cantons Vaud, Neuchâtel, Jura and Fribourg, see FISCHER S., *op. cit.*: 979.

419 The General Chiropractic and Osteopathic Councils are composed of a significant number of members outside the profession. According to the Chiropractor Act 1994, Chap. 1 (1), (11) there are twenty members. Six are not required to be chiropractors and at least one has to be a registered medical practitioner.

420 Similarly, British qualified physicians and homeopaths usually join professional associations requiring them to have insurance and to adhere to the Code of Professional Ethics.

In the Netherlands, the Dutch government has not yet established structures for the licensing of alternative practitioners. However, it not only encourages and stimulates practitioners to use alternative medicines but also their professional organisations, both non-allopathic and allopathic, to meet certain standards of quality, to develop training courses, and to set up professional codes of practice and procedures for peer review.

In the US, states have set up different administrative structures. Some states have established boards composed principally of non-physicians who are charged with exercising independent regulatory authority over the profession.[421] Other states have a medical board exercising administrative control over the profession, often with the assistance of a board or committee. Finally, some states regulate the profession above the board level within a state agency, generally with the assistance of a special unit whose authority varies from state to state.[422] Furthermore, there are interdisciplinary boards that coordinate the regulation of several professions of health care providers.[423]

7.3.6.3 Evaluation

The various structures responsible for implementing medical practice regulation may deeply shape the policy approach towards medical practice.[424]

421 In 1992, Delaware established a seven member Committee on Massage/Bodywork practitioners composed of four professional members and three representatives from the general public. No more than one of the professional members of the Committee may be from the same national organisation or school in the massage/bodywork field. Among other tasks, the Committee is allowed to compile a list of schools and certified teachers to be used as a reference source in the voluntary certification process established by law for massage/bodywork practitioners.
Sage notes that "only with effort have licensed professionals other than physicians secured the right to police their own members" (SAGE W. M., *op. cit.*: 78).

422 E.g., in Connecticut, the Homeopathic Medical Examining Board is principally an advisory unit to the State Department of Public Health and Addiction Services. However, it has independent authority to hear and decide matters concerning suspension or revocation of licenses, to adjudicate complaints against practitioners, and to impose related sanctions.

423 E.g., the State of Illinois regulates the professions of physician, chiropractor and osteopath. The Board has 7 members: 5 MDs, 1 DC (doctor in chiropractic), and 1 DO (doctor in osteopathy).

424 See SAGE W. M., *op. cit.*: 78. On the subject, see also ABBOTT A., *op. cit.* (the author stresses the importance of social organisation of a profession as an element of its development).

For example, in France, the Medical Orders do not include outside representatives. These orders have large powers and their actions have been aimed more at protecting the economic monopoly of physicians rather than protecting the safety of patients.[425] Formerly in Belgium, the position was similar. Only those Belgian physicians who were opposed to alternative medicines could sit in disciplinary courts that sentenced physicians providing alternative medicines. While such a structure may have had some validity in the past when patients had to be protected against quacks, today, it seems unnecessarily oppressive and outmoded.

In recent years, there has been a growing tendency to include external representatives within the structures dealing with the implementation of practice of medicine rules. The creation of boards with a direct or indirect control from State authorities and composed of several representatives in the alternative medicines field helps to guarantee that differing interests will be addressed in a balanced way.[426] In particular, physicians should not be the sole members of any structures regulating other professions providing health care.[427] In this respect, the approach taken by some US States, and in Great Britain should be emulated, namely the inclusion of specialists and outside members within the structure regulating the medical practice. Also, the Belgium approach which is to have the department of health advised by a multidisciplinary commission, seems more in accordance with the needs of today.[428]

425 On the subject, see GUILLOD O., *op. cit.*: 23.

426 For the US, the Pew Commission has suggested "the creation of an interdisciplinary oversight board to coordinate health professional regulation in each state, the restructuring of individuals professional boards based on practice overlap, and the expansion of public representation" (PEW HEALTH PROFESSIONS COMMISSION, *op. cit.*). For a proposal regarding Great Britain, see STONE J., *op. cit.*: 282, and for Sweden, see SWEDISH COMMISSION ON ALTERNATIVE MEDICINE, *op. cit.*: 33–34.

427 In this respect, Andrews writes that "legislators should provide for separate regulatory boards for alternative providers and should not provide any role to the medical licensing board" (ANDREWS L. B., *op. cit.*: 1315). This is particularly true when lawmakers have set up regulation allowing non-allopathic practitioners to practise. A body that is open to such practices should supervise the implementation.

428 On the subject, see JOST T. S. (III), *op. cit.*: 17–44 (critical analysis and proposals regarding ways to identify, investigate, and sanction professional incompetence in the US); KINNEY E., *op. cit.*: 103–28; RELMAN A. S., *op. cit.*: 204–210 (physician perspective regarding the reality that boards must face).

Finally, self-regulation should also be favoured, and encouraged alongside the creation of self-regulatory bodies.[429]

7.3.6.4 *Summary and Proposals*

The implementation of regulations on 'alternative' medical practice is carried out by various administrative or professional structures. These bodies will enforce and sometimes even shape State policy towards medical practice.

It is necessary to take care in how these structures are implemented as they may have been given wide powers by legislators. Indeed, the establishment of boards where only one category of (allopathic) practitioners is represented may lead to undesirable effects. For example, the potential conflict of interest that could arise between the interests of the board and those of patients. A better approach, which has recently been adopted by several Western countries consists of the inclusion of outside representatives from other professions, state authorities, or patients' organisations. Such an approach which guarantees a hearing and respects diverse concerns and needs is more in accordance with current societal needs.

7.3.7 Conclusion

In Western countries, alternative medicines have developed within a legal framework, which was not originally designed for them. For several reasons, the use and provision of alternative medicines, which was discrete until the 1970's, started to strongly increase after this period. A natural consequence of this phenomenon has been the growth in the number of alternative practitioners, and the development of alternative education. Since then, many Western countries[430] have come to a realisation that three main areas need to be focused on. First, the incapacity of biomedicine to satisfy all patient needs and the acknowledgement that alternative medicines may benefit patients, second the inefficiency of repressive regulations towards alternative practitioners, and finally the generally insufficient level of education of alternative practitioners. This awareness has resulted on the one hand in the development of research and training programs, and on the other hand in a more tolerant approach by courts, as well as establishing regulations more adapted to alternative medicines and

429 See chap. 7.3.2.3.
430 Also public authorities, courts, medical establishments, etc.

practitioners. However, this evolution remains at an early stage of development, as alternative medicines and their providers are not integrated within the health care systems yet. For example, licensing regulations do not give enough weight to education. In particular, they do not require that a practitioner holds a diploma in alternative medicines in order to obtain a licence to practise or a protected title.

The recent evolution of patients' rights, in particular the right to receive information illustrates the willingness of a new and more 'responsible' generation of patients who want to make more choices about their health. From this perspective, a more liberal view of the right to access alternative medicines and to provide them seems appropriate. However, in order to provide effective guarantees as to the quality of provided care, such liberalisation must be set up with a strict control over the information that is provided to the public. As a result, only those practitioners who have a serious educational background should benefit from title protection. Furthermore, institutions in charge of regulating the practice of alternative medicines should be established in order to more effectively represent the wishes and opinions of the various participants in the field, which includes, in particular, public authorities, patients, researchers and practitioners. Finally, those medical acts linked to substantial risks should be reserved solely to skilled practitioners who also benefit from a protected title. Nevertheless, these acts should be strictly and clearly defined, in order to forestall any reintroduction of monopoly protection. In our view, existing legal mechanisms dealing with criminal and civil liability are sufficient to guarantee a good protection of patients and to appropriately react to any potential damages suffered by patients. Finally, an efficient regulatory system requires harmonisation between regulatory and non-regulatory fields.

Education remains the key element for a consistent and effective system. In order to create high standards of care in alternative medicines, it is necessary to harmonise, and possibly unify terminology, training, and standards of practice, which today still vary widely from one technique and country to another. Such harmonisation could constitute the basis for a cross-border area of free practice for alternative practitioners.

In brief, the current trend is towards a better integration of alternative medicines. However, this shift of approach has only just commenced and will need some time and an open perspective in order to reach maturity.

7.4 Coverage Framework

7.4.1 Introduction

The coverage of a technique involves the whole community of insured people who finance the funds. Thus, some serious guarantees are necessary when deciding whether or not to cover a specific technique. In order to construct the regulatory framework for the coverage of 'alternative' treatments it is necessary to determine under which conditions a technique may be covered.

When deciding to cover a technique or not, an insurance company usually applies two principles. First, the therapeutic freedom (or freedom of choice) principle,[431] which states that practitioners may provide under the insurance policy the treatment they consider the most appropriate in each specific case. The second principle consists of effectively limiting the first one, by controlling that the technique is medically necessary, namely effective, appropriate and economically justifiable.[432] It is possible that additional parameters, based on politico-socio-historical elements, as well as constitutional rights, may balance the second principle.[433]

These two principles are analysed below in relation to their application to alternative medicines[434] and some further proposals are also made.

431 This is the criterion linked to the practitioner.
432 These are the criteria linked to the technique.
433 For an analysis of additional parameters influencing the coverage of alternative medicines, see chap. 7.2.
434 There are several articles, dissertations and books on the set of problems linked to the coverage of alternative medicines. Unfortunately, it was not possible in this research to present all the studies. The objective is to give the reader some information as to the several approaches that are available. For more details, readers may refer to the bibliographies and footnotes.

7.4.2 Therapeutic Freedom

Bibliography

GASSMANN J., *Therapiewahlfreiheit in der stationären Psychiatrie – auch für komplementäre Methoden!*, in: BORGHI M. (co-editor: GASSMAN J.), *Thérapies complémentaires ou alternatives en psychiatrie: Un défi? Un droit?*, Schriftenreihe der Schweizerischen Stiftung Pro Mente Sana n° 20, 1999, Zürich: 310–11; JOST T. S., *Health care rationing in the courts: A comparative study*, in: Hasting International and Comparative Law Review, 1998, vol. 21, n° 3: 646; MINISTRY OF HEALTH AND SOCIAL AFFAIRS (I), *Report on alternative medicine – English summary*, Norges Offentliche Utredniger NOU 1998: 21, 1998, Oslo: 274; SPAHNI M., *Le tri des prestataires de médecine alternative est un terrible casse-tête*, in: Le Temps, Jan. 10, 2000; SWEDISH COMMISSION ON ALTERNATIVE MEDICINE, *Report on alternative medicine*, Regeringskansliet, 1989, Stockholm: 35.

7.4.2.1 General Remarks

The first choice a social security system or a private insurance company makes when deciding whether to cover a treatment or not, is to decide who will provide it, namely who will benefit from therapeutic freedom.

Therapeutic freedom is usually granted to medical practitioners holding a licence to practise. The main requirement in order to obtain a licence to practise is to have a specific educational background, which certifies that the practitioner has the appropriate skills.[435]

Once it has been determined who may benefit from therapeutic freedom, it is necessary to decide how this criterion will be implemented when deciding to cover alternative medicines.

7.4.2.2 Right to Benefit from Therapeutic Freedom

A. Introduction

The level of education of practitioners is decisive when determining which category of practitioners will benefit from therapeutic freedom. Indeed, when practitioners have acquired a certain level of education, and hold a diploma, they are deemed to have mastered the technique. In other words, they have sufficient skills to correctly provide treatments, and to decide which treatment is the most appropriate in each specific case.[436]

435 Additional requirements may be necessary. On this subject, see chap. 7.3.5.

436 As we have demonstrated, the level of education can be distinguished by dividing practitioners into three main categories those having a high, medium, or basic level of education. See chap. 7.3.5.2.

Traditionally, in Western countries, alternative medicines have not been covered, irrespective of whether the practitioners providing them hold a 'university' diploma or not. Indeed, as alternative medicines usually do not satisfy classic 'biomedical' criteria dealing with the coverage of medical acts,[437] they have been excluded from insurance coverage. However, some public and private insurance companies have begun to cover, both officially or unofficially, alternative medicines when provided by alternative practitioners, whether allopathic or non-allopathic.

The impact of education on the coverage of alternative medicines provided by allopathic, and non-allopathic practitioners is analysed below.

B. Allopathic practitioners

Usually, only allopathic practitioners, namely physicians and ancillary staff are considered to have acquired sufficient knowledge to safely and properly provide health care, and thus only the treatments provided by them have been covered by public and private insurance.[438] In other words, only allopathic practitioners have traditionally benefited from therapeutic freedom.

In order to be consistent with licensing regulation, insurance policies have, as a matter of principle, permitted coverage for medical acts provided by physicians.[439] While this principle was conceived from the perspective of the practice of biomedicine, it has been, both officially and non-officially, extended to some alternative medicines.[440] When the coverage is

437 E.g., proof of effectiveness, appropriateness, and cost-effectiveness. For further discussion, see chap. 6.3 and 3 7.4.3.

438 See, however, the case of a Swiss insurance company who refused to cover medical treatments provided by a French physician because he did not hold a licence to practise in Switzerland.

439 The extent of the coverage may vary, according to the type of insurance (private or public), and policy (from minimal to extensive benefits/premiums). Sometimes medical acts are not covered, or the coverage is limited (such as new or expensive treatments). However, when the treatment is included in a policy, the holding of an allopathic diploma remains the key to the coverage.

440 In several countries (e.g., in Belgium, Finland, France, Ireland, Luxembourg, Netherlands, and Switzerland), although insurance (public or private) officially does not cover alternative medicines, allopathic practitioners (physicians and ancillary staff) may provide them under a standard appellation or as a general consultation.
Surprisingly, in some monopolistic countries where the practice of alternative medicines should in theory not exist, some alternative techniques are officially covered (e.g., in France, Luxembourg and Italy). This demonstrates the inconsistency of countries having such regulation.

official,[441] it is usually granted to allopathic practitioners, irrespective of whether they hold a specialisation title in alternative medicine or not.[442] To the best of our knowledge, Austria and Switzerland[443] are the first countries, which officially require a specialised education in alternative medicine in order to cover alternative treatments.

Thus, in relation to the above, one may note two things. First, that the coverage of alternative medicines is developing. Second, that there is a gap between the coverage of alternative medicines and the education of alternative physicians, or at least between the coverage and the requirement of education.[444] This situation is unsatisfactory as there is no real guarantee as to the quality of treatments provided by these practitioners. Indeed, while physicians or other allopathic practitioners supposedly have extensive knowledge in biomedicine permitting them to choose and correctly provide allopathic treatments, this is usually not the case when they provide alternative techniques.

The position is similar in both monopolistic and tolerant countries, and for both public and private coverage.

C. Non-allopathic practitioners

In monopolistic countries, non-allopathic practitioners and the techniques they provide should, in theory, not exist. As a result, these countries do not regulate either the education and licensing to practise of alternative

441 E.g., in Austria, Denmark, Finland, France, Germany, Great Britain, Italy, Latvia, Luxembourg, Malta, Norway, Netherlands, Switzerland and the US for techniques such as acupuncture, chiropractic and homeopathy. For a categorisation of coverage modalities, see chap. 5.2.

442 E.g., in France, acupuncture and homeopathy are covered by the social insurance when treatments are provided by "MEP" physicians (MEP means "physicians with a particular type of practice", in French: "Médecin à mode d'Exercice Particulier"). However, the MEP is neither a specialty nor a qualification. It only indicates a physician's orientation, and does not guarantee that the physician has attended training in alternative medicine.

443 In Switzerland, since July 1999, five alternative medicines (homeopathy, Chinese medicine including acupuncture, anthroposophic medicine, neural therapy and phytotherapy) are reimbursed from the compulsory social insurance when provided by physicians holding a post-graduate diploma in alternative medicines. The diploma attests that the physician successfully attended training.

444 However, one may assume that most alternative physicians providing alternative medicines are diligent persons, and have attended training, even though it is not formally required.

practitioners, or the coverage of medical acts provided by these practitioners. To the best of our knowledge, there exists no monopolistic country, which covers, officially or unofficially, medical acts provided by non-allopathic practitioners.

In tolerant countries, medical acts provided by non-allopathic practitioners are generally not covered. When insurance companies decide to provide such coverage, they always require from the practitioner the holding of diploma.[445] In Finland, for example, treatments provided by chiropractors, naprapaths and osteopaths are covered by social insurance, but only if they are appropriately trained.[446]

Two trends may be noticed in this regard. First, only those treatments which are provided by non-allopathic practitioners having a medium level of training are covered by insurance.[447] Germany remains the sole country studied in this research where some private insurance covers the acts provided by "Heilpraktikers" who receive only a basic training.

Second, private insurance companies are usually more likely to cover treatments provided by non-allopathic practitioners than social security. When they decide to cover alternative medicines, they always require that

445 With possibly other conditions, such as membership in a professional organisation. In Denmark, public insurance partially covers chiropractic treatments, as long as these treatments are provided by chiropractors recognised by the Danish Chiropractic Association. To become a member of the association, chiropractors have to be trained in a college accredited by the American Council on Chiropractic Education.

446 The situation is similar in Malta where acupuncture treatments are reimbursed when practitioners hold a foreign diploma. In Switzerland and in the US, treatments provided by authorised chiropractors (those who have passed an exam) are covered by both public and private insurance.

447 Regarding the criterion of education, the minority of the Norwegian Committee on Alternative Medicine has proposed the introduction of a refund scheme for treatment by those alternative practitioners who register in the register proposed by the Committee. The Committee adds that additional requirements should be satisfied in order to allow coverage. In particular, it stresses that co-operation should be established between doctors and alternative practitioners, and that research should be conducted. Furthermore, the treatment should be of considerable significance for the patient's functional capacity which means a positive effect should be demonstrated on patients' health and welfare (MINISTRY OF HEALTH AND SOCIAL AFFAIRS (I), *op. cit.*: 274).
For more details regarding the different levels of education that may be required, see above, chap. 7.1.5.2.

practitioners hold a diploma.[448] In the US, for example, social security covers only the treatments provided by chiropractors and podiatrists, while private health plans cover the treatments provided by a wide variety of non-allopathic practitioners such as chiropractors, osteopaths, podiatrists, yoga teachers, acupuncturists, massage therapists and nutritional counsellors, among others. These practitioners generally must have attended an appropriate training in order to be admitted to the plan.[449]

The situation in tolerant countries is not entirely satisfactory either. Indeed, while the coverage of non-allopathic practitioners is expanding, treatments provided by these practitioners are usually not covered. However, when an insurance covers such treatments, there is a concordance between coverage and education, as insurance will always condition the coverage of a specific treatment to the holding of a diploma.

D. Conclusion

Although there is a trend toward an increasing coverage for alternative medicines, there is generally no official recognition from insurances. If they do propose such coverage, they generally provide it only when allopathic practitioners provide these techniques. However, they usually do not verify whether the health care provider has been trained in the field or not.

The coverage of treatments provided by non-allopathic practitioners is slowly developing in a constructive way. Indeed, such coverage is always conditioned to the holding of a diploma. However, such coverage still remains at an early stage of development.

Alternative medicines have strongly developed over the past 25 years. Coverage of alternative medicines provided by both allopathic and non-

448 In Switzerland, several private insurance companies cover the treatments provided by non-allopathic practitioners when the health care providers have been recognised by the Register of Empirical Medicine (RME) which verifies their skills. The RME has established a database to determine which non-allopathic practitioners may have their treatments covered under a supplementary insurance. The criterion of education is decisive. 150 hours of training are usually necessary to be allowed to provide a technique under a complementary insurance (acupuncture, however, requires 600 hours). Furthermore, a basic knowledge in allopathic medicine is also required (50 hours). Additional conditions for the practice of allopathic medicine must be fulfilled as well. For more details, see SPAHNI M., *op. cit.*

449 Although practitioners may be admitted to a plan, this does not mean that treatments provided by these practitioners will be fully covered. Indeed, the practice varies widely from one insurance to another.

allopathic practitioners has developed in parallel to the increasing demand of patients to have access to these treatments, and to the relaxing of licensing regulations. However, contrary to the development of coverage of biomedical treatments, which is based on research and education, coverage of alternative treatments has developed in the biomedical framework, as an extension of classic coverage. This approach was an attempt to adapt coverage to changing needs. As a result, coverage has developed without sufficient reliance on alternative research and education. In other words, therapeutic freedom has usually not been granted on the basis of educational parameters.

7.4.2.3 Implementation of Therapeutic Freedom

In the past, as Jost states

> Health care professionals, and in particular physicians, have determined, on the basis of their professional training and experience, what diagnostic and treatment modalities would benefit their patients. In the era of fee-for-service medicine, which existed both in the United States and Germany until the recent past, the decision of a physician that a patient required a service usually meant that the service would be provided. Even British National Health Service resource allocation decisions, within the context of the national health budget, were until recently largely controlled by professionals.[450]

Thus, therapeutic freedom used to be the only parameter to decide whether a technique should be covered or not.

This principle, which was conceived from the perspective of biomedicine, has been extended, both officially and unofficially, to alternative medicines, and it has also been proposed by certain authors.[451] When insurances decide to cover alternative medicines, the coverage relies on the principle of therapeutic freedom even though, on the basis of strict criteria, medical necessity has not been demonstrated. In these cases, insurances implicitly consider that practitioners have sufficient skills to enable them to determine not only which medical act must be provided, but also how each act should be provided.[452]

450 JOST T. S., *op. cit.*: 646.

451 See GASSMANN J., *op. cit.*: 310–11 (regarding in particular methods in the psychiatric field); MINISTRY OF HEALTH AND SOCIAL AFFAIRS (I), *op. cit.*: 274.

452 See the coverage of some alternative treatments provided, e.g., by French MEP physicians, Swedish, Swiss and Italian physicians, as well as Finnish chiropractors, naprapaths and osteopaths. All these practitioners may provide health care that will be officially covered, although the efficacy of the practices have not been fully demonstrated as of yet. The situation is similar in Latvia for treatments in acupuncture and homeopathy that are provided by physicians.

More generally, when insurances cover general consultations, which do not require practitioners to indicate the type of medical act they provided, they apply the principle of therapeutic freedom. Thus, for example, in Belgium, Finland, Luxembourg, and the Netherlands, physicians may give a guarantee to their patients that the alternative treatments they provide will be – unofficially – covered by insurance funds, as part of a general consultation.[453]

7.4.2.4 Summary and Proposals

When deciding to cover a technique, it is necessary to first decide who will be permitted to provide the technique under the insurance policy, namely who will benefit from therapeutic freedom. The right to therapeutic freedom is bestowed upon those practitioners who hold a recognised title, registration by a competent body, or a licence to practise. Currently, the main condition to satisfy in order to obtain a licence to practise is to have attained a certain level of education. In other words, coverage regulation should be in relation to the licensing regulation, and therefore depend on the level of education of 'alternative' practitioners.

Although in some countries, the therapeutic freedom to provide alternative medicines under an insurance policy is granted only to those practitioners who have acquired a defined level of education, the situation remains unsatisfactory globally for the following reasons. First, the coverage has not been sufficiently developed yet, in particular for non-allopathic practitioners. Second, when an official coverage exists, such coverage does not usually depend upon the level of education of the practitioner. However, some insurance companies are showing the way forward. They have demonstrated that it is possible to cover treatments when provided by alternative practitioners having acquired a high or medium level of education. These examples may be a source of inspiration for countries deciding to develop the coverage of alternative medicines and practitioners.

Once practitioners have acquired a sufficient level of education, and as long as the other requirements are satisfied, they should be allowed to benefit from therapeutic freedom.[454] This means that when alternative

453 These cases may result in fraud. This set of problems will not be analysed in this research. For an overview of the position in the US, see COHEN M. H. (I), *op. cit.*: 104–09.

454 In this respect, the Swiss system is sensible. Here, coverage by the compulsory health insurance depends upon the holding of a diploma attesting a post-graduate training in alternative medicines.

physicians provide alternative medicines without having attended the related training, insurance coverage should not be given.[455] In our view, while the coverage of alternative treatments provided by practitioners having attended high or medium education[456] should be envisaged, this should not be the case for alternative treatments provided by practitioners who have only a basic training. Indeed, the latter do not offer the same guarantees as the former do.[457]

Although therapeutic freedom is a crucial element when deciding to cover a technique it is not sufficient as additional criteria must also be satisfied. These additional criteria will be discussed in the following section.

7.4.3 Limitations to Therapeutic Freedom

Bibliography

ANDREWS L. B., *The shadow health care system: Regulation of alternative health care providers*, in: Houston Law Review, 1996, vol. 32: 1279–310; BAERTSCHI B., *Le prix de la santé et le coût des soins – Rationnement, santé publique et justice*, in: Médecine et Hygiène, July 1999, vol. 57: 1464–66; BERG R., *Note, HMO exclusion of chiropractors*, in: S. Cal. L. Rev., 1993, vol. 66: 807, 833–34; BINDER M., *Zur Kostendeckung alternativmedizinischer Behandlungsmethoden durch die Krankenversicherung*, in: Recht der Medizin, 1997, vol. 4, n° 2: 39–44; BOOZANG K. (I), M., *Western medicine opens the door to alternative medicine*, in: American Journal of Medicine, 1998, vol. 24, n° 2/3: 202–04; BOOZANG K. M. (II), *Is the alternative medicine? Managed care apparently thinks so*, in: Connecticut Law Review, Winter 2000, vol. 32: 567–613; CLINE J. S. (co-author: ROSTEN K. A.), *The effect of policy language on the containment of health care cost*, in: Tort and Insurance Law Journal, 1985, vol. 21: 120; COHEN M. H. (I), *Complementary and alternative medicine – Legal boundaries and regulatory perspectives*, The Johns Hopkins University Press, 1998, London & Oxford: 97, 100–04; COHEN M. H. (II), *Holistic health care: Including alternative and complementary medicine in insurance and regulatory schemes*, in:

455 One cannot put forward the principle of "freedom of choice". Indeed, this principle allows physicians to provide the type of treatment (alternative or not) they want, not to provide such treatment without having attended any training.

456 In particular, when the length and quality of training for non-allopathic practitioners (e.g., chiropractor, osteopath or acupuncturist) is equivalent to the training for ancillary professionals (e.g. nurse, or physiotherapist). For further details, see chap. 7.3.5.2.

457 Private insurance companies remain (relatively) free to decide to cover treatments provided by these practitioners.

Arizona Law Review, Spring 1996, vol. 38: 83–164; COMMISSIE ALTERNATIEVE GENEESWIJZEN, *Alternative geneeswijzen in Nederland*, Staatsuitgeverij, 1981, Den Haag; COST ACTION B4, *COST action B4 unconventional medicine – Final report of the management committee, 1993–1998*, European Communities, 1998, Luxembourg: 23–24; CRAMER R., *Strafrechtliche Grenzen der Therapiefreiheit und der Heilbehandlung durch den Heilpraktiker*, Dissertation, 1995, Köln: 43; DOMENIGHETTI G. (co-authors: GRILLI R., GUILLOD O., GUTZWILLER F., QUAGLIA J.), *Usage personnel de pratiques relevant des médecines douces ou alternatives parmi les médecins suisses*, in: Médecine et Hygiène, 2000, vol. 58, n° 2291: 570–72; FRIEDMAN R. (co-authors: SEDLER M., MYERS P., BENSON H.), *Behavioral medicine, complementary medicine and integrated care: Economic implications*, in: Prim. Care, Dec. 1997, vol. 24, n° 4: 952, 956–59; FURROW B. R. (co-authors: GREANEY T. L., JOST T., SCHWARTZ R. L.) (II), *Health law: Cases, materials and problems*, West Publishing, 1997, St Paul: 37; GASPOZ J.-M., *Adéquation des procédures en cardiologie: utilisation excessive, adéquate ou insuffisante?*, in: Médecine et Hygiène, 1999, vol. 57, n° 2275: 2090–93; GOODWIN J., *A health insurance revolution*, in: New Age Journal's Guide to Holistic Medicine, 1997–1998: 69; HEUSSER P., *Kriterien zur Beurteilung des Nutzens von komplementärmedizinischen Methoden*, Bundesamt für Sozialversicherung, Mar. 1998, Bern; JAPSEN B., *Cost-conscious providers take to holistic medicine; Once scorned or banned, alternative treatments have gone mainstream as less expensive but effective cures*, in: Mos. Healthcare, Aug. 21, 1995: 140; JOST T. S., *Health care rationing in the courts: A comparative study*, in: Hasting International and Comparative Law Review, 1998, vol. 21, n° 3: 639–714; JUNOD A.-F. (II), *Définition et évaluation de l'"appropriateness"*, in: Médecine et Hygiène, 1999, vol. 57, n° 2275: 2078–81; KILGORE C., *Expanding coverage signals growing demand, acceptance for alternative care*, in: Medicine & Health Perspectives, May 4 1998: 2–4; LAMM L. C. (co-authors: WEGNER, E. COLLORD, D.), *Chiropractic scope of practice: what the law allows – Update 1993*, in: J. Manipulative Physiol. Ther., Jan. 1995, vol. 18, n° 1: 16, 19–20; LAY B. F., *Healer-patient privilege: extending the physician-patient privilege to alternative health practitioners in California*, in: Hastings Law Journal, Mar. 1997: 639–40; MINISTRY OF HEALTH AND SOCIAL AFFAIRS (I), *Report on alternative medicine – English summary*, Norges Offentliche Utredniger NOU 1998: 21, 1998, Oslo: 273–74; MITCHELL WEITZMAN S., *Insurance coverage for complementary and alternative medicine – Access, challenges, and policy*, in: HUMBER J. M. (co-editor: ALMEDER R.), *Alternative medicine and ethics*, Humana Press, 1998, Totowa: 140–41; NÜCHTERN E., *Die Begutachtung unkonventionellen Heilmethoden im Rahmen der gesetzlichen Krankenversicherung – Probleme vor dem Hintergrund der derzeitigen Rechtsprechung*, in: Gesundh.-Wes., vol. 57, 1995: 437–42; OEPEN I. (II), *Unkonventionelle medizinische Verfahren – ein Beitrag zur Kostendämpfung?*, in: Versicherungsmedizin, 1989, vol. 41: 53–57; OEPEN I. (III), *Pseudo-Naturheilverfahren und Aussenseitermethoden in der Rheumatologie*, in: Zeitschrift für Rheumatologie, 1993, vol. 52: 264–74; OFFICE FÉDÉRAL DES ASSURANCES SOCIALES, *Manuel de standardisation pour l'évaluation médicale et économique des prestations médicales*, Office Fédéral des Assurances Sociales, 1998, Bern; PÉNTEK M., *Die Leistungspflicht der Gesetzlichen Krankenversicherung bei der Anwendung von Aussenseitermethoden in der Medizin*, Dissertation, 1996, Konstanz: 71–106, 114–142; PERRIER A., *Les critères d'adéquation sont-ils bien adéquats?*, in: Médecine et Hygiène, 1999, vol. 57, n° 2275: 2082–88; POWERS MONACO G. (co-author: SMITH G.), *Healthcare plans as gatekeepers*, in: HUMBER J. M. (co-editor: ALMEDER R.), *Alternative medicine and ethics*, Humana Press, 1998, Totowa: 103ss; RICHLI P., *Hoheitliche Leistungspflichten und Leistungsbeschränkungen im Gesundheitswesen als Grundrechtsproblem*, in: Revue Suisse d'Assurances, 1998, n° 9–10: 253; SARASIN F.-P., *Méthode de mesure de l'adéquation des soins et recommandations pour la pratique clinique*, in: Médecine et Hygiène, 1999, vol. 57, n° 2275: 2098–102; SELECT COMMITTEE ON SCIENCE AND TECHNOLOGY, *Complementary and alternative medicine*, House of Lords – Session 1999–2000 6th Report, The Stationary Office, 2000, London: 110–11; SHEKELLE P. G., *What role for chiropractic in health care?*, in: The New England Journal of Medicine, 1998, vol. 339: 1074–75; SCHMIDT-RÖGNITZ A., *Die Gewährung von alternativen sowie neueren Behandlungs- und Heilmethoden durch die gesetzliche Krankenversicherung*, Dissertation, Duncker & Humblot, 1996, Berlin; SHAPIRO A. K. (co-author: SHAPIRO E.) (I), *The powerful placebo – From ancient priest to modern physician*, The Johns Hopkins University Press, 1997, Baltimore/London: 232; SIMONET L., *Adéquation des soins: Qu'en est-il du patient?*, in: Médecine et Hygiène, 1999, vol. 57, n° 2275: 2094–97; STARR P., *The social transformation of american medicine*, Basic Books, 1982: 386–87; STEFFEN G., *Droit aux soins et rationnement: Approche d'une définition des soins nécessaires*, Stämpfli, 2002, Bern; VASSALLI P., *Forum Louis-Jeantet sur les coûts de la santé 1998*, Fondation Louis-Jeantet de médecine, Genève, 1998: 15–17, 55–63; VOGEL G., *Medikation mit Aussenseitermethoden-eine Kostenfrage?*, in: RdM, 1994, n° 4; WHITE HOUSE COMMISSION ON COMPLEMENTARY AND ALTERNATIVE MEDICINE POLICY, *Final report*, March 2002, available at http://www.whccamp.hhs.gov/pdfs/fr2002_document.pdf, accessed Feb. 1 2005: 108–12, 16; WICKI M., *Komplementärmedizin im Rahmen des Rechtes*, Dissertation, Stämpfli, 1998, Bern: 185–86, 255–57.

7.4.3.1 General Remarks

A crucial problem that health care systems[458] face today is resource allocation.[459] By definition, all valuable resources are scarce, and awareness of scarcity has become more acute in recent years.[460] In the past, as Jost

458 For a presentation of the health care markets and its components, see VASSALLI P., *op. cit.*

459 On this subject, see BAERTSCHI B., *op. cit.*: 1464–66; STEFFEN G., *op. cit.*; VASSALLI P., *op. cit.*

460 The principal factors driving health care cost increases are generally the increasing demand for health care, and more specifically, the continuing progress of medical technology, the aging of the population, increasing administrative costs, as well as waste and abuse. For more details, see JOST T. S., *op. cit.*: 644ss.

notes "scarce resources have been allocated both to and within health care systems on the basis of professional judgement".[461] However, professional judgements that are based on therapeutic freedom[462] do not reach predictable or consistent results when focusing on resource allocation. Indeed, such judgements tend to benefit some patients, but dismiss the needs of others. Furthermore, medical practitioners tend to provide more, rather than fewer procedures, as there is theoretically no limit to the resources that can be allocated to health care and that have some beneficial effect. There is also the problem of over-consumption of care.[463]

Scientific and economic parameters must therefore be employed when deciding to allocate health care and in containing (or rationalising) health care expenditures. The concept of "medical necessity" then becomes of importance as usually, an act is deemed medically necessary when it is demonstrated to be effective, appropriate and economic.[464]

Thus, although those practitioners benefiting from therapeutic freedom have freedom of choice to use whichever techniques they choose,[465] the reality is that only those medical techniques that are demonstrated to be medically necessary[466] will be covered by insurance funds.[467]

461 JOST T. S., *op. cit.*: 646.

462 For more information on therapeutic freedom, see chap. 7.4.2.

463 COHEN M. H. (I), *op. cit.*: 103; JOST T. S., *op. cit.*: 644, 647; KILGORE C., *op. cit.*: 1–4; STARR P., *op. cit.*: 386–87.

464 These elements may appear under other appellations, but they always make reference to the same concepts.
The British Select Committee on Science and Technology reported a study undertaken by the British NHS. The purpose of the study was to determine which factors are important when deciding whether or not to cover a technique. The study showed the following responses: 1. evidence of effectiveness (84%); 2. evidence of cost-effectiveness (74%); 3. accreditation procedures and standards (65%); 4. resource implications (58%); 5. availability of practitioners (32%); 6. local needs assessment (30%); 6. patient demand (30%); lack of national guidance (28%) (SELECT COMMITTEE ON SCIENCE AND TECHNOLOGY, *op. cit.*: 111).
For further developments concerning rationalisation in health care, see BAERTSCHI B., *op. cit.*: 1464–66; JOST T. S., *op. cit.* See also BINDER M., *op. cit.*: 39–44 (Austria); COHEN M. H. (I), *op. cit.*: 100ss; NÜCHTERN E., *op. cit.*: 437–42 (Germany); POWERS MONACO G., *op. cit.*: 97–124; SCHMIDT-RÖGNITZ A., *op. cit.* (Germany); VASSALLI P., *op. cit.*: 15–16, 55–63; WICKI M., *op. cit.*: 185–86 (Switzerland).

465 Among all the techniques included within their scope of practice.

466 However, several medical procedures that are covered are not scientifically validated. This results in significant variations in the use of medical techniques, from one country and one practitioner to another. For more details, see chap. 6.2 and 6.3.

Various countries have adopted certain positions when deciding whether or not to limit the therapeutic freedom of practitioners who wish to use alternative medicines. These differing approaches will be analysed below with further focus being placed on the implementation of the criteria determining the medical necessity of a treatment, namely effectiveness, appropriateness, and economic character.[468]

7.4.3.2 Presentation of Coverage Criteria

A. Effectiveness[469]

Concept

The criterion of effectiveness expresses the clinical value of a medical technique. It indicates to which extent a medical technique has, in specific conditions, reached its objective.[470]

The demonstration of effectiveness of a medical technique is based on scientifically documented results, taking into consideration all indications, and contra-indications.[471]

When assessing the effectiveness of a new technique, it is necessary to make a comparison with the technique usually employed, which has the

467 Some criticise the use of evidence-based medicine when deciding whether to cover alternative medicines or not. On the subject, see Domenighetti G., *op. cit.*: 570–72.
For an analysis and critique of American Managed Care organisations that include alternative medicines within their program, without assessing their medical necessity, see Boozang K. M. (II), *op. cit.*: 567–613.
For a development regarding the institution deciding whether a technique is necessary or not, see Jost T. S., *op. cit.*: 639ss; Cline J. S., *op. cit.*

468 The role played by other parameters (constitutional rights, and parameters based on politico-socio-historical elements) has been developed in chapter 7.2.

469 For further discussion on the scientific evaluation of effectiveness, see chap. 6.3.3.

470 Heusser P., *op. cit.*: 3–7; Office Fédéral des Assurances Sociales, *op. cit.*: 8; Vassalli P., *op. cit.*: 55.

471 It is necessary here to make a distinction between theoretical and real effectiveness. Theoretical effectiveness is demonstrated by clinical testing for determined conditions, in optimal controlled conditions. Real effectiveness takes into consideration the expected results in an experimental framework, and the results observed in practice.
On the subject, see Office Fédéral des Assurances Sociales, *op. cit.*: 8, 131–32; Vassalli P., *op. cit.*: 55.

same objective, and to demonstrate that the effectiveness is similar or superior. The safety of the technique must also be demonstrated.[472]

Implementation with alternative medicines

The level of effectiveness that is required to cover a technique varies. The problem consists in fixing the bottom line. There is no definitive solution to this problem, as each technique is particular, and each insurance coverage has its own interpretation of this criterion.[473] However, examples and opinions may be given that provide some guidelines for implementation.[474]

There are several ways to demonstrate the effectiveness of a technique.[475] One approach in medicine is to use randomised controlled trials. When alternative medicines are demonstrated to be 'relatively' effective during these trials, they satisfy the condition of effectiveness that is required for coverage under insurance policies.[476] Most countries usually base their system of coverage on this principle. Some authors retain a stricter interpretation of the criterion of effectiveness. They consider that as long as a technique has not been demonstrated to be effective, it should not be covered.[477]

472 OFFICE FÉDÉRAL DES ASSURANCES SOCIALES, *op. cit.*: 59. For more information regarding safety, see chap. 6.5.

473 Boozang notes an interesting relation between coverage and effectiveness where "patients are likely to interpret health plans' inclusion of a particular treatment as an imprimatur on its efficacy, especially because patients perceive health plans in today's market to be restrictive in their coverage decisions" (BOOZANG K. M., *op. cit.*: 202–03).

474 For a presentation of the situation in Germany regarding the evaluation of effectiveness, see PÉNTEK M., *op. cit.*: 70ss.

475 The evidence that the technique is effective is sufficient to decide to cover a technique. It is not necessary to demonstrate the mechanism of action of the technique, or the scientific character of the technique. On this subject, see RICHLI P., *op. cit.*: 253.

476 See COHEN M. H. (I), *op. cit.*: 97.

477 E.g., in the past, Swiss courts rejected the coverage of techniques, whose efficacy was not demonstrated according to evidence-based medicine techniques. Oepen states that the alleged benefit of some natural methods, in particular the "Action for Biological Medicine" has never been proved. Therefore, "they must without any exception be considered as totally unnecessary" (OEPEN I. (III), *op. cit.*: 264). See also BOOZANG K. M. (II), *op. cit.*: 567–613. The majority of the Norwegian Commission on Alternative Medicines states that an "argument against introduction of a refund is also the low level of documented efficacy" (MINISTRY OF HEALTH AND SOCIAL AFFAIRS (I), *op. cit.*: 274). See also JOST T. S., *op. cit.*: 663ss (Germany); MINISTRY OF HEALTH AND SOCIAL AFFAIRS (I), *op. cit.*: 273–74 (Norway).

However, other commentators have stressed that this type of trial is not applicable to all methods.[478] In this respect, one must note that there have been attempts to adapt these trials to alternative medicines. Furthermore, new criteria and procedures are being developed to evaluate the effectiveness of these techniques. These alternatives to strict controlled trials seem to be more adapted to the specificity of alternative medicines[479] as they take more into account the relationship between the practitioner and the patient, as well as psychological factors.[480] They also rely more on the experience and opinion of physicians and other minority experts.[481] These procedures tend to demonstrate that therapies may result in a positive effect in specific cases, which may be considered as sufficient to cover a technique.[482] This approach has already been taken into account by some insurance schemes when deciding to cover alternative medicines. For example, the Swiss Federal Office of Social Insurance (FOSI) considers that, when

478 E.g., the Dutch Commission on Alternative Medicine considers that randomised controlled trials are not applicable to alternative medicines when deciding to cover or not an alternative medicine (COMMISSIE ALTERNATIEVE GENEESWIJZEN, *op. cit.*).

479 E.g., a US court stated that a treatment based on nutritional deficiencies and food allergies was not so deviant from generally accepted medical practices as to be non-medical.
The British Select Committee on Science and Technology has reported the opinions of several participants in the NHS, who are ready to undermine the importance of biomedical ways of assessing the value of 'alternative' medical techniques (SELECT COMMITTEE ON SCIENCE AND TECHNOLOGY, *op. cit.*: 110–11). They recommend "that only those CAM therapies which are statutorily regulated, or have a powerful mechanism of voluntary self-regulation, should be make available, by reference from doctors and other healthcare professionals working in primary, secondary or tertiary care, on the NHS" (idem, at 111).

480 Today, these parameters are usually excluded from classic evidence based medicine processes. On the subject, see WHITE HOUSE COMMISSION ON COMPLEMENTARY AND ALTERNATIVE MEDICINE POLICY, *op. cit.*: 116.

481 See COHEN M. H. (I), *op. cit.*: 103.

482 E.g., the minority of the Norwegian Committee on Alternative Medicine suggests that "the introduction of a refund scheme for treatment by alternative medicine practitioners who are registered in the register proposed by the Committee [...]. One criterion for refund in that case would be that co-operation is established between a doctor and the alternative therapists and that experience shows that the alternative medicine treatment has a positive effect on the patient's health and welfare. The treatment must be of considerable significance for the patient's functional capacity" (MINISTRY OF HEALTH AND SOCIAL AFFAIRS (I), *op. cit.*: 274).
See also BINDER M., *op. cit.*: 40ss.

evaluating alternative medicines, the methods must take into consideration the particularities of alternative medicines.[483] They must also evaluate these techniques as a whole, rather than considering only one parameter.[484] Thus, personals aspects must also be part of the evaluation, as well as observational studies. In addition, methods that do not modify the medical intervention[485] should be favoured over those that modify it.[486] In Austria, a court ruled that a neural and laser therapy should be covered, as it had demonstrated its effectiveness for the patient.[487] Several private insurance companies that offer coverage for alternative techniques also take into account the relative effectiveness of some alternative techniques. In Germany, for example, some private insurance companies reimburse treatments as long as their effectiveness is not completely rejected.[488]

Some commentators go further, proposing that coverage should not depend upon scientific criteria.[489] Based on the principle of therapeutic freedom, they consider that physicians can use alternative medicines, as long as they provide them diligently. Furthermore, they should only demonstrate the rationality of the process and the treatment in order to receive coverage.[490] In 1994, an Austrian court ruled that only the criterion of appropriateness and cost-effectiveness must be taken into consideration when deciding to cover homeopathy.[491] The court later ruled that a treatment must be successful or likely to be successful in order to be covered.[492]

483 See also WHITE HOUSE COMMISSION ON COMPLEMENTARY AND ALTERNATIVE MEDICINE POLICY, *op. cit.*: 109.

484 Furthermore, they must take into account the specific medical tradition (experience of alternative practitioners and developed good practices).

485 Such as the retrospective use of medical experience (interviews among alternative practitioners, reports, expertises, conclusion of lecturers, etc.), non-controlled and controlled studies or interviews among patients.

486 E.g., experimental studies on particular cases, crossover designs, double blind testing, randomised studies.
For further developments, see HEUSSER P., *op. cit.*: 7–11; WICKI M., *op. cit.*: 185–86, 255–57.

487 On this subject, see BINDER M., *op. cit.*: 40–41.

488 E.g., vitamin products, ozone-therapy or acupuncture (CRAMER R., *op. cit.*: 43).

489 See BINDER M., *op. cit.*: 41 (Austria).

490 NÜCHTERN E., *op. cit.* Binder adds that treatments should further be appropriate and economic (BINDER M., *op. cit.*: 42).

491 According to the ruling, when a less expensive allopathic treatment is available, one should demonstrate that such treatment will very likely not result in a positive effect.
Decision of the OGH of Apr. 14, 1994 (SSV-NF 8/19 = DRdA 1995, 22, Binder). See also BINDER M., *op. cit.*: 40.

Other commentators again have stated that since alternative medicines are taught within universities, they should be covered by social security. They suggest that when an allopathic treatment is not available to treat a specific condition, that the importance of the proof of effectiveness of a technique should be lowered. Therefore, since a technique has some chance of success, it should be covered.[493]

For those techniques lacking scientific proof of their effectiveness, it is possible to envisage an *a posteriori* coverage, where the medical act would be covered only if it was effective in a particular case. The criterion of effectiveness in this instance being either the recovery of the patient or at least the improvement in his or her health. Such a system would satisfy the requirement of effectiveness, and thus allow the coverage of techniques that have been demonstrated to be objectively valuable.[494] However, it could create uncertainty for patients as to the possible coverage of the treatment.

B. Appropriateness

Concept

A treatment is appropriate when it is likely to be able to treat the patient's condition. The appropriateness[495] is measured by a comparative evaluation of the medical utility of a medical technique for a patient, against

492 Decision of the OGH of Mar. 26, 1996, ARD-Betriebendienst 4770/47/96. See also BINDER M., *op. cit.*: 40.

493 This is the solution adopted by the German social security system, and in Austria. For further details, see BINDER M., *op. cit.*: 42; COHEN M. H. (I), *op. cit.*: 103–04.

494 A procedure could be set up to ensure that the improvement of the health condition was due to the effect of the specific alternative technique, and not to another cause. This would consist in determining the symptoms of the patient before and after the alternative treatment and verifying that no other treatment was provided.
On this subject, see BINDER M., *op. cit.*: 42.

495 The criterion of "appropriateness" was first developed by Brook and the RAND corporation, in cooperation with UCLA (University of California in Los Angeles). For a general criticism of the concept of appropriateness, see JUNOD A.-F. (II), *op. cit.*: 2078–81; PERRIER A., *op. cit.*: 2082–88 (the authors stress the difficulty of implementing this criterion in practice).

the risks that are related with the technique.[496] Therefore, a medical technique is deemed appropriate when the utility of the technique is greater than the risks related with the technique.[497] Thus, the appropriateness of a medical technique is estimated, first according to the rate of success and failure of a medical benefit, and the frequency of complications. Then, a comparison is made with other measures, taking into consideration the consequences of these measures.[498]

Implementation with alternative medicines

The appropriateness of a medical technique is established for each specific condition it is likely to treat. As the risks linked with the provision of alternative medicines are usually low,[499] the balance between positive effects and risks is usually positive, and therefore the treatment is appropriate. However, there is no definitive conclusion as to whether alternative medicines are appropriate or not. Schmidt-Rögnitz stresses that the

496 There is a distinction between immediate risks (i.e. risks related to the providing of the technique, frequency of early complications, undesirable side effects), and later risks, evaluated over a period of 1 or 2 years. In the hypothesis of a serious illness, one would consider the immediate safety, and the safety in the mid-term in relation to the personal level of pain caused by the illness (OFFICE FÉDÉRAL DES ASSURANCES SOCIALES, *op. cit.*: 59).
For further analysis of the risks and the concept of safety, see chap. 6.5.

497 For an example of the criterion of "appropriateness" in cardiology, see GASPOZ J.-M., *op. cit.*: 2090–93.
Regarding the appropriateness of classic biomedical treatments, FURROW notes that "the appropriateness of much medical treatment has been questioned. Wide variation has been noted in the use of laboratory tests, prescription drugs, X-rays, return appointments, and telephone consultations among similarly trained doctors in a wide variety of practice settings" (FURROW B. R. (II), *op. cit.*: 37).
Sarasin stresses that medical guidelines based on evidence of effectiveness play a decisive role in appreciating the appropriateness of a medical act. When there is no evidence-based proof, the method developed by the RAND may be an alternative. However, these two methods are limited (SARASIN F.-P., *op. cit.*: 2098–102).
For a discussion regarding the position of the patient when determining the appropriateness of a medical technique, see SIMONET L., *op. cit.*: 2094–97 (the author argues that the evaluation of the appropriateness of a technique does not take into consideration the preferences and values of patients, in particular when decisions are taken in uncertain conditions).

498 HEUSSER P., *op. cit.*: 11–12; OFFICE FÉDÉRAL DES ASSURANCES SOCIALES, *op. cit.*: 8.

499 As well as side effects and later complications. For more details, see chap. 6.5.

appropriateness is demonstrated when the positive effects of the technique are, according to the current level of science, not completely unlikely.[500] In this respect, the choice over the methods to employ in order to determine the effectiveness of the treatment is important[501] as some method may demonstrate that a technique is effective in specific situations.

Germany has adopted a sensible solution to the problem of comparing the appropriateness of alternative medicines to classic biomedical treatments. Alternative medicines are covered when an allopathic treatment and an alternative treatment are both available, but side effects are related to the allopathic treatment or there are risks, in general or in particular, for the patient.[502] Similarly, an Austrian court has ruled that when an interferon treatment has serious side effects, then an alternative medical treatment might be covered.[503]

The SFOSI has also developed guidelines to establish the appropriateness of alternative medicines,[504] namely that:[505]

a. The patient chooses an alternative technique after having been informed about all the existing possibilities, which includes both alternative and biomedical techniques;
b. The expected effect of the technique is the same as the objective to reach, i.e. the indication is correct and the technique is safe;

500 SCHMIDT-RÖGNITZ A., *op. cit.*: 166.

501 For a discussion on the criteria of effectiveness of a technique, see above, same chap. (effectiveness).

502 However, in this case, it is necessary to balance existing risks and the cost-effectiveness of the treatment.
For a criticism of the criterion of appropriateness, see NÜCHTERN E., *op. cit.*: 438, 439–40; SCHMIDT-RÖGNITZ A., *op. cit.*: 162ss.
For a German opinion regarding the problem of placebo effect and appropriateness of the treatment, see NÜCHTERN E., *op. cit.*: 440.

503 The Court added that the treatment must be likely to result in the improvement of the condition of the patient, and must be economic. On this subject, see BINDER M., *op. cit.*: 41.

504 The basic compulsory health insurance in Switzerland covers some alternative techniques.
The SFOSI states that alternative and biomedical medicines do not exclude each other. Sometimes, for the treatment of specific illnesses, the combination of alternative and biomedical techniques may be useful. These techniques therefore become complementary (HEUSSER P., *op. cit.*: 12).

505 HEUSSER P., *op. cit.*: 12. For more details regarding Switzerland see also, e.g., WICKI M., *op. cit.*: 185.

c. The objective to achieve with the alternative technique may not be achieved with another method.

All three conditions must be fulfilled to consider the treatment as appropriate.

C. Economic character

Concept[506]

The economic character of a medical technique is measured by a comparative evaluation of the expenditure caused by the medical technique to the value of its results.[507]

The main element for the estimation of the economic character is usually the evaluation of the expenditures of the technique, as well as the expenditures in relation to the preparation of the benefit and later techniques.[508]

The evaluation of the consequences, namely the medical utility, may in principle be expressed in financial terms as well. This is typically the case for cost-benefit analysis.[509]

Another possible evaluation may be made by taking into consideration such natural units as hospital prevention, reduction of hospitalisation time or the facilitation of later treatments. This approach is typical

506 For a study on the medical and economic evaluation of medical techniques, see HEUSSER P., *op. cit.*: 13–14; OFFICE FÉDÉRAL DES ASSURANCES SOCIALES, *op. cit.*

507 OFFICE FÉDÉRAL DES ASSURANCES SOCIALES, *op. cit.*: 8.
Regarding the justification of assessing the economic character of a technique, the SFOSI states that the effectiveness of a medical technique is an indication as to the quality of care. The providing of non-effective treatments is a waste of economic resources. Thus, economic parameters are used to identify medical techniques that are clinically effective, but also whose providing is economically justifiable (OFFICE FÉDÉRAL DES ASSURANCES SOCIALES, *op. cit.*: 125).

508 There is a distinction between direct (e.g. time and material) and indirect costs (loss of earning), which may be divided between primary (for direct use), and secondary costs (for additional, subsequent use).
For further discussion on this subject, see HEUSSER P., *op. cit.*: 13–14; OFFICE FÉDÉRAL DES ASSURANCES SOCIALES, *op. cit.*: 8.

509 Cost-benefit analysis makes a comparison between the costs linked to the providing of the therapy, and the economic positive effect of the therapy.
Cost-utility analysis is another technique, which consists in making a comparison between the costs linked with the providing of the therapy and clinical results, taking into consideration additional criteria regarding the quality of life.
For a definition of economic benefit, see OFFICE FÉDÉRAL DES ASSURANCES SOCIALES, *op. cit.*: 134ss.

of cost-effectiveness analysis. However, results may also be expressed as non-quantifiable (financial) benefits, such as the improvement of quality of life.[510, 511]

The cost-effectiveness analysis (CEA) is the reference technique used when evaluating a medical technique in the real practice. The costs and the consequences of medical acts are analysed. More specifically, the CEA compares the additional costs linked with a medical technique and its clinical results.[512] Thus, the CEA measures the costs linked with an effect or an expected clinical result. Expenditures are measured as quantities of used resources, expressed in monetary units. Thus, the CEA makes it possible to compare several technologies, as long as they have the same specific indication.[513]

Therefore, in order to be covered, a technique must be safe and effective. Furthermore, when the technique is more expensive than other ones, the benefits must be superior to the benefits of other techniques.[514]

510 When assessing the economic character of a medical technique, it may be necessary to make a comparison with the expenditures linked with the providing of other techniques (OFFICE FÉDÉRAL DES ASSURANCES SOCIALES, *op. cit.*: 59).

511 OFFICE FÉDÉRAL DES ASSURANCES SOCIALES, *op. cit.*: 8–9. For a development regarding these notions, see the same author, at 148ss, and 153ss. See also HEUSSER P., *op. cit.*: 14–15 (the author stresses that for alternative medicines, these costs are important, as these techniques have a holistic and prophylactic approach); VASSALLI P., *op. cit.*: 55–56 (including several examples); WHITE HOUSE COMMISSION ON COMPLEMENTARY AND ALTERNATIVE MEDICINE POLICY, *op. cit.*: 109.

512 A CEA takes into consideration the following expenditures:
1. the direct costs linked with the providing of the technique;
2. the direct costs linked with the diagnosis or the treatment of undesirable side effects or complications;
3. the costs linked with later medical acts linked with the providing of the technique;
4. the saving of costs, made possible because of the avoidance of therapeutic acts, and of unnecessary later medical acts;
5. the saving of costs, made possible because of the avoidance of diagnosis and treatments of undesirable side effects or complications;
6. the additional costs or the saving of costs, linked to the saving or loss of productivity, or of life expectancy.

On this subject, see HEUSSER P., *op. cit.*: 14–15; OFFICE FÉDÉRAL DES ASSURANCES SOCIALES, *op. cit.*: 156; VASSALLI P., *op. cit.*: 16–17, 55–58.

513 E.g., it is possible to make the ratio of cost-effectiveness: "cost per saved year of life", which is often used for surgical operations. This ratio defines the cost of a life year saved thanks to surgical operations.

514 OFFICE FÉDÉRAL DES ASSURANCES SOCIALES, *op. cit.*: 131.

Implementation with alternative medicines[515]

CEA is the method usually employed to evaluate the economic character of an alternative technique and it has been endorsed by the SFOSI.[516] A qualitative analysis of alternative medicines requires an expert knowledge of the specificities of alternative medicines. Such an analysis should take into consideration all the socio-economic benefits of alternative therapies, and also distinguish between what is wished for and what is feasible.[517]

Although the appreciation of the economic character of a technique is similar for both public and private funds, private insurance companies are more likely to cover a technique when the market is profitable. As a result, they take more into account the demand from patients as well as their general satisfaction towards alternative medicines when deciding whether to cover a technique or not, public funds are usually stricter in their interpretation of this criterion, as the whole community contributes to the fund. The present section is more focused on the public coverage aspect.

The question to determine is whether alternative medicines are economic or not and this has been the subject of innumerable articles, and of endless controversy.[518] While some authors maintain that alternative medicines are cost-effective,[519] others contend that the reverse is true. A sample of these conflicting opinions is presented below.

Studies that demonstrate the cost-effectiveness of alternative medicines include, for example, research on chiropractic to treat low back pain, which has seemed to indicate that it is more cost-effective than biomedical therapies.[520] There is also compelling evidence that treatment for chronic pain

515 For various propositions regarding the practical evaluation of alternative medicines, see HEUSSER P., *op. cit.*: 16ss.

516 On this point, see HEUSSER P., *op. cit.*: 13–15.

517 HEUSSER P., *op. cit.*: 14–15.

518 According to the COST Action B4 at the European Commission, "a general overview would suggest that the use of unconventional medicine is at the moment cost neutral" (COST ACTION B4, *op. cit.*: 23).
See FRIEDMAN R., *op. cit.*: 950; HEUSSER P., *op. cit.*: 13; KILGORE C., *op. cit.*: 2; WICKI M., *op. cit.*: 256.

519 One commentator states that "I know we are going to come up with positive outcomes and cost saving that will knock insurers' socks off [...] It is not a question of if, but when. Everything is changing, faster than imaginable" (KILGORE C., *op. cit.*: 4). See also, e.g., JAPSEN B., *op. cit.*: 140.

520 ANDREWS L. B., *op. cit.*: 1279; BERG R., *op. cit.* 833–34 (the author states that "it is economically irrational for a competitive HMO to exclude chiropractic doctors"); COST ACTION B4, *op. cit.*: 23; KILGORE C., *op. cit.*: 2; LAMM L. C., *op. cit.*: 16, 20; MITCHELL WEITZMAN S., *op. cit.*: 140–41; WHITE HOUSE COMMISSION

is less expensive when it includes a behavioural medicine intervention.[521] Friedman argues that behavioural medicine results in a positive cost-offset effect[522] and he identifies several pathways by which behavioural medicine interventions can optimise clinical care and result in significant economic benefits.[523]

ON COMPLEMENTARY AND ALTERNATIVE MEDICINE POLICY, *op. cit.*: 111 (with several examples of cost-effective treatments).

521 Friedman makes a distinction between alternative techniques, by distinguishing behavioural medicine from the main stream of alternative medicines. He states that "behavioural medicine consists of three broad intervention categories: 1. basic patient education; 2. behaviour change or lifestyle modification, and 3. stress management" (FRIEDMAN R., *op. cit.*: 952). Shapiro considers that behavioural medicine is an example of recent popular placebo (SHAPIRO A. K. (I), *op. cit.*: 232).

522 For the author, the cost-offset effect "is a simple concept that indicates that the cost of providing behavioural medicines services is offset by a subsequent reduction in biomedical utilisation" (FRIEDMAN R., *op. cit.*: 956).
See FRIEDMAN R., *op. cit.*: 956–57 (citing several examples). A study conducted in an HMO analysed the effect of a 90-minute group session led by a physician and a psychologist for 10 weeks (including biomedical and behavioural treatment strategies, yoga-type exercises, communication skills), on patients suffering from chronic pain for several years (such as headaches, backaches, stomach aches and neck pain). The study showed that clinic visits decreased by 36% in the first and second year after the program. The net saving was estimated to average $110 per year in the first year, when the costs of the program had to be subtracted, and $210 during the second year, because no supplementary behavioural medicine costs were incurred.
Another study focused on the effect of a self-management program on patients having arthritis. The result was a 20% reduction in pain and a 43% reduction in physician visits. On the basis of the reduced doctor visits, adjusted 4-year health care savings were $648 per patient with rheumatoid arthritis and $189 per patient with osteoarthritis.

523 These pathways are the following (FRIEDMAN R., *op. cit.*: 958):
1. "the information and decision-support pathway in which patients are given information about physiology of their illness and information about treatment options;
2. the psychophysiologic pathway in which patients are taught self-regulatory skills such as elicitation of the relaxation response that reduces physical symptoms and inhibits the pathogenesis of many conditions;
3. the behaviour change pathway in which patients are taught specific strategies and skills to reduce illness-promoting behaviours and to increase health-promoting behaviours;
4. the social support pathway in which patients are either directly given access to social support within the clinic environment or given information to facilitate the development of social support networks outside clinic settings;

One may also assume that the decision of some managed care organisations to offer the services of alternative practitioners within their networks is based on economic considerations as well.[524] For example, American Western Life "is happy to confirm that alternative medicine saves money for both the consumer and the insurer. Wellness, self care, self reliance, the company says, can help control health costs".[525]

Andrews also contends the use of alternative medicines can result in cost savings as non-physician providers charge less for their services.[526] Similarly, Lay states that alternative medicines are less expensive to administer than Western allopathic treatments because alternative medical treatments generate fewer side effects, and are usually cheaper to administer than conventional therapies.[527] He adds that patients who are interested in alternative medicines may tend to be healthier in the first place, and furthermore that alternative practitioners are focused on preventive care, thereby reducing future health costs for both the patient and the insurance covering the patient.[528]

In contrast, the opinion of the majority of the Norwegian Committee is that the introduction of a refund for more types of treatment would increase expenditures.[529]

Other authors, such as Shekelle, consider that chiropractic care for low back pain costs more than the usual supportive medical care delivered by health maintenance organisations.[530] He further notes, in regard

---

5. the undiagnosed psychiatric disorder pathway in which behavioural medicine programs provide effective screenings and referrals for psychiatric problems that had not been previously diagnosed within biomedical settings, and;
6. the somatization pathway in which behavioural medicine programs teach patient skills to better discriminate between symptoms that require professional attention and symptoms that do not."

524 For more details concerning the coverage proposed by managed care organisations, see BOOZANG K. M., *op. cit.*: 202–04.

525 KILGORE C., *op. cit.*: 2.

526 ANDREWS L. B., *op. cit.*: 1279.

527 The author takes the example of nutrition counselling, biofeedback, herbal remedies, and non-invasive procedures such as massage and acupuncture.

528 LAY B. F., *op. cit.*: 639–40.

529 It points out that other authorised health personnel do not necessarily receive a refund for treatment (e.g., ordinary dental treatment) (MINISTRY OF HEALTH AND SOCIAL AFFAIRS (I), *op. cit.*: 273–74).
See also, e.g., OEPEN I. (II), *op. cit.*: 53–57.

530 The author specifies that "whether the small symptomatic benefit and the enhanced satisfaction of patients, as consistently reported by studies of patients treated by chiropractors, are worth this cost is debatable. Before we judge this approach

to the treatment of other musculoskeletal problems, that there is evidence from randomised clinical trials that spinal manipulations may be efficacious for some patients with neck pain. However, the cost effectiveness of spinal manipulations has not been established nor the efficacy of other therapies.[531]

Germany has adopted an interesting solution in relation to the implementation of the cost-effectiveness criteria. Patients may choose the less expensive method, when there are safe allopathic and non-allopathic treatments at their disposal, whether alternative or allopathic. When an allopathic treatment and an alternative treatment are both available, but there are side effects related to the allopathic treatment or there are risks, in general or in particular, for the patient, then the use of alternative medicines is reimbursed.[532] However, in this case, it is necessary to balance the existing risks with the cost-effectiveness of the treatment, irrespective of whether it is allopathic or alternative.[533]

The introduction of alternative medicines in a coverage policy may be viewed as a marketing tool. Although this element does not enter into cost-effectiveness analysis, it remains an economic argument to be considered when deciding whether or not to cover an alternative technique. For example, some hospitals who offer programs that include alternative medicines have noticed that, although there were no conclusive results on the clinical efficacy or cost-effectiveness of programs integrating alternative medicines, these programs have proved extremely popular with both

too harshly, however, we must remember that many existing medical interventions currently paid for by insurance companies provide equally small benefits or even none at all (for example, ultrasonographic therapy for shoulder disorders […] and epidural injections of corticosteroids for sciatica)" (SHEKELLE P. G., *op. cit.*: 1074–75).

531 SHEKELLE P. G., *op. cit.*: 1075.
The cost-effectiveness of certain alternative medicines is currently evaluated by managed care organisations. The director for alternative medicine at Oxford Health plans believes that people are too quick to assume that certain alternative medicine approaches will save money. Then, one must remain attentive and sceptical when evaluating the cost-effectiveness of alternative medicines. He says, "there are a lot of baseless opinions floating around. Will [the modalities] be more cost-effective? Or will [costs] be additive initially and then go down? No one can say… But someone seeking acupuncture for asthma is probably going to see the pulmonogist, at least initially" (KILGORE C., *op. cit.*: 2).

532 E.g., the provision of Ney-Tumorin to treat the side effects of chemotherapies has been covered.

533 On this subject see PÉNTEK M., *op. cit.*: 114–42.

patients and hospital administrators. The administrators of these hospitals have noted the potential use of such programs as a marketing tool and as an additional source of revenue.[534]

7.4.3.3 *Summary and Proposals*[535]

A. In general

Resource allocation in health care systems has become a priority. The evaluation of the medical necessity of medical treatments through the criteria of effectiveness, appropriateness and economic character are currently the most reliable methods at our disposal. In our view, proposals to eliminate one or several of these criteria when deciding to cover alternative medicines are not realistic. However, one must be aware that these methods are limited and that efforts are made to adapt these criteria to the specificities of alternative medicines. In fact, some private and public insurance schemes have already moved some distance away from a strict interpretation of these criteria and are extending their coverage for alternative medicines.[536]

B. Effectiveness

Alternative medicines do not usually satisfy evidence-based criteria employed to establish the effectiveness of a medical technique. However, some insurance schemes are already granting coverage for some alternative medicines, based on these modified parameters of effectiveness.

534 KILGORE C., *op. cit.*: 3. He adds (idem, at 3), that at Oxford Health Plans, since it launched its pioneering alternative medicine network, an estimated 40–50% of plan members have seen at least one of the 3,000 alternative practitioners the company contract with,
Goodwin also notes that "the decision to cover is made by the purchaser, not the seller. [...] If an employee insists on reimbursement for acupuncture, for example, then it is incumbent upon the employer to insert that in its contracts. And it is happening. After all, insurers are in the business of selling coverage, and they respond to market demand. The message is clear. Consumers should demand it" (GOODWIN J., *op. cit.*: 69).
For a development regarding the satisfaction of patients towards alternative medicines, see chap. 2.6.

535 The following remarks and proposals are formulated as general guidelines. It has not been possible given the limitations of this research to make precise proposals for each technique and each medical condition.

536 E.g., various initiatives and regulations have been adopted in Germany and in the US to extend the coverage of alternative medicines.

In our view, a technique should demonstrate some level of effectiveness in order to be covered. To establish effectiveness, it is necessary not only to maintain an open mind, but also to avoid reliance on only one method of demonstrating such effectiveness. Thus, one should rely on classical randomised trials, but other means and procedures should also be considered, particularly as they may be more suited to the evaluation of alternative medicines. In this respect, it is important to consider that, although alternative medicines may not be generally scientifically recognised, they may however result in a positive effect for specific conditions. In addition, minority opinion of experts should also be considered.

When an allopathic treatment is not available to treat a specific illness, the importance of the criterion of effectiveness should be lowered, and coverage be permitted as soon as the technique has some chance of success and as long as the other conditions are fulfilled.

For techniques that do not reach an acceptable level of recognition, an *a posteriori* coverage could be envisaged.

On the other hand, the proposal by some authors to make coverage independent of scientific criteria, or to cover all alternative medicines taught within universities is not realistic.

C. Appropriateness

When implementing the criterion of appropriateness, variations may appear for both allopathic and alternative treatments. The evaluation of appropriateness in relation to alternative medicines depends upon the criteria used to determine the effectiveness of a treatment. Moreover, some countries have developed parameters to evaluate such appropriateness.

In our view, the rules to determine the appropriateness of an alternative technique should be the following:

1. the patient should have the possibility to choose the treatment he or she wishes, after having been informed about all available possibilities;
2. the expected effect of the technique should be the same as the objective to reach, i.e. the indication is correct, and the technique is safe;
3. the objective to be achieved using the alternative technique should not be attainable with another method. When two or more methods are available to reach a specific objective, one should then make an accurate evaluation of the risks linked with the providing of each medical technique. If the side effects or risks, in general or in particular, related to the allopathic treatment are greater than those linked to alternative medicines, then the alternative medical treatment should be covered.

D. Economic character

The cost-effectiveness analysis appears to be an effective method in evaluating the economic character of a medical technique. However, there have been contradictory results in terms of the economic benefits of using alternative medicines as opposed to classic allopathic treatments. For certain medical conditions, specific alternative medicines seem to be cost-effective. The satisfaction of patients with the use of alternative medicines is generally high, which constitutes a valuable argument in support of some alternative medicines being integrated into health care plans. The costs related to the administration of alternative medicines are generally lower than those linked with allopathic treatments, in particular, professional fees. In our view, all the available socio-economic aspects linked with the providing of medical techniques, based on both objective and subjective observational studies,[537] should be taken into account when assessing the economic character of a medical technique. Sociological and marketing[538] arguments could also be considered. This would result in the creation of a method that combines both cost-effectiveness and cost-utility analysis.

Some countries have sensibly assessed the cost-effectiveness of medical techniques in relation to their appropriateness in such a way that the economic criteria becomes less important when an alternative treatment is safer or more appropriate than an allopathic treatment.

Initiatives such as the one formulated by Switzerland where coverage for specific alternative medicines is included in the compulsory health insurance and their cost-effectiveness is analysed should be encouraged. Such initiatives facilitate the gathering of serious data, in real practice, on the medical utility of alternative medicines. In general, when assessing the cost-effectiveness of a medical technique for a specific condition, one must be cautious, and analyse carefully the literature on the topic. It is possible that additional studies may be required.

7.4.4 Conclusion

Coverage of an alternative technique, in particular from the social insurance perspective, is a crucial element toward a fuller integration of these techniques within the health care system. Indeed, it guarantees patients complete access to the technique, and gives assurance to practitioners that the techniques they provide will be refunded.

537 Such as life-quality criteria.
538 For private insurance companies.

Two principles are decisive when establishing a regulatory framework for the coverage of alternative medicines. First, it is necessary to decide who will be allowed to provide alternative medicines under an insurance policy, i.e. who will benefit from therapeutic freedom. The holding of a licence to practise, and therefore of an educational diploma in the field should be the decisive element in determining who will benefit from therapeutic freedom. In practice, the global situation is unsatisfactory. Nevertheless, some insurance schemes have demonstrated that it is possible to condition the right to cover under an insurance policy upon a requirement of education. In this respect, there is a distinction between practitioners having a high or medium level of education, from those having only a basic level of education. Only the first group should benefit from therapeutic freedom.

Second, given that resource allocation has now become a priority, it is necessary to impose some limits on therapeutic freedom. This consists of determining the medical necessity of 'alternative' medicines, which is determined on the basis of three parameters, namely, the effectiveness, the appropriateness and the economic character of the technique. At present, methods based on these criteria are the most reliable means at our disposal. Alternative medicines usually do not satisfy evidence based criteria, but it is important to remind that such criteria are limited. Also, there have been initiatives to adapt these criteria to alternative medicines. Indeed, some insurance schemes already cover alternative medicines, on the basis of modified methods using these parameters. These initiatives should open interesting perspectives for the future coverage of these techniques.

In brief, alternative medicines are slowly becoming integrated within Western health care systems.

7.5 Prerequisites for a Regulation

7.5.1 General Remarks

The education of health care providers and the development of standards of practice are the prerequisites for any type of regulation linked to medical activities, particularly in regard to the licensing of practitioners and the coverage of treatments. These important requirements constitute the basis on which it will be possible first to build a regulatory framework, and second to implement a regulation. They also provide guidance in the creation of effective guidelines and guarantees for an efficient regulation. These two basic requirements will be presented below.

7.5.2 Building an Educational Framework

Bibliography

ABBOTT A., *The system of professions: An essay on the division of expert labor*, University of Chicago Press, 1988, Chicago; ANONYMOUS (IV), *Integrated healthcare – A way forward for the next five years?*, Foundation for Integrated Medicine, 1997: 19–26; ARNDT K. F., *Heilpraktikerrecht – Entstehung, Funktionswandel, Berufszulassungsregelung*, Alfred Metzner Verlag, 1985, Frankfurt am Main: 92–99; BECK A., *La chaire de médecine complémentaire à l'Université de Berne: Une création récente*, in: CMS, 1996, vol. 40: 56; CONFÉRENCE DES DIRECTEURS CANTONAUX DES AFFAIRES SANITAIRES (I), *Rapport du groupe de travail "Autorisations de pratiquer les professions du domaine de la santé"*, CDS, 2000, Bern, available at: http://www.sdk-cds.ch/fr/berufsbildung-f.html, accessed July 30 2001: 27; DELUZE C. (co-author: VISCHER T.-L.), *Interactions entre médecine académique et médecines non conventionnelles*, in: CMS, 1996, vol. 40: 33–40; EHLERS A. P. F., *Medizin in den Händen von Heilpraktikern – "Nicht-Heilkundigen"*, Springer Verlag, 1995, Berlin/Heidelberg: 39, 281–86; EUROPEAN COMMITTEE FOR HOMEOPATHY, *Homeopathy in Europe – Developing standars for professionnal practice of homeopathy in the European Union*, European Committee for Homeopathy, 1994, Rotterdam; FEASBY C., *Determining standard of care in alternative contexts*, in: Health Law Journal, 1997, vol. 5: 45–65; GAIER H. (II), *Reveille for biocentric medicine*, in: LEWITH G. (co-editor: ALDRIDGE D.), *Complementary medicine and the European Community*, CW Daniel, 1991, Saffron Walden: 21–22; GUILLOD O. (I), *Rebouteux, naturopathes et guérisseurs: Pour un traitement légal alternatif*, Recueil de Jurisprudence Neuchâtelois, 1989, Neuchâtel: 38–39; KILGORE C., *Expanding coverage signals growing demand, acceptance for alternative care*, in: Medicine & Health Perspectives, May 4 1998: 3; RÖSCH B., *Die Stellung der Erfahrungsheilkundigen aus verfassungs- und verwaltungsrechtlicher Sicht, dargestellt am Beispiel der geistig Heilenden*, Dissertation, Helbing & Lichtenhahn Verlag, 1994, Basel: 355; SAGE W. M. (co-author: AIKEN L. H.), *Regulating interdisciplinary practice*, in: JOST T. S., *Regulation of the healthcare professions*, Health Administration Press, 1996, Chicago: 82–83; SELECT COMMITTEE ON SCIENCE AND TECHNOLOGY, *Complementary and alternative medicine*, House of Lords – Session 1999–2000 6th Report, The Stationary Office, 2000, London: 58–75, 113–14; SPAHNI M., *Le tri des prestataires de médecine alternative est un terrible cassetête*, in: Le Temps, Jan. 10, 2000; SELECT COMMITTEE ON SCIENCE AND TECHNOLOGY, *Complementary and alternative medicine*, House of Lords – Session 1999–2000 6th Report, The Stationary Office, 2000, London: STONE J. (co-author: MATTHEWS J.), *Complementary medicine and the law*, Oxford University Press, 1996, Oxford; SWEDISH COMMISSION ON ALTERNATIVE MEDICINE,

Report on alternative medicine, Regeringskansliet, 1989, Stockholm: 33; SWEDISH COMMISSION ON COMPETENCE, *Report on the new legislation on competence to pursue a profession within the health and medical services*, in: Statens offentliga utredningar 1996: 138, Socialdepartementet, 1996, Stockholm: 32–33; WALDBURGER N. (co-author: MARCER N.), *Définition d'un niveau de formation adéquat – Exigences d'un examen final pour l'obtention d'un diplôme reconnu par le Service de la Santé Publique*, 2001, Lausanne; WETZEL M. S. (co-authors: EISENBERG D. M., KAPTCHUK T. J., *Courses involving complementary and alternative medicine at US medical schools*, in: JAMA, 1998, vol. 280, n° 9: 784–87; WHITE HOUSE COMMISSION ON COMPLEMENTARY AND ALTERNATIVE MEDICINE POLICY, *Final report*, March 2002, available at http://www.whccamp.hhs.gov/pdfs/fr2002_document.pdf, accessed Feb. 1 2005: XX–XXII, 51–67; WHO (IV), *Guidelines on basic training and safety in acupuncture*, WHO, 1999, Geneva.

7.5.2.1 Introduction

Education is probably the most important condition to consider when assessing the licensing to practise and the coverage of medical techniques.

The current position of education in alternative medicines and the necessity of education when regulating alternative medicines, both licensing and coverage, has been addressed above.[539] However, in addition, some proposals on the content and form of education are explored below. These solutions are based on solutions already adopted in Western countries as they offer more realistic chances of success.

7.5.2.2 Proposals Regarding the Content and Form of Education

A. Introduction

The purpose of the following proposals is limited to defining a framework of education that may be of value for all alternative medicines. The precise details of such a framework will not be presented here as they may vary widely from one technique to another.

539 See chap. 3 (education), 7.3.5.2 (licensing), and 7.4.2 (coverage).

Some basic conditions have been identified when deciding to envisage education:[540]

1. the technique must be teachable, i.e. it must be possible to practise it after having acquired theoretical knowledge and practical skills, which do not involve specific natural gifts (e.g. magnetism);
2. the attention must focus on techniques that are part of comprehensive medical systems,[541] so that practitioners mastering them may provide health care within a coherent framework;[542]
3. education must be focused on techniques that research has demonstrated to be (relatively) safe and effective. In this respect, one must be aware of the limitations of biomedical parameters and equally recognise the value of other criteria such as socio-historical elements.[543]

540 At the European level, several criteria have been developed regarding the equivalence of diplomas. In particular, there are criteria in relation to:
1. the conditions necessary to fulfil in order to have access to the training, in particular the type of diploma previously obtained;
2. the type of institution delivering the training;
3. the type of training (theoretical and practical-clinical training);
4. the content of training;
5. the length of training (minimal number of hours).
Regarding more specifically osteopathy, Waldburger has completed a comparative analysis of the training in European osteopathic schools (WALDBURGER N., *op. cit.*).

541 See chap. 1.1.1.

542 Feasby has stressed that one of the conditions necessary in order to consider a practice as a profession is a substantially different treatment. The author suggests that "the idea of different treatment implicitly requires that the school of alternative medicine in question have some degree of uniformity of treatment to be recognised as a 'profession'. To constitute a school of medicine it must have rules and principles of practice for the guidance of all its members, as respects principles, diagnosis, and remedies, which each member is supposed to observe in any given case. Thus, any competent practitioner of any given school would treat a given case substantially the same as any other competent practitioner of the same school would treat it" (FEASBY C., *op. cit.*: 55–56). For a discussion of the concept of profession, see ABBOTT A., *op. cit.* See also chap. 7.3.2.3.

543 For more details, see chap. 3 and 6. See also, e.g., STONE J., *op. cit.*: 285 ("it is not feasible to regulate therapies before they have established therapeutic credibility. It would also be positively harmful to grant statutory status to a therapy which had no tenable basis for making therapeutic claims").

The practice of 'alternative' medicines can be divided into three main spheres of activities, determined by the risks that are linked to the providing of medical methods.[544] The level of education (high, medium, or basic) must be adapted to the scope of practice of each category of providers who practise in these three different spheres.[545]

As the biomedical paradigm still dominates our health care systems, all categories of health care providers should acquire not only alternative knowledge, but also some biomedical knowledge.[546] However, students should acquire a knowledge of the philosophy linked to the practice of each specific alternative technique, as it is an important feature of the therapy. Thus, the difficulty lies in developing educational programs that take into account both biomedical and alternative paradigms, so as to allow 'alternative' practitioners to properly provide alternative methods in a general

544 See chap. 7.3.2.3 and 7.3.5.2.

545 For further discussion regarding the variation of necessary education, see STONE J., *op. cit.*: 242–43.

546 On this point Stone states that: "although the amount of biomedical knowledge that practitioners require is the subject of fierce debate, a basic level of orthodox medical training is necessary for all practitioners so that, at the very least, they will be capable of recognising contra-indications to their therapy and situations in which urgent, acute medical care is required". And further, "the more medicalised a therapy is, the more medical knowledge students will require. Needless to say, where a therapy has a medical faction, the self-protective stance of its medical practitioners will push for a high degree of medical training for 'lay' practitioners" (STONE J., *op. cit.*: 275). According to the same author, "for the sake of consistency, the requirement to have some medical basis should also extend to a knowledge of psychiatry, since therapists are dealing with the patient's mental health and there may well be situations in which a therapist might need to identify patients requiring orthodox psychological or psychiatric assessment of care" (idem at 242). See also the same author at 272–73.
In Switzerland, non-allopathic practitioners who wish their practices to be covered by a complementary insurance must attend at least 50 hours of allopathic training (SPAHNI M., *op. cit.*).
One may also wonder if the therapist should have some research skills (STONE J., *op. cit.*: 274–75).
For more information regarding the inclusion of allopathic medical knowledge, see EHLERS A. P. F., *op. cit.*: 282–83; STONE J., *op. cit.*: 275; WHITE HOUSE COMMISSION ON COMPLEMENTARY AND ALTERNATIVE MEDICINE POLICY, *op. cit.*: 52–53.

biomedical framework.[547] Continuing education must also be enhanced, which would permit practitioners to provide treatments based on the latest developments in the alternative medicines field.[548]

Furthermore, even if it is likely that some alternative techniques will be taught in a similar way to biomedical techniques,[549] this should not be the case for all alternative medicines which may require a more flexible and more understanding approach.[550] Stone notes that

> It may not be possible either to teach or to examine many of the attributes of a good complementary therapist in the same way as it is possible to impart technical knowledge. Many complementary therapists rely on intuitive, not just rational, knowledge. This may not be able to be taught in the same way as rational scientific fact.[551]

547 Stone writes that "we must constantly remind ourselves of why it is that people consult complementary therapists and what it is they expect from that therapy. [...], we do not think that many patients who are consulting a complementary practitioner would want, or indeed expect, that therapist to be the source of a diagnosis in orthodox medical terms. Often, it is precisely the limitations of conventional means of diagnosis that they are seeking to transcend" (STONE J., *op. cit.*: 243; see also at 91–92). The author adds "all therapists, be they orthodox or complementary, need to cultivate qualities such as basic empathy, genuineness, warmth, and an ability to communicate. Some trainees are more talented in these areas than others. It is debatable how far these things can be formally taught. Various educational approaches are possible. These might include the intellectual approach, the didactic approach, the experiential approach, or a model which integrates all these approaches" (STONE J., *op. cit.*: 245). This statement may seem obvious, but the points it raises are crucial today. Indeed, as reported above, an increasing number of patients have voiced their concerns about the cold mechanical approach that allopathic practitioners (typically physicians) have toward their person and health (see chap. 2.5).

548 GAIER H. (II), *op. cit.*: 21–22; RÖSCH B., *op. cit.*: 355.
In Switzerland, on behalf of private insurance companies, the Register of Empirical Medicine verifies whether alternative practitioners have a sufficient training to provide specific techniques under complementary insurance policies. One of the conditions necessary to fulfil in order to be registered is to attend continuing training.

549 E.g., manipulation techniques such as chiropractic or osteopathy may be taught in a similar way to physiotherapy.

550 E.g., oriental systems of healing. In this respect Stone notes that "We should not assume though, that all therapists work from a formalised knowledge base in the way that orthodox doctors do" (STONE J., *op. cit.*: 242).

551 STONE J., *op. cit.*: 272.

B. High level of education

There are two main reasons why educational programs in graduate schools of medicine should be developed.[552] First, a high level of education is required, including possibly the holding of an allopathic degree in medicine, in order to practise alternative activities whose providing is linked with high risks.[553] Second, the importance of alternative medicines in Western societies is such that it is not possible anymore to ignore or reject them. Wetzel states that

> medical education is under constant pressure to evolve. [...] Changes in the medical interview over the past few years mirror this evolution. Where once value-laden issues about human sexual behavior, resuscitation preferences, and domestic violence were considered taboo in the physician-patient dialogue, these topics are now mandatory as a part of responsible medical care. The rapid increase of public interest in and use of complementary and alternative therapies is likewise exerting a powerful influence on medical education.[554]

However, he also stresses that there is a

> tremendous heterogeneity in content, format, and requirements among complementary and alternative medicine courses at US medical schools. This area of the medical curriculum is at an early stage of development and appears to have few guiding principles.[555]

The author concludes that

> patients are increasingly seeking to identify a physician who is solidly grounded in conventional, orthodox medicine and is also knowledgeable about the value and limitations of alternative treatments. The discussion about how best to prepare future physicians for this role is only beginning. As with most newly defined challenges, this role is temporarily ill defined and multifaceted and requires refinement. As a profession, physicians will increasingly be expected to responsibly advise patients who use, seek, or demand complementary and alternative therapies. We believe the development of a more consistent educational approach to this provocative area is essential.[556]

552 The Swiss Conference of Directors of Health Affairs has stressed the importance given to post-graduate and continuing education and the lesser importance given to basic education (CONFÉRENCE DES DIRECTEURS CANTONAUX DES AFFAIRES SANITAIRES (I), *op. cit.*: 27).

553 Such as the provision of some alternative "drugs" or preparations (typically herbal remedies), the treatment of serious illnesses, the providing of chelation therapy, etc. For an analysis of the risks related to the practice of alternative medicines, see chap. 6.5.

554 WETZEL M. S., *op. cit.*: 784–87. See also ANONYMOUS (IV), *op. cit.*: 20; SELECT COMMITTEE ON SCIENCE AND TECHNOLOGY, *op. cit.*: 8; 68ss.

555 Idem.

556 Ibidem.

It is true that the curriculum of physicians is already heavy, and that requiring them to gain knowledge of all alternative techniques would be an additional burden. However, alternative medicines are a reality that physicians are likely to come across at some stage in their professional practice.[557] As such, they should therefore acquire some knowledge during their basic training in order to be able to meet the requests of patients regarding these techniques.[558] This may also include the possibility of speciality.[559]

Therefore, research and teaching of alternative medicines should be developed within universities. Furthermore, the training programs developed in universities could be used as a reference tool for the creation of

557 The British Select Committee on Science and Technology states that "medical training is now taking full account of many aspects of healthcare, including much of what CAM [Complementary and Alternative Medicines] regards as important, with an increased emphasis on behavioural science, communication skills, counselling, patient-doctor interaction and patient-oriented practice and partnership" (SELECT COMMITTEE ON SCIENCE AND TECHNOLOGY, *op. cit.*: 23).

558 The British Medical Association notes that "doctors need to know more about non-conventional therapies, not only for appropriate delegation of care, but also in their role as trusted adviser to their patients" (BRITISH MEDICAL ASSOCIATION, *op. cit.*: 49–50). See also GRUNWALD D., *op. cit.*; SELECT COMMITTEE ON SCIENCE AND TECHNOLOGY, *op. cit.*: 9, 94ss; WHITE HOUSE COMMISSION ON COMPLEMENTARY AND ALTERNATIVE MEDICINE POLICY, *op. cit.*: XX.

559 Some authors have proposed that universities should unify the two scientific views in order to improve the interactions and the synergies between academic and alternative medicines.

According to Stone "Because of the practical and philosophical problems in including a significant amount of biomedical knowledge in complementary therapists' training, and the problems which this raises in terms of practitioners' ability to spot serious underlying conditions which may require conventional treatment, therapists should be encouraged to work as closely alongside GPs as possible. Greater integration of complementary therapy at a primary care level will no doubt be the best way of increasing understanding between practitioners working within a different conceptual framework" (STONE J., *op. cit.*: 275).

E.g., the North Western College of Chiropractic has an interdisciplinary program that "allows interns to observe the clinical practices of other health professions. This exposure provides an important understanding for interns in order to be successful participants in the emerging world of managed care. The Interdisciplinary Program shows interns the protocols of neurologists, orthopaedic surgeons, osteopaths, and medical and chiropractic radiologists" (available at http://www.nwchiro.edu, accessed Sept. 17, 1999).

See also, e.g., BECK A., *op. cit.*: 56; DELUZE C., *op. cit.*: 33–40; KILGORE C., *op. cit.*: 3; SAGE W. M., *op. cit.*: 82–83; WHITE HOUSE COMMISSION ON COMPLEMENTARY AND ALTERNATIVE MEDICINE POLICY, *op. cit.*: 53–55.

For more details regarding an integrated system, see chap. 8.

medium education programs.[560] In this respect, universities have already accomplished several steps. For example, some universities have proposed introductory courses, which are mainly optional, on alternative medicines.[561] The creation of such courses must be encouraged, but for the reasons just mentioned, they are not sufficient in and of themselves. A more consistent approach has been adopted by other universities where some have included compulsory courses providing a background knowledge of alternative medicines during the basic curriculum of physicians.[562] Others again are developing courses[563] that lead to a diploma and in-depth programs on alternative medicines.[564] Theoretically, the best solution would be the creation of speciality degree programs, similar in structure to the biomedical specialisations. Indeed, the setting up of training having the same length and structure as biomedical specialities[565] could lead to the

560 Until now, the situation has rather been the reverse. Indeed, the influence of private organisations setting up training programs in alternative medicines has been undeniable. Several courses for physicians are also available outside universities, in both tolerant and monopolistic countries (e.g., courses on homeopathy in Belgium, diploma in acupuncture proposed by the Danish Society for Medical Acupuncture).
Wetzel has proposed the incorporation of alternative medical topics appropriately into the medical curriculum and he has offered several suggestions: "Focus on critical thinking and critical reading of the literature [...]; Identify thematic content (i.e., therapies and conditions to be formally addressed) and express the chosen topics in clear, concise learning objectives. [...]; Include an experiential component [...]; Promote a willingness to communicate professionally with alternative health care clinicians [...]; Teach students to talk to patients about alternative therapies. [...]" (WETZEL M. S., *op.cit.*: 786–87).

561 E.g., the Swiss universities of Lausanne and Geneva.

562 E.g., the Swiss universities of Bern and Zürich. In Finland, acupuncture is included in the medical curriculum. In Germany, courses on alternative medicines have been integrated into the regular undergraduate education of some universities. This is also the case in several US universities.

563 E.g., in Austria, training is organised by the Council of the Order of Physicians in acupuncture, homeopathy, manual therapies and neuraltherapy. In France, there are diplomas available in several techniques at some universities (e.g., acupuncture, homeopathy, phytotherapy, osteopathy or auriculotherapy). In Great Britain, some universities have also taken similar initiatives, as have Italy, Spain, Sweden and the Ukraine.

564 E.g., in Switzerland for homeopathy and Chinese medicine (including acupuncture), anthroposophic medicine and neural therapy.

565 E.g., similar periods of theoretical courses and internships in hospitals or by individual practitioners. We are aware that even among biomedical specialities there are variations in length and structure and that the holistic approach of alternative

establishment of a category of practitioners having the same status as biomedical specialists.

C. Medium education

The practice of certain medical acts requires only a medium education.[566] In the biomedical framework, those practitioners who have acquired such a training, such as nurses and physiotherapists, are defined as ancillary professionals.[567] Some schools have developed training programs for alternative practitioners that may be considered as being equivalent to the training of ancillary professionals. For example, US schools have established training programs in manipulation techniques (mainly chiropractic and osteopathy), that may be considered as giving sufficient guarantees as to the quality of such training.

In comparing the regulation of alternative education,[568] to the training programs of several schools,[569] some main features or conditions have been identified,[570] which should be satisfied in order to consider such training as being in the medium category:[571]

---

medicines may constitute a barrier for the creation of specialities within the biomedical paradigm.
To the best of our knowledge, only Latvia has speciality training in alternative medicines (for acupuncture and homeopathy). However, it was not possible to obtain any details of the training.

566 See chap. 7.3.5.2.

567 Ancillary professionals traditionally practise upon referral by a physician, or under the supervision of a physician. For a definition of ancillary professionals, see chap. 1.1.2.

568 See chap. 3.

569 In particular, the Swiss School of Osteopathy of Belmont, Switzerland; the European School of Osteopathy of Maidstone (GB), the NorthWestern College of Chiropractic, USA; the Academy of Chinese Culture and Health Sciences of Oakland, USA; the School of Physiotherapy of Geneva, Switzerland; the School for Nurses of Neuchâtel, Switzerland.

570 These features are based on the interpretation made by the author.

571 For general propositions regarding training in alternative medicines, see SELECT COMMITTEE ON SCIENCE AND TECHNOLOGY, *op. cit.*: 64ss; WHITE HOUSE COMMISSION ON COMPLEMENTARY AND ALTERNATIVE MEDICINE POLICY, *op. cit.*: 55ss.
For propositions regarding the teaching of homeopathy in Europe, see EUROPEAN COMMITTEE FOR HOMEOPATHY, *op. cit.* For propositions regarding acupuncture, see WHO (IV), *op. cit.*
For propositions regarding osteopathic training, see WALDBURGER N., *op. cit.*

1. The training programs must be full time, and last for at least 4 years (preferably 5);[572]
2. The training must include both the theoretical and practical aspects and the practical aspects must represent a substantial part of the training;[573]
3. In addition to the practical teaching, clinical experience/internships either in hospitals, medical centres, or by individual practitioners must be included. The internships should be at least 6–12 months;[574]

572 E.g., the curriculum leading to the title of doctor of chiropractic at the NorthWestern College of Chiropractic, and the curriculum leading to the title of osteopath at the Swiss School of Osteopathy of Belmont lasts for five years (four years for the European School of Osteopathy). The Master of Science in Traditional Chinese Medicine at the Academy of Chinese Culture and Health Sciences of Oakland, US, lasts for four year. In Finland, the training of chiropractors, naprapaths and osteopaths also lasts for four years. The British School of Herbal Medicine offers a comprehensive training program lasting for four years as well.
See, however, the Swedish Commission on Competence, which considers that "medium-length training programmes for caring services" [...] "have now for the most part been extended to three years. The Committee does not propose any further extensions" (Swedish Commission on Competence, *op. cit.*: 32).
According to Waldburger the training in osteopathy should be full time. Indeed, to adapt the training to European standards, four years training as a physiotherapist are necessary, with two additional years of hospital post-graduate experience, and then a six year complementary training in osteopathy (Waldburger N., *op. cit.*).

573 According to the British Select Committee on Science and Technology, training should include teaching about holistic models of healthcare, and more specifically about alternative therapies and their potential uses, including the principles of diagnosis and practice. Furthermore, it must include professional ethics, the therapeutic relationship, the impact of social, cultural, economic, employment and environmental factors on health, counselling skills, as well as principles of quality management and audit, organisational skills including record keeping and technical skills including IT management (Select Committee on Science and Technology, *op. cit.*: 66). On this subject, see also Stone J., *op. cit.*: 242–46 where the author distinguishes between the acquisition of human and technical skills); Gaier H. (II), *op. cit.*: 21–22.
E.g., at the NorthWestern College of Chiropractic, the curriculum for the doctor of chiropractic degree includes several clinical laboratory courses (gastrointestinal system, neurodiagnosis, patient interviewing, physical diagnosis).

574 E.g., to become a member of the Danish Chiropractic Association, candidates must have completed an internship for a period of six months held by a member of the association. The osteopathic English schools (in particular the European School of Osteopathy) require at least 1,000 hours of personal contact (anamnesis, exam and treatment directly with the patient). Students must have treated at least 50 patients. See also Waldburger N., *op. cit.*

4. Students must acquire biomedical knowledge in specific fields[575] and should also have a clear understanding of evidence-based medicine and healthcare;[576]
5. Students must acquire knowledge of the general health environment, including some legal aspects.[577]

575 The British Select Committee on Science and Technology recommends "that training in anatomy, physiology, and basic biochemistry and pharmacology should be included within the education of practitioners of therapies that are likely to offer diagnostic information [...]. Although it may be useful for other therapists to understand basic biomedical science, there is no requirement for such in-depth understanding if the therapy being practised is to be used as an adjunct to conventional medicine" (SELECT COMMITTEE ON SCIENCE AND TECHNOLOGY, *op. cit.*: 64). See also, e.g., ANONYMOUS (IV), *op. cit.*: 22ss.
E.g., at the NorthWestern College of Chiropractic, the curriculum for the doctor of chiropractic degree includes courses on biochemistry, anatomy, histology, skeletal radiology, physiology, nervous system, pathology, microbiology, neuromuskoletal system, respiratory system, cardiovascular system, gastrointestinal system, genitourinary system, gynaecology, endocrinology, radiology, dermatology, obstetrics, emergency procedures, pharmacology and toxicology, mental health, paediatrics, geriatrics and eent (eyes, ear, nose, and throat).
The Swiss School of Osteopathy, in Belmont has similar courses, even if not as extensive, and provides further courses on traumatology, immunology, rheumatology, semiology and forensic medicine.
Schools such as the Academy of Chinese Culture and Health Sciences of Oakland in the US, includes less biomedical courses. In our view, even though Chinese medicine is a comprehensive medical system, the development of biomedical teaching should be encouraged.
In Switzerland, the Register of Empirical Medicine verifies, on behalf of private insurance companies, whether alternative practitioners have a sufficient training to provide specific techniques under complementary insurance policies. One of the conditions necessary to fulfil in order to be registered is to have attended a training in both allopathic and alternative medicines.

576 According to the British Select Committee on Science and Technology "an in-depth understanding of research methods may be even more important for those therapies that operate independently of medical supervision, and which attempt to make a diagnosis and to cure complaints rather than for those which offer relaxation or aim to improve the general quality of life of patients" (SELECT COMMITTEE ON SCIENCE AND TECHNOLOGY, *op. cit.*: 65). See also the same author at 66ss.

577 E.g., at the NorthWestern College of Chiropractic, the required curriculum for the doctor of chiropractic degree includes courses on infectious diseases, community health, professional issues and legal aspects.
The Swiss School of Osteopathy, in Belmont has similar courses, including the sociology of health and illness.

Ideally, a final exam testing the clinical and therapeutic qualities of the candidate should complete the training. Pre-clinical, theoretical, and less practical fields could be eliminated from the final exam by examining the annually.[578]

Once the training is completed, a therapist should have a clear understanding of the limits of his or her competences. The training should enable students to give clear guidance on when a patient should be referred to a physician. Non-allopathic practitioners should also be made aware of the other alternative therapies available to their patients and how they are practised.[579]

D. Basic education

In some countries, non-allopathic practitioners wishing to provide such techniques must pass an exam. The purpose of the exam is to establish that the practitioner does not constitute a danger to individual or public health.[580]

Even though we are not in favour of conditioning the right to practise upon the holding of a basic education,[581] one must, of course, encourage those wishing to engage in healing to be trained appropriately. In particular, non-allopathic practitioners whose technique has not yet been organised and recognised should still have the possibility to receive serious teaching. If the training satisfies specific requirements, it may gain the status of medium training. In this case, practitioners who have attended such training could provide the technique under a protected title.[582]

578 According to Waldburger, the final exam in osteopathy aims to test: 1. the fundamental medical knowledge allowing the practitioner to exclude the patient from his/her field of competence; 2. the examination of the patient and the osteopathic diagnosis; 3. the rigour of the osteopathic reasoning (indication and choice of treatment); 4. the mastery of osteopathic methods; 5. the dissertation. For more details, see WALDBURGER N., *op. cit.*

579 SELECT COMMITTEE ON SCIENCE AND TECHNOLOGY, *op. cit.*: 64.

580 E.g., in Germany or in Appenzell External Rhodes. According to the Swedish Commission on Alternative Medicine, "the best way to improve the safety and security of patients is to guarantee that those who practise alternative medicine have undergone a certain amount of basic medical training" (SWEDISH COMMISSION ON ALTERNATIVE MEDICINE, *op. cit.*: 33).

581 For further developments, see chap. 7.3.2.3 and 7.3.5.2.

582 E.g., basic education programs developed in Germany could be a starting point. The content of the exam of "Heilpraktikers" consists in verifying basic knowledge about health regulations, in particular the epidemic act. Candidates must also have a basic knowledge of anatomy, physiology, hygiene measures, pathology, sterilisation, disinfection and diagnosis. On the subject, see GUILLOD O. (I), *op. cit.*: 38–39.

7.5.2.3 *Summary*

Education is an indispensable condition when deciding to regulate alternative medicines. The right to practise should be conditioned upon the holding of a recognised diploma, and the coverage should depend upon the licensing to practise.

Such a theoretical model presupposes the development, within a regulatory framework, of training in alternative medicines for both allopathic and non-allopathic practitioners. Currently, the level of education is generally unsatisfactory. However, some schools and universities already offer serious training programs for alternative practitioners. Such programs may become a model for the development of new training programs in Western countries.

The integration of courses on alternative medicine during both graduate and post-graduate education through the means of interdisciplinary training may lead to a more open-minded class of future health care providers (in particular physicians), to an improved patient-health care provider relationship, and finally to a better satisfaction of patients' needs. Furthermore, the integration of allopathic courses with the alternative curriculum, and similarly the introduction and increasing integration of alternative medicine within the classic allopathic curriculum is likely to improve the relations and the synergies between biomedical and alternative practitioners.

7.5.3 Building Standards of Practice

Bibliography

ABBING R., *Quality of medical practice and professional misconduct in the European Union*, in: European Journal of Health Law, 1997, n° 4: 273–78; BRADFORD G. E., *The "respectable minority" doctrine in Missouri medical negligence law*, in: Journal of the Missouri Bar, Dec. 2000, vol. 56: 326–34; BRITISH MEDICAL ASSOCIATION (LAMONT T.), *Complementary medicine – New approaches to good practice*, Oxford University Press, 1993, Oxford/New York: 60–61; COHEN M. H. (I), *Complementary and alternative medicine – Legal boundaries and regulatory perspectives*, The Johns Hopkins University Press, 1998, London & Oxford: 64–67, 88–92; COST ACTION B4, *COST action B4 unconventional medicine – Final report of the management committee, 1993–1998*, European Communities, 1998, Luxembourg: 108–09; EUROPEAN COMMITTEE FOR HOMEOPATHY, *Homeopathy in Europe – Developing standars for professionnal practice of homeopathy in the European Union*, European Committee for Homeopathy, 1994, Rotterdam; FEASBY C., *Determining standard of care in alternative contexts*, in: Health Law Journal, 1997, vol. 5: 64; FURROW B. R. (co-authors: GREANEY T. L., JOST T., SCHWARTZ R. L.) (I), *Health law*, West Publishing, 1995, St Paul: 239–41; FURROW B. R. (co-authors: GREANEY T. L., JOST T., SCHWARTZ R. L.) (II), *Health law: Cases, materials and problems*, West Publishing, 1997, St Paul: 35–39, 46; GENERAL OSTEOPATHIC COUNCIL, *Standard 2000 – Standard of proficiency*, General Osteopathic Council, Mar. 1999; POZGAR G. D. (co-author: POZGAR N. S.), *Legal aspects of health care administration*, Aspen Publishers, 1996, Gaithersburg: 336–37; RÖSCH B., *Die Stellung der Erfahrungsheilkundigen aus verfassungs- und verwaltungsrechtlicher Sicht, dargestellt am Beispiel der geistig Heilenden*, Dissertation, Helbing & Lichtenhahn Verlag, 1994, Basel: 355; SELECT COMMITTEE ON SCIENCE AND TECHNOLOGY, *Complementary and alternative medicine*, House of Lords – Session 1999–2000 6th Report, The Stationary Office, 2000, London: 32, 38; STEPNO E. M., *Acupuncture – Stricter standards for those performing acupuncture*, in: M. George L. Rev., 1998, vol. 29: 411–15; STONE J. (co-author: MATTHEWS J.), *Complementary medicine and the law*, Oxford University Press, 1996, Oxford: 95; WHO (IV), *Guidelines on basic training and safety in acupuncture*, WHO, 1999, Geneva: 17ss.

7.5.3.1 General Remarks

During their training, health care providers learn how to provide care according to certain standards of practice. These standards are a "description of the conduct that is expected of an individual in a given situation. It is a measure against which a defendant's conduct is compared".[583] Such standards of practice appear during malpractice trials and criminal procedures involving health care providers,[584] but they are also present during

583 POZGAR G. D., *op. cit.*: 336–37. See also BRADFORD G. E., *op. cit.*: 326–27.
One may consider that standards of practice include ethical rules. However, these rules will not be analysed here.
For more details on civil liability, see chap. 7.2.3.

584 E.g., Furrow writes that in the US "several states have legislated the use of practice guidelines, offering tort immunities in exchange for following such guidelines. [...] Such reforms, its proponents say, will reduce physician malpractice premiums by solidifying the standard of care, reducing practice variation, and reducing the risk of suits against providers." (FURROW B. R. (I), *op. cit.*: 241). Some US states have defined malpractice in alternative medicines. In Nevada, e.g., homeopathic malpractice is defined as "failure on the part of a homeopathic physician to exercise the degree of care, diligence and skill ordinarily exercised by homeopathic physicians in good standing in the community in which he practises" (Nev. Rev. Stat. § 630A.060).
For further analysis of the use of standards of practice during malpractice trials in general, see ABBING R., *op. cit.*: 273–78; FURROW B. R. (I), *op. cit.*: 240–41.
For further analysis of the standard of care applicable in medical negligence when physicians use alternative medicines (including an analysis of the two schools of

the everyday practice of medicine.[585] As long as practitioners follow them, the quality of treatment is supposedly guaranteed. For this reason, regulation[586] should ideally be based on reliable standards of practice.[587]

However, even if standards of practice underlie the delivering of health care, it is less clear if they are a necessary condition to any decision to regulate. Indeed, first the process of creating the standards of practice, as well as the participants who establish such standards are not clearly defined. Second, it is difficult to clearly define the standards of practice, as they may vary from one place, and from one practitioner to another. Finally, standards of practice evolve more or less rapidly, and may quickly be out-of-date once they are formalised.[588]

7.5.3.2 Creation of Standards of Practice

The establishment of standards of practice is a complex process. Regarding the origins of standards, Furrow writes that they do

> not normally derive from an external authority such as a government standard. In the medical profession, as in other professions, standards develop in a complicated way involving the interaction of leaders of the profession, professionals journals and meetings, and networks of colleagues.[589]

He adds that

---

thought or respectable minority), see BRADFORD G. E., *op. cit.*: 326–34; COHEN M. H. (I), *op. cit.*: 64–67, 88–92. See also chap. 7.2.3.

585 Experts having to assess standards of practice form their opinions by combining their own personal experience and knowledge of customary practices with their knowledge of the medical literature (BRADFORD G. E., *op. cit.*: 327).

586 In particular the licensing to practise and the coverage of 'alternative' medicines.

587 RÖSCH B., *op. cit.*: 355. The British Select Committee on Science and Technology highlights the importance of the evidence of the validity of diagnostic procedures, which it considers as important as evidence supporting efficacy of a treatment (SELECT COMMITTEE ON SCIENCE AND TECHNOLOGY, *op. cit.*: 32).

588 This means that standards must be regularly updated. See the case of osteopathy in Great Britain (GENERAL OSTEOPATHIC COUNCIL, *op. cit.*).

589 In the US, FURROW notes that "neither the Food and Drug Administration, the National Institutes of Health, the Department of Health and Human Services, nor state licensing boards have had much to do with shaping medical practice" (FURROW B. R. (II), *op. cit.*: 35). One may even say that case law contributes in a significant way to the shaping of standards of practice.

> most clinical policies derive from a flow of reports in the literature, at meetings, and in peer discussions. Over a period of time, hundreds of separate comments come together to form a clinical policy. If this becomes generally accepted, we can call it "standardised practice".[590]

Thus, the creation of standards of practice involves several participants.[591] Furthermore, various approaches are available when establishing such standards. For example, one possible approach would be to rely on the forces of professional ethics and socialisation. Another would be to expand the role of the marketplace[592] or to improve the current modes of self-regulation of both the medical profession and the healthcare industry.[593] Again, the process by which a patient sues for malpractice could be improved and, finally, the intervention of government could be encouraged in order to establish standards and to demand improved processes and results.[594, 595]

Several efforts have been made to create and heighten standards of care in the field of alternative medicines. For example, the American Association of Naturopathic Physicians issued guidelines which provide general criteria for naturopathic medical practice. The guidelines list a range of techniques from which a naturopath (usually a physician) may choose and are consistent with the legislatively authorized scope of practice in the naturopath's particular state.[596] Among other things, the naturopath is obliged to keep up with changes in professional practice, to conform to the professional code of ethics, to take thorough histories, to maintain clear records, to make appropriate referrals and to perform appropriate physical and mental

590 FURROW B. R. (I), *op. cit.*: 239. The author adds: "The development of practice standards and guidelines by national medical organisations will accelerate the process of moving all medical practice towards national standards." (FURROW B. R. (I), *op. cit.*: 240).

591 In the US, clinical practice protocols (also referred to as practice parameters or guidelines) have been developed by medical societies (such as the American Academy of Paediatrics) and the National Institutes of Health, and also by individual hospitals.

592 E.g., in disseminating quality information to consumers, on the theory that prudent buyers will reject lowers quality providers.

593 This includes accreditation, medical staff privileges and medical licensing actions.

594 This is typically the case in the US where the government is a primary source of financing for much health care in the US.

595 FURROW B. R. (II), *op. cit.*: 38.

596 The therapies include homeopathy, acupuncture, massage therapy and natural childbirth.

examinations. The guidelines also establish criteria for making diagnoses using conventional and other diagnostic methods.[597]

Guidelines have even been created for techniques that are more difficult to standardise, because of their esoteric approach. For example, the American National Commission for the Certification of Acupuncturists has developed procedures such as the "clean needle technique" (CNT) as part of its national certification program. The aim is to ensure that patients are treated with safe and sterile needles and all applicants must demonstrate knowledge of CNT sufficient to maintain safe clinical procedures.[598]

In Europe, some steps have also been taken towards the creation of serious standards of practice. For example, the European Committee for Homeopathy has established standards for the professional practice of homeopathy.[599] These include definitions, indications for homeopathic treatments, guidelines for the consultation[600] and the providing of drugs, as well as recommendations regarding fundamental research and training. Suggestions have also been made concerning the standards of quality, registration schemes, right of complaint and disciplinary rules within the homeopathy field generally. In Great Britain, the General Osteopathic Council has developed standards of practice, which are regularly

597 Such as those for oriental and Ayurvedic medicine.
Similar standards exist in the chiropractic profession. For more details, see COHEN M. H. (I), *op. cit.*: 65 and references; POZGAR G. D., *op. cit.*: 336–37.

598 California has enacted a statute that establishes stricter standards for those providing acupuncture. In Great Britain, the British Acupuncture Council is seen as having led the way in establishing verifiable standards of education for acupuncturists. For more details, see STEPNO E. M., *op. cit.*: 411–15; SELECT COMMITTEE ON SCIENCE AND TECHNOLOGY, *op. cit.*: 38.
The WHO also set up some guidelines regarding safety in acupuncture (WHO (IV), *op. cit.*: 17ss.).
Cohen notes that "although the acupuncture community to date has not established written guidelines setting forth standards of care for the profession, most courts probably would view CNT as part of the standard of care because the community as a whole accepts it as a baseline for safe clinical practice. A patient injured through unsterilized or contaminated acupuncture needles will probably succeed in a malpractice claim if he or she proves that the acupuncturist violated CNT guidelines" (COHEN M. H. (I), *op. cit.*: 66).

599 EUROPEAN COMMITTEE FOR HOMEOPATHY, *op. cit.*: 27–30.

600 Divided between general medical part of the consultation and the specific homeopathic part of the consultation. The second part is divided into three phases: case taking, case analysis and data processing, and remedy selection.
Recommendations regarding follow-up consultations and the duration of consultation and treatment are also made.

updated.[601] A concern of professional boards and health authorities has been to maintain a proper referral system between the allopathic and alternative professions, in order to ensure that patients receive an appropriate treatment.[602] The COST Action B4 recommends the establishment of national and international agencies, which could be responsible for, among others, the setting up of guidelines in research, training and practice.[603]

When there is an overlap in an area of knowledge of treatment, for example where the scope of practice includes both alternative and biomedical methods, Cohen suggests that alternative practitioners could be held to a heightened, biomedical standard of care.[604]

601 The first standard consists of a number of statements related to the clinical practice of osteopathy under eleven headings of key areas of importance. The second standard is structured using sixteen areas of capability. Each area of capability is described in its osteopathic context and then further considered under a number of outcome statements related, where possible, to osteopathic practice. The second standard is therefore more comprehensive than the first and makes more explicit reference to the context as well as the content of modern osteopathic practice.
The areas of capability are the following: a. knowledge relevant for the safe and competent practice of homeopathy; b. concepts and principles of osteopathy; c. therapeutic and professional relationship; d. personal and individual skills; e. communication skills; f. information and data handling skills; g. intra and inter-professional collaboration and co-operation; h. professional identity and accountability, ethics and responsibilities; i. professional self-evaluation and development by means of reflective practice; j. identification and evaluation of the needs of the patient; k. acquisition and enhancement of the skills of osteopathic palpation; l. planning, justifying and monitoring osteopathic treatment interventions; m. conducting osteopathic treatment and patient management; n. evaluation of post treatment progress and change; o. advice and support for the promotion and maintenance of healthy living; p. managing an efficient and effective environment for the provision of osteopathic health care.
Each area of capability is presented in two parts. The first part provides a description of the area in some detail including its significance for osteopathic practice. The second part takes the form of outcome statements indicating some of the key features of the area concerned.
For more details, see GENERAL OSTEOPATHIC COUNCIL, *op. cit.*

602 On this subject, see BRITISH MEDICAL ASSOCIATION, *op. cit.*: 60–61; STONE J., *op. cit.*: 243.
For more information on the establishment of standards of practice for alternative medicines, see COHEN M. H. (I), *op. cit.*: 88–92, 112.

603 COST ACTION B4, *op. cit.*: 108–09.

604 E.g., in situation, in which chiropractors take X-rays, perform urine analysis, take or order blood tests, or perform physical examinations, failure to perform the procedure may be judged against a biomedical standard of care and may constitute malpractice. In these situations, chiropractors are judged by standards applicable to physicians.
For further discussion, see COHEN M. H. (I), *op. cit.*: 66–67.

As standards of practice are related to specific techniques, national barriers do not limit their development. This leads to two observations. First, standards develop more or less easily according to the legal framework of the country.[605] Second, it is possible to rely on standards of practice developed in other countries, when establishing standards of practice in a country. Thus, as for education, standards may evolve and develop through the contribution of international initiatives. This opens interesting perspectives regarding the setting up of standards of practice recognised as valid in an international framework.

7.5.3.3 Variation of Standards of Practice

Standards of practice may vary widely from one region, and practitioner to another. In this respect, Furrow notes that

> a national standard of practice does not exist for many procedures and tools, and the "highest and best" practice may not be the safest or most effective in the long run. Substantial regional variations exist in the use of many procedures, with no apparent differences in outcome (life expectancy, morbidity, days missed from work). [...] Different practice styles exist in different regions, and even within states, based on a local concept of good practice.[606]

The variation of standards is even greater for alternative medicines[607] for while some techniques may set up standards less removed from biomedical

605 In monopolistic countries, alternative medicines are usually not allowed, and rules (legal or paralegal) impede their development. E.g., In Italy, while physicians are permitted to practise alternative medicines, they must however assume the consequences of taking patients away from allopathic medicine (when providing alternative techniques).

606 FURROW B. R. (I), *op. cit.*: 239–40. For example, wide variation has been noted in the use of laboratory tests, X-rays, prescription drugs, return appointments, and telephone consultations among similarly trained doctors in a wide variety of practice settings (FURROW B. R. (II), *op. cit.*: 37).
Thus, as Furrow states, "the phenomenon of medical practice variation highlights the role of uncertainty in the setting up of medical standards" (FURROW B. R. (II), *op. cit.*: 36).
In this respect, one may note the doctrine of the "two schools of medical thought", or the "faith minority" defence, that aroused when defendant doctors argue that there are in effect two separate and distinct standards of care. For more details on this point, see BRADFORD G. E., *op. cit*: 326–34. See also chap. 6.3.4.

607 According to Cohen "it is often difficult to determine exactly what protocols or procedures are within the standard of care for complementary and alternative medicines. Outside of biomedicine, standards of care are more fluid, because

practice, such as naturopathy, or massage techniques, other methods (such as acupuncture) find this more difficult. Actually, the more esoteric a technique the less a formalised consensus around standards of care has developed.[608]

Furthermore, standards of practice incessantly evolve and, as such, practices that were previously not recognised may be legitimised, and vice versa.[609] Similarly, established techniques are often modified in order to make them more efficient.[610]

Another problem that needs to be addressed in relation to standards of practice is their enforcement. Indeed, the creation of standards of practice does not mean that they will, as a result, be effectively applied. In reality, the dissemination of guidelines has often very little effect on actual practitioner practice.[611] Therefore, when standards are issued, some controls

---

treatments involve widely varying schools of thought and techniques, and highly individualized or non-standardized methods. Many treatments, such as massage therapy, draw on the provider's intuitive or subjective faculties as much as on uniform, professionally prescribed practices." (COHEN M. H. (I), *op.cit.*: 65).

608 As Cohen notes, "because acupuncturists treat imbalance and chi, rather that biomedically defined conditions or diseases, they do not generally rely on standardized treatments for curing particular ailments. Individual acupuncturists may treat colitis or anxiety differently – for example, varying the number of sessions, the placement of acupuncture needles" (COHEN M. H. (I), *op.cit.*: 65).
One may add that standards of practice are partly based on research. Currently, research in alternative medicines face several problems. For a development, see chap. 6.

609 E.g., in the US, only in 1996 was acupuncture reclassified from experimental devices to devices for which performance standards exist to provide reasonable assurance of their safety and effectiveness. Similarly, doctors in various specialities have been quick to adopt new technologies such as gastric freezing of ulcers, respirator therapy and other now-discredited techniques.

610 As Furrow writes "the diffusion of new medical technologies of diagnosis and treatment poses special problems for the individual physician. Most doctors will note new ideas as they show up in the literature. But they may not be appropriately sceptical" (FURROW B. R. (II), *op.cit.*: 36).

611 E.g., a study was undertaken, whose objective was to evaluate the effect of distribution practice guidelines generated under the auspices of a national speciality association – the 1986 Canadian guidelines that advocated a lower rate of caesarean sections. The study concluded that the dissemination of guidelines had little effect on actual physician practice. Physician awareness of them was high, and the attitudes of obstetricians were positive toward the recommendations. However, only one third of obstetricians and hospitals reported changing their practices because of the guidelines (FURROW B. R. (II), *op.cit.*: 38). See also SAGE W. M., *op.cit.*: 68.

should be imposed so as to enable their enforcement. However, even if such standards are enforced, they may not be recognised by the health authorities or by the appropriate medical society within a specific jurisdiction. As Feasby notes

> Both Canadian and U.S. case law demonstrated that there is a general reluctance to place even established alternative schools on a level with conventional medicine in the process of determining standard of care. This hesitance to endorse alternative medicine is rooted in the perception that modern medicine is a preferable, or even the proper, form of treatment. While such a judicial endorsement is perhaps unfair in an increasingly pluralist society permeated by post modern values, it is one that is reflected implicitly in legislation governing health professions and in the allocation of state resources to fund conventional medicine and medical research. Given this societal bias, it is likely that standard of care will continue, to some extent at least, to be viewed through the prism of modern medical science.[612]

7.5.3.4 Summary

Today, there is a growing trend towards reliable standards of practice for both allopathic and alternative medicines.[613] There is still, however, substantial variation among existing standards of practice for alternative medicines. Further development will certainly continue the process of creating precise standard rules regarding the behaviour of alternative practitioners, and make them more accountable. This will enable a better integration of such practitioners within the health care system. For this reason, the regulatory framework should be adapted in order to allow the development and enforcement of standards of practice. Although the development of such standards of practice must be encouraged,[614] licensure regulation may not require them as a strict condition. Indeed, their content may not be precisely defined, and they are constantly evolving. However,

612 FEASBY C., *op. cit.*: 64.

613 Furrow notes that "the combined problems of variation in medical practice and lack of evidence of efficacy of many treatment approaches have launched a movement toward practice parameters.[...] The development of practice parameters or protocols has intensified in recent years, as the medical profession attempts to shift through the available research knowledge and reduce variation in medical practice" (FURROW B. R. (II), *op. cit.*: 38).

614 The British Select Committee on Science and Technology considers that "minimum standards of safety need to be defined and widely disseminated in order to protect the public" (SELECT COMMITTEE ON SCIENCE AND TECHNOLOGY, *op. cit.*: 33).

it is recommended that a search be instituted in order to ascertain whether such guidelines exist and if so, to possibly implement them.[615]

7.6 Conclusion

There is a clear move towards increased integration of alternative practitioners within Western countries. Public authorities have responded to the strong increase in the use of alternative medicines by seeking solutions in order to give patients access to alternative medicines, while also seeking to integrate the safety and quality of these techniques at the same time.

Over the past twenty years various Western countries have shifted their policy regarding the licensing to practise alternative medicines from a monopolistic approach to a more tolerant one. Restrictive policies regarding the providing of health care in Western countries may have been justified in the past, but today it is more difficult to legitimise them. Indeed, history has demonstrated the limits of (bio-) medicine as well as the inefficiency and inappropriateness of such policies in the evolving world of health care.[616] In addition, patients' rights have evolved. They are better informed and feel more responsible for the choices they must make regarding their health and their wish to have access to alternative therapies. If a more liberal vision of the right to have access to and to provide alternative medicines seems appropriate, then the corollary must be the enhancement of the quality of care. In particular, any liberalisation should be accompanied by a strict control over the information provided to the public. Indeed, only those practitioners who have a serious educational background should benefit from title protection. Furthermore, potentially dangerous medical acts should be strictly defined and restricted solely to skilled practitioners.

615 There appears to be a paradox here. Indeed, when the discussion is made to require standards of practice to license a specific practice, this presupposes that the practice has already developed in an illegal environment. However, the development of standards of practice is not limited by national barriers.
Indeed, a source of inspiration may be found from foreign standards of practice, training programs, research, guidelines and recommendation issued by associations, public authorities, hospitals and individual practitioners.

616 Obviously, this also demonstrates that biomedicine is efficient to treat a whole range of illnesses and health problems, and that techniques employed for centuries were ultimately useless.

The coverage of alternative medicines is following a similar pattern to the licensing of alternative practitioners. Public and private insurance are officially, or unofficially extending such coverage. The principle of therapeutic freedom and the criteria determining and limiting the coverage of alternative medicines, namely the effectiveness, appropriateness, and economic character, are usually not adapted to alternative medicines. Although such criteria must be applied in order to determine which treatments may be covered, they should be modulated, in order to take into consideration the specificities of alternative medicines.

The development of alternative medicines in Western countries is recent, and educational programs, particularly in universities, need more time to develop. However, various countries have already demonstrated that the right to provide alternative medicines may be conditioned upon the training of practitioners in alternative medicines. In this respect, some of those countries have based their regulation on the recognition of foreign diplomas. This opens the door to international developments in education, licensing and coverage regulation.

Although standards of practice in alternative medicines are developing and becoming more reliable, there are still variations among them. Furthermore, they are constantly evolving and, as such, it is difficult to formally require that regulatory initiatives be based upon such standards. However, when a regulation is envisaged, the search for existing standards in other jurisdictions as a guide or the creation of new standards will provide valuable indications as to the reliability, effectiveness and safety of the technique.

It is vitally important today to create a legal framework more adapted to alternative medicines. The establishment of a consistent system requires that lawmakers have a general view of the existing set of problems and that coordination is ensured between the regulatory and non-regulatory fields.[617] This may require a (re-) definition of the tasks and powers of authorities, or the setting up of new structures aimed at achieving a consistent system.

Thus, while it is true to say that the position of alternative medicines in Western countries still remains unsatisfactory, there have also been many developments and ideas that have opened up new perspectives. Above all, the move towards an increased integration of alternative practitioners within current health care systems is only at the initial stage.

617 In several countries, there is little correlation between education, licensing to practice and coverage.

8. An Integrated System of Medicine

Bibliography

ABBING R., *Quality of medical practice and professional misconduct in the European Union*, in: European Journal of Health Law, 1997, n° 4: 273–78; ABBOTT A., *The system of professions: An essay on the division of expert labor*, University of Chicago Press, 1988, Chicago; ALDRIDGE D. (I), *Unconventional medicine in Europe*, Advances, 1994, vol. 10, n° 2: 52–54; ANDREWS L. B., *The shadow health care system: Regulation of alternative health care providers*, in: Houston Law Review, 1996, vol. 32: 1273–317; ANONYMOUS (IV), *Integrated healthcare – A way forward for the next five years?*, Foundation for Integrated Medicine, 1997; BECK A., *La chaire de médecine complémentaire à l'Université de Berne: Une création récente*, in: CMS, 1996, vol. 40: 56; BERG R., *Note, HMO exclusion of chiropractors*, in: S. Cal. L. Rev., 1993, vol. 66: 827; BONVIN E. (I), *Médecine officielle et thérapies alternatives: Dialogue ou concurrence?*, in: BORGHI M. (co-editor: GASSMAN J.), *Thérapies complémentaires ou alternatives en psychiatrie: Un défi? Un droit?*, Schriftenreihe der Schweizerischen Stiftung Pro Mente Sana n° 20, 1999, Zürich: 44–56; BOOZANG K. M. (III), *National policy on CAM: The White House Commission report*, in: The Journal of Law, Medicine and Ethics, 2003, vol. 31, n° 2: 251–61; BORGHI M. (co-editor: GASSMAN J.), *Thérapies complémentaires ou alternatives en psychiatrie: Un défi? Un droit?*, Schriftenreihe der Schweizerischen Stiftung Pro Mente Sana n° 20, 1999, Zürich; BRENDSTRUP E., *Researching a holistic integrated treatment model – Used by cancer patients*, in: JOHANNESSEN H. (co-authors: LAUNSO L., OLESEN S. G., STAUGARD F.) (I), *Studies in alternative therapy 1 – Contributions from the Nordic countries*, Odense University Press, 1994, Gylling: 151–60; BRITISH MEDICAL ASSOCIATION (LAMONT T.), *Complementary medicine – New approaches to good practice*, Oxford University Press, 1993, Oxford/New York: 49–50, 51–59, 65–66; COBURN D., *State authority, medical dominance, and trends in the regulation of the health professions: The Ontario case*, in: Social-Science-and-Medicine, Oct. 1993, vol. 37, n° 7: 841–50; COHEN M. H. (I), *Complementary and alternative medicine – Legal boundaries and regulatory perspectives*, The Johns Hopkins University Press, 1998, London & Oxford; COHEN M. H. (II), *Holistic health care: Including alternative and complementary medicine in insurance and regulatory schemes*, in: Arizona Law Review, Spring 1996, vol. 38: 154ss; COST ACTION B4, *COST Action B4 Unconventional Medicine – Final report of the management committee, 1993–1998*, European Communities, 1998, Luxembourg; COURRIER INTERNATIONAL (I), *Dossier 2000–2100, Techno sapiens prend le pouvoir*, Courrier International, 1999, n° 469: 31–38; DAGUET R., *Per una cura integrata: Riflessioni su medicina moderna e terapie alternative*, in: BORGHI M., *op. cit.*: 15–21; EISENBERG D. M. and co-authors (I), *Trends in alternative medicine use in the United States, 1990–1997*, in: JAMA,

1998, vol. 280, n° 18: 1569–75; ESKINAZI D. P., *Factors that shape alternative medicine*, in: JAMA, 1998, vol. 280, n° 18: 1621–23; FAN R., *Modern Western science as a standard for traditional Chinese medicine: A critical appraisal*, in: The Journal of Law, Medicine and Ethics, 2003, vol. 31, n° 2: 213–221; FRIEDMAN R. (co-authors: SEDLER M., MYERS P., BENSON H.), *Behavioral medicine, complementary medicine and integrated care: Economic implications*, in: Prim. Care, Dec. 1997, vol. 24, n° 4: 949–62; FURROW B. R. (co-authors: GREANEY T. L., JOST T., SCHWARTZ R. L.) (I), *Health law*, West Publishing, 1995, St Paul: 7–13, 56–58, 125–35; GAIER H. (II), *Reveille for biocentric medicine*, in: LEWITH G. (co-editor: ALDRIDGE D.), *Complementary medicine and the European Community*, CW Daniel, 1991, Saffron Walden: 21–22; GASSMANN J., *Therapiewahlfreiheit in der stationären Psychiatrie – auch für komplementäre Methoden!*, in: BORGHI M., *op. cit.*: 309–13; GOODWIN J., *A health insurance revolution*, in: New Age Journal's Guide to Holistic Medicine, 1997–1998: 66; GRMEK M. D. and co-authors, *Histoire de la pensée médicale en Occident*, Editions du Seuil, 199, Paris; GROUPE DE RÉFLEXION "MÉDECINES DIFFÉRENTES", *Evaluer les médecines différentes, un défi? Rapport aux ministres des affaires sociales et de la solidarité nationale et au secrétaire d'Etat chargé de la santé*, La documentation française, 1986: 93–94; GUEX P., *La place des médecines complémentaires: Considérations générales*, in: CMS, 1996, vol. 40, n° 1: 7–9; GUILLOD O. (I), *Rebouteux, naturopathes et guérisseurs: Pour un traitement légal alternatif*, Recueil de Jurisprudence Neuchâtelois, 1989, Neuchâtel: 38; GUILLOD O. (VII), *Le droit médical: Quelques (r)évolutions récentes*, in: BERTRAND T. (co-authors: HARDING T.-W, MANDOFIA BERNY M., UMMEL M.), *Médecin et droit médical*, Editions Médecine et Hygiène, 1998, Chêne-Bourg: 21–36; HÄNGGELI C., *Une étape décisive pour la FMH*, in: Bulletin des Médecins Suisses: 1998, vol. 79, n° 48: 2447–48; HERNESNIEMI A., *Co-work between a medical doctor and a traditional healer*, in: JOHANNESSEN H. (co-authors: LAUNSO L., OLESEN S. G., STAUGARD F.) (I), *Studies in alternative therapy 1 – Contributions from the Nordic countries*, Odense University Press, 1994, Gylling: 126–38; HOFMEISTER E. (co-author: LAUNSO L., BRENDSTRUP E.), *Centers for integrated medicine in Denmark*, in: JOHANNESSEN H. (co-authors: LAUNSO L., OLESEN S. G., STAUGARD F.) (I), *Studies in alternative therapy 1 – Contributions from the Nordic countries*, Odense University Press, 1994, Gylling: 126–38; JAPSEN B., *Cost-conscious providers take to holistic medicine; Once scorned or banned, alternative treatments have gone mainstream as less expensive but effective cures*, in: Mos. Healthcare, Aug. 21, 1995: 140; JINGFENG C., *Integration of traditional Chinese medicine with Western medicine – Right or wrong?*, Social Science & Medicine, 1988, vol. 27 (5), n° 521; JOHANNESSEN H. (co-authors: LAUNSO L., OLESEN S. G., STAUGARD F.) (I), *Studies in alternative therapy 1 – Contributions from the Nordic countries*, Odense University Press, 1994, Gylling, 1994, Gylling; JOSEFEK K. J., *Alternative medicine's roadmap to mainstream*, in: American Journal of Law and Medicine, 2000, vol. 26: 295–310; KILGORE C., *Expanding coverage signals growing demand, acceptance for alternative care*, in: Medicine & Health Perspectives, May 4 1998: 2–3; KUHN T. S., *La structure des révolutions scientifiques*, Flammarion, 1983, Manchecourt; KÜNZI M. (I), *Komplementärmedizin und Gesundheitsrecht*, Helbing & Lichtenhahn Verlag AG, 1996, Basel: 74–75, 95–98; LANNOYE P., *Is there a future for complementary medicine in Europe? – European report on the status of non-conventionnal medicine*, The Natural Medicines Society, 1996, Heanor: 4–6; LAUNSO L. (co-author: BRENDSTRUP E.) (II), *Description of a holistic integrated treatment model used by cancer patients and research evaluated part I and II*, in: Townsend for Doctors, Dec. 1994 and Jan. 1995; LAY B. F., *Healer-patient privilege: Extending the physician-patient privilege to alternative health practitioners in California*, in: Hastings Law Journal, Mar. 1997: 638; LE FANU J., *Grandeur et décadence de la médecine*, in: Courrier International, 1999, n° 463: 45; MATTHIESSEN P. F., *Unkonventionelle Behandlungsmethoden im Kontext medizinischer Versorgung*, in: Zeitschrift für Sozialreform, 1994, vol. 40, n° 8: 522–36; MELCHART D. (co-authors: LINDE K., WEIDENHAMMER W., WORKU F., WAGNER H.), *The integration of natural healing procedures into research and teaching at German universities*, in: Alternative Therapies, 1995, vol. 1, n° 1: 30–33; MICHEL E., *L'hôpital de Genève fait bon ménage avec les guérisseurs à distance*, in: Le Temps, Aug. 12, 1999; MICKELSON A. A. (co-authors: DAILEY W. H., SINGH KHALSA S., FEDAK M. L.), *Managed care potpourri IV: Where is complementary/alternative care?*, in: Whittier Law Review, Fall 1997, vol. 19: 128ss; MINISTRY OF HEALTH AND SOCIAL AFFAIRS, *Report on alternative medicine – English summary*, Norges Offentliche Utredniger NOU 1998: 21, 1998, Oslo: 269, 271–74; MITCHELL WEITZMAN S., *Insurance coverage for complementary and alternative medicine – Access, challenges, and policy*, in: HUMBER J. M. (co-editor: ALMEDER R.), *Alternative medicine and ethics*, Humana Press, 1998, Totowa: 127–61; PATEL V., *Understanding the integration of alternative modalities into an emerging healthcare model in the United States*, in: HUMBER J. M. (co-editor: ALMEDER R.), *Alternative medicine and ethics*, Humana Press, 1998, Totowa: 43–96; PELLETIER K. R., (co-authors: MARIE A., KRASNER M., et al.), *Current trends in the integration and reimbursement of complementary and alternative medicine by managed care, insurance carriers, and hospital providers*, in: Am. J. Health Promot., 1997, n° 12: 112–22; PEW HEALTH PROFESSIONS COMMISSION (FINOCCHIO L. J., DOWER C. M., MCMAHON T., GRAGNOLA C. M., AND THE TASKFORCE ON HEALTH CARE WORKFORCE REGULATION), *Reforming health care workforce regulation: Policy considerations for the 21st Century*, Pew Health Professions Commission, 1995, San Francisco; ROBARD I., *La santé hors la loi: Les hors la loi de la santé*, 4th ed., Ed. de l'Ancre, 1994, Suresnes; RÖSCH B., *Die Stellung der Erfahrungsheilkundigen aus verfassungs- und verwaltungsrechtlicher Sicht, dargestellt am Beispiel der geistig Heilenden*, Dissertation, Helbing & Lichtenhahn Verlag AG, 1994, Basel: 24–27; ROSSI I. (I), *Médecine, médecines: Parallélisme ou complémentarité?*, in: CMS, 1996, vol. 40: 17–24; SAGE W. M. (co-author: AIKEN L. H.), *Regulating interdisciplinary practice*, in: JOST T. S., *Regulation of the healthcare professions*, Health Administration Press, 1996, Chicago: 71–101; SALE D. M., *Overview of legislative developments concerning alternative health care in the United States*, 1995: 53–54; SALLER R., *Médecine naturelle (Naturheilkunde) à l'Université de Zürich*, in: CMS, 1996, vol. 40: 71–74; SELECT COMMITTEE ON SCIENCE AND TECHNOLOGY, *Complementary and alternative medicine*, House of Lords – Session 1999–2000 6th Report, The Stationary Office, 2000, London; SHAPIRO A. K. (co-author: SHAPIRO E.) (I), *The powerful placebo – From ancient priest to modern physician*, The Johns Hopkins University Press, 1997, Baltimore/London; STAUGARD F. (II), *The role of traditional and complementary therapy in primary health care system*, in: JOHANNESSEN H. (co-authors: LAUNSO L., OLESEN S. G., STAUGARD F.) (I), *Studies in alternative therapy 1 – Contributions from the Nordic countries*, Odense University Press, 1994, Gylling: 84–92; STEPAN J., *Traditional and alternative systems of medicine: A comparative review of legislation*, in: International Digest of Health Legislation, 1985, vol.36, n°2, Genève: 285, 287, 303; STONE J. (co-author: MATTHEWS J.), *Complementary medicine and the law*, Oxford University Press, 1996, Oxford; SWEDISH COMMISSION ON ALTERNATIVE MEDICINE, *Report on alternative medicine*, Regeringskansliet, 1989, Stockholm: 29–33; THOMSON B., *The medical revolution*, in: Natural Health, Mar.–Apr. 1996: 98ss; WARREN D. G., *Complementary medicine and the law*, in: Journal of Legal Medicine, June 1997: 261–62; WETZEL M. S. (co-authors: EISENBERG D. M., KAPTCHUK T. J.), *Courses involving complementary and alternative medicine at US medical schools*, in: JAMA, 1998, vol.280, n°9: 784–87; WHITE HOUSE COMMISSION ON COMPLEMENTARY AND ALTERNATIVE MEDICINE POLICY, *Final report*, March 2002, available at http://www.whccamp.hhs.gov/pdfs/fr2002_document.pdf, accessed Feb. 1 2005; WHO (II), *Report of the third meeting of directors of WHO collaborating centres for traditional medicine*, WHO, 1995, Geneva; WICKI M., *Komplementärmedizin im Rahmen des Rechtes*, Dissertation, Stämpfli, 1998, Bern: 204–07.

8.1 Introduction

Until the nineteenth century, the practice of medicine was not based upon a serious scientific background.[1] Treatments were provided on the basis of non-demonstrated theories, tradition and mysticism. At that point, medicine was constituted of a broad set of techniques provided by "therapists" who may or may not have had a formal educational background, such as physicians or lay practitioners, or administered by patients themselves.

As biomedicine developed on the basis of controlled trials it differentiated itself from treatments lacking scientific legitimacy. Biomedicine was slowly recognised and it has since acquired a predominant position within Western research institutions, hospitals, academic medical training and insurance coverage funds.[2] In addition, strict policies have attempted to suppress the recourse to non-biomedical or alternative medicines, by forbidding non-allopathic practitioners to provide health care treatments, by

1 For more details, see chap. 6.2.1.
2 For an overview of the evolution of (bio-) medicine, see 6.2.2.

prohibiting the use of alternative medicines by allopathic practitioners, or by not allowing coverage for these techniques.

Although restrictive policies towards alternative medicines did not entirely succeed, non-biomedical treatments were, by the late sixties, generally excluded from Western health care systems. The emergence of a counter culture in the late sixties and seventies brought a new breath of life to alternative medicines. Since then, these techniques have slowly (re-) gained acceptance in Western countries.

Several authors have observed the "mainstreaming" of alternative medicines while others wish this phenomenon to continue until these alternative techniques are fully "integrated" within Western health care systems.[3] An integrated system of medicine is based on the idea of a unique medicine, whose purpose is to predict and prevent illness and to relieve and cure pain. All available methods must be employed to reach these objectives, irrespective of whether they are considered allopathic or alternative.[4]

While the concept of integrated medicine is appealing, an overriding concern is whether it is legitimate and realistic. As a result, an analysis of the concept of "integrated system" and its components will be presented below. Finally, current trends and evolutions will be compared with the theoretical model developed during the course of this research.[5]

3 E.g., ALDRIDGE D. (I), *op. cit.*; ANONYMOUS (IV), *op. cit.*; BONVIN E., *op. cit.*: 56; BOOZANG K. M. (III), *op. cit.*: 251; BRENDSTRUP E., *op. cit.*; COHEN M. H. (I), *op. cit.*: 95; DAGUET R., *op. cit.*; FRIEDMAN R., *op. cit.*; HOFMEISTER E., *op. cit.*; JAPSEN B., *op. cit.*; JOSEFEK K. J., *op. cit.*; LAUNSO L. (II), *op. cit.*; MELCHART D., *op. cit.*; PELLETIER K. R., *op. cit.*; JINGFENG C., *op. cit.*

4 Obviously, proponents of evidence-based-medicine have argued strenuously against the integration of techniques whose efficacy has not been demonstrated.

5 The proposed model is personal. It has been slowly shaped during the compilation of this research. Often, the various authors cited in this research have not specifically written on the idea of an integrated system of medicine. However their proposals have been identified as fitting within the concept that will be developed here below.

8.2 Concept

The concept of an "integrated system of medicine" or "integrated medicine"[6] rests on the concept of "medicine", which the Oxford English Dictionary defines as

> that department of knowledge and practice which is concerned with the cure, alleviation, and prevention of disease in human beings, and with the restoration and preservation of health. Also, in a more restricted sense, applied to that branch of this department which is the province of the physician, in the modern application of the term: the art of restoring and preserving the health of human beings by the administration of remedial substances and the regulation of diet, habits, and conditions of life; distinguished from surgery and obstetrics.[7]

As this definition suggests, the concept of medicine has acquired two meanings. In its restrictive sense, medicine is limited to biomedicine, while in its broad meaning it may be understood as the implementation of all available means, both biomedical and non-biomedical, whose purpose is to prevent, cure and alleviate diseases.[8] The broad meaning of medicine is actually an integrated vision of medicine, as it encompasses not only evidence-based-medicine, but also other medical methods having the same purpose as biomedicine. Actually, in its extensive meaning, the concept of "integrated medicine" includes the social aspect of health that requires the implementation of specific non-medical means to ensure the social well being of the person. Therefore, a crucial feature of integrated medicine is to again view patients as the central concern of medicine, rather than medicine itself.[9]

6 Hereafter, both terms will be employed.

7 *The Oxford English Dictionary*, *op. cit.*
In its broad meaning, health has been defined, by the World Health Organisation as "a state of physical, mental and social well-being" (The WHO constitution is published at Swiss RS 0.810.1), available at http://www.admin.ch, accessed on Sept. 1 2001.
For more details, regarding the concept of health, medicine, and illness, see chap. 1.1.

8 Developments in genetics add a "predictive" component to medicine.

9 See BONVIN E. (I), *op. cit.*: 52–56; BOOZANG K. M. (III), *op. cit.*: 251; ROSSI I. (I), *op. cit.*: 18–19.

Authors have used several terms to express the concept of "integrated medicine", such as "unique", "global", or "whole" medicine.[10] Stepan was the first to define one of the approaches to the regulation of medical practice as an "integrated system". In this system, official promotion of the integration of two or more systems exists within a single recognised service. Only a few countries have adopted this integrative health care policy, namely China, Nepal and North Korea.[11] Mickelson later defined "integrated medicine" as

> the concept of forming a partnership between the two often-opposing camps of conventional and alternative medicine. This partnership provides the opportunity to make available a full range of medical care, using all available medical knowledge. It will make available to each patient the care that is appropriate to his needs. Not all patients respond to medicine in the same way, even if they have the same condition. Therefore, they need access to what is appropriate on an individual basis.[12]

10 See Beck A., *op. cit.*: 56 ("pourtant, l'opposition entre médecine académique et médecine alternative, constamment remise sur le tapis et génératrice de réactions émotionnelles, doit être surmontée. Il n'y a pas deux sciences médicales. Il n'existe qu'une médecine globale, constituée d'une part de la médecine clinique mécaniste-matérialiste, quantitative et matérielle, et, d'autre part, de la médecine complémentaire biologique-cybernétique, qualitative-énergétique"); Künzi M. (I), *op. cit.*: 95 ("Gesamtmedizin"); Robard I., *op. cit.*: 36; Staugard F. (II), *op. cit.*: 84–92; White House Commission on Complementary and Alternative Medicine Policy, *op. cit.*: 3 ("A wholeness orientation in health care delivery").

11 Stepan J., *op. cit.*: 287. For further discussion, see chap. 4.2. and 4.3.5.
The World Health Organisation has defined as a key priority the setting up of integrated systems medicine, in order to ensure access to health care for the population (Stepan J., *op. cit.*: 285, 303).

12 Mickelson A. A., *op. cit.*: 128. See also Mitchell Weitzman S., *op. cit.*: 156.

8.3 Requirements for an Integrated System of Medicine

8.3.1 General Remarks

Although the concept of integrated system may be easily explained,[13] the definition of the requirements for such system is a difficult task. In this section an attempt will be made to identify them, in order that the reader may understand the set of problems linked with the concept of "integrated system".

China is a good example of a country that possesses what Stepan considers to be an integrated system. Here, traditional Chinese medicine forms an integral part of the health care delivery system. While the Chinese government has reiterated its commitment to equality of treatment for traditional Chinese medicine and modern medicine as being one of the guiding principles of health. The official policy favours integrated training of health practitioners, which combines both aspects of traditional Chinese and modern medicine. Traditional and modern medicine are practised alongside each other at every level of the health care system. Practitioners of Chinese medicine are employed in modern hospitals, where they work in cooperation with Western-style physicians and where patients may see either type of doctor. Brigade-based services carry out preventive public health measures, although some curative services provided by traditional doctors are also available.[14]

This description is only a partial one but it serves the purpose of illustrating why the establishment of an integrated system requires the conjunction of several elements.[15] The most important requirement is the need

13 For a presentation of the concept of "integrated system", see above, chap. 8.2.

14 For more details, see chap. 4.3.5.2.

15 The WHHCCAMP developed 10 principles to guide the process of making recommendations that may be taken into account here. They are the following: "1. A wholeness orientation in health care delivery; 2. Evidence of safety and efficacy; 3. The healing capacity of the person; 4. Respect for individuality; 5. The right to choose treatment; 6. An emphasis on health promotion and self-care; 7. Partnerships as essential for integrated health care; 8. Education as a fundamental health care service; 9. Dissemination of comprehensive and timely information; 10. Integral public involvement". These guiding principles are according to the WHCCAMP consistent with the 10 rules for health care reform listed by the National Academy of Sciences' Institute of Medicine on ways to improve health care in the 21st century (WHITE HOUSE COMMISSION ON COMPLEMENTARY AND ALTERNATIVE MEDICINE POLICY, *op. cit.*: 3).

for a reassessment of the medical paradigm that still dominates Western health care systems. As a change of paradigm is caused by and results[16] in modifications of established structures and beliefs so also may these modifications be viewed as many requirements to the creation of an integrated system.

8.3.2 Change of Paradigm

8.3.2.1 Introduction

Some authors argue that the current dominating biomedical paradigm has reached a state of crisis and that a new paradigm is necessary in order that medicine may accomplish new steps.

To fully appreciate these arguments, the notion of paradigm and shift of paradigm will be explained. Finally, the opinion of these authors will be presented and analysed in an attempt to determine whether the conditions of a change of paradigm have been met today.

8.3.2.2 Paradigm and Revolution

Kuhn defines a paradigm as a shared set of assumptions, by which individuals define the parameters of their reality and their investigation of this reality.[17] For example, physics was dominated until the twentieth century by the principles of Newton, and by the theories of Ptolemy on astronomy. Similarly, medicine has been centred on the theories of Galen for many centuries.[18] Those who follow the paradigm find acceptance within the community, as they are committed to the consensus reality. On the contrary, those who oppose the paradigm, or who define problems or articulate solutions outside the paradigm, are usually marginalized and not taken seriously, since their method implicitly attacks the foundational order.

Shifts of paradigms may occur by revolution. The process of a revolution follows several steps, namely: 1. awareness of anomaly leading to a crisis; 2. establishment of a new theory, resulting in observational and theoretical recognition; and 3. change of paradigm, which results in methodological

---

See also ALDRIDGE D. (I), *op. cit.*: 53; ANONYMOUS (IV), *op. cit.*: 40ss; MITCHELL WEITZMAN S., *op. cit.*: 139ss; PATEL V., *op. cit.*: 61, 77ss.

16 As one will see below, both phenomena are inextricably linked.

17 KUHN T. S., *op. cit.*: 238.

18 SHAPIRO A. K. (I), *op. cit.*: 10–11. For a development regarding the evolution of medicine in Western countries, see GRMEK M. D., *op. cit.*

and structural changes, often accompanied by resistance. A classical example is the evolution of physics. At the turn of the twentieth century, physics was stagnating. At that stage, the mechanistic vision, based on the theories of Newton, was able to explain all visible and measurable phenomena. However, its limitations became apparent after attempts were made to understand the relationship between time and space, or between energy and matter.[19] The advent of the new physics of Albert Einstein was necessary in order to escape the narrowness of the traditional way of thinking. He conceived matter and energy as two parts of the same reality and linked time and space in a relative way. Only this change of paradigm made possible the accomplishment of new steps within the field of physics.[20] Similarly, Copernicus observed that even though the theories of Ptolemy appeared to describe fairly accurately the course of stars they gave inaccurate indications as to the position of planets and equinoxes. The incapacity of the former paradigm to explain certain phenomena constituted the basis for Copernicus to create a new paradigm, later developed by Kepler and eventually recognised.[21] In the medical field, the incapacity of Galen medicine to find a solution to innumerable health conditions, combined with the emergence and acceptance of scientific methodology, has led to the shift from Galen medicine to biomedicine.[22]

8.3.2.3 Crisis of the Paradigm

Some commentators have observed that current medical research, from the epistemological point of view, is at the same point of stagnation that physics was at the beginning of the 20th century.[23] As we have seen,[24] biomedicine has its limits; it may not entirely explain the health, illness and recovery phenomena, and is not able to offer a solution to every illness it encounters.

19 In the late 17th century, some naturalist physicians criticised Newton's conception of absolute space and could almost demonstrate the absence of function regarding absolute positions and movements within Newton's system. Later on, theories of Maxwell on electromagnetism based on Newton's principle could not integrate prior conceptions. This situation led to a crisis that constituted the background for Einstein's theory of relativism.

20 DAGUET R., *op. cit.*: 20–21.

21 KUHN T. S., *op. cit.*: 102–09.

22 For more details, see chap. 6.2.

23 DAGUET R., *op. cit.*: 20–21; LE FANU J., *op. cit.*: 45.

24 See chap. 6.2. and 6.3.

Other authors have criticised the philosophical approach on which biomedicine is based.[25] As Cohen writes

> in keeping with Newtonian physics and Cartesian dualism, the biomedical model views the body as a physical system, objectively analysable in terms of mechanical parts. Mechanism (the "body as machine" metaphor) and reductionism (the reduction of illness to a set of physical symptoms) dominate biomedical thinking.[26]

This mechanical approach toward illnesses and patients,[27] has been particularly effective in some fields, but it has also been a signal failure in others. Indeed, health is a complex phenomenon, and biomedicine has two main defects that fail to take into account this complexity. First, it focuses only on certain aspects of health, without taking – enough – consideration of other elements such as psychological and environmental parameters. Second, biomedicine has a tendency to analyse each aspect of health as being independent, rather that inter-dependent and thus, it lacks a general view of the problem.[28] Indeed, biomedicine is often unable to pinpoint

25 Certain authors note that the paradigm of falsification of Poppers, to which the epistemology of the scientific method refers, is questionable for two reasons (according to Poppers, when these theories have negative results, they must be rejected). First, it is particularly difficult to formulate a non-trivial hypothesis that one may falsify, and then there are several fields of knowledge that may not be able to be subject to experimentation (such as black holes, the Big Bang, or the hole in the ozone). One may notice that there is no evidence that numerical evaluations (based on measures) are more objective than qualitative evaluation. However, the concept of the scientific method and rationality are based on this premise. See, on the subject, COHEN M. H. (I), *op. cit.*: 2–3; DAGUET R., *op. cit.*: 17–18; ESKINAZI D. P., *op. cit.*: 1621–22 (biomedicine has "the same fundamental quality as traditional systems of health: it reflects the dominant philosophical belief of the society in which it developed [...] It has not been scientifically demonstrated that physical matter is the only reality, materialism, therefore is akin to religion, i.e., a system of beliefs held to with ardour and faith"); SHAPIRO A. K. (I), *op. cit.*: 10–11, 55–60; WICKI M., *op. cit.*: 204–07.

26 COHEN M. H. (I), *op. cit.*: 2. E.g., biomedicine artificially divides mind and body. For a development on the subject, see chap. 1. See also, e.g., ESKINAZI D. P., *op. cit.*: 1621–22.

27 Current and future developments in medicine, such as bionic medicine, gene technology (in therapy, testing and pharmacy), or new techniques of transplant reinforce this mechanical approach. See COURRIER INTERNATIONAL (I), *op. cit.*: 31–38.

28 Some consider that biomedicine, in the attempt to understand the mechanism of illness instead of understanding the therapeutic relation, has lost its essential and central position during the medical and curative activity. Alternative medicines are opposed to the naturalist reduction and parcelling up of the human being. This change of paradigm reinstates the holistic vision with the subject at the central position (e.g., COHEN M. H. (I), *op. cit.*: 3–4; DAGUET R., *op. cit.*: 19–20).

the synergies and relationships between the various aspects of health and between the several factors influencing health.[29]

More specifically, the evidence-based-medicine framework has been criticised, even though it is widely accepted by the medical community. Issues of continuing debate are, for example, the absence of a real "double blind" framework during controlled trials, or the failure of most studies to match active and placebo agents adequately. Several studies have also demonstrated the lack of scientific background to several drugs and treatments, such as psychotherapies or surgery. Finally, biomedicine has also not been able to explain the placebo effect.[30]

The momentary incapacity of science to find a solution to enigmas does not automatically mean that a crisis has arisen requiring a shift of paradigm as the only appropriate response. Indeed, the purpose of scientific paradigms is to set up a framework for the development of research and not to find an immediate solution for all problems. The incapacity of science to resolve a dilemma must be serious enough to engender not only a re-examination of the existing paradigm but to lead to the formulation of a new one.[31] Therefore, it is essential to be careful when interpreting the limits of the biomedical paradigm. Indeed, there may be a considerable period between the perception of failure and the emergence of a new paradigm. This period of relative inactivity was the same prior to the emergence of the paradigm of Copernican astronomy, relativism in physics, or contemporary nuclear theory. As described earlier,[32] the biomedical paradigm had been subject to much criticism and, as such, required time before it became widely accepted. In addition, only fourty years have passed since biomedicine became the prevailing standard.[33] Therefore, this incapacity must be put into perspective, considering that the future evolution of biomedical medicine may be able to explain more fully the above-mentioned phenomenon. For example, with the aid of recent developments in medicine, such as the modern approach of the theory of systems, psycho-neuro-immunologists have been able to describe the harmony of the organism as a homeostasis, which results from a dynamic balance between hormones

29 Although there are studies regarding the interrelations between fields of medicine, they have not been developed to any meaningful extent.

30 For more details on this subject, see chap. 6.2.3.

31 KUHN T. S., *op. cit.*: 114ss. The author states that there is no clear rule as to when a crisis starts.

32 See chap. 6.2.

33 A short period when compared to the length of the former Galenic paradigm.

and other substances of the body.[34] Similar advances in psychology and psychiatry are also likely to occur in the future which will allow us to better understand certain phenomena which are still mysterious today, such as the placebo effect. In other words, the current biomedical paradigm could become more precise or more extensive in its parameters, thus integrating aspects currently neglected by biomedicine.

It is difficult to interpret the facts contained in Kuhn's perspective of a change of paradigm. For example, the proposals[35] to adapt controlled trials to alternative medicines by integrating aspects that had been eliminated from clinical testing, such as the personal or psychological aspects, may be viewed from two opposite perspectives. One is to consider it as a natural evolution of the biomedical paradigm. Another is to interpret it as a desperate attempt to make alternative medicines fit within the biomedical paradigm, or in other words as evidence of a symptom of crisis. While it is currently impossible to give a definitive interpretation of such phenomenon, it is evident, however, that a division among the medical community exists between those who (blindly) support the biomedical paradigm and those who doubt its validity. Only future developments will enable us to see whether this division will disappear, or whether the division will become wider and thus act as catalysis for the development of new theories. However, at present, criticism of the biomedical paradigm has not (yet?) reached the level to generate a crisis powerful enough to engender a shift of paradigm. This is due to the fact that faith in the biomedical paradigm remains powerful enough to hinder such a shift.

In our view, the primary cause of the current division between biomedicine and alternative medicine is due more to our presently limited medical knowledge rather than to different philosophical approaches. Future developments in medical research will certainly help to fill the existing gap between these two conceptions of medicine and also lead to a better understanding of the psychological, environmental, and social aspects of human health. In addition, explanations may be found for abstract notions such as balance of energy, or flow of energy employed by supporters of alternative medicines. While new discoveries should allow researchers to set aside some therapies and to promote new or existing therapies. In brief, the biomedical paradigm will probably evolve and integrate aspects that

34 Advances in genetics also contribute to a better understanding of the human body, such as the individual response of patients to drugs.

35 See chap. 6.3.3.

are currently neglected. From this perspective, medicine should become indivisible, combining both biomedicine and alternative medicines within one single framework.

8.3.2.4 Existence of a Replacing Paradigm

A shift of paradigm requires not only a crisis to engender the shift but also the existence of a new competitive theory that is able to replace the preceding theory.[36]

Some authors have proposed a change of paradigm in medicine, whereby aspects neglected by biomedicine and taken into account by alternative medicines are integrated. However, the holistic paradigm is blurred,[37] in that it is based more on intuition than on evidence. In the holistic paradigm the individual is considered as a whole, while the resources and the potential of self-recovery by the individual are stressed. Here, psychological factors are regarded as being more important during the complex phenomenon of recovery than they are within the current paradigm.[38] The "biomedical healing paradigm"[39] aims towards a non-mechanist and non-reductionist comprehension of the disease process. Medical conditions are viewed as having multiple causes, not only biological, but also environmental, social, and psychological, and are therefore amenable to interventions at several levels, which include pharmaceuticals, nutrition, stress management and exercise. The goal in the holistic paradigm is to find the correct balance and not only to control the symptoms of disease.

Supporters of a new paradigm allege that the introduction of a new paradigm will solve the problems that are responsible for the crisis experienced by the old paradigm.[40] For example, the superiority of the Tabulae rudolphinae of Kepler to the calculation based on the theories of Ptolemy was the crucial factor in the ultimate adherence to the Copernican model. However, proponents of a holistic paradigm are not able to avail themselves of the superiority of their new paradigm for while an abstract general theory may be held to exist, there is still a lack of proof to support such a theory.

36 KUHN T. S., *op. cit.*: 114, 117.

37 See COHEN M. H. (I), *op. cit.*: 2–14; DAGUET R., *op. cit.*: 20–21; MATTHIESSEN P. F., *op. cit.*: 522–36; WICKI M., *op. cit.*: 204–07.

38 There are numerous studies on the placebo effect, but also studies on the high capacity of recovery of athletes (their will to be cured as soon as possible plays a decisive role in the recovery process). For further details, see chap. 6.2.

39 COHEN M. H. (I), *op. cit.*: 2. See also chap. 1.1.

40 KUHN T. S., *op. cit.*: 211.

It is true that there have been developments in the methodological and clinical frameworks based on a holistic vision of health and that the integration of personal, sociological and psychological aspects within these frameworks have violated rules of evidence-based-medicine. However, such developments are still in their primary stages and, as such, have not gained sufficient enough acceptance within the medical community to lead to a re-examination of the current use of controlled trials, which form part of the current paradigm in medicine. In addition, the holistic theory, on which recent experiments have been made, has demonstrated inconsistent results and relies more on instinctual approach than on logical thought.[41]

However, other arguments may also be taken into consideration. For example, a new theory may be more elegant, or more convincing, better adapted or simpler than an old one. However, when a new candidate for a paradigm appears, it has rarely solved all the problems that existed before its emergence, and the solutions it proposes are often far from perfect.[42]

Thus, the basis for a new paradigm does not necessarily have to be rational or definitively exact. However, as Kuhn states, there has to be some basis that gives, at least to a few scientists, the feeling that the new proposal goes in the right direction.[43] It is evident that a decisive feature of a potential new paradigm lies not in its capacity to find a solution to current problems, but rather in its ability to promise solutions to problems that the current paradigm cannot solve. Thus, paradigms must be appreciated less according to past achievements and more as future pledges.[44] Given that future research in medicine will also be focused on how to better understand the relationship and synergies between the gene structure, the mind and the body, it appears that the holistic paradigm is more likely to favor investigations in this field.

41 After having divided the problem (i.e. the human being) into parts, and having understood some of its mechanisms, the holistic theory aims to gather together all the parts in order to understand the set of problems in its entire complexity, and to widen the scope in order to accept other ideas. E.g., certain neuro-endocrinologists sustain that biomedical concepts are reconcilable with several traditional concepts of oriental medicine and with the psyche (Daguet R., *op. cit.*: 21). See also Beck A., *op. cit.*: 56.

42 Kuhn T. S., *op. cit.*: 214–17. The author puts into perspective the validity of evidences. Discussions about the choice of a new theory may not result from logical or mathematical proof. Indeed, such discussions would take as their reference a pre-defined framework. In order to be effective, the questioning of a paradigm must be done outside the paradigm to question the fundaments of the paradigm itself (Kuhn T. S., *op. cit.*: 270).

43 Kuhn T. S., *op. cit.*: 217.

44 Kuhn T. S., *op. cit.*: 216.

The creation of a new paradigm requires seeing the world from a new perspective, which is always particularly difficult, as it usually requires the refutation of existing rules.[45] For example, James Lind undertook a simple and straightforward study, which showed the efficacy of oranges and lemons in the prevention of scurvy.[46] Although the results he obtained showed efficacy, Lind could not fully appreciate them. In this respect Shapiro notes that, "Perhaps the weight of tradition proved too strong and influenced his judgment".[47] Those supporters of alternative medicines who challenge the biomedical paradigm rightly sustain that a change of vision is required. However, it is difficult and sometimes impossible for strong believers in the biomedical paradigm to admit that such a change is necessary.

All in all, the arguments outlined above are likely to favor the holistic paradigm. However, one must remain critical, and not accept blindly any theory, no matter how intellectually attractive it may appear to be. Indeed, the history of medicine is full of examples of actions based on good intentions and apparently sound theories that have resulted in pain, suffering and death.[48]

By definition, paradigms are likely to evolve and shifts are an expected part of such evolution.[49] For example, light was considered as consisting of material corpuscles, following the principles of Newton's optic theory, and was then explained as a transversal wave movement. Today, light is explained as being composed of photons, namely those entities of quantum mechanic physics that possess some characteristics of waves and some characteristics of particles. Similarly, the current biomedical paradigm may also cease to be the definitive paradigm in the future. The history of medicine shows not only that different beliefs have evolved but also that various meanings and explanations have been given to explain health and disease. Although the current biomedical paradigm is relatively satisfying as it may explain some illnesses and provide solutions which cure many of them, it is not conclusive. Similarly, one may argue that the holistic paradigm is not new and that if such a paradigm was well-founded, it would have already become the standard a long time ago. However, a new paradigm might need some time to reach maturity, which was the case for the biomedical paradigm. Finally, various revolutions are likely to occur in

45 KUHN T. S., *op.cit.*: 172ss, 207.
46 SHAPIRO A. K. (I), *op.cit.*: 24, 125–26.
47 SHAPIRO A. K. (I), *op.cit.*: 126.
48 For more details, see above, chap. 6.2.
49 KUHN T. S., *op.cit.*: 31–32, 233ss.

the future, given the complexity of the human body as well as the health, illness and recovery phenomena,[50] and, as such, the current system should not be considered as being the definitive standard.

The shift from one paradigm to a new paradigm as the result of a crisis is not a cumulative process. Even though a shift of paradigm may result in the assimilation of a prior paradigm into a more comprehensive and complete paradigm,[51] it also requires the reconstruction of a field based on new fundamentals that may not only change some theoretical basis but also affect the methods and applications previously used.[52] Perhaps, a new paradigm based on new foundations will appear that integrates both the biomedical and holistic paradigms. Again, the future course of developments within medicine will determine whether the course taken leads to an integration of the holistic paradigm within the biomedicine paradigm or the reverse or whether a new and unexpected paradigm emerges that renders both unnecessary and even obsolete.[53]

In our view, the difficulty in explaining the holistic paradigm rests on the impossibility of considering it as a separate paradigm when it is, in reality, a part of the biomedical paradigm. When proponents of the holistic paradigm voice their support for a change of paradigm they are essentially demanding recognition for those aspects of health care which have been ignored within the biomedicine paradigm. Given the current limitations of medical research and medical knowledge, the hope is that future medical research will enable a better understanding and greater integration of all the components that make up the sum of human health. In this respect, it is possible to view the existing biomedical paradigm as being still incomplete and thus a puzzle whose many parts must still be understood and then integrated in order for a complete picture to emerge.

50 According to Aldridge, "meeting health care needs is a matter of social strategy and political will. True, health is not a homogenous concept; it is differentially understood. Medicine, too is not an isolated discipline but an agglomeration of concepts taken from a variety of fields only some of which belong to the natural sciences." (Aldridge D. (I), *op. cit.*: 53).

51 E.g., the theory of Einstein is considered as including Newton's principles. For more details, see Kuhn T. S., *op. cit.*: 141ss.

52 Kuhn T. S., *op. cit.*: 124.

53 Proponents of the holistic paradigm usually do not propose a complete substitution of the biomedicine paradigm with their own. Their purpose is to bring an additional light and dimension to medicine. In fact, they consider that biomedicine and alternative medicines complement each other. Such a vision may be viewed more as an enlargement of the biomedical paradigm rather than a change of paradigm.

8.3.2.5 Conclusion – Summary

Apart from the current evolution in biomedical research, there are indications that medicine itself seems to be moving along new paths. On the one hand, there are the new and potential future biomedical developments, which have aroused new hopes, but have also, in many ways, continued the mechanisation of the human being. On the other hand, and perhaps as a natural attempt to balance the first trend, medicine has re-discovered some of the ancient concepts of oriental medicine that have emerged bringing new ideas and perspectives.

Although the biomedical paradigm has its limitations, it is still unclear whether medicine itself is in a state of crisis, which is the preliminary condition necessary for a change of paradigm, or if it is still in a period of evolution seeking to better integrate those aspects that have been left aside until now. It seems evident that the current consensus of the medical community regarding the biomedical paradigm is strong enough to impede, in the short- and mid-term, a major crisis from occurring. However, the increasing failure of biomedicine to address the many deficiencies evident in the health care field may lead to a reversal of the current. Indeed, after making tremendous progress, the biomedical paradigm could be limited by its own foundations, as it has voluntary limited its scope of investigation.

In our view, the primary cause of the current division between biomedicine and alternative medicine is the limited amount of medical knowledge we possess at this point. Future developments in medical research will certainly fill the gap between these two conceptions of medicine and the biomedical paradigm should seek to extend itself so as to incorporate fully the holistic paradigm.

The change from a biomedical paradigm to a more holistic oriented paradigm is the preliminary condition necessary in order to establish an integrated system. Indeed, such a system requires that the patient is perceived as a whole and that all available methods that are likely to preserve and restore health, by acting on the biological, psychological, and social aspects of health are used.

A comprehensive and solid paradigm able to replace the current one does not yet exist. Future potential developments in medicine would seem to require at least an extension of the current paradigm. If such an extension results in incompatibility with the current biomedical paradigm, then a shift will result.

In our opinion, the holistic paradigm does not exist separately and is part of the biomedical paradigm. In the future, medical research is likely to evolve so as to better understand and eventually integrate those components of human health that are currently neglected by biomedicine and enhanced by alternative medicines. However, the questioning of the biomedical paradigm has reached a sufficient level to require a modification of the structures built around it.

8.3.3 Patient as the Focus of Medicine

A classic criticism of biomedicine is that it has a mechanistic approach towards the patient. As the biomedical paradigm is founded on biology, chemistry and physics, patients are often seen more as a subject of experimentation, rather than as human beings in need of help. In response, supporters of an integrated system of medicine have stressed the need for medicine to focus on patients rather than for medicine to focus on itself.[54]

The adoption of a more holistic approach towards patients requires the conjunction of several elements. Patients must have free access to treatments and choice over treatment and drugs. This requires the establishment of institutional mechanisms that can not only enforce such rights,[55] but also disseminate and control the flow of proper information to the public.[56]

54 Aldridge notes that "as in the United States, there has recently been a governmental call in England suggesting a radical restructuring of health care with an emphasis on consumer-based service. This emphasis reflects a growing movement throughout Europe in which health care initiatives respond to consumer demand" (ALDRIDGE D. (I), *op. cit.*: 52). Regarding the situation in the US, Andrews adds, "a more patient-centered health care practice would give patients greater options to consult alternative providers. A more patient-centered legal analysis might even privilege that choice" (ANDREWS L. B., *op. cit.*: 1312). Similarly, the Norwegian Committee on Alternative Medicine considers "that the patient's best interests, including concerns of self-determination, protection of patient security and the need for treatment, are paramount" (MINISTRY OF HEALTH AND SOCIAL AFFAIRS, *op. cit.*: 272). See also GUEX P., *op. cit.*: 7–9; ROBARD I., *op. cit.*: 106; STONE J., *op. cit.*: 3; WARREN D. G., *op. cit.*: 261–62; WHITE HOUSE COMMISSION ON COMPLEMENTARY AND ALTERNATIVE MEDICINE POLICY, *op. cit.*: 3.

55 Namely the recognition of such rights and the appropriate licensing and coverage framework.

56 E.g., regarding the way practitioners may designate themselves. For further information on this area, see chap. 7.2.2. See also, e.g., ALDRIDGE D. (I), *op. cit.*: 53; GASSMANN J., *op. cit.*: 309–11; SAGE W. M., *op.*: 91; SELECT COMMITTEE ON SCIENCE AND TECHNOLOGY, *op. cit.*: 9, 94ss; WHITE HOUSE COMMISSION ON COMPLEMENTARY AND ALTERNATIVE MEDICINE POLICY, *op. cit.*: XXII–XXIII, 3, 68–88.

The rights of patients have developed in recent years. For example, they have been integrated within recent regulations dealing with access to medical treatment. In addition, the right to have access to alternative health care and to choose an alternative practitioner are also starting to be recognised.[57] There are also incentives available to encourage physicians to provide information on alternative medicines to their patients.

This evolution is the result of a changing world of health care, where patients have become more aware of medical possibilities, and have become more responsible, and therefore require more freedom of choice. In the future, the development of patients' rights related to alternative medicines will probably contribute to the establishment of a favourable legal framework.

8.3.4 Open-minded Research Framework

In order to establish an integrated system of medicine there needs to be a research framework sufficient to support it.[58] Indeed, the results of medical research provide arguments supporting scientific legitimacy.[59]

However, strict biomedical research does not constitute a basis for scientific legitimacy, for several reasons. As demonstrated earlier,[60] evidence-based-medical methodology is often unsatisfactory, and biomedicine is often unable to explain or cure various illnesses.[61] Furthermore, biomedical research guidelines do not, often deliberately, take into account some crucial components of alternative medicines.[62]

Several authors have insisted on the need to develop a more open-minded research framework. Beck, for example,[63] states that until now only a part of medicine has benefited from the research and teaching undertaken within

57 There are interesting developments in this field in Switzerland and in the US. For more details, see chap. 7.2.2.

58 See chap. 8.2.3.2.

59 Scientific arguments are crucial when regulating medical practice. For example, there is a strong link between research, teaching and licensing.
On this subject, see GUILLOD O. (I), *op.cit.*: 38; MINISTRY OF HEALTH AND SOCIAL AFFAIRS, *op.cit.*: 272.

60 See chap. 6.2.

61 See chap. 6.2.3.

62 Such as the patient-health care provider relationship, or the environmental elements of the patient's life.

63 BECK A., *op.cit.*: 56. See also KÜNZI M. (I), *op.cit.*: 95.

universities.[64] He proposes that both medical scientific paradigms, resulting from a historical process of separation, meet to constitute, by complementing each other, an entity for the patients' good. In these conditions, he adds, research and teaching would be equally distributed according to both approaches. The WHCCAMP stresses also the importance of having alternative practitioners allowed to participate in fundamental research and clinical trials.[65] Thus, the gathering of both biomedical and social scientific methodology could lead to a unified understanding of man and nature.[66]

Alternative medical research and practice have been excluded for decades from Western academia. However, this situation is changing as evidenced by the current increase in research undertaken through various Western countries. For example, several countries[67] have launched national research programs on various aspects of alternative medicines, which involve biological, sociological, legal and economical studies. More specifically, researchers are developing effective new clinical designs in order to assess the value of medical treatments, which consider holistic elements such as psychological, social and interrelationship factors.[68]

In our view, even though the biomedical paradigm dominating current research is questioned, it still remains very strong. Thus, there is little chance that it will be disrupted in the near future. However, it is likely to evolve, through the integration of other ways of demonstrating the mechanism of action and of assessing the effectiveness of medical techniques. As a result, these potential developments could open up new and interesting research perspectives.

64 For that reason, as Beck states, the question of the frequency of chronic illnesses is not well understood.

65 White House Commission on Complementary and Alternative Medicine Policy, *op. cit.*: XIX.

66 See Anonymous (IV), *op. cit.*: 8–18, 46–47, 57–59 (necessity of research, guidelines, cooperation, and open-minded research); British Medical Association, *op. cit.*: 51–59 (research and cooperation); Cost Action B4, *op. cit.*: 8–9 (proposals regarding research); Friedman R., *op. cit.*: 954–56; Select Committee on Science and Technology, *op. cit.*: 8–9, 76ss; Swedish Commission on Alternative Medicine, *op. cit.*: 32–33 (recommending a multi-disciplinary approach).

67 E.g., the Netherlands, Switzerland, the Scandinavian countries and the US.

68 For more details, see chap. 3.2 and 6.3.3.

8.3.5 Integrated Education

The training of practitioners is a crucial element necessary in order to ensure the quality of treatments provided to patients.[69] Within an integrated system, health care providers are likely to provide both biomedical and non-biomedical treatments, or at least to work in cooperation with several categories of practitioners. As a result, therapists need an educational background, which integrates both the biomedical and holistic aspects of health care. Several authors have, for example, proposed that alternative medicines be integrated within the teaching syllabus of universities and that high quality schools be developed in order to train non-allopathic practitioners.[70]

In practice, education in alternative medicines for both physicians and non-physicians has significantly evolved during the last two decades, especially for widely accepted techniques.[71] While such techniques were initially taught only outside universities in an unregulated environment, they have begun to be better organised in parallel with fundamental and clinical research.[72]

However, even if new steps have been taken as far as the training of alternative medicines is concerned, this field still remains at an early stage of development. In Western countries, the quality of courses, as well as their

69 See chap. 7.4.5.2 and 7.5.2. See also, e.g., GUILLOD O. (I), *op. cit.*: 38; LANNOYE P., *op. cit.*: 5.

70 The British Medical Association states that "doctors need to know more about non-conventional therapies, not only for appropriate delegation of care, but also in their role as trusted adviser to their patients" (BRITISH MEDICAL ASSOCIATION, *op. cit.*: 49–50). See also BECK A., *op. cit.*: 56; COHEN M. H. (I), *op. cit.*: 95; COST ACTION B4, *op. cit.*: 28–29, 91; GAIER H. (II), *op. cit.*: 21–22; GROUPE DE RÉFLEXION "MÉDECINES DIFFÉRENTES", *op. cit.*: 93–94; HÄNGGELI C., *op. cit.*; KÜNZI M. (I), *op. cit.*: 74–75, 96–98; LANNOYE P., *op. cit.*: 5; MINISTRY OF HEALTH AND SOCIAL AFFAIRS, *op. cit.*: 274; ROBARD I., *op. cit.*: 271–72; STONE J., *op. cit.*: 95, 142–146, 271–79, WHITE HOUSE COMMISSION ON COMPLEMENTARY AND ALTERNATIVE MEDICINE POLICY, *op. cit.*: XX–XXII, 3, 44–45, 51ss. See also chap. 7.5.2.

71 Such as chiropractic, osteopathy, acupuncture, homeopathy, iridology, massage techniques, naturopathy, phytotherapy and anthroposophy.

72 Medical schools in several countries now propose education programs for physicians, under several forms, including medical specialties, diplomas or continuous education.
For non-physician training, programs in schools, such as in Great Britain, Switzerland, the Scandinavian countries and the US, have started to become more comprehensive, including allopathic knowledge and practical training

content and their length varies widely from one school to another. Indeed, there is a strong need for development and harmonisation of educational standards in these countries. In order to provide the basis necessary to build an appropriate licensing and coverage framework.[73]

8.3.6 Unification of Terminology and Standards of Practice

In order to create and maintain high standards of care, the terminology and standards of practice must be harmonised and, if possible, unified. Indeed, the necessity of good communication among the several categories of health care practitioners requires a codification of medical acts, consisting of a terminology understood by and accessible to every practitioner.[74] Similarly, a need for quality and cooperation underlies the establishment of minimum standards of practice within a specific profession. Harmonisation of the terminology and standards of practice could constitute the basis for a cross-border area of free practice for alternative practitioners. Even though alternative medical practices are more difficult to standardise, because of their esoteric approaches, several efforts have been made to create and heighten standards of care. For example, the American Association of Naturopathic Physicians has issued guidelines, which provide general criteria for naturopathic medical practice. Similar guidelines also exist for techniques such as acupuncture, chiropractic, homeopathy and osteopathy.[75]

If there is a trend toward reliable standards of practice, in both allopathic and alternative medicine, important progress may be expected in this field.

73 For more details, see chap. 7.4.5.2, and 7.6.2.

74 E.g., the American Pew Commission has proposed the establishment of consistent regulatory terminology and uniform standards for entry to practise (directly measuring knowledge and skills), with interstate reciprocal licensure by endorsement (Pew Health Professions Commission, *op. cit.*: 1–8). See also, e.g., Abbing R., *op. cit.*: 273–78; Robard I., *op. cit.*: 271; Sage W. M., *op. cit.*: 83–84; White House Commission on Complementary and Alternative Medicine Policy, *op. cit.*: XXVIII.

75 E.g., several initiatives have been taken in the US and in Great Britain. For more details, see chap. 7.5.3.

8.3.7 Safety and Quality of Health Care

The guarantee of access to treatment and drugs, as well as the freedom of choice within an integrated system is viable only if there is a guarantee that high quality medicine will be provided.[76]

Safety and quality result from the combination of several elements, such as the combination of solid research, leading to high standards in teaching and medical practice and the establishment of appropriate controls on health care providers practice by professional and/or state institutions. Certification by voluntary professional boards and the credentialing system for clinical staff privileges within hospitals and other institutions also play a decisive role. In addition, many commentators have emphasised the importance of interdisciplinary skills and coordination.[77]

Although there is still little case law on malpractice claims and criminal sanctions against alternative practitioners, this does not mean that alternative practitioners provide high quality care.[78] For example, the quality and length of training varies widely among various countries,[79] and there is a lack of reliable standards of practice for several techniques.[80] Thus, even if research, teaching, and the establishment of standards of practice have recently improved in some countries, such initiatives still remain at an early stage of development.

8.3.8 Controlled Liberalisation of Licensing to Practise Framework

The process of preventing and restoring health implies the existence of several participants and an interrelated web of relationships, with the most important being the patient-health care provider relationship.

Practitioners must be able to practise within a framework capable of ensuring the safety and quality of health care in order to allow patients to

76 WHITE HOUSE COMMISSION ON COMPLEMENTARY AND ALTERNATIVE MEDICINE POLICY, *Final op. cit.*: XXIV, 3.

77 See SAGE W. M., *op. cit.*: 88. See, also FURROW B. R. (I), *op. cit.*: 7–13, 56–58, 125–39; GASSMANN J., *op. cit.*: 309–13; LANNOYE P., *op. cit.*: 4. See also chap. 8.3.11.

78 For more details, see chap. 7.2.3 and 8.3.12.

79 For more details, see chap. 3.3.

80 For more details, see chap. 7.5.3.

receive the treatment they want.[81] In our view, this requires the establishment of a controlled liberalised licensing framework, which contains safeguards as to the providing of potentially dangerous procedures.[82] Except for this restricted area, one should avoid possible monopoly in favour of specific professions over the providing of certain acts.[83] In addition, adequate structures aiming to assess the competencies of practitioners and controlling the providing of high-quality health care should also be established.[84] Authorities should also disseminate and verify public information as to the qualifications of practitioners in order that patients choose competent practitioners. In particular, only those health care providers who have acquired a certain level of training should be able to practise under a protected title.[85] The creation of a protected title would be particularly

81 On the subjet, see White House Commission on Complementary and Alternative Medicine Policy, *op. cit.*: XXV–XXVII.

82 Aldridge states that the establishment of a consumer-based health plan is required to "promote an atmosphere of permissive legislation for the control and licensing of a broad spectrum of practitioners" (Aldridge D. (I), *op. cit.*: 53). For further discussion on this area, see chap. 7.3.2.3. See also Cohen M. H. (I), *op. cit.*: 95; Guillod O. (I), *op. cit.*: 38; Künzi M. (I), *op. cit.*: 74–75; Lannoye P., *op. cit.*: 6.

83 Indeed, in practice, monopolies impede the spreading out of cooperative skills and the creation of synergies between health care structures. Andrews notes that "letting the medical model dominate may create greater risk to patients because the licensing system may force people to choose a more harmful treatment approach. [...] The physician practitioner may lack training in areas such as prevention, nutrition, or sexual counselling [...] and thus not be fully competent to handle the individual's problem. The physician practitioner may choose intrusive and harmful tests and remedies when less intrusive approaches could achieve equal or better results" (Andrews L. B., *op. cit.*: 1310). For a development, see chap. 8.3.11.

84 Sage emphasises the importance of ensuring appropriate organisation structures. He notes that "an important determinant of success in any institutional oversight mechanism will be the stability of organisational structures. One problem with individual licensure has been the inability of resource-constrained public bodies to oversee large numbers of mobile professionals. A smaller universe of established organisations with greater interests in avoiding reputational injury and the financial resources to assist regulators in gathering and processing information might well be easier to monitor. However, the current trend toward 'virtual integration' and the proliferation of transient, poorly capitalised enterprises would tend in the opposite direction" (Sage W. M., *op. cit.*: 89).
For more details concerning the establishment of a professional/administrative structure, see chap. 7.3.6.

85 Obviously, practitioners should also satisfy classic entry requirements prior to obtaining a licence to practise, such as physical and mental abilities or morality. For more details, see chap. 7.3.5.8.

indicated and useful in the field of alternative medicines where patients are often unable to separate the wheat from the chaff. Similarly, general information[86] about alternative medicines should be provided and publicised in order that patients be better informed.[87]

Over the past three decades, there has been a clear trend towards increased tolerance and better integration of alternative practitioners within Western health care systems. This has been the result of a slow change of policy. Alternative medicines have had to exist within a legal framework, not originally intended for them. After a period of strict repression, authorities came to realise that such a policy was ineffective and ill-adapted to the situation. Since then, although in theory most regulations have continued to have a monopolistic pattern, public authorities and courts have in practice been more flexible in their approach towards and treatment of alternative practitioners. This change of attitude has resulted in the establishment of new regulations that were, at first, tolerant in their approach and then moved forward to a more precise regulation of alternative practices.[88] Thus, regulatory structures have appeared that on the one hand regulate specific alternative techniques in a similar way to allopathic techniques, and on the other hand permit, with fewer conditions, the practice of non-dangerous or non-scientific medical acts. However, medical acts involving substantial risks remain the exclusive competence of allopathic practitioners. Some practices that were once considered as alternative have now been totally integrated within most Western countries, such as chiropractic.[89] Moreover, it is important to note that no country has changed from a tolerant to a monopolistic policy.

However, although regulations of alternative medicines have evolved, they are not yet uniform in their approach and coverage. In particular, licences to practise and diplomas are not widely recognised between

86 On the subject, see SELECT COMMITTEE ON SCIENCE AND TECHNOLOGY, *op. cit.*: 94ss.

87 For more details, see chap. 7.3.2.3 and 7.3.5.8.

88 E.g., the new general regulations in Belgium, Hungary, the Netherlands, and in Swiss cantons Basel Stadt, Bern, Fribourg, Geneva, Neuchâtel, Solothurn, Ticino, Valais and Zürich. In addition, numerous alternative practices are now regulated by specific medical practice acts in several US states. In Great Britain, the government has enacted the Chiropractor and Osteopath Acts. For further details, see chap. 7.4.2.3.

89 Manipulative techniques are also completely integrated within the health care systems of Scandinavian countries.

jurisdictions. This situation impedes the development of an area of free movement of practitioners based on the mutual recognition of diplomas and licences to practise.

8.3.9 Appropriate Coverage System

In order to guarantee patients real access to the treatment they want, health care providers must be able to freely practise, and the coverage of these modalities must be ensured.[90] In the ideal integrated system, any benefiting medical act should be covered. Although such a system is unrealistic, measures may be taken to encourage the creation of a more satisfying system.

A proper coverage is ensured by appropriate action taken on several levels. First, it is necessary to decide who will be allowed to provide the care needed to patients. It is apparent that only those practitioners who have acquired a certain level of education should be allowed to benefit from therapeutic freedom.[91]

Second, it is necessary to carefully decide which conditions should apply in order to permit coverage of treatments.[92] Classic evidence-based-medicine criteria[93] should not be the sole means of evaluation, as such evaluation should also take into account other parameters, such as personal, social and psychological factors.[94] Some authors have gone further and advocated the introduction of coverage as soon as a technique is taught at

90 Sage notes that "restrictive reimbursement standards, and other legal barriers may limit access to care for large numbers of Americans. In the absence of a national commitment to universal health insurance, the potential for non-physician practitioners to supply much-needed general health services at reasonable cost should not be ignored" (Sage W. M., *op. cit.*: 91). On the subject, see also Cohen M. H. (II), *op. cit.*: 154ss; Mitchell Weitzman S., *op. cit.*: 144–46; White House Commission on Complementary and Alternative Medicine Policy, *op. cit.*: XXV–XXVII.

91 See chap. 7.4.2.

92 See chap. 7.4.3.

93 Namely, proof of the effectiveness, appropriateness and cost-effectiveness of the technique.

94 In this respect, Cohen states, "future legislative initiatives could establish insurance policy definitions of medical necessity and experimental treatment so as to support appropriate reimbursement of ACM" (Cohen M. H. (I), *op. cit.*: 94). See also Lannoye P., *op. cit.*: 6–7.

a university, or recommended *a posteriori* coverage, when the treatment has demonstrated its effectiveness in a specific case.[95]

Another requirement is that the structures providing health care be shaped appropriately.[96] Managed care organisations would be likely to fit within the integrated medical framework. Indeed, if the framework is set up appropriately, patients entering in network could access the most appropriate treatment for their medical condition. The gatekeeper (or first-contact practitioner), possessing an open approach towards health care, could either provide direct care utilising a mechanistic or holistic approach, or refer the patient to an allopathic or non-allopathic practitioner.[97] However, the establishment of appropriate mechanisms in order that patients can have access to alternative medicines within hospitals may also be appropriate.[98]

Coverage of alternative medicines by social insurance and private insurance companies follows a similar pattern of extension as licensing to practise alternative medicines. Indeed, for almost all the countries studied in this research a form of coverage, either private or public, exists for some alternative medicines.[99] This coverage may take several forms. Usually, the coverage is only partial, and a deductible is often required. Education is always a decisive criterion in order to obtain coverage from social insurance, for both allopathic practitioners, as in Italy, and non-allopathic practitioners, as in Scandinavian countries.[100]

The coverage of alternative medicines has, as with the licensing to practise, developed in a legal framework not originally developed for them. The coverage was at first unofficial and driven by pressure from patients and alternative providers. However, recently, some alternative techniques

95 For further details, see chap. 6.3.3, 7.4.3.2, 7.4.3.3.

96 See ALDRIDGE D. (I), *op. cit.*: 53; ANONYMOUS (IV), *op. cit.*: 35ss; MICKELSON A. A., *op. cit.*: 128, MINISTRY OF HEALTH AND SOCIAL AFFAIRS, *op. cit.*: 269.

97 All categories of practitioners should have a background that includes both biomedical and holistic elements, as this will allow them to assess patients' needs in a sensible way. For more details, see chap. 7.5.2.2, 8.3.5. See also KILGORE C., *op. cit.*: 2–3; SELECT COMMITTEE ON SCIENCE AND TECHNOLOGY, *op. cit.*: 109–10 (the Committee recommends that all NHS provision of alternative medicines should be through GP referral or other healthcare professionals working in primary, secondary and tertiary care).

98 See chap. 8.3.11.

99 In the US, Goodwin notes that "all of these advances have contributed to an environment in which alternative therapies are no longer viewed as fringe, so the insurance industry is more willing to accept them" (GOODWIN J., *op. cit.*: 66).

100 For more details, see chap. 7.4.2.

have received official coverage. Such coverage is usually ensured through the establishment of a positive list in a catalogue or benefits, such as has been instituted in France, Switzerland and the Scandinavian countries. In other countries, courts have established specific criteria dealing with the right to obtain a public coverage for some alternative techniques such as in Austria and Germany, when certain conditions are fulfilled.[101] Some recent regulations, namely the US mandate benefit, mandate provider, any willing provider, and freedom-of-choice statutes, have also extended the right of patients to have access to alternative practitioners.

The evaluation of alternative medicines is evolving. Recent initiatives such as those taken in Switzerland use evidence-based-medical methods, but have also stressed the need to take into account the specificities of alternative medicines. Such initiatives involve the use of both quantitative and qualitative methods.[102]

There have also been some interesting developments in the US concerning access to alternative medicines where some networks (HMO and PPO) have established a system whereby the gatekeeper may refer patients to either allopathic or non-allopathic practitioners, using his/her own opinion and the wishes of patients as guidance.[103] There have also been various initiatives in several countries seeking to establish *"integrated centers"*, where alternative and possibly biomedical treatments can be provided together.[104]

Although social security and private insurance companies are today more open and tolerant in their attitude towards alternative medicines, the integration of alternative medicines within existing health care systems

101 E.g., when allopathic techniques are not available to treat specific medical conditions, alternative treatments are covered when they have some chance of success.
For further details, see chap. 7.4.3.

102 See chap. 7.4.3.2, and 7.4.3.3.

103 However, see Berg R., *op. cit.*: 827 (exclusion of chiropractors in US HMOs); Josefek K. J., *op. cit.*: 309–310 (reluctance of some gatekeepers to refer patients to alternative practitioners). See also the decision of the Swiss Federal Court ATF 125 V 437 (insured people having a HMO insurance policy limit their freedom of choice as to chiropractors).

104 See Hofmeister E., *op. cit.*: 126–38 (Denmark); Kilgore C., *op. cit.*: 2–3 (US); Lay B. F., *op. cit.*: 638 (US); Ministry of Health and Social Affairs (I), *op. cit.*: 271 (Norway); Patel V., *op. cit.*: 67–68 (US); Saller R., *op. cit.*: 71–74 (Switzerland); Swedish Commission on Alternative Medicine, *op. cit.*: 29–31 (Sweden); Thomson B., *op. cit.*: 98ss (US); White House Commission on Complementary and Alternative Medicine Policy, *op. cit.*: 21–22 (USA); WHO (II), *op. cit.* (WHO initiatives).

is still incomplete in Western countries. The development of new ways of evaluating the potential benefit of these techniques and current experiences could have either a positive or negative effect upon their future inclusion within insurance schemes. The economical issues implied with the provision of alternative medicines will also play a decisive role in the extension of coverage of these techniques.

8.3.10 Adequate Drug Regulatory Framework

Some preparations are necessary to the provision of certain therapies. As a result, the access to drugs and other substances must be guaranteed in order that practitioners may work efficiently and correctly. This requires the establishment of adequate regulations regarding the production and marketing of therapeutic preparations.

Several initiatives have been taken in Western countries to adopt regulations that ensure adequate controls over alternative preparations and drugs. This is the area where harmonisation of alternative medicines, at least as far as Europe is concerned, has reached its highest degree, although there is still no uniformity among Western countries yet.[105]

The continuing evolution in the drug regulatory field may constitute a basis for the development of better coordination between countries. The initiatives already taken in this area are a strong indication that harmonisation in other fields is possible. Pharmaceutical companies will probably play a decisive role in the development of a free market for alternative preparations, as it already has an impressive potential in this field.[106]

8.3.11 Interdisciplinary Skills and Cooperation

The core and strength of an integrated system lies in its structure. The two fields of medicine, biomedicine and alternative medicines, must be viewed as complementing each other if patients are to be permitted access to the most appropriate health care. This requires institutions and structures to

105 The influence of European Directives on homeopathic products has played a decisive role in this field. In Switzerland and more specifically in the US, differentiated regulations apply to food products and supplements and to anthroposophic and homeopathic products.

106 For a development on the subject, see chap. 7.2.4.

take an interdisciplinary, inter-professional and cooperative perspective,[107] in order to utilise all the potential synergies.[108, 109]

Such cooperation must be particularly fluid among health care providers and between patients and practitioners.[110] However, insurance funds, hospitals,[111] associations, employers and public authorities must also become active partners.[112] The establishment of appropriate organisational

107 Abbott has emphasised the differences between public perception and reality in the work place regarding the attribution of professional tasks (Abbott A., *op. cit.*: 68ss), which presupposes to inform actors, in particular patients and insurance scheme about the competences of each category of practitioner.

108 As the WHCCAMP notes: "A dialogue between CAM [Complementary and Alternative Medicines] and conventional medicine appears to be emerging and efforts should be made to strengthen it" (White House Commission on Complementary and Alternative Medicine Policy, *op. cit.*: XIX). See also the same author at 3, 40–45.

109 From this perspective, monopolies are assimilated as non-integrative trends and should therefore be avoided.

110 Wetzel reports a speech made to the faculty and students of the Harvard Medical School, where its dean said he had "come to believe that it is through the establishment of a unique doctor–friend–patient relationship that most of the healing occurs, whether helped along by surgery, acupuncture, or regular doses of approved medicines" (Wetzel M. S., *op. cit.*: 787).
The British Select Committee on Science and Technology recommends "that each existing regulatory body in the healthcare professions should develop clear guidelines on competency and training for their members on the position they take in relation to their members' activities in well organised CAM disciplines; as well as guidelines on appropriate training courses and other relevant issues. In drawing up such guidelines the conventional regulatory bodies should communicate with the relevant complementary regulatory bodies and the Foundation for Integrated Medicine to obtain advice on training and best practice to encourage integrated practice" (Select Committee on Science and Technology, *op. cit.*: 54).

111 Several authors have suggested the introduction of alternative medicines within hospitals, together with a proper referral system. See Sale D. M., *op. cit.*: 53–54.

112 E.g., Rossi notes that the contemporary world of health care is a social field where science, economics, humanitarian issues and law, both public and private are interwoven. Thus, medicine, when viewed in a broad sense as including all other forms of therapies should not be perceived any longer as a set of activities reserved to specialists. Actually, health is today the concern of all participants. The awareness and willingness of patients to be personally more active concerning their health is an indication of this change (Rossi I. (I), *op. cit.*: 17–24). Mitchell Weitzman stresses the importance of employers in the US, as these are the primary purchasers of health insurance via employee health benefits (Mitchell Weitzman S., *op. cit.*: 132). See also the same author at 146–47.

structures will be crucial in order to achieve such an objective. For example, insurance structures or bodies aiming to ensure a proper practice within a profession should be shaped in such a way as to facilitate interdisciplinary practice and cooperation. The British Select Committee on Science and Technology recommends,

> that those practising privately accessed CAM therapies should work towards integration between CAM and conventional medicine, and CAM therapists should encourage patients with conditions that have not been previously discussed with a medical practitioner to see their GP. We also urge CAM practitioners and GPs to keep an open mind about each other's ability to help their patients, to make patients feel comfortable about integrating their healthcare provision and to exchange information about treatment programmes and their perceptions of the healthcare needs of patients.[113]

There is evidence that interdisciplinary skills are developing. For example, medical education in universities has started to include and integrate holistic components. Conversely, allopathic elements are now being integrated within serious education programs for non-allopathic practitioners.[114]

Similarly, there have been various interesting inter-professional and cooperative initiatives.[115] For example, some regulations have implemented mechanisms to ensure that non-allopathic practitioners are aware of the limits on their practice, and to ensure a proper referral to other health care providers when necessary.[116] Hospitals are also enhancing their cooperation with non-allopathic practitioners,[117] while some have been integrated non-allopathic practitioners within their structures.[118] General practitioners also seem to be less reluctant to refer patients to non-allopathic practitioners. Managed care organisations have been specially interested in the integration of alternative health care within their structures, which is not

113 SELECT COMMITTEE ON SCIENCE AND TECHNOLOGY, *op. cit.*: 107.
See also, ABBOTT A., *op. cit.*: 65ss; BRITISH MEDICAL ASSOCIATION, *op. cit.*: 65–66; FAN R., *op. cit.*: 213–221; WHITE HOUSE COMMISSION ON COMPLEMENTARY AND ALTERNATIVE MEDICINE POLICY, *op. cit.*: XIX–XX. For further details, see chap. 7.3.6, and 8.3.8.

114 See chap. 3.3.

115 See HERNESNIEMI A., *op. cit.*: 126–38; JOHANNESSEN H. (I), *op. cit.*

116 See recent regulations in Belgium, Hungary and in Swiss canton Vaud (in this canton, osteopaths must refer patients to a physician when the patient's condition requires it). For more details, see chap. 7.5.3.2.

117 See, however, SAGE W. M., *op. cit.*: 79 (regarding the control of physicians over the practices of other health professionals).

118 E.g., in Great Britain. See also KILGORE C., *op. cit.*: 3; MICHEL E., *op. cit.* (the hospital of Geneva employs healers to treat patients who have suffered burns).

surprising given their orientation on prevention. Indeed, several HMOs in the US are already experiencing such cooperation and important developments may be expected in this field. More generally, Sage notes a trend within the US health care industry towards inter-professional relationships more than inter-professional boundaries.[119] He states that

> High-quality managed care will require interdisciplinary skills and coordination, with providers of various professions assuming complementary roles in larger healthcare organisations. Efficiency considerations favor giving these organisations flexibility to accomplish their goals as cost-effectively as possible. As a practical matter, evidence suggests that legal restrictions on scope of practice are seldom determinative of actual behaviour in large healthcare organisations. Instead, organisations tend to assign tasks flexibly – sometimes in disregard of the law – relying on internal quality control to safeguard patients.[120]

Even though there is a perceptible trend towards the improvement of interdisciplinary skills and the establishment of more effective cooperation, much still remains to be done. For example, the British Select Committee on Science and Technology has noted that one weakness of the current situation in Great Britain is the lack of communication between bodies representing alternative and conventional medicine. This leads, the Committee notes "to little agreement on educational standards, little collaboration on research and, most worryingly, no clear agreement on information policies within a therapy to help the public understand their options when wishing to consult a practitioner of a particular therapy".[121] Developments in this field are likely to occur in the future, as this integrative vision of medicine should open interesting and even economic ways of treating patients.

119 Sage W. M., *op. cit.*: 88.

120 Sage W. M., *op. cit.*: 88. He notes that the solo physician practice upon which licensure standards are based has virtually disappeared, and observes that studies comparing physician assistants and advanced practice nurses to physicians have not shown differences in quality in situations within the claimed competence of each profession. He suggests also the creation of an interdisciplinary board based on practice overlap and expansion of public representation (idem at 78, 87, 88–89).
For further analysis of the requirements of cooperation and interdisciplinarity, see also, e.g., Aldridge D. (I), *op. cit.*: 54; Andrews L. B., *op. cit.*: 1310; Bonvin E., *op. cit.*: 52–56; Cohen M. H. (I), *op. cit.*: 111; Guex P., *op. cit.*; Josefek K. J., *op. cit.*: 305; Kilgore C., *op. cit.*: 2–3; Mickelson A. A., *op. cit.*: 128; Ministry of Health and Social Affairs, *op. cit.*: 269, 271–72.

121 Select Committee on Science and Technology, *op. cit.*: 55.

8.3.12 Liability Mechanisms

In a perfect system, only careful practitioners would be permitted to practice, in accordance with established standards of practice, and as a result no mistake or injury would occur. In reality, however, liability mechanisms are vital for the prevention and repair of possible injuries to patients.

In Western countries, there is little existing case law on malpractice claims, or criminal sanctions for physical injury or death concerning alternative practitioners, in particular, non-allopathic practitioners.[122] The fact that standards of care for non-allopathic professions are still not well established may play a role. However, the different expectations of patients regarding non-allopathic treatments, as well as the usually low risks involved with the provision of alternative medicines seem also to be important factors.[123]

Although generally courts no longer enforce rules aiming to punish non-allopathic practitioners when they provide alternative health care, some alternative practitioners may still face the risk of prosecution. Indeed, when such practitioners provide alternative health care, they infringe the scope of practice of protected professions, such as physicians. These protective measures (which may have been justified in the past), must today be viewed as aiming more to protect the economic monopoly of certain professions than seeking to protect public health.[124] Therefore, they should, in our view, be ended.[125] To ensure the safety of patients, potentially dangerous medical acts should be reserved to practitioners having the required skills. As a result, criminal prosecution should be limited to infringement of this restricted scope-of-practice by non-competent practitioners.[126] General criminal rules dealing with injuries or death should be sufficient preventive and punitive tools.

In our view, attention should definitively be focused on the creation of new mechanisms to deal with malpractice liability. When patients are injured, compensation is a necessary remedy, but the shape of current regulations based on the evidence of professional mistake is unsatisfactory.[127] The remedy to this situation, as some authors have proposed, is

122 For more details, see chap. 7.2.3.

123 For more details, see chap. 2.6, 6.5, 7.5.3.

124 For more details, see chap. 7.3.2.2 and 7.3.2.3.

125 Furthermore, such protective measures impede the development of interdisciplinary skills and cooperation (see chap. 8.3.11).

126 For more details, see chap. 7.3.2.3, 7.3.3.3, 7.3.4.3 and 8.3.8.

127 See chap. 7.2.3.

the creation of a compensation fund. Such funds could be financed in several ways, for example by the combined contribution and participation of insurance companies, physicians, patients, and government bodies.[128] As Sage notes,

> malpractice liability in interdisciplinary practice may be unpredictable, exposing various classes of professionals to allegations of improper delegation or inadequate supervision as well as errors in diagnosis or treatment. Successful collaborative models therefore require a mechanism for liability to be shared, apportioned, or assumed by a third party such as healthcare institution, without unduly sacrificing deterrence or jeopardizing compensation for injury. Moreover, the market for malpractice insurance will have to accommodate these changes.[129]

Although there have been various initiatives seeking to modify the system of malpractice liability, the evolution towards a better system is likely to take several years. Meanwhile, the "mainstreaming" of alternative medicines that is likely to occur in the future will probably result in an increase of malpractice cases being brought against alternative practitioners.

8.3.13 International Framework

The creation of areas of free movement, and the improvement of transport have made it easier for individuals to travel and to live in foreign countries. Thus, there is a greater risk that such individuals will face health problems while being out of their country of residence. If an integrated system of medicine was correctly implemented, then patients would be able to have access to the appropriate treatment everywhere. Similarly, health care providers would be allowed to practise in foreign countries in order that individuals could receive the treatment they require.

The emergence of an international space where practitioners and patients can freely move in order to provide and receive treatments has been one of the most interesting recent developments. For example, a friendly framework is developing at the EU level in order to regulate drugs and the licensing to practise regime. However, these developments, with the exception

128 GUILLOD O. (VII), *op. cit.*: 35.

129 SAGE W. M., *op. cit.*: 89. On the same subject, Cohen states that "legal authority can more fully and appropriately integrate complementary care if the duty to refer runs both ways: biomedical physicians should have a duty to refer the patient to a chiropractor, massage therapist, acupuncturist, or other provider when the condition is amenable to such treatment" (COHEN M. H. (I), *op. cit.*: 111).
For more development regarding criminal and malpractice liability, see chap. 7.2.3.

of chiropractic soon to be addressed, do not affect the current status of alternative medicines. In Switzerland, there is no regulation, which allows all categories of non-allopathic practitioners to practise within the country as a whole. However, there is a trend towards a better harmonisation of the conditions necessary to fulfil in order to practise 'alternative' medicines.[130] In the US, federal regulations or interstate agreements regarding the practice of alternative medicines are still non-existent.

Competence in the coverage field is still a state prerogative and future changes in this area are unlikely, given the complexity of Western health care systems, especially at the EU level.

The most interesting developments have occurred in the training field. Foreign diplomas are now gaining increased recognition from state regulatory authorities and courts. This increasing acceptance of foreign skills could lead to the foundation of an international platform supporting the introduction of an area of free practice for alternative practitioners.

8.3.14 Coordination of Regulatory and Non-regulatory Fields

The above presentation of prerequisites for an integrated system of medicine demonstrates the existing links between the various regulatory and non-regulatory fields. For example, coverage must be granted to those authorised practitioners who have been admitted by insurance funds. Their admission will depend upon licensing and educational factors and it is evident that education must be based on solid research.[131] As Aldridge states,

> If we are to implement a consumer-based health plan that emphasizes choice and includes "complementary" medicine, then it will be necessary to promote an atmosphere of permissive legislation for the control and licensing of a broad

130 Chiropractic will be included in the new Swiss statute regulating the exercise of the professions of physicians, pharmacists and veterinarians; music therapy will be regulated at the intercantonal level; there are agreements regarding the mutual recognition of naturopath training; and there is an ongoing project for an inter-cantonal agreement regarding the training and licensing of osteopathy. However, non-allopathic practitioners will not be able to rely on the principle of freedom of movement contained in the Act on the Internal Market to practise in another canton. Furthermore, there is still a need for better coordination among cantons.

131 Similarly, liability rules are likely to influence education and standards of practice. Lawmakers will need to consider malpractice liability, education and standards of practice issues when deciding to set up licensing regulations.

> spectrum of practitioners, and to develop financing and delivery arrangements for different modalities. The structure of such arrangements will depend on consumer knowledge about health care delivery and organisation. Information about competing treatments may also bring about an improvement in health care and reduce the escalation of health costs.[132]

In order to achieve a consistent system where regulatory and non-regulatory fields are appropriately coordinated, an overview of the global surrounding of health care delivery is necessary. The state should be the authority entrusted with the power and task of ensuring this proper coordination.[133]

There is no doubt that coordination between the regulatory and non-regulatory fields is improving. For example, in Switzerland, steps have been taken to ensure that post-graduate training be compatible with EU regulation regarding licensing to practise and with the requirements of the compulsory Swiss Federal Act on Health Insurance. However, coordination is also often lacking. In several countries, there is still little correlation between education, licensing to practice and coverage. In France, for example, the teaching of alternative medicines is permitted, and diplomas have been recognised by competent authorities. However, the practice of alternative medicines is forbidden to both allopathic and non-allopathic practitioners. At the same time, the French social security officially reimburses some alternative treatments and preparations, while the National Academy of Medicine does not recognise alternative techniques.

Thus, in general, there is still room for improvement in terms of ensuring effective coordination. This could require the (re-) definition of the tasks and powers of authorities, or the establishment of new structures which have as their aim the achievement of a consistent system.

132 Aldridge D. (I), *op. cit.*: 53. Similarly, Eisenberg states, "our survey confirms that alternative medicine use and expenditures have increased dramatically from 1990 to 1997. In light of these observations, we suggest that federal agencies, private corporations, foundations, and academic institutions adopt a more proactive posture concerning the implementation of clinical and basic science research, the development of relevant educational curricula, credentialing and referral guidelines, improved quality control of dietary supplements, and the establishment of postmarket surveillance of drug-herb (and drug-supplement) interactions" (Eisenberg D. M. (I), *op. cit.*: 1575). See also Cohen M. H. (I), *op. cit.*: 95.

133 Abbott A., *op. cit.*: 62–63; Coburn D., *op. cit.*: 841–50; Furrow B. R. (I), *op. cit.*: 56; Rösch B., *op. cit.*: 24–27; White House Commission on Complementary and Alternative Medicine Policy, *op. cit.*: XXXI, 136–41 (including proposals at the US level).

8.4 Conclusion

Within an integrated system of medicine, the person is the sole focus of medicine. All available methods are employed in order to predict, prevent, relieve and cure pain, irrespective of whether such methods are considered as allopathic or alternative. In this respect, the combined physical, psychological and socio-environmental components of health are taken into consideration. In order to ensure the best possible care, the health care delivery system relies on a network of competences where interdisciplinary skills and cooperation are enhanced to take advantage of potential synergies. Similarly, the right to obtain and to choose high-quality treatment is enhanced and guaranteed.

Although the ideal system portrayed above is still non-existent and would, in any case, be extremely difficult to implement, it is based on sound proposals that could be used in order to improve current Western health care systems.

The creation of such a system could require a shift of paradigm, quite apart from the question of financing its establishment. The current dominating – biomedical – model has resulted from the major change of paradigm that affected medicine, namely the shift from Galen medicine to evidence-based-medicine. A consequence of this shift has been the current division between biomedicine and alternative medicines. Developments in medicine will probably require at least an extension of the existing paradigm, as it seems crucial in current medical research that a better understanding be gained of the psychological, environmental and social aspects of human health. If such an extension results in incompatiblity with the biomedical paradigm, a shift of paradigm will occur. Future developments in medical research and related fields will determine the path that medicine will take in this respect.

In our view, the primary cause of the division between biomedicine and alternative medicine is the current limited amount of medical knowledge we have at our disposal. Future developments in medical research will almost certainly fill the gap between these two conceptions of medicine. As a result of further research in these areas, the biomedical paradigm should extend so as to achieve a full integration of the holistic paradigm.

Currently, it is evident that education, research, licensing to practise, coverage, and patients' rights are all evolving in the same direction, namely towards a better and more complete integration of alternative medicines within Western health care systems. However, the ideal theoretical model still remains out of reach, and the level of integration varies deeply from one field and from one country to another. Furthermore, even if there is still a lack of conclusive international developments in this area, it is apparent that a powerful impetus exists towards a better and more complete integration of alternative medicines at all the various regulatory and non-regulatory levels

Although it remains difficult to predict with any certainty the direction that medicine will take, it is crucial that a critical approach be maintained towards the supporters of both the biomedical and the holistic paradigm. The placing of blind faith in the biomedical paradigm leads to a limited vision of both patient and health, and impedes potential progress. On the other hand, one must view with caution the unlimited enthusiasm shown by the proponents for an integrated system, which is currently based more on speculation than on solid theory and conclusive outcomes. A more effective approach consists in first conducting a critical appraisal of the evolution in biomedicine and alternative medicines, and then to consider the ways in which the various developments in these fields can be used in order to create an improved level of health care.

Conclusion

In daily practice, alternative medicines are no longer marginalised and have acquired a position that is, in some ways, comparable to biomedicine. The existence of this "parallel" world of health care highlights the limitations inherent in current biomedicine to understand and cure patients' illnesses.

Today more than ever there is an open-minded attitude towards alternative medicines. This attitude is reflected in the current trend towards official or unofficial recognition of the role alternative medicines can play in filling various gaps in Western health care systems. Many countries are realising the importance of the contribution these techniques can make in better satisfying present and future patients' needs.

Education, research, licensing to practise, coverage and the evolution of patients' rights are all moving in the same direction, namely a better integration of alternative medicines within Western medical systems. However, the level of integration varies greatly from one field to another and among countries as well, while there is still a lack of conclusive international developments in the field. This process will probably continue in the coming years.

A few countries have already taken the first step in the process of integrating alternative medicines. Some countries not only tolerate alternative practitioners but have begun to actively promote alternative medicines by building a system of education and examination. Some governments have also begun to officially include some coverage for alternative medicines in their social insurance schemes, while accepting that some alternative treatments be unofficially covered by public funds. In addition, an increasing number of private insurance companies have proposed policies which include coverage for alternative medicines. Finally, a certain degree of coordination between education, licensing and coverage has been noted in some countries.

Switzerland is a good example of a country which reflects the current trends surrounding alternative medicines. For example, recent cantonal Public Health Acts regulate alternative medicines from a tolerant perspective, post-graduate education programs for physicians have been set up for some techniques and the five most used alternative medicines are temporarily covered in the basic social health care insurance.

Although there is a powerful trend towards better integration of alternative medicines at all regulatory and non-regulatory levels, we are still far removed from the theoretical model of an integrated system of medicine. Such a model is based on the idea of a unique medicine whose purpose is not only to relieve pain but to predict, prevent and cure illness and disease. All available methods must be employed to reach these objectives, irrespective of whether such methods are considered as allopathic or alternative. Within such a system the patient is the sole focus of medicine, with the physical, psychological and socio-environmental components of health taken into consideration. The patient has a right to obtain and to choose high-quality treatment. To ensure the best possible care, the health care delivery system relies on a network of competences where interdisciplinary structures and cooperation are enhanced to take advantage of potential synergies. This ideal model does not yet exist and would, in any case, be difficult to implement. However, the model is based on sound proposals that may be taken into consideration to improve current Western health care systems.

The contemporary world of health care is a social field where science, economics, humanitarian principles and law, both public and private, are interwoven. Hence, health and medicine should not be perceived anymore as activities reserved to specialists but as a matter of vital concern for all participants. Our societies must decide the type of medicine they want while taking into account the cost of implementation and maintenance.

Apart from the crucial question of how to finance a better integrated system of medicine, a further problem is that the creation of such a system may require a shift or extension of paradigm. The current division between biomedicine and alternative medicine has resulted from the major change of paradigm that affected medicine as a whole, namely the shift from galenic medicine to evidence-based-medicine. Now, developments in medicine seem to require a shift or at least an extension of the current paradigm, as it seems crucial that current medical research better understands the psychological, environmental and social aspects of human health.

When an extension of paradigm results in being incompatible with the biomedical paradigm, it will result in a shift of paradigm. In our view, the above-mentioned division is based less on different philosophical approaches, than on the limited amount of knowledge that we possess at present. The health, illness and recovery phenomenon is extraordinarily complex. Given that biomedical sciences have evolved greatly during the last century, one may only guess as to the potential outcomes likely to occur in the future. Thus, progress in the medical and related fields will almost certainly make this distinction disappear. However, for such progress to continue it will be necessary to remain open-minded, critical and to carefully take into consideration evolutions within and outside the biomedical framework.

Bibliography

Austria

BINDER M., *Zur Kostendeckung alternativmedizinischer Behandlungsmethoden durch die Krankenversicherung*, in: Recht der Medizin, 1997, vol. 4, n° 2: 39–44.

SCHICK P. J., *Die kriminologische und arztrechtliche Problematik unwissenschaftlicher Heilmethoden*, in: BAUHOFER S. (co-editors: BOLLE P.-H., DITTMANN V.), *Sectes et occultisme – Aspects criminologiques*, Verlag Rüegger, 1996, Zürich: 351–73.

SCHWARTZ W., *Von Exorzisten und Heilpraktikern: Geistheilungen rechtlich betrachtet*, in: Recht der Medizin, 1999, n° 1: 13–19.

Case law: Decision of the OGH of Apr. 14, 1994 (SSV-NF 8/19 = DRdA 1995, 22, Binder).

Decision of the OGH of Mar. 26, 1996, ARD-Betriebendienst 4770/47/96.

Belgium

LEMAL I., *Le succès des médecines parallèles prescrit une loi*, in: Le Soir, Jan. 23, 1998.

MIRALLES J., *Homéopathie et Ostéopathie – Pour la 1ère fois, une mutualité rembourse!*, in: La Dernière Heure, Mar. 3, 1997.

NYS H. (I), *La médecine et le droit*, Kluwer, 1995, Diegem.

NYS H. (II), *Belgium* in: *International Encyclopedia of laws* – Medical Law, Kluwer Law International, The Hague/London/Boston.

SERMEUS G., *Alternative health care in Belgium: An explanation of various social aspects*, in: LEWITH G. (co-editor: ALDRIDGE D.), *Complementary medicine and the European Community*, CW Daniel, 1991, Saffron Walden: 61–74.

SCHEPERS R., *The Belgian medical profession since the 1980s: Dominance and decline?*, in: JOHNSON T. (co-authors: LARKIN G., SAKS M.), *Health professions and the State in Europe*, Routledge, 1995, London/New York: 162–77.

SWENNEN H., *The medical profession in Belgium*, in: FURE M. (co-authors: FINSINGER J., SIEGERS J., VAN DEN BERGH R.), *Regulation of professions, a law and economics approach to the regulation of attorneys and physicians in the US, Belgium, the Netherlands, Germany and the UK*, 1993, Maklu Antwerpen: 129.

China

AKERELE O. (co-editor: STOTT G., WEIBO L.), *The role of traditional medicine in primary health care in China*, WHO, 1985, Geneva.

COMMITTEE ON TRADITIONAL CHINESE MEDICINE, *Traditional Chinese Medicine*, Ministry of Health, 1995, Singapore.

JINGFENG C., *Integration of traditional Chinese medicine with Western medicine – Right or wrong?*, in: Social Science & Medicine, vol. 27(5), 1988, n° 521.

ROSENTHAL M. M., *Modernization and health care in the people's republic of China: The period of transition*, in: ROSENTHAL M. M. (ed.), *Health care systems and their patients: An international perspective*, Westview Press, 1992, Boulder.

Denmark

HOFMEISTER E. (co-author: LAUNSO L., BRENDSTRUP E.), *Centers for integrated medicine in Denmark*, in: JOHANNESSEN H. (co-authors: LAUNSO L., OLESEN S. G., STAUGARD F.) (I), *Studies in alternative therapy 1 – Contributions from the Nordic countries*, Odense University Press, 1994, Gylling: 126–38.

RASMUSSEN N. (co-author: MORGALL J.), *The use of alternative treatments in the Danish population*, in: LEWITH G. (co-author: ALDRIDGE D.), *Complementary medicine and the European Community*, CW Daniel, 1991, Saffron Walden: 83–99.

Finland

HERNESNIEMI A., *Co-work between a medical doctor and a traditional healer*, in: JOHANNESSEN H. (co-authors: LAUNSO L., OLESEN S. G., STAUGARD F.) (I), *Studies in alternative therapy 1 – Contributions from the Nordic countries*, Odense University Press, 1994, Gylling: 126–38.

VASKILAMPI T. (I), *The role of alternative medicine: The Finnish experience*, in: LEWITH G. (co-author: ALDRIDGE D.), *Complementary medicine and the European Community*, CW Daniel, 1991, Saffron Walden: 101–12.

VASKILAMPI T. (II), *The role of alternative medicine: The Finnish experience*, in: Complementary Medical Research, 1990, vol. 4, n° 2.

VASKILAMPI T. (III), *Strategies of alternative medicine in the Finnish experience*, Jyväskylä University, Department of Social Policy, 1988.

France

ALMÉRAS J.-P. (co-author: PÉQUIGNOT H.), *La déontologie médicale*, Litec, 1996, Paris.

BOUCHAYER F., *Alternative medicines: A general approach to the French situation*, in: LEWITH G. (co-editor: ALDRIDGE D.), *Complementary medicine and the European Community*, CW Daniel, 1991, Saffron Walden: 45–60.

DE FORGES J.-M. (I), *Le droit de la santé*, PUF, Collection que sais-je?, 1997, Paris.

DE FORGES J.-M. (coauthors: TRUCHET D., PENNEAU J., VIALA G.) (II), *Codes de la santé publique de la famille et de l'aide sociale,* 10e éd., Dalloz, 1993, Paris.

GROUPE DE RÉFLEXION "MÉDECINES DIFFÉRENTES", *Evaluer les médecines différentes, un défi? Rapport aux ministres des affaires sociales et de la solidarité nationale et au secrétaire d'Etat chargé de la santé*, La documentation française, 1986, Paris.

GRUNWALD D., *Pratiques médicales non éprouvées*, Session de l'Ordre des médecins, Sept. 1997, Paris.

HARICHAUX M., *Réformes de l'assurance maladie et protection des assurés*, in: Revue de droit sanitaire et social, Oct.–Dec. 1996, vol. 43, n° 4: 842–52.

LECHAT P., *A propos du projet de création d'un diplôme interuniversitaire d'homéopathie dans les facultés de médecine*, in: Bulletin de l'Académie Nationale de Médecine, 1998, vol. 182, n° 4: 889.

LE GALLOU A., *Responsabilité pénale médicale*, in: Médecine et droit, 1997, n° 24: 26–30.

MÉMETEAU G., *The new code of medical deontology*, in: European Journal of Health Law, 1996, n° 3: 75–84.

MOREAU J. (co-author: TRUCHET D.), *Droit de la santé publique*, Mémento Dalloz, 1997, Paris.

PELLERIN D., *Sur la pratique de l'acupuncture par les sages-femmes*, in: Bulletin de l'Académie Nationale de Médecine, 1997, vol. 181, n° 9: 1909–10.

PORTELLI N., *Le délit d'exercice illégal de la médecine*, mémoire, 1994, France.

ROBARD I., *La santé hors la loi: Les hors la loi de la santé*, 4th ed., Ed. de l'Ancre, 1994, Suresnes.

SAURY R., *Manuel de droit médical*, Masson, 1989, Paris.

VÉRON M., *L'exercice illégal de la médecine*, in: AUBY J.-M., *Droit médical et hospitalier*, Litec, 1993, Paris.

Germany

ALDRIDGE D. (II), *Pluralism of medical practice in Germany*, in: LEWITH G. (co-editor: ALDRIDGE D.), *Complementary medicine and the European Community*, CW Daniel, 1991, Saffron Walden: 75–83.

ANONYMOUS (I), *Gerichtsurteil gegen die deutschen Krankenkassen – Indirekte Anerkennung von Naturheilverfahren*, in: NZZ, July 8, 1988.

ANONYMOUS (II), *Zur Leistungspflicht der Krankenkassen bei Heilbehandlung durch Heilpraktiker*, in: MedR, 1998, n° 6: 269.

ANONYMOUS (III), *Zur Leistungspflicht der Krankenkassen für alternative Heilmethoden*, in: MedR, 1998, n° 5: 230ss.

ARNDT K. F., *Heilpraktikerrecht – Entstehung, Funktionswandel, Berufszulassungsregelung*, Alfred Metzner Verlag, 1985, Frankfurt am Main.

BACKES O., *Die Rechtslage beim Einsatz wissenschaftlich nicht gesicherter Therapieverfahren*, in: MELCHART D. (co-author: WAGNER H.), *Naturheilverfahren – Grundlagen einer autoregulativen Medizin*, K. F. Schattauer Verlag, Stuttgart, 1993: 550–69.

BETTSCHART R., (co-authors: GLAESKE G., LANGBEIN K., SALLER R., SKALNIK C.) *Bittere Naturmedizin – Wirkung und Bewertung der alternativen Behandlungsmethoden, Diagnoseverfahren und Arzneimittelrecht*, Kieper & Witsch, 1995, Köln.

CRAMER R., *Strafrechtliche Grenzen der Therapiefreiheit und der Heilbehandlung durch den Heilpraktiker*, Dissertion, 1995, Köln.

EHLERS A. P. F., *Medizin in den Händen von Heilpraktikern – "Nicht-Heilkundigen"*, Springer Verlag, 1995, Berlin/Heidelberg.

FREUDENBERG U., *Der Leistungsanspruch bei alternativen Heilmethoden gegenüber der gesetzlichen Krankenversicherung, der privaten Krankenversicherung und der Beihilfe*, Dissertation, 1994, Bonn.

GRUPP K., *Rechtliche Probleme alternativer Behandlungsmethoden*, in: MedR, 1992, vol. 5: 256–63.

HAUFF M. (co-author: PRÄTORIUS R.), *Leistungsstruktur alternativer Arztpraxen*, in: Soziale Hygiene,

JUNG H. (co-author: NEUMANN J. N.), *Alternative Behandlungsmethoden*, in: ESER (co-authors: LUTTEROTTI, SPORKEN), *Lexikon Medizin – Ethik – Recht*, Freiburg, 1989: 48–63.

LANZ, *Erstattung einer Heilpraktikertherapie bei Aids-Erkrankten*, in: NJW, 1996, n° 37: 2434–35.

LAUFS A. (co-author: UHLENBRUCK W.) (I), *Handbuch des Arztrechts*, C.H. Beck'sche Verlagbuchhandlung, 1992, München.

LAUFS A. (II), *Sorgfaltspflichten des Heilpraktikers*, in: MedR, 1991, n° 4: 195–98.

LAUFS A. (III), *Wissenschaftliche und alternative Medizin. Paradigmen, Praxis, Perspektiven*, in: MedR, 1994, n° 9: 384.

MATTHIESSEN P. F., *Unkonventionelle Behandlungsmethoden im Kontext medizinischer Versorgung*, in: Zeitschrift für Sozialreform, 1994, vol. 40, n° 8: 520–36.

NARR (I), *Ausübung der Heilkunde*, in: MedR, 1990, n° 5: 283–85.

NARR (II), *Werbeverbot für Heilpraktiker*, in: MedR, 1990, n° 2: 82–83.

NARR (III), *Das Heilpraktikergesetz ist auf psychotherapeutisch tätige Diplompsychologen anwendbar*, in: MedR, 1988, n° 6: 299–304.

NÜCHTERN E., *Die Begutachtung unkonventioneller Heilmethoden im Rahmen der gesetzlichen Krankenversicherung – Probleme vor dem Hintergrund der derzeitigen Rechtsprechung*, in: Gesundh.-Wes., vol. 57, 1995, 437–42.

OEPEN I. (I), *Zur Leistungspflicht der Krankenkasse sowie zur Beihilfefähigkeit bei unkonventionellen medizinischen Verfahren*, in: Med Sach 82: 46.

OEPEN I. (II), *Unkonventionelle medizinische Verfahren – ein Beitrag zur Kostendämpfung?*, in: Versicherungsmedizin, 1989, 41: 53–57.

OEPEN I. (III), *Pseudo-Naturheilverfahren und Aussenseitermethoden in der Rheumatologie*, in: Zeitschrift für Rheumatologie, 1993, vol. 52: 264–74.

OSTENDORF G.-M., *Probleme der Alternativmedizin in der privaten Personenversicherung*, in: Versicherungsmedizin 47, 1995, n° 6: 224–31.

PÉNTEK M., *Die Leistungspflicht der Gesetzlichen Krankenversicherung bei der Anwendung von Aussenseitermethoden in der Medizin*, Dissertation, 1996, Konstanz.

REILING E. (I), *Ausübung der Heilkunde durch Heilmagnetiseur*, in: MedR, 1992, n° 1: 52–53.

REILING E. (II), *Ermächtigungsgrundlagen im Heilpraktikergesetz; Heilkundebegriff*, in: MedR, 1992, n° 1: 54–58.

SCHMIDT-RÖGNITZ A., *Die Gewährung von Alternativen sowie neueren Behandlungs- und Heilmethoden durch die gesetzliche Krankenversicherung*, Dissertation, Duncker & Humblot, 1996, Berlin.

SCHULIN B., *Alternative Medizin in der gesetzlichen Krankenversicherung*, in: Zeitschrift für Sozialreform, 1994, vol. 40, n° 8: 546–65.

SIEBERT A., *Strafrechtliche Grenzen ärztlicher Therapiefreiheit*, 1983, Berlin/Heidelberg/New York.

SCHROEDER-PRINTZER G., *"Aussenseitermethoden"*, in: MedR, 1996, n° 8: 373–79.

TAUPITZ J. (I), *Arzt und Heilpraktiker im Doppelberuf?*, in: MedR, 1993, n° 6: 219–24.

TAUPITZ J. (II), *"Geistheilen" und Heilpraktikergesetz*, in: MedR, 1994, n° 9: 369–72.

Taupitz J. (III), *Erlaubnispflichtige Ausübung der Heilkunde*, in: MedR, 1998, n° 12: 571–75.

Vogel G., *Medikation mit Aussenseitermethoden – eine Kostenfrage?*, in: RdM, 1994, n° 4: 108–11.

Wiesendanger H., *Das grosse Buch vom geistigen Heilen*, Scherz Verlag, 1994, Bern/München/Wien.

Wölk W., *Paramedizinische Therapie und Rechtsprechung*, in: MedR, 1995, vol. 13, n° 12: 492–96.

Cases: H. 6: 269: BVerfG, Beschl. v. Dec. 15, 1997 – 1 BvR 1953/97

Great Britain

Anonymous (IV), *Integrated healthcare – A way forward for the next five years?*, Foundation for Integrated Medicine, 1997.

British Medical Association (Lamont T.), *Complementary medicine – New approaches to good practice*, Oxford University Press, 1993, Oxford/New York.

General Osteopathic Council, *Standard 2000 – Standard of proficiency*, General Osteopathic Council, Mar. 1999.

McHale J. (co-authors: Fox M., Murphy J.), *Health care law: Text, cases and materials*, Sweet and Maxwell, 1997, London: 258.

Budd S. (co-author: Mills S.), *Professional organisation of complementary and alternative medicine in the UK 2000: A second report to the Department of Health*, University of Exeter, 2000, London.

Montgomery J., *Health care law*, Oxford University Press, 1997, Oxford.

National Association of Health Authorities and Trusts Research, *Complementary therapists in the NHS*, NAHAT, 1993, Paper 10, Brimingham.

Saks M. (II), *The changing response of the medical profession to alternative medicine in Britain: A case of altruism or self- interest?*, in: Johnson T. (co-authors: Larkin G., Saks M.), *Health professions and the State in Europe*, Routledge, 1995, London/New York: 103–15.

Saks M. (III), *The alternatives to medicine*, in: Gabe J. (co-editors: Kelleher D., Williams G.), *Challenging medicine*, Routledge, 1994, London/New York: 84–103.

Select Committee on Science and Technology, *Complementary and alternative medicine*, House of Lords – Session 1999–2000 6th Report, The Stationary Office, 2000, London.

Stone J. (co-author: Matthews J.), *Complementary medicine and the law*, Oxford University Press, 1996, Oxford.

Thomas K. J. (I), *Non-orthodox health care in the UK*, in: Lewith G. (co-editor: Aldridge D.), *Complementary medicine and the European Community*, CW Daniel, 1991, Saffron Walden: 125–34.

Warren D. G., *Complementary medicine and the law*, in: Journal of Legal Medicine, June 1997: 257–64.

Italy

MATTOLI P., *La legislazione omeopatica in Italia*, in: AUSSER O., *Handbuch zu den natürlichen Heilweisen und besonderen Therapierichtungen*, Alfred & Söhne, 1992, Meran.

Liechtenstein

HOCH H., *Geschichte des liechtensteinischen Sozialversicherungrechts*, Dissertation, 1991, Schaan.

SCHÄDLER P., *Die "Götter in Weiss" sollen eine Kammer bekommen*, in: Liechtensteiner Vaterland, July 22, 1997.

STOTTER H. J., *Das neue liechtensteinische Strafgesetzbuch*, ex jure Verlagsanstalt, 1988, Vaduz.

Netherlands

BOS M., *Health and health care in the Netherlands*, Zorgverzekeraars, 1998, Zeist.

COMMISSIE ALTERNATIEVE GENEESWIJZEN *Alternative geneeswijzen in Nederland*, Staatsuitgeverij, 1981, Den Haag.

DE BIJL N. (co-author: NEDERVEEN-VAN DE KRAGT I.), *Legal safeguards against medical practice by not suitably qualified persons: A comparative study in seven EU-countries*, in: European Journal of Health Law, 1997, vol. 4: 5–18.

DUTCH HEALTH COUNCIL, *Report on complementary therapies and research*, Dutch Health Care Council, 1993, The Hague.

MINISTRY OF HEALTH, WELFARE AND SPORT (I), *The Individual Health Care Professional Act*, Ministry of Health, Welfare, and Sport, 1997, Rijswijk.

MINISTRY OF HEALTH, WELFARE AND SPORT (II), *Health insurance in the Netherlands*, Ministry of Health, Welfare, and Sport, 1995, Rijswijk.

MINISTRY OF HEALTH, WELFARE AND SPORT (III), *Medical Treatment Contracts Act*, Ministry of Health, Welfare, and Sport, 1995, Rijswijk.

MINISTRY OF HEALTH, WELFARE AND SPORT (IV), *The Care Institutions Quality Act*, Ministry of Health, Welfare, and Sport, 1996, Rijswijk.

MINISTRY OF HEALTH, WELFARE AND SPORT (V), *Preventive health policy in the Netherlands*, Ministry of Health, Welfare, and Sport, 1997, Rijswijk.

SLOTTE T., *Meeste maatschappijen vergoeden alternatieve geneeswijzen*, in: Consumentengids, Feb. 1997: 40–41.

VISSER G. J., *Alternative medicine in the Netherlands*, in: LEWITH G. (co-editor: ALDRIDGE D.), *Complementary medicine and the European Community*, CW Daniel, 1991, Saffron Walden: 113–24.

Norway

MINISTRY OF HEALTH AND SOCIAL AFFAIRS (I), *Report on alternative medicine – English summary*, Norges Offentliche Utredniger NOU 1998: 21, 1998, Oslo.

MINISTRY OF HEALTH AND SOCIAL AFFAIRS (II), *Chinese-Norwegian health seminar*, Ministry of Health and Social Affairs, 2001, Oslo.

Spain

ALONSO OLEA M., *Las prestaciones sanitarias de la seguridad social*, Editorial civitas, 1994, Madrid.

ARJALAGUER X., *Los médicos daràn reconocimiento oficial a homeopatìa, acupuntura y medicina naturista*, in: La Vanguardia, Sept. 24, 1996: 25.

GUZMAN L., (co-author: CASERO J. V.), *Aproximación a la regulación juridica de la homeopatia*, Revista general de derecho, 1992, vol. 48: 3943–56.

MARTINEZ-CALCERRADA L., *Derecho medico general y especial*, Tecnos, 1986, Madrid.

ORGANIZACIÓN MEDICA COLLEGIAL, *Regulación de las medicinas alternativas – Documento de la OMC sobre la proposición de la Ley socialista*, in: Organización Medica Collegial, Feb. 1, 1993, n° 25.

PÉREZ OLIVIA M., *El código de los médicos catalanes da más poder de decisión a los pacientes*, in: El Pais, June 17, 1997.

LAGUNA T., *El quiromasajista no representa competencia deleal para el fisioterapeuta, según la Audencia*, in: Las Provincias, Mar. 19, 1997, Valencia.

ROMERO-CASABONA C. (co-authors: HERNANDEZ-PLASCENCIA J., SOLA-RECHE E.), *Spain* in: *International Encyclopedia of Laws – Medical Law*, Kluwer Law International, The Hague/London/Boston.

Sweden

SWEDISH COMMISSION ON ALTERNATIVE MEDICINE, *Report on alternative medicine*, Regeringskansliet, 1989, Stockholm.

SWEDISH COMMISSION ON COMPETENCE, *Report on the new legislation on competence to pursue a profession within the health and medical services*, in: Statens offentliga utredningar 1996: 138, Socialdepartementet, 1996, Stockholm: 29–44.

Switzerland

AMBÜHL I., *Naturheilkunde auf dem Weg zur Anerkennung*, in: Basler Zeitung, Mar. 22, 1994.

ANONYMOUS (V), *La formation postgraduée de deux ans selon la LAMal*, in: BMS, 1997, vol. 78, n° 25: 943–44.

ANONYMOUS (VI), *Nouvelle systématique des titres de spécialiste*, in: BMS, 1997, vol. 78, n° 39: 1426–27.

AUER A. (co-authors: MALINVERNI G., HOTTELIER M.), *Droit constitutionnel suisse – Volume II: Les droits fondamentaux*, Staempfli, 2000, Bern.

BAERTSCHI B., *Le prix de la santé et le coût des soins – Rationnement, santé publique et justice*, in: Médecine et Hygiène, July 1999, vol. 57: 1464–66.

BECK A., *La chaire de médecine complémentaire à l'Université de Berne: Une création récente*, in: CMS, 1996, vol. 40: 55–62.

BERNER D., *L'exercice illégal de la médecine ou les problèmes juridiques posés par les médecines parallèles*, in: *Aspects du droit médical*, Editions universitaires, 1988, Fribourg: 155–58.

Borghi M. (co-editor: Gassman J.), *Thérapies complémentaires ou alternatives en psychiatrie: Un défi? Un droit?*, Schriftenreihe der Schweizerischen Stiftung Pro Mente Sana n° 20, 1999, Zürich.

Borghi M., *Droit fondamental à des thérapies alternatives ou complémentaires en psychiatrie?*, in: Borghi M. (co-editor: Gassman J.), *Thérapies complémentaires ou alternatives en psychiatrie: Un défi? Un droit?*, Schriftenreihe der Schweizerischen Stiftung Pro Mente Sana n° 20, 1999, Zürich: 259–64.

Conférence des Directeurs cantonaux des Affaires Sanitaires (I), *Rapport du groupe de travail "Autorisations de pratiquer les professions du domaine de la santé"*, CDS, 2000, Bern, available at: http://www.sdk-cds.ch/fr/berufsbildung-f.html, accessed July 30 2001.

Conférence des Directeurs cantonaux des Affaires Sanitaires (II), *Rapport du groupe de travail "Critères pour déterminer l'aptitude d'une formation à être reconnue ou réglementée"*, CDS, 1997, Bern, available at: http://www.sdk-cds.ch/fr/berufsbildung-f.html, accessed July 30 2001.

Corboz B., *Les principales infractions – Volume II*, Stämpfli, 1999, Bern.

Cottier T. (co-author: Merkt B.) (I), *La fonction fédérative de la liberté du commerce et de l'industrie et la loi sur le marché intérieur suisse: L'influence du droit européen et du droit international économique*, in: *De la Constitution – Etudes en l'honneur de Jean-François Aubert*, Helbing & Lichtenhahn, 1996, Basel: 449–71.

Cottier T. (co-author: Wagner M.) (II), *Das neue Bundesgesetz über den Binnenmarkt (BGBM) – Übersicht und kurzer Kommentar*, in: AJP, 1995, n° 12: 1582ss.

Daguet R., *Per una cura integrata: Riflessioni su medicina moderna e terapie alternative*, in: Borghi M. (co-editor: Gassman J.), *Thérapies complémentaires ou alternatives en psychiatrie: Un défi? Un droit?*, Schriftenreihe der Schweizerischen Stiftung Pro Mente Sana n° 20, 1999, Zürich: 15–21.

Dayer P., *Le groupe multidisciplinaire d'étude des médecines non-conventionnelles de Genève*, in: CMS, 1996, vol. 40: 67–69.

Diezi J., *L'enseignement informatif sur les médecines parallèles à la faculté de médecine de Lausanne*, in: CMS, 1996, vol. 40: 63–65.

Duc J.-L., *Médecines parallèles et assurances sociales (plus spécialement au regard de la nouvelle LAMal)*, in: CMS, 1996, vol. 40, n° 1: 41–51.

Dumoulin J.-F. (co-authors: Guillod O., Méroz J.-C.), *L'impact d'une adhésion suisse à l'Union Européenne sur le droit de la santé*, in: Cottier T. (co-editor: Kopse A. R.), *L'adhésion de la Suisse à l'Union Européenne – Enjeux et conséquences*, Schulthess, 1998, Zürich: 925–48.

Feuardent R., *Qu'entend-on par médecines alternatives?*, in: RMSR, 1986, vol. 106: 93–95.

Fischer S., *Commission de surveillance des professions de la santé: La situation en Suisse romande*, in: Médecine et Hygiène, 1999, vol. 57: 979.

Fréchelin K. (II), *Conséquences de l'accord sur la libre circulation des personnes en matière d'assurance-maladie, d'assurance-accidents et d'allocations familiales*, in: Sécurité Sociale, 1999, n° 3: 132–34.

Frey F. (co-editor: Baumann P. H.), *Supplementum 62, FNRS-PNR 34: Médecines complémentaires*, Schwabe, 1994, Basel.

GASPOZ J.-M., *Adéquation des procédures en cardiologie: Utilisation excessive, adéquate ou insuffisante?*, in: Médecine et Hygiène, 1999, vol. 57, n° 2275: 2090–93.

GASSMANN J., *Therapiewahlfreiheit in der stationären Psychiatrie – auch für komplementäre Methoden!*, in: BORGHI M. (co-editor: GASSMAN J.), *Thérapies complémentaires ou alternatives en psychiatrie: Un défi? Un droit?*, Schriftenreihe der Schweizerischen Stiftung Pro Mente Sana n° 20, 1999, Zürich: 309–13.

GIGER M., *Les médecines parallèles dans le réseau de la Fédération des Médecins Suisses*, in: CMS, 1996, vol. 40: 53–54.

GROSS J., *Alternative Behandlungsmethoden in der Psychiatrie – Ist die Wahlfreiheit des Patienten noch finanzierbar?*, in: BORGHI M. (co-editor: GASSMAN J.), *Thérapies complémentaires ou alternatives en psychiatrie: Un défi? Un droit?*, Schriftenreihe der Schweizerischen Stiftung Pro Mente Sana n° 20, 1999, Zürich: 5–7.

GUGGENHEIM S., *Naturopathes et guérisseurs – Autoriser ou interdire?*, in: Argus, Feb. 7, 1997.

GUILLOD O. (I), *Rebouteux, naturopathes et guérisseurs: Pour un traitement légal alternatif*, Recueil de Jurisprudence Neuchâtelois, 1989, Neuchâtel: 9–45.

GUILLOD O. (II), *Legislation: A new Federal Act on Health Insurance*, in: European Journal of Health Law, 1995: 271–79.

GUILLOD O. (III), *Market integration in a small federal state (Switzerland): The role of public health*, in: COTTIER T., MAVROIDIS P. C. (editors), *Regulatory barriers and the principle of non-discrimination in world trade law*, The University of Michigan Press, 1999: 211–30.

GUILLOD O. (co-author: ZENGER C., RUCKSTUHL N.) (IV), *Structure et organisation de la santé publique en Suisse*, in: GUTZWILLER F. (co-editor: JEANNERET O.), *Médecine sociale et préventive – Santé publique*, Hans Huber, 1999, Bern: 229–35.

GUILLOD O. (co-author: SPRUMONT D.) (V), *Le droit à la santé: Un droit en émergence*, in: *De la Constitution, Etudes en l'honneur de Jean-François Aubert*, Basel, 1996: 337ss.

GUILLOD O. (VI), *Le consentement éclairé du patient*, Dissertation, Editions Ides et Calendes, 1986, Neuchâtel.

GUILLOD O. (VII), *Le droit médical: Quelques (r)évolutions récentes*, in: BERTRAND T. (co-authors: HARDING T.-W, MANDOFIA BERNY M., UMMEL M.), *Médecin et droit médical*, Editions Médecine et Hygiène, 1998, Chêne-Bourg: 21–36.

GUTZWILLER F. (co-editor: JEANNERET O.), *Médecine sociale et préventive – Santé publique*, Hans Huber, 1999, Bern.

HÄFELIN U. (co-author: HALLER W.), *Schweizerisches Bundesstaatrecht*, 3. Auflage, 1993.

HÄNGGELI C. (I), *Une étape décisive pour la FMH*, in: BMS: 1998, vol. 79, n° 48: 2447–48.

HÄNGGELI C. (II), *La formation postgraduée en pleine mutation: Chance ou risque?*, in: BMS, 2000, vol. 81, n° 35: 1896–98.

HEUSSER P., *Kriterien zur Beurteilung des Nutzens von komplementärmedizinischen Methoden*, Bundesamt für Sozialversicherung, Mar. 1998, Bern.

HONSELL H. (co-ed.: BÄR W.), *Handbuch des Arztrechtes*, Schulthess, 1994, Zürich.

JUNOD A.-F. (I), *Analyse décisionnelle et/ou "evidence-based medicine"?*, in: Médecine et Hygiène, 1997, vol. 55: 2027–29.

JUNOD A.-F. (II), *Définition et évaluation de l'"appropriateness"*, in: Médecine et Hygiène, 1999, vol. 57, n° 2275: 2078–81.

KAHIL-WOLFF B., *L'accord sur la libre circulation des personnes Suisse–CE et le droit des assurances sociales*, in: Semaine Judiciaire, 2001, vol. 123, n° 4: 81–135.

KOCH-WULKAN P. W., *Evaluation de l'utilité des méthodes de médecines "parallèles": on touche au but!*, in: Sécurité Sociale, 1998, n° 1: 21.

KUHN H. P., *Autorisation de pratiquer: Deux fois non, une fois oui*, in: BMS, 1999, vol. 80, n° 40: 2399–2401.

KÜNZI M. (I), *Komplementärmedizin und Gesundheitsrecht*, Helbing & Lichtenhahn Verlag AG, 1996, Basel.

KÜNZI M. (II), *Komplementärmedizin und Gesundheitsrecht*, in: FREY F. (co-editor: BAUMANN P. H.), *Supplementum 62, FNRS-PNR 34: Médecines complémentaires*, Schwabe, 1994, Basel: 7–12.

KÜNZI M. (III), *Naturheilerinnen und Naturheiler: Zulassen, dulden oder verbieten? Inventar, Kritik, Empfehlungen*, in: Schweizerische Zeitschrift für Ganzheitsmedizin, vol. 2, 1997.

KÜNZI M. (IV), *Postulats concernant la santé publique en 1996, à défaut de résultats certains, bien des choses restent (dangereusement) confinées dans le domaine théorique*, in: Der Arzt und sein Patient, Politique de la santé en Suisse, vol. 8, 1997.

MANAÏ D., *Les droits du patient face à la médecine contemporaine*, Helbing & Lichtenhahn, 1999, Basel/Genève/München.

MARTENET V. (co-author: RAPIN C.), *Le marché intérieur suisse – Les mesures restrictives du droit suisse à la lumière du droit européen*, Staempfli (Cahiers Suisse de l'Intégration Européenne), 1999, Bern.

MAURON P., *Unter den Rädern des neuen KVG*, in: Schweizer Versicherung, Feb. 1, 1996.

MÉROZ J.-C., *Les "Directives pour les médicaments homéopathiques" vers l'approbation de l'Assemblée de l'UICM*, in: Tribune Médicale, 1997, n° 47.

METTLER H., *Particularités appenzelloises*, in: Hôpital Suisse, 1989, vol. 7: 14–15.

MICHEL E., *L'hôpital de Genève fait bon ménage avec les guérisseurs à distance*, in: Le Temps, Aug. 12, 1999.

OFFICE FÉDÉRAL DES ASSURANCES SOCIALES, *Manuel de standardisation pour l'évaluation médicale et économique des prestations médicales*, Office Fédéral des Assurances Sociales, 1998, Bern.

PACCAUD F. (co-author: GUTZWILLER F.), *Structure et organisation de la santé publique en Suisse*, in: GUTZWILLER F. (co-editor: JEANNERET O.), *Médecine sociale et préventive – Santé publique*, Hans Huber, 1999, Bern: 223–28.

PERRIER A., *Les critères d'adéquation sont-ils bien adéquats?*, in: Médecine et Hygiène, 1999, vol. 57, n° 2275: 2082–88.

PETIT-PIERRE M.-C. (I), *L'homéopathie et la médecine chinoise décrochent le titre envié de spécialité*, in: Le Temps, Oct. 24, 1998.

PETIT-PIERRE M.-C. (II), *Les médecines alternatives ont six ans pour prouver leur efficacité*, in: Le Temps, July 14, 1998.

PETIT-PIERRE M.-C. (III), *Les médecines complémentaires pourraient bientôt être remboursées*, in: Le Temps, Apr. 14, 1998.

PLOTKE H., *Gegenseitige Anerkennung von Diplomen und Berufserfahrung in der EWG und Auswirkungen auf die Schweiz*, Helbing & Lichtenhahn, 1991, Basel.

POLEDNA T. (co-author: NÜESCH S.) (I), *Komplementärmedizin in der sozialen Krankenversicherung*, in: AJP, 2001: 638–44.

POLEDNA T. (co-author: BERGER B.) (II), *Öffentliches Gesundheitsrecht*, Stämpfli, 2002, Bern.

REETZ C., *Komplementärmedizin in der Grundversicherung – auch für stationäre PsychiatriepatientInnen?*, in: BORGHI M. (co-editor: GASSMAN J.), *Thérapies complémentaires ou alternatives en psychiatrie: Un défi? Un droit?*, Schriftenreihe der Schweizerischen Stiftung Pro Mente Sana n° 20, 1999, Zürich: 259–64.

DE REYNIER V. (co-author: RIVA E.), *Les effets de la loi fédérale sur le marché intérieur (LMI) sur les professionnels de la santé détenteurs d'une autorisation de pratiquer délivrée par un canton*, Conférence des Directeurs cantonaux des Affaires Sanitaires, 1998, Bern.

RICHLI P. (I), *Hoheitliche Leistungspflichten und Leistungsbeschränkungen im Gesundheitswesen als Grundrechtsproblem*, in: Revue Suisse d'Assurances, 1998, n° 9–10: 243–58.

RICHLI P. (co-author: WUNDER K.) (II), *Über die Möglichkeiten zur Beschränkung des freien Warenverkehrs nach dem Binnenmarktgesetz*, in: AJP, 1996, n° 6: 908–17.

RÖSCH B., *Die Stellung der Erfahrungsheilkundigen aus verfassungs- und verwaltungsrechtlicher Sicht, dargestellt am Beispiel der geistig Heilenden*, Dissertation, Helbing & Lichtenhahn Verlag, 1994, Basel.

SALLER R., *Médecine naturelle (Naturheilkunde) à l'Université de Zürich*, in: CMS, 1996, vol. 40: 71–74.

SARASIN F.-P., *Méthode de mesure de l'adéquation des soins et recommandations pour la pratique clinique*, in: Médecine et Hygiène, 1999, vol. 57, n° 2275: 2098–2102.

SCHLUND G.-H., *Alternativmedizin aus zivilrechtlicher Sicht*, in: Krankenhaus und Recht, 1999, n° 2: 34ss.

SIMONET L., *Adéquation des soins: Qu'en est-il du patient?*, in: Médecine et Hygiène, 1999, vol. 57, n° 2275: 2094–97.

SOCIÉTÉ NEUCHÂTELOISE DE MÉDECINE, *Les médecines dites "parallèles"*, in: SNM News, Dec. 1998, n° 20.

SOMMER J. H. (co-author: BÜRGI M.), *Gesundheitsökonomische Analyse der Wirkungen des Angebotes komplementärmedizinischer Leistungen der Krankenkassen*, in: FREY F. (co-editor: BAUMANN P. H.), *Supplementum 62, FNRS-PNR 34: Médecines complémentaires*, Schwabe, 1994, Basel: 13–17.

SPAHNI M., *Le tri des prestataires de médecine alternative est un terrible casse-tête*, in: Le Temps, Jan. 10, 2000.

SPRUMONT D. (I), *Droit des patients: Survol de la législation*, in: Plaidoyer, 1998, n° 4: 41–46.

SPRUMONT D. (II), *La protection des sujets de recherche: Notamment dans le domaine biomédical*, thèse, Stämpfli, Bern, 1993.

STEFFEN G., *Droit aux soins et rationnement: Approche d'une définition des soins nécessaires*, thèse, Stämpfli, 2002, Bern.

STRATENWERTH G., *Schweizerisches Strafrecht – Besonderer Teil I: Straftaten gegen Individualinteressen*, 5th ed., Stämpfli, 1995, Bern.

VALLENDER K. A., *Grundzüge der "neuen" Wirtschaftsverfassung*, in: AJP, 1999: n° 6.

VASSALLI P., *Forum Louis-Jeantet sur les coûts de la santé 1998*, Fondation Louis-Jeantet de médecine, Genève, 1998.

WICKI M., *Komplementärmedizin im Rahmen des Rechtes*, Dissertation, Stämpfli, 1998, Bern.

WIEGAND W., *3. Kapitel – Die Aufklärungspflicht und die Folgen ihrer Verletzung*, in: HONSELL H. (co-ed.: BÄR W.), *Handbuch des Artzrechtes*, Schulthess, 1994, Zürich: 139–41.

ZENGER C., *Geschichte und Bedeutung des eidgenössischen Freizügigkeitsgesetzes*, in: Schweizerische Ärztezeitung, 1986: 2039ss.

Cantonal cases: Decision 525/97 TA BE.
Decision 78/98 TA SZ.
Decision 467/98 TA GE.
Decision 535/98 TA TG.
Decision 663/98 Sozialversicherungsgericht ZH.
Decision 63/99 TAss VD.
Decision 187/99 Sozialversicherungsgericht ZH.
Decision 321/99 Versicherungsdreiergericht BS.
Decision 437/99 Versicherungsgericht AG.
Decision 666/99 Versicherungsgericht AG.
Decision 1/99 Versicherungsgericht SO et 479/98 TA ZG.
Decision 540/99 TAss VD.
Decision 742/99 et 743/99 TAss VD.

Federal cases: ATF 97 I 504.
ATF 103 Ia 259.
ATF 103 Ia 272.
ATF 104 Ia 486.
ATF 109 Ia 180.
ATF 110 Ia 99.
ATF 112 Ia 322.
ATF 117 Ia 440.
ATF 119 Ia 35.
ATF 119 Ia 382.
ATF 121 I 367.
ATF 122 I 101.
ATF 123 I 212.
ATF 124 I 310.
ATF 125 I 276.
ATF 125 I 322.
ATF 125 I 335.
ATF 125 II 56.
ATF 125 V 323.
ATF 125 V 437.

ATF 126 III 353.
ATF 127 III 68.
ATF 127 III 289.
Decision of June 9 1995, in RSJ 1995, 713 E. 3

United States

ABBOTT A., *The system of professions: An essay on the division of expert labor*, University of Chicago Press, 1988, Chicago.

AMERICAN CANCER SOCIETY, *Questionable methods of cancer management: The committee for freedom of choice in medicine, Inc.*, in: a Cancer Journal for Clinicians, 1993, vol. 43, n° 2: 117–23.

AMERICAN CHIROPRACTIC ASSOCIATION, *Alternative medicine: Hearing before the subcommittee on labor, health, and human services, and education and related agencies of the senate committee on appropriations*, American Chiropractic Association, 103d Congress, 1st Sess. 153.

AMERICAN MEDICAL ASSOCIATION, *Principles of medial ethics*, American Medical Association, Chicago, 1956, chap. 3.1.

ANDREWS L. B., *The shadow health care system: Regulation of alternative health care providers*, in: Houston Law Review, 1996, vol. 32: 1273–317.

ANNAS G. J., *The right of patients*, 2nd edition, Humana Press, 1992, Totawa.

BERG R., *Note, HMO exclusion of chiropractors*, in: S. Cal. L. Rev., 1993, vol. 66: 807–38.

BERMAN B. M. et al., *Physicians' attitudes toward complementary or alternative medicine: A regional survey*, in: J. Am. Board Fam. Prac, 1995, vol. 8: 361ss.

BOOZANG K. M. (I), *Western medicine opens the door to alternative medicine*, in: American Journal of Medicine, 1998, vol. 24, n° 2/3: 185–212.

BOOZANG K. M. (II), *Is the alternative medicine? Managed care apparently thinks so*, in: Connecticut Law Review, Winter 2000, vol. 32: 567–613.

BOOZANG K. M. (III), *National policy on CAM: The White House Commission report*, in: The Journal of Law, Medicine and Ethics, 2003, vol. 31, n° 2: 251–61.

BRADFORD G. E., *The "respectable minority" doctrine in Missouri medical negligence law*, in: Journal of the Missouri Bar, Dec. 2000, vol. 56: 326–34.

BRETT A. S. (co-author: MCCULLOUGH L. B.), *When patients request specific interventions*, in: New England Journal of Medicine, 1986, vol. 315: 1347ss.

CALLENDER A., *Buckeye chiropractic: Turbulence in a limited branch of medicine, 1915–1975*, in: Chiropract. Hist., Dec. 1995, vol. 15, n° 2: 1532–34.

CHERKIN D. C. (co-editor: MOOTZ R. D.), *Chiropractic in the United States: Training, practice and research*, Agency for Health Care Policy and Research, 1997, Rockville.

CLINE J. S. (co-author: ROSTEN K. A.), *The effect of policy language on the containment of health care cost*, in: Tort and Insurance Law Journal, 1985, vol. 21: 120.

COBURN D., *State authority, medical dominance, and trends in the regulation of the health professions: The Ontario case*, in: Social-Science-and-Medicine, Oct. 1993, vol. 37, n° 7: 841–50.

COHEN M. H. (I), *Complementary and alternative medicine – Legal boundaries and regulatory perspectives*, The Johns Hopkins University Press, 1998, London & Oxford.

COHEN M. H. (II), *Holistic health care: Including alternative and complementary medicine in insurance and regulatory schemes*, in: Arizona Law Review, Spring 1996, vol. 38: 83–164.

COHEN M. H. (III), *Beyond complementary medicine*, The University of Michigan Press, 2000.

COLGATE M. A., *Gaining insurance coverage for alternative therapies*, in: Journal of Health Care Marketing, 1995, vol. 15, n° 1: 24, 27.

COULTER, *Divided Legacy*, in: JAMA, vol. 36, n° 525: 430.

DANNE W. H., *Acupuncture as illegal practice of medicine*, in: A.L.R.3D, 1977–1998, vol. 72: 1257ss.

DOSSEY L. (co-author.: SWYFERS J. P.), *Alternative medicine: Expanding horizons*, NIH publication n° 94-066, 1994: XXXIX–XLI.

DRECHSLER C. T., *Physicians, surgeons and other healers*, in: American Jurisprudence, 2nd edition, Apr. 1996.

EISENBERG D. M. (III), *Advising patients who seek alternative medical therapies*, in: Ann. Intern. Med., 1997; n° 127: 61–69.

ESKINAZI D. P., *Factors that shape alternative medicine*, in: JAMA, 1998, vol. 280, n° 18: 1621–23.

FEASBY C., *Determining standard of care in alternative contexts*, in: Health Law Journal, 1997, vol. 5: 45–65.

FURROW B. R. (co-authors: GREANEY T. L., JOST T., SCHWARTZ R. L.) (I), *Health law*, West Publishing, 1995, St Paul.

FURROW B. R. (co-authors: GREANEY T. L., JOST T., SCHWARTZ R. L.) (II), *Health law: Cases, materials and problems*, West Publishing, 1997, St Paul.

FURROW B. R. (co-authors: GREANEY T. L., JOHNSON S. H., JOST T. S., SCHWARTZ R. L.) (III), *The law of health care organisation and finance*, West Publishing, 1997, St Paul.

GILHOOLEY M., *Herbal remedies and dietary boundaries of drug claims and freedom of choice*, in: Florida Law Review, 1997, vol. 49: 663ss.

GOLDBERG B. D., *As alternative increases, so malpractice claims*, in: Med. Malpractice l. & Strategy, 1999, vol. 16, n° 7: 1ss.

GOODWIN J., *A health insurance revolution*, in: New Age Journal's Guide to Holistic Medicine, 1997–1998: 66–69.

GREANEY T. L., *Public licensure, private certification, and credentialing of medical professionals: an antitrust perspective*, in: JOST T. S., *Regulation of the healthcare professions*, Health Administration Press, 1996, Chicago: 149–68.

GRIFFIN K., *Alternative care: Finally some insurance coverage*, in: Health, Oct. 1995.

HALL M., *Institutional control of physician behaviour: Legal barriers to health care cost containment*, in: U. Pa. L. Rev., 1988, vol. 137, n° 80: 451ss.

HARTLEY J. E., *Refusal to cover alternative providers or new technology*, in: *Antitrust in the healthcare field*, National Health Lawyers Association, 1992, Washington.

HOFFMEYER P., *Etats-Unis: Appel pour une réglementation plus stricte des traitements à base de plantes*, in: Médecine et Hygiène, 1998, vol. 56, n° 225: 1861.

HOLCOMBE R. G., *Eliminating scope of practice and licensing laws to improve health care*, in: The Journal of Law, Medicine and Ethics, 2003, vol. 31, n° 2: 236–46.

HOOPER (co-authors: LUNDY & BOOKMAN), *ERISA does not preempt state plan requiring alternative medicine offerings*, in: Cal. Health L. Monitor, 1998, vol. 6, n° 19: 2ss.

JACKSON R. B., *"Empyricism" in Kansas: Chiropractic's legal struggle, 1906–1915*, in: J. Manipulative Physiol. Ther., Feb. 1996, vol. 19, n° 2: 113–17.

JAPSEN B., *Cost-conscious providers take to holistic medicine; once scorned or banned, alternative treatments have gone mainstream as less expensive but effective cures*, in: Mos. Healthcare, Aug. 21, 1995: 140.

JOSEFEK K. J., *Alternative medicine's roadmap to mainstream*, in: American Journal of Law and Medicine, 2000, vol. 26: 295–310.

JOST T. S. (I), *Health care rationing in the courts: A comparative study*, in: Hasting International and Comparative Law Review, 1998, vol. 21, n° 3: 639–714.

JOST T. S. (II), *Introduction – Regulation of the health care professions*, in: JOST T. S., *Regulation of the healthcare professions*, Health Administration Press, 1996, Chicago: 1–16.

JOST T. S. (III), *Oversight of the competence of healthcare professionals*, in: JOST T. S., *Regulation of the healthcare professions*, Health Administration Press, 1996, Chicago: 17–44.

KARPMAN A., *Informed consent: Does the first amendment protect a patient's right to choose alternative treatment*, in: New York School of Human rights, Summer 2000: 933–57.

KILGORE C., *Expanding coverage signals growing demand, acceptance for alternative care*, in: Medicine & Health Perspectives, May 4, 1998: 1–4.

KINNEY E., *Administrative law issues in professional regulation*, in: JOST T. S., *Regulation of the healthcare professions*, Health Administration Press, 1996, Chicago: 103–28.

KNOTHE B. D., *New law requires health insurers to pay for chiropractic care*, in: N.Y. Health L. Update, 1997, vol. 4, n° 8: 2ss.

KOHN L. T. (co-editors: CORRIGAN J. M., DONALDSON M. S.), *To err is human: Building a safer health system*, National Academy Press, 2000, Washington D. C.

LAMM L. C. (co-authors: WEGNER E., COLLORD D.), *Chiropractic scope of practice: What the law allows – update 1993*, in: J. Manipulative Physiol. Ther., Jan. 1995, vol. 18, n° 1: 16–20.

LAWLOR J. D., *Chiropractor's liability for failure to refer patient to medical practitioner*, in: A.L.R. 3d, 1975–1998, vol. 58: 590ss.

LAY B. F., *Healer–patient privilege: Extending the physician–patient privilege to alternative health practitioners in California*, in: Hastings Law Journal, Mar. 1997: 633–66.

LIANG B. A., *Health law and policy – A survival guide to medicolegal issues for practitioners*, Butterworth-Heinemann, 2000, Woburn.

MCRAE G., *A critical overview of U.S. acupuncture regulation*, in: Journal of Health Politics, Policy and Law, 1982, vol. 7, n° 1: 163–196.

MAGNER G., *Chiropractic – The victim's perspective*, Prometheus Book, 1995, New York.

MARWICK C., *Alterations are ahead at the OAM*, in: JAMA, 1998, vol. 280, n° 18: 1553–54.

MICKELSON A. A. (co-authors: DAILEY W. H., SINGH KHALSA S., FEDAK M. L.), *Managed care potpourri IV: Where is complementary/alternative care?*, in: Whittier Law Review, Fall 1997, vol. 19: 119–33.

MILES S. H., *Informed demand for "non-beneficial" medical treatment*, in: New England Journal of Medicine, 1991, vol. 325: 512ss.

MITCHELL WEITZMAN S., *Insurance coverage for complementary and alternative medicine – Access, challenges, and policy*, in: HUMBER J. M. (co-editor: ALMEDER R.), *Alternative medicine and ethics*, Humana Press, 1998, Totowa: 127–61.

MITKA M., *FDA never promised an herb garden – But sellers and buyers eager to see one grow*, in: JAMA, 1998, vol. 280, n° 18: 1553–54.

NATIONAL INSTITUTES OF HEALTH, OFFICE OF ALTERNATIVE MEDICINE, *Alternative medicine: Expanding medical horizons: A report to the MH on alternative medical systems and practices in the United States*, National Institutes of Health, Office of Alternative Medicine, 1995, Washington.

ORENTLICHER D., *The role of professional self-regulation*, in: JOST T. S., *Regulation of the healthcare professions*, Health Administration Press, 1996, Chicago: 129–48.

PARADIS N., *Making a living off the dying*, in: New York Times, Apr. 25, 1992.

PATEL V., *Understanding the integration of alternative modalities into an emerging healthcare model in the United States*, in: HUMBER J. M. (co-editor: ALMEDER R.), *Alternative medicine and ethics*, Humana Press, 1998, Totowa: 43–96.

PATTERSON E. G., *Health care choice and the constitution: Reconciling privacy and public health*, in: Rutgers Law Review, Fall 1989, vol. 42: 1–91.

PELLETIER K. R. (co-authors: MARIE A., KRASNER M., et al.), *Current trends in the integration and reimbursement of complementary and alternative medicine by managed care, insurance carriers, and hospital providers*, in: Am. J. Health., 1997, n° 12: 112–22.

PEW HEALTH PROFESSIONS COMMISSION (FINOCCHIO L. J., DOWER C. M., MCMAHON T., GRAGNOLA C. M., AND THE TASKFORCE ON HEALTH CARE WORKFORCE REGULATION), *Reforming health care workforce regulation: Policy considerations for the 21st Century*, Pew Health Professions Commission, 1995, San Francisco.

POWERS MONACO G. (co-author: SMITH G.), *Healthcare plans as gatekeepers*, in: HUMBER J. M. (co-editor: ALMEDER R.), *Alternative medicine and ethics*, Humana Press, 1998, Totowa: 97–124.

POZGAR G. D. (co-author: POZGAR N. S.), *Legal aspects of health care administration*, Aspen Publishers, 1996, Gaithersburg.

REHM W. S., *Kansas coconuts: Legalising chiropractic in the first state, 1910–1915*, in: Chiropractic. Hist., Dec. 1995, vol. 15, n° 2: 43–50.

RELMAN A. S., *Regulation of the medical profession: A physician's perspective*, in: JOST T. S., *Regulation of the healthcare professions*, Health Administration Press, 1996, Chicago: 199–210.

RUSSEL S., *HMOs try dose of alternative medicine*, in: S. F. Chron., Jan. 22, 1996: A1, A4.

SAFRIET B. J., *Health care dollars and regulatory sense: The role of advanced practice nursing*, in: Yale Journal on Regulation, 1992, vol. 9.

SAGE W. M. (co-author: AIKEN L. H.), *Regulating interdisciplinary practice*, in: JOST T. S., *Regulation of the healthcare professions*, Health Administration Press, 1996, Chicago: 71–101.

SALE D. M., *Overview of legislative developments concerning alternative health care in the United States*, 1995.

SARNER L. (co-author: ROSA L.), *Using Daubert to aid the injured: A case of therapeutic touch?*, in: Quinnipiac Health Law Journal, 1999–2000, vol. 3: 25–35.

SENN D., *Insurance commissioner, every category of provider*, in: Washington Office of Insurance Commissioner Bulletin, Dec. 19, 1995, n° 95–9.

SHEKELLE P. G. ,*What role for chiropractic in health care?*, in: The New England Journal of Medicine, 1998, vol. 339: 1074–75.

SHULTZ M., *From informed consent to patient choice: A new protected interest*, in: Yale Law Journal, 1985, vol. 95: 219ss.

STRAHILEVITZ L. J., *Controlling the costs of alternative medicine*, in: Southwestern Universitz Law Review, 1999, vol. 28: 543–98.

STUDDERT D. M. and co-authors, *Medical malpractice implications of alternative medicine*, in: JAMA, 1998, vol. 280, n° 18: 1610–15.

SUGARMAN J. (I), *Physicians' ethical obligations regarding alternative medicine*, in: JAMA, 1998, vol. 280, n° 18: 1623–25.

SUGARMAN J. (II), *Informed consent, shared decision-making, and complementary and alternative medicine*, in: The Journal of Law, Medicine and Ethics, 2003, vol. 31, n° 2: 247–50.

STARR P., *The social transformation of american medicine*, Basic Books, 1982.

STEPNO E. M., *Acupuncture – Stricter standards for those performing acupuncture*, in: M. George L. Rev., 1998, vol. 29: 411–15.

THOMSON B., *The medical revolution*, in: Natural Health, Mar.–Apr. 1996: 98ss.

VINCLER L. A. (co-author: NICOL M. F.), *When ignorance isn't bliss: What healthcare practitioners and facilities should know about complementary and alternative medicine*, in: J. Health & Hosp. L., 1997, vol. 30: 160ss.

VYBORNY K. M., *Legal and political issues facing telemedicine*, in: Annals of Health Law, 1996, vol. 5: 61–119.

WARDWELL W. I., *Alternative medicine in the United States*, in: Social Science and Medicine, 1994, vol. 38, n° 8: 1061–68.

WARREN D. G., *Complementary medicine and the law*, in: Journal of Legal Medicine, June 1997: 257–64.

WETZEL M. S. (co-authors: EISENBERG D. M., KAPTCHUK T. J.), *Courses involving complementary and alternative medicine at US medical schools*, in: JAMA, 1998, vol. 280, n° 9: 784–87.

WEISS R., *Acupuncture gets a clean bill of health by US panel*, in: International Herald Tribune, Nov. 7, 1997.

WHITE HOUSE COMMISSION ON COMPLEMENTARY AND ALTERNATIVE MEDICINE POLICY, *Final report*, March 2002, available at http://www.whccamp.hhs.gov/pdfs/fr2002_document.pdf, accessed Feb. 1 2005.

WISHARD B., *Physicians, surgeons, and other Healers*, in: FL Jur. 2d Physicians, 1999, vol. 39.

YESSIAN M. R. (co-author: GREENLEAF M.), *The ebb and flow of federal initiatives to regulate healthcare professionals*, in: JOST T. S., *Regulation of the healthcare professions*, Health Administration Press, 1996, Chicago: 169–98.

Cases:

Acupuncture Soc'y v. Kansas State Bd. Of Healing Arts, 602 P.2d 1311 (Kan. 1979).

Andrews v. Ballard, 498 F. Supp. 1038 (S.D. Tex. 1980).

Atkins v. Guest, 601 N.Y.S.2d 234 (Sup. Ct. 1993), aff'd, 607 N.Y.S.2d 655 (App. Div. 1994).

Baderbessono v. Michels, 91 Cal. Rptr. 760, 764, 478 P.2d 480, 484 (Cal.1970).

Black v. State, 216 S.W. 181 (Tex. Crim. App. 1919).

Blue Shield of Virginia v. McCready, 457 U.S. 465 (1982).

Boyle v. Revici, 961 F.2d 1060 (2d Cir. 1992).

Burzynski v. Aetna Life Ins. Co., Inc., n° H-89-3976, 1992 U.S. Dist. LEXIS 21300 (S.D. Tex., Mar. 31, 1992).

Burzyinski v. Aetna Life Ins. Co., 967 F.2d 1063 (5th Cir. 1992), remaded, 989 F.2d 733 (5th Cir. 1993).

Chumbler v. McClure, 505 F.2d 489, 491–92 (6th Cir. 1974).

Clark v. Department of Professional Regulation, 463 So.2d 328 (Fla. App. 1985).

Commonwealth v. Dragon, 132 N.E. 356, 357 (Mass. 1921).

Day v. Aetna Employees Benefit Div., No 88CA00463, 1989 Ohio App. LEXIS 2458 (Ohio Ct. App. June 21, 1989).

Dent v. West Virginia, 129 U.S. 114 (1888).

Feingold v. Commonwealth of Pennsylvania, State Board of Chiropractic, 568 A.2d 1365 (Pa. Commw. Ct. 1980).

Foster v. Board of Chiropractic Examiners, 359 S.E.2d 877 (Ga.1987).

Gemme v. Goldberg, 626 A.2d 318 (Conn. App. Ct. 1993).

Hahn v. Oregon Physicians' Service, civil n° 78-0887-MA, 1990 U.S. Dist. Lexis 16899 (D. Or. Oct. 26, 1990).

Hawker v. New York (1898).

Hitchcock v. State, 131 A.2d 714 (Md. 1957).

Ireland v. Eckerly, 1989 Minn. App. LEXIS 13, at 3 (Minn. Ct. App., Jan. 10, 1989).

Jacobson v. Massachusetts, 197 U.S. 11 (1905).

Kerman v. Hintz, 418 N.W.2d 795, 802–03 (Wis. 1988).

Makris v. Bureau of Professional and Occupational Affairs, State Board of Psychology, 599 A.2d 279 (Comm. Ct. Pa. 1991).

McLauglin v. Connecticut Gen. Life Ins. Co., 565 F. Supp. 434 (N.D. Cal. 1983).

Ohio State Bd. Of Chiropractic Examiners v. Fulk, 617 N.E.2d 690 (Ohio C.App. 1992).

Parma v. Wolff, 635 N.E.2d, 76, 78–79 (Ohio Mun. Ct. 1993).

People v. Amber, 349 N.Y.S.2d 604 (Sup. Ct. 1973).

People v. Mastromarino, 265 N.Y.S. 864 (Sup. Ct. 1933).

People v. Steinberg, 73 N.Y.S.2d 475 (Mag. Ct. 1947).

Piazza v. Behrman Chiropractic Clinic, 601 So.2d 1378, 1379 (La. 1992).

Plumber v. Dep't of Health and Human Resources, 634 So.2d 1347 (La. Ct. App. 1994), cert. denied, 637 So.2d 1056 (La. 1994).

Prudential Ins. Co. of Am. v. Brown, n° B14-89-00695-CV (Tex. Ct. App. 1990).

Reams v. State, 279 So.2d 839 (Fla. 1973).

Reynolds v. McNichols, 488 F.2d 1378, 1382 (10th Cir. 1979).

Sabastier v. State, 504 So.2d 45 (Fla. Dist. Ct. App. 1987).
Sarchett v. Blue Shield, 729 P.2d 267, 270 (Cal. 1987).
Scalia v. Liberty Mut. Ins. Co., n° 9308, 1995 WL 296772, at *3 (Mass. App. Div., May 10, 1995).
Schneider v. Revici, 817 F.2d 987 (2d Cir. 1987).
Sermchief v. Gonzalez, 660 S.W.2d 683, 689–90 (Mo. 1983).
Shumake v. Travelers Ins. Co., 383 N.W.2d 259 (Mich. App. 1985), appeal denied, 425 Mich. 859 (1986).
Smith v. People, 117 P. 612 (Colo. 1911).
State v. Beno, 373 N.W.2d 544 (Mich. 1985).
State v. Ghadili, 175 A. 315, 318 (Del. 1933), cert. dismissed, 292 U.S. 653 (1934).
State v. Guess, 393 S.E.2d at 833 (N.C. Ct. App. 1989).
State v. Hinze, 441 N.W.2d 593, (Neb. 1989).
State v. Howard, 337 S.E.2d 598 (N.C. Ct. App. 1985).
State v. Kellogg, 568 P.2d 514 (Idaho 1977).
State v. MountJoy et al., 891 P.2d 376, 384 (Kan. 1995).
State v. Nelson, 317 S.E.2d 711, 714 (N.C. Ct. App. 1984).
State v. Rich, 44 Ohio St. 2d, 195, 73 Ohio Ops 2d 487, 339, N.E.2d 630 (1975).
State v. Wilson, 111 Wash. App. 916, 528 P.2d 279 (1974).
State v. Won, 528 P.2d 594, 72 A.L.R.3d 1253 (1974).
State Board of Chiropractic Examiners v. Clark, 713 S.W.2d 621 (Mo. Ct. App. 1986).
State Board of Medical Examiners v. Rogers, 387 So.2d 937 (Fla. 1980).
Stetina v. State, 513 N.E.2d 1234 (Ind. Ct. App. 1987).
Stockwell v. Washington State Chiropractic Disciplinary Board, 622 P.2d at 910.
Taulbee v. Travelers Company Co., 537 N.E.2d 670 (Ohio Ct. App. 1987).
Trustees of the Northwest Laundry and Dry Cleaners Health and Welfare Fund v. Burzinsky, 27 F.3d 153–55 (5th Cir. 1994), reh'g, en banc, denied, 38 F.3d 571 (5th Cir. 1994), cert. denied, 115 S. Ct. 1110 (1995).
Tudor v. Metropolitan Life insurance Company, 539 N.Y.S.2d 690 (Dist. Ct. 1989).
United States v. Burzynski Cancer Research Inst., n° H-83-2069 (S.D. Tex., May 24, 1983).
United States v. Hoxsey Cancer Clinic, 198 F.2d 273, 280 (5th Cir. 1952), cert. denied, 346 U.S. 897 (1953).
Virginia Academy of Clinical Psychologists v. Blue Shield of Virginia, 624 F.2d 476 (4th Cir. 1980), cert. denied, 450 U.S. 916 (1981).
Wait v. Metropolitan Life Ins. Co., 564 N.Y.S.2d 535 (App. Div. 1990).
Washington v. Harper, 194 U.S. 210 (1990).
Wengel, 473 N.W.2d at 744.
Williams v. State of Alabama ex rel. Medical Licensure Comm'n, 453 So.2d 1051, 1053 (Ala. Civ. App. 1984).
Wilk v. American Medical Ass'n, 719 F.2d 207 (7th Cir. 1983), cert. denied, 467 U.S. 1210 (1984), on remand, 671 F. Supp. 1465 (N.D: Ill. 1987) aff'd, 895 F.2d 352 (7th Cir. 1990).
Zabrecky v. Connecticut Board of Chiropractors, n° 0702118, 1991 Conn. Super. Ct. LEXIS 2682, at *7(Nov. 15, 1991).
Zuckerberg v. Blue Cross & Blue Shield, 490 N.E.2d 839 (N.Y. 1986).

European Union

ABBING R., *Quality of medical practice and professional misconduct in the European Union*, in: European Journal of Health Law, 1997, n° 4: 273–78.

ALDRIDGE D., *Complementary medicine in Europe: Some natural perspectives*, in: LEWITH G. (co-editor: ALDRIDGE D.), *Complementary medicine and the European Community*, CW Daniel, 1991, Saffron Walden: 35–44.

BAEYENS A., *Free movement of good and services in health care: A comment on the court cases Decker and Kohll from a Belgian point of view*, in: European Journal of Health Law, 1999, n° 6: 373–383.

BONNAMOUR M.-C. (co-author: GRANTURCO T.), *The Lannoye report on non-conventional medicines was adopted by the European Parliament*, CP Info, June 1997, Bruxelles.

BRITISH MEDICAL ASSOCIATION (LAMONT T.), *Complementary medicine – New approaches to good practice*, Oxford University Press, 1993, Oxford/New York.

BMS, *Europa-Parlament lehnt Alternativmedizin ab*, in: BMS, 1997, vol. 78, n° 36: 1290.

DE BIJL N. (co-author: NEDERVEEN-VAN DE KRAGT I.), *Legal safeguards against medical practice by not suitably qualified persons: A comparative study in seven EU-countries*, 1997, in: European Journal of Health Law, vol. 4: 5–18.

DUMOULIN J.-F. (co-authors: GUILLOD O., MÉROZ J.-C.), *L'impact d'une adhésion suisse à l'Union Européenne sur le droit de la santé*, in: COTTIER T. (co-editor: KOPSE A. R.), *L'adhésion de la Suisse à l'Union Européenne – Enjeux et conséquences*, Schulthess, 1998, Zürich: 925–48.

FRÉCHELIN K. (I), *Couverture en cas de maladie et d'accidents dans les Etats de l'UE*, in: Sécurité Sociale, 1999, n° 3: 134–36.

FRIEDEL E. (co-author: FREUNDLICH M.), *European community harmonisation of the licensing and manufacturing of medicinal products*, in: Food and Drug Law Journal, 1994, vol. 49: 141–70.

GAIER H.C. (I), *Evolving problems for natural medicines within the European Community – and the biocentric practitioners who use them*, in: Complementary Medical Research, 1991, vol. 5, n° 1: 36–41.

GAIER H. (II), *Reveille for biocentric medicine*, in: LEWITH G. (co-editor: ALDRIDGE D.), *Complementary medicine and the European Community*, CW Daniel, 1991, Saffron Walden: 9–34.

HAEHNEL P., *Les médecines parallèles au Parlement Européen: Un projet voué à l'échec*, Bulletin de l'Ordre, Sept. 1996.

HAMILTON G. J., *Competition and solidarity in European health care systems*, in: European Journal of Health Law, 1996, n° 3: 323–29.

KAHIL-WOLFF B., *L'accord sur la libre circulation des personnes Suisse–CE et le droit des assurances sociales*, in: Semaine Judiciaire, 2001, vol. 123, n° 4: 81–135.

KELLER K. (I), *Herbal medicinal products in Germany and Europe: Experiences with national and European Assessment*, in: Drug Information Journal, 1996, vol. 30: 933–48.

KELLER K. (II), *Homeopathic medicinal products in Germany and Europe: Legal requirements for registration and marketing authorisation*, in: Drug Information Journal, 1998, vol. 32: 803–11.

LANNOYE P., *Is there a future for complementary medicine in Europe? – European report on the status of non-conventional medicine*, The Natural Medicines Society, 1996, Heanor.

MULAS S., *Freizügigkeit freier Berufe im europäischen Binnenmarkt*, Dissertation, 1995, Tübingen.

PROCOMED, *Lettre d'information de l'Association pour la reconnaissance et la promotion des médecines complémentaires en Europe*, Bulletin n° 2, Dec., 1997, Bruxelles.

RICHLI P. (co-author: WUNDER K.), *Über die Möglichkeiten zur Beschränkung des freien Warenverkehrs nach dem Binnenmarktgesetz*, in: AJP, 1996, n° 6: 908–17.

SCHNEIDER H., *Die Anerkennung von Diplomen in der Europäischen Gemeinschaft*, Maklu, 1995, Uitgevers Antwerpen.

SEGEST E., *Consumer protection and the free movement of medical practitioners in the European Union*, in: European Journal of Health Law, 1997, n° 4: 267–72.

TRIBUNE POUR L'EUROPE, *Médecines non conventionnelles*, in: Tribune pour l'Europe, June 1997, Antwerpen.

Case Law: Case 120/95 *Decker v. Caisse de Maladie des Employés Privés* (1998) ECR.

Case 158/96 *Kohll v. Union des Caisses de Maladie* (1998) ECR.

Comparative and International Law

AKERELE O. (co-editor: STOTT G., WEIBO L.), *The role of traditional medicine in primary health care in China*, WHO, 1985, Geneva: 54–58.

ALBER J. (co-author: BERNARDI-CHENKLUHN B.), *Westeuropäische Gesundheitssysteme im Vergleich, Bundesrepublik Deutschland, Schweiz, Frankreich, Italien, Grossbritannien*, Campus Verlag, 1992, Frankfurt.

ALDRIDGE D. (I), *Unconventional medicine in Europe*, Advances, 1994, vol. 10, n° 2: 52–60.

ANDERSEN J. O., *Health seeking in pluralistic health care systems*, in: JOHANNESSEN H. (co-authors: LAUNSO L., OLESEN S. G., STAUGARD F.) (I), *Studies in alternative therapy 1 – Contributions from the Nordic countries*, Odense University Press, 1994, Gylling: 114–25.

BANNERMAN R. H. (co-authors: BURTON J., WEN-CHIEH C.), *Traditional medicine and health care coverage – A reader for health administrators and practitioners*, World Health Organization, 1983, Genève.

BERTHOD-WURMSER M., *La santé en Europe*, La documentation française, 1994, Paris.

BISSEL T., *United States*, in: BEDEE H. (co-authors: D'HAESE W., PETRY V., ROMPELMAN A. J.), *The international guide to social security*, Kluwer Law International, 1995, The Hague/London/Boston: 401–12.

BONNAMOUR M.-C. (co-author: GRANTURCO T.), *The Lannoye report on non-conventional medicines was adopted by the European Parliament*, CP Info, June 1997, Bruxelles.

BRITISH MEDICAL ASSOCIATION (LAMONT T.), *Complementary medicine – New approaches to good practice*, Oxford University Press, 1993, Oxford/New York.

CARTER J. P., *Racketeering in medicine – The suppression of alternatives*, Hampton Roads Publishing Co., 1993, Norfolk.

CHAPMAN-SMITH D. A., *Legislative approaches to the regulation of the chiropractic profession*, in: Journal of the Canadian Chiropractic Association, June 1996, vol. 40, n° 2: 108–14.

DE BIJL N. (co-author: NEDERVEEN-VAN DE KRAGT I.), *Legal safeguards against medical practice by not suitably qualified persons: A comparative study in seven EU-countries*, 1997, in: European Journal of Health Law, vol. 4: 5–18.

DOMMERS J., *An introduction to European Union health law*, in: European Journal of Health Law, vol. 4, n° 1, 1997: 19–41.

EUROPEAN COMMITTEE FOR HOMEOPATHY, *Homeopathy in Europe – Developing standars for professionnal practice of homeopathy in the European Union*, European Committee for Homeopathy, 1994, Rotterdam.

FISHER P. (co-author: WARD A.), *Complementary medicine in Europe*, in: BMJ, vol. 309, July 9, 1994: 107–11.

FROST AND SULLIVAN LTD, *Alternative medical practices in Europe*, Report n° E874, Sullivan House, Grosvenor Gardens, 1987, London SW1.

FULDER S., *The handbook of complementary medicine*, 2nd edition, Oxford University Press, 1988, Oxford/New York.

HOFF W. (I), *Guidelines for training traditional health practitioners in primary health care*, Divison of Strengthening of Health Services and Traditional Medicine Programme, Geneva 1995.

GUILLOD O. (I), *Rebouteux, naturopathes et guérisseurs: Pour un traitement légal alternatif*, Recueil de Jurisprudence Neuchâtelois, 1989, Neuchâtel: 9–45.

GUZMAN L. (co-author CASERO J. V.), *Aproximaciòn a la regulaciòn juridica de la homeopatia*, Revista general de derecho, 1992, vol. 48: 3943–56.

HERNESNIEMI A., *Co-work between a medical doctor and a traditional healer*, in: JOHANNESSEN H. (co-authors: LAUNSO L., OLESEN S. G., STAUGARD F.) (I), *Studies in alternative therapy 1 – Contributions from the Nordic countries*, Odense University Press, 1994, Gylling: 126–38.

JOHNSON T. (co-authors: LARKIN G., SAKS M.), *Health professions and the State in Europe*, Routledge, 1995, London/New York.

LANNOYE P., *Is there a future for complementary medicine in Europe? – European report on the status of non-conventionnal medicine*, The Natural Medicines Society, 1996, Heanor.

LEWITH G. (co-author: ALDRIDGE D.), *Complementary medicine and the European Community*, Saffron Walden, CW Daniel, 1991.

LÜSCHEN G. (co-authors: COCKERHAM W., VAN DER ZEE J., etc.), *Health systems in the European Union*, Oldenburg Verlag, 1995, München.

MADDALENA S., *The legal status of complementary medicines in Europe*, Stämpfli, 1999, Bern.

MADDALENA S., *La situation juridiques des médecines alternatives – Un aperçu de la législation en Europe*, in: BORGHI M. (co-editor: GASSMAN J.), *Thérapies complémentaires ou alternatives en psychiatrie: Un défi? Un droit?*, Schriftenreihe der Schweizerischen Stiftung Pro Mente Sana n° 20, 1999, Zürich: 223–57.

MCCARTHY M. (co-author: REES S.), *Health systems and health medicine in the European Community*, Royal College of Physicians of London, 1992, London.

Preusker U. K., *Gesundheitssysteme in Skandinavien – Eine aktuelle Darstellung des schwedischen, norwegischen und finnischen Gesundheitswesens*, Bergisch Gladbach, 1996, Heider.

Robard I., *La santé hors la loi: Les hors la loi de la santé*, 4th ed., Ed. de l'Ancre, 1994, Suresnes.

Roemer M. I., *National health systems of the World*, vol. 1, Oxford University Press, 1992, New York.

Schneider M. (co-authors: Biene-Dietrich P., Gebanyi M., Hofmann U., Huber M., Köse A., Sommer J. H.) (I), *Gesundheitssysteme im internationalen Vergleich*, ed. 1994, BASYS, 1995, Augsburg.

Schneider M. (co-authors: Hofmann U., Vasikjevic S.) (II), *Die Honorierung naturheilkundlicher Verfahren – Untersuchung für den Bundesminister für Arbeit und Sozialordnung*, Basys, 1989, Augsburg.

Steinhoff B., *Regulatory situation of herbal medicines – A world Review*, World Health Organisation, WHO/TRM/98.1, Geneva 1998.

Stepan J., *Traditional and alternative systems of medicine: A comparative review of legislation*, in: International Digest of Health Legislation, 1985, vol. 36, n° 2, Genève.

Taylor R. C. R., *Alternative medicine and the medical encounter in Britain and the United States*, in: Salmon J. W. (editors), *Alternative medicines – popular and policy perspectives*, Tavistock Publications, 1984, New York.

Treece S. J., *An evaluation of medicines regulation*, in: Medical Law International, 1997, vol. 2: 315–36.

Weber A. (co-authors: Leienbach V., Dohle A., Strunk S., Teyukov A., Schulte-Mimberg U., Angele S.), *Soziale Sicherung in West-, Mittel-, und Osteuropa*, Nomos Verlagsgesellschaft, 1994, Baden-Baden.

WHO

Akerele O. (co-editor: Stott G., Weibo L.), *The role of traditional medicine in primary health care in China*, WHO, 1985, Geneva.

Bannerman R. H. (co-authors: Burton J., Wen-Chieh C.), *Traditional medicine and health care coverage – A reader for health administrators and practitioners*, World Health Organization, 1983, Genève.

Hoff W. (I), *Guidelines for training traditional health practitioners in primary health care*, Divison of Strengthening of Health Services and Traditional Medicine Programme, Geneva 1995.

Hoff W. (II), *Traditional practitioners as primary health care workers*, Divison of Strengthening of Health Services and Traditional Medicine Programme, Geneva 1995.

Steinhoff B., *Regulatory situation of herbal medicines – A world Review*, World Health Organisation, WHO/TRM/98.1, Geneva 1998.

Traditional Medicine Programme and Global programme on AIDS, *Report of a WHO consultation on traditional medicine and AIDS: Clinical evaluation of traditional medicines and natural products*, WHO, 1990, Geneva.

WHO (I), *WHO monographs on selected medicinal plants*, vol. 1, WHO, 1999, Geneva.

WHO (II), *Report of the third meeting of directors of WHO collaborating centres for traditional medicine*, WHO, 1995, Geneva.

WHO (III), *Report of the working group on auricular acupuncture nomenclature*, WHO, 1990, Lyon.

WHO (IV), *Guidelines on basic training and safety in acupuncture*, WHO, 1999, Geneva.

WHO (V), *Legal status of traditional medicine and complementary/alternative medicine – A World overview*, WHO, 2001, Geneva.

WHO REGIONAL OFFICE FOR AFRICA, *African traditional medicine: Report of an expert group*, WHO, AFRO Technical Report Series, n° 1, 1976, Brazzaville.

WHO REGIONAL OFFICE FOR WESTERN PACIFIC (I), *Research guidelines for evaluating the safety and efficacy of herbal remedies*, WHO, 1993, Manila.

WHO REGIONAL OFFICE FOR WESTERN PACIFIC (II), *Report – Working group on herbal remedies*, WHO, 1998, Manila.

WHO SCIENTIFIC GROUP, *A proposed standard international acupuncture nomenclature*, WHO, 1991, Geneva.

Non-legal Publications

ANGELL M. (co-author: KASSIRER J. P.), *Alternative medicine – The risks of untested and unregulated medicine*, in: New England Journal of Medicine, 1998, vol. 339, n° 12: 839–41.

ANONYMOUS (VIII), *Meinungsumfrage zur Alternativmedizin*, in: Das Beste, 1997, n° 7.

ASTIN J. A., *Why patients use alternative medicine – Results of a national study*, in: JAMA, 1998, vol. 279, n° 19: 1548–53.

BALON J. and co-authors, *A comparison of active and simulated chiropractic manipulations as adjunctive treatment for childhood asthma*, in: New England Journal of Medicine, 1998, vol. 338, n° 15: 1013–27.

BATTERMAN R. C., *Appraisal of new drugs*, in: JAMA, 1955, n° 158: 1547.

BECK A., *La chaire de médecine complémentaire à l'Université de Berne: Une création récente*, in: CMS, 1996, vol. 40: 55–62.

BENFELD H. (co-author: KORNGOLD E.), *Between heaven and Earth: A guide to Chinese medicine*, Ballantine Books, 1991, New York.

BLACK N., *Why we need observational studies to evaluate the effectiveness of health care*, in: British Medical Journal, 1996, n° 312: 12215–18.

BONVIN E. (I), *Médecine officielle et thérapies alternatives: dialogue ou concurrence?*, in: BORGHI M. (co-editor: GASSMAN J.), *Thérapies complémentaires ou alternatives en psychiatrie: Un défi? Un droit?*, Schriftenreihe der Schweizerischen Stiftung Pro Mente Sana n° 20, 1999, Zürich: 43–61.

BONVIN E. (II), *Intégration de l'homéopathie dans la clinique psychiatrique ambulatoire*, in: BORGHI M. (co-editor: GASSMAN J.), *Thérapies complémentaires ou alternatives en psychiatrie: Un défi? Un droit?*, Schriftenreihe der Schweizerischen Stiftung Pro Mente Sana n° 20, 1999, Zürich: 211–18.

BORCHGREVINK C. F., *Alternative medicine in Norway*, in: JOHANNESSEN H. (co-authors: LAUNSO L., OLESEN S. G., STAUGARD F.) (I), *Studies in alternative therapy 1 – Contributions from the Nordic countries*, Odense University Press, 1994, Gylling: 51–54.

BRODY J. E., *Evaluating acupuncture: Medical profession is divided*, in: International Herald Tribune, Nov. 20, 1997.

BÜRGI M. (co-authors: SOMMER J. H., JÜRG H. AND THEISS R.), *Alternative Heilmethoden – Verbreitung in der Schweiz*, Verlag Rüegger, 1996, Zürich.

BRENDSTRUP E., *Researching a holistic integrated treatment model – used by cancer patients*, in: JOHANNESSEN H. (co-authors: LAUNSO L., OLESEN S. G., STAUGARD F.) (I), *Studies in alternative therapy 1 – Contributions from the Nordic countries*, Odense University Press, 1994, Gylling: 151–60.

BRUSET S., *Holism and individualism – The Yin and Yang in complementary medicines*, in: JOHANNESSEN H. (co-authors: LAUNSO L., OLESEN S. G., STAUGARD F.) (I), *Studies in alternative therapy 1 – Contributions from the Nordic countries*, Odense University Press, 1994, Gylling: 186–96.

BULL J. P., *The historical development of clinical therapeutic trials*, in: Journal of Chronic Diseases, 1959, vol. 10: 218–48.

BURG M. A. (co-authors: KOSCH S. G., NEIMS A. H., and al.), *Personal use of alternative medicine therapies by health science center faculty*, in JAMA, 1998, n° 280: 1563.

CAROLL K. M. (co-authors: ROUNSAVILLE B. J., NICH C.), *Blind man's bluff: Effectiveness and significance of psychotherapy and pharmacotherapy, blinding procedures in clinical trials*, in: Journal of Consulting and Clinical Psychology, 1994, vol. 62: 276–80.

CHEZ R. (co-author: JONAS W.), *The challenge of complementary and alternative medicine*, in: American Journal of Obstetrics and Gynecology, Nov. 1997, vol. 177, n° 5: 1156–61.

CREMONINI D., *La salute nelle diverse tradizioni mediche*, in: BORGHI M. (co-editor: GASSMAN J.), *Thérapies complémentaires ou alternatives en psychiatrie: Un défi? Un droit?*, Schriftenreihe der Schweizerischen Stiftung Pro Mente Sana n° 20, 1999, Zürich: 37–41.

DELUZE C. (co-author: VISCHER T.-L.), *Interactions entre médecine académique et médecines non conventionnelles*, in: CMS, 1996, vol. 40: 33–40.

DAYER P., *Le groupe multidisciplinaire d'étude des médecines non-conventionnelles de Genève*, in: CMS, 1996, vol. 40: 67–69.

DEJUNG B., *Manuelle Triggerpunktbehandlung bei chronischer Lumbosakralagie*, in: FREY F. (co-editor: BAUMANN P. H.), *Supplementum 62, FNRS-PNR 34: Médecines complémentaires*, Schwabe, 1994, Basel: 82–87.

DESCARTES R., *Discourse on method and the meditations*, Pinguin Classics, 1987.

DIEZI J., *L'enseignement informatif sur les médecines parallèles à la faculté de médecine de Lausanne*, in: CMS, 1996, vol. 40: 63–65.

DITTMANN V., *Schulmedizin und Alternativmedizin – unüberbrückbare Gegensätze?*, in: BAUHOFER S. (co-editors: BOLLE P.-H., DITTMANN V.), *Sectes et occultisme – Aspects criminologiques*, Verlag Rüegger, 1996, Zürich: 333–49.

DOMENIGHETTI G. (co-authors: GRILLI R., GUILLOD O., GUTZWILLER F., QUAGLIA J.), *Usage personnel de pratiques relevant des médecines douces ou alternatives parmi les médecins suisses*, in: Médecine et Hygiène, 2000, vol. 58, n° 2291: 570–72.

DONDEN Y., *Health through balance: An introduction to Tibetan medicine*, Snow Lion, 1986, New York.

EISENBERG D. M. and co-authors (I), *Trends in alternative medicine use in the United States, 1990–1997*, in: JAMA, 1998, vol. 280, n° 18: 1569–75.

EISENBERG D. M. and co-authors (II), *Unconventional medicine in the USA*, in: The New England Journal of Medicine, 1993, n° 328: 246–52.

EKLÖF M. (co-author: TEGERN G.), *Stockholmare och den komplementära medicinen: Befolkningsstudie angaende inställning till och användning av komplementär medicin genomförd under ar 2000 i Stockholms läns landsting*, HSN rapport nr 12/00, Stockholm läns landsting, 2001, Stockholm.

ERNST E. (ed.) (I), *Complementary medicine: An objective appraisal*, Butterworth Heinmann, 1996, Oxford.

ERNST E. (co-author: WHITE A.) (II), *The BBC survey of complementary medicine use in the UK*, in: Complementary Therapies in Medicine, 2000, n° 8: 32–36.

ESKINAZI D. P., *Factors that shape alternative medicine*, in: JAMA, 1998, vol. 280, n° 18: 1621–23.

COST ACTION B4, *COST action B4 unconventional medicine – Final report of the management committee, 1993–1998*, European Communities, 1998, Luxembourg.

FAN R. *Modern Western science as a standard for traditional Chinese medicine: A critical appraisal*, in: The Journal of Law, Medicine and Ethics, 2003, vol. 31, n° 2: 213–221.

LE FANU J., *Grandeur et décadence de la médecine*, in: Courrier International, 1999, n° 463: 45.

FEARS T. R. (co-author: SCHNEIDERMAN M. A.), *Pathologic evaluation and the blind technique*, in: Science, 1974, n° 183: 21–22.

FRIEDMAN R. (co-authors: SEDLER M., MYERS P., BENSON H.), *Behavioral medicine, complementary medicine and integrated care: Economic implications*, in: Prim. Care, Dec. 1997, vol. 24, n° 4: 949–62.

GIGER M., *Les médecines parallèles dans le réseau de la Fédération des Médecins Suisses*, in: CMS, 1996, vol. 40: 53–54.

GOLD H. (co-auhors: KWIT N. T., OTTO H.), *The xanthines (theobromine and aminophylline) in the treatment of cardiac pain*, in: JAMA, 1996, vol. 108: 2173–79.

GOLDBECK-WOOD S. (co-authors: DOROZYNSKI A., LIE L. G., et al.), *Complementary medicine is booming worldwide*, in BMJ: 1996, n° 313: 131–133.

GREINER T. H. (co-authors: GOLD H., CATTELL M. et al.), *A method for the evaluation of effects of drugs on cardiac pain in patients with angina of effort: A study of khellin (visamin)*, in: American Journal of Medicine, 1950, vol. 9: 143–55.

GRMEK M. D. and co-authors, *Histoire de la pensée médicale en Occident*, Editions du Seuil, 1999, Paris.

GUEX P., *La place des médecines complémentaires: Considérations générales*, in: CMS, 1996, vol. 40, n° 1: 7–9.

GYSIN T. (co-author: ZIEGLER C.), *Klinische Hypnotherapie/Selbsthypnose für unspezifische chronische und episodische Kopfschmerzen ohne Migräne und andere definierte Kopfschmerzarten bei Kindern und Jugendlichen*, in: FREY F. (co-editor: BAUMANN P. H.), *Supplementum 62, FNRS-PNR 34: Médecines complémentaires*, Schwabe, 1994, Basel: 64–66.

HARALDSSON E. (I), *Research on alternative therapis in Iceland*, in: JOHANNESSEN H. (co-authors: LAUNSO L., OLESEN S. G., STAUGARD F.) (I), *Studies in alternative therapy 1 – Contributions from the Nordic countries*, Odense University Press, 1994, Gylling, 1994, Gylling: 46–50.

HARALDSSON E. (II), *Spiritual healing in Iceland*, in: JOHANNESSEN H. (co-authors: LAUNSO L., OLESEN S. G., STAUGARD F.) (I), *Studies in alternative therapy 1 – Contributions from the Nordic countries*, Odense University Press, 1994, Gylling, 1994, Gylling: 103–13.

HILL A., *A visual Encyclopedia of unconventionnal medicine*, Crown publishers Inc, 1974, New York.

HILL A. B., *The clinical trial*, in: New England Journal of Medicine, 1952, n° 247: 113–19.

HOCHSTRASSER B. (co-author: MATTMANN P.), *Homöopathie und Schulmedizin in der Schwangerschafts- und Geburtsbetreuung*, in: FREY F. (co-editor: BAUMANN P. H.), *Supplementum 62, FNRS-PNR 34: Médecines complémentaires*, Schwabe, 1994, Basel: 28–35.

HOFFER A., *A theoretical examination of double-blind design*, in: Canadian Medical Association Journal, 1967, n° 97: 123–27.

HUFFORD D. J., *Evaluating complementary and alternative medicines: The limits of science and scientists*, in: The Journal of Law, Medicine and Ethics, 2003, vol. 31, n° 2: 198–212.

HÜRNY C. and co-authors, *Verbessern nicht-konventionelle Zusatztherapien die Lebensqualität von Krebspatienten?*, in: FREY F. (co-editor: BAUMANN P. H.), *Supplementum 62, FNRS-PNR 34: Médecines complémentaires*, Schwabe, 1994, Basel: 55–63.

JOHANNESSEN H. (co-authors: LAUNSO L., OLESEN S. G., STAUGARD F.) (I), *Studies in alternative therapy 1 – Contributions from the Nordic countries*, Odense University Press, 1994, Gylling, 1994, Gylling.

JOHANNESSEN H. (II), *Alternative therapies as social cultural and therapeutic phenomena*, in: JOHANNESSEN H. (co-authors: LAUNSO L., OLESEN S. G., STAUGARD F.), *Studies in alternative therapy 1 – Contributions from the Nordic countries*, Odense University Press, 1994, Gylling: 13–23.

JOHANNESSEN H. (III), *Research on alternative therapy in Denmark*, in: JOHANNESSEN H. (co-authors: LAUNSO L., OLESEN S. G., STAUGARD F.), *Studies in alternative therapy 1 – Contributions from the Nordic countries*, Odense University Press, 1994, Gylling: 30–39.

JÜTTE R., *Geschichte der Alternativen Medizin: von der Volksmedizin zu den unkonventionellen Therapien von heute*, C.H. Beck, 1996, München.

KING L. S., *The road to scientific therapy*, in JAMA, 1966, vol. 197: 92–98.

KISSEL P. (co-author: BARRUCAND D.), *Placebo and placebo effect in medicine*, Masson, 1964, Paris.

KUHN T. S., *La structure des révolutions scientifiques*, Flammarion, 1983, Manchecourt.

LAPLANTINE F. (co-author: RABEYRON P.-L.), *Les médecines parallèles*, PUF, collection Que sais-je?, 1987, Paris.

LAUNSO L. (co-author: BRENDSTRUP E.) (I), *People choose alternative therapies – The consequence for future pharmacy practice*, in: Journal of Social and Administrative Pharmacy, 1995, vol. 12, n° 1.

LAUNSO L. (co-author: BRENDSTRUP E.) (II), *Description of a holistic integrated treatment model used by cancer patients and research evaluated part I and II*, in: Townsend for Doctors, Dec. 1994 and Jan. 1995.

LAUNSO L. (co-author: BRENDSTRUP E.) (III), *Headache and reflexogical treatment*, The Council Concerning Alternative Treatment, The National Board of Health, 1997, Copenhagen.

LEMOINE P., *La mystérieuse efficacité des placebos et autre poudres de perlimpinpin*, in: Le Temps Stratégique, 1999, n° 89: 84–91.

MACLENNAN A. H. (co-authors: WILSON D. H., TAYLOR A. W.), *Prevalence and cost of alternative medicine in Australia*, in: Lancet, 1996, n° 347: 569–73.

MARGOLIN A., *Investigating alternative medicine therapies in randomized controlled trials*, in: JAMA, 1998, vol. 280, n° 18: 1626–8.

MEDICIS T. C., *Akupunktur und Bronchialasthma*, in: FREY F. (co-editor: BAUMANN P. H.), *Supplementum 62, FNRS-PNR 34: Médecines complémentaires*, Schwabe, 1994, Basel: 39–48.

MELCHART D. (co-authors: LINDE K., WEIDENHAMMER W., WORKU F., WAGNER H.), *The integration of natural healing procedures into research and teaching at German universities*, in: Alternative Therapies, 1995, vol. 1, n° 1: 30–33.

MICOZZI M. S. (ed.), *Fundamentals of complementary and alternative medicine*, CHURCHILL Livingstone, 1996, New York.

MILLAR W. J., *Use of alternative health care practitioners by Canadians*, in: Can. J. Public Health, 1997, n° 88: 155–58.

MODELL W., *Origins and development of pharmacology*, in: MODELL W. (co-editors: SCHILD H. O., WILSON H. O.), *Applied pharmacology*, W. B. Saunders, 1976, Philadelphia: 7–28.

MONTAKAB H. (co-author: LANGEL G.), *L'effet de l'acupuncture dans le traitement de l'insomnie*, in: FREY F. (co-editor: BAUMANN P. H.), *Supplementum 62, FNRS-PNR 34: Médecines complémentaires*, Schwabe, 1994, Basel: 39–48.

MORREIM E. H., *A dose of our own medicine: Alternative medicine, conventional medicine, and the standards of science*, in: The Journal of Law, Medicine and Ethics, 2003, vol. 31, n° 2: 222–35.

NASH H., *The double-blind procedure: Rationale and empirical evaluation*, in: Journal of Nervous and Mental Disease, 1962, n° 134: 34–37.

NATIONAL INSTITUTES OF HEALTH, OFFICE OF ALTERNATIVE MEDICINE, *Alternative medicine: Expanding medical horizons: A report to the NIH on alternative medical systems and practices in the United States*, National Institutes of Health, Office of Alternative Medicine, 1995, Washington.

O'CONNOR B. B. and co-authors, *Defining and describing complementary and alternative medicine*, in: Alternative Therapies, Mar. 1997, vol. 3, n° 2: 49–57.

OFFICE OF ALTERNATIVE MEDICINE HOME PAGE, *What is CAM?*, available at: http://altmed.od.nih.gov/oam/resources/present/cam-core/, accessed Oct. 1, 2001.

OMS, *Médecine traditionnelle et couverture des soins de santé*, OMS, Genève, 1983.

PERREZ M., *Möglichkeiten und Grenzen der Evaluation von alternativen Behandlungsmethoden*, in: BORGHI M. (co-editor: GASSMAN J.), *Thérapies complémentaires ou alternatives en psychiatrie: Un défi? Un droit?*, Schriftenreihe der Schweizerischen Stiftung Pro Mente Sana n° 20, 1999, Zürich: 141–56.

PFEIFFER C. C., *Critical discussion of research designs for determining the effect of therapy which may increase or decrease the schizophrenic state*, in: Modern Hospital, 1957, n° 88: 104–10.

REES R., *Complementary medicine in the Nordic countries*, in: *Alternative Therapy Health Medicine*, Sept. 1997; vol. 3, n° 3: 92–93.

RIVERS W. H. R. (I), *The influence of alcohol and other drugs*, Arnold, 1908, London.

RIVERS W. H. R. (II), *Medicine, magic, and religion*, Macmillan, 1927, London.

ROSENTHAL CENTER FOR COMPLEMENTARY AND ALTERNATIVE MEDICINE *Information Sheet: What is complementary and alternative medicine?*, available at: http://www.rosenthal.hs.columbia.edu/, accessed Sept. 1 2001.

ROSSI I., (I *Médecine, médecines: Parallélisme ou complémentarité?*, in: CMS, 1996, vol. 40: 17–24.

ROSSI I. (II), *Pluralisme médical: Les enjeux des corps possibles*, in: CMS, 1995, vol. 39: 25–31.

SAKS M. (I), *Alternative medicine in Britain*, Clarendon Press, 1992, Oxford.

SALMON J. W. (editors), *Alternative medicines – popular and policy perspectives*, Tavistock Publications, 1984, New York.

SANDIFER M. G. (co-author: HAWKINGS D. R.), *A double-blind study of the effects of drugs on mood, mentation, and sedation*, Paper presented at the convention of the American psychiatrix association, 1958, San Francisco.

SANGARE H. C., *Les déterminants de la demande des médecines alternative en Suisse*, IEMS, 2001, Lausanne.

SANTOS-EGGIMANN B., *Le recours aux médecines non-conventionnelles en Suisse*, in: CMS, 1996, vol. 40: 11–16.

SCHÄR A. (co-authors: MESSERLI-OHRBACH V., SCHUBARTH P.), *Schulmedizin oder Komplementärmedizin: Nach welchen Kriterien entscheiden sich Patientinnen und Patienten?*, in: FREY F. (co-editor: BAUMANN P. H.), *Supplementum 62, FNRS-PNR 34: Médecines complémentaires*, Schwabe, 1994, Basel.

SCHNEIDERMAN L. L., *The (alternative) medicalization of life*, in: The Journal of Law, Medicine and Ethics, 2003, vol. 31, n° 2: 191–97.

SHAPIRO A. K. (co-author: SHAPIRO E.) (I), *The powerful placebo – From ancient priest to modern physician*, The Johns Hopkins University Press, 1997, Baltimore/London.

SHAPIRO A. K. (co-authors: SHAPIRO E., STRUENING E. L.) (II), *Reliability and validity of placebo test*, in: Journal of Psychiatric Research, 1980, vol. 15: 253–90.

SHAPIRO A. K. (co-authors: SHAPIRO E., STRUENING E. L.) (III), *Diazepam: How much better than placebo?*, in: Journal of Psychiatric Research, 1980, vol. 17: 51–73.

SHARMA U., *Complementary medicine today; practitioners and patients*, Routledge, 1995, London.

SILVERMAN W. A., *The myth of informed consent: In daily practice and in clincal trials*, in: Journal of Medical Ethics, 1989, vol. 15: 6–11.

SLEISENGER M. H., *Reply to Dr. Tomenius*, in: Amercian Journal of Digestive Diseases, 1958, n° 3: 415–16.

SLOTTE T., *Meeste maatschappijen vergoeden alternatieve geneeswijzen*, in: Consumentengids, Feb. 1997.

SNM News, *Les médecines dites "parallèles"*, Dec. 1998, n° 20.

STANLEY B., *An integration of ethical and clinical considerations in the use of placebos*, in: Psychopharmacology Bulletin, 1988, vol. 24: 18–20.

SUTER B. (co-author: KISTLER A.), *Beeinflusst Akupunktur die Hautdurchblutung über das autonome Nervensystem?*, in: FREY F. (co-editor: BAUMANN P. H.), *Supplementum 62, FNRS-PNR 34: Médecines complémentaires*, Schwabe, 1994, Basel: 36–38.

TETREAULT L. (co-author: BORDELEAU J. M.), *On the usefulness of the placebo and of the double-blind technique in the evaluation of psychotropic drugs*, in: Psychopharmacology Bulletin, 1971, n° 7: 44–54.

THOMAS R. W. (II), *Evidence for an energy model-based paradigm for health and healing – Two examples*, in: JOHANNESSEN H. (co-authors: LAUNSO L., OLESEN S. G., STAUGARD F.) (I), *Studies in alternative therapy 1 – Contributions from the Nordic countries*, Odense University Press, 1994, Gylling: 240–52.

VAUTRAVERS P. (co-author: LECOQ J.), *Lombalgies communes et manipulations vertébrales – Etat des lieux*, in: Revue du Rhumatisme, 1993, n° 7–8: 518–23.

WALDBURGER N. (co-author: MARCER N.), *Définition d'un niveau de formation adéquat – Exigences d'un examen final pour l'obtention d'un diplôme reconnu par le Service de la Santé Publique*, 2001, Lausanne.

WISE T. A., *Origin and history of medicine*, in: WISE T. A., *The Hindu system of medicine*, Mittal Publications, 1986, New Delhi.

WOOLF S. H. and co-authors, *Clinical practice guidelines in complementary and alternative medicines*, in: Arch. Fam. Med., 1997, n° 6: 149–54.

YOUNG J. H. (I), *The medical messiah*, Princeton University Press, 1967, Princeton.

YOUNG J. H. (II), *American health quackery*, Princeton University Press, 1992, Princeton.

Index

B

C

D

E

M

N

O

P